SOUND DOCTRINE FOR TODAY'S CHRISTIANS; WHAT THE BIBLE SAYS

REV. PRESTON N. TOLLIVER, JR.

Order this book online at www.trafford.com
or email orders@trafford.com

Most Trafford titles are also available at major online book retailers.

Print information available on the last page.

ISBN: 978-1-4251-3557-7 (sc)
ISBN: 978-1-4251-3913-1 (e)

Library of Congress Control Number: 2009932865

Trafford rev. 08/22/2018

www.trafford.com

North America & international
toll-free: 1 888 232 4444 (USA & Canada)
fax: 812 355 4082

DEDICATORY

THE BIBLE HAS a great tendency towards supporting the notion of Christian men being utilized in the capacity of father-like figures and role models to the extent of being vital in the role of molding and training up boys to men. I have become increasingly aware of the uniqueness of my background since birth into a sound Christian home as well as the kaleidoscope of Christian men who have had a profound influence on my life. This seeks to make mention of a multitude of men, as it has been their influence that has been the tremendous difference in my empowerment now before other men, especially, and women. They all have indeed exhibited a Christ-like mentality.

I was born into a sound Christian family. This book is in part dedicated to my mother and father who celebrated 60 years of matrimony in January of 2008. My parents have exhibited the personification of Christian family values and training in the upbringing of my brother, sister and me along with providing an example to the extended family.

This book is in part dedicated to my help meet, Ruthanne, since October, 1974 as well as my son Minister Preston N. Tolliver, III, an Associate Minister, at the Broadview Baptist Church, Broadview, Illinois. Their assistance in the electronic pasting of scriptures into the text of this book was invaluable.

Other than my Father, there is no one that has had a more profound influence on my life than the late Rev. Dr. Edward Thomas, Sr., who served as Pastor of the Greater First Baptist Church of Washington, D.C., for more than fifty years. I have estimated that I absorbed over 400 always profound sermons preached by Rev. Dr. Thomas who had two earned doctorate degrees. Rev. Dr. Edward Thomas is to a large part responsible for the soundness in my doctrine. In addition, I would be remiss in not in part dedicating this book to the memory of Greater First Baptist Church Bible teachers Dea. William D. Newkirk, Dea. Lydell Burpo, Dea. Malachi Clark, Bro. Albert Cook, Bro. James Beech and the memory of gospel preachers Rev. John Lewis, Rev. William Peyton (the gift of my concordance), Rev. Carroll Jackman and Rev. Quincy McClain. Lastly with regard to men of a profound spiritual influence by their ever present example and counsel at the Greater First Baptist Church, this book is part dedicated to Bro. Reginald Osborne and Dea. Calvin Johnson and well as the memories of Robert Holmes, Wesley Prather, Trustee Nelson Roots and Dea. Thomas (from whom I got my shout).

This book is in part dedicated to the memory of my father in the Ministry, the late Rev. Lawrence E. Mosley, Sr., Pastor of the Lilydale Progressive Missionary Baptist Church, Chicago. I was nurtured and vouched for as a gospel preacher by this Man of God. Pastor Mosley took it upon himself to initiate my ordination as a gospel preacher and Youth Minister within 9 months of my initial sermon. This book is also in part dedicated to those then on the ministerial staff, Rev. Jesse L. Reason, Rev. Donald Williams, Rev. Delmece Tolefree (my pulpit dancing partner), Bro. James Patton (fellow chef, dishwasher and Men's Day Co-Chair) and Bro E.C Dodd as well as in the memory of Rev. John J. Patrick, Rev. Marcus Thomas, Dea. John Plummer, Dea. Theodore Glover and Dea. James Woodson.

The late Rev. Dr. A. William Johnson, Pastor of the St. John's Church Baptist, Chicago, who was ordained as a deacon and then a preacher of the Gospel by Rev. Dr. Edward Thomas, Sr., was to become, at the behest of Dr. Thomas, a personal advisor and confidant to me at a crucial time during my calling. This book is in part dedicated to this Man of God, a dean among Chicago pastors over recent decades.

This book is in part dedicated to the memory of my mother's brother and husband of Mary, Dea. William "Bill" Cunningham of Shreveport and Haughton, Louisiana. I was old enough to witness my uncle's maturation to the highly respected family man, educator, Deacon and Trustee known to a great many. My uncle became a man in the true biblical sense. "When I was a child, I spake as a child and understood as a child but when I became a man I put away childish things" such as unbelief, disobedience, unfaithfulness, infidelity, irresponsibility, insobriety, malice and non-fellowship. What remains of my uncle is the everlasting memory of an exemplary Christian for me and you William, Larcey Charles, Kendell, Kiel, Kourtney, Andrew, Jarred, Taylon and even Korey. All real men are in Christ and in Christian fellowship with the saints.

This book is in part dedicated to the memory of my granduncle Calvin Morrison, of Washington, D.C., husband of Birda, who is etched into my earliest memories, alongside the earliest memories of my father, as a nurturer, provider and protector in a Christian manner. He was instrumental in my care from infancy and had a tremendous influence upon my early outlook on the world.

This book is in part dedicated to my cousin Mayor L.J. Harrison of Toccoa, Georgia. He is a former Mayor of the city, educator of particular note and an encourager of this Man of God over the years as the high school sweetheart and then husband since the early 1960s to my cousin Mabel. L.J. has always exemplified Christian faithfulness and hospitality as well as providing the impeccable example and tradition that I strive to maintain in my family.

Recruited at 22 years old as a degreed engineer and just on my own, I was taken under the wings of an all-star cast of employees and Christian men at Commonwealth Edison in Chicago. These men introduced me to the corporation, Chicago, their families and their churches. This group, to whom I in part dedicate this book, includes Lester Dugus (deceased), Cordell Reed, now Judge John Steele, George Lofton, Bill Dunbar, Bob Freeman, John Hooker and now Chairman and CEO of the Corporation, Frank Clark.

Rev. Dr. George W. Waddles, Sr., Dean of Christian Education, National Baptist Conference, Inc., and my Pastor at the Zion Hill Missionary Baptist Church South, Chicago, for the last decade, taught me in a few of his spare moments, how to utilize my Strong's Concordance prior even to my membership at Zion Hill. I have learned and gleaned from his powerful doctrinal preaching. Also, any preacher of the gospel, do your self a tremendous favor and begin attending WHW Ministries Expository Preaching Conference the first week of October each year at Los Angeles (Dr. Waddles as co-founder). Now, the opinions expressed in this book are not necessarily those of Dr. Waddles, however, it is hoped that there is to him nothing offensive herein. This book is in part dedicated to my Pastor.

Lastly, Debbie Brooks, Roberta Jaburek and Lisa Lester, each of you helped when I was nearly without strength to complete the assignment.

PREFACE

TO ALL MANKIND, I hope that in completing this book, I have been an obedient servant of God our Father and the Father of our Lord and Savior, Jesus Christ. I am persuaded that we have today just what God would have us to have in terms of His Holy Word, the Bible; we are without excuse in terms of learning and embracing the truth.

I have been led by the Holy Ghost to utilize extensively Biblical scripture as I have in a direct and frank manner addressed many of the topics prevalent in the world today. The world is indeed hungry for the Living Word and maybe as never before in history. Mankind is unquestionably growing in knowledge at an incredible rate while at the same time there remains a rejection of the knowledge of true and living God.

> "This know also, that in the last days perilous times shall come. For men shall be lovers of their own selves, covetous, boasters, proud, blasphemers, disobedient to parents, unthankful, unholy, without natural affection, trucebreakers, false accusers, incontinent, fierce, despisers of those that are good, traitors, heady, highminded, lovers of pleasures more than lovers of God; having a form of godliness, but denying the power thereof: from such turn away. For of this sort are they which creep into houses, and lead captive silly women laden with sins, led away with divers lusts, ever learning, and never able to come to the knowledge of the truth." (2 Timothy 3:1-7)

I have presented herein, Bible-based Christian doctrine in a manner that attempts to back up virtually every statement made with scripture. The scriptures serve as the "commentary". I am hoping, nothwithstanding the scriptural notations, that you will read the continuous expression of the scriptures from doctrinal statement to statement, in order to experience the complete spiritual revelation of the passages. Feel free to skip throughout this book as you like; this is by no means a cover to cover reading book. Further, I would suggest that all argument in favor or against what I have expressed, be made utilizing some spiritually inspired source as well. My desire is the same as God's desire, I would have all men saved.

> "I exhort therefore, that, first of all, supplications, prayers, intercessions, and giving of thanks, be made for all men; for kings, and for all that are in authority; that we may lead a quiet and peaceable life in all godliness and honesty. For this is good and acceptable in the sight of God our Saviour; who will have all men to be saved, and to come unto the knowledge of the truth." (1 Timothy 2:1-4)

May God have mercy on my soul inasmuch as this book may speak a word of salvation to someone, even as I identify with Peter and John in having no theological credentials of particular note, but rather just one laboring in the word under the anointing of a calling in Christ.

> "Now when they saw the boldness of Peter and John, and perceived that they were unlearned and ignorant men, they marvelled; and they took knowledge of them, that they had been with Jesus." (Acts 4:13)

"Brethren, if any of you do err from the truth, and one convert him; Let him know, that he which converteth the sinner from the error of his way shall save a soul from death, and shall hide a multitude of sins." (James 5:19&20)

Contents

1   Significance in the Studying of the Bible 1

2   The Trinity/Godhead 10

3   The Preeminence of Christ 23

4   A Statement of Sound Biblical Doctrine – Baptist Articles of Faith for Examination and
     Comparison 36

5   Biblical Faith/Faith in Jesus Christ 77

6   Being Fully Persuaded in Christ 83

7   Salvation/Being Born Again 94

8   Prayer – Making a Difference 113

9   The Church – Visible (Physical) and Spiritual 120

10   Preaching, Preachers, Ministers and the Calling (The Man of God and the Woman of God) . . 138

11   Pastors (Overseers)/Men, Women or Both 153

12   Christian Tolerance 165

13   Testing of Christian Denominations – Guidance from the Bible 180

14   Differentiating Christianity from Other World Religions 203

15   Judaism – A Special Case of Unbelief 216

16   Islam Including the Nation of Islam as a Special Case of Unbelief 222

17   Fundamentals of the Best Possible Living – Christian Lives in the Understanding of Mankind's
     Purpose 241

18   True Freedom, Christian Liberty 256

19   Holy Matrimony Defined 268

20   Divorce; What has to be Wrong 277

21   A Christian Basis for Child Rearing and Discipline 280

22   Wealth and Prosperity: the Rich in God's Sight 285

23   A Christian Work Ethic 292

24   Our Appearance as Christians 297

25   Legal Matters Among Christians 301

26   Sickness, Illness and Birth Defects 304

27   Christian Sexual Morality 313

28   Sin by Biblical Definition 317

29   Abominations in the Sight of God 325

30 Damnation 329

31 Racism 336

32 Satan (a.k.a. the Devil) 340

33 Resisting the Devil. 345

34 Speaking of the Antichrist and Antichrists 351

35 Capital Punishment under Scriptural Examination. 356

36 Homosexuality. 361

37 Abortion 366

38 A Nation from a Biblical Perspective. 371

39 The Error in the Civil Rights Movement. 379

40 A Christian Perspective on Certain Celebrations and Holidays 388

Appendix 1 Brief Outline of the History of the Bible. 395

Appendix 2 The Epistle Dedicatory of the King James Version of the Bible. 397

Appendix 3 The History of the Baptist Church (greatly abbreviated) 399

Appendix 4 Baptist Church Covenant 402

Appendix 5 Prayer Meeting Outline 403

Appendix 6 My Calling. 404

Appendix 7 Open Letter to Minister Farrakhan 408

Appendix 8 TITLE 89: SOCIAL SERVICES CHAPTER III: DEPARTMENT OF CHILDREN
AND FAMILY SERVICES SUBCHAPTER a: SERVICE DELIVERY PART 300
REPORTS OF CHILD ABUSE AND NEGLECT 418

Appendix 9 Emancipation Day Sermon in Toccoa, Georgia – God's Emancipating Word. . . . 458

Appendix 10 Proposed 28th Amendment to the United States Constitution as Revised 1/20/09 –
Right of Acknowledgement 465

Appendix 11 "Franklin D. Roosevelt's D-Day Prayer" June 6, 1944 466

Appendix 12 Holiday Proclamations 468

Appendix 13 U. S. President George W. Bush's 2008 Thanksgiving Day Proclamation. 470

References 472

1

SIGNIFICANCE IN THE STUDYING OF THE BIBLE

What is the point in studying the Bible? How can something written so long ago be relevant to my life today?

Nature of the Scriptures

Holy men wrote the scriptures as they were inspired by the Holy Spirit and therefore the scriptures are not subject to interpretation except as revealed by the Sprit of God.

> *"Knowing this first, that no prophecy of the scripture is of any private interpretation. For the prophecy came not in old time by the will of man: but holy men of God spake as they were moved by the Holy Ghost."* **(2 Peter 1:20-21)**

The word of God is pure (Tsaraph – refined).

> *"Every word of God is pure: he is a shield unto them that put their trust in him."* **(Proverbs 30:5)**

The Bible is able to lead us through life.

> *"Thy word is a lamp unto my feet, and a light unto my path."* **(Psalm 119:105)**

The Bible leads us to a blessed hope in eternal salvation.

> *"For God so loved the world, that he gave his only begotten Son, that whosoever believeth in him should not perish, but have everlasting life."* **(John 3:16)**

> *"The fool hath said in his heart, There is no God. Corrupt are they, and have done abominable iniquity: there is none that doeth good."* **(Psalm 53:1)**

> *"For the wrath of God is revealed from heaven against all ungodliness and unrighteousness of men, who hold the truth in unrighteousness; Because that which may be known of God is manifest in them; for God hath shewed it unto them. For the invisible things of him from the creation of the world are clearly seen, being understood by the things that are made, even his eternal power and Godhead; so that they are without excuse: Because that, when they knew God, they glorified him not as God, neither were thankful; but became vain in their imaginations, and their foolish heart was darkened."* **(Romans 1:18-21)**

"For what is the hope of the hypocrite, though he hath gained, when God taketh away his soul? Will God hear his cry when trouble cometh upon him? Will he delight himself in the Almighty? will he always call upon God? (**Job 27:8-10**)

"For the grace of God that bringeth salvation hath appeared to all men, Teaching us that, denying ungodliness and worldly lusts, we should live soberly, righteously, and godly, in this present world; Looking for that blessed hope, and the glorious appearing of the great God and our Saviour Jesus Christ; Who gave himself for us, that he might redeem us from all iniquity, and purify unto himself a peculiar people, zealous of good works. These things speak, and exhort, and rebuke with all authority. Let no man despise thee." (**Titus 2:11-15**)

"For what is a man profited, if he shall gain the whole world, and lose his own soul? or what shall a man give in exchange for his soul?" (**Matthew 16:26**)

The Bible Reveals Christ

Jesus is the incarnate (brought to life) word.

"And the Word was made flesh, and dwelt among us, (and we beheld his glory, the glory as of the only begotten of the Father,) full of grace and truth." (**John 1:14**)

The Bible believer's faith is in Jesus Christ.

"Looking unto Jesus the author and finisher of our faith; who for the joy that was set before him endured the cross, despising the shame, and is set down at the right hand of the throne of God." (**Hebrews 12:2**)

Without faith in Christ, the preached word does not benefit unto salvation the individual.

"For unto us was the gospel preached, as well as unto them: but the word preached did not profit them, not being mixed with faith in them that heard it." (**Hebrews 4:2**)

The Bible contains eyewitness accounts of Jesus Christ.

"This is the disciple which testifieth of these things, and wrote these things: and we know that his testimony is true. And there are also many other things which Jesus did, the which, if they should be written every one, I suppose that even the world itself could not contain the books that should be written. Amen." (**John 21:24&25**)

"And many other signs truly did Jesus in the presence of his disciples, which are not written in this book: But these are written, that ye might believe that Jesus is the Christ, the Son of God; and that believing ye might have life through his name." (**John 20:30&31**)

"Forasmuch as many have taken in hand to set forth in order a declaration of those things which are most surely believed among us, Even as they delivered them unto us, which from the beginning were eyewitnesses, and ministers of the word; It seemed good to me also, having had perfect understanding of all things from the very first, to write unto thee in order, most excellent Theophilus, That thou mightest know the certainty of those things, wherein thou hast been instructed." (**Luke 1:1-4**)

"For we have not followed cunningly devised fables, when we made known unto you the power and coming of our Lord Jesus Christ, but were eyewitnesses of his majesty. For he received from God the Father honour and glory, when there came such a voice to him from the excellent glory, This is my beloved Son, in whom I am well pleased. And this voice which came from heaven we heard, when we were with him in the holy mount." (1 Peter 2:16-18)

Reasons for the Bible

The Bible exists for our blessing.

"Blessed is he that readeth, and they that hear the words of this prophecy, and keep those things which are written therein: for the time is at hand." (Revelation 1:3)

The Bible reveals the days/ages (yowm) in the creation of the universe. Modern science has no proof of the evolution of man and also the origin of all of the water on the planet earth. Note also man's definition of a day (i.e. 24 hours) is not necessarily God's definition and certainly not when creation is explained.

"Thus the heavens and the earth were finished, and all the host of them. And on the seventh day God ended his work which he had made; and he rested on the seventh day from all his work which he had made. And God blessed the seventh day, and sanctified it: because that in it he had rested from all his work which God created and made. These are the generations of the heavens and of the earth when they were created, in the day that the Lord God made the earth and the heavens, And every plant of the field before it was in the earth, and every herb of the field before it grew: for the Lord God had not caused it to rain upon the earth, and there was not a man to till the ground. But there went up a mist from the earth, and watered the whole face of the ground." (Genesis 2:1-6)

"For we have not followed cunningly devised fables, when we made known unto you the power and coming of our Lord Jesus Christ, but were eyewitnesses of his majesty. For he received from God the Father honour and glory, when there came such a voice to him from the excellent glory, This is my beloved Son, in whom I am well pleased. And this voice which came from heaven we heard, when we were with him in the holy mount." (2 Peter 3:8)

The Bible reveals our creation in the likeness of an eternal Godhead.

"In the beginning God created the heaven and the earth." (Genesis 1:1)

"And God said, Let us make man in our image, after our likeness: and let them have dominion over the fish of the sea, and over the fowl of the air, and over the cattle, and over all the earth, and over every creeping thing that creepeth upon the earth. So God created man in his own image, in the image of God created he him; male and female created he them. And God blessed them, and God said unto them, Be fruitful, and multiply, and replenish the earth, and subdue it: and have dominion over the fish of the sea, and over the fowl of the air, and over every living thing that moveth upon the earth." (Genesis 1:26-28)

"And the Lord God formed man of the dust of the ground, and breathed into his nostrils the breath of life; and man became a living soul." (Genesis 2:7)

The Bible reveals that there is only the true and living God; he is the Lord of hosts.

"See now that I, even I, am he, and there is no god with me: I kill, and I make alive; I wound, and I heal: neither is there any that can deliver out of my hand. For I lift up my hand to heaven, and say, I live for ever." (Deuteronomy 32:38&39)

"I am the Lord, and there is none else, there is no God beside me: I girded thee, though thou hast not known me: That they may know from the rising of the sun, and from the west, that there is none beside me. I am the Lord, and there is none else. I form the light, and create darkness: I make peace, and create evil: I the Lord do all these things." (Isaiah 45:5-7)

"Forasmuch as there is none like unto thee, O Lord; thou art great, and thy name is great in might. Who would not fear thee, O King of nations? for to thee doth it appertain: forasmuch as among all the wise men of the nations, and in all their kingdoms, there is none like unto thee. But they are altogether brutish and foolish: the stock is a doctrine of vanities. Silver spread into plates is brought from Tarshish, and gold from Uphaz, the work of the workman, and of the hands of the founder: blue and purple is their clothing: they are all the work of cunning men. But the Lord is the true God, he is the living God, and an everlasting king: at his wrath the earth shall tremble, and the nations shall not be able to abide his indignation. Thus shall ye say unto them, The gods that have not made the heavens and the earth, even they shall perish from the earth, and from under these heavens. He hath made the earth by his power, he hath established the world by his wisdom, and hath stretched out the heavens by his discretion. When he uttereth his voice, there is a multitude of waters in the heavens, and he causeth the vapours to ascend from the ends of the earth; he maketh lightnings with rain, and bringeth forth the wind out of his treasures. Every man is brutish in his knowledge: every founder is confounded by the graven image: for his molten image is falsehood, and there is no breath in them. They are vanity, and the work of errors: in the time of their visitation they shall perish. The portion of Jacob is not like them: for he is the former of all things; and Israel is the rod of his inheritance: The Lord of hosts is his name. (Jeremiah 10:6-16)

"And this is life eternal, that they might know thee the only true God, and Jesus Christ, whom thou hast sent." (John 17:3)

"Knowing, brethren beloved, your election of God. For our gospel came not unto you in word only, but also in power, and in the Holy Ghost, and in much assurance; as ye know what manner of men we were among you for your sake. And ye became followers of us, and of the Lord, having received the word in much affliction, with joy of the Holy Ghost: So that ye were ensamples to all that believe in Macedonia and Achaia. For from you sounded out the word of the Lord not only in Macedonia and Achaia, but also in every place your faith to God-ward is spread abroad; so that we need not to speak any thing. For they themselves shew of us what manner of entering in we had unto you, and how ye turned to God from idols to serve the living and true God; And to wait for his Son from heaven, whom he raised from the dead, even Jesus, which delivered us from the wrath to come." (1 Thessalonians 1:4-10)

The Bible reveals man's purpose in life.

"Even every one that is called by my name: for I have created him for my glory, I have formed him; yea, I have made him. Bring forth the blind people that have eyes, and the

deaf that have ears. Let all the nations be gathered together, and let the people be assembled: who among them can declare this, and shew us former things? let them bring forth their witnesses, that they may be justified: or let them hear, and say, It is truth. Ye are my witnesses, saith the Lord, and my servant whom I have chosen: that ye may know and believe me, and understand that I am he: before me there was no God formed, neither shall there be after me. I, even I, am the Lord; and beside me there is no savior." (Isaiah 43:7-11)

"If ye abide in me, and my words abide in you, ye shall ask what ye will, and it shall be done unto you. Herein is my Father glorified, that ye bear much fruit; so shall ye be my disciples." (John 15:7-8)

The Bible testifies of Christ.

"Search the scriptures; for in them ye think ye have eternal life: and they are they which testify of me." (John 5:39)

"And many other signs truly did Jesus in the presence of his disciples, which are not written in this book: But these are written, that ye might believe that Jesus is the Christ, the Son of God; and that believing ye might have life through his name." (John 20:30&31)

"This is the disciple which testifieth of these things, and wrote these things: and we know that his testimony is true. And there are also many other things which Jesus did, the which, if they should be written every one, I suppose that even the world itself could not contain the books that should be written. Amen." (John 21:24&25)

The Bible enables us to study and meditate on God's word.

"Study to shew thyself approved unto God, a workman that needeth not to be ashamed, rightly dividing the word of truth." (2 Timothy 2:15)

The Bible is profitable (Ophelimos – helpful, advantageous) to all mankind and especially provides those called to preach the word with all wisdom. It is of proof of all things pertaining to our faith in God Almighty.

"All scripture is given by inspiration of God, and is profitable for doctrine, for reproof, for correction, for instruction in righteousness: That the man of God may be perfect, throughly furnished unto all good works." (2 Timothy 3:16-17)

"Prove all things; hold fast that which is good." (1 Thessalonians 5:21)

"These were more noble than those in Thessalonica, in that they received the word with all readiness of mind, and searched the scriptures daily, whether those things were so." (Acts 17:11)

It reveals that the law from God to man was fulfilled through Christ.

"Think not that I am come to destroy the law, or the prophets: I am not come to destroy, but to fulfil." (Matthew 5:17)

No man but Christ is justified (Dikaloo – innocent, judged, righteous) under the law.

"For as many as are of the works of the law are under the curse: for it is written, Cursed is every one that continueth not in all things which are written in the book of the law to do them." (Galatians 3:10-13)

If we keep Christ's commandments, we abide (meno – continue, dwell, endure, stand) in faith.

"If ye keep my commandments, ye shall abide in my love; even as I have kept my Father's commandments, and abide in his love." (John 15:10)

The believer is to resist the devil and draw closer to God.

"Submit yourselves therefore to God. Resist the devil, and he will flee from you. Draw nigh to God, and he will draw nigh to you. Cleanse your hands, ye sinners; and purify your hearts, ye double minded." (James 4:7-8)

The Bible Reveals God's New Covenant as the Basis for the Commandments (Spiritual) Over the Law (Carnal)

The commandments are to be kept in our hearts (internalized).

"Behold, the days come, saith the Lord, that I will make a new covenant with the house of Israel, and with the house of Judah: But this shall be the covenant that I will make with the house of Israel; After those days, saith the Lord, I will put my law in their inward parts, and write it in their hearts; and will be their God, and they shall be my people." (Jeremiah 31:31, 33)

"A new heart also will I give you, and a new spirit will I put within you: and I will take away the stony heart out of your flesh, and I will give you an heart of flesh.

And I will put my spirit within you, and cause you to walk in my statutes, and ye shall keep my judgments, and do them." (Ezekiel 36:26-27)

The Bible Reveals God's Law of the Old Testament (Law of Moses)

The Ten Commandments were given to Moses.

"And God spake all these words, saying, I am the Lord thy God, which have brought thee out of the land of Egypt, out of the house of bondage. Thou shalt have no other gods before me. Thou shalt not make unto thee any graven image, or any likeness of any thing that is in heaven above, or that is in the earth beneath, or that is in the water under the earth. Thou shalt not bow down thyself to them, nor serve them: for I the Lord thy God am a jealous God, visiting the iniquity of the fathers upon the children unto the third and fourth generation of them that hate me; And shewing mercy unto thousands of them that love me, and keep my commandments. Thou shalt not take the name of the Lord thy God in vain; for the Lord will not hold him guiltless that taketh his name in vain. Remember the sabbath day, to keep it holy. Six days shalt thou labor, and do all thy work: But the seventh day is the sabbath of the Lord thy God: in it thou shalt not do any work, thou, nor thy son, nor thy daughter, thy manservant, nor thy maidservant, nor thy cattle, nor thy stranger that is within thy gates: For in six days the Lord made heaven and earth, the sea, and all that

in them is, and rested the seventh day: wherefore the Lord blessed the sabbath day, and hallowed it. Honor thy father and thy mother: that thy days may be long upon the land which the Lord thy God giveth thee. Thou shalt not kill. Thou shalt not commit adultery. Thou shalt not steal. Thou shalt not bear false witness against thy neighbor. Thou shalt not covet thy neighbor's house, thou shalt not covet thy neighbor's wife, nor his manservant, nor his maidservant, nor his ox, nor his ass, nor any thing that is thy neighbor's." (Exodus 20:1-17)

"And Moses called all Israel, and said unto them, Hear, O Israel, the statutes and judgments which I speak in your ears this day, that ye may learn them, and keep, and do them. The Lord our God made a covenant with us in Horeb. The Lord made not this covenant with our fathers, but with us, even us, who are all of us here alive this day. The Lord talked with you face to face in the mount out of the midst of the fire, (I stood between the Lord and you at that time, to shew you the word of the Lord: for ye were afraid by reason of the fire, and went not up into the mount;) saying, I am the Lord thy God, which brought thee out of the land of Egypt, from the house of bondage. Thou shalt have none other gods before me. Thou shalt not make thee any graven image, or any likeness of any thing that is in heaven above, or that is in the earth beneath, or that is in the waters beneath the earth: Thou shalt not bow down thyself unto them, nor serve them: for I the Lord thy God am a jealous God, visiting the iniquity of the fathers upon the children unto the third and fourth generation of them that hate me, And shewing mercy unto thousands of them that love me and keep my commandments. Thou shalt not take the name of the Lord thy God in vain: for the Lord will not hold him guiltless that taketh his name in vain. Keep the sabbath day to sanctify it, as the Lord thy God hath commanded thee. Six days thou shalt labor, and do all thy work: But the seventh day is the sabbath of the Lord thy God: in it thou shalt not do any work, thou, nor thy son, nor thy daughter, nor thy manservant, nor thy maidservant, nor thine ox, nor thine ass, nor any of thy cattle, nor thy stranger that is within thy gates; that thy manservant and thy maidservant may rest as well as thou. And remember that thou wast a servant in the land of Egypt, and that the Lord thy God brought thee out thence through a mighty hand and by a stretched out arm: therefore the Lord thy God commanded thee to keep the sabbath day. Honor thy father and thy mother, as the Lord thy God hath commanded thee; that thy days may be prolonged, and that it may go well with thee, in the land which the Lord thy God giveth thee. Thou shalt not kill. Neither shalt thou commit adultery. Neither shalt thou steal. Neither shalt thou bear false witness against thy neighbor. Neither shalt thou desire thy neighbor's wife, neither shalt thou covet thy neighbor's house, his field, or his manservant, or his maidservant, his ox, or his ass, or any thing that is thy neighbor's." (Deuteronomy 5:1-21)

Note that the complete Law (Law of Moses) to God's chosen people exists as the books of Genesis, Exodus, Leviticus, Numbers, and Deuteronomy.

The Bible Reveals the Difference between the Law of Moses and the Commandments of Christ

The law was our schoolmaster (Paidagogos – tutor, instructor) to bring us to faith in Christ.

"Wherefore the law was our schoolmaster to bring us unto Christ, that we might be justified by faith." (Galatians 3:24)

"Therefore we conclude that a man is justified by faith without the deeds of the law." (Romans 3:28)

Note the Christian commandments are referenced as follows:

Mark 10:17-19; Matthew Chapters 5, 6, and 7 also Luke 6:20-49; Romans 13:1-15:4; Ephesians 4:24-32; 1 Thessalonians 4:1-12 and 1 Thessalonians 5:12-23.

The Bible Teaches of Our Reconciliation to Our Creator

Reconciliation is only through Jesus Christ; he is our atonement (amends for injury or wrong, expiation, propitiation)

"For it pleased the Father that in him should all fulness dwell; And, having made peace through the blood of his cross, by him to reconcile all things unto himself; by him, I say, whether they be things in earth, or things in heaven." (Colossians 1:19-20)

The Bible reveals how it is that the promises made to Abraham, beginning with the Old Covenant, are now promised to all believers.

"And it came to pass, that, when the sun went down, and it was dark, behold a smoking furnace, and a burning lamp that passed between those pieces. In the same day the Lord made a covenant with Abram, saying, Unto thy seed have I given this land, from the river of Egypt unto the great river, the river Euphrates: The Kenites, and the Kenizzites, and the Kadmonites, And the Hittites, and the Perizzites, and the Rephaims, And the Amorites, and the Canaanites, and the Girgashites, and the Jebusites." (Genesis 15:17-21) **Read the entire 15th Chapter.**

"Know ye therefore that they which are of faith, the same are the children of Abraham. And the scripture, foreseeing that God would justify the heathen through faith, preached before the gospel unto Abraham, saying, In thee shall all nations be blessed. So then they which be of faith are blessed with faithful Abraham." (Galatians 3:7-9)

"Behold my servant, whom I have chosen; my beloved, in whom my soul is well pleased: I will put my spirit upon him, and he shall shew judgment to the Gentiles. He shall not strive, nor cry; neither shall any man hear his voice in the streets. A bruised reed shall he not break, and smoking flax shall he not quench, till he send forth judgment unto victory. And in his name shall the Gentiles trust." (Matthew 12:18-21)

"Now I say that Jesus Christ was a minister of the circumcision for the truth of God, to confirm the promises made unto the fathers: And that the Gentiles might glorify God for his mercy; as it is written, For this cause I will confess to thee among the Gentiles, and sing unto thy name. And again he saith, Rejoice, ye Gentiles, with his people. And again, Praise the Lord, all ye Gentiles; and laud him, all ye people. And again, Esaias saith, There shall be a root of Jesse, and he that shall rise to reign over the Gentiles; in him shall the Gentiles trust. Now the God of hope fill you with all joy and peace in believing, that ye may abound in hope, through the power of the Holy Ghost." (Romans 15:8-13)

Those that have been born again have put on the likeness of Christ spiritually.

"For as many of you as have been baptized into Christ have put on Christ. There is neither Jew nor Greek, there is neither bond nor free, there is neither male nor female: for ye are all one in Christ Jesus." (Galatians 3:27-28)

The Bible reveals the believer's unity with the Son and the Father. This unity is enabled only by our indwelling by the Holy Ghost.

"Neither pray I for these alone, but for them also which shall believe on me through their word; That they all may be one; as thou, Father, art in me, and I in thee, that they also may be one in us: that the world may believe that thou hast sent me." (John 17:20-21)

"There is one body, and one Spirit, even as ye are called in one hope of your calling; One Lord, one faith, one baptism, One God and Father of all, who is above all, and through all, and in you all. But unto every one of us is given grace according to the measure of the gift of Christ." (Ephesians 4:4-7)

"Know ye not that ye are the temple of God, and that the Spirit of God dwelleth in you? If any man defile the temple of God, him shall God destroy; for the temple of God is holy, which temple ye are." (1 Corinthians 3:16 & 17)

The Bible Teaches Us to Baptize and Observe the Lord's Supper as Ordinances in the Church

Concerning baptism:

"And Jesus came and spake unto them, saying, All power is given unto me in heaven and in earth. Go ye therefore, and teach all nations, baptizing them in the name of the Father, and of the Son, and of the Holy Ghost: Teaching them to observe all things whatsoever I have commanded you: and, lo, I am with you alway, even unto the end of the world." (Matthew 28:18-20)

Concerning the Lord's Supper:

"For as often as ye eat this bread, and drink this cup, ye do shew the Lord's death till he come. Wherefore whosoever shall eat this bread, and drink this cup of the Lord, unworthily, shall be guilty of the body and blood of the Lord. But let a man examine himself, and so let him eat of that bread, and drink of that cup. For he that eateth and drinketh unworthily, eateth and drinketh damnation to himself, not discerning the Lord's body. For this cause many are weak and sickly among you, and many sleep. For if we would judge ourselves, we should not be judged. But when we are judged, we are chastened of the Lord, that we should not be condemned with the world." (1 Corinthians 11:23-32)

Appendix 1 contains a brief history compiled by me of the origin of the Bible. Appendix 2 contains the Epistle Dedicatory of the King James Version of the Bible. The King James Bible exists as the basis of all modern Biblical word study visa vie the Strong's Exhaustive Concordance of the King James Bible, author James Strong, S.T.D., LL.D. As the author of "Sound Doctrine for Today's Christians", I have quoted exclusively the King James Version of the Bible. There are some other very respectable interpretations of the Bible such as the Revised King James Version; however, there are numerous amplified Bibles that are erroneous particularly in the license taken in their interpretation.

2

THE TRINITY/GODHEAD

There is only one true God right? What is meant by a Trinity which is not a word used in my bible?

CHRISTIANITY ACCEPTS THE Godhead (Trinity) as basic in defining God. The God of Abraham, Isaac and Jacob is revealed in the New Testament as the Godhead/Trinity. Any doctrine stating otherwise is not Christianity.

> *"For there are three that bear record in heaven, the Father, the Word, and the Holy Ghost: and these three are one." (1 John 5:7)*

There is reference made in the Bible within the story of creation that gives a clue as to the nature of God when it is stated let "us" make man.

> *"And God said, Let us make man in our image, after our likeness: and let them have dominion over the fish of the sea, and over the fowl of the air, and over the cattle, and over all the earth, and over every creeping thing that creepeth upon the earth. So God created man in his own image, in the image of God created he him; male and female created he them. And God blessed them, and God said unto them, Be fruitful, and multiply, and replenish the earth, and subdue it: and have dominion over the fish of the sea, and over the fowl of the air, and over every living thing that moveth upon the earth. And God said, Behold, I have given you every herb bearing seed, which is upon the face of all the earth, and every tree, in the which is the fruit of a tree yielding seed; to you it shall be for meat. And to every beast of the earth, and to every fowl of the air, and to every thing that creepeth upon the earth, wherein there is life, I have given every green herb for meat: and it was so. And God saw every thing that he had made, and, behold, it was very good. And the evening and the morning were the sixth day." (Genesis 1:26-31)*

> *"Then Paul stood in the midst of Mars' hill, and said, Ye men of Athens, I perceive that in all things ye are too superstitious. For as I passed by, and beheld your devotions, I found an altar with this inscription, TO THE UNKNOWN GOD. Whom therefore ye ignorantly worship, him declare I unto you. God that made the world and all things therein, seeing that he is Lord of heaven and earth, dwelleth not in temples made with hands; Neither is worshipped with men's hands, as though he needed any thing, seeing he giveth to all life, and breath, and all things; And hath made of one blood all nations of men for to dwell on all the face of the earth, and hath determined the times before appointed, and the bounds*

of their habitation; That they should seek the Lord, if haply they might feel after him, and find him, though he be not far from every one of us: For in him we live, and move, and have our being; as certain also of your own poets have said, For we are also his offspring. Forasmuch then as we are the offspring of God, we ought not to think that the Godhead is like unto gold, or silver, or stone, graven by art and man's device." (**Acts 17:22-29**)

"And this I say, lest any man should beguile you with enticing words. For though I be absent in the flesh, yet am I with you in the spirit, joying and beholding your order, and the sted-fastness of your faith in Christ. As ye have therefore received Christ Jesus the Lord, so walk ye in him: Rooted and built up in him, and stablished in the faith, as ye have been taught, abounding therein with thanksgiving. Beware lest any man spoil you through philosophy and vain deceit, after the tradition of men, after the rudiments of the world, and not after Christ. For in him dwelleth all the fulness of the Godhead bodily." (**Colossians 2:4-9**)

It is a fact that the scriptures reveal that there is a Heavenly Father who has a desire to have all men to live eternally in peace with him. We were in fact created to glorify our heavenly Father.

"For God so loved the world, that he gave his only begotten Son, that whosoever believeth in him should not perish, but have everlasting life." (**John 3:16**)

"Giving thanks unto the Father, which hath made us meet to be partakers of the inheri-tance of the saints in light: Who hath delivered us from the power of darkness, and hath translated us into the kingdom of his dear Son: In whom we have redemption through his blood, even the forgiveness of sins: Who is the image of the invisible God, the firstborn of ev-ery creature: For by him were all things created, that are in heaven, and that are in earth, visible and invisible, whether they be thrones, or dominions, or principalities, or powers: all things were created by him, and for him: And he is before all things, and by him all things consist. And he is the head of the body, the church: who is the beginning, the first-born from the dead; that in all things he might have the preeminence. For it pleased the Father that in him should all fulness dwell; And, having made peace through the blood of his cross, by him to reconcile all things unto himself; by him, I say, whether they be things in earth, or things in heaven. And you, that were sometime alienated and enemies in your mind by wicked works, yet now hath he reconciled, In the body of his flesh through death, to present you holy and unblameable and unreproveable in his sight: If ye continue in the faith grounded and settled, and be not moved away from the hope of the gospel, which ye have heard, and which was preached to every creature which is under heaven; whereof I Paul am made a minister; Who now rejoice in my sufferings for you, and fill up that which is behind of the afflictions of Christ in my flesh for his body's sake, which is the church:" (**Colossians 1:12-24**)

"Even every one that is called by my name: for I have created him for my glory, I have formed him; yea, I have made him." (**Isaiah 43:7**)

"Know ye therefore that they which are of faith, the same are the children of Abraham. And the scripture, foreseeing that God would justify the heathen through faith, preached before the gospel unto Abraham, saying, In thee shall all nations be blessed. So then they which be of faith are blessed with faithful Abraham." (**Galatians 3:7-9**)

"Herein is my Father glorified, that ye bear much fruit; so shall ye be my disciples. As the Father hath loved me, so have I loved you: continue ye in my love. If ye keep my commandments, ye shall abide in my love; even as I have kept my Father's commandments, and abide in his love. These things have I spoken unto you, that my joy might remain in you, and that your joy might be full." (John 15:8-11)

It is the Father that has established since creation, a plan for mankind's redemption from the penalty of sin as declared by him.

"And the Lord God said unto the woman, What is this that thou hast done? And the woman said, The serpent beguiled me, and I did eat. And the Lord God said unto the serpent, Because thou hast done this, thou art cursed above all cattle, and above every beast of the field; upon thy belly shalt thou go, and dust shalt thou eat all the days of thy life: And I will put enmity between thee and the woman, and between thy seed and her seed; it shall bruise thy head, and thou shalt bruise his heel." (Genesis 3:13-15)

"But God be thanked, that ye were the servants of sin, but ye have obeyed from the heart that form of doctrine which was delivered you. Being then made free from sin, ye became the servants of righteousness. I speak after the manner of men because of the infirmity of your flesh: for as ye have yielded your members servants to uncleanness and to iniquity unto iniquity; even so now yield your members servants to righteousness unto holiness. For when ye were the servants of sin, ye were free from righteousness. What fruit had ye then in those things whereof ye are now ashamed? for the end of those things is death. But now being made free from sin, and become servants to God, ye have your fruit unto holiness, and the end everlasting life. For the wages of sin is death; but the gift of God is eternal life through Jesus Christ our Lord." (Romans 6:17-23)

"For when we were yet without strength, in due time Christ died for the ungodly. For scarcely for a righteous man will one die: yet peradventure for a good man some would even dare to die. But God commendeth his love toward us, in that, while we were yet sinners, Christ died for us. Much more then, being now justified by his blood, we shall be saved from wrath through him. For if, when we were enemies, we were reconciled to God by the death of his Son, much more, being reconciled, we shall be saved by his life. And not only so, but we also joy in God through our Lord Jesus Christ, by whom we have now received the atonement. Wherefore, as by one man sin entered into the world, and death by sin; and so death passed upon all men, for that all have sinned: (For until the law sin was in the world: but sin is not imputed when there is no law. Nevertheless death reigned from Adam to Moses, even over them that had not sinned after the similitude of Adam's transgression, who is the figure of him that was to come. But not as the offence, so also is the free gift. For if through the offence of one many be dead, much more the grace of God, and the gift by grace, which is by one man, Jesus Christ, hath abounded unto many. And not as it was by one that sinned, so is the gift: for the judgment was by one to condemnation, but the free gift is of many offences unto justification. For if by one man's offence death reigned by one; much more they which receive abundance of grace and of the gift of righteousness shall reign in life by one, Jesus Christ.) Therefore as by the offence of one judgment came upon all men to condemnation; even so by the righteousness of one the free gift came upon all men unto justification of life. For as by one man's disobedience many were made sinners, so by the obedience of one shall many be made righteous. Moreover the law entered, that the offence might abound. But where sin abounded, grace did much more abound:

That as sin hath reigned unto death, even so might grace reign through righteousness unto eternal life by Jesus Christ our Lord." (Romans 5:6-21)

Jesus is manifested [phaneroo: appeared from, made forth from, render apparent, made external from] not a creation out of God the Father. He has testified of the Father as the True and Living God and spoken only what the Father has declared.

"In the beginning was the Word, and the Word was with God, and the Word was God. The same was in the beginning with God. All things were made by him; and without him was not any thing made that was made. In him was life; and the life was the light of men. And the light shineth in darkness; and the darkness comprehended it not. There was a man sent from God, whose name was John. The same came for a witness, to bear witness of the Light, that all men through him might believe. He was not that Light, but was sent to bear witness of that Light. That was the true Light, which lighteth every man that cometh into the world. He was in the world, and the world was made by him, and the world knew him not. He came unto his own, and his own received him not. But as many as received him, to them gave he power to become the sons of God, even to them that believe on his name: Which were born, not of blood, nor of the will of the flesh, nor of the will of man, but of God. And the Word was made flesh, and dwelt among us, (and we beheld his glory, the glory as of the only begotten of the Father,) full of grace and truth. John bare witness of him, and cried, saying, This was he of whom I spake, He that cometh after me is preferred before me: for he was before me. And of his fulness have all we received, and grace for grace. For the law was given by Moses, but grace and truth came by Jesus Christ. No man hath seen God at any time; the only begotten Son, which is in the bosom of the Father, he hath declared him." (John 1:1-18)

"That which was from the beginning, which we have heard, which we have seen with our eyes, which we have looked upon, and our hands have handled, of the Word of life; (For the life was manifested, and we have seen it, and bear witness, and shew unto you that eternal life, which was with the Father, and was manifested unto us;) That which we have seen and heard declare we unto you, that ye also may have fellowship with us: and truly our fellowship is with the Father, and with his Son Jesus Christ." (1 John 1:1-3)

"Behold, what manner of love the Father hath bestowed upon us, that we should be called the sons of God: therefore the world knoweth us not, because it knew him not. Beloved, now are we the sons of God, and it doth not yet appear what we shall be: but we know that, when he shall appear, we shall be like him; for we shall see him as he is. And every man that hath this hope in him purifieth himself, even as he is pure. Whosoever committeth sin transgresseth also the law: for sin is the transgression of the law. And ye know that he was manifested to take away our sins; and in him is no sin. Whosoever abideth in him sinneth not: whosoever sinneth hath not seen him, neither known him. Little children, let no man deceive you: he that doeth righteousness is righteous, even as he is righteous. He that committeth sin is of the devil; for the devil sinneth from the beginning. For this purpose the Son of God was manifested, that he might destroy the works of the devil." (1 John 3:1-8)

"And Jesus walked in the temple in Solomon's porch. Then came the Jews round about him, and said unto him, How long dost thou make us to doubt? If thou be the Christ, tell us plainly. Jesus answered them, I told you, and ye believed not: the works that I do in my Father's name, they bear witness of me. But ye believe not, because ye are not of my sheep,

13

as I said unto you. My sheep hear my voice, and I know them, and they follow me: And I give unto them eternal life; and they shall never perish, neither shall any man pluck them out of my hand. My Father, which gave them me, is greater than all; and no man is able to pluck them out of my Father's hand. I and my Father are one. Then the Jews took up stones again to stone him." (John 10:23-31)

"And this is life eternal, that they might know thee the only true God, and Jesus Christ, whom thou hast sent. I have glorified thee on the earth: I have finished the work which thou gavest me to do. And now, O Father, glorify thou me with thine own self with the glory which I had with thee before the world was. I have manifested thy name unto the men which thou gavest me out of the world: thine they were, and thou gavest them me; and they have kept thy word. Now they have known that all things whatsoever thou hast given me are of thee. For I have given unto them the words which thou gavest me; and they have received them, and have known surely that I came out from thee, and they have believed that thou didst send me. I pray for them: I pray not for the world, but for them which thou hast given me; for they are thine. And all mine are thine, and thine are mine; and I am glorified in them. And now I am no more in the world, but these are in the world, and I come to thee. Holy Father, keep through thine own name those whom thou hast given me, that they may be one, as we are. While I was with them in the world, I kept them in thy name: those that thou gavest me I have kept, and none of them is lost, but the son of perdition; that the scripture might be fulfilled." (John 17:3-12)

Jesus is revealed as the comfort (nacham: console, pity, ease, avenger) of Israel and the Spirit of God as the third person of the Trinity of the God in the Old Testament scriptures. Jesus confirms the advent of the Holy Ghost upon his ascension back to heaven.

"Comfort ye, comfort ye my people, saith your God. Speak ye comfortably to Jerusalem, and cry unto her, that her warfare is accomplished, that her iniquity is pardoned: for she hath received of the Lord's hand double for all her sins. The voice of him that crieth in the wilderness, Prepare ye the way of the Lord, make straight in the desert a highway for our God. Every valley shall be exalted, and every mountain and hill shall be made low: and the crooked shall be made straight, and the rough places plain: And the glory of the Lord shall be revealed, and all flesh shall see it together: for the mouth of the Lord hath spoken it. The voice said, Cry. And he said, What shall I cry? All flesh is grass, and all the goodliness thereof is as the flower of the field: The grass withereth, the flower fadeth: because the spirit of the Lord bloweth upon it: surely the people is grass. The grass withereth, the flower fadeth: but the word of our God shall stand for ever. O Zion, that bringest good tidings, get thee up into the high mountain; O Jerusalem, that bringest good tidings, lift up thy voice with strength; lift it up, be not afraid; say unto the cities of Judah, Behold your God! Behold, the Lord God will come with strong hand, and his arm shall rule for him: behold, his reward is with him, and his work before him. He shall feed his flock like a shepherd: he shall gather the lambs with his arm, and carry them in his bosom, and shall gently lead those that are with young. Who hath measured the waters in the hollow of his hand, and meted out heaven with the span, and comprehended the dust of the earth in a measure, and weighed the mountains in scales, and the hills in a balance? Who hath directed the Spirit of the Lord, or being his counseller hath taught him? With whom took he counsel, and who instructed him, and taught him in the path of judgment, and taught him knowledge, and shewed to him the way of understanding? Behold, the nations are as a drop of a

bucket, and are counted as the small dust of the balance: behold, he taketh up the isles as a very little thing. And Lebanon is not sufficient to burn, nor the beasts thereof sufficient for a burnt offering. All nations before him are as nothing; and they are counted to him less than nothing, and vanity. To whom then will ye liken God? or what likeness will ye compare unto him? The workman melteth a graven image, and the goldsmith spreadeth it over with gold, and casteth silver chains. He that is so impoverished that he hath no oblation chooseth a tree that will not rot; he seeketh unto him a cunning workman to prepare a graven image, that shall not be moved. Have ye not known? have ye not heard? hath it not been told you from the beginning? have ye not understood from the foundations of the earth? It is he that sitteth upon the circle of the earth, and the inhabitants thereof are as grasshoppers; that stretcheth out the heavens as a curtain, and spreadeth them out as a tent to dwell in: That bringeth the princes to nothing; he maketh the judges of the earth as vanity. Yea, they shall not be planted; yea, they shall not be sown: yea, their stock shall not take root in the earth: and he shall also blow upon them, and they shall wither, and the whirlwind shall take them away as stubble. To whom then will ye liken me, or shall I be equal? saith the Holy One." **(Isaiah 40:1-25)**

"If ye love me, keep my commandments. And I will pray the Father, and he shall give you another Comforter, that he may abide with you for ever; Even the Spirit of truth; whom the world cannot receive, because it seeth him not, neither knoweth him: but ye know him; for he dwelleth with you, and shall be in you. I will not leave you comfortless: I will come to you. Yet a little while, and the world seeth me no more; but ye see me: because I live, ye shall live also. At that day ye shall know that I am in my Father, and ye in me, and I in you. He that hath my commandments, and keepeth them, he it is that loveth me: and he that loveth me shall be loved of my Father, and I will love him, and will manifest myself to him. Judas saith unto him, not Iscariot, Lord, how is it that thou wilt manifest thyself unto us, and not unto the world? Jesus answered and said unto him, If a man love me, he will keep my words: and my Father will love him, and we will come unto him, and make our abode with him. He that loveth me not keepeth not my sayings: and the word which ye hear is not mine, but the Father's which sent me. These things have I spoken unto you, being yet present with you. But the Comforter, which is the Holy Ghost, whom the Father will send in my name, he shall teach you all things, and bring all things to your remembrance, whatsoever I have said unto you." **(John 14:15-26)**

The third person of the Trinity is God's spirit physically poured out upon flesh; he is the Holy Spirit or the Holy Ghost as one prefers. The Holy Ghost testifies and glorifies Christ in all things; in doing so, we are led by the Holy Ghost in all truth whereas Christ is the Logos (the Divine Expression concerning communication, doctrine, reasoning).

"Howbeit when he, the Spirit of truth, is come, he will guide you into all truth: for he shall not speak of himself; but whatsoever he shall hear, that shall he speak: and he will shew you things to come. He shall glorify me: for he shall receive of mine, and shall shew it unto you. All things that the Father hath are mine: therefore said I, that he shall take of mine, and shall shew it unto you. A little while, and ye shall not see me: and again, a little while, and ye shall see me, because I go to the Father." **(John 16:13-15)**

The Holy Ghost is rejected by the world at large, but, it is promised that he will never leave alone the believer. He is able to indwell the believer, as now understood since the day

of Pentecost, whereas, he had been active in only resting upon certain persons in times past.

> *"If ye love me, keep my commandments. And I will pray the Father, and he shall give you another Comforter, that he may abide with you for ever; Even the Spirit of truth; whom the world cannot receive, because it seeth him not, neither knoweth him: but ye know him; for he dwelleth with you, and shall be in you."* (John 14:15-17)

> *"And when the day of Pentecost was fully come, they were all with one accord in one place. And suddenly there came a sound from heaven as of a rushing mighty wind, and it filled all the house where they were sitting. And there appeared unto them cloven tongues like as of fire, and it sat upon each of them. And they were all filled with the Holy Ghost, and began to speak with other tongues, as the Spirit gave them utterance. And there were dwelling at Jerusalem Jews, devout men, out of every nation under heaven. Now when this was noised abroad, the multitude came together, and were confounded, because that every man heard them speak in his own language. And they were all amazed and marvelled, saying one to another, Behold, are not all these which speak Galilaeans? And how hear we every man in our own tongue, wherein we were born? Parthians, and Medes, and Elamites, and the dwellers in Mesopotamia, and in Judaea, and Cappadocia, in Pontus, and Asia, Phrygia, and Pamphylia, in Egypt, and in the parts of Libya about Cyrene, and strangers of Rome, Jews and proselytes, Cretes and Arabians, we do hear them speak in our tongues the wonderful works of God. And they were all amazed, and were in doubt, saying one to another, What meaneth this? Others mocking said, These men are full of new wine. But Peter, standing up with the eleven, lifted up his voice, and said unto them, Ye men of Judaea, and all ye that dwell at Jerusalem, be this known unto you, and hearken to my words: For these are not drunken, as ye suppose, seeing it is but the third hour of the day. But this is that which was spoken by the prophet Joel; And it shall come to pass in the last days, saith God,I will pour out of my Spirit upon all flesh: and your sons and your daughters shall prophesy, and your young men shall see visions, and your old men shall dream dreams: And on my servants and on my handmaidens I will pour out in those days of my Spirit; and they shall prophesy: And I will shew wonders in heaven above, and signs in the earth beneath; blood, and fire, and vapour of smoke: The sun shall be turned into darkness, and the moon into blood, before that great and notable day of the Lord come: And it shall come to pass, that whosoever shall call on the name of the Lord shall be saved."* (Acts 2:1-21)

The Holy Ghost reproves (elegcho: conflicts, admonishes, convicts, convinces, points out, and rebukes) the believer of sin and he is the interpreter of the scriptures. The Holy Ghost is not to be blasphemed (blasphemeo: defamed, railed on, reviled, speak evil of]. Believers begin moving towards that blasphemy by a grieving (cause sorrow) and then the possible eventual quenching (extinguishing) the Holy Ghost from their lives.

> *"Nevertheless I tell you the truth; It is expedient for you that I go away: for if I go not away, the Comforter will not come unto you; but if I depart, I will send him unto you. And when he is come, he will reprove the world of sin, and of righteousness, and of judgment: Of sin, because they believe not on me; Of righteousness, because I go to my Father, and ye see me no more; Of judgment, because the prince of this world is judged."* (John 16:7-11)

"Knowing this first, that no prophecy of the scripture is of any private interpretation. For the prophecy came not in old time by the will of man: but holy men of God spake as they were moved by the Holy Ghost." (2 Peter 1:20&21)

"Verily I say unto you, All sins shall be forgiven unto the sons of men, and blasphemies wherewith soever they shall blaspheme: But he that shall blaspheme against the Holy Ghost hath never forgiveness, but is in danger of eternal damnation." (Mark 3:28&29)

"And grieve not the holy Spirit of God, whereby ye are sealed unto the day of redemption." (Ephesians 4:29-30)

"Quench not the Spirit." (1 Thessalonians 5:19)

"Know ye not that they which run in a race run all, but one receiveth the prize? So run, that ye may obtain. And every man that striveth for the mastery is temperate in all things. Now they do it to obtain a corruptible crown; but we an incorruptible. I therefore so run, not as uncertainly; so fight I, not as one that beateth the air: But I keep under my body, and bring it into subjection: lest that by any means, when I have preached to others, I myself should be a castaway." (1 Corinthians 9:24-27)

Now there are wonderful spiritual fruits (karpos: plucked fruit of results, outcome) for the believer that are manifested out of the indwelling activity of the Holy Ghost. And, there is strengthening power in the Holy Ghost.

"But the fruit of the Spirit is love, joy, peace, longsuffering, gentleness, goodness, faith, Meekness, temperance: against such there is no law." (Galatians 5:22&23)

"Now the God of hope fill you with all joy and peace in believing, that ye may abound in hope, through the power of the Holy Ghost." (Romans 15:13)

"For this cause I bow my knees unto the Father of our Lord Jesus Christ, Of whom the whole family in heaven and earth is named, That he would grant you, according to the riches of his glory, to be strengthened with might by his Spirit in the inner man; That Christ may dwell in your hearts by faith; that ye, being rooted and grounded in love, May be able to comprehend with all saints what is the breadth, and length, and depth, and height; And to know the love of Christ, which passeth knowledge, that ye might be filled with all the fulness of God." (Ephesians 3:14-19)

The danger of damnation in blaspheming against the Holy Ghost is because he is the sealer of the believer until judgment having first revealed the Heavenly Father through Jesus Christ. It is impossible once the Holy Ghost has been extinguished in the believer's life to the extent of one be judged then reprobate, for that person to crucify to themselves [be born again] the Son of God again, because it belies the one time death of Jesus on the cross as sufficient.

"Blessed be the God and Father of our Lord Jesus Christ, who hath blessed us with all spiritual blessings in heavenly places in Christ: According as he hath chosen us in him before the foundation of the world, that we should be holy and without blame before him in love: Having predestinated us unto the adoption of children by Jesus Christ to himself, according to the good pleasure of his will, To the praise of the glory of his grace, wherein he hath made us accepted in the beloved. In whom we have redemption through his blood, the

forgiveness of sins, according to the riches of his grace; Wherein he hath abounded toward us in all wisdom and prudence; Having made known unto us the mystery of his will, according to his good pleasure which he hath purposed in himself: That in the dispensation of the fulness of times he might gather together in one all things in Christ, both which are in heaven, and which are on earth; even in him: In whom also we have obtained an inheritance, being predestinated according to the purpose of him who worketh all things after the counsel of his own will: That we should be to the praise of his glory, who first trusted in Christ. In whom ye also trusted, after that ye heard the word of truth, the gospel of your salvation: in whom also after that ye believed, ye were sealed with that holy Spirit of promise," (Ephesians 1:3-13)

"Even so we, when we were children, were in bondage under the elements of the world: But when the fulness of the time was come, God sent forth his Son, made of a woman, made under the law, To redeem them that were under the law, that we might receive the adoption of sons. And because ye are sons, God hath sent forth the Spirit of his Son into your hearts, crying, Abba, Father. Wherefore thou art no more a servant, but a son; and if a son, then an heir of God through Christ. Howbeit then, when ye knew not God, ye did service unto them which by nature are no gods. But now, after that ye have known God, or rather are known of God, how turn ye again to the weak and beggarly elements, whereunto ye desire again to be in bondage? (Galatians 4:3-9)

"For it is impossible for those who were once enlightened, and have tasted of the heavenly gift, and were made partakers of the Holy Ghost, And have tasted the good word of God, and the powers of the world to come, If they shall fall away, to renew them again unto repentance; seeing they crucify to themselves the Son of God afresh, and put him to an open shame." (Hebrews 6:4-6)

The Holy Ghost is given to those that are obedient to Christ. If you love Christ, then keep his commandments beginning with "believe and be baptized". Be baptized as Christ commanded i.e. emerged and in the name of the Trinity upon being taught as Christ commanded.

"Then Peter and the other apostles answered and said, We ought to obey God rather than men. The God of our fathers raised up Jesus, whom ye slew and hanged on a tree. Him hath God exalted with his right hand to be a Prince and a Saviour, for to give repentance to Israel, and forgiveness of sins. And we are his witnesses of these things; and so is also the Holy Ghost, whom God hath given to them that obey him." (Acts 5:29-32)

"He that believeth and is baptized shall be saved; but he that believeth not shall be damned." (Mark 16:16)

"And Jesus came and spake unto them, saying, All power is given unto me in heaven and in earth. Go ye therefore, and teach all nations, baptizing them in the name of the Father, and of the Son, and of the Holy Ghost: Teaching them to observe all things whatsoever I have commanded you: and, lo, I am with you alway, even unto the end of the world. Amen." (Matthew 28:18-20)

Our obedience in our Christian walk allows the Holy Ghost to strengthen our inner being because, after all, we are yet flesh trying to walk spiritually. Obedience is the evidence of being filled with the Holy Ghost not speaking in tongues which on the day

of Pentecost was the miracle of speaking in foreign languages. God undoubtedly used speaking in tongues to quench skeptics of regeneration during the very early days of the church. Believers in the New Testament church evidenced their regeneration by speaking in tongues before and after baptism. There remains no need for the evidencing of the Holy Ghost in the believer by the speaking in tongues; obedience suffices. We now understand speaking in tongues to be the least of the spiritual gifts. It is to be used with discretion and with interpretation.

> *"For this cause I bow my knees unto the Father of our Lord Jesus Christ, Of whom the whole family in heaven and earth is named, That he would grant you, according to the riches of his glory, to be strengthened with might by his Spirit in the inner man; That Christ may dwell in your hearts by faith; that ye, being rooted and grounded in love, May be able to comprehend with all saints what is the breadth, and length, and depth, and height; And to know the love of Christ, which passeth knowledge, that ye might be filled with all the fulness of God."* (Ephesians 3:14-19)

> *"This I say then, Walk in the Spirit, and ye shall not fulfill the lust of the flesh. For the flesh lusteth against the Spirit, and the Spirit against the flesh: and these are contrary the one to the other: so that ye cannot do the things that ye would. But if ye be led of the Spirit, ye are not under the law."* (Galatians 5:16-18)

> *"And they were all filled with the Holy Ghost, and began to speak with other tongues, as the Spirit gave them utterance. And there were dwelling at Jerusalem Jews, devout men, out of every nation under heaven. Now when this was noised abroad, the multitude came together, and were confounded, because that every man heard them speak in his own language."* (Acts 2:4-6)

> *"While Peter yet spake these words, the Holy Ghost fell on all them which heard the word. And they of the circumcision which believed were astonished, as many as came with Peter, because that on the Gentiles also was poured out the gift of the Holy Ghost. For they heard them speak with tongues, and magnify God. Then answered Peter, Can any man forbid water, that these should not be baptized, which have received the Holy Ghost as well as we? And he commanded them to be baptized in the name of the Lord. Then prayed they him to tarry certain days."* (Acts 10:44-48)

> *"And it came to pass, that, while Apollos was at Corinth, Paul having passed through the upper coasts came to Ephesus: and finding certain disciples, He said unto them, Have ye received the Holy Ghost since ye believed? And they said unto him, We have not so much as heard whether there be any Holy Ghost. And he said unto them, Unto what then were ye baptized? And they said, Unto John's baptism. Then said Paul, John verily baptized with the baptism of repentance, saying unto the people, that they should believe on him which should come after him, that is, on Christ Jesus. When they heard this, they were baptized in the name of the Lord Jesus. And when Paul had laid his hands upon them, the Holy Ghost came on them; and they spake with tongues, and prophesied. And all the men were about twelve."* (Acts 19:1-7)

> *"But the manifestation of the Spirit is given to every man to profit withal. For to one is given by the Spirit the word of wisdom; to another the word of knowledge by the same Spirit; To another faith by the same Spirit; to another the gifts of healing by the same Spirit; To another the working of miracles; to another prophecy; to another discerning of*

spirits; to another divers kinds of tongues; to another the interpretation of tongues: But all these worketh that one and the selfsame Spirit, dividing to every man severally as he will. For as the body is one, and hath many members, and all the members of that one body, being many, are one body: so also is Christ." (1 Corinthians 12:7-11)

"Follow after charity, and desire spiritual gifts, but rather that ye may prophesy. For he that speaketh in an unknown tongue speaketh not unto men, but unto God: for no man understandeth him; howbeit in the spirit he speaketh mysteries. But he that prophesieth speaketh unto men to edification, and exhortation, and comfort. He that speaketh in an unknown tongue edifieth himself; but he that prophesieth edifieth the church. I would that ye all spake with tongues, but rather that ye prophesied: for greater is he that prophesieth than he that speaketh with tongues, except he interpret, that the church may receive edifying. Now, brethren, if I come unto you speaking with tongues, what shall I profit you, except I shall speak to you either by revelation, or by knowledge, or by prophesying, or by doctrine? (1 Corinthians 14:1-6)

"Even so ye, forasmuch as ye are zealous of spiritual gifts, seek that ye may excel to the edifying of the church. Wherefore let him that speaketh in an unknown tongue pray that he may interpret. For if I pray in an unknown tongue, my spirit prayeth, but my understanding is unfruitful. What is it then? I will pray with the spirit, and I will pray with the understanding also: I will sing with the spirit, and I will sing with the understanding also. Else when thou shalt bless with the spirit, how shall he that occupieth the room of the unlearned say Amen at thy giving of thanks, seeing he understandeth not what thou sayest?" (1 Corinthians 14:12-16)

"Brethren, be not children in understanding: howbeit in malice be ye children, but in understanding be men. In the law it is written, With men of other tongues and other lips will I speak unto this people; and yet for all that will they not hear me, saith the Lord. Wherefore tongues are for a sign, not to them that believe, but to them that believe not: but prophesying serveth not for them that believe not, but for them which believe. If therefore the whole church be come together into one place, and all speak with tongues, and there come in those that are unlearned, or unbelievers, will they not say that ye are mad? But if all prophesy, and there come in one that believeth not, or one unlearned, he is convinced of all, he is judged of all: And thus are the secrets of his heart made manifest; and so falling down on his face he will worship God, and report that God is in you of a truth. How is it then, brethren? when ye come together, everyone of you hath a psalm, hath a doctrine, hath a tongue, hath a revelation, hath an interpretation. Let all things be done unto edifying. If any man speak in an unknown tongue, let it be by two, or at the most by three, and that by course; and let one interpret. But if there be no interpreter, let him keep silence in the church; and let him speak to himself, and to God." (1 Corinthians 14:20-28)

Finally, the Bible reveals the divine purpose in the Trinity of God. There is none besides the God of Israel. He has created everything including evil. Mankind must not strive against this True and Living God who is able to save with an everlasting salvation. All nations should look to the Everlasting God for salvation. The Trinity functions as one in the work of our assurance of salvation through a risen savior.

"I am the Lord, and there is none else, there is no God beside me: I girded thee, though thou hast not known me: That they may know from the rising of the sun, and from the west, that

there is none beside me. I am the Lord, and there is none else. I form the light, and create darkness: I make peace, and create evil: I the Lord do all these things. Drop down, ye heavens, from above, and let the skies pour down righteousness: let the earth open, and let them bring forth salvation, and let righteousness spring up together; I the Lord have created it. Woe unto him that striveth with his Maker! Let the potsherd strive with the potsherds of the earth. Shall the clay say to him that fashioneth it, What makest thou? or thy work, He hath no hands? Woe unto him that saith unto his father, What begettest thou? or to the woman, What hast thou brought forth? Thus saith the Lord, the Holy One of Israel, and his Maker, Ask me of things to come concerning my sons, and concerning the work of my hands command ye me. I have made the earth, and created man upon it: I, even my hands, have stretched out the heavens, and all their host have I commanded. I have raised him up in righteousness, and I will direct all his ways: he shall build my city, and he shall let go my captives, not for price nor reward, saith the Lord of hosts. Thus saith the Lord, The labour of Egypt, and merchandise of Ethiopia and of the Sabeans, men of stature, shall come over unto thee, and they shall be thine: they shall come after thee; in chains they shall come over, and they shall fall down unto thee, they shall make supplication unto thee, saying, Surely God is in thee; and there is none else, there is no God. Verily thou art a God that hidest thyself, O God of Israel, the Saviour. They shall be ashamed, and also confounded, all of them: they shall go to confusion together that are makers of idols. But Israel shall be saved in the Lord with an everlasting salvation: ye shall not be ashamed nor confounded world without end. For thus saith the Lord that created the heavens; God himself that formed the earth and made it; he hath established it, he created it not in vain, he formed it to be inhabited: I am the Lord; and there is none else. I have not spoken in secret, in a dark place of the earth: I said not unto the seed of Jacob, Seek ye me in vain: I the Lord speak righteousness, I declare things that are right. Assemble yourselves and come; draw near together, ye that are escaped of the nations: they have no knowledge that set up the wood of their graven image, and pray unto a god that cannot save. Tell ye, and bring them near; yea, let them take counsel together: who hath declared this from ancient time? who hath told it from that time? have not I the Lord? and there is no God else beside me; a just God and a Saviour; there is none beside me. Look unto me, and be ye saved, all the ends of the earth: for I am God, and there is none else. I have sworn by myself, the word is gone out of my mouth in righteousness, and shall not return, That unto me every knee shall bow, every tongue shall swear. Surely, shall one say, in the Lord have I righteousness and strength: even to him shall men come; and all that are incensed against him shall be ashamed. In the Lord shall all the seed of Israel be justified, and shall glory." (Isaiah 45:5-25)

"But now in Christ Jesus ye who sometimes were far off are made nigh by the blood of Christ. For he is our peace, who hath made both one, and hath broken down the middle wall of partition between us; Having abolished in his flesh the enmity, even the law of commandments contained in ordinances; for to make in himself of twain one new man, so making peace; And that he might reconcile both unto God in one body by the cross, having slain the enmity thereby: And came and preached peace to you which were afar off, and to them that were nigh. For through him we both have access by one Spirit unto the Father. Now therefore ye are no more strangers and foreigners, but fellowcitizens with the saints, and of the household of God; And are built upon the foundation of the apostles and prophets, Jesus Christ himself being the chief corner stone; In whom all the building fitly framed together groweth unto an holy temple in the Lord: In whom ye also are builded together for an habitation of God through the Spirit." (Ephesians 2:13-22)

"For there are three that bear record in heaven, the Father, the Word, and the Holy Ghost: and these three are one. And there are three that bear witness in earth, the spirit, and the water, and the blood: and these three agree in one." (**1 John 5:7-8**)

"For in him we live, and move, and have our being; as certain also of your own poets have said, For we are also his offspring. Forasmuch then as we are the offspring of God, we ought not to think that the Godhead is like unto gold, or silver, or stone, graven by art and man's device. And the times of this ignorance God winked at; but now commandeth all men every where to repent: Because he hath appointed a day, in the which he will judge the world in righteousness by that man whom he hath ordained; whereof he hath given assurance unto all men, in that he hath raised him from the dead." (**Acts 17:29-31**)

3

THE PREEMINENCE OF CHRIST

Is it Jesus, the Christ, Christ Jesus or Jesus Christ?
Why does this name seem to be seen and mentioned more than any other name that I have ever heard?

JESUS CAN BE recognized in creation when the Bible states "let us" make man in our own image. The believer is to understand this as a revelation of God the Trinity. Moreover, this is a revelation as to the role to which Christ was relegated in creation; that role gives him a preeminence (proteo: first in rank and influence).

> "And God said, Let us make man in our image, after our likeness: and let them have dominion over the fish of the sea, and over the fowl of the air, and over the cattle, and over all the earth, and over every creeping thing that creepeth upon the earth. So God created man in his own image, in the image of God created he him; male and female created he them." (Genesis 1:26 & 27)

> "In the beginning was the Word, and the Word was with God, and the Word was God. The same was in the beginning with God. All things were made by him; and without him was not any thing made that was made. In him was life; and the life was the light of men." (John 1:1-4)

> "For there are three that bear record in heaven, the Father, the Word, and the Holy Ghost: and these three are one." (1 John 5:7)

> "Giving thanks unto the Father, which hath made us meet to be partakers of the inheritance of the saints in light: Who hath delivered us from the power of darkness, and hath translated us into the kingdom of his dear Son: In whom we have redemption through his blood, even the forgiveness of sins: Who is the image of the invisible God, the firstborn of every creature: For by him were all things created, that are in heaven, and that are in earth, visible and invisible, whether they be thrones, or dominions, or principalities, or powers: all things were created by him, and for him: And he is before all things, and by him all things consist. And he is the head of the body, the church: who is the beginning, the firstborn from the dead; that in all things he might have the preeminence." (Colossians 1:12-18)

> "For we are his workmanship, created in Christ Jesus unto good works, which God hath before ordained that we should walk in them." (Ephesians 2:10)

The Bible bears witness that Jesus is the Son of God. Jesus said that he is the Son of God the Father. Are not we to believe this on the basis of what Christ did (eyewitness accounts) and/or said?

"The woman saith unto him, I know that Messias cometh, which is called Christ: when he is come, he will tell us all things. Jesus saith unto her, I that speak unto thee am he." (John 4:25 & 26)

"Search the scriptures; for in them ye think ye have eternal life: and they are they which testify of me. And ye will not come to me, that ye might have life. I receive not honor from men. But I know you, that ye have not the love of God in you. I am come in my Father's name, and ye receive me not: if another shall come in his own name, him ye will receive." (John 5:39-43)

"For I came down from heaven, not to do mine own will, but the will of him that sent me. And this is the Father's will which hath sent me, that of all which he hath given me I should lose nothing, but should raise it up again at the last day.

And this is the will of him that sent me, that every one which seeth the Son, and believeth on him, may have everlasting life: and I will raise him up at the last day." (John 6:38-40)

"I know that ye are Abraham's seed; but ye seek to kill me, because my word hath no place in you. I speak that which I have seen with my Father: and ye do that which ye have seen with your father." (John 8:37 & 38)

"Jesus answered, If I honor myself, my honor is nothing: it is my Father that honoreth me; of whom ye say, that he is your God: Yet ye have not known him; but I know him: and if I should say, I know him not, I shall be a liar like unto you: but I know him, and keep his saying. Your father Abraham rejoiced to see my day: and he saw it, and was glad." (John 8:54-56)

"Jesus answered them, I told you, and ye believed not: the works that I do in my Father's name, they bear witness of me." (John 10:25)

"If I do not the works of my Father, believe me not. But if I do, though ye believe not me, believe the works: that ye may know, and believe, that the Father is in me, and I in him." (John 10:37 & 38)

"Believest thou not that I am in the Father, and the Father in me? the words that I speak unto you I speak not of myself: but the Father that dwelleth in me, he doeth the works. Believe me that I am in the Father, and the Father in me: or else believe me for the very works' sake." (John 14:10 & 11)

The Bible reveals and foretells of Jesus Christ. He is revealed as the Prophet [nably: the inspired man].

"The Lord thy God will raise up unto thee a Prophet from the midst of thee, of thy brethren, like unto me; unto him ye shall hearken; According to all that thou desiredst of the Lord thy God in Horeb in the day of the assembly, saying, Let me not hear again the voice of the Lord my God, neither let me see this great fire any more, that I die not. I will raise them up a Prophet from among their brethren, like unto thee, and will put my words in

24

his mouth; and he shall speak unto them all that I shall command him." (Deuteronomy 18:15, 16&18)

Jesus is revealed as Immanuel [Immanuel: God is with us].

"Therefore the Lord himself shall give you a sign; Behold, a virgin shall conceive, and bear a son, and shall call his name Immanuel." (Isaiah 7:14)

There is an appearence of Jesus in the book of Daniel as he is, the Son of God [bar elahh].

"He answered and said, Lo, I see four men loose, walking in the midst of the fire, and they have no hurt; and the form of the fourth is like the Son of God. " (Daniel 3:25)

The Christ child is referred to as the personification of wonderful [pele: a miracle, a wonder, a marvelous thing], counselor [yaats: advisor, consultant, guide], the mighty God [gibbowr el: strong and valiant almighty), everlasting Father [ad ab: chief Father, advance/first/perpetual Father, without end Father].

"For unto us a child is born, unto us a son is given: and the government shall be upon his shoulder: and his name shall be called Wonderful, Counsellor, The mighty God, The everlasting Father, The Prince of Peace." (Isaiah 9:6)

The New Testament of the Bible calls our Lord and Savior, Jesus [Iesous as Greek version of Hebrew Yehowshuwa: Jehovah-saved, Jehoshua], Christ [Christos: the Messiah], Word [logos: the divine expression of reasoning, thought and doctrine], Son [hurios: male child of a father], and Master [kathegetes: the teacher, the guide and Lord] [kurios: supreme in authority God].

"But while he thought on these things, behold, the angel of the Lord appeared unto him in a dream, saying, Joseph, thou son of David, fear not to take unto thee Mary thy wife: for that which is conceived in her is of the Holy Ghost. And she shall bring forth a son, and thou shalt call his name Jesus: for he shall save his people from their sins." (Matthew 1:20 & 21)

"When Jesus came into the coasts of Caesarea Philippi, he asked his disciples, saying, Whom do men say that I the Son of man am? And they said, Some say that thou art John the Baptist: some, Elias; and others, Jeremias, or one of the prophets. He saith unto them, But whom say ye that I am? And Simon Peter answered and said, Thou art the Christ, the Son of the living God. And Jesus answered and said unto him, Blessed art thou, Simon Barjona: for flesh and blood hath not revealed it unto thee, but my Father which is in heaven." (Matthew 16:13-17)

"And the Word was made flesh, and dwelt among us, (and we beheld his glory, the glory as of the only begotten of the Father,) full of grace and truth. John bare witness of him, and cried, saying, This was he of whom I spake, He that cometh after me is preferred before me: for he was before me. And of his fulness have all we received, and grace for grace. For the law was given by Moses, but grace and truth came by Jesus Christ. No man hath seen God at any time, the only begotten Son, which is in the bosom of the Father, he hath declared him." (John 1:14-18)

"In the beginning was the Word, and the Word was with God, and the Word was God. The same was in the beginning with God. All things were made by him; and without him was not any thing made that was made. (1 John 1:1-3)

"But be not ye called Rabbi: for one is your Master, even Christ; and all ye are brethren. And call no man your father upon the earth: for one is your Father, which is in heaven. Neither be ye called masters: for one is your Master, even Christ." (**Matthew 23:8-10**)

"While the Pharisees were gathered together, Jesus asked them, Saying, What think ye of Christ? whose son is he? They say unto him, The son of David. He saith unto them, How then doth David in spirit call him Lord, saying, The LORD said unto my Lord, Sit thou on my right hand, till I make thine enemies thy footstool? If David then call him Lord, how is he his son?" (**Matthew 22:41-45**)

Speaking further to the preeminence of Jesus Christ, Jesus is declared by the Bible to be the fullness of the Godhead, all sufficient, equal to the Father, the author of faith, the author of eternal salvation, the beginning and the end, as well as worthy alone. He is both King and Priest. Also, he is to be our judge.

"Beware lest any man spoil you through philosophy and vain deceit, after the tradition of men, after the rudiments of the world, and not after Christ. For in him dwelleth all the fulness of the Godhead bodily." (**Colossians 2:8 & 9**)

"Let this mind be in you, which was also in Christ Jesus: Who, being in the form of God, thought it not robbery to be equal with God: But made himself of no reputation, and took upon him the form of a servant, and was made in the likeness of men: And being found in fashion as a man, he humbled himself, and became obedient unto death, even the death of the cross. Wherefore God also hath highly exalted him, and given him a name which is above every name:" (**Philippians 2:5-9**)

"Looking unto Jesus the author and finisher of our faith; who for the joy that was set before him endured the cross, despising the shame, and is set down at the right hand of the throne of God." (**Hebrews 12:2**)

"And being made perfect, he became the author of eternal salvation unto all them that obey him; Called of God an high priest after the order of Melchisedec." (**Hebrews 5:9 & 10**)

"God the Father commits all judgement to Jesus. For the Father judgeth no man, but hath committed all judgment unto the Son: That all men should honor the Son, even as they honor the Father. He that honoreth not the Son honoreth not the Father which hath sent him." (**John 5:22 & 23**)

According to the eyewitness record provided the God of the Bible is is that Jesus is the Father's son and that anything believed contrary is a lie.

"If we receive the witness of men, the witness of God is greater: for this is the witness of God which he hath testified of his Son. He that believeth on the Son of God hath the witness in himself: he that believeth not God hath made him a liar; because he believeth not the re-cord that God gave of his Son. And this is the record, that God hath given to us eternal life, and this life is in his Son. He that hath the Son hath life; and he that hath not the Son of

> *God hath not life. These things have I written unto you that believe on the name of the Son of God; that ye may know that ye have eternal life, and that ye may believe on the name of the Son of God. And we know that we are of God, and the whole world lieth in wickedness. And we know that the Son of God is come, and hath given us an understanding, that we may know him that is true, and we are in him that is true, even in his Son Jesus Christ. This is the true God, and eternal life.* (1 John 5:9-13, 19 &20)

Jesus Christ existed before the creation of mankind unlike any other man that has lived on earth. Note also that God the Father did not vacate his throne in heaven to come down to earth.

> *"For I came down from heaven, not to do mine own will, but the will of him that sent me. And this is the Father's will which hath sent me, that of all which he hath given me I should lose nothing, but should raise it up again at the last day.*
>
> *And this is the will of him that sent me, that every one which seeth the Son, and believeth on him, may have everlasting life: and I will raise him up at the last day."* (John 6: 38-40)
>
> *"Your father Abraham rejoiced to see my day: and he saw it, and was glad. Then said the Jews unto him, Thou art not yet fifty years old, and hast thou seen Abraham? Jesus said unto them, Verily, verily, I say unto you, Before Abraham was, I am."* (John 8:56-58)
>
> *"I have glorified thee on the earth: I have finished the work which thou gavest me to do. And now, O Father, glorify thou me with thine own self with the glory which I had with thee before the world was."* (John 17: 4 & 5)

Jesus fulfilled all forty-four Old Testament scriptural prophecies with regard to the Messiah. Eight are presented here.

> *"And I will put enmity between thee and the woman, and between thy seed and her seed; it shall bruise thy head, and thou shalt bruise his heel."* (Genesis 3:15
>
> *"But when the fulness of the time was come, God sent forth his Son, made of a woman, made under the law, To redeem them that were under the law, that we might receive the adoption of sons."* (Galatians 4:4&5)
>
> *"But thou, Bethlehem Ephratah, though thou be little among the thousands of Judah, yet out of thee shall he come forth unto me that is to be ruler in Israel; whose goings forth have been from of old, from everlasting."* (Micah 5:2)
>
> *"And Joseph also went up from Galilee, out of the city of Nazareth, into Judaea, unto the city of David, which is called Bethlehem; (because he was of the house and lineage of David:) To be taxed with Mary his espoused wife, being great with child. And she brought forth her firstborn son, and wrapped him in swaddling clothes, and laid him in a manger; because there was no room for them in the inn."* (Luke 2:4-5, 7)
>
> *"Therefore the Lord himself shall give you a sign; Behold, a virgin shall conceive, and bear a son, and shall call his name Immanuel."* (Isaiah 7:14)
>
> *"And in the sixth month the angel Gabriel was sent from God unto a city of Galilee, named Nazareth, To a virgin espoused to a man whose name was Joseph, of the house of David; and the virgin's name was Mary. And the angel said unto her, Fear not, Mary: for thou hast*

found favor with God. And, behold, thou shalt conceive in thy womb, and bring forth a son, and shalt call his name Jesus." (**Luke 1:26-27, 30 & 31**)

"The Spirit of the Lord God is upon me; because the Lord hath anointed me to preach good tidings unto the meek; he hath sent me to bind up the brokenhearted, to proclaim liberty to the captives, and the opening of the prison to them that are bound; To proclaim the acceptable year of the Lord, and the day of vengeance of our God; to comfort all that mourn;" (**Isaiah 61:1-2**)

"The Spirit of the Lord is upon me, because he hath anointed me to preach the gospel to the poor; he hath sent me to heal the brokenhearted, to preach deliverance to the captives, and recovering of sight to the blind, to set at liberty them that are bruised, To preach the acceptable year of the Lord." (**Luke 4:18-19**)

"Therefore will I divide him a portion with the great, and he shall divide the spoil with the strong; because he hath poured out his soul unto death: and he was numbered with the transgressors; and he bare the sin of many, and made intercession for the transgressors." (**Isaiah 53:12**)

"And with him they crucify two thieves; the one on his right hand, and the other on his left. And the scripture was fulfilled, which saith, And he was numbered with the transgressors." (**Mark 15:27&28**)

"He keepeth all his bones: not one of them is broken." (**Psalm 34:20**)

"Then came the soldiers, and brake the legs of the first, and of the other which was crucified with him. But when they came to Jesus, and saw that he was dead already, they brake not his legs: For these things were done, that the scripture should be fulfilled, A bone of him shall not be broken." (**John 19:32-33&36**)

"For thou wilt not leave my soul in hell; neither wilt thou suffer thine Holy One to see corruption." (**Psalm 16:10**)

"But God will redeem my soul from the power of the grave: for he shall receive me. Selah." (**Psalm 49:15**)

"And he saith unto them, Be not affrighted: Ye seek Jesus of Nazareth, which was crucified: he is risen; he is not here: behold the place where they laid him. But go your way, tell his disciples and Peter that he goeth before you into Galilee: there shall ye see him, as he said unto you." (**Mark 16:6 & 7**)

"Thou hast ascended on high, thou hast led captivity captive: thou hast received gifts for men; yea, for the rebellious also, that the Lord God might dwell among them." (**Psalm 68:18**)

"So then after the Lord had spoken unto them, he was received up into heaven, and sat on the right hand of God." (**Mark 16:19**)

"And when he had spoken these things, while they beheld, he was taken up; and a cloud received him out of their sight." (**Acts 1:9**)

"And that he was buried, and that he rose again the third day according to the scriptures:" (**1 Corinthians 15:4**)

"Wherefore he saith, When he ascended up on high, he led captivity captive, and gave gifts unto men." (Ephesians 4:8)

There are other gospels preached; check the lineage of Christ and the doctrine.

I marvel that ye are so soon removed from him that called you into the grace of Christ unto another gospel: Which is not another; but there be some that trouble you, and would pervert the gospel of Christ. But though we, or an angel from heaven, preach any other gospel unto you than that which we have preached unto you, let him be accursed. As we said before, so say I now again, if any man preach any other gospel unto you than that ye have received, let him be accursed. **Galatians 1:6-9**

But we preach Christ crucified, unto the Jews a stumblingblock, and unto the Greeks foolishness; But unto them which are called, both Jews and Greeks, Christ the power of God, and the wisdom of God. **1 Corinthians 1:23 & 24**

Note as follows, the genealogy of Christ

The book of the generation of Jesus Christ, the son of David, the son of Abraham. Abraham begat Isaac; and Isaac begat Jacob; and Jacob begat Judas and his brethren; And Judas begat Phares and Zara of Thamar; and Phares begat Esrom; and Esrom begat Aram; And Aram begat Aminadab; and Aminadab begat Naasson; and Naasson begat Salmon; And Salmon begat Booz of Rachab; and Booz begat Obed of Ruth; and Obed begat Jesse; And Jesse begat David the king; and David the king begat Solomon of her that had been the wife of Urias; And Solomon begat Roboam; and Roboam begat Abia; and Abia begat Asa; And Asa begat Josaphat; and Josaphat begat Joram; and Joram begat Ozias; And Ozias begat Joatham; and Joatham begat Achaz; and Achaz begat Ezekias; And Ezekias begat Manasses; and Manasses begat Amon; and Amon begat Josias; And Josias begat Jechonias and his brethren, about the time they were carried away to Babylon: And after they were brought to Babylon, Jechonias begat Salathiel; and Salathiel begat Zorobabel; And Zorobabel begat Abiud; and Abiud begat Eliakim; and Eliakim begat Azor; And Azor begat Sadoc; and Sadoc begat Achim; and Achim begat Eliud; And Eliud begat Eleazar; and Eleazar begat Matthan; and Matthan begat Jacob; And Jacob begat Joseph the husband of Mary, of whom was born Jesus, who is called Christ. So all the generations from Abraham to David are fourteen generations; and from David until the carrying away into Babylon are fourteen generations;and from the carrying away into Babylon (**Matthew 1:1-7**)

And Jesus himself began to be about thirty years of age, being (as was supposed) the son of Joseph, which was the son of Heli, Which was the son of Matthat, which was the son of Levi, which was the son of Melchi, which was the son of Janna, which was the son of Joseph, Which was the son of Mattathias, which was the son of Amos, which was the son of Naum, which was the son of Esli, which was the son of Nagge, Which was the son of Maath, which was the son of Mattathias, which was the son of Semei, which was the son of Joseph, which was the son of Juda, Which was the son of Joanna, which was the son of Rhesa, which was the son of Zorobabel, which was the son of Salathiel, which was the son of Neri, Which was the son of Melchi, which was the son of Addi, which was the son of Cosam, which was the son of Elmodam, which was the son of Er, Which was the son of Jose, which was the son of Eliezer, which was the son of Jorim, which was the son of Matthat, which was the son of Levi, Which was the son of Simeon, which was the son of Juda, which was the son of Joseph, which was the son of Jonan, which was the son of Eliakim, Which was the son of Melea, which was the son of Menan, which was the son of Mattatha, which was the son of Nathan, which was the son of David, Which was the son of Jesse, which was the son of Obed, which was the son of Booz, which was the son of Salmon, which was the son of Naasson, Which was the son of Aminadab, which was the son of Aram, which was the son of Esrom, which was the son of Phares, which was the son of Juda, Which was the son of Jacob, which was the son of Isaac, which was the son of Abraham, which was the son of Thara, which was the son of Nachor, Which was the son of Saruch, which was the son of Ragau, which was the son of Phalec, which was the son of Heber, which was the son of Sala, Which was the son of Cainan, which was the son of Arphaxad, which was the son of Sem, which was the son of Noe, which was the son of Lamech, Which was the son of Mathusala, which was the son of Enoch, which was the son of Jared, which was the son of Maleleel, which was the son of Cainan, Which was the son of Enos, which was the son of Seth, which was the son of Adam, which was the son of God. Luke 3:23-38

"Whosoever transgresseth, and abideth not in the doctrine of Christ, hath not God. He that abideth in the doctrine of Christ, he hath both the Father and the Son." (2 John 9)

There was in Christ's life here on earth the following purposes: (1) to bring down the gospel of kingdom of heaven to earth, (2) to reveal the true and living God, and (3) to fulfill the law and (4) die as the spotless sacrifice on the cross for the sins of all mankind.

"In those days came John the Baptist, preaching in the wilderness of Judaea, And saying, Repent ye: for the kingdom of heaven is at hand. For this is he that was spoken of by the prophet Esaias, saying, The voice of one crying in the wilderness, Prepare ye the way of the Lord, make his paths straight." (Matthew 3:1-3)

And he came to Nazareth, where he had been brought up: and, as his custom was, he went into the synagogue on the sabbath day, and stood up for to read. And there was delivered unto him the book of the prophet Esaias. And when he had opened the book, he found the place where it was written, The Spirit of the Lord is upon me, because he hath anointed me to preach the gospel to the poor; he hath sent me to heal the brokenhearted, to preach deliverance to the captives, and recovering of sight to the blind, to set at liberty them that are bruised, To preach the acceptable year of the Lord. And he closed the book, and he gave it again to the minister, and sat down. And the eyes of all them that were in the synagogue were fastened on him. And he began to say unto them, This day is this scripture fulfilled in your ears." (Luke 4:16-21)

"But if I cast out devils by the Spirit of God, then the kingdom of God is come unto you." (Matthew 12:28)

"Now after that John was put in prison, Jesus came into Galilee, preaching the gospel of the kingdom of God, And saying, The time is fulfilled, and the kingdom of God is at hand: repent ye, and believe the gospel." (Mark 1:14&15)

"And this is life eternal, that they might know thee the only true God, and Jesus Christ, whom thou hast sent." (John 17:3)

"Jesus answered, My kingdom is not of this world: if my kingdom were of this world, then would my servants fight, that I should not be delivered to the Jews: but now is my kingdom not from hence. Pilate therefore said unto him, Art thou a king then? Jesus answered, Thou

sayest that I am a king. To this end was I born, and for this cause came I into the world, that I should bear witness unto the truth. Every one that is of the truth heareth my voice." (John 18:36&37)

"Think not that I am come to destroy the law, or the prophets: I am not come to destroy, but to fulfil. For verily I say unto you, Till heaven and earth pass, one jot or one tittle shall in no wise pass from the law, till all be fulfilled." (Matthew 5:17&18)

"Then he took unto him the twelve, and said unto them, Behold, we go up to Jerusalem, and all things that are written by the prophets concerning the Son of man shall be accomplished. For he shall be delivered unto the Gentiles, and shall be mocked, and spitefully entreated, and spitted on: And they shall scourge him, and put him to death: and the third day he shall rise again." (Luke 18:31-33)

"The next day John seeth Jesus coming unto him, and saith, Behold the Lamb of God, which taketh away the sin of the world. This is he of whom I said, After me cometh a man which is preferred before me: for he was before me." (John 1:29&30)

"For he taught his disciples, and said unto them, The Son of man is delivered into the hands of men, and they shall kill him; and after that he is killed, he shall rise the third day. But they understood not that saying, and were afraid to ask him." (Mark 9:31&32)

"And he saith unto them, But whom say ye that I am? And Peter answereth and saith unto him, Thou art the Christ. And he charged them that they should tell no man of him. And he began to teach them, that the Son of man must suffer many things, and be rejected of the elders, and of the chief priests, and scribes, and be killed, and after three days rise again." (Mark 8:29-31)

Now, it is important to understand how mere mortals were able to put to death by crucifixion an immortal God. The answer goes beyond just Jesus having said that, "I lay down my life, that I might take it again", but rather also, to the fact that Jesus was relegated, here on earth, to a position of a little less than the immortality of the angels for the expressed purpose of him being able to taste of death.

I am the good shepherd, and know my sheep, and am known of mine. As the Father knoweth me, even so know I the Father: and I lay down my life for the sheep. And other sheep I have, which are not of this fold: them also I must bring, and they shall hear my voice; and there shall be one fold, and one shepherd.

Therefore doth my Father love me, because I lay down my life, that I might take it again. No man taketh it from me, but I lay it down of myself. I have power to lay it down, and I have power to take it again. This commandment have I received of my Father. John 10:14-18

"What is man, that thou art mindful of him? and the son of man, that thou visitest him? For thou hast made him a little lower than the angels, and hast crowned him with glory and honour". (Psalm 8:4-5)

"But one in a certain place testified, saying, What is man, that thou art mindful of him? or the son of man that thou visitest him? Thou madest him a little lower than the angels; thou crownedst him with glory and honor, and didst set him over the works of thy hands: Thou hast put all things in subjection under his feet. For in that he put all in subjection under him, he left nothing that is not put under him. But now we see not yet all things put

under him. But we see Jesus, who was made a little lower than the angels for the suffering of death, crowned with glory and honor; that he by the grace of God should taste death for every man." (Hebrews 2:6-9)

Further, the eye witnessed death and resurrection of Jesus Christ, as recorded, has life-altering ramifications to all mankind. There is in the death of Jesus on the cross, the redemption of all mankind from the curse of the law; the wages of sin is death, but that the gift of God through Jesus Christ is life forever. Jesus shed his precious sinless blood on the cross for the remission of the sins of all mankind; without the shedding of innocent blood there is no forgiveness of sins according to the Bible.

"For when we were yet without strength, in due time Christ died for the ungodly. For scarcely for a righteous man will one die: yet peradventure for a good man some would even dare to die. But God commendeth his love toward us, in that, while we were yet sinners, Christ died for us. Much more then, being now justified by his blood, we shall be saved from wrath through him. For if, when we were enemies, we were reconciled to God by the death of his Son, much more, being reconciled, we shall be saved by his life. And not only so, but we also joy in God through our Lord Jesus Christ, by whom we have now received the atonement. Wherefore, as by one man sin entered into the world, and death by sin; and so death passed upon all men, for that all have sinned: (For until the law sin was in the world: but sin is not imputed when there is no law. Nevertheless death reigned from Adam to Moses, even over them that had not sinned after the similitude of Adam's transgression, who is the figure of him that was to come. But not as the offence, so also is the free gift. For if through the offence of one many be dead, much more the grace of God, and the gift by grace, which is by one man, Jesus Christ, hath abounded unto many." (Romans 5:6-15)

"For all have sinned, and come short of the glory of God; Being justified freely by his grace through the redemption that is in Christ Jesus: Whom God hath set forth to be a propitiation through faith in his blood, to declare his righteousness for the remission of sins that are past, through the forbearance of God;' (Romans 3:23-25)

"For the wages of sin is death; but the gift of God is eternal life through Jesus Christ our Lord " (Romans 6:23)

"And almost all things are by the law purged with blood; and without shedding of blood is no remission. For Christ is not entered into the holy places made with hands, which are the figures of the true; but into heaven itself, now to appear in the presence of God for us: Nor yet that he should offer himself often, as the high priest entereth into the holy place every year with blood of others; For then must he often have suffered since the foundation of the world: but now once in the end of the world hath he appeared to put away sin by the sacrifice of himself." (Hebrews 9:22, 24-26)

"And he commanded us to preach unto the people, and to testify that it is he which was ordained of God to be the Judge of quick and dead. To him give all the prophets witness, that through his name whosoever believeth in him shall receive remission of sins." (Acts 10: 42-43)

"For the life of the flesh is in the blood: and I have given it to you upon the altar to make an atonement for your souls: for it is the blood that maketh an atonement for the soul." (Leviticus 17:11)

We that preach the gospel, preach of a risen (living) savior. Jesus declared himself to be the resurrection. By eyewitness accounts, Jesus Christ raised a man named Lazarus from the dead and then rose from the grave himself. Christians worship a risen Savior, otherwise, the preaching of the gospel is useless and we are most miserable as a result.

"Jesus saith unto her, Thy brother shall rise again. Martha saith unto him, I know that he shall rise again in the resurrection at the last day. Jesus said unto her, I am the resurrection, and the life: he that believeth in me, though he were dead, yet shall he live: And whosoever liveth and believeth in me shall never die. Believest thou this?" (John 11:23-26)

"And when he thus had spoken, he cried with a loud voice, Lazarus, come forth. And he that was dead came forth, bound hand and foot with graveclothes: and his face was bound about with a napkin. Jesus saith unto them, Loose him, and let him go." (John 11:43-44)

"Now if Christ be preached that he rose from the dead, how say some among you that there is no resurrection of the dead? But if there be no resurrection of the dead, then is Christ not risen: And if Christ be not risen, then is our preaching vain, and your faith is also vain. Yea, and we are found false witnesses of God; because we have testified of God that he raised up Christ: whom he raised not up, if so be that the dead rise not. For if the dead rise not, then is not Christ raised: And if Christ be not raised, your faith is vain; ye are yet in your sins. Then they also which are fallen asleep in Christ are perished. If in this life only we have hope in Christ, we are of all men most miserable. But now is Christ risen from the dead, and become the firstfruits of them that slept. For since by man came death, by man came also the resurrection of the dead. For as in Adam all die, even so in Christ shall all be made alive." (1 Corinthians 15:12-22)

"And that he was seen of Cephas, then of the twelve: After that, he was seen of above five hundred brethren at once; of whom the greater part remain unto this present, but some are fallen asleep. After that, he was seen of James; then of all the apostles. And last of all he was seen of me also, as of one born out of due time." (1 Corinthians 15:5-8)

Christians worship an all-powerful risen Savior that sits at the right hand of God the Father in heaven. Eyewitnesses received the testimony of Christ upon his resurrection and there were eyewitnesses as well that saw Jesus ascend into heaven.

"And Jesus came and spake unto them, saying, All power is given unto me in heaven and in earth. Go ye therefore, and teach all nations, baptizing them in the name of the Father, and of the Son, and of the Holy Ghost: Teaching them to observe all things whatsoever I have commanded you: and, lo, I am with you alway, even unto the end of the world. Amen." (Matthew 28:18-20)

'This is the disciple which testifieth of these things, and wrote these things: and we know that his testimony is true." (John 21:24)

And, being assembled together with them, commanded them that they should not depart from Jerusalem, but wait for the promise of the Father, which, saith he, ye have heard of me. For John truly baptized with water; but ye shall be baptized with the Holy Ghost not many days hence. When they therefore were come together, they asked of him, saying, Lord, wilt thou at this time restore again the kingdom to Israel? And he said unto them, It is not for you to know the times or the seasons, which the Father hath put in his own power. But ye shall receive power, after that the Holy Ghost is come upon you: and ye shall be witnesses unto me both in Jerusalem, and in all Judaea, and in Samaria, and unto the uttermost part of the earth. And when he had spoken these things, while they beheld, he was taken up; and a cloud received him out of their sight. And while they looked stedfastly toward heaven as he went up, behold, two men stood by them in white apparel; Which also said, Ye men of Galilee, why stand ye gazing up into heaven? this same Jesus, which is taken up from you into heaven, shall so come in like manner as ye have seen him go into heaven." (Acts 1:4-11)

"Then returned they unto Jerusalem from the mount called Olivet, which is from Jerusalem a sabbath day's journey. And when they were come in, they went up into an upper room, where abode both Peter, and James, and John, and Andrew, Philip, and Thomas, Bartholomew, and Matthew, James the son of Alphaeus, and Simon Zelotes, and Judas the brother of James. These all continued with one accord in prayer and supplication, with the women, and Mary the mother of Jesus, and with his brethren. And in those days Peter stood up in the midst of the disciples, and said, (the number of names together were about an hundred and twenty,) Men and brethren, this scripture must needs have been fulfilled, which the Holy Ghost by the mouth of David spake before concerning Judas, which was guide to them that took Jesus. For he was numbered with us, and had obtained part of this ministry. Now this man purchased a field with the reward of iniquity; and falling headlong, he burst asunder in the midst, and all his bowels gushed out." (Acts 1:12-18)

That the God of our Lord Jesus Christ, the Father of glory, may give unto you the spirit of wisdom and revelation in the knowledge of him: The eyes of your understanding being enlightened; that ye may know what is the hope of his calling, and what the riches of the glory of his inheritance in the saints, And what is the exceeding greatness of his power to usward who believe, according to the working of his mighty power, Which he wrought in Christ, when he raised him from the dead, and set him at his own right hand in the heavenly places, Far above all principality, and power, and might, and dominion, and every name that is named, not only in this world, but also in that which is to come: And hath put all things under his feet, and gave him to be the head over all things to the church, Which is his body, the fulness of him that filleth all in all." (Ephesians 1:17-23)

Jesus is the believer's propitiation (atonement) and intercessor along with the Holy Ghost.

"Herein is love, not that we loved God, but that he loved us, and sent his Son to be the propitiation for our sins." (1 John 4:10)

'My little children, these things write I unto you, that ye sin not. And if any man sin, we have an advocate with the Father, Jesus Christ the righteous: And he is the propitiation for our sins: and not for ours only, but also for the sins of the whole world." (1 John 2:1&2)

"For he testifieth, Thou art a priest for ever after the order of Melchisedec. For there is verily a disannulling of the commandment going before for the weakness and unprofitableness thereof. For the law made nothing perfect, but the bringing in of a better hope did; by the which we draw nigh unto God. And inasmuch as not without an oath he was made priest:

(For those priests were made without an oath; but this with an oath by him that said unto him, The Lord sware and will not repent, Thou art a priest for ever after the order of Melchisedec:) By so much was Jesus made a surety of a better testament. And they truly were many priests, because they were not suffered to continue by reason of death: But this man, because he continueth ever, hath an unchangeable priesthood. Wherefore he is able also to save them to the uttermost that come unto God by him, seeing he ever liveth to make intercession for them." **(Hebrews 7:17-25)**

Likewise the Spirit also helpeth our infirmities: for we know not what we should pray for as we ought: but the Spirit itself maketh intercession for us with groanings which cannot be uttered. And he that searcheth the hearts knoweth what is the mind of the Spirit, because he maketh intercession for the saints according to the will of God. And we know that all things work together for good to them that love God, to them who are the called according to his purpose. For whom he did foreknow, he also did predestinate to be conformed to the image of his Son, that he might be the firstborn among many brethren. Moreover whom he did predestinate, them he also called: and whom he called, them he also justified: and whom he justified, them he also glorified. What shall we then say to these things? If God be for us, who can be against us? He that spared not his own Son, but delivered him up for us all, how shall he not with him also freely give us all things? Who shall lay any thing to the charge of God's elect? It is God that justifieth. Who is he that condemneth? It is Christ that died, yea rather, that is risen again, who is even at the right hand of God, who also maketh intercession for us. Who shall separate us from the love of Christ? Shall tribulation, or distress, or persecution, or famine, or nakedness, or peril, or sword?" **(Romans 8:26-35)**

4

A STATEMENT OF SOUND BIBLICAL DOCTRINE – BAPTIST ARTICLES OF FAITH FOR EXAMINATION AND COMPARISON

Can anyone point me in the direction of a sound basis of Biblical doctrine?

The Importance of Sound Doctrine

The Bible reveals that the most important reason for sound doctrine (didache - instruction (the act or the matter), hath been taught) is to have a relationship with the Heavenly Father. Roundly reject unsound doctrine in your Christian homes.

> *"Whosoever transgresseth, and abideth not in the doctrine of Christ, hath not God. He that abideth in the doctrine of Christ, he hath both the Father and the Son. If there come any unto you, and bring not this doctrine, receive him not into your house, neither bid him God speed: For he that biddeth him God speed is partaker of his evil deeds." (2 John 9-11)*

Christ has given us the doctrine of our heavenly Father.

> *"Jesus answered them, and said, My doctrine is not mine, but his that sent me. If any man will do his will, he shall know of the doctrine, whether it be of God, or whether I speak of myself. He that speaketh of himself seeketh his own glory: but he that seeketh his glory that sent him, the same is true, and no unrighteousness is in him." (John 7:16 – 18)*

Scripture is given in part as a statement of doctrine.

> *"All scripture is given by inspiration of God, and is profitable for doctrine, for reproof, for correction, for instruction in righteousness: That the man of God may be perfect, throughly furnished unto all good works." (2 Timothy 3:16&17)*

Pastors (Bishops, Elders, and Overseers) are to labor in doctrine and are to be held in an esteem as recognition of that obvious labor. That laboring is a vital way in which the role of the Pastor is to be accomplished to God's delight and glorification.

> *"Let the elders that rule well be counted worthy of double honour, especially they who labour in the word and doctrine." (1 Timothy 5:17)*

"For when for the time ye ought to be teachers, ye have need that one teach you again which be the first principles of the oracles of God; and are become such as have need of milk, and not of strong meat. For every one that useth milk is unskilful in the word of righteousness: for he is a babe. But strong meat belongeth to them that are of full age, even those who by reason of use have their senses exercised to discern both good and evil." (**Hebrews 5:12-14**)

"And I will give you pastors according to mine heart, which shall feed you with knowledge and understanding." (Jeremiah 3:15)

Pastors are to hold fast to sound doctrine. Pastors are charged not to preach any other doctrine(s) than that of Christ.

"Hold fast the form of sound words, which thou hast heard of me, in faith and love which is in Christ Jesus. That good thing which was committed unto thee keep by the Holy Ghost which dwelleth in us." (2 Timothy 1:13&14)

"As I besought thee to abide still at Ephesus, when I went into Macedonia, that thou mightest charge some that they teach no other doctrine, Neither give heed to fables and endless genealogies, which minister questions, rather than godly edifying which is in faith: so do." (1 Timothy 1:3–4)

"Neglect not the gift that is in thee, which was given thee by prophecy, with the laying on of the hands of the presbytery. Meditate upon these things; give thyself wholly to them; that thy profiting may appear to all. Take heed unto thyself, and unto the doctrine; continue in them: for in doing this thou shalt both save thyself, and them that hear thee." (1 Timothy 4:14-16)

"Then spake Jesus again unto them, saying, I am the light of the world: he that followeth me shall not walk in darkness, but shall have the light of life." (John 8:12)

The sheep are to be reminded of sound doctrine in the face of so many things departing from the faith in these days. The sheep need to be reminded for it is the propensity of many others in the church, not to listen to sound doctrine in these days.

"Now the Spirit speaketh expressly, that in the latter times some shall depart from the faith, giving heed to seducing spirits, and doctrines of devils; Speaking lies in hypocrisy; having their conscience seared with a hot iron; Forbidding to marry, and commanding to abstain from meats, which God hath created to be received with thanksgiving of them which believe and know the truth. For every creature of God is good, and nothing to be refused, if it be received with thanksgiving: For it is sanctified by the word of God and prayer. If thou put the brethren in remembrance of these things, thou shalt be a good minister of Jesus Christ, nourished up in the words of faith and of good doctrine, whereunto thou hast attained. But refuse profane and old wives' fables, and exercise thyself rather unto godliness. For bodily exercise profiteth little: but godliness is profitable unto all things, having promise of the life that now is, and of that which is to come. This is a faithful saying and worthy of all acceptation. For therefore we both labour and suffer reproach, because we trust in the living God, who is the Saviour of all men, specially of those that believe. These things command and teach." (1 Timothy 4:1–11)

"Preach the word; be instant in season, out of season; reprove, rebuke, exhort with all longsuffering and doctrine. For the time will come when they will not endure sound doctrine; but after their own lusts shall they heap to themselves teachers, having itching ears; And they shall turn away their ears from the truth, and shall be turned unto fables." (2 Timothy 4:2–4)

The Bible warns of the peril in despising the scriptures.

"Whoso despiseth the word shall be destroyed: but he that feareth the commandment shall be rewarded."(Proverbs 13:13)

"Now I beseech you, brethren, mark them which cause divisions and offences contrary to the doctrine which ye have learned; and avoid them. For they that are such serve not our Lord Jesus Christ, but their own belly; and by good words and fair speeches deceive the hearts of the simple. For your obedience is come abroad unto all men. I am glad therefore on your behalf: but yet I would have you wise unto that which is good, and simple concerning evil." (Romans 16:17-19)

The true unity involved in the perfecting of those within the body of Christ, occurs when the members are no longer manipulated by doctrine not of Christ and therefore not of the Bible. The body of Christ (the spiritual church) needs to move on to a greater perfecting in knowledge and grace having mastered the basic concepts of Christian doctrine such as repentance, faith, baptism, intersession, resurrection and salvation.

And he gave some, apostles; and some, prophets; and some, evangelists; and some, pastors and teachers; For the perfecting of the saints, for the work of the ministry, for the edifying of the body of Christ: Till we all come in the unity of the faith, and of the knowledge of the Son of God, unto a perfect man, unto the measure of the stature of the fulness of Christ: That we henceforth be no more children, tossed to and fro, and carried about with every wind of doctrine, by the sleight of men, and cunning craftiness, whereby they lie in wait to deceive; But speaking the truth in love, may grow up into him in all things, which is the head, even Christ: From whom the whole body fitly joined together and compacted by that which every joint supplieth, according to the effectual working in the measure of every part, maketh increase of the body unto the edifying of itself in love." (Ephesians 4: 11–16)

"Therefore leaving the principles of the doctrine of Christ, let us go on unto perfection; not laying again the foundation of repentance from dead works, and of faith toward God, Of the doctrine of baptisms, and of laying on of hands, and of resurrection of the dead, and of eternal judgment. And this will we do, if God permit." (Hebrews 6:1–3)

Author Baptist by Choice

I am a Christian and a Baptist by choice, although, I must admit that I was born into such a household. I was born in the middle of the 20th century. I was therefore a teenager during the 1960's and grew into adult maturity during the 1970s. I am hard pressed to think of a more turbulent period in terms of biblical challenge. Jesus Christ became a "Superstar" while someone declared again that "God is dead".

My testimony is of God's ability to bring a person into knowledge of his word if we do not posture ourselves but rather continue to seek the truth. After nearly rejecting the

Bible in the early 1970's, by the late 1970's I risked imprisonment while teaching the Bible to Saudi Arabs in Saudi Arabia. Then to my amazement I was called to preach the Word (see Chapter 10, Preaching, Preachers, Ministers and the Calling (The Man of God and the Woman of God) and Appendix 6, My Calling, A Testimony) while teaching Sunday School in the early 1990's. However, if I were to be shown sounder biblical doctrine than Baptist doctrine, I would surely convert. I have studied all of the world's major religions and I have studied all of the major Christian denominations.

> *"Shew me thy ways, O Lord; teach me thy paths. Lead me in thy truth, and teach me: for thou art the God of my salvation; on thee do I wait all the day. Remember, O Lord, thy tender mercies and thy lovingkindnesses; for they have been ever of old. Remember not the sins of my youth, nor my transgressions: according to thy mercy remember thou me for thy goodness' sake, O Lord. Good and upright is the Lord: therefore will he teach sinners in the way. The meek will he guide in judgment: and the meek will he teach his way. All the paths of the Lord are mercy and truth unto such as keep his covenant and his testimonies. For thy name's sake, O Lord, pardon mine iniquity; for it is great. What man is he that feareth the Lord? him shall he teach in the way that he shall choose. His soul shall dwell at ease; and his seed shall inherit the earth."* (Psalms 25:4–13)

A Model of Sound Doctrine

There is no authorship on my part with regard to the Baptist Articles only a presentation for the sake of instruction. The scriptural references used have departed from other material I had seen with I believe greater clarity.

> *"To know wisdom and instruction; to perceive the words of understanding; To receive the instruction of wisdom, justice, and judgment, and equity; To give subtilty to the simple, to the young man knowledge and discretion. A wise man will hear, and will increase learning; and a man of understanding shall attain unto wise counsels: To understand a proverb, and the interpretation; the words of the wise, and their dark sayings. The fear of the Lord is the beginning of knowledge: but fools despise wisdom and instruction."* (Proverbs 1:2-7)

Baptist Articles of Faith – The New Hampshire Confession of Faith (1833)

This author was born into a Baptist family and yet has studied the doctrines of all of the major world religions and well as numerous Christian denominational doctrines. I studied in the quest to determine for myself the truth and found that I had been rooted in sound doctrine from childhood as have many of you from the Baptist Christian denomination. I have presented herein for target practice, Baptist Doctrine that I profess to be the closest doctrine to the Bible. The Baptist Articles of Faith as presented herein in its modified Baptist Church Manual version is essentially what is known as the New Hampshire Confession of Faith (1833). The New Hampshire Confession of Faith was framed by a committee after three years of labor and approved by the New Hampshire Baptist Convention in 1833. It has been adopted by more Baptist Churches than any other of the five (5) Baptist Confessions of Faith that have been produced. The other four (4) Baptist Confessions of Faith are: (1) The First London Baptist Confession of Faith (1644 & 1646), The Second London Baptist Confession of Faith (1833), The Philadelphia Confession and The Baptist Faith and Message (1925, 1963, 1998 and 2000 editions. All of these confessions share a continuity representative of the beliefs common to Baptist. The Baptist Articles of Faith presented herein, is recommended by many if not nearly all Baptist Handbooks.

Note: There is also a Baptist Church Covenant that is used by many Baptist Churches. See Appendix 4, The Baptist Church Covenant.

I.   *OF THE SCRIPTURES*

"We believe that the Holy Bible was written by men divinely inspired, and is a perfect treasure of heavenly instructions: that it has God for its author, salvation for its end, and truth without any mixture of error, for its matter; that it reveals the principles by which God will judge us; and therefore is, and shall remain to the end of the world, the true center of Christian union, and the supreme standard by which all human conduct, creeds, and opinions should be tried."

"All scripture is given by inspiration of God, and is profitable for doctrine, for reproof, for correction, for instruction in righteousness: That the man of God may be perfect, throughly furnished unto all good works." (2 Timothy 3:16&17)

"Knowing this first, that no prophecy of the scripture is of any private interpretation. For the prophecy came not in old time by the will of man: but holy men of God spake as they were moved by the Holy Ghost. " (2 Peter 1:20&21)

"Yea, and all that will live godly in Christ Jesus shall suffer persecution. But evil men and seducers shall wax worse and worse, deceiving, and being deceived. But continue thou in the things which thou hast learned and hast been assured of, knowing of whom thou hast learned them; And that from a child thou hast known the holy scriptures, which are able to make thee wise unto salvation through faith which is in Christ Jesus." (2 Timothy 3:12-15)

"For I am not ashamed of the gospel of Christ: for it is the power of God unto salvation to every one that believeth; to the Jew first, and also to the Greek. For therein is the righteousness of God revealed from faith to faith: as it is written, The just shall live by faith." (Romans 1:16&17)

"Sanctify them through thy truth: thy word is truth." (John 17:17)

"Who hath ascended up into heaven, or descended? who hath gathered the wind in his fists? who hath bound the waters in a garment? who hath established all the ends of the earth? what is his name, and what is his son's name, if thou canst tell? Every word of God is pure: he is a shield unto them that put their trust in him." (Proverbs 30:5&6)

"The words of the Lord are pure words: as silver tried in a furnace of earth, purified seven times. Thou shalt keep them, O Lord, thou shalt preserve them from this generation for ever." (Psalms 12:6&7)

"Thy statutes have been my songs in the house of my pilgrimage. I have remembered thy name, O Lord, in the night, and have kept thy law. This I had, because I kept thy precepts. Thou art my portion, O Lord: I have said that I would keep thy words. I intreated thy favor with my whole heart: be merciful unto me according to thy word. I thought on my ways, and turned my feet unto thy testimonies. I made haste, and delayed not to keep thy commandments. The bands of the wicked have robbed me: but I have not forgotten thy law.

At midnight I will rise to give thanks unto thee because of thy righteous judgments. I am a companion of all them that fear thee, and of them that keep thy precepts. The earth, O Lord, is full of thy mercy: teach me thy statutes." (**Psalm 119:57-64**)

"And I John saw these things, and heard them. And when I had heard and seen, I fell down to worship before the feet of the angel which shewed me these things. Then saith he unto me, See thou do it not: for I am thy fellowservant, and of thy brethren the prophets, and of them which keep the sayings of this book: worship God. And he saith unto me, Seal not the sayings of the prophecy of this book: for the time is at hand. He that is unjust, let him be unjust still: and he which is filthy, let him be filthy still: and he that is righteous, let him be righteous still: and he that is holy, let him be holy still. And, behold, I come quickly; and my reward is with me, to give every man according as his work shall be. I am Alpha and Omega, the beginning and the end, the first and the last. Blessed are they that do his commandments, that they may have right to the tree of life, and may enter in through the gates into the city. For without are dogs, and sorcerers, and whoremongers, and murderers, and idolaters, and whosoever loveth and maketh a lie." (**Revelation 22:8-15**)

"And if any man hear my words, and believe not, I judge him not: for I came not to judge the world, but to save the world. He that rejecteth me, and receiveth not my words, hath one that judgeth him: the word that I have spoken, the same shall judge him in the last day. For I have not spoken of myself; but the Father which sent me, he gave me a commandment, what I should say, and what I should speak." (**John 12:47-49**)

"For there is no respect of persons with God. For as many as have sinned without law shall also perish without law: and as many as have sinned in the law shall be judged by the law; (For not the hearers of the law are just before God, but the doers of the law shall be justified. For when the Gentiles, which have not the law, do by nature the things contained in the law, these, having not the law, are a law unto themselves: Which shew the work of the law written in their hearts, their conscience also bearing witness, and their thoughts the mean while accusing or else excusing one another); In the day when God shall judge the secrets of men by Jesus Christ according to my gospel. Behold, thou art called a Jew, and restest in the law, and makest thy boast of God, And knowest his will, and approvest the things that are more excellent, being instructed out of the law; And art confident that thou thyself art a guide of the blind, a light of them which are in darkness, An instructor of the foolish, a teacher of babes, which hast the form of knowledge and of the truth in the law. Thou therefore which teachest another, teachest thou not thyself? thou that preachest a man should not steal, dost thou steal? Thou that sayest a man should not commit adultery, dost thou commit adultery? thou that abhorrest idols, dost thou commit sacrilege? Thou that makest thy boast of the law, through breaking the law dishonorest thou God?" (**Romans 2:11-23**)

"For all flesh is as grass, and all the glory of man as the flower of grass. The grass withereth, and the flower thereof falleth away: But the word of the Lord endureth for ever. And this is the word which by the gospel is preached unto you. (**1 Peter 1:24&25**)

"Heaven and earth shall pass away: but my words shall not pass away." (**Luke 21:33**)

"Yea doubtless, and I count all things but loss for the excellency of the knowledge of Christ Jesus my Lord: for whom I have suffered the loss of all things, and do count them but dung, that I may win Christ, And be found in him, not having mine own righteousness, which is of the law, but that which is through the faith of Christ, the righteousness which is of God

by faith: That I may know him, and the power of his resurrection, and the fellowship of his sufferings, being made conformable unto his death; If by any means I might attain unto the resurrection of the dead. Not as though I had already attained, either were already perfect: but I follow after, if that I may apprehend that for which also I am apprehended of Christ Jesus. Brethren, I count not myself to have apprehended: but this one thing I do, forgetting those things which are behind, and reaching forth unto those things which are before, I press toward the mark for the prize of the high calling of God in Christ Jesus. Let us therefore, as many as be perfect, be thus minded: and if in any thing ye be otherwise minded, God shall reveal even this unto you. Nevertheless, whereto we have already attained, let us walk by the same rule, let us mind the same thing." **(Philippians 3:8-16)**

"Beloved, when I gave all diligence to write unto you of the common salvation, it was needful for me to write unto you, and exhort you that ye should earnestly contend for the faith which was once delivered unto the saints." **(Jude 3)**

"Sanctify the Lord of hosts himself; and let him be your fear, and let him be your dread. And he shall be for a sanctuary; but for a stone of stumbling and for a rock of offense to both the houses of Israel, for a gin and for a snare to the inhabitants of Jerusalem. And many among them shall stumble, and fall, and be broken, and be snared, and be taken. Bind up the testimony, seal the law among my disciples. And I will wait upon the Lord, that hideth his face from the house of Jacob, and I will look for him. Behold, I and the children whom the Lord hath given me are for signs and for wonders in Israel from the Lord of hosts, which dwelleth in mount Zion. And when they shall say unto you, Seek unto them that have familiar spirits, and unto wizards that peep, and that mutter: should not a people seek unto their God? for the living to the dead? To the law and to the testimony: if they speak not according to this word, it is because there is no light in them. And they shall pass through it, hardly bestead and hungry: and it shall come to pass, that when they shall be hungry, they shall fret themselves, and curse their king and their God, and look upward. And they shall look unto the earth; and behold trouble and darkness, dimness of anguish; and they shall be driven to darkness." **(Isaiah 8:13-22)**

II.   *OF THE TRUE GOD*

"We believe that there is one, and only one living and true God, an infinite, intelligent Spirit, whose name is Jehovah, the Maker and Supreme Ruler of heaven and earth; inexpressibly glorious in holiness, and worthy of all possible honor, confidence, and love; that in the unity of the Godhead there are three persons, the Father, the Son, and the Holy Ghost; equal in every divine perfection, and executing distinct but harmonious offices in the great work of redemption."

"But the Lord is the true God, he is the living God, and an everlasting king: at his wrath the earth shall tremble, and the nations shall not be able to abide his indignation. Thus shall ye say unto them, The gods that have not made the heavens and the earth, even they shall perish from the earth, and from under these heavens. He hath made the earth by his power, he hath established the world by his wisdom, and hath stretched out the heavens by his discretion. When he uttereth his voice, there is a multitude of waters in the heavens, and he causeth the vapours to ascend from the ends of the earth; he maketh lightnings with rain, and bringeth forth the wind out of his treasures. Every man is brutish in his knowledge: every founder is confounded by the graven image: for his molten image is falsehood,

and there is no breath in them. They are vanity, and the work of errors: in the time of their visitation they shall perish." (Jeremiah 10:10-15)

"For thy Maker is thine husband; the Lord of hosts is his name; and thy Redeemer the Holy One of Israel; The God of the whole earth shall he be called." (Isaiah 54:5)

"These words spake Jesus, and lifted up his eyes to heaven, and said, Father, the hour is come; glorify thy Son, that thy Son also may glorify thee: As thou hast given him power over all flesh, that he should give eternal life to as many as thou hast given him. And this is life eternal, that they might know thee the only true God, and Jesus Christ, whom thou hast sent.." (John 17:1-3)

"And Moses said unto God, Behold, when I come unto the children of Israel, and shall say unto them, The God of your fathers hath sent me unto you; and they shall say to me, What is his name? what shall I say unto them? And God said unto Moses, I AM THAT I AM: and he said, Thus shalt thou say unto the children of Israel, I AM hath sent me unto you. And God said moreover unto Moses, Thus shalt thou say unto the children of Israel, The Lord God of your fathers, the God of Abraham, the God of Isaac, and the God of Jacob, hath sent me unto you: this is my name for ever, and this is my memorial unto all generations." (Exodus 3:13-15)

"Then king Darius wrote unto all people, nations, and languages, that dwell in all the earth; Peace be multiplied unto you. I make a decree, That in every dominion of my kingdom men tremble and fear before the God of Daniel: for he is the living God, and stedfast for ever, and his kingdom that which shall not be destroyed, and his dominion shall be even unto the end. He delivereth and rescueth, and he worketh signs and wonders in heaven and in earth, who hath delivered Daniel from the power of the lions. So this Daniel prospered in the reign of Darius, and in the reign of Cyrus the Persian." (Daniel 6:25-28)

"Great is our Lord, and of great power: his understanding is infinite." (Psalm 147:5)

"Let them be confounded and troubled for ever; yea, let them be put to shame, and perish: That men may know that thou, whose name alone is Jehovah, art the most high over all the earth." (Psalm 83:17&18)

"And in that day thou shalt say, O Lord, I will praise thee: though thou wast angry with me, thine anger is turned away, and thou comfortedst me. Behold, God is my salvation; I will trust, and not be afraid: for the Lord Jehovah is my strength and my song; he also is become my salvation. Therefore with joy shall ye draw water out of the wells of salvation. And in that day shall ye say, Praise the Lord, call upon his name, declare his doings among the people, make mention that his name is exalted. Sing unto the Lord; for he hath done excellent things: this is known in all the earth. Cry out and shout, thou inhabitant of Zion: for great is the Holy One of Israel in the midst of thee." (Isaiah Chapter 12)

"And God spake unto Moses, and said unto him, I am the Lord: And I appeared unto Abraham, unto Isaac, and unto Jacob, by the name of God Almighty, but by my name Jehovah was I not known to them. And I have also established my covenant with them, to give them the land of Canaan, the land of their pilgrimage, wherein they were strangers." (Exodus 6:2-4)

"Tell ye, and bring them near; yea, let them take counsel together: who hath declared this from ancient time? who hath told it from that time? have not I the Lord? and there is no

God else beside me; a just God and a Savior; there is none beside me. Look unto me, and be ye saved, all the ends of the earth: for I am God, and there is none else. I have sworn by myself, the word is gone out of my mouth in righteousness, and shall not return, That unto me every knee shall bow, every tongue shall swear." **(Isaiah 45:21-23)**

"Sanctify yourselves therefore, and be ye holy: for I am the Lord your God. And ye shall keep my statutes, and do them: I am the Lord which sanctify you." **(Leviticus 20:7&8)**

Exalt the Lord our God, and worship at his holy hill; for the Lord our God is holy." **(Psalm 99:9)**

"The four and twenty elders fall down before him that sat on the throne, and worship him that liveth for ever and ever, and cast their crowns before the throne, saying, Thou art worthy, O Lord, to receive glory and honor and power: for thou hast created all things, and for thy pleasure they are and were created." **(Revelation 4:10&11)**

"But to us there is but one God, the Father, of whom are all things, and we in him; and one Lord Jesus Christ, by whom are all things, and we by him." **(1 Corinthians 8:6)**

"There is one body, and one Spirit, even as ye are called in one hope of your calling; One Lord, one faith, one baptism, One God and Father of all, who is above all, and through all, and in you all." **(Ephesians 4:4-6)**

"Wherefore remember, that ye being in time past Gentiles in the flesh, who are called Uncircumcision by that which is called the Circumcision in the flesh made by hands; That at that time ye were without Christ, being aliens from the commonwealth of Israel, and strangers from the covenants of promise, having no hope, and without God in the world: But now in Christ Jesus ye who sometimes were far off are made nigh by the blood of Christ. For he is our peace, who hath made both one, and hath broken down the middle wall of partition between us; Having abolished in his flesh the enmity, even the law of commandments contained in ordinances; for to make in himself of twain one new man, so making peace; And that he might reconcile both unto God in one body by the cross, having slain the enmity thereby: And came and preached peace to you which were afar off, and to them that were nigh. For through him we both have access by one Spirit unto the Father. Now therefore ye are no more strangers and foreigners, but fellowcitizens with the saints, and of the household of God; And are built upon the foundation of the apostles and prophets, Jesus Christ himself being the chief corner stone; In whom all the building fitly framed together groweth unto an holy temple in the Lord: In whom ye also are builded together for an habitation of God through the Spirit." **(Ephesians 2:11-22)**

"Then Paul stood in the midst of Mars' hill, and said, Ye men of Athens, I perceive that in all things ye are too superstitious. For as I passed by, and beheld your devotions, I found an altar with this inscription, TO THE UNKNOWN GOD. Whom therefore ye ignorantly worship, him declare I unto you. God that made the world and all things therein, seeing that he is Lord of heaven and earth, dwelleth not in temples made with hands; Neither is worshipped with men's hands, as though he needed any thing, seeing he giveth to all life, and breath, and all things; And hath made of one blood all nations of men for to dwell on all the face of the earth, and hath determined the times before appointed, and the bounds of their habitation; That they should seek the Lord, if haply they might feel after him, and find him, though he be not far from every one of us: For in him we live, and move, and have our being; as certain also of your own poets have said, For we are also his offspring.

Forasmuch then as we are the offspring of God, we ought not to think that the Godhead is like unto gold, or silver, or stone, graven by art and man's device. And the times of this ignorance God winked at; but now commandeth all men every where to repent: Because he hath appointed a day, in the which he will judge the world in righteousness by that man whom he hath ordained; whereof he hath given assurance unto all men, in that he hath raised him from the dead." **(Act 17:22-31)**

"For the wrath of God is revealed from heaven against all ungodliness and unrighteousness of men, who hold the truth in unrighteousness; Because that which may be known of God is manifest in them; for God hath shewed it unto them. For the invisible things of him from the creation of the world are clearly seen, being understood by the things that are made, even his eternal power and Godhead; so that they are without excuse: Because that, when they knew God, they glorified him not as God, neither were thankful; but became vain in their imaginations, and their foolish heart was darkened." **(Romans 1:18-21)**

"For there are three that bear record in heaven, the Father, the Word, and the Holy Ghost: and these three are one." **(1 John 5:7)**

"And Jesus came and spake unto them, saying, All power is given unto me in heaven and in earth. Go ye therefore, and teach all nations, baptizing them in the name of the Father, and of the Son, and of the Holy Ghost:" **(Matthew 28:18&19)**

"Jesus saith unto him, I am the way, the truth, and the life: no man cometh unto the Father, but by me. If ye had known me, ye should have known my Father also: and from henceforth ye know him, and have seen him. Philip saith unto him, Lord, shew us the Father, and it sufficeth us. Jesus saith unto him, Have I been so long time with you, and yet hast thou not known me, Philip? he that hath seen me hath seen the Father; and how sayest thou then, Shew us the Father? Believest thou not that I am in the Father, and the Father in me? the words that I speak unto you I speak not of myself: but the Father that dwelleth in me, he doeth the works. Believe me that I am in the Father, and the Father in me: or else believe me for the very works' sake. Verily, verily, I say unto you, He that believeth on me, the works that I do shall he do also; and greater works than these shall he do; because I go unto my Father. And whatsoever ye shall ask in my name, that will I do, that the Father may be glorified in the Son. If ye shall ask any thing in my name, I will do it. If ye love me, keep my commandments. And I will pray the Father, and he shall give you another Comforter, that he may abide with you for ever; Even the Spirit of truth; whom the world cannot receive, because it seeth him not, neither knoweth him: but ye know him; for he dwelleth with you, and shall be in you. I will not leave you comfortless: I will come to you. Yet a little while, and the world seeth me no more; but ye see me: because I live, ye shall live also. At that day ye shall know that I am in my Father, and ye in me, and I in you. He that hath my commandments, and keepeth them, he it is that loveth me: and he that loveth me shall be loved of my Father, and I will love him, and will manifest myself to him. These things have I spoken unto you, being yet present with you. But the Comforter, which is the Holy Ghost, whom the Father will send in my name, he shall teach you all things, and bring all things to your remembrance, whatsoever I have said unto you." **(John 14:6-21, 25&26)**

"For I came down from heaven, not to do mine own will, but the will of him that sent me. And this is the Father's will which hath sent me, that of all which he hath given me I should lose nothing, but should raise it up again at the last day. And this is the will of him that

sent me, that every one which seeth the Son, and believeth on him, may have everlasting life: and I will raise him up at the last day." (John 38-40)

"After this manner therefore pray ye: Our Father which art in heaven, Hallowed be thy name. Thy kingdom come. Thy will be done in earth, as it is in heaven." (Matthew 6:9&10)

"Heaven and earth shall pass away: but my words shall not pass away. But of that day and that hour knoweth no man, no, not the angels which are in heaven, neither the Son, but the Father." (Mark 13:31&32)

"Likewise the Spirit also helpeth our infirmities: for we know not what we should pray for as we ought: but the Spirit itself maketh intercession for us with groanings which cannot be uttered. And he that searcheth the hearts knoweth what is the mind of the Spirit, because he maketh intercession for the saints according to the will of God." (Romans 8:26&27)

"Herein is love, not that we loved God, but that he loved us, and sent his Son to be the propitiation for our sins. Beloved, if God so loved us, we ought also to love one another. No man hath seen God at any time. If we love one another, God dwelleth in us, and his love is perfected in us. Hereby know we that we dwell in him, and he in us, because he hath given us of his Spirit. And we have seen and do testify that the Father sent the Son to be the Saviour of the world. Whosoever shall confess that Jesus is the Son of God, God dwelleth in him, and he in God. And we have known and believed the love that God hath to us. God is love; and he that dwelleth in love dwelleth in God, and God in him. Herein is our love made perfect, that we may have boldness in the day of judgment: because as he is, so are we in this world. There is no fear in love; but perfect love casteth out fear: because fear hath torment. He that feareth is not made perfect in love. We love him, because he first loved us. If a man say, I love God, and hateth his brother, he is a liar: for he that loveth not his brother whom he hath seen, how can he love God whom he hath not seen? And this commandment have we from him, That he who loveth God love his brother also." (1 John 4:10-21)

"As ye have therefore received Christ Jesus the Lord, so walk ye in him: Rooted and built up in him, and stablished in the faith, as ye have been taught, abounding therein with thanksgiving. Beware lest any man spoil you through philosophy and vain deceit, after the tradition of men, after the rudiments of the world, and not after Christ. For in him dwelleth all the fulness of the Godhead bodily. And ye are complete in him, which is the head of all principality and power: In whom also ye are circumcised with the circumcision made without hands, in putting off the body of the sins of the flesh by the circumcision of Christ: Buried with him in baptism, wherein also ye are risen with him through the faith of the operation of God, who hath raised him from the dead." (Colossians 2:6-12)

III.   *OF THE FALL OF MAN*

"We believe that man was created in holiness, under the law of his Maker; but by voluntary transgression fell from that holy and happy state; in consequence of which all mankind are now sinners, not by constraint, but choice; being by nature utterly void of that holiness required by the law of God, positively inclined to evil; and therefore under just condemnation to eternal ruin, without defense or excuse."

"And God said, Let us make man in our image, after our likeness: and let them have dominion over the fish of the sea, and over the fowl of the air, and over the cattle, and over all the earth, and over every creeping thing that creepeth upon the earth. So God created man in his own image, in the image of God created he him; male and female created he them. And God blessed them, and God said unto them, Be fruitful, and multiply, and replenish the earth, and subdue it: and have dominion over the fish of the sea, and over the fowl of the air, and over every living thing that moveth upon the earth. And God said, Behold, I have given you every herb bearing seed, which is upon the face of all the earth, and every tree, in the which is the fruit of a tree yielding seed; to you it shall be for meat. And to every beast of the earth, and to every fowl of the air, and to every thing that creepeth upon the earth, wherein there is life, I have given every green herb for meat: and it was so. And God saw every thing that he had made, and, behold, it was very good. And the evening and the morning were the sixth day." (Genesis 1:26-31)

"And when the woman saw that the tree was good for food, and that it was pleasant to the eyes, and a tree to be desired to make one wise, she took of the fruit thereof, and did eat, and gave also unto her husband with her; and he did eat. And the eyes of them both were opened, and they knew that they were naked; and they sewed fig leaves together, and made themselves aprons. And they heard the voice of the Lord God walking in the garden in the cool of the day: and Adam and his wife hid themselves from the presence of the Lord God amongst the trees of the garden. And the Lord God called unto Adam, and said unto him, Where art thou? And he said, I heard thy voice in the garden, and I was afraid, because I was naked; and I hid myself. And he said, Who told thee that thou wast naked? Hast thou eaten of the tree, whereof I commanded thee that thou shouldest not eat? And the man said, The woman whom thou gavest to be with me, she gave me of the tree, and I did eat. And the Lord God said unto the woman, What is this that thou hast done? And the woman said, The serpent beguiled me, and I did eat. And the Lord God said unto the serpent, Because thou hast done this, thou art cursed above all cattle, and above every beast of the field; upon thy belly shalt thou go, and dust shalt thou eat all the days of thy life: And I will put enmity between thee and the woman, and between thy seed and her seed; it shall bruise thy head, and thou shalt bruise his heel. Unto the woman he said, I will greatly multiply thy sorrow and thy conception; in sorrow thou shalt bring forth children; and thy desire shall be to thy husband, and he shall rule over thee. And unto Adam he said, Because thou hast hearkened unto the voice of thy wife, and hast eaten of the tree, of which I commanded thee, saying, Thou shalt not eat of it: cursed is the ground for thy sake; in sorrow shalt thou eat of it all the days of thy life; Thorns also and thistles shall it bring forth to thee; and thou shalt eat the herb of the field; In the sweat of thy face shalt thou eat bread, till thou return unto the ground; for out of it wast thou taken: for dust thou art, and unto dust shalt thou return. And Adam called his wife's name Eve; because she was the mother of all living. Unto Adam also and to his wife did the Lord God make coats of skins, and clothed them. And the Lord God said, Behold, the man is become as one of us, to know good and evil: and now, lest he put forth his hand, and take also of the tree of life, and eat, and live for ever: Therefore the Lord God sent him forth from the garden of Eden, to till the ground from whence he was taken. So he drove out the man; and he placed at the east of the garden of Eden Cherubims, and a flaming sword which turned every way, to keep the way of the tree of life." (Genesis 3:6-24)

"For as by one man's disobedience many were made sinners, so by the obedience of one shall many be made righteous." (**Romans 5:19**)

"Therefore my people shall know my name: therefore they shall know in that day that I am he that doth speak: behold, it is I." (**Isaiah 53:6**)

"Now therefore fear the Lord, and serve him in sincerity and in truth: and put away the gods which your fathers served on the other side of the flood, and in Egypt; and serve ye the Lord. And if it seem evil unto you to serve the Lord, choose you this day whom ye will serve; whether the gods which your fathers served that were on the other side of the flood, or the gods of the Amorites, in whose land ye dwell: but as for me and my house, we will serve the Lord." (**Joshua 24:14&15**)

"But we are all as an unclean thing, and all our righteousnesses are as filthy rags; and we all do fade as a leaf; and our iniquities, like the wind, have taken us away. And there is none that calleth upon thy name, that stirreth up himself to take hold of thee: for thou hast hid thy face from us, and hast consumed us, because of our iniquities. But now, O Lord, thou art our father; we are the clay, and thou our potter; and we all are the work of thy hand. Be not wroth very sore, O Lord, neither remember iniquity for ever: behold, see, we beseech thee, we are all thy people." (**Isaiah 64:6-9**)

And you hath he quickened, who were dead in trespasses and sins; Wherein in time past ye walked according to the course of this world, according to the prince of the power of the air, the spirit that now worketh in the children of disobedience: Among whom also we all had our conversation in times past in the lusts of our flesh, fulfilling the desires of the flesh and of the mind; and were by nature the children of wrath, even as others." (**Ephesians 2:1-3**)

And this is the condemnation, that light is come into the world, and men loved darkness rather than light, because their deeds were evil." (**John 3:19**)

"The soul that sinneth, it shall die. The son shall not bear the iniquity of the father, neither shall the father bear the iniquity of the son: the righteousness of the righteous shall be upon him, and the wickedness of the wicked shall be upon him. But if the wicked will turn from all his sins that he hath committed, and keep all my statutes, and do that which is lawful and right, he shall surely live, he shall not die. All his transgressions that he hath committed, they shall not be mentioned unto him: in his righteousness that he hath done he shall live. Have I any pleasure at all that the wicked should die? saith the Lord God: and not that he should return from his ways, and live? But when the righteous turneth away from his righteousness, and committeth iniquity, and doeth according to all the abominations that the wicked man doeth, shall he live? All his righteousness that he hath done shall not be mentioned: in his trespass that he hath trespassed, and in his sin that he hath sinned, in them shall he die. Yet ye say, The way of the Lord is not equal. Hear now, O house of Israel; Is not my way equal? are not your ways unequal? When a righteous man turneth away from his righteousness, and committeth iniquity, and dieth in them; for his iniquity that he hath done shall he die. Again, when the wicked man turneth away from his wickedness that he hath committed, and doeth that which is lawful and right, he shall save his soul alive. Because he considereth, and turneth away from all his transgressions that he hath committed, he shall surely live, he shall not die. Yet saith the house of Israel, The way of the Lord is not equal. O house of Israel, are not my ways equal? are not your ways unequal? Therefore I will judge you, O house of Israel, every one according to his ways, saith the Lord God. Repent, and turn yourselves from all your transgressions; so iniquity shall not be

your ruin. Cast away from you all your transgressions, whereby ye have transgressed; and make you a new heart and a new spirit: for why will ye die, O house of Israel? For I have no pleasure in the death of him that dieth, saith the Lord God: wherefore turn yourselves, and live ye." (**Ezekiel 18:20-32**)

"As it is written, There is none righteous, no, not one: There is none that understandeth, there is none that seeketh after God. They are all gone out of the way, they are together become unprofitable; there is none that doeth good, no, not one. Their throat is an open sepulchre; with their tongues they have used deceit; the poison of asps is under their lips: Whose mouth is full of cursing and bitterness: Their feet are swift to shed blood: Destruction and misery are in their ways: And the way of peace have they not known: There is no fear of God before their eyes. Now we know that what things soever the law saith, it saith to them who are under the law: that every mouth may be stopped, and all the world may become guilty before God. Therefore by the deeds of the law there shall no flesh be justified in his sight: for by the law is the knowledge of sin." (**Romans 3:10-20**)

IV. *OF THE WAY OF SALVATION*

"We believe that the salvation of sinners is wholly of grace; through the mediatorial offices of the Son of God; who by the appointment of the Father, freely took upon him our nature, yet without sin; honored the divine law by his personal obedience, and by his death made a full atonement of our sins; that having risen from the dead he is now enthroned in heaven; and uniting in his wonderful person the tenderest sympathies with divine perfections, he is every way qualified to be a suitable, a compassionate, and an all-sufficient Savior."

"But God, who is rich in mercy, for his great love wherewith he loved us, Even when we were dead in sins, hath quickened us together with Christ, (by grace ye are saved;) And hath raised us up together, and made us sit together in heavenly places in Christ Jesus: That in the ages to come he might shew the exceeding riches of his grace in his kindness toward us through Christ Jesus. For by grace are ye saved through faith; and that not of yourselves: it is the gift of God: Not of works, lest any man should boast. For we are his workmanship, created in Christ Jesus unto good works, which God hath before ordained that we should walk in them." (**Ephesians 2:4-10**)

"For God so loved the world, that he gave his only begotten Son, that whosoever believeth in him should not perish, but have everlasting life." (**John 3:16**)

"Let this mind be in you, which was also in Christ Jesus: Who, being in the form of God, thought it not robbery to be equal with God: But made himself of no reputation, and took upon him the form of a servant, and was made in the likeness of men: And being found in fashion as a man, he humbled himself, and became obedient unto death, even the death of the cross." (**Philippians 2:5-8**)

"Beware lest any man spoil you through philosophy and vain deceit, after the tradition of men, after the rudiments of the world, and not after Christ. For in him dwelleth all the fulness of the Godhead bodily." (**Colossians 2:8&9**)

"Produce your cause, saith the Lord; bring forth your strong reasons, saith the King of Jacob." (**Isaiah 42:21**)

"Who hath believed our report? and to whom is the arm of the Lord revealed? For he shall grow up before him as a tender plant, and as a root out of a dry ground: he hath no form nor comeliness; and when we shall see him, there is no beauty that we should desire him. He is despised and rejected of men; a man of sorrows, and acquainted with grief: and we hid as it were our faces from him; he was despised, and we esteemed him not. Surely he hath born our griefs, and carried our sorrows: yet we did esteem him stricken, smitten of God, and afflicted. But he was wounded for our transgressions, he was bruised for our iniquities: the chastisement of our peace was upon him; and with his stripes we are healed. All we like sheep have gone astray; we have turned every one to his own way; and the Lord hath laid on him the iniquity of us all." (Isaiah 53:1-6)

"But God commendeth his love toward us, in that, while we were yet sinners, Christ died for us. Much more then, being now justified by his blood, we shall be saved from wrath through him. For if, when we were enemies, we were reconciled to God by the death of his Son, much more, being reconciled, we shall be saved by his life. And not only so, but we also joy in God through our Lord Jesus Christ, by whom we have now received the atonement. Wherefore, as by one man sin entered into the world, and death by sin; and so death passed upon all men, for that all have sinned: (For until the law sin was in the world: but sin is not imputed when there is no law. Nevertheless death reigned from Adam to Moses, even over them that had not sinned after the similitude of Adam's transgression, who is the figure of him that was to come. But not as the offense, so also is the free gift. For if through the offense of one many be dead, much more the grace of God, and the gift by grace, which is by one man, Jesus Christ, hath abounded unto many. And not as it was by one that sinned, so is the gift: for the judgment was by one to condemnation, but the free gift is of many offenses unto justification. For if by one man's offense death reigned by one; much more they which receive abundance of grace and of the gift of righteousness shall reign in life by one, Jesus Christ). Therefore as by the offense of one judgment came upon all men to condemnation; even so by the righteousness of one the free gift came upon all men unto justification of life. For as by one man's disobedience many were made sinners, so by the obedience of one shall many be made righteous. Moreover the law entered, that the offense might abound. But where sin abounded, grace did much more abound: That as sin hath reigned unto death, even so might grace reign through righteousness unto eternal life by Jesus Christ our Lord." (Romans 5:8-21)

Wherefore I also, after I heard of your faith in the Lord Jesus, and love unto all the saints, Cease not to give thanks for you, making mention of you in my prayers; That the God of our Lord Jesus Christ, the Father of glory, may give unto you the spirit of wisdom and revelation in the knowledge of him: The eyes of your understanding being enlightened; that ye may know what is the hope of his calling, and what the riches of the glory of his inheritance in the saints, And what is the exceeding greatness of his power to us-ward who believe, according to the working of his mighty power, Which he wrought in Christ, when he raised him from the dead, and set him at his own right hand in the heavenly places, Far above all principality, and power, and might, and dominion, and every name that is named, not only in this world, but also in that which is to come: And hath put all things under his feet, and gave him to be the head over all things to the church, Which is his body, the fulness of him that filleth all in all. And you hath he quickened, who were dead in trespasses and sins; Wherein in time past ye walked according to the course of this world, according to the prince of the power of the air, the spirit that now worketh in the children of disobedience:

Among whom also we all had our conversation in times past in the lusts of our flesh, fulfilling the desires of the flesh and of the mind; and were by nature the children of wrath, even as others." (Ephesians 1:15-23)

"By so much was Jesus made a surety of a better testament. And they truly were many priests, because they were not suffered to continue by reason of death: But this man, because he continueth ever, hath an unchangeable priesthood. Wherefore he is able also to save them to the uttermost that come unto God by him, seeing he ever liveth to make intercession for them. For such an high priest became us, who is holy, harmless, undefiled, separate from sinners, and made higher than the heavens; Who needeth not daily, as those high priests, to offer up sacrifice, first for his own sins, and then for the people's: for this he did once, when he offered up himself. For the law maketh men high priests which have infirmity; but the word of the oath, which was since the law, maketh the Son, who is consecrated for evermore." (Hebrews 7:22-28)

"In this was manifested the love of God toward us, because that God sent his only begotten Son into the world, that we might live through him. Herein is love, not that we loved God, but that he loved us, and sent his Son to be the propitiation for our sins. Beloved, if God so loved us, we ought also to love one another. No man hath seen God at any time. If we love one another, God dwelleth in us, and his love is perfected in us. Hereby know we that we dwell in him, and he in us, because he hath given us of his Spirit. And we have seen and do testify that the Father sent the Son to be the Savior of the world. Whosoever shall confess that Jesus is the Son of God, God dwelleth in him, and he in God. And we have known and believed the love that God hath to us. God is love; and he that dwelleth in love dwelleth in God, and God in him. Herein is our love made perfect, that we may have boldness in the day of judgment: because as he is, so are we in this world." (1 John 4:9-17)

V.   OF JUSTIFICATION

    We believe that the great gospel blessing which Christ secures to such as believe in him is justification; that justification includes the pardon of sin, and the promise of eternal life on principles of righteousness; that it is bestowed, not in consideration of any works of righteousness which we have done, but solely through faith in the Redeemers blood; by virtue of which faith his perfect righteousness is freely imputed to us of God; that it brings us into a state of most blessed peace and favor with God, and secures every other blessing needful for time and eternity.

"Even as David also describeth the blessedness of the man, unto whom God imputeth righteousness without works, Saying, Blessed are they whose iniquities are forgiven, and whose sins are covered. Blessed is the man to whom the Lord will not impute sin. And he received the sign of circumcision, a seal of the righteousness of the faith which he had yet being uncircumcised: that he might be the father of all them that believe, though they be not circumcised; that righteousness might be imputed unto them also: And the father of circumcision to them who are not of the circumcision only, but who also walk in the steps of that faith of our father Abraham, which he had being yet uncircumcised. And being fully persuaded that, what he had promised, he was able also to perform. And therefore it was imputed to him for righteousness. Now it was not written for his sake alone, that it was imputed to him; But for us also, to whom it shall be imputed, if we believe on him that raised

up Jesus our Lord from the dead; Who was delivered for our offences, and was raised again for our justification." (Romans 4:6-8,11&12, 21-25)

"Nevertheless death reigned from Adam to Moses, even over them that had not sinned after the similitude of Adam's transgression, who is the figure of him that was to come. But not as the offence, so also is the free gift. For if through the offence of one many be dead, much more the grace of God, and the gift by grace, which is by one man, Jesus Christ, hath abounded unto many. And not as it was by one that sinned, so is the gift: for the judgment was by one to condemnation, but the free gift is of many offences unto justification. For if by one man's offence death reigned by one; much more they which receive abundance of grace and of the gift of righteousness shall reign in life by one, Jesus Christ.) Therefore as by the offence of one judgment came upon all men to condemnation; even so by the righteousness of one the free gift came upon all men unto justification of life. For as by one man's disobedience many were made sinners, so by the obedience of one shall many be made righteous. Moreover the law entered, that the offence might abound. But where sin abounded, grace did much more abound: That as sin hath reigned unto death, even so might grace reign through righteousness unto eternal life by Jesus Christ our Lord." (Romans 5:14-21)

"For when we were yet without strength, in due time Christ died for the ungodly. For scarcely for a righteous man will one die: yet peradventure for a good man some would even dare to die. But God commendeth his love toward us, in that, while we were yet sinners, Christ died for us. Much more then, being now justified by his blood, we shall be saved from wrath through him." (Romans 5:6-9)

"Therefore by the deeds of the law there shall no flesh be justified in his sight: for by the law is the knowledge of sin. But now the righteousness of God without the law is manifested, being witnessed by the law and the prophets; Even the righteousness of God which is by faith of Jesus Christ unto all and upon all them that believe: for there is no difference: For all have sinned, and come short of the glory of God; Being justified freely by his grace through the redemption that is in Christ Jesus: Whom God hath set forth to be a propitiation through faith in his blood, to declare his righteousness for the remission of sins that are past, through the forbearance of God; To declare, I say, at this time his righteousness: that he might be just, and the justifier of him which believeth in Jesus." (Romans 3:20-26)

"Therefore if any man be in Christ, he is a new creature: old things are passed away; behold, all things are become new. And all things are of God, who hath reconciled us to himself by Jesus Christ, and hath given to us the ministry of reconciliation; To wit, that God was in Christ, reconciling the world unto himself, not imputing their trespasses unto them; and hath committed unto us the word of reconciliation. (2 Corinthians 5:17-19)

"Therefore being justified by faith, we have peace with God through our Lord Jesus Christ: By whom also we have access by faith into this grace wherein we stand, and rejoice in hope of the glory of God." (Romans 5:1&2)

VI.   *OF THE FREENESS OF SALVATION*

We believe that the blessings of salvation are made free to all by the gospel; that it is the immediate duty of all to accept them by a cordial, penitent, and obedient faith; and that nothing prevents the salvation of the greatest sinner on earth but his own inherent deprav-

ity and voluntary rejection of the gospel; which rejection involves him in an aggravated condemnation.

"Ho, every one that thirsteth, come ye to the waters, and he that hath no money; come ye, buy, and eat; yea, come, buy wine and milk without money and without price. Wherefore do ye spend money for that which is not bread? and your labour for that which satisfieth not? hearken diligently unto me, and eat ye that which is good, and let your soul delight itself in fatness. Incline your ear, and come unto me: hear, and your soul shall live; and I will make an everlasting covenant with you, even the sure mercies of David." (Isaiah 55:1-3)

"For by grace are ye saved through faith; and that not of yourselves: it is the gift of God:" (Ephesians 2:8)

"Now to him that is of power to stablish you according to my gospel, and the preaching of Jesus Christ, according to the revelation of the mystery, which was kept secret since the world began, But now is made manifest, and by the scriptures of the prophets, according to the commandment of the everlasting God, made known to all nations for the obedience of faith: To God only wise, be glory through Jesus Christ for ever. Amen." (Romans 16:25-27)

"O Jerusalem, Jerusalem, thou that killest the prophets, and stonest them which are sent unto thee, how often would I have gathered thy children together, even as a hen gathereth her chickens under her wings, and ye would not! Behold, your house is left unto you desolate. For I say unto you, Ye shall not see me henceforth, till ye shall say, Blessed is he that cometh in the name of the Lord." (Matthew 23:37-39)

"Wherefore he is able also to save them to the uttermost that come unto God by him, seeing he ever liveth to make intercession for them." (Hebrews 7:25)

"The Lord is not slack concerning his promise, as some men count slackness; but is long-suffering to us-ward, not willing that any should perish, but that all should come to repentance. But the day of the Lord will come as a thief in the night; in the which the heavens shall pass away with a great noise, and the elements shall melt with fervent heat, the earth also and the works that are therein shall be burned up. Seeing then that all these things shall be dissolved, what manner of persons ought ye to be in all holy conversation and godliness, Looking for and hasting unto the coming of the day of God, wherein the heavens being on fire shall be dissolved, and the elements shall melt with fervent heat? Nevertheless we, according to his promise, look for new heavens and a new earth, wherein dwelleth righteousness. Wherefore, beloved, seeing that ye look for such things, be diligent that ye may be found of him in peace, without spot, and blameless." (2 Peter 3:9-14)

"This is a faithful saying, and worthy of all acceptation, that Christ Jesus came into the world to save sinners; of whom I am chief. Howbeit for this cause I obtained mercy, that in me first Jesus Christ might shew forth all longsuffering, for a pattern to them which should hereafter believe on him to life everlasting." (1 Timothy 1:15-16)

"How long, ye simple ones, will ye love simplicity? and the scorners delight in their scorning, and fools hate knowledge? Turn you at my reproof: behold, I will pour out my spirit unto you, I will make known my words unto you. Because I have called, and ye refused; I have stretched out my hand, and no man regarded; But ye have set at nought all my counsel, and would none of my reproof: I also will laugh at your calamity; I will mock when your fear cometh; When your fear cometh as desolation, and your destruction cometh as a whirlwind; when distress and anguish cometh upon you. Then shall they call upon me,

but I will not answer; they shall seek me early, but they shall not find me: For that they hated knowledge, and did not choose the fear of the Lord: They would none of my counsel: they despised all my reproof. Therefore shall they eat of the fruit of their own way, and be filled with their own devices. For the turning away of the simple shall slay them, and the prosperity of fools shall destroy them. But whoso hearkeneth unto me shall dwell safely, and shall be quiet from fear of evil." **(Proverbs 1:22-33)**

"For God sent not his Son into the world to condemn the world; but that the world through him might be saved. He that believeth on him is not condemned: but he that believeth not is condemned already, because he hath not believed in the name of the only begotten Son of God. And this is the condemnation, that light is come into the world, and men loved darkness rather than light, because their deeds were evil. For every one that doeth evil hateth the light, neither cometh to the light, lest his deeds should be reproved. But he that doeth truth cometh to the light, that his deeds may be made manifest, that they are wrought in God." **(John 3:17-21)**

VII.   OF GRACE IN REGENERATION

We believe that, in order to be saved, sinners must be regenerated or born again; that regeneration consists in giving a holy disposition to the mind; that it is effected, in a manner above our comprehension, by the power of the Holy Spirit in connection with divine truth, so as to secure our voluntary obedience to the gospel; and that its proper evidence appears in the holy fruits of repentance and faith and newness of life.

"He that believeth and is baptized shall be saved; but he that believeth not shall be damned." **(Mark 16:16)**

"Jesus answered and said unto him, Verily, verily, I say unto thee, Except a man be born again, he cannot see the kingdom of God. Jesus answered, Verily, verily, I say unto thee, Except a man be born of water and of the Spirit, he cannot enter into the kingdom of God. That which is born of the flesh is flesh; and that which is born of the Spirit is spirit. Marvel not that I said unto thee, Ye must be born again. The wind bloweth where it listeth, and thou hearest the sound thereof, but canst not tell whence it cometh, and whither it goeth: so is every one that is born of the Spirit." **(John 3:3, 5-8)**

"For this cause I bow my knees unto the Father of our Lord Jesus Christ, Of whom the whole family in heaven and earth is named, That he would grant you, according to the riches of his glory, to be strengthened with might by his Spirit in the inner man; That Christ may dwell in your hearts by faith; that ye, being rooted and grounded in love, May be able to comprehend with all saints what is the breadth, and length, and depth, and height; And to know the love of Christ, which passeth knowledge, that ye might be filled with all the fulness of God." **(Ephesians 3:14-19)**

"And be renewed in the spirit of your mind; And that ye put on the new man, which after God is created in righteousness and true holiness. Wherefore putting away lying, speak every man truth with his neighbour: for we are members one of another. Be ye angry, and sin not: let not the sun go down upon your wrath: Neither give place to the devil. Let him that stole steal no more: but rather let him labour, working with his hands the thing which is good, that he may have to give to him that needeth. Let no corrupt communication proceed out of your mouth, but that which is good to the use of edifying, that it may minister grace

unto the hearers. And grieve not the holy Spirit of God, whereby ye are sealed unto the day of redemption. Let all bitterness, and wrath, and anger, and clamour, and evil speaking, be put away from you, with all malice: And be ye kind one to another, tenderhearted, forgiving one another, even as God for Christ's sake hath forgiven you." (Ephesians 4:23-32)

"Seeing ye have purified your souls in obeying the truth through the Spirit unto unfeigned love of the brethren, see that ye love one another with a pure heart fervently: Being born again, not of corruptible seed, but of incorruptible, by the word of God, which liveth and abideth for ever. For all flesh is as grass, and all the glory of man as the flower of grass. The grass withereth, and the flower thereof falleth away: But the word of the Lord endureth for ever. And this is the word which by the gospel is preached unto you." (1 Peter 1:22-25)

"Let no man deceive you with vain words: for because of these things cometh the wrath of God upon the children of disobedience. Be not ye therefore partakers with them. For ye were sometimes darkness, but now are ye light in the Lord: walk as children of light: (For the fruit of the Spirit is in all goodness and righteousness and truth;) Proving what is acceptable unto the Lord. And have no fellowship with the unfruitful works of darkness, but rather reprove them. For it is a shame even to speak of those things which are done of them in secret." (Ephesians 5:6-12)

VIII. OF REPENTANCE AND FAITH

We believe that Repentance and Faith are sacred duties, and also inseparable graces, wrought in our souls by the regenerating Spirit of God; whereby, being deeply convinced of our guilt, danger, and helplessness, and of the way of salvation by Christ, we turn to God with unfeigned contrition, confession, and supplication for mercy; at the same time heartily receiving the Lord Jesus Christ as our Prophet, Priest, and King, and relying on him alone as the only and all-sufficient Savior.

"And saying, The time is fulfilled, and the kingdom of God is at hand: repent ye, and believe the gospel." Mark 1:15

"Do ye think that the scripture saith in vain, The spirit that dwelleth in us lusteth to envy? But he giveth more grace. Wherefore he saith, God resisteth the proud, but giveth grace unto the humble. Submit yourselves therefore to God. Resist the devil, and he will flee from you. Draw nigh to God, and he will draw nigh to you. Cleanse your hands, ye sinners; and purify your hearts, ye double minded. Be afflicted, and mourn, and weep: let your laughter be turned to mourning, and your joy to heaviness. Humble yourselves in the sight of the Lord, and he shall lift you up." (James 4:5-10)

"Have mercy upon me, O God, according to thy lovingkindness: according unto the multitude of thy tender mercies blot out my transgressions. Wash me throughly from mine iniquity, and cleanse me from my sin. For I acknowledge my transgressions: and my sin is ever before me. Against thee, thee only, have I sinned, and done this evil in thy sight: that thou mightest be justified when thou speakest, and be clear when thou judgest. Behold, I was shapen in iniquity; and in sin did my mother conceive me. Behold, thou desirest truth in the inward parts: and in the hidden part thou shalt make me to know wisdom. Purge me with hyssop, and I shall be clean: wash me, and I shall be whiter than snow. Make me to hear joy and gladness; that the bones which thou hast broken may rejoice. Hide thy face from my sins, and blot out all mine iniquities. Create in me a clean heart, O God; and *renew a right spirit within me. Cast me not away from thy presence; and take not thy holy spirit from me. Restore unto me the joy of thy salvation; and uphold me with thy free spirit. Then will I teach transgressors thy ways; and sinners shall be converted unto thee. Deliver me from bloodguiltiness, O God, thou God of my salvation: and my tongue shall sing aloud of thy righteousness. O Lord, open thou my lips; and my mouth shall shew forth thy praise. For thou desirest not sacrifice; else would I give it: thou delightest not in burnt offering. The sacrifices of God are a broken spirit: a broken and a contrite heart, O God, thou wilt not despise."* **(Psalm 51:1-17)**

"And the publican, standing afar off, would not lift up so much as his eyes unto heaven, but smote upon his breast, saying, God be merciful to me a sinner. I tell you, this man went down to his house justified rather than the other: for every one that exalteth himself shall be abased; and he that humbleth himself shall be exalted." **(Luke 18:13&14)**

"Jesus saith unto him, I am the way, the truth, and the life: no man cometh unto the Father, but by me." **(John 14:6)**

"Let no man deceive you with vain words: for because of these things cometh the wrath of God upon the children of disobedience. Be not ye therefore partakers with them. For ye were sometimes darkness, but now are ye light in the Lord: walk as children of light: (For the fruit of the Spirit is in all goodness and righteousness and truth;)" **(Ephesians 5:6-9)**

"He that believeth on him is not condemned: but he that believeth not is condemned already, because he hath not believed in the name of the only begotten Son of God. And this is the condemnation, that light is come into the world, and men loved darkness rather than light, because their deeds were evil. For every one that doeth evil hateth the light, neither cometh to the light, lest his deeds should be reproved." **(John 3:18-20)**

"Whereof the Holy Ghost also is a witness to us: for after that he had said before, This is the covenant that I will make with them after those days, saith the Lord, I will put my laws into their hearts, and in their minds will I write them; And their sins and iniquities will I remember no more. Now where remission of these is, there is no more offering for sin. Having therefore, brethren, boldness to enter into the holiest by the blood of Jesus, By a new and living way, which he hath consecrated for us, through the veil, that is to say, his flesh; And having an high priest over the house of God; Let us draw near with a true heart in full assurance of faith, having our hearts sprinkled from an evil conscience, and our bodies washed with pure water. Let us hold fast the profession of our faith without wavering; (for he is faithful that promised;) And let us consider one another to provoke unto love and to good works: Not forsaking the assembling of ourselves together, as the manner of some is; but exhorting one another: and so much the more, as ye see the day approaching. For if we sin wilfully after that we have received the knowledge of the truth, there remaineth no more sacrifice for sins, But a certain fearful looking for of judgment and fiery indignation, which shall devour the adversaries." **(Hebrews 10:15-27)**

"This is a faithful saying, and worthy of all acceptation, that Christ Jesus came into the world to save sinners; of whom I am chief. Howbeit for this cause I obtained mercy, that in me first Jesus Christ might shew forth all longsuffering, for a pattern to them which should hereafter believe on him to life everlasting. Now unto the King eternal, immortal, invisible, the only wise God, be honour and glory for ever and ever. Amen." **(1 Timothy 1:15-17)**

"Let this mind be in you, which was also in Christ Jesus: Who, being in the form of God, thought it not robbery to be equal with God: But made himself of no reputation, and took upon him the form of a servant, and was made in the likeness of men: And being found in fashion as a man, he humbled himself, and became obedient unto death, even the death of the cross. Wherefore God also hath highly exalted him, and given him a name which is above every name: That at the name of Jesus every knee should bow, of things in heaven, and things in earth, and things under the earth; And that every tongue should confess that Jesus Christ is Lord, to the glory of God the Father." (**Philippians 2:5-11**)

IX.   OF GOD'S PURPOSE OF GRACE

We believe that Election is the eternal purpose of God, according to which he graciously regenerates, sanctifies, and saves sinners; that being perfectly consistent with the free agency of man, it comprehends all the means in connection with the end; that it is a most glorious display of God's sovereign goodness, being infinitely free, wise, holy, and unchangeable; that it utterly excludes boasting, and promotes humility, love, prayer, praise, trust in God, and active imitation of his free mercy; that it encourages the use of means in the highest degree; that it may be ascertained by its effects in all who truly believe the gospel; that it is the foundation of Christian assurance; and that to ascertain it with regard to ourselves demands and deserves the utmost diligence.

"Wherein in time past ye walked according to the course of this world, according to the prince of the power of the air, the spirit that now worketh in the children of disobedience: Among whom also we all had our conversation in times past in the lusts of our flesh, fulfilling the desires of the flesh and of the mind; and were by nature the children of wrath, even as others. But God, who is rich in mercy, for his great love wherewith he loved us, Even when we were dead in sins, hath quickened us together with Christ, (by grace ye are saved;) And hath raised us up together, and made us sit together in heavenly places in Christ Jesus: That in the ages to come he might shew the exceeding riches of his grace in his kindness toward us through Christ Jesus. For by grace are ye saved through faith; and that not of yourselves: it is the gift of God: Not of works, lest any man should boast." (**Ephesians 2:2-9**)

"Even so then at this present time also there is a remnant according to the election of grace. And if by grace, then is it no more of works: otherwise grace is no more grace. But if it be of works, then is it no more grace: otherwise work is no more work." (**Romans 11:5-6**)

"And he said, I beseech thee, shew me thy glory. And he said, I will make all my goodness pass before thee, and I will proclaim the name of the Lord before thee; and will be gracious to whom I will be gracious, and will shew mercy on whom I will shew mercy." (**Exodus 33:18&19**)

"For we are his workmanship, created in Christ Jesus unto good works, which God hath before ordained that we should walk in them. Wherefore remember, that ye being in time past Gentiles in the flesh, who are called Uncircumcision by that which is called the Circumcision in the flesh made by hands; That at that time ye were without Christ, being aliens from the commonwealth of Israel, and strangers from the covenants of promise, having no hope, and without God in the world: But now in Christ Jesus ye who sometimes were far off are made nigh by the blood of Christ. For he is our peace, who hath made both one, and hath broken down the middle wall of partition between us; Having abolished in

his flesh the enmity, even the law of commandments contained in ordinances; for to make in himself of twain one new man, so making peace; And that he might reconcile both unto God in one body by the cross, having slain the enmity thereby: And came and preached peace to you which were afar off, and to them that were nigh. For through him we both have access by one Spirit unto the Father. Now therefore ye are no more strangers and for-eigners, but fellowcitizens with the saints, and of the household of God; And are built upon the foundation of the apostles and prophets, Jesus Christ himself being the chief corner stone; In whom all the building fitly framed together groweth unto an holy temple in the Lord: In whom ye also are builded together for an habitation of God through the Spirit." (Ephesians 2:10-22)

"Knowing, brethren beloved, your election of God. For our gospel came not unto you in word only, but also in power, and in the Holy Ghost, and in much assurance; as ye know what manner of men we were among you for your sake. And ye became followers of us, and of the Lord, having received the word in much affliction, with joy of the Holy Ghost: So that ye were ensamples to all that believe in Macedonia and Achaia. For from you sounded out the word of the Lord not only in Macedonia and Achaia, but also in every place your faith to God-ward is spread abroad; so that we need not to speak any thing. For they themselves shew of us what manner of entering in we had unto you, and how ye turned to God from idols to serve the living and true God; And to wait for his Son from heaven, whom he raised from the dead, even Jesus, which delivered us from the wrath to come." (1 Thessalonians 1:4-10)

"Grace and peace be multiplied unto you through the knowledge of God, and of Jesus our Lord, According as his divine power hath given unto us all things that pertain unto life and godliness, through the knowledge of him that hath called us to glory and virtue: Whereby are given unto us exceeding great and precious promises: that by these ye might be partak-ers of the divine nature, having escaped the corruption that is in the world through lust. And beside this, giving all diligence, add to your faith virtue; and to virtue knowledge; And to knowledge temperance; and to temperance patience; and to patience godliness; And to godliness brotherly kindness; and to brotherly kindness charity. For if these things be in you, and abound, they make you that ye shall neither be barren nor unfruitful in the knowledge of our Lord Jesus Christ. But he that lacketh these things is blind, and cannot see afar off, and hath forgotten that he was purged from his old sins. Wherefore the rather, brethren, give diligence to make your calling and election sure: for if ye do these things, ye shall never fall: For so an entrance shall be ministered unto you abundantly into the ever-lasting kingdom of our Lord and Saviour Jesus Christ." (2 Peter 1:2-11)

X.   OF SANCTIFICATION

We believe that Sanctification is the process by which, according to the will of God, we are made partakers of his holiness; that it is a progressive work; that it is begun in regen-eration; and that it is carried on in the hearts of believers by the presence and power of the Holy Spirit, the Sealer and Comforter, in the continual use of the appointed means, espe-cially the word of God, self-examination, self-denial, watchfulness, and prayer.

"Furthermore then we beseech you, brethren, and exhort you by the Lord Jesus, that as ye have received of us how ye ought to walk and to please God, so ye would abound more and more. For ye know what commandments we gave you by the Lord Jesus. For this is the will

of God, even your sanctification, that ye should abstain from fornication: That every one of you should know how to possess his vessel in sanctification and honour; Not in the lust of concupiscence, even as the Gentiles which know not God: That no man go beyond and defraud his brother in any matter: because that the Lord is the avenger of all such, as we also have forewarned you and testified. For God hath not called us unto uncleanness, but unto holiness." (1 **Thessalonians 4:1-7**)

"Be not thou therefore ashamed of the testimony of our Lord, nor of me his prisoner: but be thou partaker of the afflictions of the gospel according to the power of God; Who hath saved us, and called us with an holy calling, not according to our works, but according to his own purpose and grace, which was given us in Christ Jesus before the world began, But is now made manifest by the appearing of our Saviour Jesus Christ, who hath abolished death, and hath brought life and immortality to light through the gospel: Whereunto I am appointed a preacher, and an apostle, and a teacher of the Gentiles." (2 **Timothy 1:8-11**)

"Sanctify yourselves therefore, and be ye holy: for I am the Lord your God." (**Leviticus 20:7**)

"For this cause I bow my knees unto the Father of our Lord Jesus Christ, Of whom the whole family in heaven and earth is named, That he would grant you, according to the riches of his glory, to be strengthened with might by his Spirit in the inner man; That Christ may dwell in your hearts by faith; that ye, being rooted and grounded in love, May be able to comprehend with all saints what is the breadth, and length, and depth, and height; And to know the love of Christ, which passeth knowledge, that ye might be filled with all the fulness of God. Now unto him that is able to do exceeding abundantly above all that we ask or think, according to the power that worketh in us," (**Ephesians 3:14-20**)

"Wherein he hath abounded toward us in all wisdom and prudence; Having made known unto us the mystery of his will, according to his good pleasure which he hath purposed in himself: That in the dispensation of the fulness of times he might gather together in one all things in Christ, both which are in heaven, and which are on earth; even in him: In whom also we have obtained an inheritance, being predestinated according to the purpose of him who worketh all things after the counsel of his own will: That we should be to the praise of his glory, who first trusted in Christ. In whom ye also trusted, after that ye heard the word of truth, the gospel of your salvation: in whom also after that ye believed, ye were sealed with that holy Spirit of promise, Which is the earnest of our inheritance until the redemption of the purchased possession, unto the praise of his glory." (**Ephesians 1:8-14**)

"For I have received of the Lord that which also I delivered unto you, That the Lord Jesus the same night in which he was betrayed took bread: And when he had given thanks, he brake it, and said, Take, eat: this is my body, which is broken for you: this do in remembrance of me. After the same manner also he took the cup, when he had supped, saying, This cup is the new testament in my blood: this do ye, as oft as ye drink it, in remembrance of me. For as often as ye eat this bread, and drink this cup, ye do shew the Lord's death till he come. Wherefore whosoever shall eat this bread, and drink this cup of the Lord, unworthily, shall be guilty of the body and blood of the Lord. But let a man examine himself, and so let him eat of that bread, and drink of that cup. For he that eateth and drinketh unworthily, eateth and drinketh damnation to himself, not discerning the Lord's body. For this cause many are weak and sickly among you, and many sleep. For if we would judge ourselves, we should not be judged." (1 **Corinthians 11:23-31**)

"Wherefore, my beloved, as ye have always obeyed, not as in my presence only, but now much more in my absence, work out your own salvation with fear and trembling. For it is God which worketh in you both to will and to do of his good pleasure. Do all things without murmurings and disputings: That ye may be blameless and harmless, the sons of God, without rebuke, in the midst of a crooked and perverse nation, among whom ye shine as lights in the world; Holding forth the word of life; that I may rejoice in the day of Christ, that I have not run in vain, neither laboured in vain. Yea, and if I be offered upon the sacrifice and service of your faith, I joy, and rejoice with you all." **(Philippians 2:12-17)**

"Take ye heed, watch and pray: for ye know not when the time is. For the Son of man is as a man taking a far journey, who left his house, and gave authority to his servants, and to every man his work, and commanded the porter to watch. Watch ye therefore: for ye know not when the master of the house cometh, at even, or at midnight, or at the cockcrowing, or in the morning: Lest coming suddenly he find you sleeping. And what I say unto you I say unto all, Watch." **(Mark 13:33-37)**

XI.   *OF THE PERSEVERANCE OF SAINTS*

We believe that such only are real believers as endure unto the end; that their persevering attachment to Christ is the grand mark which distinguishes them from superficial professors; that a special Providence watches over their welfare; and that they are kept by the power of God through faith unto righteousness.

"Then said Jesus to those Jews which believed on him, If ye continue in my word, then are ye my disciples indeed; And ye shall know the truth, and the truth shall make you free." **(John 8:31-32)**

"Whosoever believeth that Jesus is the Christ is born of God: and every one that loveth him that begat loveth him also that is begotten of him. By this we know that we love the children of God, when we love God, and keep his commandments. For this is the love of God, that we keep his commandments: and his commandments are not grievous. For whatsoever is born of God overcometh the world: and this is the victory that overcometh the world, even our faith. Who is he that overcometh the world, but he that believeth that Jesus is the Son of God?" **(1 John 5:1-5)**

"Little children, it is the last time: and as ye have heard that antichrist shall come, even now are there many antichrists; whereby we know that it is the last time. They went out from us, but they were not of us; for if they had been of us, they would no doubt have continued with us: but they went out, that they might be made manifest that they were not all of us. But ye have an unction from the Holy One, and ye know all things. I have not written unto you because ye know not the truth, but because ye know it, and that no lie is of the truth. Who is a liar but he that denieth that Jesus is the Christ? He is antichrist, that denieth the Father and the Son. Whosoever denieth the Son, the same hath not the Father: (but) he that acknowledgeth the Son hath the Father also. Let that therefore abide in you, which ye have heard from the beginning. If that which ye have heard from the beginning shall remain in you, ye also shall continue in the Son, and in the Father. And this is the promise that he hath promised us, even eternal life." **(1 John 2:18-25)**

"Being confident of this very thing, that he which hath begun a good work in you will perform it until the day of Jesus Christ:" **(Philippians 1:6)**

"For we are saved by hope: but hope that is seen is not hope: for what a man seeth, why doth he yet hope for? But if we hope for that we see not, then do we with patience wait for it. Likewise the Spirit also helpeth our infirmities: for we know not what we should pray for as we ought: but the Spirit itself maketh intercession for us with groanings which cannot be uttered. And he that searcheth the hearts knoweth what is the mind of the Spirit, because he maketh intercession for the saints according to the will of God. And we know that all things work together for good to them that love God, to them who are the called according to his purpose. For whom he did foreknow, he also did predestinate to be conformed to the image of his Son, that he might be the firstborn among many brethren. Moreover whom he did predestinate, them he also called: and whom he called, them he also justified: and whom he justified, them he also glorified. What shall we then say to these things? If God be for us, who can be against us?" (**Romans 8:24-31**)

XII.   *OF THE HARMONY OF THE LAW AND THE GOSPEL*

We believe that the Law of God is the eternal and unchangeable rule of his moral government; that it is holy, just and good; that the inability which the scriptures ascribe to fallen men is love of sin; to deliver them from which, and to restore them through a mediator to unfeigned obedience to the holy law, is one great end of the gospel, and of the means of grace connected with establishment of the visible church.

"And it shall come to pass, if thou shalt hearken diligently unto the voice of the Lord thy God, to observe and to do all his commandments which I command thee this day, that the Lord thy God will set thee on high above all nations of the earth: And all these blessings shall come on thee, and overtake thee, if thou shalt hearken unto the voice of the Lord thy God. Blessed shalt thou be in the city, and blessed shalt thou be in the field. Blessed shall be the fruit of thy body, and the fruit of thy ground, and the fruit of thy cattle, the increase of thy kine, and the flocks of thy sheep. Blessed shall be thy basket and thy store. Blessed shalt thou be when thou comest in, and blessed shalt thou be when thou goest out. The Lord shall cause thine enemies that rise up against thee to be smitten before thy face: they shall come out against thee one way, and flee before thee seven ways. The Lord shall command the blessing upon thee in thy storehouses, and in all that thou settest thine hand unto; and he shall bless thee in the land which the Lord thy God giveth thee. The Lord shall establish thee an holy people unto himself, as he hath sworn unto thee, if thou shalt keep the commandments of the Lord thy God, and walk in his ways. And all people of the earth shall see that thou art called by the name of the Lord; and they shall be afraid of thee. And the Lord shall make thee plenteous in goods, in the fruit of thy body, and in the fruit of thy cattle, and in the fruit of thy ground, in the land which the Lord sware unto thy fathers to give thee. The Lord shall open unto thee his good treasure, the heaven to give the rain unto thy land in his season, and to bless all the work of thine hand: and thou shalt lend unto many nations, and thou shalt not borrow. And the Lord shall make thee the head, and not the tail; and thou shalt be above only, and thou shalt not be beneath; if that thou hearken unto the commandments of the Lord thy God, which I command thee this day, to observe and to do them: And thou shalt not go aside from any of the words which I command thee this day, to the right hand, or to the left, to go after other gods to serve them." (**Deuteronomy 28:1-14**)

"Good and upright is the Lord: therefore will he teach sinners in the way. The meek will he guide in judgment: and the meek will he teach his way. All the paths of the Lord are mercy

and truth unto such as keep his covenant and his testimonies. The secret of the Lord is with them that fear him; and he will shew them his covenant." (**Psalm 25:8-10,14**)

"Love worketh no ill to his neighbour: therefore love is the fulfilling of the law." (**Romans 13:10**)

"For, brethren, ye have been called unto liberty; only use not liberty for an occasion to the flesh, but by love serve one another. For all the law is fulfilled in one word, even in this; Thou shalt love thy neighbour as thyself. But if ye bite and devour one another, take heed that ye be not consumed one of another. This I say then, Walk in the Spirit, and ye shall not fulfill the lust of the flesh." (**Galatians 5:13-16**)

"Wherefore, my brethren, ye also are become dead to the law by the body of Christ; that ye should be married to another, even to him who is raised from the dead, that we should bring forth fruit unto God. For when we were in the flesh, the motions of sins, which were by the law, did work in our members to bring forth fruit unto death. But now we are delivered from the law, that being dead wherein we were held; that we should serve in newness of spirit, and not in the oldness of the letter. What shall we say then? Is the law sin? God forbid. Nay, I had not known sin, but by the law: for I had not known lust, except the law had said, Thou shalt not covet. But sin, taking occasion by the commandment, wrought in me all manner of concupiscence. For without the law sin was dead. For I was alive without the law once: but when the commandment came, sin revived, and I died. And the commandment, which was ordained to life, I found to be unto death. For sin, taking occasion by the commandment, deceived me, and by it slew me. Wherefore the law is holy, and the commandment holy, and just, and good." (**Romans 7:4-12**)

Because the carnal mind is enmity against God: for it is not subject to the law of God, neither indeed can be. So then they that are in the flesh cannot please God." (**Romans 8:7&8**)

"But evil men and seducers shall wax worse and worse, deceiving, and being deceived. But continue thou in the things which thou hast learned and hast been assured of, knowing of whom thou hast learned them; And that from a child thou hast known the holy scriptures, which are able to make thee wise unto salvation through faith which is in Christ Jesus." (**2 Timothy 3:13-15**)

"And this I say, that the covenant, that was confirmed before of God in Christ, the law, which was four hundred and thirty years after, cannot disannul, that it should make the promise of none effect. For if the inheritance be of the law, it is no more of promise: but God gave it to Abraham by promise. Wherefore then serveth the law? It was added because of transgressions, till the seed should come to whom the promise was made; and it was ordained by angels in the hand of a mediator. Now a mediator is not a mediator of one, but God is one. Is the law then against the promises of God? God forbid: for if there had been a law given which could have given life, verily righteousness should have been by the law. But the scripture hath concluded all under sin, that the promise by faith of Jesus Christ might be given to them that believe. But before faith came, we were kept under the law, shut up unto the faith which should afterwards be revealed. Wherefore the law was our schoolmaster to bring us unto Christ, that we might be justified by faith. But after that faith is come, we are no longer under a schoolmaster. For ye are all the children of God by faith in Christ Jesus. For as many of you as have been baptized into Christ have put on Christ There is

neither Jew nor Greek, there is neither bond nor free, there is neither male nor female: for ye are all one in Christ Jesus." (Galatians 3:17-28)

"Do we then make void the law through faith? God forbid: yea, we establish the law." (Romans 3:31)

"Forasmuch then as Christ hath suffered for us in the flesh, arm yourselves likewise with the same mind: for he that hath suffered in the flesh hath ceased from sin; That he no longer should live the rest of his time in the flesh to the lusts of men, but to the will of God. For the time past of our life may suffice us to have wrought the will of the Gentiles, when we walked in lasciviousness, lusts, excess of wine, revellings, banquetings, and abominable idolatries: Wherein they think it strange that ye run not with them to the same excess of riot, speaking evil of you: Who shall give account to him that is ready to judge the quick and the dead. For for this cause was the gospel preached also to them that are dead, that they might be judged according to men in the flesh, but live according to God in the spirit." (1 Peter 4:1-6)

"Husbands, love your wives, even as Christ also loved the church, and gave himself for it; That he might sanctify and cleanse it with the washing of water by the word, That he might present it to himself a glorious church, not having spot, or wrinkle, or any such thing; but that it should be holy and without blemish." (Ephesians 5:25-27)

XIII.   OF A GOSPEL CHURCH

We believe that a visible church of Christ is a congregation of baptized believers associated by covenant in the faith and fellowship of the gospel; observing the ordinances of Christ; governed by his laws; and exercising the gifts, rights, and privileges invested in them by his word; that its only Scriptural officers are Bishops, or Pastors, and Deacons, whose qualifications, claims, and duties are defined in the epistles to Timothy and Titus.

"Then Peter said unto them, Repent, and be baptized every one of you in the name of Jesus Christ for the remission of sins, and ye shall receive the gift of the Holy Ghost. For the promise is unto you, and to your children, and to all that are afar off, even as many as the Lord our God shall call. And with many other words did he testify and exhort, saying, Save yourselves from this untoward generation. Then they that gladly received his word were baptized: and the same day there were added unto them about three thousand souls. And they continued stedfastly in the apostles' doctrine and fellowship, and in breaking of bread, and in prayers." (Acts 2:38-42)

"Moreover if thy brother shall trespass against thee, go and tell him his fault between thee and him alone: if he shall hear thee, thou hast gained thy brother. But if he will not hear thee, then take with thee one or two more, that in the mouth of two or three witnesses every word may be established. And if he shall neglect to hear them, tell it unto the church: but if he neglect to hear the church, let him be unto thee as an heathen man and a publican." (Matthew 18:15-17)

"And Jesus came and spake unto them, saying, All power is given unto me in heaven and in earth. Go ye therefore, and teach all nations, baptizing them in the name of the Father, and of the Son, and of the Holy Ghost: Teaching them to observe all things whatsoever I have commanded you: and, lo, I am with you alway, even unto the end of the world. Amen." (Matthew 28:18-20)

"Be ye followers of me, even as I also am of Christ. Now I praise you, brethren, that ye remember me in all things, and keep the ordinances, as I delivered them to you." (1 Corinthians 11:1&2)

"And he gave some, apostles; and some, prophets; and some, evangelists; and some, pastors and teachers; For the perfecting of the saints, for the work of the ministry, for the edifying of the body of Christ: Till we all come in the unity of the faith, and of the knowledge of the Son of God, unto a perfect man, unto the measure of the stature of the fulness of Christ: That we henceforth be no more children, tossed to and fro, and carried about with every wind of doctrine, by the sleight of men, and cunning craftiness, whereby they lie in wait to deceive; But speaking the truth in love, may grow up into him in all things, which is the head, even Christ: From whom the whole body fitly joined together and compacted by that which every joint supplieth, according to the effectual working in the measure of every part, maketh increase of the body unto the edifying of itself in love." (Ephesians 4:11-16)

"For I say, through the grace given unto me, to every man that is among you, not to think of himself more highly than he ought to think; but to think soberly, according as God hath dealt to every man the measure of faith. For as we have many members in one body, and all members have not the same office: So we, being many, are one body in Christ, and every one members one of another. Having then gifts differing according to the grace that is given to us, whether prophecy, let us prophesy according to the proportion of faith; Or ministry, let us wait on our ministering: or he that teacheth, on teaching; Or he that exhorteth, on exhortation: he that giveth, let him do it with simplicity; he that ruleth, with diligence; he that sheweth mercy, with cheerfulness. Let love be without dissimulation. Abhor that which is evil; cleave to that which is good. Be kindly affectioned one to another with brotherly love; in honour preferring one another; Not slothful in business; fervent in spirit; serving the Lord; Rejoicing in hope; patient in tribulation; continuing instant in prayer; Distributing to the necessity of saints; given to hospitality." (Romans 12:3-13)

"Now there are diversities of gifts, but the same Spirit. And there are differences of administrations, but the same Lord. And there are diversities of operations, but it is the same God which worketh all in all. But the manifestation of the Spirit is given to every man to profit withal. For to one is given by the Spirit the word of wisdom; to another the word of knowledge by the same Spirit; To another faith by the same Spirit; to another the gifts of healing by the same Spirit; To another the working of miracles; to another prophecy; to another discerning of spirits; to another divers kinds of tongues; to another the interpretation of tongues: But all these worketh that one and the selfsame Spirit, dividing to every man severally as he will. For as the body is one, and hath many members, and all the members of that one body, being many, are one body: so also is Christ. For by one Spirit are we all baptized into one body, whether we be Jews or Gentiles, whether we be bond or free; and have been all made to drink into one Spirit. For the body is not one member, but many." (1 Corinthians 12:4-14)

Turn, O backsliding children, saith the Lord; for I am married unto you: and I will take you one of a city, and two of a family, and I will bring you to Zion: And I will give you pastors according to mine heart, which shall feed you with knowledge and understanding." (Jeremiah 3:14&15)

"And in those days, when the number of the disciples was multiplied, there arose a murmuring of the Grecians against the Hebrews, because their widows were neglected in the

daily ministration. Then the twelve called the multitude of the disciples unto them, and said, It is not reason that we should leave the word of God, and serve tables. Wherefore, brethren, look ye out among you seven men of honest report, full of the Holy Ghost and wisdom, whom we may appoint over this business. But we will give ourselves continually to prayer, and to the ministry of the word. And the saying pleased the whole multitude: and they chose Stephen, a man full of faith and of the Holy Ghost, and Philip, and Prochorus, and Nicanor, and Timon, and Parmenas, and Nicolas a proselyte of Antioch: Whom they set before the apostles: and when they had prayed, they laid their hands on them. And the word of God increased; and the number of the disciples multiplied in Jerusalem greatly; and a great company of the priests were obedient to the faith." (Acts 6:1-7)

"Take heed therefore unto yourselves, and to all the flock, over the which the Holy Ghost hath made you overseers, to feed the church of God, which he hath purchased with his own blood. For I know this, that after my departing shall grievous wolves enter in among you, not sparing the flock. Also of your own selves shall men arise, speaking perverse things, to draw away disciples after them." (Acts 20:28-30)

"Let the elders that rule well be counted worthy of double honour, especially they who labour in the word and doctrine. For the scripture saith, Thou shalt not muzzle the ox that treadeth out the corn. And, The labourer is worthy of his reward." (1 Timothy 5:17&18)

"A bishop then must be blameless, the husband of one wife, vigilant, sober, of good behaviour, given to hospitality, apt to teach; Not given to wine, no striker, not greedy of filthy lucre; but patient, not a brawler, not covetous; One that ruleth well his own house, having his children in subjection with all gravity; (For if a man know not how to rule his own house, how shall he take care of the church of God?) Not a novice, lest being lifted up with pride he fall into the condemnation of the devil. Moreover he must have a good report of them which are without; lest he fall into reproach and the snare of the devil. Likewise must the deacons be grave, not doubletongued, not given to much wine, not greedy of filthy lucre; Holding the mystery of the faith in a pure conscience. And let these also first be proved; then let them use the office of a deacon, being found blameless. Even so must their wives be grave, not slanderers, sober, faithful in all things. Let the deacons be the husbands of one wife, ruling their children and their own houses well. For they that have used the office of a deacon well purchase to themselves a good degree, and great boldness in the faith which is in Christ Jesus." (1 Timothy 3:2-13)

"To Titus, mine own son after the common faith: Grace, mercy, and peace, from God the Father and the Lord Jesus Christ our Saviour. For this cause left I thee in Crete, that thou shouldest set in order the things that are wanting, and ordain elders in every city, as I had appointed thee: If any be blameless, the husband of one wife, having faithful children not accused of riot or unruly. For a bishop must be blameless, as the steward of God; not selfwilled, not soon angry, not given to wine, no striker, not given to filthy lucre; But a lover of hospitality, a lover of good men, sober, just, holy, temperate; Holding fast the faithful word as he hath been taught, that he may be able by sound doctrine both to exhort and to convince the gainsayers." (Titus 1:4-9)

XIV.   *OF BAPTISM AND THE LORDS SUPPER*

We believe that Christian Baptism is the immersion in water of a believer, in the name of the Father, the Son, and the Holy Ghost; to show forth, in a solemn and beautiful emblem,

our faith in the crucified, buried, and risen Savior, with its effect in our death to sin and resurrection to a new life; that it is prerequisite to the privileges of a church relation; and to the Lord's Super; in which the members of the church, by the sacred use of bread and wine are to commemorate together the dying love of Christ; preceded always by solemn self-examination.

"And Jesus came and spake unto them, saying, All power is given unto me in heaven and in earth. Go ye therefore, and teach all nations, baptizing them in the name of the Father, and of the Son, and of the Holy Ghost: Teaching them to observe all things whatsoever I have commanded you: and, lo, I am with you alway, even unto the end of the world. Amen." (Matthew 28:18-20)

"And as they went on their way, they came unto a certain water: and the eunuch said, See, here is water; what doth hinder me to be baptized? And Philip said, If thou believest with all thine heart, thou mayest. And he answered and said, I believe that Jesus Christ is the Son of God. And he commanded the chariot to stand still: and they went down both into the water, both Philip and the eunuch; and he baptized him. And when they were come up out of the water, the Spirit of the Lord caught away Philip, that the eunuch saw him no more: and he went on his way rejoicing." (Acts 8:36-39)

Then Peter said unto them, Repent, and be baptized every one of you in the name of Jesus Christ for the remission of sins, and ye shall receive the gift of the Holy Ghost. For the promise is unto you, and to your children, and to all that are afar off, even as many as the Lord our God shall call. And with many other words did he testify and exhort, saying, Save yourselves from this untoward generation. Then they that gladly received his word were baptized: and the same day there were added unto them about three thousand souls. And they continued stedfastly in the apostles' doctrine and fellowship, and in breaking of bread, and in prayers. And fear came upon every soul: and many wonders and signs were done by the apostles. And all that believed were together, and had all things common; And sold their possessions and goods, and parted them to all men, as every man had need. And they, continuing daily with one accord in the temple, and breaking bread from house to house, did eat their meat with gladness and singleness of heart, Praising God, and having favour with all the people. And the Lord added to the church daily such as should be saved." (Acts 2:38-47)

"And the keeper of the prison awaking out of his sleep, and seeing the prison doors open, he drew out his sword, and would have killed himself, supposing that the prisoners had been fled. But Paul cried with a loud voice, saying, Do thyself no harm: for we are all here. Then he called for a light, and sprang in, and came trembling, and fell down before Paul and Silas, And brought them out, and said, Sirs, what must I do to be saved? And they said, Believe on the Lord Jesus Christ, and thou shalt be saved, and thy house. And they spake unto him the word of the Lord, and to all that were in his house. And he took them the same hour of the night, and washed their stripes; and was baptized, he and all his, straightway. And when he had brought them into his house, he set meat before them, and rejoiced, believing in God with all his house." (Acts 16:27-34)

"For I have received of the Lord that which also I delivered unto you, That the Lord Jesus the same night in which he was betrayed took bread: And when he had given thanks, he brake it, and said, Take, eat: this is my body, which is broken for you: this do in remembrance of me. After the same manner also he took the cup, when he had supped, saying,

This cup is the new testament in my blood: this do ye, as oft as ye drink it, in remembrance of me. For as often as ye eat this bread, and drink this cup, ye do shew the Lord's death till he come. Wherefore whosoever shall eat this bread, and drink this cup of the Lord, unworthily, shall be guilty of the body and blood of the Lord. But let a man examine himself, and so let him eat of that bread, and drink of that cup. For he that eateth and drinketh unworthily, eateth and drinketh damnation to himself, not discerning the Lord's body." (1 Corinthians 11:23-29)

"Wherefore, my dearly beloved, flee from idolatry. I speak as to wise men; judge ye what I say. The cup of blessing which we bless, is it not the communion of the blood of Christ? The bread which we break, is it not the communion of the body of Christ? For we being many are one bread, and one body: for we are all partakers of that one bread. Behold Israel after the flesh: are not they which eat of the sacrifices partakers of the alter? What say I then? that the idol is any thing, or that which is offered in sacrifice to idols is any thing? But I say, that the things which the Gentiles sacrifice, they sacrifice to devils, and not to God: and I would not that ye should have fellowship with devils. Ye cannot drink the cup of the Lord, and the cup of devils: ye cannot be partakers of the Lord's table, and of the table of devils." (1 Corinthians 10:14-21)

XV.   *OF THE CHRISTIAN SABBATH*

We believe that the first day of the week is the Lords' Day, or Christian Sabbath; and is to be kept sacred to religious purposes, by abstaining from all secular labor and sinful recreations; by the devout observance of all the means of grace, both private and public; and by preparation for that rest that remaineth for the people of God.

"And upon the first day of the week, when the disciples came together to break bread, Paul preached unto them, ready to depart on the morrow; and continued his speech until midnight." (Acts 20:7)

"Now concerning the collection for the saints, as I have given order to the churches of Galatia, even so do ye. Upon the first day of the week let every one of you lay by him in store, as God hath prospered him, that there be no gatherings when I come. And when I come, whomsoever ye shall approve by your letters, them will I send to bring your liberality unto Jerusalem." (1 Corinthians 16:2)

"Remember the sabbath day, to keep it holy." (Exodus 20:8)

"Keep the sabbath day to sanctify it, as the Lord thy God hath commanded thee. Six days thou shalt labour, and do all thy work: But the seventh day is the sabbath of the Lord thy God: in it thou shalt not do any work, thou, nor thy son, nor thy daughter, nor thy manservant, nor thy maidservant, nor thine ox, nor thine ass, nor any of thy cattle, nor thy stranger that is within thy gates; that thy manservant and thy maidservant may rest as well as thou." (Deuteronomy 5:12-14)

"If thou turn away thy foot from the sabbath, from doing thy pleasure on my holy day; and call the sabbath a delight, the holy of the Lord, honourable; and shalt honour him, not doing thine own ways, nor finding thine own pleasure, nor speaking thine own words: Then shalt thou delight thyself in the Lord; and I will cause thee to ride upon the high places of the earth, and feed thee with the heritage of Jacob thy father: for the mouth of the Lord hath spoken it." (Isaiah 58:13&14)

Let no man therefore judge you in meat, or in drink, or in respect of an holyday, or of the new moon, or of the sabbath days: Which are a shadow of things to come; but the body is of Christ. Let no man beguile you of your reward in a voluntary humility and worshipping of angels, intruding into those things which he hath not seen, vainly puffed up by his fleshly mind, And not holding the Head, from which all the body by joints and bands having nourishment ministered, and knit together, increaseth with the increase of God. Wherefore if ye be dead with Christ from the rudiments of the world, why, as though living in the world, are ye subject to ordinances, (Touch not; taste not; handle not; Which all are to perish with the using;) after the commandments and doctrines of men?" **(Colossians 2:16-22)**

"And it came to pass, that he went through the corn fields on the sabbath day; and his disciples began, as they went, to pluck the ears of corn. And the Pharisees said unto him, Behold, why do they on the sabbath day that which is not lawful? And he said unto them, Have ye never read what David did, when he had need, and was an hungred, he, and they that were with him? How he went into the house of God in the days of Abiathar the high priest, and did eat the shewbread, which is not lawful to eat but for the priests, and gave also to them which were with him? And he said unto them, The sabbath was made for man, and not man for the sabbath: Therefore the Son of man is Lord also of the sabbath." **(Mark 2:23-28)**

"For this man was counted worthy of more glory than Moses, inasmuch as he who hath builded the house hath more honour than the house. For every house is builded by some man; but he that built all things is God. And Moses verily was faithful in all his house, as a servant, for a testimony of those things which were to be spoken after; But Christ as a son over his own house; whose house are we, if we hold fast the confidence and the rejoicing of the hope firm unto the end. Wherefore (as the Holy Ghost saith, To day if ye will hear his voice, Harden not your hearts, as in the provocation, in the day of temptation in the wilderness: When your fathers tempted me, proved me, and saw my works forty years. Wherefore I was grieved with that generation, and said, They do alway err in their heart; and they have not known my ways. So I sware in my wrath, They shall not enter into my rest.)" **(Hebrews 4:3-11)**

XVI.   *OF CIVIL GOVERNMENT*

We believe that civil government is of divine appointment, for the interests and good order of human society; and that magistrates are to be prayed for, conscientiously honored and obeyed; except only in things opposed to the will of our Lord Jesus Christ, who is the only Lord of the conscience, and the Prince of the Kings of the earth.

"Let every soul be subject unto the higher powers. For there is no power but of God: the powers that be are ordained of God. Whosoever therefore resisteth the power, resisteth the ordinance of God: and they that resist shall receive to themselves damnation. For rulers are not a terror to good works, but to the evil. Wilt thou then not be afraid of the power? do that which is good, and thou shalt have praise of the same: For he is the minister of God to thee for good. But if thou do that which is evil, be afraid; for he beareth not the sword in vain: for he is the minister of God, a revenger to execute wrath upon him that doeth evil. Wherefore ye must needs be subject, not only for wrath, but also for conscience sake. For for this cause pay ye tribute also: for they are God's ministers, attending continually upon

this very thing. Render therefore to all their dues: tribute to whom tribute is due; custom to whom custom; fear to whom fear; honour to whom honour." (**Romans 13:1-7**)

"I exhort therefore, that, first of all, supplications, prayers, intercessions, and giving of thanks, be made for all men; For kings, and for all that are in authority; that we may lead a quiet and peaceable life in all godliness and honesty." (**1 Timothy 2:1&2**)

"Put them in mind to be subject to principalities and powers, to obey magistrates, to be ready to every good work," (**Titus 3:1**)

"Having your conversation honest among the Gentiles: that, whereas they speak against you as evildoers, they may by your good works, which they shall behold, glorify God in the day of visitation. Submit yourselves to every ordinance of man for the Lord's sake: whether it be to the king, as supreme; Or unto governors, as unto them that are sent by him for the punishment of evildoers, and for the praise of them that do well. For so is the will of God, that with well doing ye may put to silence the ignorance of foolish men:" (**1 Peter 2 :13-15**)

"Then Peter and the other apostles answered and said, We ought to obey God rather than men." (**Acts 5:29**)

"And what is the exceeding greatness of his power to usward who believe, according to the working of his mighty power, Which he wrought in Christ, when he raised him from the dead, and set him at his own right hand in the heavenly places, Far above all principality, and power, and might, and dominion, and every name that is named, not only in this world, but also in that which is to come:" (**Ephesians 1:19-21**)

"Wherefore God also hath highly exalted him, and given him a name which is above every name: That at the name of Jesus every knee should bow, of things in heaven, and things in earth, and things under the earth; And that every tongue should confess that Jesus Christ is Lord, to the glory of God the Father." (**Philippians 2:9-11**)

"For unto us a child is born, unto us a son is given: and the government shall be upon his shoulder: and his name shall be called Wonderful, Counseller, The mighty God, The everlasting Father, The Prince of Peace. Of the increase of his government and peace there shall be no end, upon the throne of David, and upon his kingdom, to order it, and to establish it with judgment and with justice from henceforth even for ever. The zeal of the Lord of hosts will perform this." (**Isaiah 9:6&7**)

"John to the seven churches which are in Asia: Grace be unto you, and peace, from him which is, and which was, and which is to come; and from the seven Spirits which are before his throne; And from Jesus Christ, who is the faithful witness, and the first begotten of the dead, and the prince of the kings of the earth. Unto him that loved us, and washed us from our sins in his own blood, And hath made us kings and priests unto God and his Father; to him be glory and dominion for ever and ever. Amen." (**Revelation 1:4-6**)

XVII.   OF THE RIGHTEOUS AND THE WICKED

We believe that there is a radical and essential difference between the righteous and the wicked; that such only as through faith are justified in the name of the Lord Jesus, and sanctified by the Spirit of our God, are truly righteous in his esteem; while all such as continue in impenitence and unbelief are in his sight wicked, and under the curse; and this distinction holds among men both in and after death.

"For God so loved the world, that he gave his only begotten Son, that whosoever believeth in him should not perish, but have everlasting life. For God sent not his Son into the world to condemn the world; but that the world through him might be saved. He that believeth on him is not condemned: but he that believeth not is condemned already, because he hath not believed in the name of the only begotten Son of God." (**John 3:16-18**)

"He that believeth and is baptized shall be saved; but he that believeth not shall be damned." (**Mark 16:16**)

"But it shall come to pass, if thou wilt not hearken unto the voice of the Lord thy God, to observe to do all his commandments and his statutes which I command thee this day; that all these curses shall come upon thee, and overtake thee: Cursed shalt thou be in the city, and cursed shalt thou be in the field." (**Deuteronomy 28:15&16**)

"Blessed is the man that walketh not in the counsel of the ungodly, nor standeth in the way of sinners, nor sitteth in the seat of the scornful. But his delight is in the law of the Lord; and in his law doth he meditate day and night. And he shall be like a tree planted by the rivers of water, that bringeth forth his fruit in his season; his leaf also shall not wither; and whatsoever he doeth shall prosper. The ungodly are not so: but are like the chaff which the wind driveth away. Therefore the ungodly shall not stand in the judgment, nor sinners in the congregation of the righteous. For the Lord knoweth the way of the righteous: but the way of the ungodly shall perish." (**Psalm 1**)

"For the wrath of God is revealed from heaven against all ungodliness and unrighteousness of men, who hold the truth in unrighteousness; Because that which may be known of God is manifest in them; for God hath shewed it unto them. For the invisible things of him from the creation of the world are clearly seen, being understood by the things that are made, even his eternal power and Godhead; so that they are without excuse: Because that, when they knew God, they glorified him not as God, neither were thankful; but became vain in their imaginations, and their foolish heart was darkened. Professing themselves to be wise, they became fools, And changed the glory of the uncorruptible God into an image made like to corruptible man, and to birds, and fourfooted beasts, and creeping things. Wherefore God also gave them up to uncleanness through the lusts of their own hearts, to dishonour their own bodies between themselves: Who changed the truth of God into a lie, and worshipped and served the creature more than the Creator, who is blessed for ever. Amen. For this cause God gave them up unto vile affections: for even their women did change the natural use into that which is against nature: And likewise also the men, leaving the natural use of the woman, burned in their lust one toward another; men with men working that which is unseemly, and receiving in themselves that recompence of their error which was meet. And even as they did not like to retain God in their knowledge, God gave them over to a reprobate mind, to do those things which are not convenient; Being filled with all unrighteousness, fornication, wickedness, covetousness, maliciousness; full of envy, murder, debate, deceit, malignity; whisperers, Backbiters, haters of God, despiteful, proud, boasters, inventors of evil things, disobedient to parents, Without understanding, covenantbreakers, without natural affection, implacable, unmerciful: Who knowing the judgment of God, that they which commit such things are worthy of death, not only do the same, but have pleasure in them that do them." (**Romans 1:18-32**)

"And I saw a great white throne, and him that sat on it, from whose face the earth and the heaven fled away; and there was found no place for them." (**Revelation 20:11**)

"And there shall be no more curse: but the throne of God and of the Lamb shall be in it; and his servants shall serve him:" (**Revelation 22:3**)

XVIII. *OF THE WORLD TO COME*

We believe that the end of the world is approaching; that at the last day Christ will descend from heaven, and raise the dead from the grave to final retribution; that a solemn separation will then take place; that the wicked will be adjudged to endless punishment, and the righteous to endless joy; and that this judgment will fix forever the final state of men in heaven or hell, on principles of righteousness.

"But the end of all things is at hand: be ye therefore sober, and watch unto prayer." (**1 Peter 4:7**)

"Which also said, Ye men of Galilee, why stand ye gazing up into heaven? this same Jesus, which is taken up from you into heaven, shall so come in like manner as ye have seen him go into heaven." (**Acts 1:11**)

"But I would not have you to be ignorant, brethren, concerning them which are asleep, that ye sorrow not, even as others which have no hope. For if we believe that Jesus died and rose again, even so them also which sleep in Jesus will God bring with him. For this we say unto you by the word of the Lord, that we which are alive and remain unto the coming of the Lord shall not prevent them which are asleep. For the Lord himself shall descend from heaven with a shout, with the voice of the archangel, and with the trump of God: and the dead in Christ shall rise first: Then we which are alive and remain shall be caught up together with them in the clouds, to meet the Lord in the air: and so shall we ever be with the Lord. Wherefore comfort one another with these words." (**1 Thessalonians 4:13-18**)

"But this I confess unto thee, that after the way which they call heresy, so worship I the God of my fathers, believing all things which are written in the law and in the prophets: And have hope toward God, which they themselves also allow, that there shall be a resurrection of the dead, both of the just and unjust. (**Acts 24:14&15**)

"As therefore the tares are gathered and burned in the fire; so shall it be in the end of this world." (**Matthew 13:40**)

"And I saw heaven opened, and behold a white horse; and he that sat upon him was called Faithful and True, and in righteousness he doth judge and make war. His eyes were as a flame of fire, and on his head were many crowns; and he had a name written, that no man knew, but he himself. And he was clothed with a vesture dipped in blood: and his name is called The Word of God. And the armies which were in heaven followed him upon white horses, clothed in fine linen, white and clean. And out of his mouth goeth a sharp sword, that with it he should smite the nations: and he shall rule them with a rod of iron: and he treadeth the winepress of the fierceness and wrath of Almighty God. And he hath on his vesture and on his thigh a name written, KING OF KINGS, AND LORD OF LORDS. And I saw an angel standing in the sun; and he cried with a loud voice, saying to all the fowls that fly in the midst of heaven, Come and gather yourselves together unto the supper of the great God; That ye may eat the flesh of kings, and the flesh of captains, and the flesh of mighty men, and the flesh of horses, and of them that sit on them, and the flesh of all men, both free and bond, both small and great. And I saw the beast, and the kings of the earth, and their armies, gathered together to make war against him that sat on the horse, and

against his army. And the beast was taken, and with him the false prophet that wrought miracles before him, with which he deceived them that had received the mark of the beast, and them that worshipped his image. These both were cast alive into a lake of fire burning with brimstone. And the remnant were slain with the sword of him that sat upon the horse, which sword proceeded out of his mouth: and all the fowls were filled with their flesh." **(Revelation 19:11-21)**

"And the devil that deceived them was cast into the lake of fire and brimstone, where the beast and the false prophet are, and shall be tormented day and night for ever and ever. And I saw a great white throne, and him that sat on it, from whose face the earth and the heaven fled away; and there was found no place for them. And I saw the dead, small and great, stand before God; and the books were opened: and another book was opened, which is the book of life: and the dead were judged out of those things which were written in the books, according to their works. And the sea gave up the dead which were in it; and death and hell delivered up the dead which were in them: and they were judged every man according to their works. And death and hell were cast into the lake of fire. This is the second death. And whosoever was not found written in the book of life was cast into the lake of fire." **(Revelation 20:10-15)**

"So shall it be at the end of the world: the angels shall come forth, and sever the wicked from among the just, And shall cast them into the furnace of fire: there shall be wailing and gnashing of teeth." **(Matthew 13:49&50)**

"When the Son of man shall come in his glory, and all the holy angels with him, then shall he sit upon the throne of his glory: And before him shall be gathered all nations: and he shall separate them one from another, as a shepherd divideth his sheep from the goats: And he shall set the sheep on his right hand, but the goats on the left. Then shall the King say unto them on his right hand, Come, ye blessed of my Father, inherit the kingdom prepared for you from the foundation of the world: For I was an hungred, and ye gave me meat: I was thirsty, and ye gave me drink: I was a stranger, and ye took me in: Naked, and ye clothed me: I was sick, and ye visited me: I was in prison, and ye came unto me. Then shall the righteous answer him, saying, Lord, when saw we thee an hungred, and fed thee? or thirsty, and gave thee drink? When saw we thee a stranger, and took thee in? or naked, and clothed thee? Or when saw we thee sick, or in prison, and came unto thee? And the King shall answer and say unto them, Verily I say unto you, Inasmuch as ye have done it unto one of the least of these my brethren, ye have done it unto me. Then shall he say also unto them on the left hand, Depart from me, ye cursed, into everlasting fire, prepared for the devil and his angels: For I was an hungred, and ye gave me no meat: I was thirsty, and ye gave me no drink: I was a stranger, and ye took me not in: naked, and ye clothed me not: sick, and in prison, and ye visited me not. Then shall they also answer him, saying, Lord, when saw we thee an hungred, or athirst, or a stranger, or naked, or sick, or in prison, and did not minister unto thee? Then shall he answer them, saying, Verily I say unto you, Inasmuch as ye did it not to one of the least of these, ye did it not to me. And these shall go away into everlasting punishment: but the righteous into life eternal." **(Matthew 25:31-46)**

"And I saw a new heaven and a new earth: for the first heaven and the first earth were passed away; and there was no more sea. And I John saw the holy city, new Jerusalem, coming down from God out of heaven, prepared as a bride adorned for her husband. And I heard a great voice out of heaven saying, Behold, the tabernacle of God is with men, and

he will dwell with them, and they shall be his people, and God himself shall be with them, and be their God. And God shall wipe away all tears from their eyes; and there shall be no more death, neither sorrow, nor crying, neither shall there be any more pain: for the former things are passed away. And he that sat upon the throne said, Behold, I make all things new. And he said unto me, Write: for these words are true and faithful. And he said unto me, It is done. I am Alpha and Omega, the beginning and the end. I will give unto him that is athirst of the fountain of the water of life freely. He that overcometh shall inherit all things; and I will be his God, and he shall be my son. But the fearful, and unbelieving, and the abominable, and murderers, and whoremongers, and sorcerers, and idolaters, and all liars, shall have their part in the lake which burneth with fire and brimstone: which is the second death." (**Revelation 21:1-8**)

"Knowing this first, that there shall come in the last days scoffers, walking after their own lusts, And saying, Where is the promise of his coming? for since the fathers fell asleep, all things continue as they were from the beginning of the creation. For this they willingly are ignorant of, that by the word of God the heavens were of old, and the earth standing out of the water and in the water: Whereby the world that then was, being overflowed with water, perished: But the heavens and the earth, which are now, by the same word are kept in store, reserved unto fire against the day of judgment and perdition of ungodly men. But, beloved, be not ignorant of this one thing, that one day is with the Lord as a thousand years, and a thousand years as one day. The Lord is not slack concerning his promise, as some men count slackness; but is longsuffering to us-ward, not willing that any should perish, but that all should come to repentance. But the day of the Lord will come as a thief in the night; in the which the heavens shall pass away with a great noise, and the elements shall melt with fervent heat, the earth also and the works that are therein shall be burned up. Seeing then that all these things shall be dissolved, what manner of persons ought ye to be in all holy conversation and godliness, Looking for and hasting unto the coming of the day of God, wherein the heavens being on fire shall be dissolved, and the elements shall melt with fervent heat? Nevertheless we, according to his promise, look for new heavens and a new earth, wherein dwelleth righteousness. Wherefore, beloved, seeing that ye look for such things, be diligent that ye may be found of him in peace, without spot, and blameless. And account that the longsuffering of our Lord is salvation; even as our beloved brother Paul also according to the wisdom given unto him hath written unto you; As also in all his epistles, speaking in them of these things; in which are some things hard to be understood, which they that are unlearned and unstable wrest, as they do also the other scriptures, unto their own destruction. Ye therefore, beloved, seeing ye know these things before, beware lest ye also, being led away with the error of the wicked, fall from your own stedfastness. But grow in grace, and in the knowledge of our Lord and Saviour Jesus Christ. To him be glory both now and for ever. Amen." (**2 Peter 3:3-18**)

Shortcomings of the Articles of faith

Baptism is more than just an emblem (See Chapter 7, Salvation/Being Born Again):

"Know ye not, that so many of us as were baptized into Jesus Christ were baptized into his death? Therefore we are buried with him by baptism into death: that like as Christ was raised up from the dead by the glory of the Father, even so we also should walk in newness of life. For if we have been planted together in the likeness of his death, we shall be also

in the likeness of his resurrection: Knowing this, that our old man is crucified with him, that the body of sin might be destroyed, that henceforth we should not serve sin." (**Romans 6:3-6**)

"For as many of you as have been baptized into Christ have put on Christ. For ye are all the children of God by faith in Christ Jesus." (**Galatians 3:27&26**)

"Go ye therefore, and teach all nations, baptizing them in the name of the Father, and of the Son, and of the Holy Ghost: Teaching them to observe all things whatsoever I have commanded you: and, lo, I am with you alway, even unto the end of the world. Amen." (Mathew 28:19&20)

Salvation can not be stolen but can be lost by the behavior of the individual (See Chapter 7, Salvation/Being Born Again):

"Quench not the Spirit." (1 Thessalonians 5:19)

"For it is impossible for those who were once enlightened, and have tasted of the heavenly gift, and were made partakers of the Holy Ghost, And have tasted the good word of God, and the powers of the world to come, If they shall fall away, to renew them again unto repentance; seeing they crucify to themselves the Son of God afresh, and put him to an open shame." (Hebrews 6:4)

"For I have received of the Lord that which also I delivered unto you, That the Lord Jesus the same night in which he was betrayed took bread: And when he had given thanks, he brake it, and said, Take, eat: this is my body, which is broken for you: this do in remembrance of me. After the same manner also he took the cup, when he had supped, saying, This cup is the new testament in my blood: this do ye, as oft as ye drink it, in remembrance of me. For as often as ye eat this bread, and drink this cup, ye do shew the Lord's death till he come. Wherefore whosoever shall eat this bread, and drink this cup of the Lord, unworthily, shall be guilty of the body and blood of the Lord. But let a man examine himself, and so let him eat of that bread, and drink of that cup. For he that eateth and drinketh unworthily, eateth and drinketh damnation to himself, not discerning the Lord's body." (1 Corinthians 11:23-29)

"Let not sin therefore reign in your mortal body, that ye should obey it in the lusts thereof. Neither yield ye your members as instruments of unrighteousness unto sin: but yield yourselves unto God, as those that are alive from the dead, and your members as instruments of righteousness unto God. For sin shall not have dominion over you: for ye are not under the law, but under grace. What then? shall we sin, because we are not under the law, but under grace? God forbid. Know ye not, that to whom ye yield yourselves servants to obey, his servants ye are to whom ye obey; whether of sin unto death, or of obedience unto righteousness? (Romans 6:12-16)

The spiritual Church, that is the body of Christ, is not mentioned:

"For as we have many members in one body, and all members have not the same office: So we, being many, are one body in Christ, and every one members one of another." (Romans 12:4&5)

The Rapture is not mentioned with regard to the Last Days:

"For then shall be great tribulation, such as was not since the beginning of the world to this time, no, nor ever shall be. And except those days should be shortened, there should no flesh be saved: but for the elect's sake those days shall be shortened. Then if any man shall say unto you, Lo, here is Christ, or there; believe it not. For there shall arise false Christs, and false prophets, and shall shew great signs and wonders; insomuch that, if it were possible, they shall deceive the very elect. Behold, I have told you before. Wherefore if they shall say unto you, Behold, he is in the desert; go not forth: behold, he is in the secret chambers; believe it not. For as the lightning cometh out of the east, and shineth even unto the west; so shall also the coming of the Son of man be. For wheresoever the carcase is, there will the eagles be gathered together. Immediately after the tribulation of those days shall the sun be darkened, and the moon shall not give her light, and the stars shall fall from heaven, and the powers of the heavens shall be shaken: And then shall appear the sign of the Son of man in heaven: and then shall all the tribes of the earth mourn, and they shall see the Son of man coming in the clouds of heaven with power and great glory. And he shall send his angels with a great sound of a trumpet, and they shall gather together his elect from the four winds, from one end of heaven to the other. Now learn a parable of the fig tree; When his branch is yet tender, and putteth forth leaves, ye know that summer is nigh: So likewise ye, when ye shall see all these things, know that it is near, even at the doors. Verily I say unto you, This generation shall not pass, till all these things be fulfilled. Heaven and earth shall pass away, but my words shall not pass away. But of that day and hour knoweth no man, no, not the angels of heaven, but my Father only. But as the days of Noe were, so shall also the coming of the Son of man be. For as in the days that were before the flood they were eating and drinking, marrying and giving in marriage, until the day that Noe entered into the ark, And knew not until the flood came, and took them all away; so shall also the coming of the Son of man be. Then shall two be in the field; the one shall be taken, and the other left. Two women shall be grinding at the mill; the one shall be taken, and the other left. Watch therefore: for ye know not what hour your Lord doth come. But know this, that if the goodman of the house had known in what watch the thief would come, he would have watched, and would not have suffered his house to be broken up. Therefore be ye also ready: for in such an hour as ye think not the Son of man cometh. Who then is a faithful and wise servant, whom his lord hath made ruler over his household, to give them meat in due season? Blessed is that servant, whom his lord when he cometh shall find so doing." (Matthew 24:21-46)

"For yourselves know perfectly that the day of the Lord so cometh as a thief in the night. For when they shall say, Peace and safety; then sudden destruction cometh upon them, as travail upon a woman with child; and they shall not escape. But ye, brethren, are not in darkness, that that day should overtake you as a thief. Ye are all the children of light, and the children of the day: we are not of the night, nor of darkness. Therefore let us not sleep, as do others; but let us watch and be sober. For they that sleep sleep in the night; and they that be drunken are drunken in the night. But let us, who are of the day, be sober, putting on the breastplate of faith and love; and for an helmet, the hope of salvation. For God hath not appointed us to wrath, but to obtain salvation by our Lord Jesus Christ, Who died for us, that, whether we wake or sleep, we should live together with him." (1 Thessalonians 5:2-10)

"Behold, I come as a thief. Blessed is he that watcheth, and keepeth his garments, lest he walk naked, and they see his shame. And he gathered them together into a place called in the Hebrew tongue Armageddon." (**Revelations 16:15&16**)

The Thousand Years of Christ's Rule on Earth (the Millennium) in the Last Days is not mentioned:

"And I saw an angel come down from heaven, having the key of the bottomless pit and a great chain in his hand. And he laid hold on the dragon, that old serpent, which is the Devil, and Satan, and bound him a thousand years, And cast him into the bottomless pit, and shut him up, and set a seal upon him, that he should deceive the nations no more, till the thousand years should be fulfilled: and after that he must be loosed a little season. And I saw thrones, and they sat upon them, and judgment was given unto them: and I saw the souls of them that were beheaded for the witness of Jesus, and for the word of God, and which had not worshipped the beast, neither his image, neither had received his mark upon their foreheads, or in their hands; and they lived and reigned with Christ a thousand years. But the rest of the dead lived not again until the thousand years were finished. This is the first resurrection. Blessed and holy is he that hath part in the first resurrection: on such the second death hath no power, but they shall be priests of God and of Christ, and shall reign with him a thousand years. And when the thousand years are expired, Satan shall be loosed out of his prison, And shall go out to deceive the nations which are in the four quarters of the earth, Gog and Magog, to gather them together to battle: the number of whom is as the sand of the sea." (**Revelation 20:1-8**)

The incorruptible (aphthartos - undecaying in essence or continuance) and immortal nature of our existence forever in heaven upon a resurrection to eternal life is not mentioned.

"Behold, I shew you a mystery; We shall not all sleep, but we shall all be changed, In a moment, in the twinkling of an eye, at the last trump: for the trumpet shall sound, and the dead shall be raised incorruptible, and we shall be changed. For this corruptible must put on incorruption, and this mortal must put on immortality. So when this corruptible shall have put on incorruption, and this mortal shall have put on immortality, then shall be brought to pass the saying that is written, Death is swallowed up in victory. O death, where is thy sting? O grave, where is thy victory? The sting of death is sin; and the strength of sin is the law. But thanks be to God, which giveth us the victory through our Lord Jesus Christ. Therefore, my beloved brethren, be ye stedfast, unmoveable, always abounding in the work of the Lord, forasmuch as ye know that your labour is not in vain in the Lord." (**1 Corinthians 15:51-58**)

5

BIBLICAL FAITH/FAITH IN JESUS CHRIST

Faith based is a universal term used today. How is faith defined in the Bible?

FAITH (PISTIS) ORIGINATES in hearing of the word. Pistis is to give credence or conviction in the hearing of the word (of religious truth or truthfulness or truthfulness of God or a religious teacher) especially reliance upon Jesus Christ for salvation with consistency in such a profession. Pistis is the acceptance of the gospel as truth itself. Pistis is the assurance, belief, believing faith, and/or fidelity in the Lord.

> *"For with the heart man believeth unto righteousness; and with the mouth confession is made unto salvation. For the scripture saith, Whosoever believeth on him shall not be ashamed. For there is no difference between the Jew and the Greek: for the same Lord over all is rich unto all that call upon him. For whosoever shall call upon the name of the Lord shall be saved. How then shall they call on him in whom they have not believed? and how shall they believe in him of whom they have not heard? and how shall they hear without a preacher? And how shall they preach, except they be sent? as it is written, How beautiful are the feet of them that preach the gospel of peace, and bring glad tidings of good things! But they have not all obeyed the gospel. For Esaias saith, Lord, who hath believed our report? So then faith cometh by hearing, and hearing by the word of God."* (Romans 10:10-17)

> *"For I would that ye knew what great conflict I have for you, and for them at Laodicea, and for as many as have not seen my face in the flesh; That their hearts might be comforted, being knit together in love, and unto all riches of the full assurance of understanding, to the acknowledgement of the mystery of God, and of the Father, and of Christ; In whom are hid all the treasures of wisdom and knowledge. And this I say, lest any man should beguile you with enticing words. For though I be absent in the flesh, yet am I with you in the spirit, joying and beholding your order, and the stedfastness of your faith in Christ. As ye have therefore received Christ Jesus the Lord, so walk ye in him: Rooted and built up in him, and stablished in the faith, as ye have been taught, abounding therein with thanksgiving. Beware lest any man spoil you through philosophy and vain deceit, after the tradition of men, after the rudiments of the world, and not after Christ."* (Colossians 2:1-8)

Every human being is given a measure (a degree) of faith in Christ. Jesus Christ is the originator and completer of our faith.

> *"For I say, through the grace given unto me, to every man that is among you, not to think of himself more highly than he ought to think; but to think soberly, according as God hath dealt to every man the measure of faith."* (Romans 12:3)

> *"Looking unto Jesus the author and finisher of our faith; who for the joy that was set before him endured the cross, despising the shame, and is set down at the right hand of the throne of God."* (Hebrews 12:2)

Without our faith we cannot please God. Sin exists in the absence of faith. Whatsoever is not of faith is sin to a righteous God.

> *"But without faith it is impossible to please him: for he that cometh to God must believe that he is, and that he is a rewarder of them that diligently seek him."* (Hebrews 11:6)

> *"And he that doubteth is damned if he eat, because he eateth not of faith: for whatsoever is not of faith is sin."* (Romans 14:23)

We are only justified (Daikyo - show or regard as innocent, righteous) to God, i.e. judged righteous to God, by our faith as exemplified by the faith of Abraham.

> *"Blessed is the man to whom the Lord will not impute sin. Cometh this blessedness then upon the circumcision only, or upon the uncircumcision also? for we say that faith was reckoned to Abraham for righteousness."* (Romans 4:8-9)

> *"And the scripture, foreseeing that God would justify the heathen through faith, preached before the gospel unto Abraham, saying, In thee shall all nations be blessed. So then they which be of faith are blessed with faithful Abraham."* (Galatians 3: 8-9).

We, in and of ourselves, are judged without righteousness (unjustified before God) and therefore can have no fellowship with a holy and Almighty God.

> *"As it is written, There is none righteous, no, not one: There is none that understandeth, there is none that seeketh after God. They are all gone out of the way, they are together become unprofitable; there is none that doeth good, no, not one. Their throat is an open sepulchre; with their tongues they have used deceit; the poison of asps is under their lips: Whose mouth is full of cursing and bitterness: Their feet are swift to shed blood: Destruction and misery are in their ways: And the way of peace have they not known: There is no fear of God before their eyes. Now we know that what things soever the law saith, it saith to them who are under the law: that every mouth may be stopped, and all the world may become guilty before God. Therefore by the deeds of the law there shall no flesh be justified in his sight: for by the law is the knowledge of sin. "* (Romans 3:10-20)

Biblical faith is based upon our belief in Jesus Christ.

> *"But now the righteousness of God without the law is manifested, being witnessed by the law and the prophets; Even the righteousness of God which is by faith of Jesus Christ unto all and upon all them that believe: for there is no difference: For all have sinned, and come short of the glory of God; Being justified freely by his grace through the redemption that is in Christ Jesus: Whom God hath set forth to be a propitiation through faith in his blood, to*

declare his righteousness for the remission of sins that are past, through the forbearance of God; To declare, I say, at this time his righteousness: that he might be just, and the justifier of him which believeth in Jesus." (**Romans 3:21-25**)

Now Christ is the Christian's hope.

"For we through the Spirit wait for the hope of righteousness by faith." (**Galatians 5:5**)

"Behold, what manner of love the Father hath bestowed upon us, that we should be called the sons of God: therefore the world knoweth us not, because it knew him not. Beloved, now are we the sons of God, and it doth not yet appear what we shall be: but we know that, when he shall appear, we shall be like him; for we shall see him as he is. And every man that hath this hope in him purifieth himself, even as he is pure." (**I John 3: 1-3**)

There needs to be the self examination of our faith.

"Examine yourselves, whether ye be in the faith; prove your own selves. Know ye not your own selves, how that Jesus Christ is in you, except ye be reprobates? But I trust that ye shall know that we are not reprobates. Now I pray to God that ye do no evil; not that we should appear approved, but that ye should do that which is honest, though we be as reprobates." (**2 Corinthians 13:5-7**)

Note that Christ sits bodily at the right hand of the Heavenly Father in heaven. He is alive.

"Wherefore I also, after I heard of your faith in the Lord Jesus, and love unto all the saints, Cease not to give thanks for you, making mention of you in my prayers; That the God of our Lord Jesus Christ, the Father of glory, may give unto you the spirit of wisdom and revelation in the knowledge of him: The eyes of your understanding being enlightened; that ye may know what is the hope of his calling, and what the riches of the glory of his inheritance in the saints, And what is the exceeding greatness of his power to us-ward who believe, according to the working of his mighty power, Which he wrought in Christ, when he raised him from the dead, and set him at his own right hand in the heavenly places," (**Ephesians 1:15-20**)

However, faith allows Christ to dwell (Kaitoke – house permanently, reside (in the authoritative spiritual sense) in our hearts.

"That Christ may dwell in your hearts by faith; that ye, being rooted and grounded in love, May be able to comprehend with all saints what is the breadth, and length, and depth, and height; And to know the love of Christ, which passeth knowledge, that ye might be filled with all the fulness of God." (**Ephesians 3:17-19**)

"And let the peace of God rule in your hearts, to the which also ye are called in one body; and be ye thankful. Let the word of Christ dwell in you richly in all wisdom; teaching and admonishing one another in psalms and hymns and spiritual songs, singing with grace in your hearts to the Lord. And whatsoever ye do in word or deed, do all in the name of the Lord Jesus, giving thanks to God and the Father by him." (**Colossians 3:15-17**)

Now, it is the Holy Ghost the physically dwells in the believer and the Holy Ghost always

testifies of Christ.

> *"But ye are not in the flesh, but in the Spirit, if so be that the Spirit of God dwell in you. Now if any man have not the Spirit of Christ, he is none of his. And if Christ be in you, the body is dead because of sin; but the Spirit is life because of righteousness. But if the Spirit of him that raised up Jesus from the dead dwell in you, he that raised up Christ from the dead shall also quicken your mortal bodies by his Spirit that dwelleth in you."* (Romans 8:9-11)

> *"But when the Comforter is come, whom I will send unto you from the Father, even the Spirit of truth, which proceedeth from the Father, he shall testify of me: And ye also shall bear witness, because ye have been with me from the beginning."* (John 15:26&27)

Hypocrites in the visible church, those that pretend to be indwelled and led by God's Spirit, offer only lip service.

> *"Ye hypocrites, well did Esaias prophesy of you, saying, This people draweth nigh unto me with their mouth, and honoreth me with their lips; but their heart is far from me. But in vain they do worship me, teaching for doctrines the commandments of men."* (Matthew 15:7-9)

There is no salvation without faith for it is by faith that the saving unmerited favor (grace) of God is bestowed upon the believer.

> *"For by grace are ye saved through faith; and that not of yourselves: it is the gift of God."* (Ephesians 2:8)

Faith allows the unity of Christians in the spiritual body of Christ (the church).

> *"And he gave some, apostles; and some, prophets; and some, evangelists; and some, pastors and teachers; For the perfecting of the saints, for the work of the ministry, for the edifying of the body of Christ: Till we all come in the unity of the faith, and of the knowledge of the Son of God, unto a perfect man, unto the measure of the stature of the fulness of Christ: That we henceforth be no more children, tossed to and fro, and carried about with every wind of doctrine, by the sleight of men, and cunning craftiness, whereby they lie in wait to deceive; But speaking the truth in love, may grow up into him in all things, which is the head, even Christ: From whom the whole body fitly joined together and compacted by that which every joint supplieth, according to the effectual working in the measure of every part, maketh increase of the body unto the edifying of itself in love."* (Ephesians 4:11-16)

Now, finally, to have faith is to be sure in our hearts and minds of the hope in our salvation to the point of being certain of things that we cannot see because of the evidence we have been already given (already seen).

> *"Now faith is the substance of things hoped for, the evidence of things not seen. For by it the elders obtained a good report. Through faith we understand that the worlds were framed by the word of God, so that things which are seen were not made of things which do appear."* (Hebrews 11:1-3)

"For I am not ashamed of the gospel of Christ: for it is the power of God unto salvation to every one that believeth; to the Jew first, and also to the Greek. For therein is the righteousness of God revealed from faith to faith: as it is written, The just shall live by faith. For the wrath of God is revealed from heaven against all ungodliness and unrighteousness of men, who hold the truth in unrighteousness; Because that which may be known of God is manifest in them; for God hath shewed it unto them. For the invisible things of him from the creation of the world are clearly seen, being understood by the things that are made, even his eternal power and Godhead; so that they are without excuse:" (Romans 1:16-20)

"Believe me that I am in the Father, and the Father in me: or else believe me for the very works' sake." (John 14:11)

How are those of faith determined? It is established through the two ordinances of the church. To be apart of the spiritual body of Christ, one must be baptized and then, must be partakers of the Lord's Supper (Holy Communion). Baptism allows us to become spiritual partakers with Christ in his suffering, death, burial, and resurrection. Holy Communion calls for our self-examination as to whether we are relying upon Christ in our lives.

"He that believeth and is baptized shall be saved; but he that believeth not shall be damned." (Mark 16:16)

"Go ye therefore, and teach all nations, baptizing them in the name of the Father, and of the Son, and of the Holy Ghost: Teaching them to observe all things whatsoever I have commanded you: and, lo, I am with you alway, even unto the end of the world. Amen." (Matthew 28:19-20)

"For as many of you as have been baptized into Christ have put on Christ." (Galatians 3:27)

"Know ye not, that so many of us as were baptized into Jesus Christ were baptized into his death? Therefore we are buried with him by baptism into death: that like as Christ was raised up from the dead by the glory of the Father, even so we also should walk in newness of life. For if we have been planted together in the likeness of his death, we shall be also in the likeness of his resurrection: Knowing this, that our old man is crucified with him, that the body of sin might be destroyed, that henceforth we should not serve sin. For he that is dead is freed from sin. Now if we be dead with Christ, we believe that we shall also live with him: Knowing that Christ being raised from the dead dieth no more; death hath no more dominion over him." (Romans 6:3-9)

"And let the peace of God rule in your hearts, to the which also ye are called in one body; and be ye thankful." (Colossians 3:15)

"For I have received of the Lord that which also I delivered unto you, That the Lord Jesus the same night in which he was betrayed took bread: And when he had given thanks, he brake it, and said, Take, eat: this is my body, which is broken for you: this do in remembrance of me. After the same manner also he took the cup, when he had supped, saying, This cup is the new testament in my blood: this do ye, as oft as ye drink it, in remembrance of me. For as often as ye eat this bread, and drink this cup, ye do shew the Lord's death till he come. Wherefore whosoever shall eat this bread, and drink this cup of the Lord, unworthily, shall be guilty of the body and blood of the Lord. But let a man examine himself,

and so let him eat of that bread, and drink of that cup. For he that eateth and drinketh unworthily, eateth and drinketh damnation to himself, not discerning the Lord's body. For this cause many are weak and sickly among you, and many sleep. For if we would judge ourselves, we should not be judged. But when we are judged, we are chastened of the Lord, that we should not be condemned with the world." (**1 Corinthians 11:23-32**)

6

BEING FULLY PERSUADED IN CHRIST

I want to know on what basis I can trust in Jesus Christ as others say that I ought.

IN THE BOOK of Romans, the Christian is admonished not to judge their brother. Christians are to be held accountable for their own actions as well as any hindrances that they have presented to others.

> *"For whether we live, we live unto the Lord; and whether we die, we die unto the Lord: whether we live therefore, or die, we are the Lord's. For to this end Christ both died, and rose, and revived, that he might be Lord both of the dead and living. But why dost thou judge thy brother? or why dost thou set at nought thy brother? for we shall all stand before the judgment seat of Christ. Let us not therefore judge one another any more: but judge this rather, that no man put a stumblingblock or an occasion to fall in his brother's way."* (Romans 14:8-10, 13)

> *"Him that is weak in the faith receive ye, but not to doubtful disputations. For one believeth that he may eat all things: another, who is weak, eateth herbs. Let not him that eateth despise him that eateth not; and let not him which eateth not judge him that eateth: for God hath received him. Who art thou that judgest another man's servant? to his own master he standeth or falleth. Yea, he shall be holden up: for God is able to make him stand."* (Romans 14:1-4)

This admonishment can be considered further amplification of Christ's teaching with regard to the hypocrisy in judging another.

> *"Judge not, that ye be not judged. For with what judgment ye judge, ye shall be judged: and with what measure ye mete, it shall be measured to you again."* (Matthew 7:1&2)

Rather, buried in the scriptures is a profound statement that is apropos today to the believing and even the unbeliever. Being fully persuaded in Christ is obtainable in the manner as prescribed in the Bible.

> *"One man esteemeth one day above another: another esteemeth every day alike. Let every man be fully persuaded in his own mind."* (Romans 14:5)

Every human being should consider Christ. Jesus is preeminent in all aspects of salvation to all of the deities in the imagination of man. There is no harm in making comparisons. Jesus Christ is able to withstand the scrutiny.

> *"Wherefore seeing we also are compassed about with so great a cloud of witnesses, let us lay aside every weight, and the sin which doth so easily beset us, and let us run with patience the race that is set before us, Looking unto Jesus the author and finisher of our faith; who for the joy that was set before him endured the cross, despising the shame, and is set down at the right hand of the throne of God. For consider him that endured such contradiction of sinners against himself, lest ye be wearied and faint in your minds."* (Hebrews 12:1-3)

Mankind is given a very real choice in whom to spiritually serve.

> *"I call heaven and earth to record this day against you, that I have set before you life and death, blessing and cursing: therefore choose life, that both thou and thy seed may live:"* (Deuteronomy 30:19)

God respects our choosing and our being confident enough to say yea or nay with regard to all matters of concern or contemplation.

> *"But above all things, my brethren, swear not, neither by heaven, neither by the earth, neither by any other oath: but let your yea be yea; and your nay, nay; lest ye fall into condemnation."* (James 5:12)

Those double-minded are judged by the scriptures to be unstable in all aspects of life.

> *"Draw nigh to God, and he will draw nigh to you. Cleanse your hands, ye sinners; and purify your hearts, ye double minded."* (James 4:8)

> *"A double minded man is unstable in all his ways."* (James 1:8)

The Bible makes a clear statement with regard to unbelief and disregard of Jesus Christ. Judgment is to begin within the hypocrisy of the church leaving those outside of the church in a very precarious position with regard to eternal salvation.

> *"For I have received of the Lord that which also I delivered unto you, That the Lord Jesus the same night in which he was betrayed took bread: For as often as ye eat this bread, and drink this cup, ye do shew the Lord's death till he come. Wherefore whosoever shall eat this bread, and drink this cup of the Lord, unworthily, shall be guilty of the body and blood of the Lord. For he that eateth and drinketh unworthily, eateth and drinketh damnation to himself, not discerning the Lord's body."* (1 Corinthians 11:23, 26, 27 & 29)

> *"Yet if any man suffer as a Christian, let him not be ashamed; but let him glorify God on this behalf. For the time is come that judgment must begin at the house of God: and if it first begin at us, what shall the end be of them that obey not the gospel of God? And if the righteous scarcely be saved, where shall the ungodly and the sinner appear? Wherefore let them that suffer according to the will of God commit the keeping of their souls to him in well doing, as unto a faithful Creator. "* (1 Peter 4:16-19)

"He that believeth on him is not condemned: but he that believeth not is condemned already, because he hath not believed in the name of the only begotten Son of God." (John 3:18)

Being fully persuaded involves self-examination of one's faith, according to the scriptures. According to the Bible, we are only saved by God's grace as a result of our faith in Jesus Christ.

"But let a man examine himself, and so let him eat of that bread, and drink of that cup. For if we would judge ourselves, we should not be judged. But when we are judged, we are chastened of the Lord, that we should not be condemned with the world." (1 Corinthians 11:28, 31, 32)

"For by grace are ye saved through faith; and that not of yourselves: it is the gift of God: Not of works, lest any man should boast." (Ephesians 2:8 & 9)

Everyone needs to trust in the Creator rather than their own mindset; of course this is a nonsensical statement to all that believe in evolution rather than creation.

"Trust in the Lord with all thine" heart; and lean not unto thine own understanding. In all thy ways acknowledge him, and he shall direct thy paths. Be not wise in thine own eyes: fear the Lord, and depart from evil."* (Proverbs 3:5-7)

"In the beginning God created the heaven and the earth." (Genesis 1:1)

"Praise ye the Lord. Praise ye the Lord from the heavens: praise him in the heights. Praise ye him, all his angels: praise ye him, all his hosts. Praise ye him, sun and moon: praise him, all ye stars of light. Praise him, ye heavens of heavens, and ye waters that be above the heavens. Let them praise the name of the Lord: for he commanded, and they were created. He hath also stablished them for ever and ever: he hath made a decree which shall not pass. Praise the Lord from the earth, ye dragons, and all deeps: Fire, and hail; snow, and vapors; stormy wind fulfilling his word: Mountains, and all hills; fruitful trees, and all cedars: Beasts, and all cattle; creeping things, and flying fowl: Kings of the earth, and all people; princes, and all judges of the earth: Both young men, and maidens; old men, and children: Let them praise the name of the Lord: for his name alone is excellent; his glory is above the earth and heaven." (Psalm 148)

"Giving thanks unto the Father, which hath made us meet to be partakers of the inheritance of the saints in light: Who hath delivered us from the power of darkness, and hath translated us into the kingdom of his dear Son: In whom we have redemption through his blood, even the forgiveness of sins: Who is the image of the invisible God, the firstborn of every creature: For by him were all things created, that are in heaven, and that are in earth, visible and invisible, whether they be thrones, or dominions, or principalities, or powers: all things were created by him, and for him: And he is before all things, and by him all things consist." (Colossians 1:12-17)

Does one need to be persuaded of the existence of the living God our creator; even demons are convinced and believe? He has revealed himself over the ages.

"Thou believest that there is one God; thou doest well: the devils also believe, and tremble." (James 2:19)

"The fool hath said in his heart, There is no God. They are corrupt, they have done abominable works, there is none that doeth good." (**Psalm 14:1**)

"For the wrath of God is revealed from heaven against all ungodliness and unrighteousness of men, who hold the truth in unrighteousness; Because that which may be known of God is manifest in them; for God hath shewed it unto them. For the invisible things of him from the creation of the world are clearly seen, being understood by the things that are made, even his eternal power and Godhead; so that they are without excuse: Because that, when they knew God, they glorified him not as God, neither were thankful; but became vain in their imaginations, and their foolish heart was darkened. Professing themselves to be wise, they became fools, And changed the glory of the uncorruptible God into an image made like to corruptible man, and to birds, and fourfooted beasts, and creeping things. Wherefore God also gave them up to uncleanness through the lusts of their own hearts, to dishonor their own bodies between themselves: Who changed the truth of God into a lie, and worshipped and served the creature more than the Creator, who is blessed for ever. Amen. For this cause God gave them up unto vile affections: for even their women did change the natural use into that which is against nature: And likewise also the men, leaving the natural use of the woman, burned in their lust one toward another; men with men working that which is unseemly, and receiving in themselves that recompence of their error which was meet. And even as they did not like to retain God in their knowledge, God gave them over to a reprobate mind, to do those things which are not convenient; Being filled with all unrighteousness, fornication, wickedness, covetousness, maliciousness; full of envy, murder, debate, deceit, malignity; whisperers, Backbiters, haters of God, despiteful, proud, boasters, inventors of evil things, disobedient to parents, Without understanding, covenantbreakers, without natural affection, implacable, unmerciful: Who knowing the judgment of God, that they which commit such things are worthy of death, not only do the same, but have pleasure in them that do them." (**Romans 1:18-32**)

As a matter of practicality, we cannot trust in God and have our lives directed unless we are led by the Creator's Spirit.

"This I say then, Walk in the Spirit, and ye shall not fulfil the lust of the flesh." (**Galatians 5:16**)

"Whereby, when ye read, ye may understand my knowledge in the mystery of Christ) Which in other ages was not made known unto the sons of men, as it is now revealed unto his holy apostles and prophets by the Spirit; That the Gentiles should be fellowheirs, and of the same body, and partakers of his promise in Christ by the gospel: Whereof I was made a minister, according to the gift of the grace of God given unto me by the effectual working of his power. Unto me, who am less than the least of all saints, is this grace given, that I should preach among the Gentiles the unsearchable riches of Christ And to make all men see what is the fellowship of the mystery, which from the beginning of the world hath been hid in God, who created all things by Jesus Christ: To the intent that now unto the principalities and powers in heavenly places might be known by the church the manifold wisdom of God, According to the eternal purpose which he purposed in Christ Jesus our Lord: In whom we have boldness and access with confidence by the faith of him. Wherefore I desire that ye faint not at my tribulations for you, which is your glory. For this cause I bow my knees unto the Father of our Lord Jesus Christ, Of whom the whole family in heaven and earth is named, That he would grant you, according to the riches of his glory, to be

> *strengthened with might by his Spirit in the inner man; That Christ may dwell in your hearts by faith; that ye, being rooted and grounded in love, May be able to comprehend with all saints what is the breadth, and length, and depth, and height; And to know the love of Christ, which passeth knowledge, that ye might be filled with all the fulness of God."* **(Ephesians 3:4-19)**

God's Spirit, the third person of the Trinity (Godhead), leads the believer in all things and he always testifies as what Christ would desire in every situation.

> *"If ye love me, keep my commandments. And I will pray the Father, and he shall give you another Comforter, that he may abide with you for ever; Even the Spirit of truth; whom the world cannot receive, because it seeth him not, neither knoweth him: but ye know him; for he dwelleth with you, and shall be in you. I will not leave you comfortless: I will come to you."* (John 14:15-18)

> *"Howbeit when he, the Spirit of truth, is come, he will guide you into all truth: for he shall not speak of himself; but whatsoever he shall hear, that shall he speak: and he will shew you things to come. He shall glorify me: for he shall receive of mine, and shall shew it unto you."* (John 16:13&14)

> *Ye have not chosen me, but I have chosen you, and ordained you, that ye should go and bring forth fruit, and that your fruit should go and bring forth fruit, and that your fruit should remain: that whatsoever ye shall ask of the Father in my name, he may give it you."* (John 15:16)

The Bible attests to the factor that makes every human being receptive to the gospel of Jesus Christ; everyone is given in creation a receptiveness in belief.

> *"For I say, through the grace given unto me, to every man that is among you, not to think of himself more highly than he ought to think; but to think soberly, according as God hath dealt to every man the measure of faith."* (Romans 12:3)

Further that measure of faith, that is given to all mankind, I am pursuaded, is designed to bring us ultimately into a unity in the faith in Jesus Christ, no longer tossed to and fro in life by unsound doctrine.

> *"And he gave some, apostles; and some, prophets; and some, evangelists; and some, pastors and teachers; For the perfecting of the saints, for the work of the ministry, for the edifying of the body of Christ: Till we all come in the unity of the faith, and of the knowledge of the Son of God, unto a perfect man, unto the measure of the stature of the fulness of Christ: That we henceforth be no more children, tossed to and fro, and carried about with every wind of doctrine, by the sleight of men, and cunning craftiness, whereby they lie in wait to deceive; But speaking the truth in love, may grow up into him in all things, which is the head, even Christ: From whom the whole body fitly joined together and compacted by that which every joint supplieth, according to the effectual working in the measure of every part, maketh increase of the body unto the edifying of itself in love."* (Ephesians 4:11-16)

Now, the Christian must study. Studying of the Bible is to be encouraged and recognized as the manner in which to unashamedly demonstrate the desire to win God's approval by

studying and correctly dividing (orths: expounding, dissect correctly) the truth(s) of the Bible.

> *"Study to shew thyself approved unto God, a workman that needeth not to be ashamed, rightly dividing the word of truth."* (2 Timothy 2:15)

Rather than mankind, it is the Holy Spirit that correctly interprets the Bible and the process is to build biblical precept upon precept and line upon line as prayed for and led by God.

> *"Knowing this first, that no prophecy of the scripture is of any private interpretation. For the prophecy came not in old time by the will of man: but holy men of God spake as they were moved by the Holy Ghost."* (1 Peter 1:20&21)

> *"Whom shall he teach knowledge? and whom shall he make to understand doctrine? them that are weaned from the milk, and drawn from the breasts. For precept must be upon precept, precept upon precept; line upon line, line upon line; here a little, and there a little: For with stammering lips and another tongue will he speak to this people. To whom he said, This is the rest wherewith ye may cause the weary to rest; and this is the refreshing: yet they would not hear. But the word of the Lord was unto them precept upon precept, precept upon precept; line upon line, line upon line; here a little, and there a little; that they might go, and fall backward, and be broken, and snared, and taken. Wherefore hear the word of the Lord, ye scornful men, that rule this people which is in Jerusalem."* (Isaiah 28:9-14)

Even as we may hear the preached word, we need to receive the sermon readily but then examine the scriptures; those meditations are blessed by God according to the Bible.

> *"These were more noble than those in Thessalonica, in that they received the word with all readiness of mind, and searched the scriptures daily, whether those things were so."* (Acts 17:11)

> *"Blessed is the man that walketh not in the counsel of the ungodly, nor standeth in the way of sinners, nor sitteth in the seat of the scornful. But his delight is in the law of the Lord; and in his law doth he meditate day and night."* (Psalm1:1-2)

> *"Wherewithal shall a young man cleanse his way? by taking heed thereto according to thy word. With my whole heart have I sought thee: O let me not wander from thy commandments. Thy word have I hid in mine heart, that I might not sin against thee. Blessed art thou, O Lord: teach me thy statutes. With my lips have I declared all the judgments of thy mouth. I have rejoiced in the way of thy testimonies, as much as in all riches. I will meditate in thy precepts, and have respect unto thy ways. I will delight myself in thy statutes: I will not forget thy word. Deal bountifully with thy servant, that I may live, and keep thy word. Open thou mine eyes, that I may behold wondrous things out of thy law. I am a stranger in the earth: hide not thy commandments from me. My soul breaketh for the longing that it hath unto thy judgments at all times. Thou hast rebuked the proud that are cursed, which do err from thy commandments. Remove from me reproach and contempt; for I have kept thy testimonies. Princes also did sit and speak against me: but thy servant did meditate in thy statutes".* (Psalm 119:9-23)

"O how I love thy law! it is my meditation all the day. Thou through thy commandments hast made me wiser than mine enemies: for they are ever with me. I have more understanding than all my teachers: for thy testimonies are my meditation. I understand more than the ancients, because I keep thy precepts. I have refrained my feet from every evil way, that I might keep thy word. I have not departed from thy judgments: for thou hast taught me. How sweet are thy words unto my taste! yea, sweeter than honey to my mouth! Through thy precepts I get understanding: therefore I hate every false way." (Psalm 119:97-104)

"Give ear to my words, O Lord, consider my meditation. Hearken unto the voice of my cry, my King, and my God: for unto thee will I pray. For thou, Lord, wilt bless the righteous; with favor wilt thou compass him as with a shield." (Psalm 5:1, 2 &12)

Now, as for persuasion of the unbeliever, God is mindful of the sinner to bring the sinner unto salvation. Seek first the kingdom of God and its righteousness and everything else in life will follow. Draw closer to God and resist the devil as opposed to the other way around.

"Good and upright is the Lord: therefore will he teach sinners in the way." (Psalm 25:8)

"Therefore take no thought, saying, What shall we eat? or, What shall we drink? or, Wherewithal shall we be clothed? For after all these things do the Gentiles seek:) for your heavenly Father knoweth that ye have need of all these things. But seek ye first the kingdom of God, and his righteousness; and all these things shall be added unto you." (Matthew 6:31-33)

"Submit yourselves therefore to God. Resist the devil, and he will flee from you. Draw nigh to God, and he will draw nigh to you. Cleanse your hands, ye sinners; and purify your hearts, ye double minded." (James 4:7&8)

Seek salvation with a mindset of being reverent to God.

"Wherefore, my beloved, as ye have always obeyed, not as in my presence only, but now much more in my absence, work out your own salvation with fear and trembling." (Philippians 2:12)

Beware and be persuaded by what is being commanded by God in the Bible as opposed to what has been taught purely by man. There are those that persist in abiding in doctrines that are not of Christ.

"Let no man beguile you of your reward in a voluntary humility and worshipping of angels, intruding into those things which he hath not seen, vainly puffed up by his fleshly mind, And not holding the Head, from which all the body by joints and bands having nourishment ministered, and knit together, increaseth with the increase of God. Wherefore if ye be dead with Christ from the rudiments of the world, why, as though living in the world, are ye subject to ordinances, (Touch not; taste not; handle not; Which all are to perish with the using;) after the commandments and doctrines of men? Which things have indeed a shew of wisdom in will worship, and humility, and neglecting of the body: not in any honor to the satisfying of the flesh." (Colossians 2:18-23)

"Now the Spirit speaketh expressly, that in the latter times some shall depart from the faith, giving heed to seducing spirits, and doctrines of devils; (1 Timothy 4:1)

For many deceivers are entered into the world, who confess not that Jesus Christ is come in the flesh. This is a deceiver and an antichrist. Look to yourselves, that we lose not those things which we have wrought, but that we receive a full reward. Whosoever transgresseth, and abideth not in the doctrine of Christ, hath not God. He that abideth in the doctrine of Christ, he hath both the Father and the Son." (2 John 7-9)

For every human being, let not wisdom originate out of your own minds; we are to be persuaded if not already postured.

"Be of the same mind one toward another. Mind not high things, but condescend to men of low estate. Be not wise in your own conceits." (Romans 12:16)

Now there is a relationship between our being fully persuaded, accepting Jesus Christ, the doctrine Christ and obtaining knowledge with an understanding of the truth. In being fully persuaded in our relationship with Christ and his doctrine, we have found wisdom out of the mouth of God.

"But of him are ye in Christ Jesus, who of God is made unto us wisdom, and righteousness, and sanctification, and redemption: That, according as it is written, He that glorieth, let him glory in the Lord." (1 Corinthians 1:30- 31)

"My son, if thou wilt receive my words, and hide my commandments with thee; So that thou incline thine ear unto wisdom, and apply thine heart to understanding; Yea, if thou criest after knowledge, and liftest up thy voice for understanding; If thou seekest her as silver, and searchest for her as for hid treasures; Then shalt thou understand the fear of the Lord, and find the knowledge of God. For the Lord giveth wisdom: out of his mouth cometh knowledge and understanding." (Proverbs 2:1- 6)

Pray for more the Holy Ghost if you lack wisdom. The Holy Ghost indwells the believer bodily and always testifies of Jesus Christ.

"If any of you lack wisdom, let him ask of God, that giveth to all men liberally, and upbraideth not; and it shall be given him." (James 1:5)

"For every one that asketh receiveth; and he that seeketh findeth; and to him that knocketh it shall be opened. If a son shall ask bread of any of you that is a father, will he give him a stone? or if he ask a fish, will he for a fish give him a serpent? Or if he shall ask an egg, will he offer him a scorpion? If ye then, being evil, know how to give good gifts unto your children: how much more shall your heavenly Father give the Holy Spirit to them that ask him?" (Luke 11:10-13)

"But when the Comforter is come, whom I will send unto you from the Father, even the Spirit of truth, which proceedeth from the Father, he shall testify of me: And ye also shall bear witness, because ye have been with me from the beginning." (John 15:26 & 27)

"Now there are diversities of gifts, but the same Spirit. And there are differences of administrations, but the same Lord. And there are diversities of operations, but it is the same God which worketh all in all. But the manifestation of the Spirit is given to every man to profit withal. For to one is given by the Spirit the word of wisdom; to another the word of knowledge by the same Spirit; To another faith by the same Spirit; to another the gifts of

healing by the same Spirit; To another the working of miracles; to another prophecy; to another discerning of spirits; to another divers kinds of tongues; to another the interpretation of tongues: But all these worketh that one and the selfsame Spirit, dividing to every man severally as he will. For as the body is one, and hath many members, and all the members of that one body, being many, are one body: so also is Christ." (**1 Corinthians 12:4-12**)

The scriptures provide instruction in righteous living.

"All scripture is given by inspiration of God, and is profitable for doctrine, for reproof, for correction, for instruction in righteousness:" (**2 Timothy 3:16**)

Hear instruction out of the Bible. Love that instruction.

"Hear instruction, and be wise, and refuse it not. Blessed is the man that heareth me, watching daily at my gates, waiting at the posts of my doors. For whoso findeth me findeth life, and shall obtain favor of the Lord. But he that sinneth against me wrongeth his own soul: all they that hate me love death." (**Proverbs 8:33-36**)

"Whoso loveth instruction loveth knowledge: but he that hateth reproof is brutish." (**Proverbs 12:1**)

Now very specifically, among those that call Christ our Savior, we should seek the doctrine of Christ and not just what we want to hear. Be careful not to judge but rather examine our own doctrine. Be careful of being in fellowship just anywhere. Some houses of worship have been labeled by the Bible as "Synagogues of Satan".

"For the time will come when they will not endure sound doctrine; but after their own lusts shall they heap to themselves teachers, having itching ears;" (**2 Timothy 4:3**)

"Woe unto you, scribes and Pharisees, hypocrites! for ye pay tithe of mint and anise and cummin, and have omitted the weightier matters of the law, judgment, mercy, and faith: these ought ye to have done, and not to leave the other undone. Ye blind guides, which strain at a gnat, and swallow a camel. Woe unto you, scribes and Pharisees, hypocrites! for ye make clean the outside of the cup and of the platter, but within they are full of extortion and excess. Thou blind Pharisee, cleanse first that which is within the cup and platter, that the outside of them may be clean also. Woe unto you, scribes and Pharisees, hypocrites! for ye are like unto whited sepulchres, which indeed appear beautiful outward, but are within full of dead men's bones, and of all uncleanness. Even so ye also outwardly appear righteous unto men, but within ye are full of hypocrisy and iniquity. Woe unto you, scribes and Pharisees, hypocrites! because ye build the tombs of the prophets, and garnish the sepulchres of the righteous, And say, If we had been in the days of our fathers, we would not have been partakers with them in the blood of the prophets. Wherefore ye be witnesses unto yourselves, that ye are the children of them which killed the prophets. Fill ye up then the measure of your fathers. Ye serpents, ye generation of vipers, how can ye escape the damnation of hell?" (**Matthew 23:23-33**)

"Therefore leaving the principles of the doctrine of Christ, let us go on unto perfection; not laying again the foundation of repentance from dead works, and of faith toward God, Of the doctrine of baptisms, and of laying on of hands, and of resurrection of the dead, and of eternal judgment. And this will we do, if God permit. For it is impossible for those who

were once enlightened, and have tasted of the heavenly gift, and were made partakers of the Holy Ghost, And have tasted the good word of God, and the powers of the world to come, If they shall fall away, to renew them again unto repentance; seeing they crucify to themselves the Son of God afresh, and put him to an open shame. For the earth which drinketh in the rain that cometh oft upon it, and bringeth forth herbs meet for them by whom it is dressed, receiveth blessing from God: But that which beareth thorns and briers is rejected, and is nigh unto cursing; whose end is to be burned. But, beloved, we are persuaded better things of you, and things that accompany salvation, though we thus speak. For God is not unrighteous to forget your work and labor of love, which ye have shewed toward his name, in that ye have ministered to the saints, and do minister. And we desire that every one of you do shew the same diligence to the full assurance of hope unto the end: That ye be not slothful, but followers of them who through faith and patience inherit the promises." (Hebrews 6:1-12)

"Let no man therefore judge you in meat, or in drink, or in respect of an holyday, or of the new moon, or of the sabbath days: Which are a shadow of things to come; but the body is of Christ." (Colossians 2:16 & 17)

"And unto the angel of the church in Smyrna write; These things saith the first and the last, which was dead, and is alive; I know thy works, and tribulation, and poverty, (but thou art rich) and I know the blasphemy of them which say they are Jews, and are not, but are the synagogue of Satan." (Revelation 2:8 & 9)

"And to the angel of the church in Philadelphia write; These things saith he that is holy, he that is true, he that hath the key of David, he that openeth, and no man shutteth; and shutteth, and no man openeth; I know thy works: behold, I have set before thee an open door, and no man can shut it: for thou hast a little strength, and hast kept my word, and hast not denied my name. Behold, I will make them of the synagogue of Satan, which say they are Jews, and are not, but do lie; behold, I will make them to come and worship before thy feet, and to know that I have loved thee." (Revelation 3:7-9)

Be persuaded and speak the things that comprise sound doctrine. Stay in prayer letting your requests be made known to God and he is careful to keep our hearts and minds; this is the basis of the new covenant, through Christ Jesus.

"But speak thou the things which become sound doctrine" (Titus 2:1)

"Be careful for nothing; but in every thing by prayer and supplication with thanksgiving let your requests be made known unto God. And the peace of God, which passeth all understanding, shall keep your hearts and minds through Christ Jesus." (Philippians 4:6-7)

"Howbeit then, when ye knew not God, ye did service unto them which by nature are no gods. But now, after that ye have known God, or rather are known of God, how turn ye again to the weak and beggarly elements, whereunto ye desire again to be in bondage?" (Galatians 4:8&9)

"Whereof the Holy Ghost also is a witness to us: for after that he had said before, This is the covenant that I will make with them after those days, saith the Lord, I will put my laws into their hearts, and in their minds will I write them; And their sins and iniquities will I remember no more." (Hebrews 10:15-17)

"But this shall be the covenant that I will make with the house of Israel; After those days, saith the Lord, I will put my law in their inward parts, and write it in their hearts; and will be their God, and they shall be my people. And they shall teach no more every man his neighbor, and every man his brother, saying, Know the Lord: for they shall all know me, from the least of them unto the greatest of them, saith the Lord: for I will forgive their iniquity, and I will remember their sin no more." (Jeremiah 31:33 & 34)

7

SALVATION/BEING BORN AGAIN

What in the world is this being born again business and what does it have to do with me going to heaven when I die?

Origin of Salvation

Salvation (Soteria – deliverance, save, saving) is of the Jews, the Bible declares.

> *"Ye worship ye know not what: we know what we worship: for salvation is of the Jews."* (John 4:22)

Why? The Jews were God's chosen people and Jesus Christ, the truth, the way and the resurrection, was Jewish.

> *"For thou art an holy people unto the Lord thy God: the Lord thy God hath chosen thee to be a special people unto himself, above all people that are upon the face of the earth. The Lord did not set his love upon you, nor choose you, because ye were more in number than any people; for ye were the fewest of all people: But because the Lord loved you, and because he would keep the oath which he had sworn unto your fathers, hath the Lord brought you out with a mighty hand, and redeemed you out of the house of bondmen, from the hand of Pharaoh king of Egypt."* (Deuteronomy 7:6-8)

> *"Now the birth of Jesus Christ was on this wise: When as his mother Mary was espoused to Joseph, before they came together, she was found with child of the Holy Ghost. Then Joseph her husband, being a just man, and not willing to make her a publick example, was minded to put her away privily. But while he thought on these things, behold, the angel of the Lord appeared unto him in a dream, saying, Joseph, thou son of David, fear not to take unto thee Mary thy wife: for that which is conceived in her is of the Holy Ghost. And she shall bring forth a son, and thou shalt call his name Jesus: for he shall save his people from their sins. Now all this was done, that it might be fulfilled which was spoken of the Lord by the prophet, saying, Behold, a virgin shall be with child, and shall bring forth a son, and they shall call his name Emmanuel, which being interpreted is, God with us."* (Matthew 1:18-23)

Christ came unto the Jews and was not received; that made a way for gentiles, as it had been foretold from the days of the prophets, to be brought into salvation along with Jews as the chosen of God.

"Behold my servant, whom I uphold; mine elect, in whom my soul delighteth; I have put my spirit upon him: he shall bring forth judgment to the Gentiles. He shall not cry, nor lift up, nor cause his voice to be heard in the street. A bruised reed shall he not break, and the smoking flax shall he not quench: he shall bring forth judgment unto truth. He shall not fail nor be discouraged, till he have set judgment in the earth: and the isles shall wait for his law. Thus saith God the Lord, he that created the heavens, and stretched them out; he that spread forth the earth, and that which cometh out of it; he that giveth breath unto the people upon it, and spirit to them that walk therein: I the Lord have called thee in righteousness, and will hold thine hand, and will keep thee, and give thee for a covenant of the people, for a light of the Gentiles; To open the blind eyes, to bring out the prisoners from the prison, and them that sit in darkness out of the prison house. I am the Lord: that is my name: and my glory will I not give to another, neither my praise to graven images." (Isaiah 42:1-8)

"In the beginning was the Word, and the Word was with God, and the Word was God. The same was in the beginning with God. All things were made by him; and without him was not any thing made that was made. In him was life; and the life was the light of men. And the light shineth in darkness; and the darkness comprehended it not. There was a man sent from God, whose name was John. The same came for a witness, to bear witness of the Light, that all men through him might believe. He was not that Light, but was sent to bear witness of that Light. That was the true Light, which lighteth every man that cometh into the world. He was in the world, and the world was made by him, and the world knew him not." (John 1:10-12)

"And the angel of the Lord called unto Abraham out of heaven the second time, And said, By myself have I sworn, saith the Lord, for because thou hast done this thing, and hast not withheld thy son, thine only son: That in blessing I will bless thee, and in multiplying I will multiply thy seed as the stars of the heaven, and as the sand which is upon the sea shore; and thy seed shall possess the gate of his enemies; And in thy seed shall all the nations of the earth be blessed; because thou hast obeyed my voice." (Genesis 22:15-18)

"And in that day there shall be a root of Jesse, which shall stand for an ensign of the people; to it shall the Gentiles seek: and his rest shall be glorious." (Isaiah 11:10)

"Thus saith the Lord, the Redeemer of Israel, and his Holy One, to him whom man despiseth, to him whom the nation abhorreth, to a servant of rulers, Kings shall see and arise, princes also shall worship, because of the Lord that is faithful, and the Holy One of Israel, and he shall choose thee. Thus saith the Lord, In an acceptable time have I heard thee, and in a day of salvation have I helped thee: and I will preserve thee, and give thee for a covenant of the people, to establish the earth, to cause to inherit the desolate heritages; That thou mayest say to the prisoners, Go forth; to them that are in darkness, Shew yourselves. They shall feed in the ways, and their pastures shall be in all high places." (Isaiah 49:7-9)

"For whosoever shall call upon the name of the Lord shall be saved. How then shall they call on him in whom they have not believed? and how shall they believe in him of whom they have not heard? and how shall they hear without a preacher? And how shall they preach, except they be sent? as it is written, How beautiful are the feet of them that preach the gospel of peace, and bring glad tidings of good things! But they have not all obeyed the gospel. For Esaias saith, Lord, who hath believed our report? So then faith cometh by hearing, and hearing by the word of God. But I say, Have they not heard? Yes verily, their sound

went into all the earth, and their words unto the ends of the world. But I say, Did not Israel know? First Moses saith, I will provoke you to jealousy by them that are no people, and by a foolish nation I will anger you. But Esaias is very bold, and saith, I was found of them that sought me not; I was made manifest unto them that asked not after me. But to Israel he saith, All day long I have stretched forth my hands unto a disobedient and gainsaying people." (Romans 10:13-21)

Those in rejection of Christ are already condemned to the second death (eternal damnation) according to the Bible.

"For God sent not his Son into the world to condemn the world; but that the world through him might be saved. He that believeth on him is not condemned: but he that believeth not is condemned already, because he hath not believed in the name of the only begotten Son of God. John 3:17-18

"And I saw the dead, small and great, stand before God; and the books were opened: and another book was opened, which is the book of life: and the dead were judged out of those things which were written in the books, according to their works. And the sea gave up the dead which were in it; and death and hell delivered up the dead which were in them: and they were judged every man according to their works. And death and hell were cast into the lake of fire. This is the second death. And whosoever was not found written in the book of life was cast into the lake of fire." (Revelation 20:12-15)

"And he said unto me, It is done. I am Alpha and Omega, the beginning and the end. I will give unto him that is athirst of the fountain of the water of life freely. He that overcometh shall inherit all things; and I will be his God, and he shall be my son. But the fearful, and unbelieving, and the abominable, and murderers, and whoremongers, and sorcerers, and idolaters, and all liars, shall have their part in the lake which burneth with fire and brimstone: which is the second death." (Revelation 21:6-8)

Those not having had the opportunity to have had Christ preached to them, I am persuaded, are to be judged differently. Jesus has the power to save to the uttermost.

"For there is no respect of persons with God. For as many as have sinned without law shall also perish without law: and as many as have sinned in the law shall be judged by the law; (For not the hearers of the law are just before God, but the doers of the law shall be justified. For when the Gentiles, which have not the law, do by nature the things contained in the law, these, having not the law, are a law unto themselves: Which shew the work of the law written in their hearts, their conscience also bearing witness, and their thoughts the mean while accusing or else excusing one another;) In the day when God shall judge the secrets of men by Jesus Christ according to my gospel." (Romans 2:11-16)

"And they truly were many priests, because they were not suffered to continue by reason of death: But this man, because he continueth ever, hath an unchangeable priesthood. Wherefore he is able also to save them to the uttermost that come unto God by him, seeing he ever liveth to make intercession for them." (Hebrews 7:23-25)

Christ is the savior and judge of all mankind, according to the bible.

"For as the Father raiseth up the dead, and quickeneth them; even so the Son quickeneth whom he will. For the Father judgeth no man, but hath committed all judgment unto the Son: That all men should honour the Son, even as they honour the Father. He that honoureth not the Son honoureth not the Father which hath sent him. Verily, verily, I say unto you, He that heareth my word, and believeth on him that sent me, hath everlasting life, and shall not come into condemnation; but is passed from death unto life. Verily, verily, I say unto you, The hour is coming, and now is, when the dead shall hear the voice of the Son of God: and they that hear shall live. For as the Father hath life in himself; so hath he given to the Son to have life in himself; And hath given him authority to execute judgment also, because he is the Son of man. Marvel not at this: for the hour is coming, in the which all that are in the graves shall hear his voice, And shall come forth; they that have done good, unto the resurrection of life; and they that have done evil, unto the resurrection of damnation." (John 5:21-29)

I would say to all not believing in Christ today, make sure of your consideration.

"For consider him that endured such contradiction of sinners against himself, lest ye be wearied and faint in your minds." (Hebrews 12:3)

"Remember them which have the rule over you, who have spoken unto you the word of God: whose faith follow, considering the end of their conversation. Jesus Christ the same yesterday, and to day, and for ever. Be not carried about with divers and strange doctrines. For it is a good thing that the heart be established with grace; not with meats, which have not profited them that have been occupied therein. We have an altar, whereof they have no right to eat which serve the tabernacle." (Hebrews 13:7-10)

Must be Born Again

God is a spirit and we must be transformed spiritually, while yet in the flesh, in order to be justified before God. In the flesh, we battle against a spiritual warfare; that we must understand.

"God is a Spirit: and they that worship him must worship him in spirit and in truth." (John 4:24)

"Jesus answered and said unto him, Verily, verily, I say unto thee, Except a man be born again, he cannot see the kingdom of God." (John 3:3)

"Therefore by the deeds of the law there shall no flesh be justified in his sight: for by the law is the knowledge of sin. But now the righteousness of God without the law is manifested, being witnessed by the law and the prophets; Even the righteousness of God which is by faith of Jesus Christ unto all and upon all them that believe: for there is no difference: For all have sinned, and come short of the glory of God; Being justified freely by his grace through the redemption that is in Christ Jesus: Whom God hath set forth to be a propitiation through faith in his blood, to declare his righteousness for the remission of sins that are past, through the forbearance of God; To declare, I say, at this time his righteousness: that he might be just, and the justifier of him which believeth in Jesus." (Romans 3:20-26)

"For though we walk in the flesh, we do not war after the flesh: (For the weapons of our warfare are not carnal, but mighty through God to the pulling down of strong holds;) Casting

down imaginations, and every high thing that exalteth itself against the knowledge of God, and bringing into captivity every thought to the obedience of Christ; And having in a readiness to revenge all disobedience, when your obedience is fulfilled." (2 Corinthians 10:3-6)

"Finally, my brethren, be strong in the Lord, and in the power of his might. Put on the whole armor of God, that ye may be able to stand against the wiles of the devil. For we wrestle not against flesh and blood, but against principalities, against powers, against the rulers of the darkness of this world, against spiritual wickedness in high places. Wherefore take unto you the whole armor of God, that ye may be able to withstand in the evil day, and having done all, to stand." (Ephesians 6:10-13)

Being born again is as Christ prescribes.

"Jesus answered, Verily, verily, I say unto thee, Except a man be born of water and of the Spirit, he cannot enter into the kingdom of God." (John 3:5)

"For we ourselves also were sometimes foolish, disobedient, deceived, serving divers lusts and pleasures, living in malice and envy, hateful, and hating one another But after that the kindness and love of God our Savior toward man appeared, Not by works of righteousness which we have done, but according to his mercy he saved us, by the washing of regeneration, and renewing of the Holy Ghost; Which he shed on us abundantly through Jesus Christ our Savior; That being justified by his grace, we should be made heirs according to the hope of eternal life." (Titus 3:3-7)

The water, I am persuaded, makes reference to the water of the baptism of John and identification with the spiritual aspects of Christ's burial along with the known aspects of Jewish ritual cleaning.

"I indeed baptize you with water unto repentance. but he that cometh after me is mightier than I, whose shoes I am not worthy to bear: he shall baptize you with the Holy Ghost, and with fire:" (Matthew 3:11)

Therefore we are buried with him by baptism into death: that like as Christ was raised up from the dead by the glory of the Father, even so we also should walk in newness of life. For if we have been planted together in the likeness of his death, we shall be also in the likeness of his resurrection: Knowing this, that our old man is crucified with him, that the body of sin might be destroyed, that henceforth we should not serve sin." (Romans 6:4-6)

"And thou shalt bring Aaron and his sons unto the door of the tabernacle of the congregation, and wash them with water. And thou shalt put upon Aaron the holy garments, and anoint him, and sanctify him; that he may minister unto me in the priest's office." (Exodus 40:12&13)

The spirit refers to the Holy Spirit/Holy Ghost in the context of the spiritual nature of the conversion from walking in the flesh with a carnal mentality to walking in the flesh with a spiritual mentality. The physical control of out hearts and minds is accomplished by the physical indwelling of the Holy Spirit/Holy Ghost upon our mental regeneration and water baptism.

"This I say then, Walk in the Spirit, and ye shall not fulfil the lust of the flesh. For the flesh lusteth against the Spirit, and the Spirit against the flesh: and these are contrary the one to the other: so that ye cannot do the things that ye would. But if ye be led of the Spirit, ye are not under the law. Now the works of the flesh are manifest, which are these; Adultery, fornication, uncleanness, lasciviousness, Idolatry, witchcraft, hatred, variance, emulations, wrath, strife, seditions, heresies, Envyings, murders, drunkenness, revellings, and such like: of the which I tell you before, as I have also told you in time past, that they which do such things shall not inherit the kingdom of God. But the fruit of the Spirit is love, joy, peace, longsuffering, gentleness, goodness, faith, Meekness, temperance: against such there is no law." (**Galatians 5:16-23**)

"What? know ye not that your body is the temple of the Holy Ghost which is in you, which ye have of God, and ye are not your own? For ye are bought with a price: therefore glorify God in your body, and in your spirit, which are God's." (**1 Corinthians 6:19-20**)

"And what agreement hath the temple of God with idols? for ye are the temple of the living God; as God hath said, I will dwell in them, and walk in them; and I will be their God, and they shall be my people. Wherefore come out from among them, and be ye separate, saith the Lord, and touch not the unclean thing; and I will receive you. And will be a Father unto you, and ye shall be my sons and daughters, saith the Lord Almighty." (**2 Corinthians 6:16-18**)

"Know ye not that ye are the temple of God, and that the Spirit of God dwelleth in you? (**1 Corinthians 3:16**)

Christ raised the question to Nicodemus as to how he could be a master of Israel and not understand a spiritual rebirth in order to accomplish our spiritual conversion, i.e., the new covenant.

"But this shall be the covenant that I will make with the house of Israel; After those days, saith the Lord, I will put my law in their inward parts, and write it in their hearts; and will be their God, and they shall be my people." (**Jeremiah 31:33**)

A person must be born again in order to be brought into a reconciled relationship with a holy God who is a spirit and does not accept our carnality.

"But the hour cometh, and now is, when the true worshippers shall worship the Father in spirit and in truth: for the Father seeketh such to worship him. God is a Spirit: and they that worship him must worship him in spirit and in truth. The woman saith unto him, I know that Messias cometh, which is called Christ: when he is come, he will tell us all things. Jesus saith unto her, I that speak unto thee am he." (**John 4:24**)

"Have mercy upon me, O God, according to thy lovingkindness: according unto the multitude of thy tender mercies blot out my transgressions. Wash me throughly from mine iniquity, and cleanse me from my sin. For I acknowledge my transgressions: and my sin is ever before me. Against thee, thee only, have I sinned, and done this evil in thy sight: that thou mightest be justified when thou speakest, and be clear when thou judgest. Behold, I was shapen in iniquity; and in sin did my mother conceive me. Behold, thou desirest truth in the inward parts: and in the hidden part thou shalt make me to know wisdom. Purge me with hyssop, and I shall be clean: wash me, and I shall be whiter than snow. Make me to hear joy and gladness; that the bones which thou hast broken may rejoice. Hide thy face

from my sins, and blot out all mine iniquities. Create in me a clean heart, O God; and renew a right spirit within me. Cast me not away from thy presence; and take not thy holy spirit from me. Restore unto me the joy of thy salvation; and uphold me with thy free spirit. For thou desirest not sacrifice; else would I give it: thou delightest not in burnt offering. The sacrifices of God are a broken spirit: a broken and a contrite heart, O God, thou wilt not despise." (Psalm 51:1-12, 16&17)

"There is therefore now no condemnation to them which are in Christ Jesus, who walk not after the flesh, but after the Spirit. For the law of the Spirit of life in Christ Jesus hath made me free from the law of sin and death. For what the law could not do, in that it was weak through the flesh, God sending his own Son in the likeness of sinful flesh, and for sin, condemned sin in the flesh: That the righteousness of the law might be fulfilled in us, who walk not after the flesh, but after the Spirit. For they that are after the flesh do mind the things of the flesh; but they that are after the Spirit the things of the Spirit. For to be carnally minded is death; but to be spiritually minded is life and peace. Because the carnal mind is enmity against God: for it is not subject to the law of God, neither indeed can be. So then they that are in the flesh cannot please God. But ye are not in the flesh, but in the Spirit, if so be that the Spirit of God dwell in you. Now if any man have not the Spirit of Christ, he is none of his. And if Christ be in you, the body is dead because of sin; but the Spirit is life because of righteousness. But if the Spirit of him that raised up Jesus from the dead dwell in you, he that raised up Christ from the dead shall also quicken your mortal bodies by his Spirit that dwelleth in you." (Romans 8:1-11)

How to be Born Again

Being born again is as simple as should be the simplicity in our presentation of Jesus Christ to the world. One must believe on Jesus and be baptized in order to be born again. Being born again is not accomplished through a prayer of salvation alone and neither is it accomplished through belief or baptism by themselves.

"He that believeth and is baptized shall be saved; but he that believeth not shall be damned." (Mark 16:16)

"For I am jealous over you with godly jealousy: for I have espoused you to one husband, that I may present you as a chaste virgin to Christ. But I fear, lest by any means, as the serpent beguiled Eve through his subtilty, so your minds should be corrupted from the simplicity that is in Christ." (2 Corinthians 11:2-3)

Jesus said to go and teach all nations to observe (tereo - holdfast, keep) whatever he had commanded (entellomail – give charge) and to baptize in the name of the Father, and of the Son, and of the Holy Ghost being the Trinity. This instruction is inferred in the nature of the preaching demanded by Jesus as well. Note also an instance as recorded in the book of Acts where instead of the Trinity, "only they were baptized in the name of the Lord Jesus".

"Go ye therefore, and teach all nations, baptizing them in the name of the Father, and of the Son, and of the Holy Ghost: Teaching them to observe all things whatsoever I have commanded you: and, lo, I am with you alway, even unto the end of the world. Amen." (Matthew 28:19-20)

"For there are three that bear record in heaven, the Father, the Word, and the Holy Ghost: and these three are one." (1 John 5:7)

"Then opened he their understanding, that they might understand the scriptures, And said unto them, Thus it is written, and thus it behoved Christ to suffer, and to rise from the dead the third day: "And that repentance and remission of sins should be preached in his name among all nations, beginning at Jerusalem." (Luke 24:45-47)

"Beware lest any man spoil you through philosophy and vain deceit, after the tradition of men, after the rudiments of the world, and not after Christ. For in him dwelleth all the fulness of the Godhead bodily." (Colossians 2:8&9)

"But there was a certain man, called Simon, which beforetime in the same city used sorcery, and bewitched the people of Samaria, giving out that himself was some great one: To whom they all gave heed, from the least to the greatest, saying, This man is the great power of God. And to him they had regard, because that of long time he had bewitched them with sorceries. But when they believed Philip preaching the things concerning the kingdom of God, and the name of Jesus Christ, they were baptized, both men and women. Then Simon himself believed also: and when he was baptized, he continued with Philip, and wondered, beholding the miracles and signs which were done. Now when the apostles which were at Jerusalem heard that Samaria had received the word of God, they sent unto them Peter and John: Who, when they were come down, prayed for them, that they might receive the Holy Ghost: (For as yet he was fallen upon none of them: only they were baptized in the name of the Lord Jesus.) Then laid they their hands on them, and they received the Holy Ghost." (Acts 8:9-17)

Jesus in responding to Nicodemus spoke in the symbolic terms of the "water" and the "spirit" in a dissertation before an acknowledged master (teacher) of Israel.

"Jesus answered and said unto him, Verily, verily, I say unto thee, Except a man be born again, he cannot see the kingdom of God. Nicodemus saith unto him, How can a man be born when he is old? can he enter the second time into his mother's womb, and be born? Jesus answered, Verily, verily, I say unto thee, Except a man be born of water and of the Spirit, he cannot enter into the kingdom of God. That which is born of the flesh is flesh; and that which is born of the Spirit is spirit. Marvel not that I said unto thee, Ye must be born again. The wind bloweth where it listeth, and thou hearest the sound thereof, but canst not tell whence it cometh, and whither it goeth: so is every one that is born of the Spirit. Nicodemus answered and said unto him, How can these things be? Jesus answered and said unto him, Art thou a master of Israel, and knowest not these things? Verily, verily, I say unto thee, We speak that we do know, and testify that we have seen; and ye receive not our witness. If I have told you earthly things, and ye believe not, how shall ye believe, if I tell you of heavenly things?" (John 3:3-12)

Now, to believe (pistevo – have faith, trust in Christ) is as it was presented on the day of Pentecost.

"Ye men of Israel, hear these words; Jesus of Nazareth, a man approved of God among you by miracles and wonders and signs, which God did by him in the midst of you, as ye yourselves also know: Him, being delivered by the determinate counsel and foreknowledge of God, ye have taken, and by wicked hands have crucified and slain: Whom God hath

raised up, having loosed the pains of death: because it was not possible that he should be holden of it. For David speaketh concerning him, I foresaw the Lord always before my face, for he is on my right hand, that I should not be moved: Therefore did my heart rejoice, and my tongue was glad; moreover also my flesh shall rest in hope: Because thou wilt not leave my soul in hell, neither wilt thou suffer thine Holy One to see corruption. Thou hast made known to me the ways of life; thou shalt make me full of joy with thy countenance. Men and brethren, let me freely speak unto you of the patriarch David, that he is both dead and buried, and his sepulchre is with us unto this day. Therefore being a prophet, and know-ing that God had sworn with an oath to him, that of the fruit of his loins, according to the flesh, he would raise up Christ to sit on his throne; He seeing this before spake of the resur-rection of Christ, that his soul was not left in hell, neither his flesh did see corruption. This Jesus hath God raised up, whereof we all are witnesses. Therefore being by the right hand of God exalted, and having received of the Father the promise of the Holy Ghost, he hath shed forth this, which ye now see and hear. For David is not ascended into the heavens: but he saith himself, The Lord said unto my Lord, Sit thou on my right hand, Until I make thy foes thy footstool. Therefore let all the house of Israel know assuredly, that God hath made the same Jesus, whom ye have crucified, both Lord and Christ." (Acts 2:22-36)

Note that infants cannot be held accountable as believers. Older children, having been taught, accepting and then desiring baptism, are accountable. It is obvious; infants were only touched (blessed) by Christ.

"And they brought unto him also infants, that he would touch them: but when his disciples saw it, they rebuked them. But Jesus called them unto him, and said, Suffer little children to come unto me, and forbid them not: for of such is the kingdom of God. Verily I say unto you, Whosoever shall not receive the kingdom of God as a little child shall in no wise enter therein." (Luke 18:15-17)

Baptism as an Essential Element of Salvation

The baptism spoken of by Christ in the proclaiming the process of being saved in "he that believeth and is baptized", was at that time the "baptism of John" (John the Baptist). Remission (aphesis: pardon, forgiveness, deliverance) of sin, with regard to the "baptism of John", was through repentance. The "baptism of John" was performed even by the twelve Disciples of Christ, but not Jesus.

"Now in the fifteenth year of the reign of Tiberius Caesar, Pontius Pilate being governor of Judaea, and Herod being tetrarch of Galilee, and his brother Philip tetrarch of Ituraea and of the region of Trachonitis, and Lysanias the tetrarch of Abilene, Annas and Caiaphas being the high priests, the word of God came unto John the son of Zacharias in the wilder-ness. And he came into all the country about Jordan, preaching the baptism of repentance for the remission of sins; As it is written in the book of the words of Esaias the prophet, saying, The voice of one crying in the wilderness, Prepare ye the way of the Lord, make his paths straight." (Luke 3:1-4)

I indeed baptize you with water unto repentance. but he that cometh after me is mightier than I, whose shoes I am not worthy to bear: he shall baptize you with the Holy Ghost, and with fire: Matthew 3:11

"John did baptize in the wilderness, and preach the baptism of repentance for the remission of sins." (**Mark 1:4**)

"And all the people that heard him, and the publicans, justified God, being baptized with the baptism of John. But the Pharisees and lawyers rejected the counsel of God against themselves, being not baptized of him." (**Luke 7:29-30**)

"When therefore the Lord knew how the Pharisees had heard that Jesus made and baptized more disciples than John, (Though Jesus himself baptized not, but his disciples,) He left Judae and departed again in Galilee." (**John 4:1-2**)

Lacking in the baptism of John is the Holy Ghost and the fire that Christ would indeed with baptize upon his resurrection and God's outpouring of his spirit upon mankind; note that John and Jesus are saying the same thing.

"I have yet many things to say unto you, but ye cannot bear them now. Howbeit when he, the Spirit of truth, is come, he will guide you into all truth: for he shall not speak of himself; but whatsoever he shall hear, that shall he speak: and he will shew you things to come." (**John 16:12&13**))

"I am come to send fire on the earth; and what will I if it be already kindled? But I have a baptism to be baptized with; and how am I straitened till it be accomplished! Suppose ye that I am come to give peace on earth? I tell you, Nay; but rather division: For from henceforth there shall be five in one house divided, three against two, and two against three. The father shall be divided against the son, and the son against the father; the mother against the daughter, and the daughter against the mother; the mother in law against her daughter in law, and the daughter in law against her mother in law." (**Luke 12:49-50**)

"Whosoever therefore shall confess me before men, him will I confess also before my Father which is in heaven. But whosoever shall deny me before men, him will I also deny before my Father which is in heaven. Think not that I am come to send peace on earth: I came not to send peace, but a sword. For I am come to set a man at variance against his father, and the daughter against her mother, and the daughter in law against her mother in law. And a man's foes shall be they of his own household." (**Matthew 10:32-36**)

"And when the day of Pentecost was fully come, they were all with one accord in one place. And suddenly there came a sound from heaven as of a rushing mighty wind, and it filled all the house where they were sitting. And there appeared unto them cloven tongues like as of fire, and it sat upon each of them. And they were all filled with the Holy Ghost, and began to speak with other tongues, as the Spirit gave them utterance. But this is that which was spoken by the prophet Joel; And it shall come to pass in the last days, saith God, I will pour out of my Spirit upon all flesh: and your sons and your daughters shall prophesy, and your young men shall see visions, and your old men shall dream dreams: And on my servants and on my handmaidens I will pour out in those days of my Spirit; and they shall prophesy: And I will shew wonders in heaven above, and signs in the earth beneath; blood, and fire, and vapour of smoke: The sun shall be turned into darkness, and the moon into blood, before that great and notable day of the Lord come: And it shall come to pass, that whosoever shall call on the name of the Lord shall be saved. Ye men of Israel, hear these words; Jesus of Nazareth, a man approved of God among you by miracles and wonders and signs, which God did by him in the midst of you, as ye yourselves also know: Him, be-

ing delivered by the determinate counsel and foreknowledge of God, ye have taken, and by wicked hands have crucified and slain: Whom God hath raised up, having loosed the pains of death: because it was not possible that he should be holden of it. For David speaketh concerning him, I foresaw the Lord always before my face, for he is on my right hand, that I should not be moved: Therefore did my heart rejoice, and my tongue was glad; moreover also my flesh shall rest in hope: Because thou wilt not leave my soul in hell, neither wilt thou suffer thine Holy One to see corruption. Thou hast made known to me the ways of life; thou shalt make me full of joy with thy countenance. Men and brethren, let me freely speak unto you of the patriarch David, that he is both dead and buried, and his sepulchre is with us unto this day. Therefore being a prophet, and knowing that God had sworn with an oath to him, that of the fruit of his loins, according to the flesh, he would raise up Christ to sit on his throne; He seeing this before spake of the resurrection of Christ, that his soul was not left in hell, neither his flesh did see corruption. This Jesus hath God raised up, whereof we all are witnesses. Therefore being by the right hand of God exalted, and having received of the Father the promise of the Holy Ghost, he hath shed forth this, which ye now see and hear. For David is not ascended into the heavens: but he saith himself, The Lord said unto my Lord, Sit thou on my right hand, Until I make thy foes thy footstool. Therefore let all the house of Israel know assuredly, that God hath made that same Jesus, whom ye have crucified, both Lord and Christ." (Acts 2:1-4, 16-24)

The water of which Christ spoke refers to the water of the baptism of John, which is a spiritual washing inclusive of belief and repentance prior to Christ's fulfillment of the scriptures in his death, burial and resurrection. The water also is symbolic of the burial tomb from which Christ rose and allows the believer spiritually to be partakers in his death, burial and resurrection.

"That word, I say, ye know, which was published throughout all Judaea, and began from Galilee, after the baptism which John preached; How God anointed Jesus of Nazareth with the Holy Ghost and with power: who went about doing good, and healing all that were oppressed of the devil; for God was with him. And we are witnesses of all things which he did both in the land of the Jews, and in Jerusalem; whom they slew and hanged on a tree: Him God raised up the third day, and shewed him openly; Not to all the people, but unto witnesses chosen before God, even to us, who did eat and drink with him after he rose from the dead. And he commanded us to preach unto the people, and to testify that it is he which was ordained of God to be the Judge of quick and dead. To him give all the prophets witness, that through his name whosoever believeth in him shall receive remission of sins. While Peter yet spake these words, the Holy Ghost fell on all them which heard the word. And they of the circumcision which believed were astonished, as many as came with Peter, because that on the Gentiles also was poured out the gift of the Holy Ghost. For they heard them speak with tongues, and magnify God. Then answered Peter, Can any man forbid water, that these should not be baptized, which have received the Holy Ghost as well as we? And he commanded them to be baptized in the name of the Lord. Then prayed they him to tarry certain days." (Acts 10:37-48)

"Know ye not, that so many of us as were baptized into Jesus Christ were baptized into his death? Therefore we are buried with him by baptism into death: that like as Christ was raised up from the dead by the glory of the Father, even so we also should walk in newness of life." (Romans 6:3-4)

The Spirit of which Christ spoke is the same Holy Ghost referred by John and the fire represents our God as a consuming fire and tester of every man's works.

> *"But ye are not in the flesh, but in the Spirit, if so be that the Spirit of God dwell in you. Now if any man have not the Spirit of Christ, he is none of his."* (**Romans 8:9**)

> *"That good thing which was committed unto thee keep by the Holy Ghost which dwelleth in us."* (**2 Timothy 1:14**)

> *"Behold, I will send my messenger, and he shall prepare the way before me: and the Lord, whom ye seek, shall suddenly come to this temple, even the messenger of the covenant, whom ye delight in: behold, he shall come, saith the Lord of hosts. But who may abide the day of his coming? and who shall stand when he appeareth? for he is like a refiner's fire, and like fullers' soap: And he shall sit as a refiner and purifer of silver: and he shall purify the sons of Levi, and purge them as gold and silver, that they may offer unto the Lord an offering in righteousness."* (**Malachi 3:1-7**)

> *"Every man's work shall be made manifest: for the day shall declare it, because it shall be revealed by fire; and the fire shall try every man's work of what sort it is. If any man's work abide which he hath built thereupon, he shall receive a reward. If any man's work shall be burned, he shall suffer loss: but he himself shall be saved; yet so as by fire."* (**1 Corinthians 3:13-15**)

> *"For our God is a consuming fire."* (**Hebrews 12:29**)

The Spiritual Significance of Baptism

Note now what occurs spiritually in the baptism as commanded by Jesus in the name of the Trinity.

> *"Go ye therefore, and teach all nations, baptizing them in the name of the Father, and of the Son, and of the Holy Ghost: Teaching them to observe all things whatsoever I have commanded you: and, lo, I am with you alway, even unto the end of the world. Amen."* (**Mathew 28: 19&20**)

> *"For as many of you as have been baptized into Christ have put on Christ. For ye are all the children of God by faith in Christ Jesus."* (**Galatians 3:27&26**)

It is of a necessity that in the sight of a holy and just God, that we be transformed from the carnal to a spiritual nature. Being born again accomplishes that through both the spiritual regeneration of our mind and our partaking in the death and burial of Jesus Christ.

> *"For we ourselves also were sometimes foolish, disobedient, deceived, serving divers lusts and pleasures, living in malice and envy, hateful, and hating one another. But after that the kindness and love of God our Saviour toward man appeared, Not by works of righteousness which we have done, but according to his mercy he saved us, by the washing of regeneration, and renewing of the Holy Ghost; Which he shed on us abundantly through Jesus Christ our Saviour; That being justified by his grace, we should be made heirs according to the hope of eternal life."* (**Titus 3:3-7**)

> *"For they that are after the flesh do mind the things of the flesh; but they that are after the Spirit the things of the Spirit. For to be carnally minded is death; but to be spiritu-*

ally minded is life and peace. Because the carnal mind is enmity against God: for it is not subject to the law of God, neither indeed can be. So then they that are in the flesh cannot please God." (**Romans 8:5-8**)

"Know ye not that the unrighteous shall not inherit the kingdom of God? Be not deceived: neither fornicators, nor idolaters, nor adulterers, nor effeminate, nor abusers of themselves with mankind, Nor thieves, nor covetous, nor drunkards, nor revilers, nor extortioners, shall inherit the kingdom of God. And such were some of you: but ye are washed, but ye are sanctified, but ye are justified in the name of the Lord Jesus, and by the Spirit of our God." (**1 Corinthians 6:9-11**)

"Wherefore come out from among them, and be ye separate, saith the Lord, and touch not the unclean thing; and I will receive you." (**2 Corinthians 6:17**)

I am persuaded that both the baptism of Jesus by John the Baptist and the death of the thief on the cross reinforce certain vital aspects of the being born again process. The thief repented and was accepted by Christ. The thief's death and burial was in Christ just as Jesus had demonstrated obedience in being baptized in spite of being sinless. When Jesus was baptized, God the Father spoke from heaven of his pleasure in his son and the Holy Spirit descended upon Christ. Therein is the representation of our indwelling upon rising as new creatures in Christ from our spiritual death, burial, and resurrection in baptism.

"And one of the malefactors which were hanged railed on him, saying, If thou be Christ, save thyself and us. But the other answering rebuked him, saying, Dost not thou fear God, seeing thou art in the same condemnation? And we indeed justly; for we receive the due reward of our deeds: but this man hath done nothing amiss. And he said unto Jesus, Lord, remember me when thou comest into thy kingdom. And Jesus said unto him, Verily I say unto thee, To day shalt thou be with me in paradise." (**Luke 23:39-43**)

"For I have given you an example, that ye should do as I have done to you. Verily, verily, I say unto you, The servant is not greater than his Lord; neither he that is sent greater than he that sent him." (**John13:15-16**)

"And Jesus answering said unto him, Suffer it to be so now: for thus it becometh us to fulfil all righteousness. Then he suffered him. And Jesus, when he was baptized, went up straightway out of the water: and, lo, the heavens were opened unto him, and he saw the Spirit of God descending like a dove, and lighting upon him: And lo a voice from heaven, saying, This is my beloved Son, in whom I am well pleased." (**Matthew 3:15-17**)

"Fear not, little flock; for it is your Father's good pleasure to give you the kingdom." (**Luke 12:32**)

Baptize (Baptizo: to make whelmed (fully wet), of ceremonial ablution, and ordinance of Christianity, wash) is by definition and act of emerging in water. Baptizo is the only word used for baptize, baptized, baptizest, baptizeth and baptizing in the new testament.

In those days came John the Baptist, preaching in the wilderness of Judaea, And saying, Repent ye: for the kingdom of heaven is at hand. I indeed baptize you with water unto repentance: but he that cometh after me is mightier than I, whose shoes I am not worthy to bear: he shall baptize you with the Holy Ghost, and with fire: Whose fan is in his hand, and he will throughly purge his floor, and gather his wheat into the garner; but he will burn up the chaff with unquenchable fire. (**Matthew 3: 1&2, 11&12**)

"But Jesus said unto them, Ye know not what ye ask: can ye drink of the cup that I drink of? and be baptized with the baptism that I am baptized with? And they said unto him, We can. And Jesus said unto them, Ye shall indeed drink of the cup that I drink of; and with the baptism that I am baptized withal shall ye be baptized: But to sit on my right hand and on my left hand is not mine to give; but it shall be given to them for whom it is prepared." (**Mark 10: 38-40**)

"And they which were sent were of the Pharisees. And they asked him, and said unto him, Why baptizest thou then, if thou be not that Christ, nor Elias, neither that prophet? John answered them, saying, I baptize with water: but there standeth one among you, whom ye know not; He it is, who coming after me is preferred before me, whose shoe's latchet I am not worthy to unloose. These things were done in Bethabara beyond Jordan, where John was baptizing. The next day John seeth Jesus coming unto him, and saith, Behold the Lamb of God, which taketh away the sin of the world. This is he of whom I said, After me cometh a man which is preferred before me: for he was before me. And I knew him not: but that he should be made manifest to Israel, therefore am I come baptizing with water. And John bare record, saying, I saw the Spirit descending from heaven like a dove, and it abode upon him. And I knew him not: but he that sent me to baptize with water, the same said unto me, Upon whom thou shalt see the Spirit descending, and remaining on him, the same is he which baptizeth with the Holy Ghost. And I saw, and bare record that this is the Son of God." (**John 1: 24-34**)

"Go ye therefore, and teach all nations, baptizing them in the name of the Father, and of the Son, and of the Holy Ghost." (**Matthew 28: 19**)

Baptism is symbolic of burial with an awesome spiritual purpose; ordinarily, salvation is not achieved without baptism which is done in faithful obedience.

"He that believeth and is baptized shall be saved; but he that believeth not shall be damned." (**Mark 16:16**)

"Jesus answered and said unto him, Verily, verily, I say unto thee, Except a man be born again, he cannot see the kingdom of God. Nicodemus saith unto him, How can a man be born when he is old? can he enter the second time into his mother's womb, and be born? Jesus answered, Verily, verily, I say unto thee, Except a man be born of water and of the Spirit, he cannot enter into the kingdom of God. That which is born of the flesh is flesh; and that which is born of the Spirit is spirit." (**John 3:3-6**)

"For by one Spirit are we all baptized into one body, whether we be Jews or Gentiles, whether we be bond or free; and have been all made to drink into one Spirit." (**1 Corinthians 12:13**)

"And ye are complete in him, which is the head of all principality and power: In whom also ye are circumcised with the circumcision made without hands, in putting off the body of the sins of the flesh by the circumcision of Christ: Buried with him in baptism, wherein also ye are risen with him through the faith of the operation of God, who hath raised him from the dead. And you, being dead in your sins and the uncircumcision of your flesh, hath he quickened together with him, having forgiven you all trespasses; Blotting out the handwrit-

ing of ordinances that was against us, which was contrary to us, and took it out of the way, nailing it to his cross; And having spoiled principalities and powers, he made a shew of them openly, triumphing over them in it. (Colossians 2:10-15)

"Therefore being justified by faith, we have peace with God through our Lord Jesus Christ: By whom also we have access by faith into this grace wherein we stand, and rejoice in hope of the glory of God." (Romans 5:1-2)

We are baptized by the Holy Spirit who testifies of Christ and interprets the scriptures.

"There is one body, and one Spirit, even as ye are called in one hope of your calling; One Lord, one faith, one baptism, One God and Father of all, who is above all, and through all, and in you all." (Ephesians 4:4-6)

"Knowing this first, that no prophecy of the scripture is of any private interpretation. For the prophecy came not in old time by the will of man: but holy men of God spake as they were moved by the Holy Ghost." (2 Peter 1:20&21)

Baptism is not a work (ergo: toil, deed, doing, labor); it is commanded by Jesus Christ and is therefore one of the two (Lord's Supper/Communion the other) ordinances (an authoritative order or command, a practice or custom established by long usage, a religious rite) in the Church. Any work done in baptism is done by the Baptizer and God the Father. We are to follow the example of Christ, the Lamb of God.

"And Jesus came and spake unto them, saying, All power is given unto me in heaven and in earth. Go ye therefore, and teach all nations, baptizing them in the name of the Father, and of the Son, and of the Holy Ghost: Teaching them to observe all things whatsoever I have commanded you: and, lo, I am with you alway, even unto the end of the world. Amen." (Matthew 28:18-20)

"John did baptize in the wilderness, and preach the baptism of repentance for the remission of sins. And there went out unto him all the land of Judaea, and they of Jerusalem, and were all baptized of him in the river of Jordan, confessing their sins. And John was clothed with camel's hair, and with a girdle of a skin about his loins; and he did eat locusts and wild honey; And preached, saying, There cometh one mightier than I after me, the latchet of whose shoes I am not worthy to stoop down and unloose. I indeed have baptized you with water: but he shall baptize you with the Holy Ghost. And it came to pass in those days, that Jesus came from Nazareth of Galilee, and was baptized of John in Jordan." (Mark 1: 4-9)

"And ye are complete in him, which is the head of all principality and power: In whom also ye are circumcised with the circumcision made without hands, in putting off the body of the sins of the flesh by the circumcision of Christ: Buried with him in baptism, wherein also ye are risen with him through the faith of the operation of God, who hath raised him from the dead. And you, being dead in your sins and the uncircumcision of your flesh, hath he quickened together with him, having forgiven you all trespasses; Blotting out the handwriting of ordinances that was against us, which was contrary to us, and took it out of the way, nailing it to his cross; And having spoiled principalities and powers, he made a shew of them openly, triumphing over them in it." (Colossians 2: 10-15)

"The next day John seeth Jesus coming unto him, and saith, Behold the Lamb of God, which taketh away the sin of the world. This is he of whom I said, After me cometh a man which is preferred before me: for he was before me. And I knew him not: but that he should be made manifest to Israel, therefore am I come baptizing with water. And John bare record, saying, I saw the Spirit descending from heaven like a dove, and it abode upon him. And I knew him not: but he that sent me to baptize with water, the same said unto me, Upon whom thou shalt see the Spirit descending, and remaining on him, the same is he which baptizeth with the Holy Ghost. And I saw, and bare record that this is the Son of God." (John 1:29-34)

Baptism is to be done in the name of the Trinity as per Jesus Christ's instruction. The book of Acts tells stories of what happened on the occasions of numerous baptisms but not precisely how they were done except in one instance. Many have misinterrupted these occurances even as Jesus has commanded that we baptize in the name of the Trinity.

"Then Peter said unto them, Repent, and be baptized every one of you in the name of Jesus Christ for the remission of sins, and ye shall receive the gift of the Holy Ghost. For the promise is unto you, and to your children, and to all that are afar off, even as many as the Lord our God shall call. And with many other words did he testify and exhort, saying, Save yourselves from this untoward generation. Then they that gladly received his word were baptized: and the same day there were added unto them about three thousand souls." (Acts 2:38-41)

"While Peter yet spake these words, the Holy Ghost fell on all them which heard the word. And they of the circumcision which believed were astonished, as many as came with Peter, because that on the Gentiles also was poured out the gift of the Holy Ghost. For they heard them speak with tongues, and magnify God. Then answered Peter, Can any man forbid water, that these should not be baptized, which have received the Holy Ghost as well as we? And he commanded them to be baptized in the name of the Lord. Then prayed they him to tarry certain days." (Acts 10:44-48)

"And it came to pass, that, while Apollos was at Corinth, Paul having passed through the upper coasts came to Ephesus: and finding certain disciples, He said unto them, Have ye received the Holy Ghost since ye believed? And they said unto him, We have not so much as heard whether there be any Holy Ghost. And he said unto them, Unto what then were ye baptized? And they said, Unto John's baptism. Then said Paul, John verily baptized with the baptism of repentance, saying unto the people, that they should believe on him which should come after him, that is, on Christ Jesus. When they heard this, they were baptized in the name of the Lord Jesus. And when Paul had laid his hands upon them, the Holy Ghost came on them; and they spake with tongues, and prophesied. And all the men were about twelve." (Acts 19:1-7)

But when they believed Philip preaching the things concerning the kingdom of God, and the name of Jesus Christ, they were baptized, both men and women. Then Simon himself believed also: and when he was baptized, he continued with Philip, and wondered, beholding the miracles and signs which were done. Now when the apostles which were at Jerusalem heard that Samaria had received the word of God, they sent unto them Peter and John: Who, when they were come down, prayed for them, that they might receive the Holy Ghost: (For as yet he was fallen upon none of them: only they were baptized in the name of the Lord Jesus.) Then laid they their hands on them, and they received the Holy Ghost." (**Acts 8:12-17**)

Can Salvation be Lost?

By no other name than Jesus are men saved according to the Bible.

> "Neither is there salvation in any other: for there is none other name under heaven given among men, whereby we must be saved." (**Acts 4:12**)

Salvation can never be taken away by anybody or anything, however, it can certainly be lost through obedience to sin and therefore being judged reprobate by God.

> "My sheep hear my voice, and I know them, and they follow me: And I give unto them eternal life; and they shall never perish, neither shall any man pluck them out of my hand. My Father, which gave them me, is greater than all; and no man is able to pluck them out of my Father's hand." (**John 10:27-29**)

> "For by grace are ye saved through faith; and that not of yourselves: it is the gift of God: Not of works, lest any man should boast." (**Ephesians 2:8-9**)

> "What shall we say then? Shall we continue in sin, that grace may abound? God forbid. How shall we, that are dead to sin, live any longer therein?" (**Romans 6:1-2**)

> "Let not sin therefore reign in your mortal body, that ye should obey it in the lusts thereof. Neither yield ye your members as instruments of unrighteousness unto sin: but yield yourselves unto God, as those that are alive from the dead, and your members as instruments of righteousness unto God. For sin shall not have dominion over you: for ye are not under the law, but under grace. What then? shall we sin, because we are not under the law, but under grace? God forbid. Know ye not, that to whom ye yield yourselves servants to obey, his servants ye are to whom ye obey; whether of sin unto death, or of obedience unto righteousness?" (**Romans 6:12-16**)

> "For it is impossible for those who were once enlightened, and have tasted of the heavenly gift, and were made partakers of the Holy Ghost, And have tasted the good word of God, and the powers of the world to come, If they shall fall away, to renew them again unto repentance; seeing they crucify to themselves the Son of God afresh, and put him to an open shame." (**Hebrews 6:4-6**)

> "Unto the pure all things are pure: but unto them that are defiled and unbelieving is nothing pure; but even their mind and conscience is defiled. They profess that they know God; but in works they deny him, being abominable, and disobedient, and unto every good work reprobate." (**Titus 1:15&16**)

> "Take heed, brethren, lest there be in any of you an evil heart of unbelief, in departing from the living God. But exhort one another daily, while it is called To day; lest any of you be hardened through the deceitfulness of sin." (**Hebrews 3:12&13**)

> "For it had been better for them not to have known the way of righteousness, than, after they have known it, to turn from the holy commandment delivered unto them. But it is happened unto them according to the true proverb, The dog is turned to his own vomit again; and the sow that was washed to her wallowing in the mire." (**2 Peter 2:21&22**)

There should be self-examination, which should lead to confession and repentance of sin one to another rather than lack of spiritual discernment (diakrino – withdraw from) of the Christ's death on the cross. On the cross, Jesus's blood was shed for the remission (aphesis: pardon, forgiveness, deliverance) of our sins, this discern.

"Examine yourselves, whether ye be in the faith; prove your own selves. Know ye not your own selves, how that Jesus Christ is in you, except ye be reprobates? But I trust that ye shall know that we are not reprobates." (2 Corinthians 13:5&6)

"Confess your faults one to another, and pray one for another, that ye may be healed. The effectual fervent prayer of a righteous man availeth much." (James 5:16)

"Now I rejoice, not that ye were made sorry, but that ye sorrowed to repentance: for ye were made sorry after a godly manner, that ye might receive damage by us in nothing. For godly sorrow worketh repentance to salvation not to be repented of: but the sorrow of the world worketh death." (2 Corinthians 7:9-10)

"For this is my blood of the new testament, which is shed for many for the remission of sins." (Matthew 26:28)

"Forasmuch as ye know that ye were not redeemed with corruptible things, as silver and gold, from your vain conversation received by tradition from your fathers; But with the precious blood of Christ, as of a lamb without blemish and without spot: Who verily was foreordained before the foundation of the world, but was manifest in these last times for you, Who by him do believe in God, that raised him up from the dead, and gave him glory; that your faith and hope might be in God. Seeing ye have purified your souls in obeying the truth through the Spirit unto unfeigned love of the brethren, see that ye love one another with a pure heart fervently: Being born again, not of corruptible seed, but of incorruptible, by the word of God, which liveth and abideth for ever." (1 Peter 1:18-23)

Judgment is to begin in the house of God (church house) first.

"For the time is come that judgment must begin at the house of God: and if it first begin at us, what shall the end be of them that obey not the gospel of God? And if the righteous scarcely be saved, where shall the ungodly and the sinner appear?" (1 Peter 4:17-18)

"For, lo, I begin to bring evil on the city which is called by my name, and should ye be utterly unpunished? Ye shall not be unpunished: for I will call for a sword upon all the inhabitants of the earth, saith the Lord of hosts." (Jeremiah 25:29)

"Another parable put he forth unto them, saying, The kingdom of heaven is likened unto a man which sowed good seed in his field: But while men slept, his enemy came and sowed tares among the wheat, and went his way. But when the blade was sprung up, and brought forth fruit, then appeared the tares also. So the servants of the householder came and said unto him, Sir, didst not thou sow good seed in thy field? from whence then hath it tares? He said unto them, An enemy hath done this. The servants said unto him, Wilt thou then that we go and gather them up? But he said, Nay; lest while ye gather up the tares, ye root up also the wheat with them. Let both grow together until the harvest: and in the time of harvest I will say to the reapers, Gather ye together first the tares, and bind them in bundles to burn them: but gather the wheat into my barn." (Matthew 13:24-30)

"Not every one that saith unto me, Lord, Lord, shall enter into the kingdom of heaven; but he that doeth the will of my Father which is in heaven. Many will say to me in that day, Lord, Lord, have we not prophesied in thy name? and in thy name have cast out devils? And in thy name done many wonderful works? And then will I profess unto them, I never knew you: depart from me, ye that work iniquity." (**Matthew 7:21-23**)

Consider what Christ has spoken to the churches.

"Unto the angel of the church of Ephesus write; These things saith he that holdeth the seven stars in his right hand, who walketh in the midst of the seven golden candlesticks; I know thy works, and thy labor, and thy patience, and how thou canst not bear them which are evil: and thou hast tried them which say they are apostles, and are not, and hast found them liars: And hast born, and hast patience, and for my name's sake hast labored, and hast not fainted. Nevertheless I have somewhat against thee, because thou hast left thy first love. Remember therefore from whence thou art fallen, and repent, and do the first works; or else I will come unto thee quickly, and will remove thy candlestick out of his place, except thou repent." (**Revelation 2:1-5**)

"And unto the angel of the church of the Laodiceans write; These things saith the Amen, the faithful and true witness, the beginning of the creation of God; I know thy works, that thou art neither cold nor hot: I would thou wert cold or hot. So then because thou art luke-warm, and neither cold nor hot, I will spue thee out of my mouth. Because thou sayest, I am rich, and increased with goods, and have need of nothing; and knowest not that thou art wretched, and miserable, and poor, and blind, and naked: I counsel thee to buy of me gold tried in the fire, that thou mayest be rich; and white raiment, that thou mayest be clothed, and that the shame of thy nakedness do not appear; and anoint thine eyes with eyesalve, that thou mayest see. As many as I love, I rebuke and chasten: be zealous therefore, and repent." (**Revelation 3:14-19**)

8

PRAYER – MAKING A DIFFERENCE

What is prayer? How should I pray and does prayer make any difference at all?

WHAT IS PRAYER? The Bible answers, as I am persuaded, that it is access to the peace of God. Our state of peace in God is a key defense against the forces of evil and puts us under God's control. The church, God's House, is proclaimed to be a house of prayer. See Appendix 4, A Prayer Meeting Outline.

> *"Be careful for nothing; but in every thing by prayer and supplication with thanksgiving let your requests be made known unto God. And the peace of God, which passeth all understanding, shall keep your hearts and minds through Christ Jesus."* (Philippians 4:6&7)

> *"Finally, brethren, pray for us, that the word of the Lord may have free course, and be glorified, even as it is with you: And that we may be delivered from unreasonable and wicked men: for all men have not faith. But the Lord is faithful, who shall stablish you, and keep you from evil."* (2 Thessalonians 3:1-3)

> *"If ye then, being evil, know how to give good gifts unto your children: how much more shall your heavenly Father give the Holy Spirit to them that ask him?"* (Luke 11:13)

> *"For this cause I bow my knees unto the Father of our Lord Jesus Christ, Of whom the whole family in heaven and earth is named, That he would grant you, according to the riches of his glory, to be strengthened with might by his Spirit in the inner man; That Christ may dwell in your hearts by faith; that ye, being rooted and grounded in love, May be able to comprehend with all saints what is the breadth, and length, and depth, and height; And to know the love of Christ, which passeth knowledge, that ye might be filled with all the fulness of God."* (Ephesians 3:14-19)

> *"Thus saith the Lord, Keep ye judgment, and do justice: for my salvation is near to come, and my righteousness to be revealed. Blessed is the man that doeth this, and the son of man that layeth hold on it; that keepeth the sabbath from polluting it, and keepeth his hand from doing any evil. Neither let the son of the stranger, that hath joined himself to the Lord, speak, saying, The Lord hath utterly separated me from his people: neither let the eunuch say, Behold, I am a dry tree. For thus saith the Lord unto the eunuchs that keep my sabbaths, and choose the things that please me, and take hold of my covenant; Even unto them will I give in mine house and within my walls a place and a name better than of sons and of daughters: I will give them an everlasting name, that shall not be cut*

off. Also the sons of the stranger, that join themselves to the Lord, to serve him, and to love the name of the Lord, to be his servants, every one that keepeth the sabbath from polluting it, and taketh hold of my covenant; Even them will I bring to my holy mountain, and make them joyful in my house of prayer: their burnt offerings and their sacrifices shall be accepted upon mine altar; for mine house shall be called an house of prayer for all people. (Isaiah 56:1-7)

Prayer [tephillah: hymn of intercession and/or supplication] in the Old Testament is seen as a song or celebration as reflected in the book of Psalms.

"Have respect therefore to the prayer of thy servant, and to his supplication, O Lord my God, to hearken unto the cry and the prayer which thy servant prayeth before thee: That thine eyes may be open upon this house day and night, upon the place whereof thou hast said that thou wouldest put thy name there; to hearken unto the prayer which thy servant prayeth toward this place. Hearken therefore unto the supplications of thy servant, and of thy people Israel, which they shall make toward this place: hear thou from thy dwelling place, even from heaven; and when thou hearest, forgive. If a man sin against his neighbour, and an oath be laid upon him to make him swear, and the oath come before thine altar in this house; Then hear thou from heaven, and do, and judge thy servants, by requiting the wicked, by recompensing his way upon his own head; and by justifying the righteous, by giving him according to his righteousness. And if thy people Israel be put to the worse before the enemy, because they have sinned against thee; and shall return and confess thy name, and pray and make supplication before thee in this house; Then hear thou from the heavens, and forgive the sin of thy people Israel, and bring them again unto the land which thou gavest to them and to their fathers. When the heaven is shut up, and there is no rain, because they have sinned against thee; yet if they pray toward this place, and confess thy name, and turn from their sin, when thou dost afflict them; Then hear thou from heaven, and forgive the sin of thy servants, and of thy people Israel, when thou hast taught them the good way, wherein they should walk; and send rain upon thy land, which thou hast given unto thy people for an inheritance. If there be dearth in the land, if there be pestilence, if there be blasting, or mildew, locusts, or caterpillers; if their enemies besiege them in the cities of their land; whatsoever sore or whatsoever sickness there be: Then what prayer or what supplication soever shall be made of any man, or of all thy people Israel, when every one shall know his own sore and his own grief, and shall spread forth his hands in this house: Then hear thou from heaven thy dwelling place, and forgive, and render unto every man according unto all his ways, whose heart thou knowest; (for thou only knowest the hearts of the children of men:) That they may fear thee, to walk in thy ways, so long as they live in the land which thou gavest unto our fathers." (2 Chronicles 6:19-31)

"And it came to pass, when I heard these words, that I sat down and wept, and mourned certain days, and fasted, and prayed before the God of heaven, and said, I beseech thee, O Lord God of heaven, the great and terrible God, that keepeth covenant and mercy for them that love him and observe his commandments: Let thine ear now be attentive, and thine eyes open, that thou mayest hear the prayer of thy servant, which I pray before thee now, day and night, for the children of Israel thy servants, and confess the sins of the children of Israel, which we have sinned against thee: both I and my father's house have sinned." (Nehemiah 1:4-6)

"Give ear to my prayer, O God; and hide not thyself from my supplication. Attend unto me, and hear me: I mourn in my complaint, and make a noise; because of the voice of the enemy, because of the oppression of the wicked: for they cast iniquity upon me, and in wrath they hate me." (Psalm 55:1-3)

In the New Testament there are many more variations of prayer such as proseuche, an oratory in earnest. Deesis is a prayer as a petition/request. Euche is a prayer as a wish expressed petition to God or in votive obligation [a vow]. Then, there is just calling on the name of the Lord; Father or Jesus help us, can undoubtedly be a sacred prayer.

"And all things, whatsoever ye shall ask in prayer, believing, ye shall receive." (Matthew 21:22)

"For I know that this shall turn to my salvation through your prayer, and the supply of the Spirit of Jesus Christ, According to my earnest expectation and my hope, that in nothing I shall be ashamed, but that with all boldness, as always, so now also Christ shall be magnified in my body, whether it be by life, or by death." (Philippians 1:19&20)

"And the prayer of faith shall save the sick, and the Lord shall raise him up; and if he have committed sins, they shall be forgiven him." (James 5:15)

"Flee also youthful lusts: but follow righteousness, faith, charity, peace, with them that call on the Lord out of a pure heart." (2 Timothy 2:22)

"Call unto me, and I will answer thee, and shew thee great and mighty things, which thou knowest not." (Jeremiah 33:3)

Jesus taught us in the Bible to pray in his name to our Heavenly Father.

"Ye have not chosen me, but I have chosen you, and ordained you, that ye should go and bring forth fruit, and that your fruit should remain: that whatsoever ye shall ask of the Father in my name, he may give it you." (John 15:16)

"And in that day ye shall ask me nothing. Verily, verily, I say unto you, Whatsoever ye shall ask the Father in my name, he will give it you. Hitherto have ye asked nothing in my name: ask, and ye shall receive, that your joy may be full." (John 16:23&24)

Prayer can certainly be for certain needs and with praise and thanksgiving for rightful things; it is an indication of faith.

"Finally, brethren, pray for us, that the word of the Lord may have free course, and be glorified, even as it is with you: And that we may be delivered from unreasonable and wicked men: for all men have not faith. But the Lord is faithful, who shall stablish you, and keep you from evil." (2 Thessalonians 3:1-3)

"Ask, and it shall be given you; seek, and ye shall find; knock, and it shall be opened unto you: For every one that asketh receiveth; and he that seeketh findeth; and to him that knocketh it shall be opened. Or what man is there of you, whom if his son ask bread, will he give him a stone? Or if he ask a fish, will he give him a serpent? If ye then, being evil, know how to give good gifts unto your children, how much more shall your Father which is in heaven give good things to them that ask him?" (Matthew 7:7-11)

"And it came to pass, when king Hezekiah heard it, that he rent his clothes, and covered himself with sackcloth, and went into the house of the Lord. And he sent Eliakim, which was over the household, and Shebna the scribe, and the elders of the priests, covered with sackcloth, to Isaiah the prophet the son of Amoz. And they said unto him, Thus saith Hezekiah, This day is a day of trouble, and of rebuke, and blasphemy: for the children are come to the birth, and there is not strength to bring forth. It may be the Lord thy God will hear all the words of Rab-shakeh, whom the king of Assyria his master hath sent to reproach the living God; and will reprove the words which the Lord thy God hath heard: wherefore lift up thy prayer for the remnant that are left. So the servants of king Hezekiah came to Isaiah. And Isaiah said unto them, Thus shall ye say to your master, Thus saith the Lord, Be not afraid of the words which thou hast heard, with which the servants of the king of Assyria have blasphemed me. Behold, I will send a blast upon him, and he shall hear a rumour, and shall return to his own land; and I will cause him to fall by the sword in his own land." (2 Kings 19:1-7)

"Is any among you afflicted? let him pray. Is any merry? let him sing psalms. Is any sick among you? let him call for the elders of the church; and let them pray over him, anointing him with oil in the name of the Lord: And the prayer of faith shall save the sick, and the Lord shall raise him up; and if he have committed sins, they shall be forgiven him." (James 5:13-15)

"From whence come wars and fightings among you? come they not hence, even of your lusts that war in your members? Ye lust, and have not: ye kill, and desire to have, and cannot obtain: ye fight and war, yet ye have not, because ye ask not. Ye ask, and receive not, because ye ask amiss, that ye may consume it upon your lusts." (James 4:1-4)

"For the Lord will not forsake his people for his great name's sake: because it hath pleased the Lord to make you his people. Moreover as for me, God forbid that I should sin against the Lord in ceasing to pray for you: but I will teach you the good and the right way: Only fear the Lord, and serve him in truth with all your heart: for consider how great things he hath done for you. But if ye shall still do wickedly, ye shall be consumed, both ye and your king." (1 Samuel 12:22-25)

"And when they were come to the multitude, there came to him a certain man, kneeling down to him, and saying, Lord, have mercy on my son: for he is lunatick, and sore vexed: for ofttimes he falleth into the fire, and oft into the water. And I brought him to thy disciples, and they could not cure him. Then Jesus answered and said, O faithless and perverse generation, how long shall I be with you? how long shall I suffer you? bring him hither to me. And Jesus rebuked the devil; and he departed out of him: and the child was cured from that very hour. Then came the disciples to Jesus apart, and said, Why could not we cast him out? And Jesus said unto them, Because of your unbelief: for verily I say unto you, If ye have faith as a grain of mustard seed, ye shall say unto this mountain, Remove hence to yonder place; and it shall remove; and nothing shall be impossible unto you. Howbeit this kind goeth not out but by prayer and fasting." (Matthew 17:21)

The Holy Ghost was ushered into the world by the prayers of the saints in the upper room.

"These all continued with one accord in prayer and supplication, with the women, and Mary the mother of Jesus, and with his brethren." (Acts 1:14)

Prayer can be private or corporate, general in nature, intercessions or petitions before God.

"And when thou prayest, thou shalt not be as the hypocrites are: for they love to pray standing in the synagogues and in the corners of the streets, that they may be seen of men. Verily I say unto you, they have their reward. But thou, when thou prayest, enter into thy closet, and when thou hast shut thy door, pray to thy Father which is in secret; and thy Father which seeth in secret shall reward thee openly. But when ye pray, use not vain repetitions, as the heathen do: for they think that they shall be heard for their much speaking. Be not ye therefore like unto them: for your Father knoweth what things ye have need of, before ye ask him." (Matthew 6:5-8)

"And straightway Jesus constrained his disciples to get into a ship, and to go before him unto the other side, while he sent the multitudes away. And when he had sent the multitudes away, he went up into a mountain apart to pray: and when the evening was come, he was there alone." (Matthew 14:22&23)

"I will therefore that men pray every where, lifting up holy hands, without wrath and doubting." (1 Timothy 2:8)

"I exhort therefore, that, first of all, supplications, prayers, intercessions, and giving of thanks, be made for all men; for kings, and for all that are in authority; that we may lead a quiet and peaceable life in all godliness and honesty. For this is good and acceptable in the sight of God our Savior; Who will have all men to be saved, and to come unto the knowledge of the truth." (1 Timothy 2:1-4)

Continue in prayer as to not let feelings of guilt or frustrations keep you from praying.

"And Samson said unto the lad that held him by the hand, Suffer me that I may feel the pillars whereupon the house standeth, that I may lean upon them. Now the house was full of men and women; and all the lords of the Philistines were there; and there were upon the roof about three thousand men and women, that beheld while Samson made sport. And Samson called unto the Lord, and said, O Lord God, remember me, I pray thee, and strengthen me, I pray thee, only this once, O God, that I may be at once avenged of the Philistines for my two eyes. And Samson took hold of the two middle pillars upon which the house stood, and on which it was borne up, of the one with his right hand, and of the other with his left. And Samson said, Let me die with the Philistines. And he bowed himself with all his might; and the house fell upon the lords, and upon all the people that were therein. So the dead which he slew at his death were more than they which he slew in his life." (Judges 16:28-30)

"Pray without ceasing." (1 Thessalonians 5:17)

The asking in thanksgiving, of God's blessing upon our food, relates to the model prayer by which Christ instructed his disciples in how to pray.

"Now the Spirit speaketh expressly, that in the latter times some shall depart from the faith, giving heed to seducing spirits, and doctrines of devils; Speaking lies in hypocrisy; having their conscience seared with a hot iron; Forbidding to marry, and commanding to abstain from meats, which God hath created to be received with thanksgiving of them which believe and know the truth. For every creature of God is good, and nothing to be re-

fused, if it be received with thanksgiving: For it is sanctified by the word of God and prayer."
(1 Timothy 4:1-5)

"And I heard a voice saying unto me, Arise, Peter; slay and eat. But I said, not so, Lord:
for nothing common or unclean hath at any time entered into my mouth. But the voice
answered me again from heaven, What God hath cleansed, that call not thou common."
(Acts 11:7-9)

"And Jesus saith unto them, How many loaves have ye? And they said, Seven, and a few
little fishes. And he commanded the multitude to sit down on the ground. And he took the
seven loaves and the fishes, and gave thanks, and brake them, and gave to his disciples,
and the disciples to the multitude. And they did all eat, and were filled: and they took up
of the broken meat that was left seven baskets full. And they that did eat were four thousand men, beside women and children." (Mathew 15:34-38)

"After this manner therefore pray ye:Our Father which art in heaven, Hallowed be thy
name. Thy kingdom come, Thy will be done in earth, as it is in heaven. Give us this day our
daily bread. And forgive us our debts, as we forgive our debtors. And lead us not into temptation, but deliver us from evil: For thine is the kingdom, and the power, and the glory, for
ever. Amen." (Matthew 6:9-13)

Every believer should pray.

"And Jesus said unto them, Because of your unbelief: for verily I say unto you, If ye have
faith as a grain of mustard seed, ye shall say unto this mountain, Remove hence to yonder
place; and it shall remove; and nothing shall be impossible unto you. Howbeit this kind
goeth not out but by prayer and fasting." (Matthew 17:20&21)

"For the eyes of the Lord are over the righteous, and his ears are open unto their prayers:
but the face of the Lord is against them that do evil." (1 Peter 3:12)

"And when he looked on him, he was afraid, and said, What is it, Lord? And he said unto
him, Thy prayers and thine alms are come up for a memorial before God." (Acts 10:4)

Those resisting God can have their prayers cut off.

"He that turneth away his ear from hearing the law, even his prayer shall be abomination."
(Proverbs 28:9)

"And now, because ye have done all these works, saith the Lord, and I spake unto you,
rising up early and speaking, but ye heard not; and I called you, but ye answered not;
Therefore will I do unto this house, which is called by my name, wherein ye trust, and unto
the place which I gave to you and to your fathers, as I have done to Shiloh. And I will cast
you out of my sight, as I have cast out all your brethren, even the whole seed of Ephraim.
Therefore pray not thou for this people, neither lift up cry nor prayer for them, neither
make intercession to me: for I will not hear thee." (Jeremiah 7:16)

**We should humble ourselves in prayer before God. Spiritually we need to be contrite
and, when in private especially, in physical posture of bowing or kneeling as exampled in
the Bible.**

"O come, let us worship and bow down: let us kneel before the Lord our maker." (**Psalm 95:6**)

"And he came out, and went, as he was wont, to the mount of Olives; and his disciples also followed him. And when he was at the place, he said unto them, Pray that ye enter not into temptation. And he was withdrawn from them about a stone's cast, and kneeled down, and prayed, Saying, Father, if thou be willing, remove this cup from me: nevertheless not my will, but thine, be done. And there appeared an angel unto him from heaven, strengthening him." (**Luke 22:39-43**)

"Then Peter arose and went with them. When he was come, they brought him into the upper chamber: and all the widows stood by him weeping, and shewing the coats and garments which Dorcas made, while she was with them. But Peter put them all forth, and kneeled down, and prayed; and turning him to the body said, Tabitha, arise. And she opened her eyes: and when she saw Peter, she sat up. And he gave her his hand, and lifted her up, and when he had called the saints and widows, presented her alive." (**Acts 9:39-41**)

The Bible states God's ability and willingness to answer a prayer before it is even uttered.

"And it shall come to pass, that before they call, I will answer; and while they are yet speaking, I will hear." (**Isaiah 65:24**)

Note The Gospel of John Chapter 17, the High Priestly Prayer of Jesus.

9

THE CHURCH –
VISIBLE (PHYSICAL) AND SPIRITUAL

What is meant by "the church" and why should I be concerned about "belonging" to the church?

THE VISIBLE CHURCH came into existence on the Day of Pentecost in 30 A.D. (fifty days after the eye witnessed crucifixion of Jesus and ten days after his eye witnessed ascension). The visible church was ushered in by the prayers of the 120 men and women in the upper room at Jerusalem.

"And when the day of Pentecost was fully come, they were all with one accord in one place. And suddenly there came a sound from heaven as of a rushing mighty wind, and it filled all the house where they were sitting. And there appeared unto them cloven tongues like as of fire, and it sat upon each of them. And they were all filled with the Holy Ghost, and began to speak with other tongues, as the Spirit gave them utterance. And there were dwelling at Jerusalem Jews, devout men, out of every nation under heaven. Now when this was noised abroad, the multitude came together, and were confounded, because that every man heard them speak in his own language. And they were all amazed, and were in doubt, saying one to another, What meaneth this? Others mocking said, These men are full of new wine. But Peter, standing up with the eleven, lifted up his voice, and said unto them, Ye men of Judaea, and all ye that dwell at Jerusalem, be this known unto you, and hearken to my words: For these are not drunken, as ye suppose, seeing it is but the third hour of the day. But this is that which was spoken by the prophet Joel; And it shall come to pass in the last days, saith God, I will pour out of my Spirit upon all flesh: and your sons and your daughters shall prophesy, and your young men shall see visions, and your old men shall dream dreams: And on my servants and on my handmaidens I will pour out in those days of my Spirit; and they shall prophesy: And I will shew wonders in heaven above, and signs in the earth beneath; blood, and fire, and vapour of smoke: The sun shall be turned into darkness, and the moon into blood, before that great and notable day of the Lord come: And it shall come to pass, that whosoever shall call on the name of the Lord shall be saved." (Acts 2:1-6 & 12-21)

"And it shall come to pass afterward, that I will pour out my spirit upon all flesh; and your sons and your daughters shall prophesy, your old men shall dream dreams, your young men shall see visions: And also upon the servants and upon the handmaids in those days will I pour out my spirit. And I will shew wonders in the heavens and in the earth, blood,

and fire, and pillars of smoke. The sun shall be turned into darkness, and the moon into blood, before the great and the terrible day of the Lord come. And it shall come to pass, that whosoever shall call on the name of the Lord shall be delivered: for in mount Zion and in Jerusalem shall be deliverance, as the Lord hath said, and in the remnant whom the Lord shall call." (Joel 2:28-32)

"Then returned they unto Jerusalem from the mount called Olivet, which is from Jerusalem a sabbath day's journey. And when they were come in, they went up into an upper room, where abode both Peter, and James, and John, and Andrew, Philip, and Thomas, Bartholomew, and Matthew, James the son of Alphaeus, and Simon Zelotes, and Judas the brother of James. These all continued with one accord in prayer and supplication, with the women, and Mary the mother of Jesus, and with his brethren. And in those days Peter stood up in the midst of the disciples, and said, (the number of names together were about an hundred and twenty,) Men and brethren, this scripture must needs have been fulfilled, which the Holy Ghost by the mouth of David spake before concerning Judas, which was guide to them that took Jesus." (Acts 1:12-16)

The visible (physical) church (Ekklesia: popular place especially a religious congregation, religious assembly, community of members on earth and/or saints in heaven) is the body of baptized believers in Jesus Christ as they assemble together

"Then they that gladly received his word were baptized: and the same day there were added unto them about three thousand souls. And they continued stedfastly in the apostles' doctrine and fellowship, and in breaking of bread, and in prayers...praising God, and having favour with all the people. And the Lord added to the church daily such as should be saved." (Acts 2:41, 42&47)

"Let us draw near with a true heart in full assurance of faith, having our hearts sprinkled from an evil conscience, and our bodies washed with pure water. Let us hold fast the profession of our faith without wavering; (for he is faithful that promised;) and let us consider one another to provoke unto love and to good works: not forsaking the assembling of ourselves together, as the manner of some is; but exhorting one another: and so much the more, as ye see the day approaching." (Hebrews 10:22-25)

The visible church is headed by the bishop [priest, pastor, elder, episkope, episkopos: superintendent, officer in charge, overseer]. The overseer is under the chief shepherd Christ and very much accountable to God.

"And I will give you pastors according to mine heart, which shall feed you with knowledge and understanding." (Jeremiah 3:15)

"Take heed therefore unto yourselves, and to all the flock, over the which the Holy Ghost hath made you overseers, to feed the church of God, which he hath purchased with his own blood. For I know this, that after my departing shall grievous wolves enter in among you, not sparing the flock. Also of your own selves shall men arise, speaking perverse things, to draw away disciples after them." (Acts 20:28-30)

"The elders which are among you I exhort, who am also an elder, and a witness of the sufferings of Christ, and also a partaker of the glory that shall be revealed: feed the flock of God which is among you, taking the oversight thereof, not by constraint, but willingly; not

for filthy lucre, but of a ready mind; neither as being lords over God's heritage, but being ensamples to the flock. And when the chief Shepherd shall appear, ye shall receive a crown of glory that fadeth not away." (**1 Peter 5:1-4**)

"Obey them that have the rule over you, and submit yourselves: for they watch for your souls, as they that must give account, that they may do it with joy, and not with grief: for that is unprofitable for you. Pray for us: for we trust we have a good conscience, in all things willing to live honestly." (**Hebrews 13:17-18**)

"Woe be unto the pastors that destroy and scatter the sheep of my pasture! saith the Lord. Therefore thus saith the Lord God of Israel against the pastors that feed my people; ye have scattered my flock, and driven them away, and have not visited them: behold, I will visit upon you the evil of your doings, saith the Lord." (**Jeremiah 23:1&2**)

There is one other office in the visible church. The only other biblical office is that of the deacon [Diakoneo: an attendant especially to run errands, menial duties, waiter, waiter upon, to minister]. The deacon is to be as blameless as the bishop. The bishop is called by God while the deacon should be called out of the congregation.

"Likewise must the deacons be grave, not doubletongued, not given to much wine, not greedy of filthy lucre; holding the mystery of the faith in a pure conscience. And let these also first be proved; then let them use the office of a deacon, being found blameless. Even so must their wives be grave, not slanderers, sober, faithful in all things. Let the deacons be the husbands of one wife, ruling their children and their own houses well. For they that have used the office of a deacon well purchase to themselves a good degree, and great boldness in the faith which is in Christ Jesus." (**1 Timothy 3:8-13**)

"For Christ sent me not to baptize, but to preach the gospel: not with wisdom of words, lest the cross of Christ should be made of none effect. For the preaching of the cross is to them that perish foolishness; but unto us which are saved it is the power of God...For ye see your calling, brethren, how that not many wise men after the flesh, not many mighty, not many noble, are called: but God hath chosen the foolish things of the world to confound the wise; and God hath chosen the weak things of the world to confound the things which are mighty; and base things of the world, and things which are despised, hath God chosen, yea, and things which are not, to bring to nought things that are: that no flesh should glory in his presence." (**1 Corinthians 1:17,18,26-29**)

"Then the twelve called the multitude of the disciples unto them, and said, it is not reason that we should leave the word of God, and serve tables. Wherefore, brethren, look ye out among you seven men of honest report, full of the Holy Ghost and wisdom, whom we may appoint over this business. But we will give ourselves continually to prayer, and to the ministry of the word." (**Acts 6:2-4**)

The church house is to be a house of prayer for all persons. It is not God's desire that one soul should be lost. The temple of the Old Testament has become now the church house.

"And Jesus went into the temple of God, and cast out all them that sold and bought in the temple, and overthrew the tables of the moneychangers, and the seats of them that sold doves, and said unto them, 'It is written, My house shall be called the house of prayer; but

ye have made it a den of thieves.' And the blind and the lame came to him in the temple; and he healed them." (Matthew 21:12-14)

"And he taught, saying unto them, 'Is it not written, My house shall be called of all nations the house of prayer? But ye have made it a den of thieves.' And the scribes and chief priests heard it, and sought how they might destroy him: for they feared him, because all the people was astonished at his doctrine." (Mark 11:17-18)

"Even them will I bring to my holy mountain, and make them joyful in my house of prayer: their burnt offerings and their sacrifices shall be accepted upon mine altar; for mine house shall be called an house of prayer for all people." (Isaiah 56:7)

"For from the rising of the sun even unto the going down of the same my name shall be great among the Gentiles; and in every place incense shall be offered unto my name, and a pure offering: for my name shall be great among the heathen, saith the Lord of hosts." (Malachi 1:11)

"I exhort therefore, that, first of all, supplications, prayers, intercessions, and giving of thanks, be made for all men; for kings, and for all that are in authority; that we may lead a quiet and peaceable life in all godliness and honesty. For this is good and acceptable in the sight of God our Saviour; who will have all men to be saved, and to come unto the knowledge of the truth." (1 Timothy 2:1-4)

The visible church is to be a place of sanctuary [miqdash: a consecrated thing or place, chapel, holy place] for God and his people.

"David also commanded all the princes of Israel to help Solomon his son, saying, 'Is not the Lord your God with you? And hath he not given you rest on every side? For he hath given the inhabitants of the land into mine hand; and the land is subdued before the Lord, and before his people. Now set your heart and your soul to seek the Lord your God; arise therefore, and build ye the sanctuary of the Lord God, to bring the ark of the covenant of the Lord, and the holy vessels of God, into the house that is to be built to the name of the Lord." (1 Chronicles 22:17-19)

"Behold, bless ye the Lord, all ye servants of the Lord, which by night stand in the house of the Lord. Lift up your hands in the sanctuary, and bless the Lord." (Psalm 134:1-2)

"For the Lord is great, and greatly to be praised: he is to be feared above all gods. For all the gods of the nations are idols: but the Lord made the heavens. Honour and majesty are before him: strength and beauty are in his sanctuary." (Psalm 96:4-6)

"For all the day long have I been plagued, and chastened every morning. If I say, I will speak thus; behold, I should offend against the generation of thy children. When I thought to know this, it was too painful for me; until I went into the sanctuary of God; then understood I their end." (Psalm 73:14-17)

The church exists for the edification of the body of Christ, the saints.

"And he gave some, apostles; and some, prophets; and some, evangelists; and some, pastors and teachers; for the perfecting of the saints, for the work of the ministry, for the edifying of the body of Christ: till we all come in the unity of the faith, and of the knowledge of the Son of God, unto a perfect man, unto the measure of the stature of the fulness of Christ: that

we henceforth be no more children, tossed to and fro, and carried about with every wind of doctrine, by the sleight of men, and cunning craftiness, whereby they lie in wait to deceive; but speaking the truth in love, may grow up into him in all things, which is the head, even Christ." (**Ephesians 4:11-15**)

"And the heavens shall praise thy wonders, O Lord: thy faithfulness also in the congregation of the saints. For who in the heaven can be compared unto the Lord? Who among the sons of the mighty can be likened unto the Lord? God is greatly to be feared in the assembly of the saints, and to be had in reverence of all them that are about him." (**Psalms 89:5-7**)

"The fear of the Lord is the beginning of wisdom: and the knowledge of the holy is understanding." (**Proverbs 9:10**)

"How is it then, brethren? When ye come together, every one of you hath a psalm, hath a doctrine, hath a tongue, hath a revelation, hath an interpretation. Let all things be done unto edifying." (**1 Corinthians 14:26**)

The church exists for the work and support of the ministry of the spreading of the gospel throughout the world.

"And Jesus went about all the cities and villages, teaching in their synagogues, and preaching the gospel of the kingdom, and healing every sickness and every disease among the people. But when he saw the multitudes, he was moved with compassion on them, because they fainted and were scattered abroad, as sheep having no shepherd. Then saith he unto his disciples, 'The harvest truly is plenteous, but the labourers are few; pray ye therefore the Lord of the harvest, that he will send forth labourers into his harvest." (**Matthew 9:35-38**)

"I therefore, the prisoner of the Lord, beseech you that ye walk worthy of the vocation wherewith ye are called, with all lowliness and meekness, with longsuffering, forbearing one another in love; endeavouring to keep the unity of the Spirit in the bond of peace." (Ephesians 4:1-3)

"Then shall the King say unto them on his right hand, Come, ye blessed of my Father, inherit the kingdom prepared for you from the foundation of the world: for I was an hungred, and ye gave me meat: I was thirsty, and ye gave me drink: I was a stranger, and ye took me in: naked, and ye clothed me: I was sick, and ye visited me: I was in prison, and ye came unto me. Then shall the righteous answer him, saying, Lord, when saw we thee an hungred, and fed thee? Or thirsty, and gave thee drink? When saw we thee a stranger, and took thee in? Or naked, and clothed thee? Or when saw we thee sick, or in prison, and came unto thee? And the King shall answer and say unto them, Verily I say unto you, Inasmuch as ye have done it unto one of the least of these my brethren, ye have done it unto me." (**Matthew 25:34-40**)

"Be not deceived; God is not mocked: for whatsoever a man soweth, that shall he also reap. For he that soweth to his flesh shall of the flesh reap corruption; but he that soweth to the Spirit shall of the Spirit reap life everlasting. And let us not be weary in well doing: for in due season we shall reap, if we faint not. As we have therefore opportunity, let us do good unto all men, especially unto them who are of the household of faith." (**Galatians 6:7-10**)

"What doth it profit, my brethren, though a man say he hath faith, and have not works? Can faith save him? If a brother or sister be naked, and destitute of daily food, and one

of you say unto them, depart in peace, be ye warmed and filled; notwithstanding ye give them not those things which are needful to the body; what doth it profit? Even so faith, if it hath not works, is dead, being alone. Yea, a man may say, Thou hast faith, and I have works: shew me thy faith without thy works, and I will shew thee my faith by my works." (James 2:14-18)

The visible church is given a charge by Jesus that recognizes his power to us since the day of Pentecost. That charge is to teach his doctrine to all the earth, baptize as he has commanded and by example observe the commandments.

"And Jesus came and spake unto them, saying, 'All power is given unto me in heaven and in earth. Go ye therefore, and teach all nations, baptizing them in the name of the Father, and of the Son, and of the Holy Ghost: teaching them to observe all things whatsoever I have commanded you: and, lo, I am with you alway, even unto the end of the world.' Amen." (Matthew 28:18-20)

"And he said unto them, 'Go ye into all the world, and preach the gospel to every creature. He that believeth and is baptized shall be saved; but he that believeth not shall be damned." (Mark 16:15-16)

"And said unto them, 'Thus it is written, and thus it behoved Christ to suffer, and to rise from the dead the third day:and that repentance and remission of sins should be preached in his name among all nations, beginning at Jerusalem. And ye are witnesses of these things. And, behold, I send the promise of my Father upon you: but tarry ye in the city of Jerusalem, until ye be endued with power from on high." (Luke 24:46-49)

"Now then we are ambassadors for Christ, as though God did beseech you by us: we pray you in Christ's stead, be ye reconciled to God." (2 Corinthians 5:20)

"Did I make a gain of you by any of them whom I sent unto you? I desired Titus, and with him I sent a brother. Did Titus make a gain of you? Walked we not in the same spirit? Walked we not in the same steps? Again, think ye that we excuse ourselves unto you? We speak before God in Christ: but we do all things, dearly beloved, for your edifying. For I fear, lest, when I come, I shall not find you such as I would, and that I shall be found unto you such as ye would not: lest there be debates, envyings, wraths, strifes, backbitings, whisperings, swellings, tumults: and lest, when I come again, my God will humble me among you, and that I shall bewail many which have sinned already, and have not repented of the uncleanness and fornication and lasciviousness which they have committed." (2 Corinthians 12:17-21)

There is to be the word of God in the church. This is to be an edifying word and likened as to Jesus himself preaching in the temple. This prophesying is to be enlightening and sustaining; not watered down.

"The high priest then asked Jesus of his disciples, and of his doctrine. Jesus answered him, 'I spake openly to the world; I ever taught in the synagogue, and in the temple, whither the Jews always resort; and in secret have I said nothing. Why askest thou me? Ask them which heard me, what I have said unto them: behold, they know what I said." (John 18:19-21)

"Now the God of hope fill you with all joy and peace in believing, that ye may abound in hope, through the power of the Holy Ghost. And I myself also am persuaded of you, my

brethren, that ye also are full of goodness, filled with all knowledge, able also to admonish one another. Nevertheless, brethren, I have written the more boldly unto you in some sort, as putting you in mind, because of the grace that is given to me of God, that I should be the minister of Jesus Christ to the Gentiles, ministering the gospel of God, that the offering up of the Gentiles might be acceptable, being sanctified by the Holy Ghost. I have therefore whereof I may glory through Jesus Christ in those things which pertain to God. For I will not dare to speak of any of those things which Christ hath not wrought by me, to make the Gentiles obedient, by word and deed, through mighty signs and wonders, by the power of the Spirit of God; so that from Jerusalem, and round about unto Illyricum, I have fully preached the gospel of Christ." (**Romans 15:13-19**)*

"Then tidings of these things came unto the ears of the church which was in Jerusalem: and they sent forth Barnabas, that he should go as far as Antioch. Who, when he came, and had seen the grace of God, was glad, and exhorted them all, that with purpose of heart they would cleave unto the Lord. For he was a good man, and full of the Holy Ghost and of faith: and much people was added unto the Lord." (**Acts 11:22-24**)*

"Take heed therefore unto yourselves, and to all the flock, over the which the Holy Ghost hath made you overseers, to feed the church of God, which he hath purchased with his own blood. For I know this, that after my departing shall grievous wolves enter in among you, not sparing the flock. Also of your own selves shall men arise, speaking perverse things, to draw away disciples after them." (**Acts 20:28-30**)*

"But he that prophesieth speaketh unto men to edification, and exhortation, and comfort. He that speaketh in an unknown tongue edifieth himself; but he that prophesieth edifieth the church. I would that ye all spake with tongues, but rather that ye prophesied: for greater is he that prophesieth than he that speaketh with tongues, except he interpret, that the church may receive edifying." (**1 Corinthians 14:3-5**)*

"Salute the brethren which are in Laodicea, and Nymphas, and the church which is in his house. And when this epistle is read among you, cause that it be read also in the church of the Laodiceans; and that ye likewise read the epistle from Laodicea." (**Colossians 4:15&16**)*

"For when for the time ye ought to be teachers, ye have need that one teach you again which be the first principles of the oracles of God; and are become such as have need of milk, and not of strong meat. For every one that useth milk is unskilful in the word of righteousness: for he is a babe. But strong meat belongeth to them that are of full age, even those who by reason of use have their senses exercised to discern both good and evil." (**Hebrews 5:12-14**)*

"Moreover, brethren, I would not that ye should be ignorant, how that all our fathers were under the cloud, and all passed through the sea; And were all baptized unto Moses in the cloud and in the sea; And did all eat the same spiritual meat; And did all drink the same spiritual drink: for they drank of that spiritual Rock that followed them: and that Rock was Christ. But with many of them God was not well pleased: for they were overthrown in the wilderness. Now these things were our examples, to the intent we should not lust after evil things, as they also lusted." (**1 Corinthians 10:1-6**)*

There is, in the visible church, a necessity for an invitation to discipleship after the

preaching. Essential in the invitation is the call to repentance and baptism of those yet to be born again. Note that an invitation should also be made to those born again but at the time living apart from church fellowship. Note also that, there are no biblical stipulations for membership prerequisites such as new membership training, financial statements or background checks. Voting in members should be more of a rudimentary process with the understanding that members in a fellowship can be put out.

"So then faith cometh by hearing, and hearing by the word of God." (Romans 10:17)

"And Jesus came and spake unto them, saying, All power is given unto me in heaven and in earth. Go ye therefore, and teach all nations, baptizing them in the name of the Father, and of the Son, and of the Holy Ghost: Teaching them to observe all things whatsoever I have commanded you: and, lo, I am with you alway, even unto the end of the world. Amen." (Matthew 28:18-20)

"Then Peter said unto them, Repent, and be baptized every one of you in the name of Jesus Christ for the remission of sins, and ye shall receive the gift of the Holy Ghost. For the promise is unto you, and to your children, and to all that are afar off, even as many as the Lord our God shall call. And with many other words did he testify and exhort, saying, Save yourselves from this untoward generation. Then they that gladly received his word were baptized: and the same day there were added unto them about three thousand souls. And they continued stedfastly in the apostles' doctrine and fellowship, and in breaking of bread, and in prayers." (Acts 2:38-42)

"Moreover if thy brother shall trespass against thee, go and tell him his fault between thee and him alone: if he shall hear thee, thou hast gained thy brother. But if he will not hear thee, then take with thee one or two more, that in the mouth of two or three witnesses every word may be established. And if he shall neglect to hear them, tell it unto the church: but if he neglect to hear the church, let him be unto thee as an heathen man and a publican. Verily I say unto you, Whatsoever ye shall bind on earth shall be bound in heaven: and whatsoever ye shall loose on earth shall be loosed in heaven. Again I say unto you, That if two of you shall agree on earth as touching any thing that they shall ask, it shall be done for them of my Father which is in heaven. For where two or three are gathered together in my name, there am I in the midst of them." (Matthew 18:15-20)

There is to be praise for God in the church.

"Praise ye the Lord. Praise God in his sanctuary: praise him in the firmament of his power. Praise him for his mighty acts: praise him according to his excellent greatness. Praise him with the sound of the trumpet: praise him with the psaltery and harp. Praise him with the timbrel and dance: praise him with stringed instruments and organs. Praise him upon the loud cymbals: praise him upon the high sounding cymbals. Let every thing that hath breath praise the Lord. Praise ye the Lord." (Psalm 150)

"Praise ye the Lord. Praise ye the name of the Lord; praise him, O ye servants of the Lord. Ye that stand in the house of the Lord, in the courts of the house of our God, Praise the Lord; for the Lord is good: sing praises unto his name; for it is pleasant." (Psalm 135:1-3)

"Rejoice in the Lord, O ye righteous: for praise is comely for the upright. Praise the Lord with harp: sing unto him with the psaltery and an instrument of ten strings." (Psalm 33:1&2).

"Also I shook my lap, and said, So God shake out every man from his house, and from his labour, that performeth not this promise, even thus be he shaken out, and emptied. And all the congregation said, Amen, and praised the Lord. And the people did according to this promise." (Nehemiah 5:13)

"O give thanks unto the Lord; for he is good; for his mercy endureth for ever. And say ye, save us, O God of our salvation, and gather us together, and deliver us from the heathen, that we may give thanks to thy holy name, and glory in thy praise. Blessed be the Lord God of Israel for ever and ever. And all the people said, Amen, and praised the Lord." (1 Chronicles 16:34-36)

As a part of the praise in the church, there should be clapping, shouting, lifting of hands and the exclamation in agreement of Amen if not Alleluia.

"O clap your hands, all ye people; shout unto God with the voice of triumph. For the Lord most high is terrible; he is a great King over all the earth. He shall subdue the people under us, and the nations under our feet." (Psalm 47:1-3)

"But let all those that put their trust in thee rejoice: let them ever shout for joy, because thou defendest them: let them also that love thy name be joyful in thee." (Psalm 5:11)

"Be glad in the Lord, and rejoice, ye righteous: and shout for joy, all ye that are upright in heart." (Psalm 32:11)

"I will therefore that men pray every where, lifting up holy hands, without wrath and doubting." (1 Timothy 2:8)

"Save us, O Lord our God, and gather us from among the heathen, to give thanks unto thy holy name, and to triumph in thy praise. Blessed be the Lord God of Israel from everlasting to everlasting: and let all the people say, Amen. Praise ye the Lord." (Psalm 106:47&48)

"After this I beheld, and, lo, a great multitude, which no man could number, of all nations, and kindreds, and people, and tongues, stood before the throne, and before the Lamb, clothed with white robes, and palms in their hands; And cried with a loud voice, saying, Salvation to our God which sitteth upon the throne, and unto the Lamb. And all the angels stood round about the throne, and about the elders and the four beasts, and fell before the throne on their faces, and worshipped God, Saying, Amen: Blessing, and glory, and wisdom, and thanksgiving, and honour, and power, and might, be unto our God for ever and ever. Amen." (Revelation 7:9-12)

"And after these things I heard a great voice of much people in heaven, saying, Alleluia; Salvation, and glory, and honour, and power, unto the Lord our God: For true and righteous are his judgments: for he hath judged the great whore, which did corrupt the earth with her fornication, and hath avenged the blood of his servants at her hand. And again they said, Alleluia. And her smoke rose up for ever and ever. And the four and twenty elders and the four beasts fell down and worshipped God that sat on the throne, saying, Amen; Alleluia. And a voice came out of the throne, saying, Praise our God, all ye his servants, and ye that fear him, both small and great. And I heard as it were the voice of a great multitude, and as the voice of many waters, and as the voice of mighty thunderings, saying, Alleluia: for the Lord God omnipotent reigneth." (Revelation 19:1-6)

Songs are to be sung in the church. Songs rooted and grounded in the word of God such as hymns, psalms and spiritual songs are in order. There has to be a spiritual familiarity in the sound of the music that will bring about a godly response among the congregation. The music is to be accomplished with skill and joy.

> *" Let the word of Christ dwell in you richly in all wisdom; teaching and admonishing one another in psalms and hymns and spiritual songs, singing with grace in your hearts to the Lord."* (Colossians 3:16)

> *"And be not drunk with wine, wherein is excess; but be filled with the Spirit; Speaking to yourselves in psalms and hymns and spiritual songs, singing and making melody in your heart to the Lord; Giving thanks always for all things unto God and the Father in the name of our Lord Jesus Christ; Submitting yourselves one to another in the fear of God."* (Ephesians 5:18-21)

> *"And even things without life giving sound, whether pipe or harp, except they give a distinction in the sounds, how shall it be known what is piped or harped? For if the trumpet give an uncertain sound, who shall prepare himself to the battle?* (1 Corinthians 14:7&8)

> *"Sing unto him a new song; play skilfully with a loud noise. For the word of the Lord is right; and all his works are done in truth."* (Psalm 33:3&4)

> *"Make a joyful noise unto the Lord, all ye lands. Serve the Lord with gladness: come before his presence with singing. Know ye that the Lord he is God: it is he that hath made us, and not we ourselves; we are his people, and the sheep of his pasture. Enter into his gates with thanksgiving, and into his courts with praise: be thankful unto him, and bless his name."* (Psalm 100:1-4)

Dancing has a place in the worship experience. Remember that everything should be done with decency and in order unto the Lord.

> *"Praise ye the Lord. Sing unto the Lord a new song, and his praise in the congregation of saints. Let Israel rejoice in him that made him: let the children of Zion be joyful in their King. Let them praise his name in the dance: let them sing praises unto him with the timbrel and harp."* (Psalm 149:1-3)

> *"Praise him with the timbrel and dance: praise him with stringed instruments and organs."* (Psalm 150)

There is to be giving in the visible church for the support of the ministry and God is faithful to bless such giving. Every Christian should understand that a tenth of our income is holy unto the Lord. If the tithe is used rather than given to the Lord, then that amount used plus 20% belongs to God. This is tithing as the Bible teaches. There is another avenue of giving referred to as the offering (minchah: gift, oblation, meat, present, sacrifice). The offering does not have a percentage requirement and conversely, there is no limitation on the amount of the offering. How much more should the rich be able to give an offering? Incidentally, giving is out of our increase (tebuwah: fruit, gain, revenue) and, therefore, after taxes with tax refunds becoming revenue all over again (just compare the 10% of the take home income of a person with tax exempt income versus a person that has taxable income).

"Will a man rob God? Yet ye have robbed me. But ye say, Wherein have we robbed thee? In tithes and offerings. Ye are cursed with a curse: for ye have robbed me, even this whole nation. Bring ye all the tithes into the storehouse, that there may be meat in mine house, and prove me now herewith, saith the Lord of hosts, if I will not open you the windows of heaven, and pour you out a blessing, that there shall not be room enough to receive it. And I will rebuke the devourer for your sakes, and he shall not destroy the fruits of your ground; neither shall your vine cast her fruit before the time in the field, saith the Lord of hosts. And all nations shall call you blessed: for ye shall be a delightsome land, saith the Lord of hosts." (**Malachi 3:8-12**)

"And all the tithe of the land, whether of the seed of the land, or of the fruit of the tree, is the Lord's: it is holy unto the Lord. And if a man will at all redeem ought of his tithes, he shall add thereto the fifth part thereof. And concerning the tithe of the herd, or of the flock, even of whatsoever passeth under the rod, the tenth shall be holy unto the Lord." (**Leviticus 27:30-32**)

"Honour the Lord with thy substance, and with the firstfruits of all thine increase: So shall thy barns be filled with plenty, and thy presses shall burst out with new wine." (**Proverbs 3:9&10**)

"Give, and it shall be given unto you; good measure, pressed down, and shaken together, and running over, shall men give into your bosom. For with the same measure that ye mete withal it shall be measured to you again." (**Luke 6:38**)

The poor should be sacrificially included in our giving; look at the principal of gleaning.

"And when ye reap the harvest of your land, thou shalt not wholly reap the corners of thy field, neither shalt thou gather the gleanings of thy harvest. And thou shalt not glean thy vineyard, neither shalt thou gather every grape of thy vineyard; thou shalt leave them for the poor and stranger: I am the Lord your God." (**Leviticus 19:9&10**)

"When thou cuttest down thine harvest in thy field, and hast forgot a sheaf in the field, thou shalt not go again to fetch it: it shall be for the stranger, for the fatherless, and for the widow: that the Lord thy God may bless thee in all the work of thine hands. When thou beatest thine olive tree, thou shalt not go over the boughs again: it shall be for the stranger, for the fatherless, and for the widow. When thou gatherest the grapes of thy vineyard, thou shalt not glean it afterward: it shall be for the stranger, for the fatherless, and for the widow. And thou shalt remember that thou wast a bondman in the land of Egypt: therefore I command thee to do this thing." (**Deuteronomy 24:19-2**)

God loves our willingness and cheerfulness in giving in the church.

"And Jesus sat over against the treasury, and beheld how the people cast money into the treasury: and many that were rich cast in much. And there came a certain poor widow, and she threw in two mites, which make a farthing. And he called unto him his disciples, and saith unto them, Verily I say unto you, That this poor widow hath cast more in, than all they which have cast into the treasury: For all they did cast in of their abundance; but she of her want did cast in all that she had, even all her living." (**Mark 12:41-44**)

"But this I say, He which soweth sparingly shall reap also sparingly; and he which soweth bountifully shall reap also bountifully. Every man according as he purposeth in his heart,

so let him give; not grudgingly, or of necessity: for God loveth a cheerful giver. And God is able to make all grace abound toward you; that ye, always having all sufficiency in all things, may abound to every good work: (As it is written, He hath dispersed abroad; he hath given to the poor: his righteousness remaineth for ever. Now he that ministereth seed to the sower both minister bread for your food, and multiply your seed sown, and increase the fruits of your righteousness;) Being enriched in every thing to all bountifulness, which causeth through us thanksgiving to God." (2 Corinthians 9:6-11)

For the edification of the church fellowship, the worship service in the church should be carried out in the simplicity that is Christ.

"For I am jealous over you with godly jealousy: for I have espoused you to one husband, that I may present you as a chaste virgin to Christ. But I fear, lest by any means, as the serpent beguiled Eve through his subtilty, so your minds should be corrupted from the simplicity that is in Christ. For if he that cometh preacheth another Jesus, whom we have not preached, or if ye receive another spirit, which ye have not received, or another gospel, which ye have not accepted, ye might well bear with him." (2 Corinthians 11:2-4)

"Brethren, be not children in understanding: howbeit in malice be ye children, but in understanding be men. In the law it is written, With men of other tongues and other lips will I speak unto this people; and yet for all that will they not hear me, saith the Lord. Wherefore tongues are for a sign, not to them that believe, but to them that believe not: but prophesying serveth not for them that believe not, but for them which believe. If therefore the whole church be come together into one place, and all speak with tongues, and there come in those that are unlearned, or unbelievers, will they not say that ye are mad? But if all prophesy, and there come in one that believeth not, or one unlearned, he is convinced of all, he is judged of all: And thus are the secrets of his heart made manifest; and so falling down on his face he will worship God, and report that God is in you of a truth. How is it then, brethren? when ye come together, everyone of you hath a psalm, hath a doctrine, hath a tongue, hath a revelation, hath an interpretation. Let all things be done unto edifying. If any man speak in an unknown tongue, let it be by two, or at the most by three, and that by course; and let one interpret. But if there be no interpreter, let him keep silence in the church; and let him speak to himself, and to God." (1 Corinthians 14:20-28)

"As every man hath received the gift, even so minister the same one to another, as good stewards of the manifold grace of God. If any man speak, let him speak as the oracles of God; if any man minister, let him do it as of the ability which God giveth: that God in all things may be glorified through Jesus Christ, to whom be praise and dominion for ever and ever. Amen." (1 Peter 4:10&11)

"As ye have therefore received Christ Jesus the Lord, so walk ye in him: Rooted and built up in him, and stablished in the faith, as ye have been taught, abounding therein with thanksgiving. Beware lest any man spoil you through philosophy and vain deceit, after the tradition of men, after the rudiments of the world, and not after Christ." (Colossians 2:6-8)

"These things write I unto thee, hoping to come unto thee shortly: But if I tarry long, that thou mayest know how thou oughtest to behave thyself in the house of God, which is the church of the living God, the pillar and ground of the truth. And without controversy great is the mystery of godliness: God was manifest in the flesh, justified in the Spirit, seen of

angels, preached unto the Gentiles, believed on in the world, received up into glory." (1 Timothy 3:14-16)

It is of utmost importance that the worship service, in the sanctuary of the house of the Lord, maintains a level of decency and order, notwithstanding the joyful celebration of the Lord.

> *"Make a joyful noise unto the Lord, all ye lands. Serve the Lord with gladness: come before his presence with singing. Know ye that the Lord he is God: it is he that hath made us, and not we ourselves; we are his people, and the sheep of his pasture. Enter into his gates with thanksgiving, and into his courts with praise: be thankful unto him, and bless his name.* (Psalm 100:1-4)

> *" Let all things be done decently and in order."* (1 Corinthians 14:40)

> *"For God is not the author of confusion, but of peace, as in all churches of the saints."* (1 Corinthians 14:33)

There are two things prescribed by Christ and therefore considered ordinances in the physical church. The first is baptism and the second is the Holy Communion/Lord's Supper.

> *"Go ye therefore, and teach all nations, baptizing them in the name of the Father, and of the Son, and of the Holy Ghost."* (Matthew 28:19)

> *"And he took the cup, and gave thanks, and said, 'Take this, and divide it among yourselves: for I say unto you, I will not drink of the fruit of the vine, until the kingdom of God shall come.' And he took bread, and gave thanks, and brake it, and gave unto them, saying, 'This is my body which is given for you: this do in remembrance of me.' Likewise also the cup after supper, saying, 'This cup is the new testament in my blood, which is shed for you."* (Luke 22:17-20)

Now there needs to be recognition of the spiritual body of Christ as the spiritual church aside from the various assemblies/congregations existing as the visible church. Unfortunately, not all visible church members shall see God.

> *"Another parable put he forth unto them, saying, 'The kingdom of heaven is likened unto a man which sowed good seed in his field: but while men slept, his enemy came and sowed tares among the wheat, and went his way. But when the blade was sprung up, and brought forth fruit, then appeared the tares also. So the servants of the householder came and said unto him, Sir, didst not thou sow good seed in thy field? From whence then hath it tares? He said unto them, An enemy hath done this. The servants said unto him, Wilt thou then that we go and gather them up? But he said, Nay; lest while ye gather up the tares, ye root up also the wheat with them. Let both grow together until the harvest: and in the time of harvest I will say to the reapers, Gather ye together first the tares, and bind them in bundles to burn them: but gather the wheat into my barn."* (Matthew 13:24-30)

> *"And unto the angel of the church of the Laodiceans write; These things saith the Amen, the faithful and true witness, the beginning of the creation of God; I know thy works, that thou art neither cold nor hot: I would thou wert cold or hot. So then because thou art luke-*

warm, and neither cold nor hot, I will spue thee out of my mouth. Because thou sayest, I am rich, and increased with goods, and have need of nothing; and knowest not that thou art wretched, and miserable, and poor, and blind, and naked: I counsel thee to buy of me gold tried in the fire, that thou mayest be rich; and white raiment, that thou mayest be clothed, and that the shame of thy nakedness do not appear; and anoint thine eyes with eyesalve, that thou mayest see. As many as I love, I rebuke and chasten: be zealous therefore, and repent. Behold, I stand at the door, and knock: if any man hear my voice, and open the door, I will come in to him, and will sup with him, and he with me. To him that overcometh will I grant to sit with me in my throne, even as I also overcame, and am set down with my Father in his throne. He that hath an ear, let him hear what the Spirit saith unto the churches." (**Revelation 3:14-22**)

"Beware of false prophets, which come to you in sheep's clothing, but inwardly they are ravening wolves. Ye shall know them by their fruits. Do men gather grapes of thorns, or figs of thistles? Even so every good tree bringeth forth good fruit; but a corrupt tree bringeth forth evil fruit. A good tree cannot bring forth evil fruit, neither can a corrupt tree bring forth good fruit. Every tree that bringeth not forth good fruit is hewn down, and cast into the fire. Wherefore by their fruits ye shall know them. Not every one that saith unto me, Lord, Lord, shall enter into the kingdom of heaven; but he that doeth the will of my Father which is in heaven. Many will say to me in that day, Lord, Lord, have we not prophesied in thy name? And in thy name have cast out devils? And in thy name done many wonderful works? And then will I profess unto them, I never knew you: depart from me, ye that work iniquity." (**Matthew 7:15-23**)

"But what I do, that I will do, that I may cut off occasion from them which desire occasion; that wherein they glory, they may be found even as we. For such are false apostles, deceitful workers, transforming themselves into the apostles of Christ. And no marvel; for Satan himself is transformed into an angel of light. Therefore it is no great thing if his ministers also be transformed as the ministers of righteousness; whose end shall be according to their works." (**2 Corinthians 11:12-15**)

"Yet if any man suffer as a Christian, let him not be ashamed; but let him glorify God on this behalf. For the time is come that judgment must begin at the house of God: and if it first begin at us, what shall the end be of them that obey not the gospel of God? And if the righteous scarcely be saved, where shall the ungodly and the sinner appear?" (**1 Peter 4:16-18**)

The key to establishment in the spiritual church lies in the two ordinances of the church. One must indeed be born again. One must also go through the periodical self-examination of the Holy Communion/the Lord's Supper. This is obedience and power.

"Jesus answered and said unto him, 'Verily, verily, I say unto thee, Except a man be born again, he cannot see the kingdom of God.' Nicodemus saith unto him, 'How can a man be born when he is old? Can he enter the second time into his mother's womb, and be born?' Jesus answered, 'Verily, verily, I say unto thee, Except a man be born of water and of the Spirit, he cannot enter into the kingdom of God. That which is born of the flesh is flesh; and that which is born of the Spirit is spirit." (**John 3:3-6**)

"For as often as ye eat this bread, and drink this cup, ye do shew the Lord's death till he come. Wherefore whosoever shall eat this bread, and drink this cup of the Lord, unwor-

thily, shall be guilty of the body and blood of the Lord. But let a man examine himself, and so let him eat of that bread, and drink of that cup. For he that eateth and drinketh unworthily, eateth and drinketh damnation to himself, not discerning the Lord's body." (1 Corinthians 11:26-29)

"Then Peter and the other apostles answered and said, We ought to obey God rather than men. The God of our fathers raised up Jesus, whom ye slew and hanged on a tree. Him hath God exalted with his right hand to be a Prince and a Saviour, for to give repentance to Israel, and forgiveness of sins. And we are his witnesses of these things; and so is also the Holy Ghost, whom God hath given to them that obey him." (Acts 5:29-32)

"Blessed be the God and Father of our Lord Jesus Christ, who hath blessed us with all spiritual blessings in heavenly places in Christ: according as he hath chosen us in him before the foundation of the world, that we should be holy and without blame before him in love: having predestinated us unto the adoption of children by Jesus Christ to himself, according to the good pleasure of his will, to the praise of the glory of his grace, wherein he hath made us accepted in the beloved. In whom we have redemption through his blood, the forgiveness of sins, according to the riches of his grace; wherein he hath abounded toward us in all wisdom and prudence; having made known unto us the mystery of his will, according to his good pleasure which he hath purposed in himself: that in the dispensation of the fulness of times he might gather together in one all things in Christ, both which are in heaven, and which are on earth; even in him: in whom also we have obtained an inheritance, being predestinated according to the purpose of him who worketh all things after the counsel of his own will: that we should be to the praise of his glory, who first trusted in Christ. In whom ye also trusted, after that ye heard the word of truth, the gospel of your salvation: in whom also after that ye believed, ye were sealed with that holy Spirit of promise." (Ephesians 1:3-13)

The spiritual church, that is, the spiritual body of Christ without spot or blemish consists of those that worship [proskuneo: spiritually prostrate in homage, do reverence to, adore] God in spirit [pneuma: Holy Ghost] and in truth [aletheia: verity].

"The woman saith unto him, Sir, I perceive that thou art a prophet. Our fathers worshipped in this mountain; and ye say, that in Jerusalem is the place where men ought to worship. Jesus saith unto her, Woman, believe me, the hour cometh, when ye shall neither in this mountain, nor yet at Jerusalem, worship the Father. Ye worship ye know not what: we know what we worship: for salvation is of the Jews. But the hour cometh, and now is, when the true worshippers shall worship the Father in spirit and in truth: for the Father seeketh such to worship him. God is a Spirit: and they that worship him must worship him in spirit and in truth." (John 4:19-24)

"For as the body is one, and hath many members, and all the members of that one body, being many, are one body: so also is Christ. For by one Spirit are we all baptized into one body, whether we be Jews or Gentiles, whether we be bond or free; and have been all made to drink into one Spirit. For the body is not one member, but many. If the foot shall say, Because I am not the hand, I am not of the body; is it therefore not of the body? And if the ear shall say, Because I am not the eye, I am not of the body; is it therefore not of the body? If the whole body were an eye, where were the hearing? If the whole were hearing, where were the smelling? But now hath God set the members every one of them in the body, as it hath pleased him. And if they were all one member, where were the body? But now are they

many members, yet but one body. And the eye cannot say unto the hand, I have no need of thee: nor again the head to the feet, I have no need of you. Nay, much more those members of the body, which seem to be more feeble, are necessary: And those members of the body, which we think to be less honourable, upon these we bestow more abundant honour; and our uncomely parts have more abundant comeliness. For our comely parts have no need: but God hath tempered the body together, having given more abundant honour to that part which lacked: That there should be no schism in the body; but that the members should have the same care one for another. And whether one member suffer, all the members suffer with it; or one member be honoured, all the members rejoice with it. Now ye are the body of Christ, and members in particular. And God hath set some in the church, first apostles, secondarily prophets, thirdly teachers, after that miracles, then gifts of healings, helps, governments, diversities of tongues." (1 Corinthians 12:12-28)

"I therefore, the prisoner of the Lord, beseech you that ye walk worthy of the vocation wherewith ye are called, With all lowliness and meekness, with longsuffering, forbearing one another in love; Endeavouring to keep the unity of the Spirit in the bond of peace. There is one body, and one Spirit, even as ye are called in one hope of your calling; One Lord, one faith, one baptism, One God and Father of all, who is above all, and through all, and in you all." (Ephesians 4:1-6)

"Therefore as the church is subject unto Christ, so let the wives be to their own husbands in every thing. Husbands, love your wives, even as Christ also loved the church, and gave himself for it; That he might sanctify and cleanse it with the washing of water by the word, That he might present it to himself a glorious church, not having spot, or wrinkle, or any such thing; but that it should be holy and without blemish." (Ephesians 5:24-27)

God wants hearers and doers of the word not our "lip service".

"Wherefore lay apart all filthiness and superfluity of naughtiness, and receive with meekness the engrafted word, which is able to save your souls. But be ye doers of the word, and not hearers only, deceiving your own selves. For if any be a hearer of the word, and not a doer, he is like unto a man beholding his natural face in a glass: for he beholdeth himself, and goeth his way, and straightway forgetteth what manner of man he was. But whoso looketh into the perfect law of liberty, and continueth therein, he being not a forgetful hearer, but a doer of the work, this man shall be blessed in his deed." (James 1:21-25)

The spiritual body of Christ rather discerns [diakrino: be partial, differs, separates him thoroughly] Christ.

"For I determined not to know any thing among you, save Jesus Christ, and him crucified." (1 Corinthians 2:2)

"The cup of blessing which we bless, is it not the communion of the blood of Christ? The bread which we break, is it not the communion of the body of Christ? For we being many are one bread, and one body: for we are all partakers of that one bread." (1 Corinthians 10:16&17)

"For he that eateth and drinketh unworthily, eateth and drinketh damnation to himself, not discerning the Lord's body." (1 Corinthians 11:29)

The spiritual church is sound in the doctrine of Christ.

"Look to yourselves, that we lose not those things which we have wrought, but that we receive a full reward. Whosoever transgresseth, and abideth not in the doctrine of Christ, hath not God. He that abideth in the doctrine of Christ, he hath both the Father and the Son. If there come any unto you, and bring not this doctrine, receive him not into your house, neither bid him God speed: for he that biddeth him God speed is partaker of his evil deeds." (2 John 8-11)

"Preach the word; be instant in season, out of season; reprove, rebuke, exhort with all longsuffering and doctrine. For the time will come when they will not endure sound doctrine; but after their own lusts shall they heap to themselves teachers, having itching ears; and they shall turn away their ears from the truth, and shall be turned unto fables." (2 Timothy 4:2-4)

The spiritual church consists of a body of believers judged by God as servants of righteousness unto holiness.

"Likewise reckon ye also yourselves to be dead indeed unto sin, but alive unto God through Jesus Christ our Lord. Let not sin therefore reign in your mortal body, that ye should obey it in the lusts thereof. Neither yield ye your members as instruments of unrighteousness unto sin: but yield yourselves unto God, as those that are alive from the dead, and your members as instruments of righteousness unto God. For sin shall not have dominion over you: for ye are not under the law, but under grace. What then? Shall we sin, because we are not under the law, but under grace? God forbid. Know ye not, that to whom ye yield yourselves servants to obey, his servants ye are to whom ye obey; whether of sin unto death, or of obedience unto righteousness? But God be thanked, that ye were the servants of sin, but ye have obeyed from the heart that form of doctrine which was delivered you. Being then made free from sin, ye became the servants of righteousness. I speak after the manner of men because of the infirmity of your flesh: for as ye have yielded your members servants to uncleanness and to iniquity unto iniquity; even so now yield your members servants to righteousness unto holiness." (Romans 6:11-19)

"Wherefore gird up the loins of your mind, be sober, and hope to the end for the grace that is to be brought unto you at the revelation of Jesus Christ; as obedient children, not fashioning yourselves according to the former lusts in your ignorance: but as he which hath called you is holy, so be ye holy in all manner of conversation; because it is written, Be ye holy; for I am holy." (1 Peter 1:13-16)

The gates of hell shall not prevail against God's spiritual church not the visible church . The spiritual church is built upon the rock exhibited by Peter's faith.

"When Jesus came into the coasts of Caesarea Philippi, he asked said, Whom do men say that I the Son of man am? And they said, Some say that thou art John the Baptist: some, Elias; and others, Jeremias, or one of the prophets. He saith unto them, But whom say ye that I am? And Simon Peter answered and said, Thou art the Christ, the Son of the living God. And Jesus answered and said unto him, Blessed art thou, Simon Barjona: for flesh and blood hath not revealed it unto thee, but my Father which is in heaven. And I say also unto thee, That thou art Peter, and upon this rock I will build my church; and the gates of hell shall not prevail against it." (Matthew 16:13-18)

And Christ shall present the victorious spiritual church, his bride, to our heavenly Father as a chaste virgin without spot or blemish.

> *"Husbands, love your wives, even as Christ also loved the church, and gave himself for it; That he might sanctify and cleanse it with the washing of water by the word, That he might present it to himself a glorious church, not having spot, or wrinkle, or any such thing; but that it should be holy and without blemish."* **(Ephesians 5:25-27)**

> *"And I John saw the holy city, new Jerusalem, coming down from God out of heaven, prepared as a bride adorned for her husband. And I heard a great voice out of heaven saying, Behold, the tabernacle of God is with men, and he will dwell with them, and they shall be his people, and God himself shall be with them, and be their God. And God shall wipe away all tears from their eyes; and there shall be no more death, neither sorrow, nor crying, neither shall there be any more pain: for the former things are passed away."* **(Revelation 21:2-4)**

10

PREACHING, PREACHERS, MINISTERS AND THE CALLING (THE MAN OF GOD AND THE WOMAN OF GOD)

How does a person become a preacher of the Word of God? What can be expected in a "calling" to preach?

THE BIBLE QUESTIONS how shall the Jew and Gentiles (everybody) be made believers and learn to call on the name of the Lord except that they hear of the Lord via the preacher (Kerusso: public crier especially of diving truth, proclaimer of divine truth, publisher of divine truth (the gospel). Furthermore the preacher is sent (apostello; set-a-part, on a mission, put in, send forth, send out).

"For the scripture saith, Whosoever believeth on him shall not be ashamed. For there is no difference between the Jew and the Greek: for the same Lord over all is rich unto all that call upon him. For whosoever shall call upon the name of the Lord shall be saved. How then shall they call on him in whom they have not believed? and how shall they believe in him of whom they have not heard? and how shall they hear without a preacher? And how shall they preach, except they be sent? as it is written, How beautiful are the feet of them that preach the gospel of peace, and bring glad tidings of good things!" (Romans 10:11-15)

"What I tell you in darkness, that speak ye in light: and what ye hear in the ear, that preach ye upon the housetops." (Matthew 10:27)

God has chosen the "foolishness" of preaching by which faith comes to mankind by hearing the word of God proclaimed.

"For after that in the wisdom of God the world by wisdom knew not God, it pleased God by the foolishness of preaching to save them that believe. For the Jews require a sign, and the Greeks seek after wisdom: but we preach Christ crucified, unto the Jews a stumblingblock, and unto the Greeks foolishness; but unto them which are called, both Jews and Greeks, Christ the power of God, and the wisdom of God. Because the foolishness of God is wiser than men; and the weakness of God is stronger than men." (1 Corinthians 1:21-25)

"So then faith cometh by hearing, and hearing by the word of God." (Romans 10:17)

There is a calling (Klesis: and invitation, vocation) upon preaching. It is a constraint. It is a gift of God to some, for the edification of the body of believers, the church.

> *"For ye see your calling, brethren, how that not many wise men after the flesh, not many mighty, not many noble, are called: but God hath chosen the foolish things of the world to confound the wise; and God hath chosen the weak things of the world to confound the things which are mighty, And base things of the world, and things which are despised, hath God chosen, yea, and things which are not, to bring to nought things that are: That no flesh should glory in his presence."* (1 Corinthians 1:26-29)

> *"For if I do this thing willingly, I have a reward: but if against my will, a dispensation of the gospel is committed unto me. What is my reward then? Verily that, when I preach the gospel, I may make the gospel of Christ without charge, that I abuse not my power in the gospel. For though I be free from all men, yet have I made myself servant unto all, that I might gain the more."* (1 Corinthians 9:17-19)

> *"Therefore seeing we have this ministry, as we have received mercy, we faint not; but have renounced the hidden things of dishonesty, not walking in craftiness, nor handling the word of God deceitfully; but by manifestation of the truth commending ourselves to every man's conscience in the sight of God. But if our gospel be hid, it is hid to them that are lost: in whom the god of this world hath blinded the minds of them which believe not, lest the light of the glorious gospel of Christ, who is the image of God, should shine unto them. For we preach not ourselves, but Christ Jesus the Lord; and ourselves your servants for Jesus' sake. For God, who commanded the light to shine out of darkness, hath shined in our hearts, to give the light of the knowledge of the glory of God in the face of Jesus Christ. But we have this treasure in earthen vessels, that the excellency of the power may be of God, and not of us."* (2 Corinthians 4:1-7)

> *"For though I should boast somewhat more of our authority, which the Lord hath given us for edification, and not for your destruction, I should not be ashamed: that I may not seem as if I would terrify you by letters. For his letters, say they, are weighty and powerful; but his bodily presence is weak, and his speech contemptible."* (2 Corinthians 10:8-10)

> *"And I intreat thee also, true yokefellow, help those women which laboured with me in the gospel, with Clement also, and with other my fellowlabourers, whose names are in the book of life."* (Philippians 4:3)

Jesus establishes the preaching of the gospel when he appears in the temple at Nazareth and reads from the book of the prophet Isaiah. Notice that the last part of the Isaiah prophecy is yet to be fulfilled. Also, there is no further, messiah or revelation to come from God. This nullifies any further scriptural revelation according to the Bible.

> *"And Jesus returned in the power of the Spirit into Galilee: and there went out a fame of him through all the region round about. And he taught in their synagogues, being glorified of all. And he came to Nazareth, where he had been brought up: and, as his custom was, he went into the synagogue on the sabbath day, and stood up for to read. And there was delivered unto him the book of the prophet Esaias. And when he had opened the book, he found the place where it was written, the Spirit of the Lord is upon me, because he hath anointed me to preach the gospel to the poor; he hath sent me to heal the brokenhearted, to preach deliverance to the captives, and recovering of sight to the blind, to set at liberty*

them that are bruised, to preach the acceptable year of the Lord. And he closed the book, and he gave it again to the minister, and sat down. And the eyes of all them that were in the synagogue were fastened on him. And he began to say unto them, this day is this scripture fulfilled in your ears." (**Luke 4:14-21**)

"The Spirit of the Lord God is upon me; because the Lord hath anointed me to preach good tidings unto the meek; he hath sent me to bind up the brokenhearted, to proclaim liberty to the captives, and the opening of the prison to them that are bound; To proclaim the acceptable year of the Lord, and the day of vengeance of our God; to comfort all that mourn; To appoint unto them that mourn in Zion, to give unto them beauty for ashes, the oil of joy for mourning, the garment of praise for the spirit of heaviness; that they might be called trees of righteousness, the planting of the Lord, that he might be glorified." (**Isaiah 61:1-3**)

"And John calling unto him two of his disciples sent them to Jesus, saying, Art thou he that should come? or look we for another? When the men were come unto him, they said, John Baptist hath sent us unto thee, saying, Art thou he that should come? or look we for another? And in that same hour he cured many of their infirmities and plagues, and of evil spirits; and unto many that were blind he gave sight. Then Jesus answering said unto them, Go your way, and tell John what things ye have seen and heard; how that the blind see, the lame walk, the lepers are cleansed, the deaf hear, the dead are raised, to the poor the gospel is preached. And blessed is he, whosoever shall not be offended in me." (**Luke 7:19-23**)

"God is a Spirit: and they that worship him must worship him in spirit and in truth. The woman saith unto him, I know that Messias cometh, which is called Christ: when he is come, he will tell us all things. Jesus saith unto her, I that speak unto thee am he. And upon this came his disciples, and marvelled that he talked with the woman: yet no man said, What seekest thou? or, Why talkest thou with her? The woman then left her waterpot, and went her way into the city, and saith to the men, Come, see a man, which told me all things that ever I did: is not this the Christ?" (**John 4:25-29**)

"And now, O Father, glorify thou me with thine own self with the glory which I had with thee before the world was. I have manifested thy name unto the men which thou gavest me out of the world: thine they were, and thou gavest them me; and they have kept thy word. Now they have known that all things whatsoever thou hast given me are of thee. For I have given unto them the words which thou gavest me; and they have received them, and have known surely that I came out from thee, and they have believed that thou didst send me. I pray for them: I pray not for the world, but for them which thou hast given me; for they are thine. And all mine are thine, and thine are mine; and I am glorified in them. And now I am no more in the world, but these are in the world, and I come to thee. Holy Father, keep through thine own name those whom thou hast given me, that they may be one, as we are. While I was with them in the world, I kept them in thy name: those that thou gavest me I have kept, and none of them is lost, but the son of perdition; that the scripture might be fulfilled. And now come I to thee; and these things I speak in the world, that they might have my joy fulfilled in themselves. I have given them thy word; and the world hath hated them, because they are not of the world, even as I am not of the world. I pray not that thou shouldest take them out of the world, but that thou shouldest keep them from the evil. They are not of the world, even as I am not of the world. Sanctify them through thy truth: thy word is truth. As thou hast sent me into the world, even so have I also sent them into the world. And for their sakes I sanctify myself, that they also might be sanctified through the truth.

Neither pray I for these alone, but for them also which shall believe on me through their word; That they all may be one; as thou, Father, art in me, and I in thee, that they also may be one in us: that the world may believe that thou hast sent me. (John 17:5-21)

"The Revelation of Jesus Christ, which God gave unto him, to shew unto his servants things which must shortly come to pass; and he sent and signified it by his angel unto his servant John: Who bare record of the word of God, and of the testimony of Jesus Christ, and of all things that he saw. Blessed is he that readeth, and they that hear the words of this prophecy, and keep those things which are written therein: for the time is at hand. John to the seven churches which are in Asia: Grace be unto you, and peace, from him which is, and which was, and which is to come; and from the seven Spirits which are before his throne; And from Jesus Christ, who is the faithful witness, and the first begotten of the dead, and the prince of the kings of the earth. Unto him that loved us, and washed us from our sins in his own blood, And hath made us kings and priests unto God and his Father; to him be glory and dominion for ever and ever. Amen." (**Revelation 1:1-6**)

"And the Spirit and the bride say, Come. And let him that heareth say, Come. And let him that is athirst come. And whosoever will, let him take the water of life freely. For I testify unto every man that heareth the words of the prophecy of this book, If any man shall add unto these things, God shall add unto him the plagues that are written in this book: And if any man shall take away from the words of the book of this prophecy, God shall take away his part out of the book of life, and out of the holy city, and from the things which are written in this book. He which testifieth these things saith, Surely I come quickly. Amen. Even so, come, Lord Jesus." (**Revelation 22:17-21**)

Jesus provided an example of the spiritual calling upon men and women when he calls, ordains to preach and sends out the twelve and then the seventy notwithstanding that they were all men.

"Then he called his twelve disciples together, and gave them power and authority over all devils, and to cure diseases. And he sent them to preach the kingdom of God, and to heal the sick." (Luke 9:1-2)

And he ordained twelve, that they should be with him, and that he might send them forth to preach, And to have power to heal sicknesses, and to cast out devils: And Simon he surnamed Peter; And James the son of Zebedee, and John the brother of James; and he surnamed them Boanerges, which is, The sons of thunder: And Andrew, and Philip, and Bartholomew, and Matthew, and Thomas, and James the son of Alphaeus, and Thaddaeus, and Simon the Canaanite, And Judas Iscariot, which also betrayed him: and they went into an house. And the multitude cometh together again, so that they could not so much as eat bread. And when his friends heard of it, they went out to lay hold on him: for they said, He is beside himself." (**Mark 3:14-21**)

"These twelve Jesus sent forth, and commanded them, saying, Go not into the way of the Gentiles, and into any city of the Samaritans enter ye not: But go rather to the lost sheep of the house of Israel. And as ye go, preach, saying, The kingdom of heaven is at hand." (**Matthew 10:5-7**)

"After these things the Lord appointed other seventy also, and sent them two and two before his face into every city and place, whither he himself would come. Therefore said he

unto them, The harvest truly is great, but the labourers are few: pray ye therefore the Lord of the harvest, that he would send forth labourers into his harvest. Go your ways: behold, I send you forth as lambs among wolves. Carry neither purse, nor scrip, nor shoes: and salute no man by the way. And into whatsoever house ye enter, first say, Peace be to this house. And if the son of peace be there, your peace shall rest upon it: if not, it shall turn to you again. And in the same house remain, eating and drinking such things as they give: for the labourer is worthy of his hire. Go not from house to house. And into whatsoever city ye enter, and they receive you, eat such things as are set before you: And heal the sick that are therein, and say unto them, The kingdom of God is come nigh unto you." (Luke 10:1-9)

"Afterward he appeared unto the eleven as they sat at meat, and upbraided them with their unbelief and hardness of heart, because they believed not them which had seen him after he was risen. And he said unto them, Go ye into all the world, and preach the gospel to every creature. He that believeth and is baptized shall be saved; but he that believeth not shall be damned." (Mark 16:14-16)

Preaching has through the Holy Spirit, been given to men and women as it has pleased God. The overseeing of the church and the subsequent usurping of the man as the head in the church by the woman, is another issue (See Chapter 11, Pastors (Overseers)/Men, Women or Both).

"And ye shall know that I am in the midst of Israel, and that I am the Lord your God, and none else: and my people shall never be ashamed. And it shall come to pass afterward, that I will pour out my spirit upon all flesh; and your sons and your daughters shall prophesy, your old men shall dream dreams, your young men shall see visions: And also upon the servants and upon the handmaids in those days will I pour out my spirit." (Joel 2:27-29)

"And they were all amazed, and were in doubt, saying one to another, What meaneth this? Others mocking said, These men are full of new wine. But Peter, standing up with the eleven, lifted up his voice, and said unto them, Ye men of Judaea, and all ye that dwell at Jerusalem, be this known unto you, and hearken to my words: For these are not drunken, as ye suppose, seeing it is but the third hour of the day. But this is that which was spoken by the prophet Joel; And it shall come to pass in the last days, saith God,I will pour out of my Spirit upon all flesh: and your sons and your daughters shall prophesy, and your young men shall see visions, and your old men shall dream dreams: And on my servants and on my handmaidens I will pour out in those days of my Spirit; and they shall prophesy: And I will shew wonders in heaven above, and signs in the earth beneath; blood, and fire, and vapour of smoke:The sun shall be turned into darkness, and the moon into blood, before that great and notable day of the Lord come: And it shall come to pass, that whosoever shall call on the name of the Lord shall be saved." (Acts 2:12-21)

"And verily they that are of the sons of Levi, who receive the office of the priesthood, have a commandment to take tithes of the people according to the law, that is, of their brethren, though they come out of the loins of Abraham: but he whose descent is not counted from them received tithes of Abraham, and blessed him that had the promises." (Hebrews 7:5-6)

"For it is evident that our Lord sprang out of Juda; of which tribe Moses spake nothing concerning priesthood. And it is yet far more evident: for that after the similitude of Melchisedec there ariseth another priest, who is made, not after the law of a carnal com-

142

mandment, but after the power of an endless life. For he testifieth, Thou art a priest for ever after the order of Melchisedec...For there is verily a disannulling of the commandment going before for the weakness and unprofitableness thereof. By so much was Jesus made a surety of a better testament. And they truly were many priests, because they were not suffered to continue by reason of death: but this man, because he continueth ever, hath an unchangeable priesthood.” (Hebrews 7:14-18, 22-24)

“This is a true saying, If a man desire the office of a bishop, he desireth a good work. A bishop then must be blameless, the husband of one wife, vigilant, sober, of good behaviour, given to hospitality, apt to teach; Not given to wine, no striker, not greedy of filthy lucre; but patient, not a brawler, not covetous; One that ruleth well his own house, having his children in subjection with all gravity; (For if a man know not how to rule his own house, how shall he take care of the church of God?) Not a novice, lest being lifted up with pride he fall into the condemnation of the devil.” (1 Timothy 3:1-6)

“Let the woman learn in silence with all subjection. But I suffer not a woman to teach, nor to usurp authority over the man, but to be in silence. For Adam was first formed, then Eve.” (1 Timothy 2:11-13)

Prophesy (Propheteuo: to foretell events, speak under divine inspiration, exercise the prophetic office) is a gift given and there is no error in the desiring the gift of prophecy which is high among the spiritual gifts to the Church. Beware of the accountability that comes with the gift.

“Follow after charity, and desire spiritual gifts, but rather that ye may prophesy. For he that speaketh in an unknown tongue speaketh not unto men, but unto God: for no man understandeth him; howbeit in the spirit he speaketh mysteries. But he that prophesieth speaketh unto men to edification, and exhortation, and comfort. He that speaketh in an unknown tongue edifieth himself; but he that prophesieth edifieth the church.” (1 Corinthians 14:1-4)

“For as we have many members in one body, and all members have not the same office: so we, being many, are one body in Christ, and every one members one of another. Having then gifts differing according to the grace that is given to us, whether prophecy, let us prophesy according to the proportion of faith; or ministry, let us wait on our ministering: or he that teacheth, on teaching; or he that exhorteth, on exhortation: he that giveth, let him do it with simplicity; he that ruleth, with diligence; he that sheweth mercy, with cheerfulness.” (Romans 12: 4-8)

“Now there are diversities of gifts, but the same Spirit. And there are differences of administrations, but the same Lord. And there are diversities of operations, but it is the same God which worketh all in all. But the manifestation of the Spirit is given to every man to profit withal. For to one is given by the Spirit the word of wisdom; to another the word of knowledge by the same Spirit; to another faith by the same Spirit; to another the gifts of healing by the same Spirit; to another the working of miracles; to another prophecy; to another discerning of spirits; to another divers kinds of tongues; to another the interpretation of tongues: but all these worketh that one and the selfsame Spirit, dividing to every man severally as he will. For as the body is one, and hath many members, and all the members of that one body, being many, are one body: so also is Christ. For by one Spirit are we all

baptized into one body, whether we be Jews or Gentiles, whether we be bond or free; and have been all made to drink into one Spirit." (**1 Corinthians 12:4-13**)

"Now ye are the body of Christ, and members in particular. And God hath set some in the church, first apostles, secondarily prophets, thirdly teachers, after that miracles, then gifts of healings, helps, governments, diversities of tongues. Are all apostles? Are all prophets? Are all teachers? Are all workers of miracles? Have all the gifts of healing? Do all speak with tongues? Do all interpret? But covet earnestly the best gifts: and yet shew I unto you a more excellent way." (**1 Corinthians 12: 27-31**)

"Remember them which have the rule over you, who have spoken unto you the word of God: whose faith follow, considering the end of their conversation. Jesus Christ the same yesterday, and to day, and for ever. Be not carried about with divers and strange doctrines. For it is a good thing that the heart be established with grace; not with meats, which have not profited them that have been occupied therein. We have an altar, whereof they have no right to eat which serve the tabernacle. For the bodies of those beasts, whose blood is brought into the sanctuary by the high priest for sin, are burned without the camp. Wherefore Jesus also, that he might sanctify the people with his own blood, suffered without the gate. Let us go forth therefore unto him without the camp, bearing his reproach. For here have we no continuing city, but we seek one to come. By him therefore let us offer the sacrifice of praise to God continually, that is, the fruit of our lips giving thanks to his name. But to do good and to communicate forget not: for with such sacrifices God is well pleased. Obey them that have the rule over you, and submit yourselves: for they watch for your souls, as they that must give account, that they may do it with joy, and not with grief: for that is unprofitable for you." (**Hebrew 13: 7-17**)

Again, there is a calling associated with the gift of prophecy/preaching.

"Wherefore the rather, brethren, give diligence to make your calling and election sure: for if ye do these things, ye shall never fall: For so an entrance shall be ministered unto you abundantly into the everlasting kingdom of our Lord and Saviour Jesus Christ. Wherefore I will not be negligent to put you always in remembrance of these things, though ye know them, and be established in the present truth. Yea, I think it meet, as long as I am in this tabernacle, to stir you up by putting you in remembrance; Knowing that shortly I must put off this my tabernacle, even as our Lord Jesus Christ hath shewed me. Moreover I will endeavour that ye may be able after my decease to have these things always in remembrance. For we have not followed cunningly devised fables, when we made known unto you the power and coming of our Lord Jesus Christ, but were eyewitnesses of his majesty. For he received from God the Father honour and glory, when there came such a voice to him from the excellent glory, This is my beloved Son, in whom I am well pleased. And this voice which came from heaven we heard, when we were with him in the holy mount. We have also a more sure word of prophecy; whereunto ye do well that ye take heed, as unto a light that shineth in a dark place, until the day dawn, and the day star arise in your hearts: Knowing this first, that no prophesy of scripture is of any private interpretation." (**2 Peter 1: 10-20**)

"Wherefore, holy brethren, partakers of the heavenly calling, consider the Apostle and High Priest of our profession, Christ Jesus; who was faithful to him that appointed him, as also Moses was faithful in all his house. For this man was counted worthy of more glory than Moses, inasmuch as he who hath builded the house hath more honour than the house. For

every house is builded by some man; but he that built all things is God. And Moses verily was faithful in all his house, as a servant, for a testimony of those things which were to be spoken after; but Christ as a son over his own house; whose house are we, if we hold fast the confidence and the rejoicing of the hope firm unto the end." (Hebrews 3: 1-6)

The ministry of preaching is to be to the point of the biblical Jesus, rather than anything convoluted, as God has given differing preaching abilities.

"For I am jealous over you with godly jealousy: for I have espoused you to one husband, that I may present you as a chaste virgin to Christ. But I fear, lest by any means, as the serpent beguiled Eve through his subtilty, so your minds should be corrupted from the simplicity that is in Christ." (2 Corinthians 11:3)

"If any man speak, let him speak as the oracles of God; if any man minister, let him do it as of the ability which God giveth: that God in all things may be glorified through Jesus Christ, to whom be praise and dominion for ever and ever. Amen." (1 Peter 4:11)

The Bible provides examples of the calling to preach process. One of the most detailed accounts is with regard to Paul. The calling of Samuel, Jonah, Isaiah and Joshua are provided as well. I have attached Appendix 6, My Calling, as a personal testimony of the process. Obviously the process can vary; however, it is always spiritual. If you are called, then preach. If you are not called, then leave it alone; this includes becoming a priest because they deliver sermons.

"And Saul, yet breathing out threatenings and slaughter against the disciples of the Lord, went unto the high priest, And desired of him letters to Damascus to the synagogues, that if he found any of this way, whether they were men or women, he might bring them bound unto Jerusalem. And as he journeyed, he came near Damascus: and suddenly there shined round about him a light from heaven: And he fell to the earth, and heard a voice saying unto him, Saul, Saul, why persecutest thou me? And he said, Who art thou, Lord? And the Lord said, I am Jesus whom thou persecutest: it is hard for thee to kick against the pricks. And he trembling and astonished said, Lord, what wilt thou have me to do? And the Lord said unto him, Arise, and go into the city, and it shall be told thee what thou must do... And there was a certain disciple at Damascus, named Ananias; and to him said the Lord in a vision, Ananias. And he said, Behold, I am here, Lord. And the Lord said unto him, Arise, and go into the street which is called Straight, and inquire in the house of Judas for one called Saul, of Tarsus: for, behold, he prayeth, And hath seen in a vision a man named Ananias coming in, and putting his hand on him, that he might receive his sight. Then Ananias answered, Lord, I have heard by many of this man, how much evil he hath done to thy saints at Jerusalem: And here he hath authority from the chief priests to bind all that call on thy name. But the Lord said unto him, Go thy way: for he is a chosen vessel unto me, to bear my name before the Gentiles, and kings, and the children of Israel: For I will shew him how great things he must suffer for my name's sake. And Ananias went his way, and entered into the house; and putting his hands on him said, Brother Saul, the Lord, even Jesus, that appeared unto thee in the way as thou camest, hath sent me, that thou mightest receive thy sight, and be filled with the Holy Ghost...And straightway he preached Christ in the synagogues, that he is the Son of God." (Acts 9: 1-6, 10-17, 20)

"Yea doubtless, and I count all things but loss for the excellency of the knowledge of Christ Jesus my Lord: for whom I have suffered the loss of all things, and do count them but dung,

that I may win Christ, and be found in him, not having mine own righteousness, which is of the law, but that which is through the faith of Christ, the righteousness which is of God by faith: that I may know him, and the power of his resurrection, and the fellowship of his sufferings, being made conformable unto his death; if by any means I might attain unto the resurrection of the dead. Not as though I had already attained, either were already perfect: but I follow after, if that I may apprehend that for which also I am apprehended of Christ Jesus. Brethren, I count not myself to have apprehended: but this one thing I do, forgetting those things which are behind, and reaching forth unto those things which are before, I press toward the mark for the prize of the high calling of God in Christ Jesus." **(Philippians 3:8-14)**

"For God hath not given us the spirit of fear; but of power, and of love, and of a sound mind. Be not thou therefore ashamed of the testimony of our Lord, nor of me his prisoner: but be thou partaker of the afflictions of the gospel according to the power of God; Who hath saved us, and called us with an holy calling, not according to our works, but according to his own purpose and grace, which was given us in Christ Jesus before the world began, But is now made manifest by the appearing of our Saviour Jesus Christ, who hath abolished death, and hath brought life and immortality to light through the gospel: Whereunto I am appointed a preacher, and an apostle, and a teacher of the Gentiles. For the which cause I also suffer these things: nevertheless I am not ashamed: for I know whom I have believed, and am persuaded that he is able to keep that which I have committed unto him against that day. Hold fast the form of sound words, which thou hast heard of me, in faith and love which is in Christ Jesus. That good thing which was committed unto thee keep by the Holy Ghost which dwelleth in us." **(2 Timothy 1: 7-14)**

"And it came to pass at that time, when Eli was laid down in his place, and his eyes began to wax dim, that he could not see; and ere the lamp of God went out in the temple of the Lord, where the ark of God was, and Samuel was laid down to sleep; that the Lord called Samuel: and he answered, Here am I. And he ran unto Eli, and said, Here am I; for thou calledst me. And he said, I called not; lie down again. And he went and lay down. And the Lord called yet again, Samuel. And Samuel arose and went to Eli, and said, Here am I; for thou didst call me. And he answered, I called not, my son; lie down again. Now Samuel did not yet know the Lord, neither was the word of the Lord yet revealed unto him. And the Lord called Samuel again the third time. And he arose and went to Eli, and said, Here am I; for thou didst call me. And Eli perceived that the Lord had called the child. Therefore Eli said unto Samuel, Go, lie down: and it shall be, if he call thee, that thou shalt say, Speak, Lord; for thy servant heareth. So Samuel went and lay down in his place. And the Lord came, and stood, and called as at other times, Samuel, Samuel. Then Samuel answered, Speak; for thy servant heareth. And the Lord said to Samuel, Behold, I will do a thing in Israel, at which both the ears of every one that heareth it shall tingle." **(1 Samuel 3:2-11)**

"Now the word of the Lord came unto Jonah the son of Amittai, saying, Arise, go to Nineveh, that great city, and cry against it; for their wickedness is come up before me. But Jonah rose up to flee unto Tarshish from the presence of the Lord, and went down to Joppa; and he found a ship going to Tarshish: so he paid the fare thereof, and went down into it, to go with them unto Tarshish from the presence of the Lord." **(Jonah 1: 1-3)**

"In the year that king Uzziah died I saw also the Lord sitting upon a throne, high and lifted up, and his train filled the temple. Above it stood the seraphims: each one had six wings;

with twain he covered his face, and with twain he covered his feet, and with twain he did fly. And one cried unto another, and said, Holy, holy, holy, is the Lord of hosts: the whole earth is full of his glory. And the posts of the door moved at the voice of him that cried, and the house was filled with smoke. Then said I, Woe is me! for I am undone; because I am a man of unclean lips, and I dwell in the midst of a people of unclean lips: for mine eyes have seen the King, the Lord of hosts. Then flew one of the seraphims unto me, having a live coal in his hand, which he had taken with the tongs from off the altar: And he laid it upon my mouth, and said, Lo, this hath touched thy lips; and thine iniquity is taken away, and thy sin purged. Also I heard the voice of the Lord, saying, Whom shall I send, and who will go for us? Then said I, Here am I; send me. And he said, Go, and tell this people, Hear ye indeed, but understand not; and see ye indeed, but perceive not. Make the heart of this people fat, and make their ears heavy, and shut their eyes; lest they see with their eyes, and hear with their ears, and understand with their heart, and convert, and be healed. Then said I, Lord, how long? And he answered, Until the cities be wasted without inhabitant, and the houses without man, and the land be utterly desolate, And the Lord have removed men far away, and there be a great forsaking in the midst of the land. But yet in it shall be a tenth, and it shall return, and shall be eaten: as a teil tree, and as an oak, whose substance is in them, when they cast their leaves: so the holy seed shall be the substance thereof." (Isaiah Chapter 6)

"And he shewed me Joshua the high priest standing before the angel of the Lord, and Satan standing at his right hand to resist him. And the Lord said unto Satan, The Lord rebuke thee, O Satan; even the Lord that hath chosen Jerusalem rebuke thee: is not this a brand plucked out of the fire? Now Joshua was clothed with filthy garments, and stood before the angel. And he answered and spake unto those that stood before him, saying, Take away the filthy garments from him. And unto him he said, Behold, I have caused thine iniquity to pass from thee, and I will clothe thee with change of raiment. And I said, Let them set a fair mitre upon his head. So they set a fair mitre upon his head, and clothed him with garments. And the angel of the Lord stood by. And the angel of the Lord protested unto Joshua, saying, thus saith the Lord of hosts; If thou wilt walk in my ways, and if thou wilt keep my charge, then thou shalt also judge my house, and shalt also keep my courts, and I will give thee places to walk among these that stand by." (Zechariah 3: 1-7)

"For though I preach the gospel, I have nothing to glory of: for necessity is laid upon me; yea, woe is unto me, if I preach not the gospel!" (1 Corinthians 9:16)

"Neglect not the gift that is in thee, which was given thee by prophecy, with the laying on of the hands of the presbytery. Meditate upon these things; give thyself wholly to them; that thy profiting may appear to all. Take heed unto thyself, and unto the doctrine; continue in them: for in doing this thou shalt both save thyself, and them that hear thee. " (1 Timothy 4:14-16)

Preach at all times what God has revealed without regard for what people may think or say. Be the evangelist (euggelistes: preacher of the gospel, declare glad tidings) as well. This is the biblical charge to the preacher.

"I charge thee therefore before God, and the Lord Jesus Christ, who shall judge the quick and the dead at his appearing and his kingdom; Preach the word; be instant in season, out of season; reprove, rebuke, exhort with all longsuffering and doctrine. For the time will

come when they will not endure sound doctrine; but after their own lusts shall they heap to themselves teachers, having itching ears; And they shall turn away their ears from the truth, and shall be turned unto fables. But watch thou in all things, endure afflictions, do the work of an evangelist, make full proof of thy ministry." (**2 Timothy 4: 1-5**)

"For now will I break his yoke from off thee, and will burst thy bonds in sunder. And the Lord hath given a commandment concerning thee, that no more of thy name be sown: out of the house of thy gods will I cut off the graven image and the molten image: I will make thy grave; for thou art vile. Behold upon the mountains the feet of him that bringeth good tidings, that publisheth peace! O Judah, keep thy solemn feasts, perform thy vows: for the wicked shall no more pass through thee; he is utterly cut off." (**Nahum 1:13-15**)

"And how shall they preach, except they be sent? As it is written, how beautiful are the feet of them that preach the gospel of peace, and bring glad tidings of good things!" (**Romans 10:15**)

"For thus saith the Lord God, My people went down aforetime into Egypt to sojourn there; and the Assyrian oppressed them without cause. Now therefore, what have I here, saith the Lord, that my people is taken away for nought? they that rule over them make them to howl, saith the Lord; and my name continually every day is blasphemed. Therefore my people shall know my name: therefore they shall know in that day that I am he that doth speak: behold, it is I. How beautiful upon the mountains are the feet of him that bringeth good tidings, that publisheth peace; that bringeth good tidings of good, that publisheth salvation; that saith unto Zion, Thy God reigneth!" (**Isaiah 52: 4-7**)

Preachers are to preach about Christ and the salvation in his life, death, burial, resurrection and doctrine.

"And he said unto them, These are the words which I spake unto you, while I was yet with you, that all things must be fulfilled, which were written in the law of Moses, and in the prophets, and in the psalms, concerning me. Then opened he their understanding, that they might understand the scriptures, And said unto them, Thus it is written, and thus it behoved Christ to suffer, and to rise from the dead the third day: And that repentance and remission of sins should be preached in his name among all nations, beginning at Jerusalem." (**Luke 24:44-47**)

"Use hospitality one to another without grudging. As every man hath received the gift, even so minister the same one to another, as good stewards of the manifold grace of God. If any man speak, let him speak as the oracles of God; if any man minister, let him do it as of the ability which God giveth: that God in all things may be glorified through Jesus Christ, to whom be praise and dominion for ever and ever. Amen. Beloved, think it not strange concerning the fiery trial which is to try you, as though some strange thing happened unto you: But rejoice, inasmuch as ye are partakers of Christ's sufferings; that, when his glory shall be revealed, ye may be glad also with exceeding joy. If ye be reproached for the name of Christ, happy are ye; for the spirit of glory and of God resteth upon you: on their part he is evil spoken of, but on your part he is glorified." (**1 Peter 4: 9-14**)

Let the elders that rule well be counted worthy of double honour, especially they who labour in the word and doctrine." (**1 Timothy 5:17**)

Preachers are in touch with God as God has ordained with the exception of the situation in the case of Moses as declared by the Bible.

"And Miriam and Aaron spake against Moses because of the Ethiopian woman whom he had married: for he had married an Ethiopian woman. And they said, Hath the Lord indeed spoken only by Moses? hath he not spoken also by us? And the Lord heard it. (Now the man Moses was very meek, above all the men which were upon the face of the earth.) And the Lord spake suddenly unto Moses, and unto Aaron, and unto Miriam, Come out ye three unto the tabernacle of the congregation. And they three came out. And the Lord came down in the pillar of the cloud, and stood in the door of the tabernacle, and called Aaron and Miriam: and they both came forth. And he said, Hear now my words: If there be a prophet among you, I the Lord will make myself known unto him in a vision, and will speak unto him in a dream. My servant Moses is not so, who is faithful in all mine house. With him will I speak mouth to mouth, even apparently, and not in dark speeches; and the similitude of the Lord shall he behold: wherefore then were ye not afraid to speak against my servant Moses?" (Numbers 12:1-8)

Now, there are false preachers and hirelings among us. They scatter the flock. They have gone and were not sent. They speak even though they have been told nothing to say. Jesus has never really known them. Even as Satan can transform himself, there are false prophets transformed into pulpits today.

"Woe be unto the pastors that destroy and scatter the sheep of my pasture! saith the Lord. Therefore thus saith the Lord God of Israel against the pastors that feed my people; Ye have scattered my flock, and driven them away, and have not visited them: behold, I will visit upon you the evil of your doings, saith the Lord." (Jeremiah 23:1-2)

"But there were false prophets also among the people, even as there shall be false teachers among you, who privily shall bring in damnable heresies, even denying the Lord that bought them, and bring upon themselves swift destruction. And many shall follow their pernicious ways; by reason of whom the way of truth shall be evil spoken of. And through covetousness shall they with feigned words make merchandise of you: whose judgment now of a long time lingereth not, and their damnation slumbereth not." (2 Peter 2:1-3)

"For thus saith the Lord of hosts, the God of Israel; Let not your prophets and your diviners, that be in the midst of you, deceive you, neither hearken to your dreams which ye cause to be dreamed. For they prophesy falsely unto you in my name: I have not sent them, saith the Lord." (Jeremiah 29:8-9)

"Beware of false prophets, which come to you in sheep's clothing, but inwardly they are ravening wolves. Ye shall know them by their fruits. Do men gather grapes of thorns, or figs of thistles? Even so every good tree bringeth forth good fruit; but a corrupt tree bringeth forth evil fruit. A good tree cannot bring forth evil fruit, neither can a corrupt tree bring forth good fruit. Every tree that bringeth not forth good fruit is hewn down, and cast into the fire. Wherefore by their fruits ye shall know them. Not every one that saith unto me, Lord, Lord, shall enter into the kingdom of heaven; but he that doeth the will of my Father which is in heaven. Many will say to me in that day, Lord, Lord, have we not prophesied in thy name? and in thy name have cast out devils? and in thy name done many wonderful works? And then will I profess unto them, I never knew you: depart from me, ye that work iniquity." (Matthew 7: 15-23)

"I am the good shepherd: the good shepherd giveth his life for the sheep. But he that is an hireling, and not the shepherd, whose own the sheep are not, seeth the wolf coming, and leaveth the sheep, and fleeth: and the wolf catcheth them, and scattereth the sheep. The hireling fleeth, because he is an hireling, and careth not for the sheep." (John 10:11-13)

"For such are false apostles, deceitful workers, transforming themselves into the apostles of Christ. And no marvel; for Satan himself is transformed into an angel of light. Therefore it is no great thing if his ministers also be transformed as the ministers of righteousness; whose end shall be according to their works." (2 Corinthians 11:13-15)

But the true man or woman of God is to labor, suffer and warn the people of their sins as did the Apostle Paul and even as Jonas. And, God's ministers are to be energized by the Holy Ghost.

"Whereof I am made a minister, according to the dispensation of God which is given to me for you, to fulfil the word of God; Even the mystery which hath been hid from ages and from generations, but now is made manifest to his saints: To whom God would make known what is the riches of the glory of this mystery among the Gentiles; which is Christ in you, the hope of glory: Whom we preach, warning every man, and teaching every man in all wisdom; that we may present every man perfect in Christ Jesus: Whereunto I also labour, striving according to his working, which worketh in me mightily." (Colossians 1: 25-29)

"Then certain of the scribes and of the Pharisees answered, saying, Master, we would see a sign from thee. But he answered and said unto them, An evil and adulterous generation seeketh after a sign; and there shall no sign be given to it, but the sign of the prophet Jonas: For as Jonas was three days and three nights in the whale's belly; so shall the Son of man be three days and three nights in the heart of the earth. The men of Nineveh shall rise in judgment with this generation, and shall condemn it: because they repented at the preaching of Jonas; and, behold, a greater than Jonas is here." (Matthew 12: 38-41)

"And every one that hath forsaken houses, or brethren, or sisters, or father, or mother, or wife, or children, or lands, for my name's sake, shall receive an hundredfold, and shall inherit everlasting life. But many that are first shall be last; and the last shall be first." (Matthew 19: 29&30)

"And it came to pass, that, as they went in the way, a certain man said unto him, Lord, I will follow thee whithersoever thou goest. And Jesus said unto him, Foxes have holes, and birds of the air have nests; but the Son of man hath not where to lay his head. And he said unto another, Follow me. But he said, Lord, suffer me first to go and bury my father. Jesus said unto him, Let the dead bury their dead: but go thou and preach the kingdom of God. And another also said, Lord, I will follow thee; but let me first go bid them farewell, which are at home at my house. And Jesus said unto him, No man, having put his hand to the plough, and looking back, is fit for the kingdom of God." (Luke 9: 57-62)

"And of the angels he saith, Who maketh his angels spirits, and his ministers a flame of fire." (Hebrews 1:7)

Good ministers (attendant waiter in the menial duties, Servant, Teacher, Pastor of Jesus Christ) are to be good examples rather the lords over the flock. The Bible notes the good example of a minister as being in the Word (Logos: the divine expression (Christ) con-

cerning doctrine, reasoning speech), conversation (Anastrophe: behavior), charity (Agape: Affection, Benevolence, Love), spirit (Pneuma: Christ's Spirit, the Holy Spirit, Holy Ghost), faith (Pistis: reliance upon Christ for salvation, assurance in Christ, belief in Christ), purity (hagenia: cleanliness, chastity), reading (anagnosis: act of reading) and exhortation (paraklesis: comfort, consolation, intreaty). It is also ordained by God that those that preach the gospel should be able to be supported by that endeavor.

"And whosoever will be chief among you, let him be your servant: Even as the Son of man came not to be ministered unto, but to minister, and to give his life a ransom for many." (Matthew 20:27&28)

"This is a true saying, If a man desire the office of a bishop, he desireth a good work. A bishop then must be blameless, the husband of one wife, vigilant, sober, of good behaviour, given to hospitality, apt to teach; Not given to wine, no striker, not greedy of filthy lucre; but patient, not a brawler, not covetous; One that ruleth well his own house, having his children in subjection with all gravity; (For if a man know not how to rule his own house, how shall he take care of the church of God?)" (1 Timothy 3: 1-5)

"The elders which are among you I exhort, who am also an elder, and a witness of the sufferings of Christ, and also a partaker of the glory that shall be revealed: Feed the flock of God which is among you, taking the oversight thereof, not by constraint, but willingly; not for filthy lucre, but of a ready mind; Neither as being lords over God's heritage, but being ensamples to the flock. And when the chief Shepherd shall appear, ye shall receive a crown of glory that fadeth not away. (1 Peter 5:1-4)

"For therefore we both labour and suffer reproach, because we trust in the living God, who is the Saviour of all men, specially of those that believe. These things command and teach. Let no man despise thy youth; but be thou an example of the believers, in word, in conversation, in charity, in spirit, in faith, in purity. Till I come, give attendance to reading, to exhortation, to doctrine." (1 Timothy 4:10-13)

"Do ye not know that they which minister about holy things live of the things of the temple? And they which wait at the alter are partakers with the alter? Even so hath the Lord ordained that they which preach the gospel should live of the gospel." (1 Corinthians 9:13-14)

"After these things the Lord appointed other seventy also, and sent them two and two before his face into every city and place, whither he himself would come. Therefore said he unto them, The harvest truly is great, but the labourers are few: pray ye therefore the Lord of the harvest, that he would send forth labourers into his harvest. Go your ways: behold, I send you forth as lambs among wolves. Carry neither purse, nor scrip, nor shoes: and salute no man by the way. And into whatsoever house ye enter, first say, Peace be to this house. And if the son of peace be there, your peace shall rest upon it: if not, it shall turn to you again. And in the same house remain, eating and drinking such things as they give: for the labourer is worthy of his hire. Go not from house to house. And into whatsoever city ye enter, and they receive you, eat such things as are set before you: And heal the sick that are therein, and say unto them, The kingdom of God is come nigh unto you." (Luke 10:1-9)

"For the scripture saith, Thou shalt not muzzle the ox that treadeth out the corn. And, The labourer is worthy of his reward." (1 Timothy 5:18)

The Bible points to the bad example and the "marking" (skopeo: take aim at, regard, consider, take heed, look at) of that bad example of a minister.

> *"Brethren, be followers together of me, and mark them which walk so as ye have us for an ensample. (For many walk, of whom I have told you often, and now tell you even weeping, that they are the enemies of the cross of Christ: whose end is destruction, whose God is their belly, and whose glory is in their shame, who mind earthly things.)"* (Philippians 3: 17-19)

> *"But though we, or an angel from heaven, preach any other gospel unto you than that which we have preached unto you, let him be accursed. As we said before, so say I now again, If any man preach any other gospel unto you than that ye have received, let him be accursed."* (Galatians 1: 8-9)

The ordaining of ministers is left to those that have been called by God and followed in the long succession of others in the ministry since the Apostles of Jesus. As an historical fact that Jesus existed and so did these specific Apostles. God does the calling and those called and established in serving do the ordaining.

> *"Paul, a servant of God, and an apostle of Jesus Christ, according to the faith of God's elect, and the acknowledging of the truth which is after godliness; In hope of eternal life, which God, that cannot lie, promised before the world began; But hath in due times manifested his word through preaching, which is committed unto me according to the commandment of God our Saviour; To Titus, mine own son after the common faith: Grace, mercy, and peace, from God the Father and the Lord Jesus Christ our Saviour. For this cause left I thee in Crete, that thou shouldest set in order the things that are wanting, and ordain elders in every city, as I had appointed thee:"* (Titus 1:1-5)

> *"I charge thee before God, and the Lord Jesus Christ, and the elect angels, that thou observe these things without preferring one before another, doing nothing by partiality. Lay hands suddenly on no man, neither be partaker of other men's sins: keep thyself pure."* (1 Timothy 5:21&22)

The world should be very careful in its treatment of the preacher of the gospel.

> *"And when they went from nation to nation, and from one kingdom to another people; He suffered no man to do them wrong: yea, he reproved kings for their sakes, Saying, Touch not mine anointed, and do my prophets no harm."* (1 Chronicles 16:20-22)

11

PASTORS (OVERSEERS)/MEN, WOMEN OR BOTH

What does the Bible say; should women be Pastors?

The Position of Christ and Men in the Church

God (the Father) is the head of Christ and Christ should be head of every man. The head of the woman is the man.

> *"But I would have you know, that the head of every man is Christ; and the head of every woman is the man; and the head of Christ is God."* (1 Corinthians 11:3)

The scriptures reveal that there is in creation by God's divine order, a fundamental difference between men and women; the man is first in creation.

> *"And the Lord God caused a deep sleep to fall upon Adam, and he slept; and he took one of his ribs, and closed up the flesh instead thereof; and the rib, which the Lord God had taken from man, made he a woman, and brought her unto the man. And Adam said, This is now bone of my bones, and flesh of my flesh; she shall be called Woman because she was taken out of man."* (Genesis 2:21-23)

> *"For the man is not of the woman; but the woman of the man. Neither was the man created for the woman, but the woman for the man."* (1 Corinthians 11:8&9)

Man is created in image and glory of God the woman is the glory of man.

> *"For the man indeed ought not to cover his head, forasmuch as he is the image of the glory of God; but the woman is the glory for the man."* (1 Corinthians 11:7)

> *"And the Lord said, it is not good that the man should be alone; I will make him a help meet for him."* (Genesis 2:18)

The husband is the head of the wife just as Christ is the head of the Church.

"For the husband is the head of the wife, even as Christ is the head of the church; and he is the savior of the body." Therefore as the church is subject unto Christ, so let the wives be to their own husbands in every thing." (Ephesians 5:23&24)

The scriptures reveal the woman to be the weaker (asthenes: more feeble, impotent, sick, without as much strength) of the two vessels, male and female.

"Likewise, ye husbands dwell with them according to knowledge, giving honor unto the wife, as unto the weaker vessel, and as being heirs together of the grace of life; that your prayers be not hindered." (1 Peter 3:7)

There is a biblical reason for the God given esteem of the man in the church.

"For Adam was first formed then Eve. And Adam was not deceived, but the woman being deceived was in the transgression." (1 Timothy 2:13&14)

Sign of the Times

The Bible speaks of an apostasy in the latter days; a time of a falling away from the truth for reasons such as persecution, false teachers, temptation, worldliness, as well as other reasons to include unbelief and the forsaking of spiritual living. In all of these situations, some shall depart from faith and therefore will not accept the sound doctrine that is taught and accepted in the church.

"Now the Spirit speaketh expressly, that in the latter times some shall depart from the faith, giving heed to seducing spirits, and doctrines of devils." (1 Timothy 4:1)

The inclination by individuals in the latter days shall be towards the selecting of what they want to hear rather than an inclination towards the hearing of sound doctrine.

"Preach the word; be instant in season, out of season; reprove, rebuke, exhort with all long-suffering and doctrine. For the time will come when they will not endure sound doctrine; but after their own lusts shall they heap unto themselves teachers, having itching ears; and they shall turn away their ears from the truth, and shall be turned unto fables." (2 Timothy 4:2-4)

Lean not on our own understanding. We should not suspect that God is confused with regard to gender nor should he rather be held to man's doctrine of equal opportunity with its tendencies towards a unisex outlook upon men and women.

"Trust in the Lord with all thine heart; and lean not unto thine own understanding. In all thy ways acknowledge him, and he shall direct thy paths. Be not wise in thine own eyes: fear the Lord, and depart from evil." (Proverbs 3:5-7)

Doctrine is vital to our walk in Christ and our reconciliation to our heavenly Father.

"For a bishop must be blameless, as the steward of God; not self-willed, not soon angry, not given to wine, no striker, not given to filthy lucre; but a lover of hospitality, a lover of good men, sober, just, holy temperate; holding fast the faithful word as he hath been taught,

that he may be able to sound doctrine both to exhort and to convince the gainsayers." (1 Titus 1:7-9)

"Whosoever transgresseth, and abideth not in the doctrine of Christ, hath not God. He that abideth in the doctrine of Christ, he hath both the Father and the Son. If there come unto you, and bring not this doctrine, receive him not into your house, neither bid him God speed." (2 John 9&10)

Least we forget, <u>for the truth</u>, our reliance <u>must</u> be upon the scriptures knowing their origin, purpose and the Holy Ghost as unifier in interpretation.

"These were more noble than those in Thessalonica, in that they received the word with all readiness of mind, and searched the scriptures daily, whether those things were so." (Acts 17:11) *"All scripture is given by inspiration of God, and is profitable for doctrine, for reproof, for correction, for instruction in righteousness: That the man of God may be perfect, throughly furnished unto all good works."* (2 Timothy 3:16&17)

"Knowing this first, that no prophecy of the scripture is of any private interpretation. For the prophecy came not in old time by the will of man: but holy men of God spake as they were moved by the Holy Ghost." (2 Peter 1:20&21)

"Study to shew thyself approved unto God, a workman that needeth not be ashamed, rightly dividing the word of truth. " 2 Timothy 2:15

Did not Isaiah say "build precept upon precept and line upon line"? Therein is the implication that the truth in the scriptures is revealed spiritually and not by our private interpretations. In many cases, we must surround a particular scripture with a body of scriptural evidence to reveal the spiritual truth. If this cannot be done, something is most probably wrong with the interpretation.

"Whom shall he teach knowledge? And whom shall he make to understand doctrine? Then that are weaned from milk, and drawn from the breasts. For precept must be upon precept, precept upon precept; line upon line, line upon line; here a little and there a little. For with stammering lips and another tongue will he speak to this people? To whom he said, this is the rest wherewith ye cause the weary to rest; and this is the refreshing; yet they would not hear. But the word of the Lord was unto them precept upon precept; line upon line; here a little, and there a little; that they might go, and fall backward, and be broken, and snared, and taken. Wherefore hear the word of the Lord, ye scornful men, that rule this people, which is in Jerusalem. Because ye have said, we have made a covenant with death, and with hell are we at agreement; when the overflowing scourge shall pass through, it shall not come unto us; for we have made lies our refuge, and under falsehood have we hid ourselves." (Isaiah 28:9-15)

Definitions to be Relied upon for a Deeper Scriptural Understanding

(All definitions from Strong's Exhaustive Concordance of the Bible)
priest:
> **kohen** (Hebrew Old Testament) – one officiating, a priest, an acting priest, chief ruler, prince, principal officer
> **hiereus** (Greek New Testament) – a priest, high priest

priestess:

Hebrew Old Testament – not found

Greek New Testament – not found

chief & high priest:

rosh (Hebrew Old Testament) – captain, chapiter, first, principal, ruler, sum, top

gadowl (Hebrew Old Testament) – great, older,mighty, more noble

archiereus (Greek New Testament) – high priest, high priests of the Jews, Christ, a chief priest, chief (high) priest, chief of the priests

priesthood:

khunnah (Hebrew Old Testament) – priesthood, priest's office

hierosune (Greek New Testament) – sacredness, the priestly office, priesthood

Example of use: the book of Hebrews

hierateuma (Greek New Testament) – priestly fraternity, a sacerdotal, priesthood

Example of use: the book of 1 Peter

prophet:

nabiy (Greek New Testament) – a prophet, inspired man, a sacerdotal, priesthood

prophetess (Greek New Testament) – a male foreteller, an inspired speaker, a poet, prophet

prophetess:

nbiyah (Hebrew Old Testament) – a female of Nabiy, a Prophetess inspired woman, a poetess, by association a prophet's wife.

prophetes (Greek New Testament) – a female foreteller or an inspired woman, prophetess

pastor:

raah (Hebrew Old Testament) – to tend to flock, to rule, to associate with as a friend, companion, keep company with, devour, eat up, evil entreat, feed, use as a friend, make friendship with, herdsman, keep sheep, pastor, shepherd, wander, waste.

poimen (Greek New Testament) – a shepherd, pastor

preacher:

goheleth (Hebrew Old Testament) – assembler, preaching

kerux (Greek New Testament) – a herald of divine truth especially of the gospel, preacher

apostle:

Hebrew Old Testament – not found

apostolos (Greek New Testament) – a delegate, an ambassador of the Gospel, officially a commissioner of Christ with miraculous powers, apostle, messenger, he that is sent.

ordain:

yacad (Hebrew Old Testament) – to set, to set down together, settle, consult, appoint, take counsel, establish, lay, lay for a foundation, found, instruct, ordain, set, sure

kathistemi (Greek new Testament) – to place down permanently, to designate, constitute, convey, appoint, be, conduct, make, ordain, set

ordained:

amad (Hebrew Old Testament) – to stand, in various relations, abide behind, appoint, arise, cease, confirm, continue, dwell, be employed, endure, establish, leave, make, ordain, be over, place, be present, raise up, remain, repair, serve set, set forth, set over, make to, make to be a, withstand, standby, stand fast, stand firm, standstill, be at a, stay, stay up, tarry

cheirotoneo (Greek New Testament) – to be a hand-reacher or voter, to select, appoint, choose, ordain

bishop:

Hebrew Old Testament – not found

episkope & episkospos (Greek New Testament) – superintendence, office of bishop & a superintendent, office in general charge of a church, overseer

elder:

zaqen (Hebrew) – old ancient man, elder, eldest man, men or women, senator

presbuteros, presbus (Greek New Testament) – elderly, older, a senior, Sanhedrist, member of the celestial council, church presbyter, elder old

minister:

sharath– as a menial or worshipper, contribute to, minister unto, do, serve, wait on

diakonos (Greek New Testament) – an attendant, a waiter, a church teacher and pastor, deacon or deaconess, minister servant

evangelist:

Hebrew Old Testament – not found

euaggelistes (Greek New Testament) – a preacher of the gospel, evangelist

prophesy:

naba (Hebrew Old Testament) - to speak or sing inspiration (inspiration or simple discourse, make self a prophet)

propheteus (Greek New Testament) – foretell events, devine, speak under inspiration, exercise the prophetic office.

Further Dividing of the Word on the Issue:

Armed with the definitions supplied herein, we are able to put additional scriptures in perspective as we labor further in the word. There is a carryover that must be recognized from the Old Testament to the New Testament that explains the true divine order in the church and it must be accepted by faith.

> *"And Simon Peter answered and said, Thou art the Christ, the Son of the living God. And I say unto thee, that thou art Peter, and upon this rock I will build my church; and the gates of hell shall not prevail against it."* **(Matthew 16:16-18)**

> *"Think not that I am come to destroy the law, or the prophets; I am not come to destroy, but to fulfill. For verily I say unto you, till heaven and earth pass, one jot or one tittle shall in no wise pass from the law, till all is fulfilled. Whosoever therefore shall break one of these least commandments, and shall teach men so, he shall be called the least in the kingdom*

of heaven; but whosoever shall do and teach them, the same shall be called great in the kingdom of heaven." (Matthew 5:17-19)

Christ is established under the New Testament as the Great Shepherd, High Priest, Intercessor and the Bishop of our souls. Christ is our Propitiation (hilasmos: atonement, an expiator).

"Now the God of peace that brought again from the dead our Lord Jesus, that great shepherd of the sheep, through the blood of the everlasting covenant." (Hebrews 13:20)

For we were sheep going astray; but are now returned unto the Shepherd and Bishop of your souls." (1 Peter 2:25)

"And no man taketh this honour unto himself, but he that is called of God, as was Aaron. So also Christ glorified not himself to be made an high priest; but he that said unto him, Thou art my Son, to day have I begotten thee. As he saith also in another place, Thou art a priest for ever after the order of Melchisedec. Who in the days of his flesh, when he had offered up prayers and supplications with strong crying and tears unto him that was able to save him from death, and was heard in that he feared; Though he were a Son, yet learned he obedience by the things which he suffered; and being made perfect, he became the author of eternal salvation unto all them that obey him; called of God an high priest after the order of Melchisedec." (Hebrews 5:8-10)

"Now of the things which we have spoken this is the sum: We have such an high priest, who is set on the right hand of the throne of the Majesty in the heavens; a minister of the sanctuary, and of the true tabernacle, which the Lord pitched, and not man." (Hebrews 8:1-2)

Who shall lay any thing to the charge of God's elect? It is God that justifieth. Who is he that condemneth? It is Christ that died, yea rather, that is risen again, who is even at the right hand of God, who also maketh intercession for us." (Romans 8:33-34)

"And he is the propitiation for our sins; and not for ours only, but also for the sins of the whole world." (1 John 2:2)

"Herein is love, not that we loved God, but that he loved us, and sent his Son to be the propitiation for our sins." (1 John 4:10)

There was in the establishment a priestly line, of which Christ is now forever designated as the High Priest, a <u>gender specification as male</u>, that carries over to the gender designation of the earthly <u>overseers</u> of the church today. Note that there were prophetess but no priestess under the old covenant, the law and/or Old Testament. Consider the scriptural basis of the establishment of the "<u>office</u>" (khunnah as the Hebrew word; hierosune as the Greek word) of the priest as an everlasting priesthood. Christ is the unchangeable priesthood (hierosune) established in the New Covenant.

"And for Aaron's sons thou shalt make coats, and thou shalt make for them girdles, and bonnets shalt thou make for them, for glory and for beauty. And thou shalt put them upon Aaron thy brother, and his sons with him; and shalt anoint them, and consecrate them, and sanctify them, that they may minister unto me in the priest's office." (Exodus 28:40-41)

"This is the portion of the anointing of Aaron, and of the anointing of his sons, out of the offerings of the Lord made by fire, in the day when he presented them to minister unto the Lord in the priest's office; which the Lord commanded to be given them of the children of Israel, in the day that he anointed them, by a statute for ever throughout their generations." (Leviticus 7:35-36)

"And thou shalt give the Levites unto Aaron and to his sons; they are wholly given unto him out of the children of Israel. And thou shalt appoint Aaron and his sons, and they shall wait on their priest's office: and the stranger that cometh nigh shall be put to death." (Number 3:9-10)

"For the Lord thy God hath chosen him out of all thy tribes, to stand to minister in the name of the Lord, him and his sons for ever. Then he shall minister in the name of the Lord his God, as all his brethren the Levites do, which stand there before the Lord." (Deuteronomy 18:5&7)

"And the Lord spake unto Aaron saying, do not drink wine nor strong drink, thou, not thy sons with thee, when ye go into the tabernacle of the congregation, lest ye die; it shall be a statute for ever throughout your generations: and that ye may put difference between holy and unholy, and between unclean and clean; and that ye may teach the children of Israel all the statues which the Lord hath spoken unto them by the hand of Moses." (Leviticus 10:8-11)

"And verily they that are of the sons of Levi, who receive the office of the priesthood, have a commandment to take tithes of the people according to the law, that is, of their brethren, though they come out of the lions of Abraham." But he whose descent is not counted from them received tithes of Abraham, and blessed him that had the promises. And without all contradiction the less is blessed of the better. And here men that die receive tithes; but there he receiveth them, of whom it is witnessed that he liveth. And as I may so say, Levi also, who receiveth tithes, payed tithes in Abraham. For he was yet in the loins of his father, when Melchisedec met him. If therefore perfection were by the Levitical priesthood, (for under it the people received the law,) what further need was there that another priest should rise after the order of Melchisedec, and not be called after the order of Aaron? For the priesthood being changed, there is made of necessity a change also of the law. For he of whom these things are spoken pertaineth to another tribe, of which no man gave attendance at the altar. For it is evident that our Lord sprang out of Juda; of which tribe Moses spake nothing concerning priesthood. And it is yet far more evident: for that after the similitude of Melchisedec there ariseth another priest, Who is made, not after the law of a carnal commandment, but after the power of an endless life. For he testifieth, Thou art a priest for ever after the order of Melchisedec." (Hebrews 7:5-17)

The New Testament clearly establishes the role of the man in the overseeing of the church today. As a starting point, Christ, our example, chose men as the Apostles. Paul was made an Apostle by God as well.

"And when it was day, he called unto him his disciples: and of them he chose twelve, whom also he named apostles; Simon, (whom he also named Peter,) and Andrew his brother, James and John, Philip and Bartholomew, Matthew and Thomas, James the son of Alphaeus, and Simon called Zelotes, And Judas the brother of James, and Judas Iscariot, which also was the traitor." (Luke 6:13-16)

"Paul, called to be an apostle of Jesus Christ through the will of God, and Sosthenes our brother, Unto the church of God which is at Corinth, to them that are sanctified in Christ Jesus, called to be saints, with all that in every place call upon the name of Jesus Christ our Lord, both theirs and ours: Grace be unto you, and peace, from God our Father, and from the Lord Jesus Christ." (1 Corinthians 1:1-3)

The apostles ordained (appointed) other men in obedience to Christ's example and for the establishment of order in the church.

"For this cause I left thee in Crete, that thou shouldest set in order the things that are wanting, and ordain elders in every city, as I had appointed thee: If any be blameless, the husband of one wife, having faithful children not accused of riot or unruly." (Titus 1:5-6)

"And when they had ordained them elders in every church, and had prayed with fasting, they commended them to the Lord, on whom they believed." (Acts 14:23)

"This is a true saying, If a man desire the office of a bishop, he desireth a good work. A bishop then must be blameless, the husband of one wife, vigilant, sober, of good behaviour, given to hospitality, apt to teach; Not given to wine, no striker, not greedy of filthy lucre; but patient, not a brawler, not covetous; One that ruleth well his own house, having his children in subjection with all gravity; (For if a man know not how to rule his own house, how shall he take care of the church of God?) Not a novice, lest being lifted up with pride he fall into the condemnation of the devil." (1 Timothy 3:1-6)

"And as they went through the cities, they delivered them the decrees for to keep, that were ordained of the apostles and elders which were at Jerusalem. And so were the churches established in the faith, and increased in number daily." (Acts 16:4&5)

There is doctrinal basis for women in the proclaiming of the gospel. There is a place clearly established under the Old Testament. A place is established within the service of the prophet and/or prophetess. In the case of the prophetess (nbiyah), the name connotes both an inspired woman and/or wife of a prophet.

"Thou shalt be perfect with the Lord thy God. For these nations, which thou shalt possess, hearkened unto observers of times, and unto diviners: but as for thee, the Lord thy God hath not suffered thee so to do. The Lord thy God will raise up unto thee a Prophet from the midst of thee, of thy brethren, like unto me; unto him ye shall hearken; According to all that thou desiredst of the Lord thy God in Horeb in the day of the assembly, saying, Let me not hear again the voice of the Lord my God, neither let me see this great fire any more, that I die not. And the Lord said unto me, They have well spoken that which they have spoken. I will raise them up a Prophet from among their brethren, like unto thee, and will put my words in his mouth; and he shall speak unto them all that I shall command him. And it shall come to pass, that whosoever will not hearken unto my words which he shall speak in my name, I will require it of him." (Deuteronomy18:13-19)

"And Miriam the prophetess, the sister of Aaron, took a timbrel in her hand; and all the women went out after her with timbrels and with dances." (Exodus 15:20)

"And Deborah, a prophetess, the wife of Lapidoth, she judged Israel at that time." (Judges 4:4)

Other Scriptural Conclusions of Note:

There is a doctrinal basis for the existence of male and female ministers, preachers, evangelists, teachers and prophets of God that was established in the Old Testament and carried over to the church today. There is the priestly fraternity (hierateuma) of all baptized believers. The prophet Joel had prophesized that God would pour out his spirit on all flesh and we know that to have been fulfilled on the day of Pentecost. Both men and women were present at Pentecost. Ministers have a tremendous role in the support of the overseers that is not for the laity to perform. And women need not usurp the authority of the man in the overseeing of the church; the woman is charged by the Bible, in this regard (1 Timothy), to "be in silence" (kerma: without gain as in lurce). In the New Testament, Lydia provides an example of a woman in a position of church leadership that submits to the authority of the Apostles being men; as a result of her submitting herself, the beautiful church of Philippi was established. Lydia was not ordained as the Overseer by the Apostles.

> *"And it shall come to pass afterward, that I will pour out my spirit upon all flesh; and your sons and your daughters shall prophesy, your old men shall dream dreams, your young men shall see visions: And also upon the servants and upon the handmaids in those days will I pour out my spirit."* (Joel 2:28&29)

> *"And when the day of Pentecost was fully come, they were all with one accord in one place. And suddenly there came a sound from heaven as of a rushing mighty wind, and it filled all the house where they were sitting. And there appeared unto them cloven tongues like as of fire, and it sat upon each of them. And they were all filled with the Holy Ghost, and began to speak with other tongues, as the Spirit gave them utterance. But this is that which was spoken by the prophet Joel;"* (Acts 2:1-4,16)

> *"Ye also, as lively stones, are built up a spiritual house, an holy priesthood, to offer up spiritual sacrifices, acceptable to God by Jesus Christ. Wherefore also it is contained in the scripture, Behold, I lay in Sion a chief corner stone, elect, precious: and he that believeth on him shall not be confounded."* (1 Peter 2:5&6)

> *"But ye are a chosen generation, a royal priesthood, an holy nation, a peculiar people; that ye should shew forth the praises of him who hath called you out of darkness into his marvellous light: Which in time past were not a people, but are now the people of God: which had not obtained mercy, but now have obtained mercy."* (1 Peter 2:9&10)

> *"Then the twelve called the multitude of the disciples unto them, and said, It is not reason that we should leave the word of God, and serve tables. Wherefore, brethren, look ye out among you seven men of honest report, full of the Holy Ghost and wisdom, whom we may appoint over this business. But we will give ourselves continually to prayer, and to the ministry of the word."* (Acts 6:2-4)

> *"But I suffer not a woman to teach, nor to usurp authority over the man, but to be in silence."* (1 Timothy 2:12)

> *"And on the Sabbath we went out of the city by a river side, where prayer was wont to be made; and we sat down, and spake unto the women which resorted thither. And a certain woman named Lydia, a seller of purple, of the city of Thyatira, which worshipped God, heard us; whose heart the Lord opened, that she attended unto the things which were spo-*

ken of Paul. And when she was baptized, and here household, she besought us, saying, if ye
have judged me to be faithful to the Lord, come in to my house, and abide there, and she
constrained us." (Acts 16:13-15)

"Paul and Timotheus, the servants of Jesus Christ, to all the saints in Christ Jesus which
are at Philippi, with the bishops and deacons: Grace be unto you, and peace, from God our
Father, and from the Lord Jesus Christ." (Philippians 1:1&2)

"Now ye Philippians know also, that in the beginning of the gospel, when I departed from
Macedonia, no church communicated with me as concerning giving and receiving, but ye
only. For even in Thessalonica ye sent once and again unto my necessity." (Philippians
4:15&16)

**Pastors must seek to be strong in doctrine and apt to teach the unadulterated word of
God. Ministers need to be able to address with the meat of the word and not just milk with
regard to the issues of the world today. Those using the milk are babes and in that they are
weak in the doctrine of Jesus Christ, can cause those under their rule to error.**

"For every one that useth milk is unskillful in the word of righteousness: for is a babe. But
strong meat belongeth to them that are of full age, even those who by reason of use have
their senses exercised to discern both good and evil." (Hebrews 5:13-14)

"Not a novice, lest being lifted up with pride he fall into condemnation of the devil.
Moreover he must have a good report of them which are without; lest he fall into reproach
and the snare of the devil." (1 Timothy 3:6-7)

"Let the elders that rule well be counted worthy of double honor, especially they who labor
in the word and doctrine." (1 Timothy 5:17)

"Remember them which have the rule over you, who have spoken the word of God: whose
faith follow, considering the end of their conversation. Jesus Christ the same yesterday, and
today, and forever. Be not carried about with divers and strange doctrines. For it is good
thing that the heart be established with grace; not with meats, which have not profited
them that have been occupied therein." (Hebrews 13:7-9)

"Obey them that have rule over you, and submit yourselves: for they watch for your souls
as they must give account, that they may do it with joy, and not with grief: for that is unprofitable for you. Pray for us: for we trust have a good conscience, in all things willing to
live honestly." (Hebrews 13:17-18)

**Pastors can not serve in the capacity of elected public servant; there are two constituen-
cies (masters) created in the entities of the voting public and Almighty God.**

"No man can serve two masters: for either he will hate the one, and love the other; or
else he will hold to the one, and despise the other. Ye cannot serve God and mammon."
(Matthew 6:24)

**And those fearful of losing the support of women in their congregations are probably
just as inclined to be ruled by women in their homes. For example, how can a man rule his
home when his wife is his Pastor or even his co-Pastor?**

"For after this manner in the old time the holy women also, who trusted in God, adorned themselves, being in subjection unto their own husbands: Even as Sara obeyed Abraham, calling him lord: whose daughters ye are, as long as ye do well, and are not afraid with any amazement." (1 Peter 3:5&6)

"Nevertheless let every one of you in particular so love his wife even as himself; and the wife see that she reverence her husband." (Ephesians 5:33)

"For is a man know not how to rule his own house, how shall he take care of the church of God?" (1 Timothy 3:5)

If we fail to recognize the truth in God's word with regard to the role of God fearing men in addition to the ordination of women as pastors, we are at further risk of experiencing the conditions as described by the prophet Isaiah.

"For, behold, the Lord, the Lord of hosts, doth take away from Jerusalem and from Judah the stay and the staff, the whole stay of bread, and the whole stay of water. The almighty man and the man of war, the judge, and the prophet, and the prudent, and the ancient. The captain of fifty, and the honorable man, and the counselor, and the cunning artificer, and the eloquent orator. And I will give children to be their princes, and babes shall rule over them. And the people shall be oppressed, every one by another, and every one by his neighbor: the child shall behave himself proudly against the ancient, and the base against the honorable. As for my people, children are their oppressors, and women rule over them, O my people, they which lead thee cause thee to err, and destroy the way of thy paths." (Isaiah 3:1-5,12)

In this day and age, however, there are those that have turned away from very basic scriptural teachings and proclaim a new status of the woman in the church that is not supported by the scriptures. Arguments have prevailed based upon man conceived doctrines of equal employment and the equality of the sexes. There is a difference between the everlasting priesthood of the Levitical order over which Christ now sits as the High Priest and the priesthood of a fraternal order of those others chosen to assist in the spreading of the Holy Ghost through the preaching of the Gospel. The fraternal priesthood (Hierateuma), as referenced in 1 Peter, was established on the day of Pentecost. The everlasting priesthood of the Levitical order (Hierosune), as referenced in Hebrews 7, was established back in the Old Testament in order to eventually oversee the church. This unchangeable priesthood exists in the sons of man and the Son of God, out of the tribe of Judah. God is not confused regarding gender. Christ remains as the bishop of our souls and the man remains as the bishop in the home and the church fellowship.

"Wherefore laying aside all malice, and all guile, and hypocrisies, and envies, and all evil speakings, As newborn babes, desire the sincere milk of the word, that ye may grow thereby: If so be ye have tasted that the Lord is gracious. To whom coming, as unto a living stone, disallowed indeed of men, but chosen of God, and precious, Ye also, as lively stones, are built up a spiritual house, an holy priesthood, to offer up spiritual sacrifices, acceptable to God by Jesus Christ. Wherefore also it is contained in the scripture, Behold, I lay in Sion a chief corner stone, elect, precious: and he that believeth on him shall not be confounded. Unto you therefore which believe he is precious: but unto them which be disobedient, the stone which the builders disallowed, the same is made the head of the corner, And a stone

of stumbling, and a rock of offence, even to them which stumble at the word, being disobedient: whereunto also they were appointed. But ye are a chosen generation, a royal priesthood, an holy nation, a peculiar people; that ye should shew forth the praises of him who hath called you out of darkness into his marvellous light: Which in time past were not a people, but are now the people of God: which had not obtained mercy, but now have obtained mercy." (**1 Peter 2:1-10**)

"But thou, Bethlehem Ephratah, though thou be little among the thousands of Judah, yet out of thee shall he come forth unto me that is to be ruler in Israel; whose goings forth have been from of old, from everlasting." (**Micah 5:2**)

"The Lord said unto my Lord, Sit thou at my right hand, until I make thine enemies thy footstool. The Lord shall send the rod of thy strength out of Zion: rule thou in the midst of thine enemies. Thy people shall be willing in the day of thy power, in the beauties of holiness from the womb of the morning: thou hast the dew of thy youth. The Lord hath sworn, and will not repent, Thou art a priest for ever after the order of Melchizedek. The Lord at thy right hand shall strike through kings in the day of his wrath. He shall judge among the heathen, he shall fill the places with the dead bodies; he shall wound the heads over many countries. He shall drink of the brook in the way: therefore shall he lift up the head. (**Psalms 110**)

"By so much was Jesus made a surety of a better testament. And they were many priests, because they were not suffered to continue by reason of death: but this man, because he continueth ever, hath an unchangeable priesthood. Wherefore he is able to save them to the uttermost that come unto God by him, seeing he ever liveth to make intercession for them. For such a high priest come unto God by him, seeing he ever liveth to make intercession for them. For such an high priest became us, who is holy, harmless, undefiled, separate from sinners, and made higher than the heavens; Who needeth not only daily, as those high priests, to offer up sacrifice, first for his own sins, and then for the people's: for this he did once, when he offered up himself. For the law maketh men high priests which have infirmity; but the word of the oath, which was since the law, maketh the Son consecrated for evermore." (**Hebrews 7:22-28**)

"And when he had taken the book, the four beasts and four and twenty elders fell down before the Lamb, having every one of them harps, and golden vials full of odours, which are the prayers of saints. And they sung a new song, saying, Thou art worthy to take the book, and to open the seals thereof: for thou wast slain, and hast redeemed us to God by thy blood out of every kindred, and tongue, and people, and nation; And hast made us unto our God kings and priests: and we shall reign on the earth. And I beheld, and I heard the voice of many angels round about the throne and the beasts and the elders: and the number of them was ten thousand times ten thousand, and thousands of thousands; Saying with a loud voice, Worthy is the Lamb that was slain to receive power, and riches, and wisdom, and strength, and honour, and glory, and blessing. And every creature which is in heaven, and on the earth, and under the earth, and such as are in the sea, and all that are in them, heard I saying, Blessing, and honour, and glory, and power, be unto him that sitteth upon the throne, and unto the Lamb for ever and ever." (**Revelations 5:8-13**)

12

CHRISTIAN TOLERANCE

Isn't Christianity intolerant of others?

General

Christians should share the basic crucial biblical belief, with regard to mankind, and that is that we all have a Heavenly Father.

> *"Have we not all one father? Hath not one God created us? Why do we deal treacherously every man against his brother, by profaning the covenant of our fathers?"* (Malachi 2:10)

As a consequence of our belief that we all share the same heavenly father/creator, how can we then hate other human beings?

> *"If a man says, I love God, and hateth his brother, he is a liar: for he that loveth not his brother whom he hath seen, how can he love God whom he hath not seen?"* (1 John 4:20)

> *"By this we know that we love the children of God, when we love God, and keep his commandments."* (1 John 5:2)

Christian tolerance and the understanding of creation with regard to mankind, does not allow for a preference of certain people.

> *"And hath made of one blood all nations of men for to dwell on all the face of the earth, and hath determined the times before appointed, and the bounds of their habitation; That they should seek the Lord, if haply they might feel after him, and find him, though he be not far from every one of us: For in him we live, and move, and have our being; as certain also of your own poets have said, For we are also his offspring."* (Acts 17:26-28)

> *"Then Peter opened his mouth, and said, Of a truth I perceive that God is no respecter of persons: "But in every nation he that feareth him, and worketh righteousness, is accepted with him."* (Acts 10:34-35)

> *"If ye fulfil the royal law according to the scripture, Thou shalt love thy neighbor as thyself, ye do well: But if ye have respect to persons, ye commit sin, and are convinced of the law as transgressors."* (James 2:8&9)

> *"For there is no respect of persons with God."* (Romans 2:11)

Our love should apply to all of our neighbors as we love God and love ourselves.

"Honor thy father and thy mother: and, Thou shalt love thy neighbor as thyself." (**Matthew 19:19**)

"Jesus said unto him, Thou shalt love the Lord thy God with all thy heart, and with all thy soul, and with all thy mind. This is the first and great commandment. And the second is like unto it, Thou shalt love thy neighbor as thyself. On these two commandments hang all the law and the prophets." (**Matthew 22:37-40**)

Even the world speaks of a "Golden Rule" which appears as a commandment to all believers in the Bible.

"Therefore all things whatsoever ye would that men should do to you, do ye even so to them: for this is the law and the prophets." (**Matthew 7:12**)

And as ye would that men should do to you, do ye also to them likewise. For if ye love them which love you, what thank have ye? for sinners also love those that love them. And if ye do good to them which do good to you, what thank have ye? for sinners also do even the same." (**Luke 6:31-33**)

Now, understand that the basis of Christian tolerance rooted in the belief that Almighty God, as the Father/Creator of all mankind, loves everyone. There should be a basic love that mankind should have for each other as God loves all creation. There is an even deeper revelation(s) with regard to Christian tolerance; as Christians, we represent Christ, the Son of God and all sufficient savior, who would have all men saved. Note that tolerance is defined in the Webster's II New Riverside University Dictionary as "recognition and respect for the opinions, practices or behavior of others" as well as "the amount of variation from a standard that is allowed".

"For God so loved the world, that he gave his only begotten Son, that whosoever believeth in him should not perish, but have everlasting life." (**John 3: 16**)

"Wherefore he is able also to save them to the uttermost that come unto God by him, seeing he ever liveth to make intercession for them." (**Hebrews 7:25**)

"I say unto you, that likewise joy shall be in heaven over one sinner that repenteth, more than over ninety and nine just persons, which need no repentance. Likewise, I say unto you, there is joy in the presence of the angels of God over one sinner that repenteth." (**Luke 15:7&10**)

"Now then we are ambassadors for Christ, as though God did beseech you by us: we pray you in Christ's stead, be ye reconciled to God." (**2 Corinthians 5:20**)

"I exhort therefore, that, first of all, supplications, prayers, intercessions, and giving of thanks, be made for all men; For kings, and for all that are in authority; that we may lead a quiet and peaceable life in all godliness and honesty. For this is good and acceptable in the sight of God our Saviour; Who will have all men to be saved, and to come unto the knowledge of the truth." (**1 Timothy 2:1-4**)

It is not God's desire that any person should perish [i.e., eternal damnation] and, in fact, heaven is joyful over the saving of one lost soul.

"The Lord is not slack concerning his promise, as some men count slackness; but is long-suffering to us-ward, not willing that any should perish, but that all should come to repentance." (**2 Peter 3:9**)

"I say unto you, that likewise joy shall be in heaven over one sinner that repenteth, more than over ninety and nine just persons, which need no repentance." (**Luke 15:7**)

We as Christians, are to do our part in the planting of the seeds of salvation among all men and in doing so, some of our own sins are blotted out (hidden) according to the Bible.

"So then neither is he that planteth any thing, neither he that watereth; but God that giveth the increase." (**1 Corinthians 3:7**)

"Let him know that he, which converteth the sinner from the error of his way, shall save a soul from death, and shall hide a multitude of sins." (**James 5:20**)

And in terms of works, Jesus would have us to do for even the least among us, as he would.

"When the Son of man shall come in his glory, and all the holy angels with him, then shall he sit upon the throne of his glory: And before him shall be gathered all nations: and he shall separate them one from another, as a shepherd divideth his sheep from the goats: And he shall set the sheep on his right hand, but the goats on the left. Then shall the King say unto them on his right hand, Come, ye blessed of my Father, inherit the kingdom prepared for you from the foundation of the world: For I was an hungered, and ye gave me meat: I was thirsty, and ye gave me drink: I was a stranger, and ye took me in: Naked, and ye clothed me: I was sick, and ye visited me: I was in prison, and ye came unto me. Then shall the righteous answer him, saying, Lord, when saw we thee and hungered, and fed thee? or thirsty, and gave thee drink? When saw we thee a stranger, and took thee in? or naked, and clothed thee? Or when saw we thee sick, or in prison, and came unto thee? And the King shall answer and say unto them, Verily I say unto you, Inasmuch as ye have done it unto one of the least of these my brethren, ye have done it unto me." (**Matthew 25:31-40**)

The reason for our attitude as Christians of tolerance towards others, comes out of the biblical understanding that even as some of the most nefarious individuals throughout the history of the world, all believers were at some point in their lives alienated from God (i.e., enemies of God).

"Wherefore remember, that ye being in time past Gentiles in the flesh, who are called Uncircumcision by that which is called the Circumcision in the flesh made by hands; That at that time ye were without Christ, being aliens from the commonwealth of Israel, and strangers from the covenants of promise, having no hope, and without God in the world: But now in Christ Jesus ye who sometimes were far off are made nigh by the blood of Christ." (**Ephesians 2:11-13**)

"And you hath he quickened, who were dead in trespasses and sins; Wherein in time past ye walked according to the course of this world, according to the prince of the power of the air, the spirit that now worketh in the children of disobedience: Among whom also we all had our conversation in times past in the lusts of our flesh, fulfilling the desires of the flesh

and of the mind; and were by nature the children of wrath, even as others." (Ephesians 2:1-3)

Even those that were once thieves among the believers, are now called upon to labor and have the ability to give to the needy.

"Let him that stole steal no more: but rather let him labour, working with his hands the thing which is good, that he may have to give to him that needeth." (Ephesians 4:28)

Now that what follows is a grouping together of scripture by tolerance groups in an effort to refute the notion alive in the world today that Christianity is intolerant.

Tolerance of Enemies

The believer is commanded to love even our enemies as a reflection upon our creator.

"But I say unto you, which hear, love your enemies, do good to them that hate you, Bless them that curse you, and pray for them which despitefully use you." (Luke 6:27&28)

"But love ye your enemies, and do well, and lend, hoping for nothing again; and your reward shall be great, and ye shall be the children of the Highest: for he is kind unto the unthankful and to the evil. Be ye therefore merciful, as your Father also is merciful." (Luke 6:35&36)

Even in the case of open hostilities, believers are commanded, to the extent possible, to live peaceably with all men.

"Recompense to no man evil for evil. Provide things honest in the sight of all men. If it be possible, as much as lieth in you, live peaceably with all men." (Romans 12:17&18)

The believer is commanded to pray, bless and do good even for our enemies; this reflects the mercy our heavenly Father.

"But I say unto you, Love your enemies, bless them that curse you, do good to them that hate you, and pray for them which despitefully use you, and persecute you; That ye may be the children of your Father which is in heaven: for he maketh his sun to rise on the evil and on the good, and sendeth rain on the just and on the unjust." (Matthew 5:44&45)

Vengeance upon the believer's enemies belongs to God; we are to be compassionate towards our enemies using good to overcome evil.

"Dearly beloved, avenge not yourselves, but rather give place unto wrath: for it is written, Vengeance is mine; I will repay, saith the Lord. Therefore if thine enemy hunger, feed him; if he thirst, give him drink: for in so doing thou shalt heap coals of fire on his head. Be not overcome of evil, but overcome evil with good." (Romans 12:19-21)

Believers have no need for building personal arsenals of weapons to use against their enemies.

"And he said unto them, When I sent you without purse, and scrip, and shoes, lacked ye any thing? And they said, Nothing. Then said he unto them, But now, he that hath a purse,

let him take it, and likewise his scrip: and he that hath no sword, let him sell his garment, and buy one. And they said, Lord, behold, here are two swords. And he said unto them, It is enough." (Luke 22:35, 36 &38)

Tolerance of Sinners

Believers are saved by God's unmerited favor [grace] through our faith; however, Christ died for us while we were sinners.

"For by grace are ye saved through faith; and that not of yourselves: it is the gift of God: Not of works, lest any man should boast." (Ephesians 2:8&9)

"For when we were yet without strength, in due time Christ died for the ungodly. For scarcely for a righteous man wills one die: yet peradventure for a good man some would even dare to die. But God commendeth his love toward us, in that, while we were yet sinners, Christ died for us." (Romans 5:6-8)

Jesus is the propitiation (hilasmos: atonement or hilasterion, expiatory thing, means of atonement) for the sins of the whole world.

"My little children, these things write I unto you, that ye sin not. And if any man sin, we have an advocate with the Father, Jesus Christ the righteous: And he is the propitiation for our sins: and not for ours only, but also for the sins of the whole world." (1 John 2:1&2)

Believers understand that we are merely sinners saved by grace through faith, therefore, that should be taken into account in our tolerance of other sinners.

"Wherein in time past ye walked according to the course of this world, according to the prince of the power of the air, the spirit that now worketh in the children of disobedience: Among whom also we all had our conversation in times past in the lusts of our flesh, fulfilling the desires of the flesh and of the mind; and were by nature the children of wrath, even as others. But God, who is rich in mercy, for his great love wherewith he loved us, Even when we were dead in sins, hath quickened us together with Christ, (by grace ye are saved;)" (Ephesians 2:2-5)

God will, through Christ, guide the sinner that seeks him.

"Good and upright is the Lord: therefore will he teach sinners in the way. The meek will he guide in judgment: and the meek will he teach his way." (Psalm 25:8&9)

"Draw nigh to God, and he will draw nigh to you. Cleanse your hands, ye sinners; and purify your hearts, ye double minded." (James 4:8)

Tolerance of the Poor

GIVE TO THE POOR.

"Give to him that asketh thee, and from him that would borrow of thee turn not thou away." (Matthew 5:42)

Believers are to be discerning with regard to matters concerning the poor and demonstrate our faith through works.

"My brethren, have not the faith of our Lord Jesus Christ, the Lord of glory, with respect of persons. For if there come unto your assembly a man with a gold ring, in goodly apparel, and there come in also a poor man in vile raiment; And ye have respect to him that weareth the gay clothing, and say unto him, Sit thou here in a good place; and say to the poor, Stand thou there, or sit here under my footstool: Are ye not then partial in yourselves, and are become judges of evil thoughts? Hearken, my beloved brethren, Hath not God chosen the poor of this world rich in faith, and heirs of the kingdom which he hath promised to them that love him? But ye have despised the poor. Do not rich men oppress you, and draw you before the judgment seats? Do not they blaspheme that worthy name by which ye are called? If ye fulfil the royal law according to the scripture, Thou shalt love thy neighbor as thyself, ye do well: But if ye have respect to persons, ye commit sin, and are convinced of the law as transgressors. For whosoever shall keep the whole law, and yet offend in one point, he is guilty of all. For he that said, Do not commit adultery, said also, Do not kill. Now if thou commit no adultery, yet if thou kill, thou art become a transgressor of the law. So speak ye, and so do, as they that shall be judged by the law of liberty. For he shall have judgment without mercy, that hath shewed no mercy; and mercy rejoiceth against judgment. What doth it profit, my brethren, though a man say he hath faith, and have not works? can faith save him? If a brother or sister be naked, and destitute of daily food, And one of you say unto them, Depart in peace, be ye warmed and filled; notwithstanding ye give them not those things which are needful to the body; what doth it profit? Even so faith, if it hath not works, is dead, being alone." (James 2:1-17)

Those having pity upon the poor unite with God in that cause.

"He that hath pity upon the poor lendeth unto the Lord; and that which he hath given will he pay him again." (Proverbs 19:17)

Yet, the believer is not expected to support bums.

"For even when we were with you, this we commanded you, that if any would not work, neither should he eat. For we hear that there are some which walk among you disorderly, working not at all, but are busybodies. Now them that are such we command and exhort by our Lord Jesus Christ, that with quietness they work, and eat their own bread." (2 Thessalonians 3:10-12)

Tolerance of the Rich

God is in control with regard to matters of wealth and poverty.

"The Lord maketh poor, and maketh rich: he bringeth low, and lifteth up. He raiseth up the poor out of the dust, and lifteth up the beggar from the dunghill, to set them among princes, and to make them inherit the throne of glory: for the pillars of the earth are the Lord's, and he hath set the world upon them." (1 Samuel 2:7&8)

The believer need not curse the rich and from a practical biblical standpoint, there should be an appreciation of not doing so; somehow they may find out if you have cursed them.

"Curse not the king, no not in thy thought; and curse not the rich in thy bedchamber: for a bird of the air shall carry the voice, and that which hath wings shall tell the matter." (Ecclesiastes 10:20)

God has made both the rich as the poor and they are mingled together.

"The rich and poor meet together: the Lord is the maker of them all." (Proverbs 22:2)

Tolerance of the Simple Minded/Weak

The believer is to be tolerant of the simple minded to the extent of helping in the easing of their burdens.

"We then that are strong ought to bear the infirmities of the weak, and not to please our-selves." (Romans 15:1)

Yet there is another simple mindedness and weakness that is characterized by those that would despise wisdom and instruction; the believer is to tolerate, with self-restraint, as God will deal with that sort.

"Then shalt thou understand the fear of the Lord, and find the knowledge of God. For the Lord giveth wisdom: out of his mouth cometh knowledge and understanding. He layeth up sound wisdom for the righteous: he is a buckler to them that walk uprightly. When wisdom entereth into thine heart, and knowledge is pleasant unto thy soul; Whose ways are crooked, and they froward in their paths: But the wicked shall be cut off from the earth, and the transgressors shall be rooted out of it." (Proverbs 2:5-7,10,15,22)

Tolerance of Unbelievers

The believer is commanded to exercise gentleness with regard to leading others to Christ.

"And the servant of the Lord must not strive; but be gentle unto all men, apt to teach, patient, In meekness instructing those that oppose themselves; if God peradventure will give them repentance to the acknowledging of the truth; And that they may recover themselves out of the snare of the devil, who are taken captive by him at his will." (2 Timothy 2:24-26)

Yet, Christians need not walk in fellowship with the unbeliever.

"Can two walk together, except they be agreed?" (Amos 3:3)

"And have no fellowship with the unfruitful works of darkness, but rather reprove them. For it is a shame even to speak of those things which are done of them in secret. But all things that are reproved are made manifest by the light: for whatsoever doth make manifest is light. Wherefore he saith, Awake thou that sleepest, and arise from the dead, and Christ shall give thee light." (Ephesians 5:11-14)

Christians need not adapt to nor bless the unbeliever.

"Whosoever transgresseth, and abideth not in the doctrine of Christ, hath not God. He that abideth in the doctrine of Christ, he hath both the Father and the Son. If there come any unto you, and bring not this doctrine, receive him not into your house, neither bid him God speed: For he that biddeth him God speed is partaker of his evil deeds." (2 John 9-11)

"And if any man obey not our word by this epistle, note that man, and have no company with him, that he may be ashamed. Yet count him not as an enemy, but admonish him as a brother." (2 Thessalonians 3:14&15)

Even in the case of the ungodly who would distort the message of the grace of God in order to excuse their immoral ways and reject Jesus Christ, through prayer in the Holy Ghost [which builds up love and faith], show a gentleness, as spiritually discerned to some, while others save with fear.

"Beloved, when I gave all diligence to write unto you of the common salvation, it was needful for me to write unto you, and exhort you that ye should earnestly contend for the faith which was once delivered unto the saints. For there are certain men crept in unawares, who were before of old ordained to this condemnation, ungodly men, turning the grace of our God into lasciviousness, and denying the only Lord God, and our Lord Jesus Christ. These are murmurers, complainers, walking after their own lusts; and their mouth speaketh great swelling words, having men's persons in admiration because of advantage. But, beloved, remember ye the words which were spoken before of the apostles of our Lord Jesus Christ; How that they told you there should be mockers in the last time, who should walk after their own ungodly lusts. But ye, beloved, building up yourselves on your most holy faith, praying in the Holy Ghost, Keep yourselves in the love of God, looking for the mercy of our Lord Jesus Christ unto eternal life. And of some have compassion, making a difference: And others save with fear, pulling them out of the fire; hating even the garment spotted by the flesh." (Jude 3, 4, 16-18, 20-23)

Believers, as taught by the scriptures, should understand that by God's mercy, even the Jews are in effect, in a special category of unbelief as (1) salvation has its origins in Judaism and (2) that out of Israel, that is proclaimed to be slumbering, there shall be a remnant saved purely by the election of God's grace. See Chapter 15, Judaism – A Special Case of Unbelief.

"Jesus saith unto her, Woman, believe me, the hour cometh, when ye shall neither in this mountain, nor yet at Jerusalem, worship the Father. Ye worship ye know not what: we know what we worship: for salvation is of the Jews. But the hour cometh, and now is, when the true worshippers shall worship the Father in spirit and in truth: for the Father seeketh such to worship him. God is a Spirit: and they that worship him must worship him in spirit and in truth." (John 4:21-24)

"In the beginning was the Word, and the Word was with God, and the Word was God. The same was in the beginning with God. All things were made by him; and without him was not any thing made that was made. In him was life; and the life was the light of men. And the light shineth in darkness; and the darkness comprehended it not. That was the true Light, which lighteth every man that cometh into the world. He was in the world, and the world was made by him, and the world knew him not. He came unto his own, and his own received him not. But as many as received him, to them gave he power to become the

sons of God, even to them that believe on his name: Which were born, not of blood, nor of the will of the flesh, nor of the will of man, but of God. And the Word was made flesh, and dwelt among us, (and we beheld his glory, the glory as of the only begotten of the Father,) full of grace and truth." (John 1:1-5, 9-14)

"I say then, Hath God cast away his people? God forbid. For I also am an Israelite, of the seed of Abraham, of the tribe of Benjamin. God hath not cast away his people which he foreknew. What ye not what the scripture saith of Elias? how he maketh intercession to God against Israel, saying, Lord, they have killed thy prophets, and digged down thine altars; and I am left alone, and they seek my life. Even so then at this present time also there is a remnant according to the election of grace. What then? Israel hath not obtained that which he seeketh for; but the election hath obtained it, and the rest were blinded. (According as it is written, God hath given them the spirit of slumber, eyes that they should not see, and ears that they should not hear;) unto this day. And David saith, Let their table be made a snare, and a trap, and a stumbling block, and a recompence unto them: Let their eyes be darkened, that they may not see, and bow down their back alway. I say then, Have they stumbled that they should fall? God forbid: but rather through their fall salvation is come unto the Gentiles, for to provoke them to jealousy." (Romans 11:1-3, 5, 7-11)

Christians should pray for Israel's salvation.

"Brethren, my heart's desire and prayer to God for Israel is, that they might be saved. For I bear them record that they have a zeal of God, but not according to knowledge. For they being ignorant of God's righteousness, and going about to establish their own righteousness, have not submitted themselves unto the righteousness of God. For Christ is the end of the law for righteousness to every one that believeth." (Romans 10:1-4)

Mankind would due well to understand the wisdom in tolerating others of a different belief from the practical standpoint of building friendships that one may need to call upon at a critical time. Also, in our tolerance others, they may find their way to salvation.

"And I say unto you, Make to yourselves friends of the mammon of unrighteousness; that, when ye fail, they may receive you into everlasting habitations. He that is faithful in that which is least is faithful also in much: and he that is unjust in the least is unjust also in much. If therefore ye have not been faithful in the unrighteous mammon, who will commit to your trust the true riches? And if ye have not been faithful in that which is another man's, who shall give you that which is your own?" (Luke 16:9-12)

"A man that hath friends must shew himself friendly: and there is a friend that sticketh closer than a brother." (Proverbs 18:24)

"Whether therefore ye eat, or drink, or whatsoever ye do, do all to the glory of God. Give none offence, neither to the Jews, nor to the Gentiles, nor to the church of God: Even as I please all men in all things, not seeking mine own profit, but the profit of many, that they may be saved." (1 Corinthians 10:31-33)

Tolerance of Other Believers
(those of other Christian denominations not true to the Bible)

Jesus taught a simple principle that is so appropriate today with regard to so many Christian denominations; if Christ is being preached, then those are not against us but for us.

> *"And John answered and said, Master, we saw one casting out devils in thy name; and we forbade him, because he followeth not with us. And Jesus said unto him, Forbid him not: for he that is not against us is for us."* (Luke 9:49&50)

There are greater spiritual concerns among believers in Jesus Christ as Lord and Savior.

> *"Let no man therefore judge you in meat, or in drink, or in respect of an holiday, or of the new moon, or of the Sabbath days: Which are a shadow of things to come; but the body is of Christ."* (Colossians 2:16&17)

Believers are most assuredly commanded to do good but even more so for those in the belief (faith).

> *"And let us not be weary in well doing: for in due season we shall reap, if we faint not. As we have therefore opportunity, let us do good unto all men, especially unto them who are of the household of faith."* (Galatians 6:9&10)

God is to be the judge of all, beginning in the church, therefore, we need not concern ourselves with the judging of even believers for we cannot root out bogus Christians by any means.

> *"Another parable put he forth unto them, saying, The kingdom of heaven is likened unto a man which sowed good seed in his field: But while men slept, his enemy came and sowed tares among the wheat, and went his way. But when the blade was sprung up, and brought forth fruit, then appeared the tares also. So the servants of the householder came and said unto him, Sir, didst not thou sow good seed in thy field? from whence then hath it tares? He said unto them, An enemy hath done this. The servants said unto him, Wilt thou then that we go and gather them up? But he said, Nay; lest while ye gather up the tares, ye root up also the wheat with them. Let both grow together until the harvest: and in the time of harvest I will say to the reapers, Gather ye together first the tares, and bind them in bundles to burn them: but gather the wheat into my barn. Then Jesus sent the multitude away, and went into the house: and his disciples came unto him, saying, Declare unto us the parable of the tares of the field. He answered and said unto them, He that soweth the good seed is the Son of man; The field is the world; the good seed are the children of the kingdom; but the tares are the children of the wicked one; The enemy that sowed them is the devil; the harvest is the end of the world; and the reapers are the angels. As therefore the tares are gathered and burned in the fire; so shall it be in the end of this world. The Son of man shall send forth his angels, and they shall gather out of his kingdom all things that offend, and them which do iniquity; And shall cast them into a furnace of fire: there shall be wailing and gnashing of teeth. Then shall the righteous shine forth as the sun in the kingdom of their Father. Who hath ears to hear, let him hear."* (Matthew 13:24-30, 36-43)

> *"For the time is come that judgment must begin at the house of God: and if it first begin at us, what shall the end be of them that obey not the gospel of God?"* (1 Peter 4:17)

Above all people, Christians should be reconciliatory and just towards each other.

"Moreover if thy brother shall trespass against thee, go and tell him his fault between thee and him alone: if he shall hear thee, thou hast gained thy brother. But if he will not hear thee, then take with thee one or two more, that in the mouth of two or three witnesses every word may be established. And if he shall neglect to hear them, tell it unto the church: but if he neglect to hear the church, let him be unto thee as a heathen man and a publican. Verily I say unto you, Whatsoever ye shall bind on earth shall be bound in heaven: and whatsoever ye shall loose on earth shall be loosed in heaven. Again I say unto you, That if two of you shall agree on earth as touching any thing that they shall ask, it shall be done for them of my Father which is in heaven. For where two or three are gathered together in my name, there am I in the midst of them." (**Matthew 18:15-20**)

"Dare any of you, having a matter against another, go to law before the unjust, and not before the saints? Do ye not know that the saints shall judge the world? And if the world shall be judged by you, are ye unworthy to judge the smallest matters? Know ye not that we shall judge angels? how much more things that pertain to this life? If then ye have judgments of things pertaining to this life, set them to judge who are least esteemed in the church." (**1 Corinthians 6:1-4**)

Tolerance in Our Families

The believer is forewarned that our enemies can be those of our own household; Christ brandished a sword (the word of God) and the variance it causes.

"Think not that I am come to send peace on earth: I came not to send peace, but a sword. For I am come to set a man at variance against his father, and the daughter against her mother, and the daughter in law against her mother in law. And a man's foes shall be they of his own household." (**Matthew 10:34-36**)

As a matter of fact, the believer's family is not necessarily those of our own family (blood) but rather other believers.

"There came then his brethren and his mother, and, standing without, sent unto him, calling him. And the multitude sat about him, and they said unto him, Behold, thy mother and thy brethren without seek for thee. And he answered them, saying, Who is my mother, or my brethren? And he looked round about on them which sat about him, and said, Behold my mother and my brethren! For whosoever shall do the will of God, the same is my brother, and my sister, and mother." (**Mark 3:31-35**)

Christians must provide for their families (relatives) and in doing so affirm their faith.

"But if any provide not for his own, and specially for those of his own house, he hath denied the faith, and is worse than an infidel." (**1 Timothy 5:8**)

Tolerance of the World in General

Christians should be able to identify worthwhile endeavors in which to be involved with mankind aside from Christian fellowship and service.

"Finally, brethren, whatsoever things are true, whatsoever things are honest, whatsoever things are just, whatsoever things are pure, whatsoever things are lovely, whatsoever things are of good report; if there be any virtue, and if there be any praise, think on these things. Those things, which ye have both learned, and received, and heard, and seen in me, do: and the God of peace shall be with you." (Philippians 4:8&9)

"And have no fellowship with the unfruitful works of darkness, but rather reprove them." (Ephesians 5:11)

Lastly, as Christians, it is commanded that we forgive in order to be forgiven by God.

"For if ye forgive men their trespasses, your heavenly Father will also forgive you: But if ye forgive not men their trespasses, neither will your Father forgive your trespasses." (Matthew 6:14&15)

"Judge not and ye shall not be judged: condemn not, and ye shall not be condemned: forgive, and ye shall be forgiven:" (Luke 6:37)

Attributes In Our Christian Tolerance

I have drawn out herein scriptures that I am persuaded point to key attributes in our Christian tolerance.

MEEKNESS

The scriptures reveal a blessing in being meek [humble].

"Blessed are the meek: for they shall inherit the earth." (Matthew 5:5)

Moses was noted in the scriptures as being very meek [lowly, humble, and especially saintly].

"(Now the man Moses was very meek, above all the men which were upon the face of the earth.)" (Numbers 12:3)

Christians as ambassadors of Christ need to be meek.

"Take my yoke upon you, and learn of me; for I am meek and lowly in heart: and ye shall find rest unto your souls." (Matthew 11:29)

PEACEMAKING

The scriptures reveal a blessing in being a peacemaker.

"Blessed are the peacemakers: for they shall be called the children of God." (Matthew 5:9)

Justification is sprung up in mankind out of the gains by the saints that promote reconciliation to God.

"And the fruit of righteousness is sown in peace of them that make peace." (James 3:18)

COURTESY

Mankind needs to operate in a compassion towards one another that would not render evil for evil; Christians should set the example.

"Finally, be ye all of one mind, having compassion one of another, love as brethren, be pitiful, be courteous: Not rendering evil for evil, or railing for railing: but contrariwise blessing; knowing that ye are thereunto called, that ye should inherit a blessing. For he that will love life, and see good days, let him refrain his tongue from evil, and his lips that they speak no guile: Let him eschew evil, and do good; let him seek peace, and ensue it." (1 Peter 3:8-11)

TEACHING

Christ commanded all believers to teach all nations and baptize them in the name of the Trinity.

"Go ye therefore, and teach all nations, baptizing them in the name of the Father, and of the Son, and of the Holy Ghost: Teaching them to observe all things whatsoever I have commanded you: and, lo, I am with you alway, even unto the end of the world. Amen." (Matthew 28:19-20)

Christians are to plant and water the seeds of righteousness while God provides the nurturing for maturation.

"I have planted, Apollos watered; but God gave the increase. So then neither is he that planteth any thing, neither he that watereth; but God that giveth the increase. Now he that planteth and he that watereth are one: and every man shall receive his own reward according to his own labour. For we are labourers together with God: ye are God's husbandry, ye are God's building." (1 Corinthians 3:6-9)

Christians, and especially the man of God, are commanded to be willing and prepared to teach.

"And the servant of the Lord must not strive; but be gentle unto all men, apt to teach, patient, In meekness instructing those that oppose themselves; if God peradventure will give them repentance to the acknowledging of the truth; And that they may recover themselves out of the snare of the devil, who are taken captive by him at his will." (2 Timothy 2:24-26)

We as believers should look to the model for the preacher as the example in tolerant teaching to the saints [baptized believers].

"Whereof I am made a minister, according to the dispensation of God which is given to me for you, to fulfil the word of God; Even the mystery which hath been hid from ages and from generations, but now is made manifest to his saints: To whom God would make known what is the riches of the glory of this mystery among the Gentiles; which is Christ in you, the hope of glory: Whom we preach, warning every man, and teaching every man in all wisdom; that we may present every man perfect in Christ Jesus: Whereunto I also labour, striving according to his working, which worketh in me mightily." (Colossians 1:25-29)

WISDOM

True wisdom comes from above.

"Who is a wise man and endued with knowledge among you? let him shew out of a good conversation his works with meekness of wisdom. But if ye have bitter envying and strife in your hearts, glory not, and lie not against the truth. This wisdom descendeth not from above, but is earthly, sensual, devilish. For where envying and strife is, there is confusion and every evil work. But the wisdom that is from above is first pure, then peaceable, gentle, and easy to be intreated, full of mercy and good fruits, without partiality, and without hypocrisy." (James 3:13-17)

Jesus Christ has been made wisdom to us. He is the incarnate word (logos: sum total of all truth) to the world.

"In the beginning was the Word, and the Word was with God, and the Word was God. The same was in the beginning with God. All things were made by him; and without him was not any thing made that was made. He was in the world, and the world was made by him, and the world knew him not. And the Word was made flesh, and dwelt among us, (and we beheld his glory, the glory as of the only begotten of the Father,) full of grace and truth." (John 1:1-3,10,14)

"But of him are ye in Christ Jesus, who of God is made unto us wisdom, and righteousness, and sanctification, and redemption: That, according as it is written, He that glorieth, let him glory in the Lord." (1 Corinthians 1:30-31)

Wisdom can be increased through the power of God's Spirit (Holy Spirit/Holy Ghost) that physically indwells the believer.

"If any of you lack wisdom, let him ask of God, that giveth to all men liberally, and up-braideth not; and it shall be given him." (Colossians 1:25-29)

"But the Comforter, which is the Holy Ghost, whom the Father will send in my name, he shall teach you all things, and bring all things to your remembrance, whatsoever I have said unto you." (John 14:26)

"But ye shall receive power, after that the Holy Ghost is come upon you: and ye shall be witnesses unto me both in Jerusalem, and in all Judaea, and in Samaria, and unto the uttermost part of the earth." (Acts 1:8)

"Know ye not that ye are the temple of God, and that the Spirit of God dwelleth in you? If any man defile the temple of God, him shall God destroy; for the temple of God is holy, which temple ye are." (1 Corinthians 3:16&17)

"If ye then, being evil, know how to give good gifts unto your children: how much more shall your heavenly Father give the Holy Spirit to them that ask him?" (Luke 11:13)

Heavenly wisdom reveals that worldly wisdom in comparison amounts to foolishness.

"For it is written, I will destroy the wisdom of the wise, and will bring to nothing the understanding of the prudent. Where is the wise? where is the scribe? where is the disputer of this world? hath not God made foolish the wisdom of this world?" (1 Corinthians 1:19-20)

TESTING OF CHRISTIAN DENOMINATIONS — GUIDANCE FROM THE BIBLE

How can I determine the validity of a particular church? It is so confusing.

THE DENOMINATION IS not Christianity without the Trinity.

> "For there are three that bear record in heaven, the Father, the Word, and the Holy Ghost: and these three are one." (1 John 5:7)

Certainly there is no such thing, as non-denominational in Christianity because of the biblical need to know the professed doctrinal basis of any particular Christian denomination (i.e. doctrine of Christ, Biblical teaching).

> "And this is love, that we walk after his commandments. This is the commandment, That, as ye have heard from the beginning, ye should walk in it. For many deceivers are entered into the world, who confess not that Jesus Christ is come in the flesh. This is a deceiver and an antichrist. Look to yourselves, that we lose not those things which we have wrought, but that we receive a full reward. Whosoever transgresseth, and abideth not in the doctrine of Christ, hath not God. He that abideth in the doctrine of Christ, he hath both the Father and the Son. If there come any unto you, and bring not this doctrine, receive him not into your house, neither bid him God speed: For he that biddeth him God speed is partaker of his evil deeds." (2 John 6-11)

Christians have been born again as prescribed by Christ. There is a regeneration that occurs in the mind upon believing on Jesus as the Christ and a spiritual change in the body upon the renewing of Baptism.

> "He that believeth and is baptized shall be saved; but he that believeth not shall be damned." (Mark 16:16)

> "For we ourselves also were sometimes foolish, disobedient, deceived, serving divers lusts and pleasures, living in malice and envy, hateful, and hating one another. But after that the kindness and love of God our Saviour toward man appeared, Not by works of righteousness which we have done, but according to his mercy he saved us, by the washing of regeneration, and renewing of the Holy Ghost; Which he shed on us abundantly through

Jesus Christ our Saviour;That being justified by his grace, we should be made heirs according to the hope of eternal life." (**Titus 3:3-7**)

Baptism [Baptizo: to make whelmed (fully wet), of ceremonial ablution, and ordinance of Christianity, wash] is to be fully emerged in water in the name of the Father, the Son and the Holy Ghost.

"Go ye therefore, and teach all nations, baptizing them in the name of the Father, and of the Son, and of the Holy Ghost: Teaching them to observe all things whatsoever I have commanded you: and, lo, I am with you alway, even unto the end of the world. Amen." (**Matthew 28:19-20**)

There is no salvation in baptism alone.

"For by grace are ye saved through faith; and that not of yourselves: it is the gift of God: Not of works, lest any man should boast." (**Ephesians 2:8&9**)

Baptism is symbolic with an awesome spiritual purpose; ordinarily, salvation is not achieved without baptism which done in faithful obedience.

"Jesus answered and said unto him, Verily, verily, I say unto thee, Except a man be born again, he cannot see the kingdom of God. Nicodemus saith unto him, How can a man be born when he is old? can he enter the second time into his mother's womb, and be born? Jesus answered, Verily, verily, I say unto thee, Except a man be born of water and of the Spirit, he cannot enter into the kingdom of God. That which is born of the flesh is flesh; and that which is born of the Spirit is spirit." (**John 3:3-6**)

"Know ye not, that so many of us as were baptized into Jesus Christ were baptized into his death? Therefore we are buried with him by baptism into death: that like as Christ was raised up from the dead by the glory of the Father, even so we also should walk in newness of life. For if we have been planted together in the likeness of his death, we shall be also in the likeness of his resurrection: Knowing this, that our old man is crucified with him, that the body of sin might be destroyed, that henceforth we should not serve sin." (**Romans 6:3-6**)

"For by one Spirit are we all baptized into one body, whether we be Jews or Gentiles, whether we be bond or free; and have been all made to drink into one Spirit." (**1 Corinthians 12:13**)

"And ye are complete in him, which is the head of all principality and power: In whom also ye are circumcised with the circumcision made without hands, in putting off the body of the sins of the flesh by the circumcision of Christ: Buried with him in baptism, wherein also ye are risen with him through the faith of the operation of God, who hath raised him from the dead. And you, being dead in your sins and the uncircumcision of your flesh, hath he quickened together with him, having forgiven you all trespasses; Blotting out the handwriting of ordinances that was against us, which was contrary to us, and took it out of the way, nailing it to his cross; And having spoiled principalities and powers, he made a shew of them openly, triumphing over them in it." (**Colossians 2:10-15**)

"Therefore being justified by faith, we have peace with God through our Lord Jesus Christ: By whom also we have access by faith into this grace wherein we stand, and rejoice in hope of the glory of God." (Romans 5:1-2)

Infants need not be baptized because they cannot know and recognize sin in order to repent. Underlying the practice of infant baptism is the apostate doctrine of salvation in baptism alone. Rather, infants can be presented for dedication/blessing by their Christian parents. Provision for salvation is also made for all those not in rejection of the preached Gospel.

"Then were there brought unto him little children, that he should put his hands on them, and pray: and the disciples rebuked them. But Jesus said, Suffer little children, and forbid them not, to come unto me: for of such is the kingdom of heaven. And he laid his hands on them, and departed thence." (Matthew 19: 13-15)

"Therefore thou art inexcusable, O man, whosoever thou art that judgest: for wherein thou judgest another, thou condemnest thyself; for thou that judgest doest the same things. But we are sure that the judgment of God is according to truth against them which commit such things. And thinkest thou this, O man, that judgest them which do such things, and doest the same, that thou shalt escape the judgment of God? Or despisest thou the riches of his goodness and forbearance and longsuffering; not knowing that the goodness of God leadeth thee to repentance? But after thy hardness and impenitent heart treasurest up unto thyself wrath against the day of wrath and revelation of the righteous judgment of God; Who will render to every man according to his deeds: To them who by patient continuance in well doing seek for glory and honour and immortality, eternal life: But unto them that are contentious, and do not obey the truth, but obey unrighteousness, indignation and wrath, Tribulation and anguish, upon every soul of man that doeth evil, of the Jew first, and also of the Gentile; But glory, honour, and peace, to every man that worketh good, to the Jew first, and also to the Gentile: For there is no respect of persons with God. For as many as have sinned without law shall also perish without law: and as many as have sinned in the law shall be judged by the law; (For not the hearers of the law are just before God, but the doers of the law shall be justified. For when the Gentiles, which have not the law, do by nature the things contained in the law, these, having not the law, are a law unto themselves: Which shew the work of the law written in their hearts, their conscience also bearing witness, and their thoughts the mean while accusing or else excusing one another;) In the day when God shall judge the secrets of men by Jesus Christ according to my gospel." (Romans 2: 1-16)

Re-baptism, other than for those baptized in error as an infant or those only sprinkled, is an exercise in futility.

"For it is impossible for those who were once enlightened, and have tasted of the heavenly gift, and were made partakers of the Holy Ghost, And have tasted the good word of God, and the powers of the world to come, If they shall fall away, to renew them again unto repentance; seeing they crucify to themselves the Son of God afresh, and put him to an open shame." (Hebrews 6:4-6)

Avoid confusion in the Church between the Son of God and our heavenly Father in heaven. Our heavenly father has never vacated his throne in heaven.

"And this is the Father's will which hath sent me, that of all which he hath given me I should lose nothing, but should raise it up again at the last day. And this is the will of him that sent me, that every one which seeth the Son, and believeth on him, may have everlasting life: and I will raise him up at the last day. The Jews then murmured at him, because he said, I am the bread which came down from heaven." (John 6: 39-41)

"How shall we escape, if we neglect so great salvation; which at the first began to be spoken by the Lord, and was confirmed unto us by them that heard him; God also bearing them witness, both with signs and wonders, and with divers miracles, and gifts of the Holy Ghost, according to his own will? For unto the angels hath he not put in subjection the world to come, whereof we speak. But one in a certain place testified, saying, What is man, that thou art mindful of him? or the son of man, that thou visitest him? Thou madest him a little lower than the angels; thou crownedst him with glory and honour, and didst set him over the works of thy hands: Thou hast put all things in subjection under his feet. For in that he put all in subjection under him, he left nothing that is not put under him. But now we see not yet all things put under him. But we see Jesus, who was made a little lower than the angels for the suffering of death, crowned with glory and honour; that he by the grace of God should taste death for every man." (Hebrews 2:3-9)

"And they were in the way going up to Jerusalem; and Jesus went before them: and they were amazed; and as they followed, they were afraid. And he took again the twelve, and began to tell them what things should happen unto him, Saying, Behold, we go up to Jerusalem; and the Son of man shall be delivered unto the chief priests, and unto the scribes; and they shall condemn him to death, and shall deliver him to the Gentiles: And they shall mock him, and shall scourge him, and shall spit upon him, and shall kill him: and the third day he shall rise again." (Mark 10: 32-34)

"And Jesus answered them, saying, The hour is come, that the Son of man should be glorified. Verily, verily, I say unto you, Except a corn of wheat fall into the ground and die, it abideth alone: but if it die, it bringeth forth much fruit. He that loveth his life shall lose it; and he that hateth his life in this world shall keep it unto life eternal. If any man serve me, let him follow me; and where I am, there shall also my servant be: if any man serve me, him will my Father honour. Now is my soul troubled; and what shall I say? Father, save me from this hour: but for this cause came I unto this hour. Father, glorify thy name. Then came there a voice from heaven, saying, I have both glorified it, and will glorify it again." (John 12:23-28)

"And he came out, and went, as he was wont, to the mount of Olives; and his disciples also followed him. And when he was at the place, he said unto them, Pray that ye enter not into temptation. And he was withdrawn from them about a stone's cast, and kneeled down, and prayed, Saying, Father, if thou be willing, remove this cup from me: nevertheless not my will, but thine, be done. And there appeared an angel unto him from heaven, strengthening him. And being in an agony he prayed more earnestly: and his sweat was as it were great drops of blood falling down to the ground." (Luke 22: 39-44)

"And it was about the sixth hour, and there was a darkness over all the earth until the ninth hour. And the sun was darkened, and the veil of the temple was rent in the midst. And when Jesus had cried with a loud voice, he said, Father, into thy hands I commend my spirit: and having said thus, he gave up the ghost." (Luke 23: 44-46)

"Wherefore I also, after I heard of your faith in the Lord Jesus, and love unto all the saints, Cease not to give thanks for you, making mention of you in my prayers; That the God of our Lord Jesus Christ, the Father of glory, may give unto you the spirit of wisdom and revelation in the knowledge of him: The eyes of your understanding being enlightened; that ye may know what is the hope of his calling, and what the riches of the glory of his inheritance in the saints, And what is the exceeding greatness of his power to us-ward who believe, according to the working of his mighty power, Which he wrought in Christ, when he raised him from the dead, and set him at his own right hand in the heavenly places, Far above all principality, and power, and might, and dominion, and every name that is named, not only in this world, but also in that which is to come: And hath put all things under his feet, and gave him to be the head over all things to the church, Which is his body, the fulness of him that filleth all in all." (Ephesians 1:15-23)

Those saved are indwelled physically by the Spirit of God, the Holy Ghost, and this is evidenced by obedience not by the necessity of speaking in tongues, which is merely a gift in this age. Christ, and note that the Father is always in the Son, dwells in our hearts as well, spiritually, through the Holy Spirit.

"What? know ye not that your body is the temple of the Holy Ghost which is in you, which ye have of God, and ye are not your own? For ye are bought with a price: therefore glorify God in your body, and in your spirit, which are God's." (1 Corinthians 6:19-20)

"And we are his witnesses of these things; and so is also the Holy Ghost, whom God hath given to them that obey him." (Acts 5:32)

"For this cause I bow my knees unto the Father of our Lord Jesus Christ, Of whom the whole family in heaven and earth is named, That he would grant you, according to the riches of his glory, to be strengthened with might by his Spirit in the inner man; That Christ may dwell in your hearts by faith; that ye, being rooted and grounded in love, May be able to comprehend with all saints what is the breadth, and length, and depth, and height; And to know the love of Christ, which passeth knowledge, that ye might be filled with all the fulness of God." (Ephesians 3:14-19)

"And be not drunk with wine, wherein is excess; but be filled with the Spirit; Speaking to yourselves in psalms and hymns and spiritual songs, singing and making melody in your heart to the Lord; Giving thanks always for all things unto God and the Father in the name of our Lord Jesus Christ; Submitting yourselves one to another in the fear of God." (John 10:37&38)

"No man hath seen God at any time. If we love one another, God dwelleth in us, and his love is perfected in us. Hereby know we that we dwell in him, and he in us, because he hath given us of his Spirit. And we have seen and do testify that the Father sent the Son to be the Saviour of the world. Whosoever shall confess that Jesus is the Son of God, God dwelleth in him, and he in God. And we have known and believed the love that God hath to us. God is love; and he that dwelleth in love dwelleth in God, and God in him." (1 John 4:12-16)

"Be ye not unequally yoked together with unbelievers: for what fellowship hath righteousness with unrighteousness? and what communion hath light with darkness? And what concord hath Christ with Belial? or what part hath he that believeth with an infidel? And what agreement hath the temple of God with idols? for ye are the temple of the living God;

as God hath said, I will dwell in them, and walk in them; and I will be their God, and they shall be my people. Wherefore come out from among them, and be ye separate, saith the Lord, and touch not the unclean thing; and I will receive you, And will be a Father unto you, and ye shall be my sons and daughters, saith the Lord Almighty." (2 Corinthians 6:14-18)

All Christians are to be ambassadors of Jesus Christ. There is no such thing as a "Holy Father" here on earth as Christ's "representative".

"Therefore if any man be in Christ, he is a new creature: old things are passed away; behold, all things are become new. And all things are of God, who hath reconciled us to himself by Jesus Christ, and hath given to us the ministry of reconciliation; To wit, that God was in Christ, reconciling the world unto himself, not imputing their trespasses unto them; and hath committed unto us the word of reconciliation. Now then we are ambassadors for Christ, as though God did beseech you by us: we pray you in Christ's stead, be ye reconciled to God. For he hath made him to be sin for us, who knew no sin; that we might be made the righteousness of God in him." (2 Corinthians 5: 17-21)

"But be not ye called Rabbi: for one is your Master, even Christ; and all ye are brethren. And call no man your father upon the earth: for one is your Father, which is in heaven. Neither be ye called masters: for one is your Master, even Christ." (Matthew 23:8-10)

In the Church, there is no need for Priests. Christ is now High Priest and remission of sin is in the blood shed by Jesus on the cross.

"Now of the things which we have spoken this is the sum: We have such an high priest, who is set on the right hand of the throne of the Majesty in the heavens; A minister of the sanctuary, and of the true tabernacle, which the Lord pitched, and not man." (Hebrews 8:1-2)

"For it is not possible that the blood of bulls and of goats should take away sins. Wherefore when he cometh into the world, he saith, Sacrifice and offering thou wouldest not, but a body hast thou prepared me: In burnt offerings and sacrifices for sin thou hast had no pleasure. Then said I, Lo, I come (in the volume of the book it is written of me,) to do thy will, O God. Above when he said, Sacrifice and offering and burnt offerings and offering for sin thou wouldest not, neither hadst pleasure therein; which are offered by the law; Then said he, Lo, I come to do thy will, O God. He taketh away the first, that he may establish the second. By the which will we are sanctified through the offering of the body of Jesus Christ once for all. And every priest standeth daily ministering and offering oftentimes the same sacrifices, which can never take away sins: But this man, after he had offered one sacrifice for sins for ever, sat down on the right hand of God; From henceforth expecting till his enemies be made his footstool. For by one offering he hath perfected for ever them that are sanctified. Whereof the Holy Ghost also is a witness to us: for after that he had said before, This is the covenant that I will make with them after those days, saith the Lord, I will put my laws into their hearts, and in their minds will I write them; And their sins and iniquities will I remember no more. Now where remission of these is, there is no more offering for sin. Having therefore, brethren, boldness to enter into the holiest by the blood of Jesus, By a new and living way, which he hath consecrated for us, through the veil, that is to say, his flesh; And having an high priest over the house of God; Let us draw near with a

true heart in full assurance of faith, having our hearts sprinkled from an evil conscience, and our bodies washed with pure water." (**Hebrews 10:4-22**)

"And now, O ye priests, this commandment is for you. If ye will not hear, and if ye will not lay it to heart, to give glory unto my name, saith the Lord of hosts, I will even send a curse upon you, and I will curse your blessings: yea, I have cursed them already, because ye do not lay it to heart. Behold, I will corrupt your seed, and spread dung upon your faces, even the dung of your solemn feasts; and one shall take you away with it. And ye shall know that I have sent this commandment unto you, that my covenant might be with Levi, saith the Lord of hosts. My covenant was with him of life and peace; and I gave them to him for the fear wherewith he feared me, and was afraid before my name. The law of truth was in his mouth, and iniquity was not found in his lips: he walked with me in peace and equity, and did turn many away from iniquity. For the priest's lips should keep knowledge, and they should seek the law at his mouth: for he is the messenger of the Lord of hosts. But ye are departed out of the way; ye have caused many to stumble at the law; ye have corrupted the covenant of Levi, saith the Lord of hosts. Therefore have I also made you contemptible and base before all the people, according as ye have not kept my ways, but have been partial in the law." (**Malachi 2:1-9**)

Mary the Mother of Jesus remained a virgin until the birth of Jesus as per the Bible. Jesus had brothers and sisters; they were not his cousins as was John the Baptist.

"Moreover the Lord spake again unto Ahaz, saying, Ask thee a sign of the Lord thy God; ask it either in the depth, or in the height above. But Ahaz said, I will not ask, neither will I tempt the Lord. And he said, Hear ye now, O house of David; Is it a small thing for you to weary men, but will ye weary my God also? Therefore the Lord himself shall give you a sign; Behold, a virgin shall conceive, and bear a son, and shall call his name Immanuel. Butter and honey shall he eat, that he may know to refuse the evil, and choose the good." (**Isaiah 7:10-15**)

"Now the birth of Jesus Christ was on this wise: When as his mother Mary was espoused to Joseph, before they came together, she was found with child of the Holy Ghost. Then Joseph her husband, being a just man, and not willing to make her a publick example, was minded to put her away privily. But while he thought on these things, behold, the angel of the Lord appeared unto him in a dream, saying, Joseph, thou son of David, fear not to take unto thee Mary thy wife: for that which is conceived in her is of the Holy Ghost. And she shall bring forth a son, and thou shalt call his name Jesus: for he shall save his people from their sins. Now all this was done, that it might be fulfilled which was spoken of the Lord by the prophet, saying, Behold, a virgin shall be with child, and shall bring forth a son, and they shall call his name Emmanuel, which being interpreted is, God with us. Then Joseph being raised from sleep did as the angel of the Lord had bidden him, and took unto him his wife: And knew her not till she had brought forth her firstborn son: and he called his name Jesus." (**Matthew 1:18-25**)

"And he went out from thence, and came into his own country; and his disciples follow him. And when the sabbath day was come, he began to teach in the synagogue: and many hearing him were astonished, saying, From whence hath this man these things? and what wisdom is this which is given unto him, that even such mighty works are wrought by his hands? Is not this the carpenter, the son of Mary, the brother of James, and Joses, and of

Juda, and Simon? and are not his sisters here with us? And they were offended at him." (Mark 6:1-3)

"And in the sixth month the angel Gabriel was sent from God unto a city of Galilee, named Nazareth, To a virgin espoused to a man whose name was Joseph, of the house of David; and the virgin's name was Mary. And the angel came in unto her, and said, Hail, thou that art highly favoured, the Lord is with thee: blessed art thou among women. And when she saw him, she was troubled at his saying, and cast in her mind what manner of salutation this should be. And the angel said unto her, Fear not, Mary: for thou hast found favour with God. And, behold, thou shalt conceive in thy womb, and bring forth a son, and shalt call his name Jesus. He shall be great, and shall be called the Son of the Highest: and the Lord God shall give unto him the throne of his father David: And he shall reign over the house of Jacob for ever; and of his kingdom there shall be no end. Then said Mary unto the angel, How shall this be, seeing I know not a man? And the angel answered and said unto her, The Holy Ghost shall come upon thee, and the power of the Highest shall overshadow thee: therefore also that holy thing which shall be born of thee shall be called the Son of God. And, behold, thy cousin Elisabeth, she hath also conceived a son in her old age: and this is the sixth month with her, who was called barren. For with God nothing shall be impossible." (Luke 1:26-37)

Regarding the Holy Communion, the second ordinance of the Church, the communion wine and bread are symbolic of Christ's body. Spiritually, they are indeed his body as he is the bread of life and as he had instructed his disciples to eat the flesh of the Son of Man even before the Lord's Supper was first celebrated. There is no mystical changing in the communion of the bread and the wine into the Lord Jesus' actual body; this is apostate.

"Verily, verily, I say unto you, He that believeth on me hath everlasting life. I am that bread of life. Your fathers did eat manna in the wilderness, and are dead. This is the bread which cometh down from heaven, that a man may eat thereof, and not die. I am the living bread which came down from heaven: if any man eat of this bread, he shall live for ever: and the bread that I will give is my flesh, which I will give for the life of the world. The Jews therefore strove among themselves, saying, How can this man give us his flesh to eat? Then Jesus said unto them, Verily, verily, I say unto you, Except ye eat the flesh of the Son of man, and drink his blood, ye have no life in you. Whoso eateth my flesh, and drinketh my blood, hath eternal life; and I will raise him up at the last day. For my flesh is meat indeed, and my blood is drink indeed. He that eateth my flesh, and drinketh my blood, dwelleth in me, and I in him. As the living Father hath sent me, and I live by the Father: so he that eateth me, even he shall live by me. This is that bread which came down from heaven: not as your fathers did eat manna, and are dead: he that eateth of this bread shall live for ever. These things said he in the synagogue, as he taught in Capernaum. Many therefore of his disciples, when they had heard this, said, This is an hard saying; who can hear it? When Jesus knew in himself that his disciples murmured at it, he said unto them, Doth this offend you? What and if ye shall see the Son of man ascend up where he was before? It is the spirit that quickeneth; the flesh profiteth nothing: the words that I speak unto you, they are spirit, and they are life. But there are some of you that believe not. For Jesus knew from the beginning who they were that believed not, and who should betray him. And he said, Therefore said I unto you, that no man can come unto me, except it were given unto him

of my Father. From that time many of his disciples went back, and walked no more with him." (John 6: 47-66)

"And they went, and found as he had said unto them: and they made ready the passover. And when the hour was come, he sat down, and the twelve apostles with him. And he said unto them, With desire I have desired to eat this passover with you before I suffer: For I say unto you, I will not any more eat thereof, until it be fulfilled in the kingdom of God. And he took the cup, and gave thanks, and said, Take this, and divide it among yourselves:For I say unto you, I will not drink of the fruit of the vine, until the kingdom of God shall come. And he took bread, and gave thanks, and brake it, and gave unto them, saying, This is my body which is given for you: this do in remembrance of me. Likewise also the cup after supper, saying, This cup is the new testament in my blood, which is shed for you. But, behold, the hand of him that betrayeth me is with me on the table. And truly the Son of man goeth, as it was determined: but woe unto that man by whom he is betrayed!" (Luke 22:13-22)

Beware of Church doctrines that would test salvation visa vie imparted righteousness rather than imputed righteousness.

"Therefore by the deeds of the law there shall no flesh be justified in his sight: for by the law is the knowledge of sin. But now the righteousness of God without the law is manifested, being witnessed by the law and the prophets; Even the righteousness of God which is by faith of Jesus Christ unto all and upon all them that believe: for there is no difference: For all have sinned, and come short of the glory of God; Being justified freely by his grace through the redemption that is in Christ Jesus: Whom God hath set forth to be a propitiation through faith in his blood, to declare his righteousness for the remission of sins that are past, through the forbearance of God; To declare, I say, at this time his righteousness: that he might be just, and the justifier of him which believeth in Jesus. Where is boasting then? It is excluded. By what law? of works? Nay: but by the law of faith. Therefore we conclude that a man is justified by faith without the deeds of the law." (Romans 3:20-28)

"Therefore if any man be in Christ, he is a new creature: old things are passed away; behold, all things are become new. And all things are of God, who hath reconciled us to himself by Jesus Christ, and hath given to us the ministry of reconciliation; To wit, that God was in Christ, reconciling the world unto himself, not imputing their trespasses unto them; and hath committed unto us the word of reconciliation. Now then we are ambassadors for Christ, as though God did beseech you by us: we pray you in Christ's stead, be ye reconciled to God. For he hath made him to be sin for us, who knew no sin; that we might be made the righteousness of God in him." (2 Corinthians 5:17-21)

Beware of Church doctrines and hypocracies that base salvation upon customs, traditions and/or apostolic succession.

"Ye hypocrites, well did Esaias prophesy of you, saying, This people draweth nigh unto me with their mouth, and honoureth me with their lips; but their heart is far from me. But in vain they do worship me, teaching for doctrines the commandments of men." (Matthew 15:7-9)

"Let no man therefore judge you in meat, or in drink, or in respect of an holyday, or of the new moon, or of the sabbath days: Which are a shadow of things to come; but the body is of Christ. Let no man beguile you of your reward in a voluntary humility and worship-

ping of angels, intruding into those things which he hath not seen, vainly puffed up by his fleshly mind, And not holding the Head, from which all the body by joints and bands having nourishment ministered, and knit together, increaseth with the increase of God." (Colossians 2:16-19)

"For a bishop must be blameless, as the steward of God; not selfwilled, not soon angry, not given to wine, no striker, not given to filthy lucre; But a lover of hospitality, a lover of good men, sober, just, holy, temperate; Holding fast the faithful word as he hath been taught, that he may be able by sound doctrine both to exhort and to convince the gainsayers. For there are many unruly and vain talkers and deceivers, specially they of the circumcision: Whose mouths must be stopped, who subvert whole houses, teaching things which they ought not, for filthy lucre's sake. One of themselves, even a prophet of their own, said, The Cretians are alway liars, evil beasts, slow bellies. This witness is true. Wherefore rebuke them sharply, that they may be sound in the faith; Not giving heed to Jewish fables, and commandments of men, that turn from the truth. Unto the pure all things are pure: but unto them that are defiled and unbelieving is nothing pure; but even their mind and conscience is defiled. They profess that they know God; but in works they deny him, being abominable, and disobedient, and unto every good work reprobate." (Titus 1:7-16)

Beware of impossibly complicated Church doctrinal statements.

"For I am jealous over you with godly jealousy: for I have espoused you to one husband, that I may present you as a chaste virgin to Christ. But I fear, lest by any means, as the serpent beguiled Eve through his subtilty, so your minds should be corrupted from the simplicity that is in Christ." (2 Corinthians 11: 2-3)

There is no purgatory.

"And as it is appointed unto men once to die, but after this the judgment:" (Hebrews 9:27)

"And I saw a great white throne, and him that sat on it, from whose face the earth and the heaven fled away; and there was found no place for them. And I saw the dead, small and great, stand before God; and the books were opened: and another book was opened, which is the book of life: and the dead were judged out of those things which were written in the books, according to their works. And the sea gave up the dead which were in it; and death and hell delivered up the dead which were in them: and they were judged every man according to their works. And death and hell were cast into the lake of fire. This is the second death. And whosoever was not found written in the book of life was cast into the lake of fire." (Revelation 20:11-15)

Know that "saints" are living believers and, unless Christ returns in their lifetime, will die but not achieve sainthood in death as determined by those saints that remain.

"The Lord maketh poor, and maketh rich: he bringeth low, and lifteth up. He raiseth up the poor out of the dust, and lifteth up the beggar from the dunghill, to set them among princes, and to make them inherit the throne of glory: for the pillars of the earth are the Lord's, and he hath set the world upon them. He will keep the feet of his saints, and the wicked shall be silent in darkness; for by strength shall no man prevail." (1 Samuel 2:7-9)

"Now therefore arise, O Lord God, into thy resting place, thou, and the ark of thy strength: let thy priests, O Lord God, be clothed with salvation, and let thy saints rejoice in goodness. O Lord God, turn not away the face of thine anointed: remember the mercies of David thy servant." (2 Chronicles 6:41-42)

"Preserve me, O God: for in thee do I put my trust. O my soul, thou hast said unto the Lord, Thou art my Lord: my goodness extendeth not to thee; But to the saints that are in the earth, and to the excellent, in whom is all my delight. Their sorrows shall be multiplied that hasten after another god: their drink offerings of blood will I not offer, nor take up their names into my lips." (Psalm 16:1-4)

"Precious in the sight of the Lord is the death of his saints." (Psalm 116:15)

In the spiritual realm, <u>only</u> Jesus Christ and the Holy Ghost make intersession for the saints (believers). Other living Christians can function as prayer intercessors and are encouraged to do so.

"Who hath believed our report? and to whom is the arm of the Lord revealed? For he shall grow up before him as a tender plant, and as a root out of a dry ground: he hath no form nor comeliness; and when we shall see him, there is no beauty that we should desire him. He is despised and rejected of men; a man of sorrows, and acquainted with grief: and we hid as it were our faces from him; he was despised, and we esteemed him not. Surely he hath borne our griefs, and carried our sorrows: yet we did esteem him stricken, smitten of God, and afflicted. But he was wounded for our transgressions, he was bruised for our iniquities: the chastisement of our peace was upon him; and with his stripes we are healed. All we like sheep have gone astray; we have turned every one to his own way; and the Lord hath laid on him the iniquity of us all. He was oppressed, and he was afflicted, yet he opened not his mouth: he is brought as a lamb to the slaughter, and as a sheep before her shearers is dumb, so he openeth not his mouth. He was taken from prison and from judgment: and who shall declare his generation? for he was cut off out of the land of the living: for the transgression of my people was he stricken. And he made his grave with the wicked, and with the rich in his death; because he had done no violence, neither was any deceit in his mouth. Yet it pleased the Lord to bruise him; he hath put him to grief: when thou shalt make his soul an offering for sin, he shall see his seed, he shall prolong his days, and the pleasure of the Lord shall prosper in his hand. He shall see of the travail of his soul, and shall be satisfied: by his knowledge shall my righteous servant justify many; for he shall bear their iniquities. Therefore will I divide him a portion with the great, and he shall divide the spoil with the strong; because he hath poured out his soul unto death: and he was numbered with the transgressors; and he bare the sin of many, and made intercession for the transgressors." (Isaiah 53:1-12)

"Who is he that condemneth? It is Christ that died, yea rather, that is risen again, who is even at the right hand of God, who also maketh intercession for us." (Romans 8:34)

"But this man, because he continueth ever, hath an unchangeable priesthood. Wherefore he is able also to save them to the uttermost that come unto God by him, seeing he ever liveth to make intercession for them. For such an high priest became us, who is holy, harmless, undefiled, separate from sinners, and made higher than the heavens; Who needeth not daily, as those high priests, to offer up sacrifice, first for his own sins, and then for the people's: for this he did once, when he offered up himself." (Hebrews 7:24-27)

"Likewise the Spirit also helpeth our infirmities: for we know not what we should pray for as we ought: but the Spirit itself maketh intercession for us with groanings which cannot be uttered. And he that searcheth the hearts knoweth what is the mind of the Spirit, because he maketh intercession for the saints according to the will of God." (**Romans 8: 26-27**)

Confess your faults one to another, and pray one for another, that ye may be healed. The effectual fervent prayer of a righteous man availeth much." (**James 5:16**)

Prayer is to be made to the Father asking all requests in the name of Jesus.

"And in that day ye shall ask me nothing. Verily, verily, I say unto you, Whatsoever ye shall ask the Father in my name, he will give it you." (**John 16:23**)

Beware of the lack of fervency in the prayers in worship services, prayer meetings and the prayer ministry.

"Even them will I bring to my holy mountain, and make them joyful in my house of prayer: their burnt offerings and their sacrifices shall be accepted upon mine altar; for mine house shall be called an house of prayer for all people." (**Isaiah 56:7**)

"And Jesus went into the temple of God, and cast out all them that sold and bought in the temple, and overthrew the tables of the moneychangers, and the seats of them that sold doves, And said unto them, It is written, My house shall be called the house of prayer; but ye have made it a den of thieves. And the blind and the lame came to him in the temple; and he healed them." (**Matthew 21:12-14**)

"Watch ye therefore, and pray always, that ye may be accounted worthy to escape all these things that shall come to pass, and to stand before the Son of man." (**Luke 21:36**)

"I exhort therefore, that, first of all, supplications, prayers, intercessions, and giving of thanks, be made for all men; For kings, and for all that are in authority; that we may lead a quiet and peaceable life in all godliness and honesty. For this is good and acceptable in the sight of God our Saviour; Who will have all men to be saved, and to come unto the knowledge of the truth. For there is one God, and one mediator between God and men, the man Christ Jesus; Who gave himself a ransom for all, to be testified in due time." (**1 Timothy 2:1-6**)

"Is any sick among you? let him call for the elders of the church; and let them pray over him, anointing him with oil in the name of the Lord: And the prayer of faith shall save the sick, and the Lord shall raise him up; and if he have committed sins, they shall be forgiven him. Confess your faults one to another, and pray one for another, that ye may be healed. The effectual fervent prayer of a righteous man availeth much.' (**James 5:14-16**)

Beware of the lack of praise in worship services.

"Praise ye the Lord. Praise God in his sanctuary: praise him in the firmament of his power. Praise him for his mighty acts: praise him according to his excellent greatness. Praise him with the sound of the trumpet: praise him with the psaltery and harp. Praise him with the timbrel and dance: praise him with stringed instruments and organs. Praise him upon

the loud cymbals: praise him upon the high sounding cymbals. Let every thing that hath breath praise the Lord. Praise ye the Lord." (**Psalm 150**)

"Praise ye the Lord. Sing unto the Lord a new song, and his praise in the congregation of saints. Let Israel rejoice in him that made him: let the children of Zion be joyful in their King. Let them praise his name in the dance: let them sing praises unto him with the timbrel and harp. For the Lord taketh pleasure in his people: he will beautify the meek with salvation. Let the saints be joyful in glory: let them sing aloud upon their beds." (**Psalm 149:1-5**)

"And when the builders laid the foundation of the temple of the Lord, they set the priests in their apparel with trumpets, and the Levites the sons of Asaph with cymbals, to praise the Lord, after the ordinance of David king of Israel. And they sang together by course in praising and giving thanks unto the Lord; because he is good, for his mercy endureth for ever toward Israel. And all the people shouted with a great shout, when they praised the Lord, because the foundation of the house of the Lord was laid. But many of the priests and Levites and chief of the fathers, who were ancient men, that had seen the first house, when the foundation of this house was laid before their eyes, wept with a loud voice; and many shouted aloud for joy: So that the people could not discern the noise of the shout of joy from the noise of the weeping of the people: for the people shouted with a loud shout, and the noise was heard afar off." (**Ezra 3: 10-13**)

"But let all those that put their trust in thee rejoice: let them ever shout for joy, because thou defendest them: let them also that love thy name be joyful in thee. For thou, Lord, wilt bless the righteous; with favour wilt thou compass him as with a shield." (**Psalm 5:11-12**)

Beware of the lack of joy in worship services.

"Be glad in the Lord, and rejoice, ye righteous: and shout for joy, all ye that are upright in heart." (**Psalm 32: 11**)

"Make a joyful noise unto the Lord, all ye lands. Serve the Lord with gladness: come before his presence with singing. Know ye that the Lord he is God: it is he that hath made us, and not we ourselves; we are his people, and the sheep of his pasture. Enter into his gates with thanksgiving, and into his courts with praise: be thankful unto him, and bless his name." (**Psalm 100:1-4**)

"Then he said unto them, Go your way, eat the fat, and drink the sweet, and send portions unto them for whom nothing us prepared: for this day is holy unto our Lord: neither be ye sorry; for the joy of the Lord is your strength." (**Nehemiah 8:10**)

Be particularly conscious of the music that is made a part of worship. The Bible gives a tremendous guideline with regard to the music that is to be made a part of worship.

"For the horse of Pharaoh went in with his chariots and with his horsemen into the sea, and the Lord brought again the waters of the sea upon them; but the children of Israel went on dry land in the midst of the sea. And Miriam the prophetess, the sister of Aaron, took a timbrel in her hand; and all the women went out after her with timbrels and with dances. And Miriam answered them, Sing ye to the Lord, for he hath triumphed gloriously; the horse and his rider hath he thrown into the sea." (**Exodus 15:19-21**)

"And even things without life giving sound, whether pipe or harp, except they give a distinction in the sounds, how shall it be known what is piped or harped? For if the trumpet give an uncertain sound, who shall prepare himself to the battle?" (1 Corinthians 14:7&8)

"Let the word of Christ dwell in you richly in all wisdom; teaching and admonishing one another in psalms and hymns and spiritual songs, singing with grace in your hearts to the Lord." (Colossians 3:16)

"And be not drunk with wine, wherein is excess; but be filled with the Spirit; Speaking to yourselves in psalms and hymns and spiritual songs, singing and making melody in your heart to the Lord; Giving thanks always for all things unto God and the Father in the name of our Lord Jesus Christ; Submitting yourselves one to another in the fear of God." (Ephesians 5:18-21)

Beware of quiet and pious worship.

"O clap your hands, all ye people; shout unto God with the voice of triumph. For the Lord most high is terrible; he is a great King over all the earth." (Psalm 47: 1-2)

"Rejoice in the Lord, O ye righteous: for praise is comely for the upright. Praise the Lord with harp: sing unto him with the psaltery and an instrument of ten strings. Sing unto him a new song; play skillfully with a loud noise." (Psalm 33:1-3)

Shouting, lifting holy hands and acknowledging agreement by uttering (if not shouting) Amen are most apropos in the sanctuary.

"Unto thee will I cry, O Lord my rock; be not silent to me: lest, if thou be silent to me, I become like them that go down into the pit. Hear the voice of my supplications, when I cry unto thee, when I lift up my hands toward thy holy oracle." (Psalm 28:1&2)

"I will therefore that men pray every where, lifting up holy hands, without wrath and doubting." (1 Timothy 2:8)

Beware of the speaking in tongues without interpretation in worship services.

"If any man speak in an unknown tongue, let it be by two, or at the most by three, and that by course; and let one interpret. But if there be no interpreter, let him keep silence in the church; and let him speak to himself, and to God. Let the prophets speak two or three, and let the other judge. If any thing be revealed to another that sitteth by, let the first hold his peace. For ye may all prophesy one by one, that all may learn, and all may be comforted. And the spirits of the prophets are subject to the prophets. For God is not the author of confusion, but of peace, as in all churches of the saints." (1 Corinthians 14:27-33)

"O give thanks unto the Lord; for he is good; for his mercy endureth for ever. And say ye, Save us, O God of our salvation, and gather us together, and deliver us from the heathen, that we may give thanks to thy holy name, and glory in thy praise. Blessed be the Lord God of Israel for ever and ever. And all the people said, Amen, and praised the Lord." (1 Chronicles 16:34-36)

Ministers are to be on spiritual fire as opposed to dull and lacking in emotion.

"Bless the Lord, O my soul. O lord my God, thou art very great; thou art clothed with honour and majesty. Who coverest thyself with light as with a garment: who stretchest out the heavens like a curtain: Who layeth the beams of his chambers in the waters: who maketh the clouds his chariot: who walketh upon the wings of the wind: Who maketh his angels spirits; his ministers a flaming fire: Who laid the foundations of the earth, that it should not be removed for ever." (**Psalm 104: 1-5**)

"And again, when he bringeth in the first begotten into the world, he saith, And let all the angels of God worship him. And of the angels he saith, Who maketh his angels spirits, and his ministers a flame of fire." (**Hebrews 1:6-7**)

"O Lord, thou hast deceived me, and I was deceived: thou art stronger than I, and hast prevailed: I am in derision daily, every one mocketh me. For since I spake, I cried out, I cried violence and spoil; because the word of the Lord was made a reproach unto me, and a derision, daily. Then I said, I will not make mention of him, nor speak any more in his name. But his word was in mine heart as a burning fire shut up in my bones, and I was weary with forbearing, and I could not stay." (**Jeremiah 20:7-9**)

There is no vow of poverty for the man or woman of God. There is no vow of celibacy as in not to marry.

"Therefore said he unto them, The harvest truly is great, but the labourers are few: pray ye therefore the Lord of the harvest, that he would send forth labourers into his harvest. Go your ways: behold, I send you forth as lambs among wolves. Carry neither purse, nor scrip, nor shoes: and salute no man by the way. And into whatsoever house ye enter, first say, Peace be to this house. And if the son of peace be there, your peace shall rest upon it: if not, it shall turn to you again. And in the same house remain, eating and drinking such things as they give: for the labourer is worthy of his hire. Go not from house to house. And into whatsoever city ye enter, and they receive you, eat such things as are set before you:" (**Luke 10:2-8**)

"Do ye not know that they which minister about holy things live of the things of the temple? and they which wait at the alter are partakers with the alter? Even so hath the Lord ordained that they which preach the gospel should live of the gospel." (**1 Corinthians 9:13-14**)

"Now concerning the things whereof ye wrote unto me: It is good for a man not to touch a woman. Nevertheless, to avoid fornication, let every man have his own wife, and let every woman have her own husband. Let the husband render unto the wife due benevolence: and likewise also the wife unto the husband. The wife hath not power of her own body, but the husband: and likewise also the husband hath not power of his own body, but the wife." (**1 Corinthians 7:1-4**)

"Marriage is honourable in all, and the bed undefiled: but whoremongers and adulterers God will judge." (**Hebrews 13:4**)

"Now the Spirit speaketh expressly, that in the latter times some shall depart from the faith, giving heed to seducing spirits, and doctrines of devils; Speaking lies in hypocrisy; having their conscience seared with a hot iron; Forbidding to marry, and commanding to abstain from meats, which God hath created to be received with thanksgiving of them which believe and know the truth." (**1 Timothy 4:1-3**)

Beware of any church that does not see the necessity of an invitation to discipleship after the word has been preached.

"So then faith cometh by hearing, and hearing by the word of God." (**Romans 10:17**)

"Then Peter said unto them, Repent, and be baptized every one of you in the name of Jesus Christ for the remission of sins, and ye shall receive the gift of the Holy Ghost. For the promise is unto you, and to your children, and to all that are afar off, even as many as the Lord our God shall call. And with many other words did he testify and exhort, saying, Save yourselves from this untoward generation. Then they that gladly received his word were baptized: and the same day there were added unto them about three thousand souls. And they continued stedfastly in the apostles' doctrine and fellowship, and in breaking of bread, and in prayers." (**Acts 2:38-42**)

Beware of women Pastors and Co-Pastors (See Chapter 11, Pastors (Overseers) Men, Women or Both).

"And thou shalt put upon Aaron the holy garments, and anoint him, and sanctify him; that he may minister unto me in the priest's office. And thou shalt bring his sons, and clothe them with coats: And thou shalt anoint them, as thou didst anoint their father, that they may minister unto me in the priest's office: for their anointing shall surely be an everlasting priesthood throughout their generations." (**Exodus 40:13-15**)

"This is a true saying, If a man desire the office of a bishop, he desireth a good work. A bishop then must be blameless, the husband of one wife, vigilant, sober, of good behaviour, given to hospitality, apt to teach; Not given to wine, no striker, not greedy of filthy lucre; but patient, not a brawler, not covetous; One that ruleth well his own house, having his children in subjection with all gravity; (For if a man know not how to rule his own house, how shall he take care of the church of God?). (**1 Timothy 3:1-5**)

"But I would have you know, that the head of every man is Christ; and the head of the woman is the man; and the head of Christ is God." (**1 Corinthians 11: 3**)

"But I suffer not a woman to teach, nor to usurp authority over the man, but to be in silence." (**1 Timothy 2:12**)

"Likewise, ye wives, be in subjection to your own husbands; that, if any obey not the word, they also may without the word be won by the conversation of the wives; While they behold your chaste conversation coupled with fear. Whose adorning let it not be that outward adorning of plaiting the hair, and of wearing of gold, or of putting on of apparel; But let it be the hidden man of the heart, in that which is not corruptible, even the ornament of a meek and quiet spirit, which is in the sight of God of great price. For after this manner in the old time the holy women also, who trusted in God, adorned themselves, being in subjection unto their own husbands:" (**1 Peter 3:1-5**)

Pastors and ministers are to be examples rather than lords over the flock.

The elders which are among you I exhort, who am also an elder, and a witness of the sufferings of Christ, and also a partaker of the glory that shall be revealed: Feed the flock of God which is among you, taking the oversight thereof, not by constraint, but willingly; not for filthy lucre, but of a ready mind; Neither as being lords over God's heritage, but being ensamples to the flock. And when the chief Shepherd shall appear, ye shall receive a crown of glory that fadeth not away." (1 Peter 5:1-4)

Obey them that have the rule over you, and submit yourselves: for they watch for your souls, as they that must give account, that they may do it with joy, and not with grief: for that is unprofitable for you. Pray for us: for we trust we have a good conscience, in all things willing to live honestly." (Hebrews 13:17-18)

Beware of prophets/founders of denominations. Learn the basis upon which a particular denomination was established and whether the prophesies of the prophet/founder have been fulfilled (they have not).

"When a prophet speaketh in the name of the Lord, if the thing follow not, nor come to pass, that is the thing which the Lord hath not spoken, but the prophet hath spoken it presumptuously: thou shalt not be afraid of him." (Deuteronomy 18:22)

"These were more noble than those in Thessalonica, in that they received the word with all readiness of mind, and searched the scriptures daily, whether those things were so." (Acts 17:11)

"Beware of false prophets, which come to you in sheep's clothing, but inwardly they are ravening wolves. Ye shall know them by their fruits. Do men gather grapes of thorns, or figs of thistles? Even so every good tree bringeth forth good fruit; but a corrupt tree bringeth forth evil fruit. A good tree cannot bring forth evil fruit, neither can a corrupt tree bring forth good fruit. Every tree that bringeth not forth good fruit is hewn down, and cast into the fire. Wherefore by their fruits ye shall know them. Not every one that saith unto me, Lord, Lord, shall enter into the kingdom of heaven; but he that doeth the will of my Father which is in heaven." (Matthew 7:15-21)

Follow the Bible rather than teachings/writings as a substitute.

"O generation of vipers, how can ye, being evil, speak good things? for out of the abundance of the heart the mouth speaketh. A good man out of the good treasure of the heart bringeth forth good things: and an evil man out of the evil treasure bringeth forth evil things. But I say unto you, That every idle word that men shall speak, they shall give account thereof in the day of judgment. For by thy words thou shalt be justified, and by thy words thou shalt be condemned." (Matthew 12:34-37)

"As ye have therefore received Christ Jesus the Lord, so walk ye in him: Rooted and built up in him, and stablished in the faith, as ye have been taught, abounding therein with thanksgiving. Beware lest any man spoil you through philosophy and vain deceit, after the tradition of men, after the rudiments of the world, and not after Christ." (Colossians 2:6-8)

"Study to shew thyself approved unto God, a workman that needeth not to be ashamed, rightly dividing the word of truth." (2 Timothy 2:15)

"For I testify unto every man that heareth the words of the prophecy of this book, If any man shall add unto these things, God shall add unto him the plagues that are written in this book: And if any man shall take away from the words of the book of this prophecy, God

shall take away his part out of the book of life, and out of the holy city, and from the things which are written in this book." (**Revelation 22:18-19**)

Beware of any prophecy beyond biblical prophecy and revelation.

"Wherefore seeing we also are compassed about with so great a cloud of witnesses, let us lay aside every weight, and the sin which doth so easily beset us, and let us run with patience the race that is set before us, Looking unto Jesus the author and finisher of our faith; who for the joy that was set before him endured the cross, despising the shame, and is set down at the right hand of the throne of God." (**Hebrews 12:1-2**)

"I am Alpha and Omega, the beginning and the ending, saith the Lord, which is, and which was, and which is to come, the Almighty." (**Revelation 1:8**)

"Now when John had heard in the prison the works of Christ, he sent two of his disciples, And said unto him, Art thou he that should come, or do we look for another? Jesus answered and said unto them, Go and shew John again those things which ye do hear and see: The blind receive their sight, and the lame walk, the lepers are cleansed, and the deaf hear, the dead are raised up, and the poor have the gospel preached to them. And blessed is he, whosoever shall not be offended in me." (**Matthew 11:2-6**)

There is only biblical theology not other theologies to include Black Liberation theology, Catholic theology, Women theology, Hispanic theology, Scientific theology etc., etc, or anything other than Jesus Christ centered theology.

"Moreover, brethren, I declare unto you the gospel which I preached unto you, which also ye have received, and wherein ye stand; By which also ye are saved, if ye keep in memory what I preached unto you, unless ye have believed in vain. For I delivered unto you first of all that which I also received, how that Christ died for our sins according to the scriptures; And that he was buried, and that he rose again the third day according to the scriptures: And that he was seen of Cephas, then of the twelve: After that, he was seen of above five hundred brethren at once; of whom the greater part remain unto this present, but some are fallen asleep. After that, he was seen of James; then of all the apostles. And last of all he was seen of me also, as of one born out of due time. For I am the least of the apostles, that am not meet to be called an apostle, because I persecuted the church of God. But by the grace of God I am what I am: and his grace which was bestowed upon me was not in vain; but I laboured more abundantly than they all: yet not I, but the grace of God which was with me. Therefore whether it were I or they, so we preach, and so ye believed." (**1 Corinthians 15:1-11**)

"Yea doubtless, and I count all things but loss for the excellency of the knowledge of Christ Jesus my Lord: for whom I have suffered the loss of all things, and do count them but dung, that I may win Christ, And be found in him, not having mine own righteousness, which is of the law, but that which is through the faith of Christ, the righteousness which is of God by faith: That I may know him, and the power of his resurrection, and the fellowship of his sufferings, being made conformable unto his death; If by any means I might attain unto the resurrection of the dead. Not as though I had already attained, either were already perfect: but I follow after, if that I may apprehend that for which also I am apprehended of Christ Jesus. Brethren, I count not myself to have apprehended: but this one thing I do, forgetting those things which are behind, and reaching forth unto those things which are

before, I press toward the mark for the prize of the high calling of God in Christ Jesus. Let us therefore, as many as be perfect, be thus minded: and if in any thing ye be otherwise minded, God shall reveal even this unto you." (**Philippians 3:8-14**)

"And I, brethren, when I came to you, came not with excellency of speech or of wisdom, declaring unto you the testimony of God. For I determined not to know any thing among you, save Jesus Christ, and him crucified. And I was with you in weakness, and in fear, and in much trembling. And my speech and my preaching was not with enticing words of man's wisdom, but in demonstration of the Spirit and of power: That your faith should not stand in the wisdom of men, but in the power of God." (**1 Corinthians 2:1-5**)

"If any man speak, let him speak as the oracles of God; if any man minister, let him do it as of the ability which God giveth: that God in all things may be glorified through Jesus Christ, to whom be praise and dominion for ever and ever. Amen." (**1 Peter 4:11**)

Hold in esteem the church that places in prominence the cross; that is the cross not the crucifix. We preach an empty cross and a risen savior not a savior still nailed to a cross; this is to have and exhibit understanding.

"For the preaching of the cross is to them that perish foolishness; but unto us which are saved it is the power of God." (**1 Corinthians 1:18**)

"Nevertheless, whereto we have already attained, let us walk by the same rule, let us mind the same thing. Brethren, be followers together of me, and mark them which walk so as ye have us for an ensample. (For many walk, of whom I have told you often, and now tell you even weeping, that they are the enemies of the cross of Christ: Whose end is destruction, whose God is their belly, and whose glory is in their shame, who mind earthly things.) For our conversation is in heaven; from whence also we look for the Saviour, the Lord Jesus Christ: Who shall change our vile body, that it may be fashioned like unto his glorious body, according to the working whereby he is able even to subdue all things unto himself." (**Philippians 3:16-21**)

"But God, who is rich in mercy, for his great love wherewith he loved us, Even when we were dead in sins, hath quickened us together with Christ, (by grace ye are saved;) And hath raised us up together, and made us sit together in heavenly places in Christ Jesus: That in the ages to come he might shew the exceeding riches of his grace in his kindness toward us through Christ Jesus." (**Ephesians 2:4-7**)

"Now upon the first day of the week, very early in the morning, they came unto the sepulchre, bringing the spices which they had prepared, and certain others with them. And they found the stone rolled away from the sepulchre. And they entered in, and found not the body of the Lord Jesus. And it came to pass, as they were much perplexed thereabout, behold, two men stood by them in shining garments: And as they were afraid, and bowed down their faces to the earth, they said unto them, Why seek ye the living among the dead? He is not here, but is risen: remember how he spake unto you when he was yet in Galilee, Saying, The Son of man must be delivered into the hands of sinful men, and be crucified, and the third day rise again." (**Luke 24:1-7**)

"And if Christ be not risen, then is our preaching vain, and your faith is also vain. Yea, and we are found false witnesses of God; because we have testified of God that he raised up Christ: whom he raised not up, if so be that the dead rise not. For if the dead rise not, then

is not Christ raised: And if Christ be not raised, your faith is vain; ye are yet in your sins. Then they also which are fallen asleep in Christ are perished. If in this life only we have hope in Christ, we are of all men most miserable. But now is Christ risen from the dead, and become the firstfruits of them that slept. (1 Corinthians 15:14-20)

Now, notwithstanding a strictness in the preaching of the gospel of Jesus Christ, the Bible recognizes a certain aspect of acceptability in the mere instance of Christ being preached at all; be careful!

"And John answered and said, Master, we saw one casting out devils in thy name; and we forbad him, because he followeth not with us. And Jesus said unto him, Forbid him not: for he that is not against us is for us." (Luke 9:49&50)

"And John answered him, saying, Master, we saw one casting out devils in thy name, and he followeth not us: and we forbad him, because he followeth not us. But Jesus said, Forbid him not: for there is no man which shall do a miracle in my name, that can lightly speak evil of me. For he that is not against us is on our part." (Mark 9:38-40)

"He that is not with me is against me: and he that gathereth not with me scattereth." (Luke 11:23)

"Some indeed preach Christ even of envy and strife; and some also of good will: The one preach Christ of contention, not sincerely, supposing to add affliction to my bonds: But the other of love, knowing that I am set for the defence of the gospel. What then? notwithstanding, every way, whether in pretence, or in truth, Christ is preached; and I therein do rejoice, yea, and will rejoice." (Philippians 1:15-18)

"Beware of false prophets, which come to you in sheep's clothing, but inwardly they are ravening wolves. Ye shall know them by their fruits. Do men gather grapes of thorns, or figs of thistles? Even so every good tree bringeth forth good fruit; but a corrupt tree bringeth forth evil fruit. A good tree cannot bring forth evil fruit, neither can a corrupt tree bring forth good fruit. Every tree that bringeth not forth good fruit is hewn down, and cast into the fire. Wherefore by their fruits ye shall know them. Not every one that saith unto me, Lord, Lord, shall enter into the kingdom of heaven; but he that doeth the will of my Father which is in heaven. Many will say to me in that day, Lord, Lord, have we not prophesied in thy name? and in thy name have cast out devils? and in thy name done many wonderful works? And then will I profess unto them, I never knew you: depart from me, ye that work iniquity." (Matthew 7:15-23)

Beware of the overemphasis and/or concentration upon a particular teaching or ministry such as healing, prosperity, social action or suffering.

"And Jesus returned in the power of the Spirit into Galilee: and there went out a fame of him through all the region round about. And he taught in their synagogues, being glorified of all. And he came to Nazareth, where he had been brought up: and, as his custom was, he went into the synagogue on the sabbath day, and stood up for to read. And there was delivered unto him the book of the prophet Esaias. And when he had opened the book, he found the place where it was written, The Spirit of the Lord is upon me, because he hath anointed me to preach the gospel to the poor; he hath sent me to heal the brokenhearted,

to preach deliverance to the captives, and recovering of sight to the blind, to set at liberty them that are bruised, To preach the acceptable year of the Lord." (**Luke 4:14-19**)

"For the preaching of the cross is to them that perish foolishness; but unto us which are saved it is the power of God. For it is written, I will destroy the wisdom of the wise, and will bring to nothing the understanding of the prudent. Where is the wise? where is the scribe? where is the disputer of this world? hath not God made foolish the wisdom of this world? For after that in the wisdom of God the world by wisdom knew not God, it pleased God by the foolishness of preaching to save them that believe." (**1 Corinthians 1:18-21**)

Look to be fed biblical knowledge with understanding as championed by Jesus Christ and as stated by the Bible, by the Pastor in the Church. This is vital to Christian maturation.

"Then opened he their understanding, that they might understand the scriptures, And said unto them, Thus it is written, and thus it behoved Christ to suffer, and to rise from the dead the third day: And that repentance and remission of sins should be preached in his name among all nations, beginning at Jerusalem." (**Luke 24:45-47**)

"And I will give you pastors according to mine heart, which shall feed you with knowledge and understanding." (**Jeremiah 3:15**)

"Knowing this first, that there shall come in the last days scoffers, walking after their own lusts, And saying, Where is the promise of his coming? for since the fathers fell asleep, all things continue as they were from the beginning of the creation. For this they willingly are ignorant of, that by the word of God the heavens were of old, and the earth standing out of the water and in the water: Whereby the world that then was, being overflowed with water, perished: But the heavens and the earth, which are now, by the same word are kept in store, reserved unto fire against the day of judgment and perdition of ungodly men." (**2 Peter 3:3-7**)

"Yea, if thou criest after knowledge, and liftest up thy voice for understanding; If thou seekest her as silver, and searchest for her as for hid treasures; Then shalt thou understand the fear of the Lord, and find the knowledge of God. For the Lord giveth wisdom: out of his mouth cometh knowledge and understanding." (**Proverbs 2:3-6**)

"The fear of the Lord is the beginning of wisdom: and the knowledge of the holy is understanding." (**Proverbs 9:10**)

"And there shall come forth a rod out of the stem of Jesse, and a Branch shall grow out of his roots: And the spirit of the Lord shall rest upon him, the spirit of wisdom and understanding, the spirit of counsel and might, the spirit of knowledge and of the fear of the Lord; And shall make him of quick understanding in the fear of the Lord: and he shall not judge after the sight of his eyes, neither reprove after the hearing of his ears: But with righteousness shall he judge the poor, and reprove with equity for the meek of the earth: and he shall smite the earth with the rod of his mouth, and with the breath of his lips shall he slay the wicked. And righteousness shall be the girdle of his loins, and faithfulness the girdle of his reins." (**Isaiah 11:1-5**)

"Wherefore he saith, Awake thou that sleepest, and arise from the dead, and Christ shall give thee light. See then that ye walk circumspectly, not as fools, but as wise, Redeeming the

time, because the days are evil. Wherefore be ye not unwise, but understanding what the will of the Lord is." (**Ephesians 5:17**)

"Brethren, be not children in understanding: howbeit in malice be ye children, but in understanding be men." (**1 Corinthians 14:20**)

"When I was a child, I spake as a child, I understood as a child, I thought as a child: but when I became a man, I put away childish things." (**1 Corinthians 13:11**)

"We give thanks to God and the Father of our Lord Jesus Christ, praying always for you, Since we heard of your faith in Christ Jesus, and of the love which ye have to all the saints, For the hope which is laid up for you in heaven, whereof ye heard before in the word of the truth of the gospel; Which is come unto you, as it is in all the world; and bringeth forth fruit, as it doth also in you, since the day ye heard of it, and knew the grace of God in truth: As ye also learned of Epaphras our dear fellowservant, who is for you a faithful minister of Christ; Who also declared unto us your love in the Spirit. For this cause we also, since the day we heard it, do not cease to pray for you, and to desire that ye might be filled with the knowledge of his will in all wisdom and spiritual understanding; That ye might walk worthy of the Lord unto all pleasing, being fruitful in every good work, and increasing in the knowledge of God; Strengthened with all might, according to his glorious power, unto all patience and longsuffering with joyfulness; Giving thanks unto the Father, which hath made us meet to be partakers of the inheritance of the saints in light: Who hath delivered us from the power of darkness, and hath translated us into the kingdom of his dear Son: In whom we have redemption through his blood, even the forgiveness of sins: Who is the image of the invisible God, the firstborn of every creature: For by him were all things created, that are in heaven, and that are in earth, visible and invisible, whether they be thrones, or dominions, or principalities, or powers: all things were created by him, and for him: And he is before all things, and by him all things consist." (**Colossians 1:3-17**)

The Bible does not permit multiple wives. Conversely, the Bible excludes no man from having a wife. Both beliefs are as such are a part of the cults of Christianity.

"Therefore shall a man leave his father and his mother, and shall cleave unto his wife: and they shall be one flesh." (**Genesis 2:24**)

"Now concerning the things whereof ye wrote unto me: It is good for a man not to touch a woman. Nevertheless, to avoid fornication, let every man have his own wife, and let every woman have her own husband." (**1 Corinthians 7:1-2**)

"Neither shall he multiply wives to himself, that his heart turn not away: neither shall he greatly multiply to himself silver and gold." (**Deuteronomy 17:17**)

For there are some eunuchs, which were so born from their mother's womb: and there are some eunuchs, which were made eunuchs of men: and there be eunuchs, which have made themselves eunuchs for the kingdom of heaven's sake. He that is able to receive it, let him receive it." (**Matthew 19:12**)

"Marriage is honourable in all, and the bed undefiled: but whoremongers and adulterers God will judge." (**Hebrews 13:4**)

"And when Jesus was come into Peter's house, he saw his wife's mother laid, and sick of a fever. And he touched her hand, and the fever left her: and she arose, and ministered unto them." (**Matthew 8:14&15**)

"A bishop then must be blameless, the husband of one wife, vigilant, sober, of good behaviour, given to hospitality, apt to teach;" (**1 Timothy 3:2**)

14

DIFFERENTIATING CHRISTIANITY FROM OTHER WORLD RELIGIONS

What differentiates Christianity from other World Religions?

CHRISTIANITY BASES ITS beliefs upon the fulfillment of the prophecies and eye witnessed accounts of the Bible

> *"Then he took unto him the twelve, and said unto them, Behold, we go up to Jerusalem, and all things that are written by the prophets concerning the Son of man shall be accomplished. For he shall be delivered unto the Gentiles, and shall be mocked, and spitefully entreated, and spitted on: and they shall scourge him, and put him to death: and the third day he shall rise again." (Luke 18: 31-33)*

> *"For I delivered unto you first of all that which I also received, how that Christ died for our sins according to the scriptures; And that he was buried, and that he rose again the third day according to the scriptures: And that he was seen of Cephas, then of the twelve: After that, he was seen of above five hundred brethren at once; of whom the greater part remain unto this present, but some are fallen asleep. After that, he was seen of James; then of all the apostles. And last of all he was seen of me also, as of one born out of due time. For I am the least of the apostles, that am not meet to be called an apostle, because I persecuted the church of God." (1 Corinthians 15:3-9)*

> *And many other signs truly did Jesus in the presence of his disciples, which are not written in this book: but these are written, that ye might believe that Jesus is the Christ, the Son of God; and that believing ye might have life through his name." (John 20:30-31)*

> *"And, being assembled together with them, commanded them that they should not depart from Jerusalem, but wait for the promise of the Father, which, saith he, ye have heard of me. For John truly baptized with water; but ye shall be baptized with the Holy Ghost not many days hence. When they therefore were come together, they asked of him, saying, Lord, wilt thou at this time restore again the kingdom to Israel? And he said unto them, It is not for you to know the times or the seasons, which the Father hath put in his own power. But ye shall receive power, after that the Holy Ghost is come upon you: and ye shall be witnesses unto me both in Jerusalem, and in all Judaea, and in Samaria, and unto the uttermost part of the earth." (Acts 1:4-8)*

The Bible (66 book cannon) provides the complete revelation of Christianity without appendage. There is no other such book.

"All scripture is given by inspiration of God, and is profitable for doctrine, for reproof, for correction, for instruction in righteousness; " (**2 Timothy 3:16**)

"For I testify unto every man that heareth the words of the prophecy of this book, If any man shall add unto these things, God shall add unto him the plagues that are written in this book: and if any man shall take away from the words of the book of this prophecy, God shall take away his part out of the book of life, and out of the holy city, and from the things which are written in this book." (**Revelation 22:18-19**)

"Knowing this first, that no prophecy of the scripture is of any private interpretation. For the prophecy came not in old time by the will of man: but holy men of God spake as they were moved by the Holy Ghost." (**2 Peter 1:20-21**)

Christianity reveals creation.

"In the beginning God created the heaven and the earth. And the earth was without form, and void; and darkness was upon the face of the deep. And the Spirit of God moved upon the face of the waters." (**Genesis 1:1-2**)

And God saw every thing that he had made, and, behold, it was very good. And the evening and the morning were the sixth day. Thus the heavens and the earth were finished, and all the host of them. And on the seventh day God ended his work which he had made; and he rested on the seventh day from all his work which he had made. And God blessed the seventh day, and sanctified it: because that in it he had rested from all his work which God created and made. These are the generations of the heavens and of the earth when they were created, in the day that the Lord God made the earth and the heavens;" (**Genesis 1:31-2:4**)

Christianity reveals man's creation in the likeness of Almighty God and man's purpose as being to glorify our Father, Almighty God.

"And God said, Let the earth bring forth the living creature after his kind, cattle, and creeping thing, and beast of the earth after his kind: and it was so. And God made the beast of the earth after his kind, and cattle after their kind, and every thing that creepeth upon the earth after his kind: and God saw that it was good. And God said, Let us make man in our image, after our likeness: and let them have dominion over the fish of the sea, and over the fowl of the air, and over the cattle, and over all the earth, and over every creeping thing that creepeth upon the earth. So God created man in his own image, in the image of God created he him; male and female created he them." (**Genesis 1:24-27**)

"For I am the Lord thy God, the Holy One of Israel, thy Saviour: I gave Egypt for thy ransom, Ethiopia and Seba for thee. Since thou wast precious in my sight, thou hast been honourable, and I have loved thee: therefore will I give men for thee, and people for thy life. Fear not: for I am with thee: I will bring thy seed from the east, and gather thee from the west; I will say to the north, Give up; and to the south, Keep not back: bring my sons from far, and my daughters from the ends of the earth; Even every one that is called by my name: for I have created him for my glory, I have formed him; yea, I have made him. Bring forth the blind people that have eyes, and the deaf that have ears. Let all the nations be gathered

together, and let the people be assembled: who among them can declare this, and shew us former things? Let them bring forth their witnesses, that they may be justified: or let them hear, and say, It is truth. Ye are my witnesses, saith the Lord, and my servant whom I have chosen: that ye may know and believe me, and understand that I am he: before me there was no God formed, neither shall there be after me." (Isaiah 43:3-10)

"Herein is my Father glorified, that ye bear much fruit; so shall ye be my disciples. As the Father hath loved me, so have I loved you: continue ye in my love." (John 15:8&9)

"For ye are all the children of God by faith in Christ Jesus." (Galatians 3:26)

Christianity worships an Almighty God that will indwell a person with his Spirit thereby enabling overcoming power.

"But ye shall receive power, after that the Holy Ghost is come upon you: and ye shall be witnesses unto me both in Jerusalem, and in all Judaea, and in Samaria, and unto the uttermost part of the earth." (Acts 1:8)

"And it shall come to pass afterward, that I will pour out my spirit upon all flesh; and your sons and your daughters shall prophesy, your old men shall dream dreams, your young men shall see visions: and also upon the servants and upon the handmaids in those days will I pour out my spirit." (Joel 2:28-29)

"And, being assembled together with them, commanded them that they should not depart from Jerusalem, but wait for the promise of the Father, which, saith he, ye have heard of me. For John truly baptized with water; but ye shall be baptized with the Holy Ghost not many days hence." (Acts 1:4-5)

"For whatsoever is born of God overcometh the world: and this is the victory that overcometh the world, even our faith. Who is he that overcometh the world, but he that believeth that Jesus is the Son of God? This is he that came by water and blood, even Jesus Christ; not by water only, but by water and blood. And it is the Spirit that beareth witness, because the Spirit is truth." (1 John 5:4-6)

Christianity proclaims that good overcomes evil.

"Be not overcome of evil, but overcome evil with good." (Romans 12: 21)

In Christianity, salvation is based upon a belief in a risen savior that compels good works rather than salvation through works.

"For God sent not his Son into the world to condemn the world; but that the world through him might be saved. He that believeth on him is not condemned: but he that believeth not is condemned already, because he hath not believed in the name of the only begotten Son of God." (John 3:17-18)

"For by grace are ye saved through faith; and that not of yourselves: it is the gift of God: not of works, lest any man should boast. For we are his workmanship, created in Christ Jesus unto good works, which God hath before ordained that we should walk in them." (Ephesians 2:8-10)

"What doth it profit, my brethren, though a man say he hath faith, and have not works? Can faith save him? If a brother or sister be naked, and destitute of daily food, and one

of you say unto them, Depart in peace, be ye warmed and filled; notwithstanding ye give them not those things which are needful to the body; what doth it profit? Even so faith, if it hath not works, is dead, being alone. Yea, a man may say, Thou hast faith, and I have works: shew me thy faith without thy works, and I will shew thee my faith by my works. Thou believest that there is one God; thou doest well: the devils also believe, and tremble. But wilt thou know, O vain man, that faith without works is dead?" (James 2:14-20)

"But thanks be to God, which giveth us the victory through our Lord Jesus Christ. Therefore, my beloved brethren, be ye stedfast, unmoveable, always abounding in the work of the Lord, forasmuch as ye know that your labour is not in vain in the Lord." (1 Corinthians 15:57&58)

Christianity reveals our relationship to the Almighty God as offsprings. In accepting the Father's sacrificial gift of his only begotten son in atonement for our sins, the righteousness of the Son of God is imputed upon the believer.

"Be ye therefore followers of God, as dear children; and walk in love, as Christ also hath loved us, and hath given himself for us an offering and a sacrifice to God for a sweetsmelling savour." (Ephesians 5:1-2)

"He that believeth and is baptized shall be saved; but he that believeth not shall be damned." (Mark 16:16)

"But God commendeth his love toward us, in that, while we were yet sinners, Christ died for us. Much more then, being now justified by his blood, we shall be saved from wrath through him. For if, when we were enemies, we were reconciled to God by the death of his Son, much more, being reconciled, we shall be saved by his life. And not only so, but we also joy in God through our Lord Jesus Christ, by whom we have now received the atonement. Wherefore, as by one man sin entered into the world, and death by sin; and so death passed upon all men, for that all have sinned: (For until the law sin was in the world: but sin is not imputed when there is no law." (Romans 5:8-13)

"Therefore it is of faith, that it might be by grace; to the end the promise might be sure to all the seed; not to that only which is of the law, but to that also which is of the faith of Abraham; who is the father of us all, (As it is written, I have made thee a father of many nations,) before him whom he believed, even God, who quickeneth the dead, and calleth those things which be not as though they were. Who against hope believed in hope, that he might become the father of many nations; according to that which was spoken, So shall thy seed be. And being not weak in faith, he considered not his own body now dead, when he was about an hundred years old, neither yet the deadness of Sara's womb: He staggered not at the promise of God through unbelief; but was strong in faith, giving glory to God; And being fully persuaded that, what he had promised, he was able also to perform. And therefore it was imputed to him for righteousness. Now it was not written for his sake alone, that it was imputed to him; But for us also, to whom it shall be imputed, if we believe on him that raised up Jesus our Lord from the dead; Who was delivered for our offences, and was raised again for our justification." (Romans 4:16-25)

Christianity worships a savior that pre-existed and was resurrected from a death in the flesh.

"Then Jesus said unto them, verily, verily, I say unto you, Moses gave you not that bread from heaven; but my Father giveth you the true bread from heaven. For the bread of God is he which cometh down from heaven, and giveth life unto the world." (John 6:32-33)

"And the Word was made flesh, and dwelt among us, (and we beheld his glory, the glory as of the only begotten of the Father,) full of grace and truth. John bare witness of him, and cried, saying, This was he of whom I spake, He that cometh after me is preferred before me: for he was before me. And of his fulness have all we received, and grace for grace. For the law was given by Moses, but grace and truth came by Jesus Christ." (John 1:14-17)

"For I came down from heaven, not to do mine own will, but the will of him that sent me. And this is the Father's will which hath sent me, that of all which he hath given me I should lose nothing, but should raise it up again at the last day. And this is the will of him that sent me, that every one which seeth the Son, and believeth on him, may have everlasting life: and I will raise him up at the last day." (John 6: 38-40)

"Jesus saith unto her, Thy brother shall rise again. Martha saith unto him, I know that he shall rise again in the resurrection at the last day. Jesus said unto her, I am the resurrection, and the life: he that believeth in me, though he were dead, yet shall he live: and whosoever liveth and believeth in me shall never die. Believest thou this? She saith unto him, Yea, Lord: I believe that thou art the Christ, the Son of God, which should come into the world." (John 11:23-27)

"In the beginning was the Word, and the Word was with God, and the Word was God. The same was in the beginning with God. All things were made by him; and without him was not any thing made that was made. In him was life; and the life was the light of men. And the light shineth in darkness; and the darkness comprehended it not." (John 1:1-5)

"Now upon the first day of the week, very early in the morning, they came unto the sepulchre, bringing the spices which they had prepared, and certain others with them. And they found the stone rolled away from the sepulchre. And they entered in, and found not the body of the Lord Jesus. And it came to pass, as they were much perplexed thereabout, behold, two men stood by them in shining garments: and as they were afraid, and bowed down their faces to the earth, they said unto them, Why seek ye the living among the dead? He is not here, but is risen: remember how he spake unto you when he was yet in Galilee, Saying, The Son of man must be delivered into the hands of sinful men, and be crucified, and the third day rise again." (Luke 24:1-7)

"But one in a certain place testified, saying, What is man, that thou art mindful of him? or the son of man, that thou visitest him? Thou madest him a little lower than the angels; thou crownedst him with glory and honour, and didst set him over the works of thy hands: Thou hast put all things in subjection under his feet. For in that he put all in subjection under him, he left nothing that is not put under him. But now we see not yet all things put under him. But we see Jesus, who was made a little lower than the angels for the suffering of death, crowned with glory and honour; that he by the grace of God should taste death for every man." (Hebrews 2:6-9)

The Christian savior, Jesus, was prophesized over centuries and he fulfilled all biblical prophecy.

"Thou shalt be perfect with the Lord thy God. For these nations, which thou shalt possess, hearkened unto observers of times, and unto diviners: but as for thee, the Lord thy God hath not suffered thee so to do. The Lord thy God will raise up unto thee a Prophet from the midst of thee, of thy brethren, like unto me; unto him ye shall hearken; according to all that thou desiredst of the Lord thy God in Horeb in the day of the assembly, saying, Let me not hear again the voice of the Lord my God, neither let me see this great fire any more, that I die not. And the Lord said unto me, They have well spoken that which they have spoken. I will raise them up a Prophet from among their brethren, like unto thee, and will put my words in his mouth; and he shall speak unto them all that I shall command him. And it shall come to pass, that whosoever will not hearken unto my words which he shall speak in my name, I will require it of him." (Deuteronomy 18:13-19)

Psalm 22 (entirety)

Men and brethren, children of the stock of Abraham, and whosoever among you feareth God, to you is the word of this salvation sent. For they that dwell at Jerusalem, and their rulers, because they knew him not, nor yet the voices of the prophets which are read every sabbath day, they have fulfilled them in condemning him. And though they found no cause of death in him, yet desired they Pilate that he should be slain. And when they had fulfilled all that was written of him, they took him down from the tree, and laid him in a sepulchre. But God raised him from the dead: and he was seen many days of them which came up with him from Galilee to Jerusalem, who are his witnesses unto the people. And we declare unto you glad tidings, how that the promise which was made unto the fathers, God hath fulfilled the same unto us their children, in that he hath raised up Jesus again; as it is also written in the second psalm, Thou art my Son, this day have I begotten thee. And as concerning that he raised him up from the dead, now no more to return to corruption, he said on this wise, I will give you the sure mercies of David. Wherefore he saith also in another psalm, Thou shalt not suffer thine Holy One to see corruption. For David, after he had served his own generation by the will of God, fell on sleep, and was laid unto his fathers, and saw corruption: but he, whom God raised again, saw no corruption. Be it known unto you therefore, men and brethren, that through this man is preached unto you the forgiveness of sins: and by him all that believe are justified from all things, from which ye could not be justified by the Law of Moses. Beware therefore, lest that come upon you, which is spoken of in the prophets; Behold, ye despisers, and wonder, and perish: for I work a work in your days, a work which ye shall in no wise believe, though a man declare it unto you." (Acts 13: 26-41)

Christianity worships a savior that was involved in creation.

"In the beginning was the Word, and the Word was with God, and the Word was God. The same was in the beginning with God. All things were made by him; and without him was not any thing made that was made. In him was life; and the life was the light of men." (John 1:1-4)

"For we are his workmanship, created in Christ Jesus unto good works, which God hath before ordained that we should walk in them." (Ephesians 2:10)

The Christian savior is worshipped as the Word of God incarnate. No other religion has a savior not to mention a savior that embodies their deity's spoken word.

"And the Word was made flesh, and dwelt among us, (and we beheld his glory, the glory as of the only begotten of the Father,) full of grace and truth.' (John 1:14)

Jesus proved himself to be the Messiah with words and works.

"Jesus answered them, I told you, and ye believed not: the works that I do in my Father's name, they bear witness of me. But ye believe not, because ye are not of my sheep, as I said unto you. My sheep hear my voice, and I know them, and they follow me: And I give unto them eternal life; and they shall never perish, neither shall any man pluck them out of my hand. My Father, which gave them me, is greater than all; and no man is able to pluck them out of my Father's hand. I and my Father are one. Then the Jews took up stones again to stone him. Jesus answered them, Many good works have I shewed you from my Father; for which of those works do ye stone me? The Jews answered him, saying, For a good work we stone thee not; but for blasphemy; and because that thou, being a man, makest thyself God. Jesus answered them, Is it not written in your law, I said, Ye are gods? If he called them gods, unto whom the word of God came, and the scripture cannot be broken; Say ye of him, whom the Father hath sanctified, and sent into the world, Thou blasphemest; because I said, I am the Son of God? If I do not the works of my Father, believe me not. But if I do, though ye believe not me, believe the works: that ye may know, and believe, that the Father is in me, and I in him. Therefore they sought again to take him: but he escaped out of their hand, And went away again beyond Jordan into the place where John at first baptized; and there he abode." (John 10:25-40)

Jesus performed among a multitude of miracles, some in particular that have otherwise never been accomplished even in this technological age.

"And as Jesus passed by, he saw a man which was blind from his birth. And his disciples asked him, saying, Master, who did sin, this man, or his parents, that he was born blind? Jesus answered, Neither hath this man sinned, nor his parents: but that the works of God should be made manifest in him. I must work the works of him that sent me, while it is day: the night cometh, when no man can work. As long as I am in the world, I am the light of the world. When he had thus spoken, he spat on the ground, and made clay of the spittle, and he anointed the eyes of the blind man with the clay, And said unto him, Go, wash in the pool of Siloam, (which is by interpretation, Sent.) He went his way therefore, and washed, and came seeing." (John 9:1-7)

"Then when Mary was come where Jesus was, and saw him, she fell down at his feet, saying unto him, Lord, if thou hadst been here, my brother had not died. When Jesus therefore saw her weeping, and the Jews also weeping which came with her, he groaned in the spirit, and was troubled, And said, Where have ye laid him? They said unto him, Lord, come and see. Jesus wept. Then said the Jews, Behold how he loved him! And some of them said, Could not this man, which opened the eyes of the blind, have caused that even this man should not have died? Jesus therefore again groaning in himself cometh to the grave. It was a cave, and a stone lay upon it. Jesus said, Take ye away the stone. Martha, the sister of him that was dead, saith unto him, Lord, by this time he stinketh: for he hath been dead four days. Jesus saith unto her, Said I not unto thee, that, if thou wouldest believe, thou shouldest see the glory of God? Then they took away the stone from the place where the dead was laid. And Jesus lifted up his eyes, and said, Father, I thank thee that thou hast heard me. And I knew that thou hearest me always: but because of the people which stand by I said it, that they may believe that thou hast sent me. And when he thus had spoken,

he cried with a loud voice, Lazarus, come forth. And he that was dead came forth, bound hand and foot with graveclothes: and his face was bound about with a napkin. Jesus saith unto them, Loose him, and let him go." (John 11:32- 44)

Jesus proclaims in the Bible the Heavenly Father, his Father, as the true God and that he is alive.

"These words spake Jesus, and lifted up his eyes to heaven, and said, Father, the hour is come; glorify thy Son, that thy Son also may glorify thee: As thou hast given him power over all flesh, that he should give eternal life to as many as thou hast given him. And this is life eternal, that they might know thee the only true God, and Jesus Christ, whom thou hast sent. I have glorified thee on the earth: I have finished the work which thou gavest me to do." (John 17:1-4)

Jesus is the fullness (best representation) of the Godhead (Trinity) of the heavenly Father, the Son and the Holy Ghost.

"As ye have therefore received Christ Jesus the Lord, so walk ye in him: Rooted and built up in him, and stablished in the faith, as ye have been taught, abounding therein with thanksgiving. Beware lest any man spoil you through philosophy and vain deceit, after the tradition of men, after the rudiments of the world, and not after Christ. For in him dwelleth all the fulness of the Godhead bodily. And ye are complete in him, which is the head of all principality and power: In whom also ye are circumcised with the circumcision made without hands, in putting off the body of the sins of the flesh by the circumcision of Christ: Buried with him in baptism, wherein also ye are risen with him through the faith of the operation of God, who hath raised him from the dead." (Colossians 2:6-12)

Jesus is proclaimed to be the author of eternal life.

"As he saith also in another place, Thou art a priest for ever after the order of Melchisedec. Who in the days of his flesh, when he had offered up prayers and supplications with strong crying and tears unto him that was able to save him from death, and was heard in that he feared; Though he were a Son, yet learned he obedience by the things which he suffered; And being made perfect, he became the author of eternal salvation unto all them that obey him;" (Hebrew 5: 6-9)

"Wherefore seeing we also are compassed about with so great a cloud of witnesses, let us lay aside every weight, and the sin which doth so easily beset us, and let us run with patience the race that is set before us, Looking unto Jesus the author and finisher of our faith; who for the joy that was set before him endured the cross, despising the shame, and is set down at the right hand of the throne of God." (Hebrews 12:1-2)

Jesus Christ is proclaimed as a risen savior and our propitiation. Jesus's ascension to heaven was eye witnessed.

"In this was manifested the love of God toward us, because that God sent his only begotten Son into the world, that we might live through him. Herein is love, not that we loved God, but that he loved us, and sent his Son to be the propitiation for our sins." (1 John 4:9-10)

"My little children, these things write I unto you, that ye sin not. And if any man sin, we have an advocate with the Father, Jesus Christ the righteous: And he is the propitiation for our sins: and not for ours only, but also for the sins of the whole world. And hereby we

do know that we know him, if we keep his commandments. He that saith, I know him, and keepeth not his commandments, is a liar, and the truth is not in him. But whoso keepeth his word, in him verily is the love of God perfected: hereby know we that we are in him. He that saith he abideth in him ought himself also so to walk, even as he walked." (**1 John 2:1-6**)

"But now the righteousness of God without the law is manifested, being witnessed by the law and the prophets; Even the righteousness of God which is by faith of Jesus Christ unto all and upon all them that believe: for there is no difference: For all have sinned, and come short of the glory of God; Being justified freely by his grace through the redemption that is in Christ Jesus: Whom God hath set forth to be a propitiation through faith in his blood, to declare his righteousness for the remission of sins that are past, through the forbearance of God; To declare, I say, at this time his righteousness: that he might be just, and the justifier of him which believeth in Jesus." (**Romans 3:21-26**)

"The former treatise have I made, O Theophilus, of all that Jesus began both to do and teach...And when he had spoken these things, while they beheld, he was taken up; and a cloud received him out of their sight...Then returned they unto Jerusalem from the mount called Olivet, which is from Jerusalem a sabbath day's journey." (**Acts 1:1, 9&12**)

"And what is the exceeding greatness of his power to us-ward who believe, according to the working of his mighty power, Which he wrought in Christ, when he raised him from the dead, and set him at his own right hand in the heavenly places, Far above all principality, and power, and might, and dominion, and every name that is named, not only in this world, but also in that which is to come: And hath put all things under his feet, and gave him to be the head over all things to the church, Which is his body, the fulness of him that filleth all in all." (**Ephesians 1:19-23**)

Christianity holds no animals scared and requires no animal sacrifice.

"For the invisible things of him from the creation of the world are clearly seen, being understood by the things that are made, even his eternal power and Godhead; so that they are without excuse: Because that, when they knew God, they glorified him not as God, neither were thankful; but became vain in their imaginations, and their foolish heart was darkened. Professing themselves to be wise, they became fools, And changed the glory of the uncorruptible God into an image made like to corruptible man, and to birds, and fourfooted beasts, and creeping things. Wherefore God also gave them up to uncleanness through the lusts of their own hearts, to dishonour their own bodies between themselves: Who changed the truth of God into a lie, and worshipped and served the creature more than the Creator, who is blessed for ever. Amen." (**Romans 1:20-25**)

"By so much was Jesus made a surety of a better testament. And they truly were many priests, because they were not suffered to continue by reason of death: But this man, because he continueth ever, hath an unchangeable priesthood. Wherefore he is able also to save them to the uttermost that come unto God by him, seeing he ever liveth to make intercession for them. For such an high priest became us, who is holy, harmless, undefiled, separate from sinners, and made higher than the heavens; Who needeth not daily, as those high priests, to offer up sacrifice, first for his own sins, and then for the people's: for this he did once, when he offered up himself." (**Hebrews 7:22-27**)

Christianity thoroughly reveals marriage and its purpose.

"And Adam gave names to all cattle, and to the fowl of the air, and to every beast of the field; but for Adam there was not found an help meet for him. And the Lord God caused a deep sleep to fall upon Adam and he slept: and he took one of his ribs, and closed up the flesh instead thereof; And the rib, which the Lord God had taken from man, made he a woman, and brought her unto the man. And Adam said, This is now bone of my bones, and flesh of my flesh: she shall be called Woman, because she was taken out of Man. Therefore shall a man leave his father and his mother, and shall cleave unto his wife: and they shall be one flesh." (**Genesis 2:20-24**)

"So God created man in his own image, in the image of God created he him; male and female created he them. And God blessed them, and God said unto them, Be fruitful, and multiply, and replenish the earth, and subdue it: and have dominion over the fish of the sea, and over the fowl of the air, and over every living thing that moveth upon the earth." (**Genesis 1:27-28**)

"Now concerning the things whereof ye wrote unto me: It is good for a man not to touch a woman. Nevertheless, to avoid fornication, let every man have his own wife, and let every woman have her own husband. Let the husband render unto the wife due benevolence: and likewise also the wife unto the husband. The wife hath not power of her own body, but the husband: and likewise also the husband hath not power of his own body, but the wife. Defraud ye not one the other, except it be with consent for a time, that ye may give yourselves to fasting and prayer; and come together again, that Satan tempt you not for your incontinency." (**1 Corinthians 7:1-5**)

"Marriage is honourable in all, and the bed undefiled: but whoremongers and adulterers God will judge." (**Hebrew 13:4**)

"Whoso findeth a wife findeth a good thing, and obtaineth favour of the Lord." (**Proverbs 18:22**)

Jesus is on his way back according to the Bible and as believed by Christians. No other man in history is prophesized to return and judge humanity.

"Now we beseech you, brethren, by the coming of our Lord Jesus Christ, and by our gathering together unto him, That ye be not soon shaken in mind, or be troubled, neither by spirit, nor by word, nor by letter as from us, as that the day of Christ is at hand. Let no man deceive you by any means: for that day shall not come, except there come a falling away first, and that man of sin be revealed, the son of perdition; Who opposeth and exalteth himself above all that is called God, or that is worshipped; so that he as God sitteth in the temple of God, shewing himself that he is God. Remember ye not, that, when I was yet with you, I told you these things? And now ye know what withholdeth that he might be revealed in his time. For the mystery of iniquity doth already work: only he who now letteth will let, until he be taken out of the way. And then shall that Wicked be revealed, whom the Lord shall consume with the spirit of his mouth, and shall destroy with the brightness of his coming: Even him, whose coming is after the working of Satan with all power and signs and lying wonders, And with all deceivableness of unrighteousness in them that perish; because they received not the love of the truth, that they might be saved. And for this cause God shall send them strong delusion, that they should believe a lie: That they all might be damned

who believed not the truth, but had pleasure in unrighteousness." (2 Thessalonians 2:1-12)

"And I saw a great white throne, and him that sat on it, from whose face the earth and the heaven fled away; and there was found no place for them. And I saw the dead, small and great, stand before God; and the books were opened: and another book was opened, which is the book of life: and the dead were judged out of those things which were written in the books, according to their works." (Revelation 20:11&12)

Christianity proclaims Jesus as the deity that shall judge men with regard to everlasting life.

"For the Father judgeth no man, but hath committed all judgment unto the Son: That all men should honour the Son, even as they honour the Father. He that honoureth not the Son honoureth not the Father which hath sent him." (John 5: 22-23)

"And I saw a great white throne, and him that sat on it, from whose face the earth and the heaven fled away; and there was found no place for them. And I saw the dead, small and great, stand before God; and the books were opened: and another book was opened, which is the book of life: and the dead were judged out of those things which were written in the books, according to their works. And the sea gave up the dead which were in it; and death and hell delivered up the dead which were in them: and they were judged every man according to their works. And death and hell were cast into the lake of fire. This is the second death. And whosoever was not found written in the book of life was cast into the lake of fire." (Revelation 20:11-15)

Christianity reveals an exclusion rather that and inclusion in eternal life. This is undoubtedly why Jesus is proclaimed to save to the uttermost. Christianity reveals God's desire to have no one eternally separated from him.

"And if any man shall take away from the words of the book of this prophecy, God shall take away his part out of the book of life, and out of the holy city, and from the things which are written in this book." (Revelation 22:19)

"He that overcometh, the same shall be clothed in white raiment; and I will not blot out his name out of the book of life, but I will confess his name before my Father, and before his angels. He that hath an ear, let him hear what the Spirit saith unto the churches." (Revelation 3:5&6)

"Yet now, if thou wilt forgive their sin--; and if not, blot me, I pray thee, out of thy book which thou hast written. And the Lord said unto Moses, Whosoever hath sinned against me, him will I blot out of my book." (Exodus 32:32-33)

"The Lord will not spare him, but then the anger of the Lord and his jealousy shall smoke against that man, and all the curses that are written in this book shall lie upon him, and the Lord shall blot out his name from under heaven." (Deuteronomy 29:20)

"Hear me, O Lord; for thy lovingkindness is good: turn unto me according to the multitude of thy tender mercies. And hide not thy face from thy servant; for I am in trouble: hear me speedily. Draw nigh unto my soul, and redeem it: deliver me because of mine enemies. Thou hast known my reproach, and my shame, and my dishonour: mine adversaries are

all before thee. Reproach hath broken my heart; and I am full of heaviness: and I looked for some to take pity, but there was none; and for comforters, but I found none. They gave me also gall for my meat; and in my thirst they gave me vinegar to drink. Let their table become a snare before them: and that which should have been for their welfare, let it become a trap. Let their eyes be darkened, that they see not; and make their loins continually to shake. Pour out thine indignation upon them, and let thy wrathful anger take hold of them. Let their habitation be desolate; and let none dwell in their tents. For they persecute him whom thou hast smitten; and they talk to the grief of those whom thou hast wounded. Add iniquity unto their iniquity: and let them not come into thy righteousness. Let them be blotted out of the book of the living, and not be written with the righteous." (**Psalm 69:16-28**)

"Hold not thy peace, O God of my praise; For the mouth of the wicked and the mouth of the deceitful are opened against me: they have spoken against me with a lying tongue. They compassed me about also with words of hatred; and fought against me without a cause. For my love they are my adversaries: but I give myself unto prayer. And they have rewarded me evil for good, and hatred for my love. Set thou a wicked man over him: and let Satan stand at his right hand. When he shall be judged, let him be condemned: and let his prayer become sin. Let his days be few; and let another take his office. Let his children be fatherless, and his wife a widow. Let his children be continually vagabonds, and beg: let them seek their bread also out of their desolate places. Let the extortioner catch all that he hath; and let the strangers spoil his labour. Let there be none to extend mercy unto him: neither let there be any to favour his fatherless children. Let his posterity be cut off; and in the generation following let their name be blotted out." (**Psalm 109:1-13**)

"For God so loved the world, that he gave his only begotten Son, that whosoever believeth in him should not perish, but have everlasting life." (**John 3:16**)

"My little children, these things write I unto you, that ye sin not. And if any man sin, we have an advocate with the Father, Jesus Christ the righteous: and he is the propitiation for our sins: and not for ours only, but also for the sins of the whole world." (**1 John 2:1-2**)

"Wherefore he is able also to save them to the uttermost that come unto God by him, seeing he ever liveth to make intercession for them." (**Hebrews 7:25**)

"The Lord is not slack concerning his promise, as some men count slackness; but is long-suffering to us-ward, not willing that any should perish, but that all should come to repentance." (**2 Peter 3:9**)

The Bible reveals that everyone is given, in an innate sense, a willing to accept Jesus the Christ and be saved.

"For I say, through the grace given unto me, to every man that is among you, not to think of himself more highly than he ought to think; but to think soberly, according as God hath dealt to every man the measure of faith." (**Romans 12:3**)

"Shew me thy ways, O Lord; teach me thy paths. Lead me in thy truth, and teach me: for thou art the God of my salvation; on thee do I wait all the day. Remember, O Lord, thy tender mercies and thy lovingkindnesses; for they have been ever of old. Remember not the sins of my youth, nor my transgressions: according to thy mercy remember thou me for thy goodness' sake, O Lord. Good and upright is the Lord: therefore will he teach sinners in the

way. The meek will he guide in judgment: and the meek will he teach his way. All the paths of the Lord are mercy and truth unto such as keep his covenant and his testimonies. For thy name's sake, O Lord, pardon mine iniquity; for it is great. What man is he that feareth the Lord? him shall he teach in the way that he shall choose. His soul shall dwell at ease; and his seed shall inherit the earth. The secret of the Lord is with them that fear him; and he will shew them his covenant." **(Psalm 25: 4-14)**

15

JUDAISM – A SPECIAL CASE OF UNBELIEF

How does belief in Judaism differ from belief in Christianity?
Jesus was Jewish; are Jews considered believers in Christ as he was Jewish?

ACCORDING TO THE Bible, Christ declared that salvation is of the Jews.

"But the hour cometh, and now is, when the true worshippers shall worship the Father in spirit and in truth: for the Father seeketh such to worship him." (John 4:23)

To God's chosen people, as the scriptures had revealed in Jewish books of the law and the prophets, there would be a Messiah to deliver Jews and Gentiles alike.

"For thou art an holy people unto the Lord thy God: the Lord thy God hath chosen thee to be a special people unto himself, above all people that are upon the face of the earth." (Deuteronomy 7:6)

"Behold, I will send my messenger, and he shall prepare the way before me: and the Lord, whom ye seek, shall suddenly come to this temple, even the messenger of the covenant, whom ye delight in: behold, he shall come, saith the Lord of hosts. But who may abide the day of his coming? and who shall stand when he appeareth? for he is like a refiner's fire, and like fullers' soap: And he shall sit as a refiner and purifer of silver: and he shall purify the sons of Levi, and purge them as gold and silver, that they may offer unto the Lord an offering in righteousness." (Malachi 3:1-3)

"And in that day there shall be a root of Jesse, which shall stand for an ensign of the people; to it shall the Gentiles seek: and his rest shall be glorious." (Isaiah 11:10)

"Behold my servant, whom I uphold; mine elect, in whom my soul delighteth; I have put my spirit upon him: he shall bring forth judgment to the Gentiles. He shall not cry, nor lift up, nor cause his voice to be heard in the street. A bruised reed shall he not break, and the smoking flax shall he not quench: he shall bring forth judgment unto truth. He shall not fail nor be discouraged, till he have set judgment in the earth: and the isles shall wait for his law. Thus saith God the Lord, he that created the heavens, and stretched them out; he that spread forth the earth, and that which cometh out of it; he that giveth breath unto the people upon it, and spirit to them that walk therein: I the Lord have called thee in righteousness, and will hold thine hand, and will keep thee, and give thee for a covenant

of the people, for a light of the Gentiles; To open the blind eyes, to bring out the prisoners from the prison, and them that sit in darkness out of the prison house. I am the Lord: that is my name: and my glory will I not give to another, neither my praise to graven images." (Isaiah 42:1-8)

"Seventy weeks are determined upon thy people and upon thy holy city, to finish the transgression, and to make an end of sins, and to make reconciliation for iniquity, and to bring in everlasting righteousness, and to seal up the vision and prophecy, and to anoint the most Holy. Know therefore and understand, that from the going forth of the commandment to restore and to build Jerusalem unto the Messiah the Prince shall be seven weeks, and threescore and two weeks: the street shall be built again, and the wall, even in troublous times. And after threescore and two weeks shall Messiah be cut off, but not for himself: and the people of the prince that shall come shall destroy the city and the sanctuary; and the end thereof shall be with a flood, and unto the end of the war desolations are determined." (Daniel 9:24-26)

Israel, the Jewish nation, was chosen by God to be servants in whom God would be glorified and also used to lead non-Jews (gentiles) to God for his glory as well.

"Listen, O isles, unto me; and hearken, ye people, from far; The Lord hath called me from the womb; from the bowels of my mother hath he made mention of my name. And he hath made my mouth like a sharp sword; in the shadow of his hand hath he hid me, and made me a polished shaft; in his quiver hath he hid me; And said unto me, Thou art my servant, O Israel, in whom I will be glorified. Then I said, I have laboured in vain, I have spent my strength for nought, and in vain: yet surely my judgment is with the Lord, and my work with my God. And now, saith the Lord that formed me from the womb to be his servant, to bring Jacob again to him, Though Israel be not gathered, yet shall I be glorious in the eyes of the Lord, and my God shall be my strength. And he said, It is a light thing that thou shouldest be my servant to raise up the tribes of Jacob, and to restore the preserved of Israel: I will also give thee for a light to the Gentiles, that thou mayest be my salvation unto the end of the earth. Thus saith the Lord, the Redeemer of Israel, and his Holy One, to him whom man despiseth, to him whom the nation abhorreth, to a servant of rulers, Kings shall see and arise, princes also shall worship, because of the Lord that is faithful, and the Holy One of Israel, and he shall choose thee." (Isaiah 49:1-7)

Now Jesus Christ was Jewish and was sent with the message of salvation (saved, saving, deliverance) first to the Jews. Jesus is the <u>cornerstone</u> of God's spiritual house. Jesus was prophesized to Israel, yet, upon his appearance, in fulfillment of all scripture, he was and remains rejected by his own, God's chosen people of the Old Testament.

"The stone which the builders refused is become the head stone of the corner." (Psalms 118:22)

"Therefore thus saith the Lord God, Behold, I lay in Zion for a foundation a stone, a tried stone, a precious corner stone, a sure foundation: he that believeth shall not make haste." (Isaiah 28:16)

"He came unto his own, and his own received him not. But as many as received him, to them gave he power to become the sons of God, even to them that believe on his name:

Which were born, not of blood, nor of the will of the flesh, nor of the will of man, but of God." (John 1:11-13)

"Now when they were going, behold, some of the watch came into the city, and shewed unto the chief priests all the things that were done. And when they were assembled with the elders, and had taken counsel, they gave large money unto the soldiers, Saying, Say ye, His disciples came by night, and stole him away while we slept. And if this come to the governor's ears, we will persuade him, and secure you. So they took the money, and did as they were taught: and this saying is commonly reported among the Jews until this day." (Matthew 28:11-15)

Jews remain in rejection of Jesus Christ as their living sacrifice and therefore it is presumed by this author that, since animal sacrifice is outlawed in nearly the entire world, their sacrifice to God is offered up at the time of the slaughter of animals by them for food.

"By so much was Jesus made a surety of a better testament. And they truly were many priests, because they were not suffered to continue by reason of death: But this man, because he continueth ever, hath an unchangeable priesthood. Wherefore he is able also to save them to the uttermost that come unto God by him, seeing he ever liveth to make intercession for them. For such an high priest became us, who is holy, harmless, undefiled, separate from sinners, and made higher than the heavens; Who needeth not daily, as those high priests, to offer up sacrifice, first for his own sins, and then for the people's: for this he did once, when he offered up himself." (Hebrews 7:22-27)

Yet, God has made provision for his chosen people in spite of their rejection of his only begotten son. Wrapped up in God's provision for his chosen people is the choice also of the balance of humanity because of God's promises to the Jews.

"What then? Israel hath not obtained that which he seeketh for; but the election hath obtained it, and the rest were blinded (According as it is written, God hath given them the spirit of slumber, eyes that they should not see, and ears that they should not hear;) unto this day. And David saith, Let their table be made a snare, and a trap, and a stumbling block, and a recompence unto them: Let their eyes be darkened, that they may not see, and bow down their back alway. I say then, Have they stumbled that they should fall? God forbid: but rather through their fall salvation is come unto the Gentiles, for to provoke them to jealousy." (Romans 11:7-11)

"And they also, if they abide not still in unbelief, shall be graffed in: for God is able to graff them in again. For if thou wert cut out of the olive tree which is wild by nature, and wert graffed contrary to nature into a good olive tree: how much more shall these, which be the natural branches, be graffed into their own olive tree?" (Romans 11: 23&24)

"For all have sinned, and come short of the glory of God; Being justified freely by his grace through the redemption that is in Christ Jesus: Whom God hath set forth to be a propitiation through faith in his blood, to declare his righteousness for the remission of sins that are past, through the forbearance of God; To declare, I say, at this time his righteousness: that he might be just, and the justifier of him which believeth in Jesus." (Romans 3: 23-26)

By God's declaration of all in unbelief, provision was made for non-Jews as well to be brought into a relationship as chosen with God. Provision is made thereby for all to be considered as a chosen and obedient people glorifying their creator.

> *"He that believeth on him is not condemned: but he that believeth not is condemned already, because he hath not believed in the name of the only begotten Son of God."* (John 3:18)

> *"For God hath concluded them all in unbelief, that he might have mercy upon all."* (Romans 11:32)

> *"And if some of the branches be broken off, and thou, being a wild olive tree, wert graffed in among them, and with them partakest of the root and fatness of the olive tree; Boast not against the branches. But if thou boast, thou bearest not the root, but the root thee. Thou wilt say then, The branches were broken off, that I might be graffed in."* (Romans 11:17-19)

> *"Even the righteousness of God which is by faith of Jesus Christ unto all and upon all them that believe: for there is no difference:"* (Romans 3:22)

Gentiles should be in a posture of prayer for Israel, according to the Bible, and belief in God without animosity towards the Jews.

> *"Brethren, my heart's desire and prayer to God for Israel is, that they might be saved. For I bear them record that they have a zeal of God, but not according to knowledge. For they being ignorant of God's righteousness, and going about to establish their own righteousness, have not submitted themselves unto the righteousness of God. For Christ is the end of the law for righteousness to every one that believeth."* (Roman 10:1-4)

> *"Boast not against the branches. But if thou boast, thou bearest not the root, but the root thee."* (Romans 11:18)

> *"What advantage then hath the Jew? or what profit is there of circumcision? Much every way: chiefly, because that unto them were committed the oracles of God. For what if some did not believe? shall their unbelief make the faith of God without effect? God forbid: yea, let God be true, but every man a liar; as it is written, That thou mightest be justified in thy sayings, and mightest overcome when thou art judged. But if our unrighteousness commend the righteousness of God, what shall we say? Is God unrighteous who taketh vengeance? (I speak as a man) God forbid: for then how shall God judge the world? For if the truth of God hath more abounded through my lie unto his glory; why yet am I also judged as a sinner? And not rather, (as we be slanderously reported, and as some affirm that we say,) Let us do evil, that good may come? whose damnation is just. What then? are we better than they? No, in no wise: for we have before proved both Jews and Gentiles, that they are all under sin; As it is written, There is none righteous, no, not one: There is none that understandeth, there is none that seeketh after God."* (Romans 3: 1-11)

God had demonstrated his mercy for all mankind by his mercy upon Israel.

> *"Therefore will I give thanks unto thee, O Lord, among the heathen, and sing praises unto thy name."* (Psalms 18:49)

> *"Now the God of patience and consolation grant you to be likeminded one toward another according to Christ Jesus: That ye may with one mind and one mouth glorify God, even the*

Father of our Lord Jesus Christ. Wherefore receive ye one another, as Christ also received us to the glory of God. Now I say that Jesus Christ was a minister of the circumcision for the truth of God, to confirm the promises made unto the fathers: And that the Gentiles might glorify God for his mercy; as it is written, For this cause I will confess to thee among the Gentiles, and sing unto thy name." (Romans 15:5-9)

Jesus is indeed the cornerstone of Almighty God's spiritual house.

"Jesus saith unto them, Did ye never read in the scriptures, The stone which the builders rejected, the same is become the head of the corner: this is the Lord's doing, and it is marvellous in our eyes?" (Matthew 21:42)

"And have ye not read this scripture; The stone which the builders rejected is become the head of the corner: This was the Lord's doing, and it is marvellous in our eyes?" (Mark 12:10&11)

"And he beheld them, and said, What is this then that is written, The stone which the builders rejected, the same is become the head of the corner?" (Luke 20:17)

"This is the stone which was set at nought of you builders, which is become the head of the corner." (Acts 4:11)

"For the king knoweth of these things, before whom also I speak freely: for I am persuaded that none of these things are hidden from him; for this thing was not done in a corner." (Acts 26:26)

"And are built upon the foundation of the apostles and prophets, Jesus Christ himself being the chief corner stone; In whom all the building fitly framed together groweth unto an holy temple in the Lord: In whom ye also are builded together for an habitation of God through the Spirit." (Ephesians 2:20-22)

"Wherefore also it is contained in the scripture, Behold, I lay in Sion a chief corner stone, elect, precious: and he that believeth on him shall not be confounded. Unto you therefore which believe he is precious: but unto them which be disobedient, the stone which the builders disallowed, the same is made the head of the corner, And a stone of stumbling, and a rock of offence, even to them which stumble at the word, being disobedient: whereunto also they were appointed." (1 Peter 2: 6-8)

Therefore, there should remain no longer Jews and Gentiles but rather Christians baptized with the same baptism and receiving the same word of salvation.

"For ye are all the children of God by faith in Christ Jesus. For as many of you as have been baptized into Christ have put on Christ. There is neither Jew nor Greek, there is neither bond nor free, there is neither male nor female: for ye are all one in Christ Jesus. And if ye be Christ's, then are ye Abraham's seed, and heirs according to the promise." (Galatians 3:26-29)

"Then departed Barnabas to Tarsus, for to seek Saul: And when he had found him, he brought him unto Antioch. And it came to pass, that a whole year they assembled themselves with the church, and taught much people. And the disciples were called Christians first in Antioch. And in these days came prophets from Jerusalem unto Antioch." (Acts 11:25-27)

"Wherefore lay apart all filthiness and superfluity of naughtiness, and receive with meekness the engrafted word, which is able to save your souls. But be ye doers of the word, and not hearers only, deceiving your own selves. For if any be a hearer of the word, and not a doer, he is like unto a man beholding his natural face in a glass: For he beholdeth himself, and goeth his way, and straightway forgetteth what manner of man he was. But whoso looketh into the perfect law of liberty, and continueth therein, he being not a forgetful hearer, but a doer of the work, this man shall be blessed in his deed." (James 1:21-25)

From the Rock and Chief Cornerstone, that is Jesus, and because of all that has occurred as a result of Christ's mission on earth, there are now to be many lively stones created in the likeness of God's only begotten son.

"And a stone of stumbling, and a rock of offence, even to them which stumble at the word, being disobedient: whereunto also they were appointed." (1 Peter 2:8)

"They shall bear thee up in their hands, lest thou dash thy foot against a stone." (Psalms 91:12)

"Ye also, as lively stones, are built up a spiritual house, an holy priesthood, to offer up spiritual sacrifices, acceptable to God by Jesus Christ." (1 Peter 2:5)

I am persuaded that there is, however, a number fixed by God out of those Israelites crossing the Red Sea from captivity in Egypt, that will enter into eternal life. There is a multitude of all others, including the present day descendents of the Israel that will repent, accept Christ, be baptized and will enter into eternal salvation along with the multitude of saints that have gone on before.

"And I heard the number of them which were sealed: and there were sealed an hundred and forty and four thousand of all the tribes of the children of Israel. Of the tribe of Juda were sealed twelve thousand. Of the tribe of Reuben were sealed twelve thousand. Of the tribe of Gad were sealed twelve thousand. Of the tribe of Aser were sealed twelve thousand. Of the tribe of Nepthalim were sealed twelve thousand. Of the tribe of Manasses were sealed twelve thousand. Of the tribe of Simeon were sealed twelve thousand. Of the tribe of Levi were sealed twelve thousand. Of the tribe of Issachar were sealed twelve thousand. Of the tribe of Zabulon were sealed twelve thousand. Of the tribe of Joseph were sealed twelve thousand. Of the tribe of Benjamin were sealed twelve thousand. After this I beheld, and, lo, a great multitude, which no man could number, of all nations, and kindreds, and people, and tongues, stood before the throne, and before the Lamb, clothed with white robes, and palms in their hands; And cried with a loud voice, saying, Salvation to our God which sitteth upon the throne, and unto the Lamb." (Revelation 7:4-10)

"Wherefore seeing we also are compassed about with so great a cloud of witnesses, let us lay aside every weight, and the sin which doth so easily beset us, and let us run with patience the race that is set before us, Looking unto Jesus the author and finisher of our faith; who for the joy that was set before him endured the cross, despising the shame, and is set down at the right hand of the throne of God. For consider him that endured such contradiction of sinners against himself, lest ye be wearied and faint in your minds." (Hebrews 12:1-3)

16

Islam Including the Nation of Islam as a Special Case of Unbelief

My Muslim friends tell me that they belief in Jesus and revere his name. What then separates Christian beliefs from Islam and/or the Black Muslims?

There are six doctrines that every Muslim, from Morocco to the Philippines, is required to believe.

God	There is only one true God and His name is Allah. Allah is all-seeing, all-knowing, and all-powerful.
Angels	The chief angel is Gabriel, who is said to have appeared to Muhammad. There is also a fallen angel named Shaitan (from the Hebrew, Satan), as well as the followers of Shaitan, the djinn (demons).
Scripture	Muslims believe in four God-inspired books; the Torah of Moses (that Christians call the Pentateuch), the Zabur (Psalms of David), the Injil (Gospel) of Jesus, and the Noble Qur'an. But the Noble Qur'an is Allah's final word to mankind, so it supersedes and overrules all previous writings.
Muhammad	The Noble Qur'an lists 28 prophets of Allah. These include Adam, Noah, Abraham, Moses, David, Jonah, and Jesus. To the Muslim, the last and greatest prophet is Muhammad.
The end times	On the "last day", the dead will be resurrected. Allah will be the judge and each person will be sent to heaven or hell. Heaven is a place for those who did not oppose Allah and his prophet, Muhammad.
Predestination	God has determined what He pleases and no one can change what He has decreed.

The five pillars of the faith

Besides the six doctrines to be believed, there are five duties to be performed.

Statement of belief	To become a Muslim, a person must publicly repeat the Shahadah: "There is no God but Allah and Muhammad is the prophet of Allah."
Prayers	This ritual must be performed five times a day. The Muslim must kneel and

	bow in the direction of the holy city, Mecca.
Alms	Muslim law today requires the believer to give one-fortieth of his income. This offering goes to widows, orphans, the sick and other unfortunates.
Ramadan	The ninth month of the Muslim lunar year is called Ramadan. It is the highest of holy seasons. Muslims are required to fast for the entire month, but only during daylight hours. As soon as the sun sets, the feasting begins. During Ramadan, the believer must not commit any unworthy act. If he does, his fasting is meaningless.
Pilgrimage to Mecca	This is called the Hajj and must be performed at least once in a Muslim's lifetime. However, if the pilgrimage is too difficult or dangerous for the believer, he can send someone in his place.

The Great Gulf between the Noble Qur'an and the Bible; Between Muslims and Christians

It is my not my intention herein to be inflammatory. I am of a mind, as persuaded by God through the Holy Ghost, that would have no man perish eternally (See Chapter 1, Significance in the Study of the Bible and also Chapter 7, Salvation/Being Born Again). There exists a great gulf between what the Noble Qur'an states and what is stated in the Bible. As a result, there is a great gulf between Islam and Christianity. I present herein differences sufficient in order to substantiate the great gulf that exists. The chapters and verses of the Noble Qur'an presented herein, are from The Interpretation of the Meanings of the Noble Qur'an in the English Language by Dr. Muhammad Taqi-ud-Din and Dr. Muhammadad Muhsin Khan, Dar-us-Salam Publications, Riyadh, Saudi Arabia.

God is called Allah and his anger is has been earned by both Jews and Christians who have gone astray.

> **Surat 1 :1-7** *In the Name of Allah, the Most Beneficent, the Most Merciful. All the praises and thanks be to Allah, the Lord of the Alamin (mankind, jinns and all that exists). The Most Beneficent, the Most Merciful. The Only Owner (and the Only Ruling Judge) of the Day of Recompense (i.e. the Day of Resurrection). You (Alone) we worship, and You (Alone) we ask for help (for each and everything). Guide us to the Straight Way. The Way of those on whom You have bestowed Your Grace, not (the way) of those who earned Your Anger (such as the Jews), nor of those who went astray (such as the Christians).*

> **Surah 3:1-5** *Alif—Lam—Mim. [These letters are one of the miracles of the Qur'an, and none but Allah (Alone) knows their meanings]. Allah! La ilaha illa Huwa (none has the right to be worshipped but He), the Ever Living, the One Who sustains and protects all that exists. It is He Who has sent down the Book (the Qur'an) to you (Muhammad) with truth, confirming what came before it. And he sent down the Taurat (Torah) and the Injeel (Gospel). Aforetime, as a guidance to mankind, And He sent down the criterion [of judgement between right and wrong (this Qur'an)]. Truly, those who disbelieve in the Ayat (proofs, evidences, verses, lessons, signs, revelations, etc). of Allah. For them there is a severe torment; and Allah is All-Mighty, All-Able of Retribution. Truly, nothing is hidden from Allah, in the earth or in the heavens.*

The Noble Qur'an is the truth.

Surah 22:54 And that those who have been given knowledge may know that it (this Qur'an) is the truth from your Lord, and that they may believe therein, and their hearts may submit to it with humility. And verily, Allah is the Guide of those who believe, to the Straight Path.

Muhammad was given the Noble Qur'an and the Al-Hikmah (Islamic laws, knowledge of legal and illegal things i.e. the Prophet's Sunnah-legal ways).

Surah 4:113 Had not the Grace of Allah and His Mercy been upon you (O Muhammad), a party of them would certainly have made a decision to mislead you, but (in fact) they mislead none except their own selves, and no harm can they do to you in the least. Allah has sent down to you the Book (The Qur'an), and Al-Hikamah (Islamic laws, knowledge of legal and illegal things, i.e. the Prophet's Sunnah—legal ways), and taught you that which you knew not. And Ever Great is the Grace of Allah unto you (O Muhammad).

Muslims are to have no friends among Jews and Christians.

Surah 5:51 O you who believe! Take not the Jews and the Christians as Auliya (friends, protectors, helpers, etc). They are but Auliya to one another. And if any amongst you takes them as Auliya, then surely he is one of them. Verily, Allah guides not these people who are the Zalimun (polytheists and wrong-doers and unjust).

Further, Muslims are to treat with harshness and deception those that reject Allah.

Surah 7:182 Those who reject Our Ayat (proofs, evidences, versus, lessons, signs, revelations, etc). We shall gradually seize them with punishment in ways they perceive not.

Surah 9:123 O you who believe! Fight those of the disbelievers who are close to you, and let them find harshness in you, and know that Allah is with those who are the Al-Muttaqun (the pious--see V 2:2).

Surah 10:13 And indeed, We destroyed generations before you, when they did wrong while their Messengers came to them with clear proofs, but they were not such as to believe! Thus do We requite the people who are Mujrimun (disbelievers, polytheists, sinners, criminals, etc).

Through struggle, Islam is to be the only religion.

Surah 8:39 And fight them until there is no more Fitnah (disbelief and polytheism: i.e. worshipping others besides Allah) and the religion (worship) will all be for Allah Alone [in the whole of the world]. But if they cease (worshipping others besides Allah), then certainly, Allah is All-Seer of what they do.

Surah 8:59-60 And let not those who disbelieve think that they can outstrip (escape from punishment), Verily, they will never be able to save themselves (from Allah's Punishment). And make ready against them all you can of power, including steeds of war (tanks, planes, missiles, artillery, etc) to threaten the enemy of Allah and your enemy, and others besides whom, you may not know but whom Allah does know. And whatever you shall spend in the Cause of Allah shall be repaid unto you, and you shall not be treated unjustly.

Surah 8:65 O Prophet (Muhammad)! Urge the believers to fight. If there are twenty steadfast persons amongst you, they will overcome two hundred, and if there be a hundred steadfast persons they will overcome a thousand of those who disbelieve, because they (the disbelievers) are people who do not understand.

God has no Son.

Surah 19: 88-92 *And they say: "The Most Beneficent (Allah) has begotten a son (or offspring or children) [as the Jews say: 'Uzair (Ezra) is the son of Allah, and the Christians say that He has begotten a son ['Iesa (Christ)], and the pagan Arabs say that He has begotten daughters (angels, etc.)]." Indeed you have brought forth (said) a terrible evil thing. Whereby the heavens are almost torn, and the earth is split asunder, and the mountains fall in ruins, That they ascribe a son (or offspring or children) to the Most Beneficent (Allah). But it is not suitable for (the Majesty of) the Most Beneficent (Allah) that He should beget a son (or offspring or children).*

Surah 2:116 *And they (Jews, Christians and pagans) say: Allah has begotten a son (children or offspring). Glory to Him (Exalted be He above all that they associate with Him). Nay, to Him belongs all that is in the heavens and on earth, and all surrender with obedience (in worship) to Him.*

Surah 10:68-70 *They (Jews, Christians and pagans) say: "Allah has begotten a son (children)." Glory be to Him! He is Rich (Free of all wants). His is all that is in the heavens and all that is in the earth. No warrant you have for this. Do you say against Allah what you know not. Say: "Verily, those who invent lie against Allah will never be successful. A brief enjoyment in this world! - and then unto Us will be their return, then We shall make them taste the severest torment because they used to disbelieve [in Allah, belie His Messengers, deny and challenge His Ayat (proofs, signs, verses, etc.)]*

Surah 18:1-5 *All the praises and thanks be to Allah, Who has sent down to His slave (Muhammad) the Book (the Qur'an), and has not placed therein any crookedness. (He has made it) Straight to give warning (to the disbelievers) of a severe punishment from Him, and to give glad tidings to the believers (in the Oneness of Allah – Islamic Monotheism), who work righteous deeds, that they shall have a fair reward (i.e. Paradise). They shall abide therein forever. And to warn those (Jews, Christians, and pagans) who say, "Allah has begotten a son (or offspring or children)." No knowledge have they of such a thing, not had their fathers. Mighty is the word that comes out of their mouths [i.e. He begot (took) sons and daughters]. They utter nothing but a lie.*

Surah 3:59 *Verily, the likeness of 'Iesa (Jesus) before Allah is the likeness of Adam. He created him from dust, then (He) said to him; "Be!" – and he was.*

There is no Trinity (the Islamic notion of the Christian Trinity rejected appears to be Allah, Jesus and the Mother of Jesus).

Surah 5: 72-75 *Surely, they have disbelieved who say "Allah is the Messiah ['Isea (Jesus)], son of Maryam (Mary)". But the Messiah ['Isea (Jesus)] said: "O Children of Isreal! Worship Allah, my Lord and your Lord." Verily, whosoever sets up partners in worhsip with Allah, then Allah has forbidden Paradise for him, and the Fire will be his abode. And for the Zalimun (polytheists and wrong-doers) there are no helpers. Surely, disbelievers are those who said: "Allah is the third of the three (in a Trinity)." But there is no ilah (god) (none who has the right to be worshipped) but One Ilah (God – Allah). And if they cease not from what they say, verily, a painful torment will befall the disbelievers among them. Will they not repent to Allah and ask His Forgiveness? For Allah is Oft-Forgiving, Most Merciful. The Messiah ['Isea (Jesus)], son of Maryam (Mary), was no more than a Messenger; many were the Messengers that passed away before him. His mother [Maryam (Mary)] was a*

Siddiqah [i.e. she believed in the words of Allah and His Books (see Verse 66:12)]. They both used to eat food (any other human being, while Allah does not eat). Look how We make the Ayat (proofs, evidences, verses, lessons, signs, revelations, etc.) clear to them, yet look how they are deluded away (from the truth).

Surah 4:48 *Verily, Allah forgives not that partners should be set up with him in worship, but He forgives except that (anything else) to whom He pleases, and whoever sets up partners with Allah in worship, he has indeed invented a tremendous sin.*

Surah 23:90-91 *Nay, son (or offspring or children) did Allah beget, nor is there any ilah (god) along with Him; (if there had been many gods), behold, each god would have taken away what he had created, and some would have tried to overcome others! Glorified be Allah above all that they attribute to Him! And when the son of Maryam (Mary) is quoted as an example [i.e. 'Isea (Jesus) is worshipped like their idols), behold! Your people cry aloud (laugh out at the example).*

Jesus is not Alpha and Omega. Muhammad is exalted over Jesus.

Surah 43:57-63 *And when the son of Maryam (Mary) is quoted as an example (i.e. 'Iesa (Jesus) is worshipped like their idols), behold! Your people cry aloud (laugh out at the example) And say: "Are our aliha (gods) better or is he ['Iesa (Jesus)]? They quoted not the above example except for argument. Nay! But they are a quarrelsome people. [(See VV. 21:97-101) – The Qur'an]. He ['Iesa (Jesus)] was not more than a slave. We granted Our Favour to him, and We made him an example to the Children of Isreal (i.e, his creation without a father). And if it were Our Will, We would have [destroyed you (makind) all, and] made angels to replace you on the earth. [Tasfir At-Tabari, Vol:25, Page 89]. And he ['Iesa (Jesus), son of Maryam (Mary) shall be a known sign for (the coming of) the Hour (Day of Resurrection) [i.e. "Iesa's)Jesus) descent on the earth]. Therefore have no doubt concerning it (i.e, the Day of Resurrection). And follow Me (Allah) (i.e. be obedient to Allah and do what He orders you to do, O Mankind)! This is the Straight Path (of Islamic Monotheism, leading to Allah and to His Paradise). And let not Shaitan (Satan) hinder you (from the right religion, i.e., Islamic Monotheism), Verily, he (Satan) to you is a plain enemy. And when "Iesa (Jesus) came with (Our) clear Proofs, he said: "I have come to you with Al-Hikmah (Prophethood), and in order to make clear to you some of the (points) in which you differ, therefore fear Allah and obey me.*

Surah 61:6 *And (remember) when 'Iesa (Jesus), son of Maryam (Mary), said: "O Children of Isreal! I am the Messenger of Allah unto you confirming the Taurat [(Torah) which came] before me, and giving glad tidings of a Messenger to come after me, whose name shall be Ahmed. But when he (Ahmed i.e, Muhammad came to them with clear proofs, they said: "This is plain magic."*

Surah 25:1&2 *Blessed be He Who sent down the criterion (of right and wrong, i.e. this Qur'an) to His slave (Muhammad) that he may be a warner to the Alamin (mankind and jinns). He to Whom belongs the dominion of the heavens and the earth, and Who has begotten no son (children or offspring) and for Whom there is no partner in the dominion. He has created everything, and has measured it exactly according to its due measurements.*

Jesus was born of a barren woman Maryam and her husband was Zakariya. Jesus is a creation as opposed to a manifestation.

Surah 3:35-56 (repeated in Surah 19) *(Remember) when the wife of 'Imran said: "O my Lord! I have vowed to You what (the child that) is in my womb to be dedicated for Your services (free from all worldly work; to serve Your Place of worship), so accept this, from me. Verily, You are the All-Hearer, the All-Knowing."Then when she delivered her [child Maryam (Mary)], she said: "O my Lord! I have delivered a female child," – and Allah knew better what she delivered, -- "And the male is not like the female, and I seek refuge with You (Allah) for her and for her offspring from Shaitan (Satan), the outcast."So he Lord (Allah) accepted her with godly acceptance. He made her grow in a good manner and put her under the care of Zakariya (Zachariya). Every time he entered Al-Mihrab to visit her, he found her suplied with sustenance. He said: "O Mayam (Mary)! From where have you got this?" She said: "This is from Allah. "Verily, Allah provides sustenance to whom He wills, without limit. " At that time Zakariya (Zachariya) invoked Lord, saying: "O my Lord! Grant me from You, a good offspring. You are indeed the All-Hearer of invocation." Then the angels called him, while he was standing in prayer in Al-Mihrab a praying place or a private room), (saying): "Allah gives you glad tidings of Yahya (John), confirming (believing in) the Word from Allah [i.e. the creation of 'Isea (Jesus) the Word from Allah ("Be! – and he was!)], noble keeping away from sexual relations with women, a Prophet, from among the righteous." He said: "O my Lord! How can I have a son when I am very old, and my wife is barren?" Allah said: "Thus Allah does what He wills." He said: "O my Lord! Make me a sign for me." Allah said: "Your sign is that you shall not speak to mankind for three days except with signals. And remember your Lord much (by praising Him again and again), and glorify (Him) in the afternoon and in the morning."*

And (remember) when the angels said: "O Maryam (Mary)! Verily, Allah has chosen you, purified you (from polytheism and disbelief), and chosen you above the women of the 'Alamin (mankind and jinns) (of her lifetime)." O Mary! "Submit yourself with obedience to your Lord (Allah, by worshipping none but Him alone) and prostrate yourself, and Irka'I (bow down etc) along with Ar-Raki'un (those who bow down etc)." This is a part of the news of the Ghaib (unseen, i.e. the news of the past nations of which you have no knowledge) which We inspire you with (O Muhammad). You were not with them, when they cast lots with their pens as to which of them should be charged with the care of Maryam (Mary); nor were you with them when they disputed. (Remember) when the angels said: "O Maryam (Mary)! Verily, Allah gives you the glad tidings of a Word ["Be!" – and he was! i.e, 'Isea (Jesus) the son of Maryam (Mary)] from Him, his name will be the Messiah 'Isea (Jesus), the son of Maryam (Mary), held in honour in this world and in the Hereafter, and will be one of those who are near to Allah." And I have come confirming that which was before me of the Taurat (Torah), and to make lawful to you part of what was forbidden to you, and I have come to you with a proof from your Lord. So fear Allah and obey me. Truly! Allah is my Lord and your Lord, so worship Him (Alone). This is the Straight Path. Then when 'Isea (Jesus) came to know of their disbelief, he said: "Who will be my helpers in Allah's Cause?" Al-Hawariun (the disciples) said: "We are the helpers of Allah: we believe in Allah, and bear witness that we are Muslims (i.e. we submit to Allah)." Our Lord! We believe in what You have sent down, and we follow the Messenger ['Isea (Jesus)]; so write us down among those who bear witness (to the truth i.e. La ilaha ill-Allah – none has the right to be worshipped but Allah).

And they (disbelievers) plotted to kill 'Isea (Jesus) and Allah planned too. And Allah is the Best of the planners. And (remember) when Allah said: "O 'Isea (Jesus)! I will take you and raise you to Myself and clear you [of the forged statement that 'Isea (Jesus) is Allah's son] of those who disbelieve, and I will make those who follow you (Monotheists, who worship none but Allah) superior to those who disbelieve [in the Oneness of Allah, or disbelieve in some of His Messengers, e.g. Muhammad, 'Isea (Jesus), Musa (Moses), etc. or in His Holy Books, e.g. the Taurat (Torah), the Injeel (Gospel), the Qur'an] till the Day of Resurrection. Then you will return to Me and I will judge between you in the matters in which you used to dispute." As to those who disbelieve, I will punish them with a severe torment in this world and in the Hereafter, and they will have no helpers."

Jesus did not die on the cross; there is ascension to heaven by Jesus without resurrection. Please forgive me but where is the eyewitness testimony with regard to someone disguised as Christ dying on the cross and the repudiating testimony of the resurrected Christ ascending to heaven. Is Mohammed the Resurrection; is he risen from the dead? Who is it then that can assure mankind of resurrection from the dead into eternal life. If the resurrection of Christ is a lie and Mohammad, who is greater than Christ, is bodily in the grave, how shall we overcome death?

Surah 4:157-158 *And because of their saying (in boast), "We killed Messiah 'Isea (Jesus), son of Maryam (Mary), the Messenger of Allah," – but they killed him not, nor crucified him, but the resemblance of 'Isea (Jesus) was put over another man (and they killed that man), and those who differ therein are full of doubts. They have no (certain) knowledge, they follow nothing but conjecture. For surely; they killed him not [i.e. 'Isea (Jesus), son of Maryam (Mary): But Allah raised him ['Isea (Jesus)] up (with his body and soul) unto Himself (and he is in the heavens). And Allah is Ever All-Powerful, All-Wise.*

Muslim apostates are to be physically stopped from making criticism of Islam.

Surah 9:12-13 *But if they violate their oaths after their covenant, and attack your religion with disapproval and criticism then fight (you) the leaders of disbelief (chiefs of Quraish – pagans of Makkah) – for surely their oaths are nothing to them – so that they may stop (evil actions). Will you not fight a people who have violated their oaths (pagans of Makkah) and intended to expel the Messenger, while they did attack you first? Do you fear them? Allah has more right that you should fear Him, if you are believers.*

All Muslims in authority are to obey Allah.

Surah 4:59 *O you who believe! Obey Allah and obey the Messenger (Muhammad) and those of you (Muslims) who are in authority. (And) if you differ in anything amongst yourselves, refer it to Allah and his Messenger, if you believe in Allah and in the Last Day. This is better and more suitable for final determination.*

What the Black Muslims Believe

1. WE BELIEVE in the One God whose proper name is Allah.

2. WE BELIEVE in the Holy Qur'an and in the scriptures of all the Prophets of God.

3. WE BELIEVE in the truth of the Bible, but we believe that it has been tampered with and must be reinterpreted so that mankind will not be snared by the falsehoods that have been added to it.

4. WE BELIEVE in Allah's Prophets and the Scriptures they brought to the people.

5. WE BELIEVE in the resurrection of the dead—not in physical resurrec-

tion—but in mental resurrection. We believe that the so-called Negroes are most in need of mental resurrection, therefore, they will be resurrected first.

Furthermore, we believe we are the people of God's choice, as it is been written, that God would choose the rejected and the despised. We can find no other persons fitting this description in these last days more than the so-called Negroes in America. We believe in the resurrection of the righteous.

6. WE BELIEVE in the judgement; we believe this first judgement will take place as God revealed, in America.

7. WE BELIEVE this is the time in history the separation for the so-called Negroes and the so-called white Americans. We believe the Black man should be freed in name as well as in fact. By this we mean that he should be freed from the names imposed upon him by his former slave masters. We believe that if we are free indeed, we should go in our own people's names—the Black peoples of the Earth.

8. WE BELIEVE in justice for all, whether in God or not; we believe as others, that we are due equal justice as human beings. We believe in equality—as a nation—of equals. We do not believe that we are equal with our slave masters in the status of "freed slaves."

We recognize and respect American citizens as independent peoples and we respect their laws which govern this nation.

9. WE BELIEVE that the offer of integration is hypocritical and is made by those who are trying to deceive the black peoples into believing that heir 400-year-old open enemies of freedom, justice, and equality are, all of a sudden, their "friends". Furthermore, we believe that such deception is intended to prevent black people from realizing that the time in history has arrived for the separation from the whites of this nation.

If the white people are truthful about their professed friendship toward the so-called Negro, they can prove it by dividing up America with their slaves.

We do not believe that America will ever be able to furnish enough jobs for her own millions of unemployed, in addition to jobs for the 20,000,000 black people as well.

10. WE BELIEVE that we who declare ourselves to be righteous Muslims, should not participate in wars which take the lives of humans. We do not believe this nation should force us to take part in such wars, for we have nothing to gain from it unless America agrees to give us the necessary territory wherein we may have something to fight for.

11. WE BELIEVE our women should be respected and protected as the women of other nationalities are respected and protected.

12. WE BELIEVE that Allah (God) appeared in the Person of Master W. Fard Muhammad, July, 1930; the long-awaited "Messiah" of the Christians and the "Mahdi" of the Muslims.

We believe further and lastly that Allah is God and besides HIM there is no God and He will bring about a universal government of peace wherein we all can live in peace together.

The Author's Refutation by Point concerning "What the Black Muslims Believe"

POINT 1:

The Bible does not use the name Allah for God or Lord thy God. There are 9 words, Elohiym, El, Yehovih, Yehovah (Jehovah), Elahh, Tsuwr, Adonay and Theos respectively, are used in the following 9 sets of biblical scriptures.

"And Moses said unto God, Behold, when I come unto the children of Israel, and shall say unto them, The God of your fathers hath sent me unto you; and they shall say to me, What is his name? what shall I say unto them? And God said unto Moses, I AM THAT I AM: and he said, Thus shalt thou say unto the children of Israel, I AM hath sent me unto you. And God said moreover unto Moses, Thus shalt thou say unto the children of Israel, The Lord God of your fathers, the God of Abraham, the God of Isaac, and the God of Jacob, hath sent me unto you: this is my name for ever, and this is my memorial unto all generations." (Exodus 3:13-15)

"Then the Lord said unto Moses, Now shalt thou see what I will do to Pharaoh: for with a strong hand shall he let them go, and with a strong hand shall he drive them out of his land." And God spake unto Moses, and said unto him, I am the Lord: And I appeared unto Abraham, unto Isaac, and unto Jacob, by the name of God Almighty, but by my name JEHOVAH was I not known to them." (Exodus 6:1-3)

"And thou hast said unto me, O Lord God, Buy thee the field for money, and take witnesses; for the city is given into the hand of the Chaldeans." (Jeremiah 32:25)

"Three times in the year all thy males shall appear before the Lord God." (Exodus 23:17)

"Then the prophets, Haggai the prophet, and Zechariah the son of Iddo, prophesied unto the Jews that were in Judah and Jerusalem in the name of the God of Israel, even unto them." (Ezra 5:1)

"I am as one mocked of his neighbour, who calleth upon God, and he answereth him: the just upright man is laughed to scorn." (Job 12:4)

"Fear ye not, neither be afraid: have not I told thee from that time, and have declared it? ye are even my witnesses. Is there a God beside me? yea, there is no God; I know not any." (Isaiah 44:8)

"The Lord God is my strength, and he will make my feet like hinds' feet, and he will make me to walk upon mine high places. To the chief singer on my stringed instruments." (Habakkuk 3:19)

"And think not to say within yourselves, We have Abraham to our father: for I say unto you, that God is able of these stones to raise up children unto Abraham." (Matthew 3:9)

Note that the name Allah as God pre-dates Islam. Allah was known, pre-Islam, as Chief among as many as 360 Arab pagan gods with some worship that even centered around the present day Ka'aba in Mecca. In Hebrew, the word allah is a word derived from the word elah meaning an oak or other strong tree. Elah in turn is derived from ayil which means anything strong particularly a chief politically, a ram or a mighty man. Ayil is also derived from uwl which is to say to twist or be strong as the body being rolled together, strong support, powerful, mighty strength, a ram and chief (politically). At the time of Muhammad and the advent of Islam (622 A.D.), Christians used the word Theos for God with the understanding of the Old Testament words used for God as well. Allah was never used by Jews or Christians for God, however, it was used among Arabs who considered the God of the Jews, Christians and Arabs as one God.

Note also, from the Webster's II New riverside University Dictionary, Jehovah is an alteration of Hebrew Yahweh for God, especially in the Christian translations of the Old Testament. Jehovah did not exist as a Hebrew word. It is actually a conflation of two Hebrew forms that came about through a peculiarity of the Hebrew writing systems. The Hebrew alphabet consists only of characters for consonants; vowels are indicated as dots or "points" written in characteristic positions above or below the consonants. The Hebrew name for God, the consonants of which are transliterated YHWH, was considered so sacred that is was never pronounced and its proper vowel points were never written. In some text vowel points for a completely different word, Adonai, "lord", were written with YHWH to indicate that the word Adonai was to be spoken whenever the reader came upon the word YHWH. YHWH was never intended to be pronounced with the vowels of Adonai, but Christian scholars of the Renaissance made exactly that mistake, and the forms Iehovah (using the classical Latin equivalents of the Hebrew letters) and Jehovah (substituting, in English, J for consonantal I) came into common use.

POINT 2:

The Bible states that it is for the purpose of instruction in righteous living and is not to be added to or taken from; this word is pure and testifies of Christ according to the scriptures.

> *"Now therefore hearken, O Israel, unto the statutes and unto the judgments, which I teach you, for to do them, that ye may live, and go in and possess the land which the Lord God of your fathers giveth you. Ye shall not add unto the word which I command you, neither shall ye diminish ought from it, that ye may keep the commandments of the Lord your God which I command you."* (Deuteronomy 4:1-2)

> *"All scripture is given by inspiration of God, and is profitable for doctrine, for reproof, for correction, for instruction in righteousness: That the man of God may be perfect, throughly furnished unto all good works."* (2 Timothy 3:16-17)

> *"Every word of God is pure: he is a shield unto them that put their trust in him."* (Proverbs 30:5)

> *"Search the scriptures; for in them ye think ye have eternal life: and they are they which testify of me."* (John 5:39)

POINT 3:

Muslims have never shown what has been tampered with in the Bible or has replaced other than their attempt to replace the whole Bible and reduce Jesus to merely a good man. If Christ did not do or say what the Bible says then, according to the Muslims, what did he do or say since they acknowledge the existence of a Jesus? Also, Muhammad is not prophesied in the Bible or elsewhere.

Note that in the Interpretation of the Meanings of the Noble Qur'an in the English

Language, it is stated that (reference Biblical Prohecy on the Advent of Muhammad) Muslim theologians have stated that "another Comforter" in John 14:15-16, of the Bible, refers to Muhammad; this overlooks John 14:26 which explains that the other (another) Comforter is the Holy Ghost (Holy Spirit).

"And the disciples of John shewed him of all these things. And John calling unto him two of his disciples sent them to Jesus, saying, Art thou he that should come? or look we for another? When the men were come unto him, they said, John Baptist hath sent us unto thee, saying, Art thou he that should come? or look we for another? And in that same hour he cured many of their infirmities and plagues, and of evil spirits; and unto many that were blind he gave sight. Then Jesus answering said unto them, Go your way, and tell John what things ye have seen and heard; how that the blind see, the lame walk, the lepers are cleansed, the deaf hear, the dead are raised, to the poor the gospel is preached. And blessed is he, whosoever shall not be offended in me." (Luke 7:18-23)

"Jesus answered, My kingdom is not of this world: if my kingdom were of this world, then would my servants fight, that I should not be delivered to the Jews: but now is my kingdom not from hence. Pilate therefore said unto him, Art thou a king then? Jesus answered, Thou sayest that I am a king. To this end was I born, and for this cause came I into the world, that I should bear witness unto the truth. Every one that is of the truth heareth my voice." (John 18:36&37)

POINT 4:

Christ is the Alpha and Omega. Christians are to expect his return and nothing else according to the Bible.

"I am Alpha and Omega, the beginning and the ending, saith the Lord, which is, and which was, and which is to come, the Almighty. John, who also am your brother, and companion in tribulation, and in the kingdom and patience of Jesus Christ, was in the isle that is called Patmos, for the word of God, and for the testimony of Jesus Christ. I was in the Spirit on the Lord's day, and heard behind me a great voice, as of a trumpet, Saying, I am Alpha and Omega, the first and the last: and, What thou seest, write in a book, and send it unto the seven churches which are in Asia; unto Ephesus, and unto Smyrna, and unto Pergamos, and unto Thyatira, and unto Sardis, and unto Philadelphia, and unto Laodicea." (Revelation 1:8-11)

"And he saith unto me, Seal not the sayings of the prophecy of this book: for the time is at hand. He that is unjust, let him be unjust still: and he which is filthy, let him be filthy still: and he that is righteous, let him be righteous still: and he that is holy, let him be holy still. And, behold, I come quickly; and my reward is with me, to give every man according as his work shall be. I am Alpha and Omega, the beginning and the end, the first and the last. Blessed are they that do his commandments, that they may have right to the tree of life, and may enter in through the gates into the city. For without are dogs, and sorcerers, and whoremongers, and murderers, and idolaters, and whosoever loveth and maketh a lie. I Jesus have sent mine angel to testify unto you these things in the churches. I am the root and the offspring of David, and the bright and morning star. And the Spirit and the bride say, Come. And let him that heareth say, Come. And let him that is athirst come. And whosoever will, let him take the water of life freely. For I testify unto every man that heareth the words of the prophecy of this book, If any man shall add unto these things, God

shall add unto him the plagues that are written in this book: And if any man shall take away from the words of the book of this prophecy, God shall take away his part out of the book of life, and out of the holy city, and from the things which are written in this book. He which testifieth these things saith, Surely I come quickly. Amen. Even so, come, Lord Jesus." (Revelation 22:10-20)

POINT 5:

Christians believe in the regeneration (turn from unbelief) of the mind and a physical resurrection. Today, believers are the people of God's choice according to the Bible. Christians are spiritually a part of the body of Christ, the only Savior according to the Bible.

"For we ourselves also were sometimes foolish, disobedient, deceived, serving divers lusts and pleasures, living in malice and envy, hateful, and hating one another. But after that the kindness and love of God our Saviour toward man appeared, Not by works of righteousness which we have done, but according to his mercy he saved us, by the washing of regeneration, and renewing of the Holy Ghost; Which he shed on us abundantly through Jesus Christ our Saviour; That being justified by his grace, we should be made heirs according to the hope of eternal life. (Titus 3:3-7)

"But God giveth it a body as it hath pleased him, and to every seed his own body. All flesh is not the same flesh: but there is one kind of flesh of men, another flesh of beasts, another of fishes, and another of birds. There are also celestial bodies, and bodies terrestrial: but the glory of the celestial is one, and the glory of the terrestrial is another. There is one glory of the sun, and another glory of the moon, and another glory of the stars: for one star differeth from another star in glory. So also is the resurrection of the dead. It is sown in corruption; it is raised in incorruption: It is sown in dishonour; it is raised in glory: it is sown in weakness; it is raised in power: It is sown a natural body; it is raised a spiritual body. There is a natural body, and there is a spiritual body. And so it is written, The first man Adam was made a living soul; the last Adam was made a quickening spirit. Howbeit that was not first which is spiritual, but that which is natural; and afterward that which is spiritual. The first man is of the earth, earthy: the second man is the Lord from heaven. As is the earthy, such are they also that are earthy: and as is the heavenly, such are they also that are heavenly. And as we have borne the image of the earthy, we shall also bear the image of the heavenly. Now this I say, brethren, that flesh and blood cannot inherit the kingdom of God; neither doth corruption inherit incorruption. Behold, I shew you a mystery; We shall not all sleep, but we shall all be changed, In a moment, in the twinkling of an eye, at the last trump: for the trumpet shall sound, and the dead shall be raised incorruptible, and we shall be changed. For this corruptible must put on incorruption, and this mortal must put on immortality. So when this corruptible shall have put on incorruption, and this mortal shall have put on immortality, then shall be brought to pass the saying that is written, Death is swallowed up in victory." (1 Corinthians 15:38-54)

"For I know that my redeemer liveth, and that he shall stand at the latter day upon the earth: And though after my skin worms destroy this body, yet in my flesh shall I see God: Whom I shall see for myself, and mine eyes shall behold, and not another; though my reins be consumed within me." (Job 19:25-27)

"And when he had found him, he brought him unto Antioch. And it came to pass, that a whole year they assembled themselves with the church, and taught much people. And the disciples were called Christians first in Antioch." (**Acts 11:26**)

"For ye are all the children of God by faith in Christ Jesus. For as many of you as have been baptized into Christ have put on Christ. There is neither Jew nor Greek, there is neither bond nor free, there is neither male nor female: for ye are all one in Christ Jesus. And if ye be Christ's, then are ye Abraham's seed, and heirs according to the promise." (**Galatians 3:26-29**)

"For this cause we also, since the day we heard it, do not cease to pray for you, and to desire that ye might be filled with the knowledge of his will in all wisdom and spiritual understanding; That ye might walk worthy of the Lord unto all pleasing, being fruitful in every good work, and increasing in the knowledge of God; Strengthened with all might, according to his glorious power, unto all patience and longsuffering with joyfulness; Giving thanks unto the Father, which hath made us meet to be partakers of the inheritance of the saints in light: Who hath delivered us from the power of darkness, and hath translated us into the kingdom of his dear Son: In whom we have redemption through his blood, even the forgiveness of sins: Who is the image of the invisible God, the firstborn of every creature: For by him were all things created, that are in heaven, and that are in earth, visible and invisible, whether they be thrones, or dominions, or principalities, or powers: all things were created by him, and for him: And he is before all things, and by him all things consist. And he is the head of the body, the church: who is the beginning, the firstborn from the dead; that in all things he might have the preeminence. For it pleased the Father that in him should all fulness dwell; And, having made peace through the blood of his cross, by him to reconcile all things unto himself; by him, I say, whether they be things in earth, or things in heaven. (**Colossians 1:9-20**)

POINT 6:

The Bible states that all judgment is committed unto the Son. Judgment is to begin in the House of God (the church) first. The small and great of all mankind shall be judged.

"For the Father judgeth no man, but hath committed all judgment unto the Son: That all men should honour the Son, even as they honour the Father. He that honoureth not the Son honoureth not the Father which hath sent him." (**John 5:22&23**)

"For the time is come that judgment must begin at the house of God: and if it first begin at us, what shall the end be of them that obey not the gospel of God?" (**1 Peter 4:17**)

"And I saw a great white throne, and him that sat on it, from whose face the earth and the heaven fled away; and there was found no place for them. And I saw the dead, small and great, stand before God; and the books were opened: and another book was opened, which is the book of life: and the dead were judged out of those things which were written in the books, according to their works." (**Revelation 20:11-12**)

POINT 7:

Let others talk of segregation for the Bible speaks of every nation, kindred, people, and tongues as comprising the saints in heaven. Whereas we are freed from the bondage of sin

by Christ, we are free indeed. Where the spirit of the Lord is, there is liberty (freedom).

> *"And they sung a new song, saying, Thou art worthy to take the book, and to open the seals thereof: for thou wast slain, and hast redeemed us to God by thy blood out of every kindred, and tongue, and people, and nation; And hast made us unto our God kings and priests: and we shall reign on the earth."* (Revelation 5:9)

> *"After this I beheld, and, lo, a great multitude, which no man could number, of all nations, and kindreds, and people, and tongues, stood before the throne, and before the Lamb, clothed with white robes, and palms in their hands; And cried with a loud voice, saying, Salvation to our God which sitteth upon the throne, and unto the Lamb."* (Revelation 7:9)

> *"If the Son therefore shall make you free, ye shall be free indeed."* (John 8:36)

> *"But if the Spirit of him that raised up Jesus from the dead dwell in you, he that raised up Christ from the dead shall also quicken your mortal bodies by his Spirit that dwelleth in you. Therefore, brethren, we are debtors, not to the flesh, to live after the flesh. For if ye live after the flesh, ye shall die: but if ye through the Spirit do mortify the deeds of the body, ye shall live. For as many as are led by the Spirit of God, they are the sons of God. For ye have not received the spirit of bondage again to fear; but ye have received the Spirit of adoption, whereby we cry, Abba, Father. The Spirit itself beareth witness with our spirit, that we are the children of God: And if children, then heirs; heirs of God, and joint-heirs with Christ; if so be that we suffer with him, that we may be also glorified together. For I reckon that the sufferings of this present time are not worthy to be compared with the glory which shall be revealed in us. For the earnest expectation of the creature waiteth for the manifestation of the sons of God. For the creature was made subject to vanity, not willingly, but by reason of him who hath subjected the same in hope, Because the creature itself also shall be delivered from the bondage of corruption into the glorious liberty of the children of God. For we know that the whole creation groaneth and travaileth in pain together until now."* (Romans 6:11-22)

POINT 8:

The just shall live by faith in Jesus. Christians must be just in matters against each other; the saints shall judge the world. The ungodly cannot be expected to be able to be just or to love mercy. We are expected to obey all ordinances (laws/rules). See Chapter 18 - Christian Liberty/True Freedom, Chapter 5 - Biblical Faith/Faith in Jesus Christ, Chapter 12 - Christian Tolerance, and Chapter 38 - A Nation from a Christian Perspective.

> *"Behold, his soul which is lifted up is not upright in him: but the just shall live by his faith."* (Habakkuk 2:4)

> *"Dare any of you, having a matter against another, go to law before the unjust, and not before the saints? Do ye not know that the saints shall judge the world? and if the world shall be judged by you, are ye unworthy to judge the smallest matters? Know ye not that we shall judge angels? how much more things that pertain to this life? If then ye have judgments of things pertaining to this life, set them to judge who are least esteemed in the church. I speak to your shame. Is it so, that there is not a wise man among you? no, not one that shall be able to judge between his brethren? But brother goeth to law with brother, and that before the unbelievers.* (1 Corinthians 6:1-6)

"Blessed is the man that walketh not in the counsel of the ungodly, nor standeth in the way of sinners, nor sitteth in the seat of the scornful. But his delight is in the law of the Lord; and in his law doth he meditate day and night. And he shall be like a tree planted by the rivers of water, that bringeth forth his fruit in his season; his leaf also shall not wither; and whatsoever he doeth shall prosper. The ungodly are not so: but are like the chaff which the wind driveth away. Therefore the ungodly shall not stand in the judgment, nor sinners in the congregation of the righteous. For the Lord knoweth the way of the righteous: but the way of the ungodly shall perish." **(Psalm 1)**

"And the remnant of Jacob shall be in the midst of many people as a dew from the Lord, as the showers upon the grass, that tarrieth not for man, nor waiteth for the sons of men. And the remnant of Jacob shall be among the Gentiles in the midst of many people as a lion among the beasts of the forest, as a young lion among the flocks of sheep: who, if he go through, both treadeth down, and teareth in pieces, and none can deliver. Thine hand shall be lifted up upon thine adversaries, and all thine enemies shall be cut off." **(Micah 5:7-9)**

"Wherefore if ye be dead with Christ from the rudiments of the world, why, as though living in the world, are ye subject to ordinances, (Touch not; taste not; handle not; Which all are to perish with the using;) after the commandments and doctrines of men? **(Colossians 2:20)**

"They answered him, Jesus of Nazareth. Jesus saith unto them, I am he. And Judas also, which betrayed him, stood with them. As soon then as he had said unto them, I am he, they went backward, and fell to the ground." **(John 18:5-6)**

POINT 9:

Put your trust in God and lean not on your understanding of white people. Almighty God as our provider is the strength behind our wealth and good gifts. America needs to see the Lord God Almighty as such and the same for any Christian nation (Australia and Canada make such a claim). See Chapter 38, A Nation from a Christian Perspective.

"Trust in the Lord with all thine heart; and lean not unto thine own understanding. In all thy ways acknowledge him, and he shall direct thy paths. Be not wise in thine own eyes: fear the Lord, and depart from evil." **(Proverbs 3:5-7)**

"And thou say in thine heart, My power and the might of mine hand hath gotten me this wealth. But thou shalt remember the Lord thy God: for it is he that giveth thee power to get wealth, that he may establish his covenant which he sware unto thy fathers, as it is this day." **(Deuteronomy 8:17-19)**

Do not err, my beloved brethren. Every good gift and every perfect gift is from above, and cometh down from the Father of lights, with whom is no variableness, neither shadow of turning. Of his own will begat he us with the word of truth, that we should be a kind of firstfruits of his creatures. Wherefore, my beloved brethren, let every man be swift to hear, slow to speak, slow to wrath: For the wrath of man worketh not the righteousness of God." (James 1:16-18)

POINT 10:

The Bible would suggest that Black Muslims, in the same manner as Jews, are going

about establishing their own righteousness and never coming into the knowledge of God.

> *"For they being ignorant of God's righteousness, and going about to establish their own righteousness, have not submitted themselves unto the righteousness of God. For Christ is the end of the law for righteousness to every one that believeth."* (**Romans 10:3-4**)

> *"If any man teach otherwise, and consent not to wholesome words, even the words of our Lord Jesus Christ, and to the doctrine which is according to godliness; He is proud, knowing nothing, but doting about questions and strifes of words, whereof cometh envy, strife, railings, evil surmisings, Perverse disputings of men of corrupt minds, and destitute of the truth, supposing that gain is godliness: from such withdraw thyself."* (**1 Timothy 6:3-5**)

> *"Jesus saith unto him, I am the way, the truth, and the life: no man cometh unto the Father, but by me. If ye had known me, ye should have known my Father also: and from henceforth ye know him, and have seen him. Philip saith unto him, Lord, shew us the Father, and it sufficeth us. Jesus saith unto him, Have I been so long time with you, and yet hast thou not known me, Philip? he that hath seen me hath seen the Father; and how sayest thou then, Shew us the Father? Believest thou not that I am in the Father, and the Father in me? the words that I speak unto you I speak not of myself: but the Father that dwelleth in me, he doeth the works. Believe me that I am in the Father, and the Father in me: or else believe me for the very works' sake."* (**John 14:6-11**)

> *"And he said, Therefore said I unto you, that no man can come unto me, except it were given unto him of my Father. From that time many of his disciples went back, and walked no more with him. Then said Jesus unto the twelve, Will ye also go away? Then Simon Peter answered him, Lord, to whom shall we go? thou hast the words of eternal life. And we believe and are sure that thou art that Christ, the Son of the living God."* (**John 6:65-69**)

POINT 11:

Love thy neighbor as thyself. Also, the man is the head of the woman, the weaker vessel.

> *"Honour thy father and thy mother: and, Thou shalt love thy neighbour as thyself."* (**Matthew 19:19**)

> *"Then one of them, which was a lawyer, asked him a question, tempting him, and saying, Master, which is the great commandment in the law? Jesus said unto him, Thou shalt love the Lord thy God with all thy heart, and with all thy soul, and with all thy mind. This is the first and great commandment. And the second is like unto it, Thou shalt love thy neighbour as thyself."* (**Matthew 22:35-39**)

> *"And the second is like, namely this, Thou shalt love thy neighbour as thyself. There is none other commandment greater than these."* (**Mark 12:31**)

> *"Owe no man any thing, but to love one another: for he that loveth another hath fulfilled the law."* (**Romans 13:8**)

> *"For, brethren, ye have been called unto liberty; only use not liberty for an occasion to the flesh, but by love serve one another."* (**Galatians 5:13**)

"If ye fulfil the royal law according to the scripture, Thou shalt love thy neighbour as thyself, ye do well: But if ye have respect to persons, ye commit sin, and are convinced of the law as transgressors." (James 2:8-9)

"But I would have you know, that the head of every man is Christ; and the head of the woman is the man; and the head of Christ is God." (1 Corinthians 11:3)

"Likewise, ye husbands, dwell with them according to knowledge, giving honour unto the wife, as unto the weaker vessel, and as being heirs together of the grace of life; that your prayers be not hindered." (1 Peter 3:7)

POINT 12:

This statement is anti-Christ (against Christ). Black Muslims should be honest, they do not believe in Christ as the Son of God. They do not believe in the Bible as we know it. They say that the Bible has been tampered with yet they cannot tell Christians what has been changed in the Bible. And, the worst of the matter is that Black Muslims do not agree doctrinally with Islam (for example, Master W. Fard Muhammad being the Messiah of the Christians and the Mahdi of the Muslims). To put it plainly, they follow neither the teachings of the Bible or The Noble Qur'an but rather "Message to the Black Man" which is not universally recognized as holy. God is not the author of confusion.

"For many deceivers are entered into the world, who confess not that Jesus Christ is come in the flesh. This is a deceiver and an antichrist. Look to yourselves, that we lose not those things which we have wrought, but that we receive a full reward. Whosoever transgresseth, and abideth not in the doctrine of Christ, hath not God. He that abideth in the doctrine of Christ, he hath both the Father and the Son. If there come any unto you, and bring not this doctrine, receive him not into your house, neither bid him God speed: For he that biddeth him God speed is partaker of his evil deeds." (2 John 7-11)

"Knowing this first, that no prophecy of the scripture is of any private interpretation. For the prophecy came not in old time by the will of man: but holy men of God spake as they were moved by the Holy Ghost." (2 Peter 1:20-21)

"And Elijah came unto all the people, and said, How long halt ye between two opinions? if the Lord be God, follow him: but if Baal, then follow him. And the people answered him not a word." (1 Kings 18:21)

"A double minded man is unstable in all his ways.' (James 1:8)

"For God is not the author of confusion, but of peace, as in all churches of the saints." (1 Corinthians 14:33)

What the Muslims (Nation of Islam) Want

(PRESENTED HEREIN WITHOUT COMMENT)

We want freedom. We want a full and complete freedom.

We want justice. Equal justice under the law. We want justice applied equally to all, regardless of creed, class or color.

We want equality of opportunity. We want equal membership in society with the best in civilized society.

We want our people in America whose parents or grandparents were descendents from slaves, to be allowed in establish a separate state or territory of their own – either on this continent or elsewhere. We believe that our former slave masters are obligated to provide such land and that the area must be fertile and minerally rally rich. We believe that our former slave masters are obligated to maintain and supply our needs in this separate territory for the next 20 to 25 years – until we are able to produce and supply our own needs.

Since we cannot get along with them in peace and equality, after giving them 400 years of our sweat and blood and receiving in return some of the worst treatment human beings have ever experienced, we believe our contributions to this land and the suffering forced upon us by white America, justifies our demand for complete separation in a state or territory of our own.

We want freedom for all Believers of Islam now held in federal prisons. We want freedom for all black men and women now under death sentence in innumerable prisons in the North as well as the South.

We want every black man and woman to have the freedom to accept or reject being separated from the slave master's children and establish a land of their own.

We know that the above plan for the solution of black and white conflict is best and only answer the problem between two people.

We want immediate end to police brutality and mob attacks against the so-called Negro throughout the United States.

We believe that the Federal government should intercede to see that black men and women tried in white courts receive justice in accordance with the laws of the land – or allow us to build a new nation for ourselves, dedicated to justice, freedom and liberty.

As long as we are not allowed to establish a state or territory of our own we demand no only equal justice under the laws of the United States, but equal employment opportunities – NOW!

We do not believe that after 400 years of free or nearly free labor, sweat and blood, which has helped American, become rich and powerful, that so many thousands of black people should have to subsist on relief, charity or live in poor houses.

We want the government of the United States to exempt our people from ALL taxation as long as we are deprived of equal justice under the laws of the land.

We want equal education – but separate schools up to 16 for boys and 18 for girls on the condition that the girls are sent to women's colleges and universities. We want all black children educated, taught and trained by their own teachers.

Under such schooling system we believe we will make a better nation of people. The United States government should provide, free, all necessary text books and equipment, schools and college buildings. The Muslim teachers shall be left free to teach and train their people in the way of righteousness, decency and self respect.

We believe that intermarriage or race mixing should be prohibited. We want the religion of Islam taught without hindrance or suppression.

These are some of the things that we, the Muslims, want for our people in North America.

Finally, it is an Islamic conjecture that there has been tampering with regard to the Bible. In actuality, Muhammed presents a completely different reality, that includes a different Jesus in the Qur'an, without anyone ever producing any tangible proof of the substitutability of The Noble Qur'an for the Bible. The Noble Qur'an fails to substitute wholesale portions of the Bible; greater substitution would tend to expose the claimed erroneous and/or tampered portions of the Bible. Regardless, Islamic scholars have quoted innumerable Bible verses in an effort to exalt Islam. It is an historical fact that Muhammed died while still receiving the revelation of the Noble Qur'an. Also, the Bible stands by itself whereas The Noble Qur'an does not.

17

FUNDAMENTALS OF THE BEST POSSIBLE LIVING – CHRISTIAN LIVES IN THE UNDERSTANDING OF MANKIND'S PURPOSE

Seriously, what is the prescription for the best possible outcome in my life regardless of my present circumstances?

THE BIBLE IS clear in stating that out first priority in life ought to be to find God.

> *"Therefore take no thought, saying, What shall we eat? Or, What shall we drink? Or, Wherewithal shall we be clothed? (For after all these things do the Gentiles seek:) for your heavenly Father knoweth that ye have need of all these things. But seek ye first the kingdom of God, and his righteousness; and all these things shall be added unto you. Take therefore no thought for the morrow: for the morrow shall take thought for the things of itself. Sufficient unto the day is the evil thereof." (Matthew 6:31-34)*

> *"Remember now thy Creator in the days of thy youth, while the evil days come not, nor the years draw nigh, when thou shalt say, I have no pleasure in them; While the sun, or the light, or the moon, or the stars, be not darkened, nor the clouds return after the rain: In the day when the keepers of the house shall tremble, and the strong men shall bow themselves, and the grinders cease because they are few, and those that look out of the windows be darkened, And the doors shall be shut in the streets, when the sound of the grinding is low, and he shall rise up at the voice of the bird, and all the daughters of musick shall be brought low; Also when they shall be afraid of that which is high, and fears shall be in the way, and the almond tree shall flourish, and the grasshopper shall be a burden, and desire shall fail: because man goeth to his long home, and the mourners go about the streets: Or ever the silver cord be loosed, or the golden bowl be broken, or the pitcher be broken at the fountain, or the wheel broken at the cistern." (Ecclesiastes 12:1-6)*

Christians are to abide under a philosophy of personal choice of the faith for ourselves as well as others. The <u>forcing</u> of converts to Christianity is and has <u>always been</u> apostate.

> *"All the paths of the Lord are mercy and truth unto such as keep his covenant and his testimonies. For thy name's sake, O Lord, pardon mine iniquity; for it is great. What man is he that feareth the Lord? him shall he teach in the way that he shall choose. His soul shall*

dwell at ease; and his seed shall inherit the earth. The secret of the Lord is with them that fear him; and he will shew them his covenant. Mine eyes are ever toward the Lord; for he shall pluck my feet out of the net. Turn thee unto me, and have mercy upon me; for I am desolate and afflicted. The troubles of my heart are enlarged: O bring thou me out of my distresses. Look upon mine affliction and my pain; and forgive all my sins. Consider mine enemies; for they are many; and they hate me with cruel hatred. O keep my soul, and deliver me: let me not be ashamed; for I put my trust in thee." (**Psalms 25:10-20**)

"Now therefore fear the Lord, and serve him in sincerity and in truth: and put away the gods which your fathers served on the other side of the flood, and in Egypt; and serve ye the Lord. And if it seem evil unto you to serve the Lord, choose you this day whom ye will serve; whether the gods which your fathers served that were on the other side of the flood, or the gods of the Amorites, in whose land ye dwell: but as for me and my house, we will serve the Lord." (**Joshua 24:14&15**)

"And the servant of the Lord must not strive; but be gentle unto all men, apt to teach, patient, In meekness instructing those that oppose themselves; if God peradventure will give them repentance to the acknowledging of the truth; And that they may recover themselves out of the snare of the devil, who are taken captive by him at his will." (**2 Timothy 2:24-26**)

For our exhortation was not of deceit, nor of uncleanness, nor in guile: But as we were allowed of God to be put in trust with the gospel, even so we speak; not as pleasing men, but God, which trieth our hearts. For neither at any time used we flattering words, as ye know, nor a cloke of covetousness; God is witness: Nor of men sought we glory, neither of you, nor yet of others, when we might have been burdensome, as the apostles of Christ. But we were gentle among you, even as a nurse cherisheth her children: So being affectionately desirous of you, we were willing to have imparted unto you, not the gospel of God only, but also our own souls, because ye were dear unto us. For ye remember, brethren, our labour and travail: for labouring night and day, because we would not be chargeable unto any of you, we preached unto you the gospel of God. Ye are witnesses, and God also, how holily and justly and unblameably we behaved ourselves among you that believe: As ye know how we exhorted and comforted and charged every one of you, as a father doth his children, That ye would walk worthy of God, who hath called you unto his kingdom and glory." (**1 Thessalonians 2:3-12**)

A basic desire of man is to live and to do so with a reasonable abundance. Jesus Christ says, according to the scriptures, that he came that we might have life with abundance.

"The thief cometh not, but for to steal, and to kill, and to destroy: I am come that they might have life, and that they might have it more abundantly." (**John 10:10**)

"I know both how to be abased, and I know how to abound: every where and in all things I am instructed both to be full and to be hungry, both to abound and to suffer need. I can do all things through Christ which strengtheneth me." (**Philippians 4:12&13**)

"But my God shall supply all your need according to his riches in glory by Christ Jesus." (**Philippians 4:19**)

"Furthermore then we beseech you, brethren, and exhort you by the Lord Jesus, that as ye have received of us how ye ought to walk and to please God, so ye would abound more and more." (1 Thessalonians 4:1)

"Now unto him that is able to do exceeding abundantly above all that we ask or think, according to the power that worketh in us, unto him be glory in the church by Christ Jesus throughout all ages, world without end. Amen." (Ephesians 3:20-21)

"Delight thyself also in the Lord; and he shall give thee the desires of thine heart." (Psalm 37:4)

Christianity acknowledges our purpose in life as having been established by the Creator in whose image we have been made as living souls (the soul eternal like God). The Bible says that true and living God created us to give him glory through the glorified lives of his people.

"In the beginning God created the heaven and the earth." (Genesis 1:1)

"And God said, Let us make man in our image, after our likeness: and let them have dominion over the fish of the sea, and over the fowl of the air, and over the cattle, and over all the earth, and over every creeping thing that creepeth upon the earth. So God created man in his own image, in the image of God created he him; male and female created he them. And God blessed them, and God said unto them, Be fruitful, and multiply, and replenish the earth, and subdue it: and have dominion over the fish of the sea, and over the fowl of the air, and over every living thing that moveth upon the earth." (Genesis 1:26-28)

"And the Lord God formed man of the dust of the ground, and breathed into his nostrils the breath of life; and man became a living soul." (Genesis 2:7)

"Even every one that is called by my name: for I have created him for my glory, I have formed him; yea, I have made him." (Isaiah 43:7)

"Then departed Barnabas to Tarsus, for to seek Saul: and when he had found him, he brought him unto Antioch. And it came to pass, that a whole year they assembled themselves with the church, and taught much people. And the disciples were called Christians first in Antioch. And in these days came prophets from Jerusalem unto Antioch." (Acts 11:25-27)

"I form the light, and create darkness: I make peace, and create evil: I the Lord do all these things." (Isaiah 45:7)

"Woe unto him that striveth with his Maker! Let the potsherd strive with the potsherds of the earth. Shall the clay say to him that fashioneth it, What makest thou? Or thy work, He hath no hands? Woe unto him that saith unto his father, What begettest thou? Or to the woman, What hast thou brought forth? Thus saith the Lord, the Holy One of Israel, and his Maker, Ask me of things to come concerning my sons, and concerning the work of my hands command ye me. I have made the earth, and created man upon it: I, even my hands, have stretched out the heavens, and all their host have I commanded." (Isaiah 45:9-12)

"Behold my servant, whom I uphold; mine elect, in whom my soul delighteth; I have put my spirit upon him: he shall bring forth judgment to the Gentiles. He shall not cry, nor lift up, nor cause his voice to be heard in the street. A bruised reed shall he not break, and the smoking flax shall he not quench: he shall bring forth judgment unto truth. He shall not

fail nor be discouraged, till he have set judgment in the earth: and the isles shall wait for his law. Thus saith God the Lord, he that created the heavens, and stretched them out; he that spread forth the earth, and that which cometh out of it; he that giveth breath unto the people upon it, and spirit to them that walk therein: I the Lord have called thee in righteousness, and will hold thine hand, and will keep thee, and give thee for a covenant of the people, for a light of the Gentiles; To open the blind eyes, to bring out the prisoners from the prison, and them that sit in darkness out of the prison house. I am the Lord: that is my name: and my glory will I not give to another, neither my praise to graven images." (Isaiah 42:1-8)

"If ye abide in me, and my words abide in you, ye shall ask what ye will, and it shall be done unto you. Herein is my Father glorified, that ye bear much fruit; so shall ye be my disciples. As the Father hath loved me, so have I loved you: continue ye in my love. If ye keep my commandments, ye shall abide in my love; even as I have kept my Father's commandments, and abide in his love. These things have I spoken unto you, that my joy might remain in you, and that your joy might be full." (John 15:7-11)

Mankind has been blessed with a written document that was prepared over the course of hundreds of years by approximately 40 different writers that were all inspired by the Holy Spirit. The Bible addresses life's issues with our salvation as its purpose. Those of the faith, study your Bibles! Those of other religions need to read the Bible as guided by a preacher who is strong in biblical understanding and in doing so will "consider" Jesus Christ.

"These were more noble than those in Thessalonica, in that they received the word with all readiness of mind, and searched the scriptures daily, whether those things were so." (Acts 17:11)

"All scripture is given by inspiration of God, and is profitable for doctrine, for reproof, for correction, for instruction in righteousness: that the man of God may be perfect, throughly furnished unto all good works." (2 Timothy 3:16-17)

"Knowing this first, that no prophecy of the scripture is of any private interpretation. For the prophecy came not in old time by the will of man: but holy men of God spake as they were moved by the Holy Ghost." (2 Peter 1:20-21)

"Study to shew thyself approved unto God, a workman that needeth not to be ashamed, rightly dividing the word of truth." (2 Timothy 2:15)

"Remember them which have the rule over you, who have spoken unto you the word of God: whose faith follow, considering the end of their conversation. Jesus Christ the same yesterday, and to day, and for ever." (Hebrews 13:7&8)

"For every one that useth milk is unskilful in the word of righteousness: for he is a babe. But strong meat belongeth to them that are of full age, even those who by reason of use have their senses exercised to discern both good and evil." (Hebrews 5:13&14)

"For consider him that endured such contradiction of sinners against himself, lest ye be wearied and faint in your minds." (Hebrews 12:3)

Mankind needs to worship the God of Abraham, Isaac, and Jacob [Israel]. The Bible de-

clares his salvation.

> *"And God said unto Moses, I AM THAT I AM: and he said, Thus shalt thou say unto the children of Israel, I AM hath sent me unto you. And God said moreover unto Moses, Thus shalt thou say unto the children of Israel, The Lord God of your fathers, the God of Abraham, the God of Isaac, and the God of Jacob, hath sent me unto you: this is my name for ever, and this is my memorial unto all generations."* (**Exodus 3:14-15**)

> *"Even as Abraham believed God, and it was accounted to him for righteousness. Know ye therefore that they which are of faith, the same are the children of Abraham. And the scripture, foreseeing that God would justify the heathen through faith, preached before the gospel unto Abraham, saying, In thee shall all nations be blessed. So then they which be of faith are blessed with faithful Abraham...For as many of you as have been baptized into Christ have put on Christ. There is neither Jew nor Greek, there is neither bond nor free, there is neither male nor female: for ye are all one in Christ Jesus. And if ye be Christ's, then are ye Abraham's seed, and heirs according to the promise."* (**Galatians 3:6-9, 27-29**)

> *"Shew me thy ways, O Lord; teach me thy paths. Lead me in thy truth, and teach me: for thou art the God of my salvation; on thee do I wait all the day."* (**Psalm 25:4&5**)

> *"And Moses said unto the people, Fear ye not, stand still, and see the salvation of the Lord, which he will shew to you to day: for the Egyptians whom ye have seen to day, ye shall see them again no more for ever. The Lord shall fight for you, and ye shall hold your peace. And the Lord said unto Moses, Wherefore criest thou unto me? speak unto the children of Israel, that they go forward: but lift thou up thy rod, and stretch out thine hand over the sea, and divide it: and the children of Israel shall go on dry ground through the midst of the sea."* (**Exodus 14:13-16**)

> *"Sing unto the Lord, all the earth; shew forth from day to day his salvation. Declare his glory among the heathen; his marvellous works among all nations. For great is the Lord, and greatly to be praised: he also is to be feared above all gods. For all the gods of the people are idols: but the Lord made the heavens. Glory and honour are in his presence; strength and gladness are in his place. Give unto the Lord, ye kindreds of the people, give unto the Lord glory and strength. Give unto the Lord the glory due unto his name: bring an offering, and come before him: worship the Lord in the beauty of holiness. Fear before him, all the earth: the world also shall be stable, that it be not moved. Let the heavens be glad, and let the earth rejoice: and let men say among the nations, The Lord reigneth."* (**1 Chronicles 16:23-31**)

> *"The woman saith unto him, Sir, I perceive that thou art a prophet. Our fathers worshipped in this mountain; and ye say, that in Jerusalem is the place where men ought to worship. Jesus saith unto her, Woman, believe me, the hour cometh, when ye shall neither in this mountain, nor yet at Jerusalem, worship the Father. Ye worship ye know not what: we know what we worship: for salvation is of the Jews. But the hour cometh, and now is, when the true worshippers shall worship the Father in spirit and in truth: for the Father seeketh such to worship him. God is a Spirit: and they that worship him must worship him in spirit and in truth."* (**John 4:19-24**)

This true and living God, that has declared "there is none but me", sent his Son into the world to reconcile sinful mankind to himself. The Bible declares that Jesus Christ, the Son

of God, paid the penalty for man's sin by dying on the cross but then he rose from the dead. The believer has forgiveness of sin in the blood of Jesus because of his willing sacrifice.

"Let all the nations be gathered together, and let the people be assembled: who among them can declare this, and shew us former things? let them bring forth their witnesses, that they may be justified: or let them hear, and say, It is truth. Ye are my witnesses, saith the Lord, and my servant whom I have chosen: that ye may know and believe me, and understand that I am he: before me there was no God formed, neither shall there be after me. I, even I, am the Lord; and beside me there is no saviour. I have declared, and have saved, and I have shewed, when there was no strange god among you: therefore ye are my witnesses, saith the Lord, that I am God. Yea, before the day was I am he; and there is none that can deliver out of my hand: I will work, and who shall let it?" (Isaiah 43:9-13)

"Therefore if any man be in Christ, he is a new creature: old things are passed away; behold, all things are become new. And all things are of God, who hath reconciled us to himself by Jesus Christ, and hath given to us the ministry of reconciliation; to wit, that God was in Christ, reconciling the world unto himself, not imputing their trespasses unto them; and hath committed unto us the word of reconciliation." (2 Corinthians 5:17-19)

"But Christ being come an high priest of good things to come, by a greater and more perfect tabernacle, not made with hands, that is to say, not of this building; neither by the blood of goats and calves, but by his own blood he entered in once into the holy place, having obtained eternal redemption for us. For if the blood of bulls and of goats, and the ashes of an heifer sprinkling the unclean, sanctifieth to the purifying of the flesh: how much more shall the blood of Christ, who through the eternal Spirit offered himself without spot to God, purge your conscience from dead works to serve the living God? And for this cause he is the mediator of the new testament, that by means of death, for the redemption of the transgressions that were under the first testament, they which are called might receive the promise of eternal inheritance. For where a testament is, there must also of necessity be the death of the testator. For a testament is of force after men are dead: otherwise it is of no strength at all while the testator liveth. Whereupon neither the first testament was dedicated without blood. For when Moses had spoken every precept to all the people according to the law, he took the blood of calves and of goats, with water, and scarlet wool, and hyssop, and sprinkled both the book, and all the people, saying, This is the blood of the testament which God hath enjoined unto you. Moreover he sprinkled with blood both the tabernacle, and all the vessels of the ministry. And almost all things are by the law purged with blood; and without shedding of blood is no remission. It was therefore necessary that the patterns of things in the heavens should be purified with these; but the heavenly things themselves with better sacrifices than these. For Christ is not entered into the holy places made with hands, which are the figures of the true; but into heaven itself, now to appear in the presence of God for us: nor yet that he should offer himself often, as the high priest entereth into the holy place every year with blood of others; for then must he often have suffered since the foundation of the world: but now once in the end of the world hath he appeared to put away sin by the sacrifice of himself. And as it is appointed unto men once to die, but after this the judgment: so Christ was once offered to bear the sins of many; and unto them that look for him shall he appear the second time without sin unto salvation." (Hebrews 9:11-28)

"For God so loved the world, that he gave his only begotten Son, that whosoever believeth in him should not perish, but have everlasting life." (John 3:16)

Jesus Christ did not just appear, he fulfilled prophecy of old.

"But I have greater witness than that of John: for the works which the Father hath given me to finish, the same works that I do, bear witness of me, that the Father hath sent me. And the Father himself, which hath sent me, hath borne witness of me. Ye have neither heard his voice at any time, nor seen his shape. And ye have not his word abiding in you: for whom he hath sent, him ye believe not. Search the scriptures; for in them ye think ye have eternal life: and they are they which testify of me." (John 5:36-39)

"In the last day, that great day of the feast, Jesus stood and cried, saying, 'If any man thirst, let him come unto me, and drink. He that believeth on me, as the scripture hath said, out of his belly shall flow rivers of living water.' (But this spake he of the Spirit, which they that believe on him should receive: for the Holy Ghost was not yet given; because that Jesus was not yet glorified.) Many of the people therefore, when they heard this saying, said, Of a truth this is the Prophet. Others said, This is the Christ. But some said, Shall Christ come out of Galilee? Hath not the scripture said, That Christ cometh of the seed of David, and out of the town of Bethlehem, where David was?" (John 7:37-42)

The Bible identifies the authorship of eternal salvation. Mankind has nothing else that gives us such particulars concerning redemption.

"Though he were a Son, yet learned he obedience by the things which he suffered; and being made perfect, he became the author of eternal salvation unto all them that obey him; called of God an high priest after the order of Melchisedec." (Hebrews 5:8-10)

"Looking unto Jesus the author and finisher of our faith; who for the joy that was set before him endured the cross, despising the shame, and is set down at the right hand of the throne of God. For consider him that endured such contradiction of sinners against himself, lest ye be wearied and faint in your minds." (Hebrews 12:2-3)

"Giving thanks unto the Father, which hath made us meet to be partakers of the inheritance of the saints in light: who hath delivered us from the power of darkness, and hath translated us into the kingdom of his dear Son: in whom we have redemption through his blood, even the forgiveness of sins: Who is the image of the invisible God, the firstborn of every creature: for by him were all things created, that are in heaven, and that are in earth, visible and invisible, whether they be thrones, or dominions, or principalities, or powers: all things were created by him, and for him: and he is before all things, and by him all things consist." (Colossians 1:12-17)

"Know ye not that the unrighteous shall not inherit the kingdom of God? Be not deceived: neither fornicators, nor idolaters, nor adulterers, nor effeminate, nor abusers of themselves with mankind, Nor thieves, nor covetous, nor drunkards, nor revilers, nor extortioners, shall inherit the kingdom of God. And such were some of you: but ye are washed, but ye are sanctified, but ye are justified in the name of the Lord Jesus, and by the Spirit of our God." (1 Corinthians 6:9-11)

What does it matter for a person to gain much wealth and fame in life and lose their

soul? Further, Jesus said, "if you are ashamed of me I will be ashamed of you". Therefore, to live the best life, a life of faith, Christ needs to be evident in our lives. Those of the faith are called Christians.

> *"And when he had called the people unto him with his disciples also, he said unto them, 'Whosoever will come after me, let him deny himself, and take up his cross, and follow me. For whosoever will save his life shall lose it; but whosoever shall lose his life for my sake and the gospel's, the same shall save it. For what shall it profit a man, if he shall gain the whole world, and lose his own soul? Or what shall a man give in exchange for his soul? Whosoever therefore shall be ashamed of me and of my words in this adulterous and sinful generation; of him also shall the Son of man be ashamed, when he cometh in the glory of his Father with the holy angels."* (**Mark 8:34-38**)

> *"For whosoever shall be ashamed of me and of my words, of him shall the Son of man be ashamed, when he shall come in his own glory, and in his Father's, and of the holy angels."* (**Luke 9:26**)

> *"Now they which were scattered abroad upon the persecution that arose about Stephen travelled as far as Phenice, and Cyprus, and Antioch, preaching the word to none but unto the Jews only. And some of them were men of Cyprus and Cyrene, which, when they were come to Antioch, spake unto the Grecians, preaching the Lord Jesus. And the hand of the Lord was with them: and a great number believed, and turned unto the Lord. Then tidings of these things came unto the ears of the church which was in Jerusalem: and they sent forth Barnabas, that he should go as far as Antioch. Who, when he came, and had seen the grace of God, was glad, and exhorted them all, that with purpose of heart they would cleave unto the Lord. For he was a good man, and full of the Holy Ghost and of faith: and much people was added unto the Lord. Then departed Barnabas to Tarsus, for to seek Saul: And when he had found him, he brought him unto Antioch. And it came to pass, that a whole year they assembled themselves with the church, and taught much people. And the disciples were called Christians first in Antioch."* (**Acts 11:19-26**)

> *"Now then we are ambassadors for Christ, as though God did beseech you by us: we pray you in Christ's stead, be ye reconciled to God. For he hath made him to be sin for us, who knew no sin; that we might be made the righteousness of God in him."* (**2 Corinthians 5:20&21**)

It is promised that Christians shall lead and will not have to follow in worldly status.

> *"And the Lord shall make thee the head, and not the tail; and thou shalt be above only, and thou shalt not be beneath; if that thou hearken unto the commandments of the Lord thy God, which I command thee this day, to observe and to do them: and thou shalt not go aside from any of the words which I command thee this day, to the right hand, or to the left, to go after other gods to serve them."* (**Deuteronomy 28:13-14**)

> *"Know ye therefore that they which are of faith, the same are the children of Abraham. And the scripture, foreseeing that God would justify the heathen through faith, preached before the gospel unto Abraham, saying, In thee shall all nations be blessed. So then they which be of faith are blessed with faithful Abraham."* (**Galatians 3:7-9**)

Now, given mankind's depravity, spiritual power is needed to overcome even ourselves. It is impossible for mankind to save itself as even history can attest to our depravity.

"And God saw that the wickedness of man was great in the earth, and that every imagination of the thoughts of his heart was only evil continually. And it repented the Lord that he had made man on the earth, and it grieved him at his heart. And the Lord said, I will destroy man whom I have created from the face of the earth; both man, and beast, and the creeping thing, and the fowls of the air; for it repenteth me that I have made them. But Noah found grace in the eyes of the Lord." (**Genesis 6:5-8**)

"If my people, which are called by my name, shall humble themselves, and pray, and seek my face, and turn from their wicked ways; then will I hear from heaven, and will forgive their sin, and will heal their land." (**2 Chronicles 7:14**)

"See now that I, even I, am he, and there is no god with me: I kill, and I make alive; I wound, and I heal: neither is there any that can deliver out of my hand. For I lift up my hand to heaven, and say, I live for ever." (**Deuteronomy 32:39-40**)

"Only be thou strong and very courageous, that thou mayest observe to do according to all the law, which Moses my servant commanded thee: turn not from it to the right hand or to the left, that thou mayest prosper whithersoever thou goest. This book of the law shall not depart out of thy mouth; but thou shalt meditate therein day and night, that thou mayest observe to do according to all that is written therein: for then thou shalt make thy way prosperous, and then thou shalt have good success." (**Joshua 1:7-9**)

"For by grace are ye saved through faith; and that not of yourselves: it is the gift of God: Not of works, lest any man should boast." (**Ephesians 2:8-10**)

For the best possible life, mankind needs to operate in God's blessings not vanity [hebel: superficial, empty, vain heart].

"And it shall come to pass, if thou shalt hearken diligently unto the voice of the Lord thy God, to observe and to do all his commandments which I command thee this day, that the Lord thy God will set thee on high above all nations of the earth: and all these blessings shall come on thee, and overtake thee, if thou shalt hearken unto the voice of the Lord thy God. The Lord shall establish thee an holy people unto himself, as he hath sworn unto thee, if thou shalt keep the commandments of the Lord thy God, and walk in his ways. And all people of the earth shall see that thou art called by the name of the Lord; and they shall be afraid of thee." (**Deuteronomy 28:1,2,9-10**)

"Wealth gotten by vanity shall be diminished: but he that gathereth by labour shall increase." (**Proverbs 13:11**)

"A good man leaveth an inheritance to his children's children: and the wealth of the sinner is laid up for the just." (**Proverbs 13:22**)

Man must be spiritually born again, as is every Christian, because the carnal mind offends God. Spiritually we walk in power above the satanic principalities and power of the flesh. The weapons of our warfare in life now become mighty in the Spirit. God fights life's battles rendering all other weapons powerless in our eternal destruction.

"For the law of the Spirit of life in Christ Jesus hath made me free from the law of sin and death. For what the law could not do, in that it was weak through the flesh, God sending his own Son in the likeness of sinful flesh, and for sin, condemned sin in the flesh: that the

righteousness of the law might be fulfilled in us, who walk not after the flesh, but after the Spirit. For they that are after the flesh do mind the things of the flesh; but they that are after the Spirit the things of the Spirit. For to be carnally minded is death; but to be spiritually minded is life and peace. Because the carnal mind is enmity against God: for it is not subject to the law of God, neither indeed can be. So then they that are in the flesh cannot please God. But ye are not in the flesh, but in the Spirit, if so be that the Spirit of God dwell in you. Now if any man have not the Spirit of Christ, he is none of his." (**Romans 8:2-9**)

"This I say then, Walk in the Spirit, and ye shall not fulfil the lust of the flesh. For the flesh lusteth against the Spirit, and the Spirit against the flesh: and these are contrary the one to the other: so that ye cannot do the things that ye would. But if ye be led of the Spirit, ye are not under the law." (**Galatians 5:16-18**)

"And you, being dead in your sins and the uncircumcision of your flesh, hath he quickened together with him, having forgiven you all trespasses; blotting out the handwriting of ordinances that was against us, which was contrary to us, and took it out of the way, nailing it to his cross; and having spoiled principalities and powers, he made a shew of them openly, triumphing over them in it." (**Colossians 2:13-15**)

"And he said, Hearken ye, all Judah, and ye inhabitants of Jerusalem, and thou king Jehoshaphat, Thus saith the Lord unto you, Be not afraid nor dismayed by reason of this great multitude; for the battle is not yours, but God's." (**2 Chronicles 20:15**)

"For though we walk in the flesh, we do not war after the flesh: (For the weapons of our warfare are not carnal, but mighty through God to the pulling down of strong holds;) casting down imaginations, and every high thing that exalteth itself against the knowledge of God, and bringing into captivity every thought to the obedience of Christ; and having a readiness to revenge all disobedience, when your obedience is fulfilled." (**2 Corinthians 10:3-5**)

"No weapon that is formed against thee shall prosper; and every tongue that shall rise against thee in judgment thou shalt condemn. This is the heritage of the servants of the Lord, and their righteousness is of me, saith the Lord." (**Isaiah 54:17**)

The believer's walk in the spirit is to be not only as children but rather dear (agapetos: beloved) children. As such, we are spiritually broken (contrite) before God. In our spiritual vulnerability and weakness, God is able to move by the Holy Ghost to strengthen us against the buffeting of Satan in our lives. God is then at his maximized strength in our lives and able to make us mighty in his will.

"But the fruit of the Spirit is love, joy, peace, longsuffering, gentleness, goodness, faith, Meekness, temperance: against such there is no law. And they that are Christ's have crucified the flesh with the affections and lusts. If we live in the Spirit, let us also walk in the Spirit." (**Galatians 5:22-25**)

"Be ye therefore followers of God, as dear children; And walk in love, as Christ also hath loved us, and hath given himself for us an offering and a sacrifice to God for a sweetsmelling savour." (**Ephesians 5:1&2**)

"Create in me a clean heart, O God; and renew a right spirit within me. Cast me not away from thy presence; and take not thy holy spirit from me. Restore unto me the joy of thy salvation; and uphold me with thy free spirit. Then will I teach transgressors thy ways; and

sinners shall be converted unto thee. Deliver me from bloodguiltiness, O God, thou God of my salvation: and my tongue shall sing aloud of thy righteousness. O Lord, open thou my lips; and my mouth shall shew forth thy praise. For thou desirest not sacrifice; else would I give it: thou delightest not in burnt offering. The sacrifices of God are a broken spirit: a broken and a contrite heart, O God, thou wilt not despise." (Psalm 51:10-17)

"And lest I should be exalted above measure through the abundance of the revelations, there was given to me a thorn in the flesh, the messenger of Satan to buffet me, lest I should be exalted above measure. For this thing I besought the Lord thrice, that it might depart from me. And he said unto me, My grace is sufficient for thee: for my strength is made perfect in weakness. Most gladly therefore will I rather glory in my infirmities, that the power of Christ may rest upon me." (2 Corinthians 12:7-9)

"For the Father loveth the Son, and sheweth him all things that himself doeth: and he will shew him greater works than these, that ye may marvel. For as the Father raiseth up the dead, and quickeneth them; even so the Son quickeneth whom he will." (John 5:20&21)

The believer is assured of overcoming the world as demonstrated by Jesus Christ.

"These things I have spoken unto you, that in me ye might have peace. In the world ye shall have tribulation: but be of good cheer; I have overcome the world." (John 16:33)

"For whatsoever is born of God overcometh the world: and this is the victory that overcometh the world, even our faith. Who is he that overcometh the world, but he that believeth that Jesus is the Son of God?" (1 John 5:4&5) "Finally, my brethren, be strong in the Lord, and in the power of his might. Put on the whole armour of God, that ye may be able to stand against the wiles of the devil. For we wrestle not against flesh and blood, but against principalities, against powers, against the rulers of the darkness of this world, against spiritual wickedness in high places. Wherefore take unto you the whole armour of God, that ye may be able to withstand in the evil day, and having done all, to stand." (Ephesians 6:10-13)

"He that overcometh shall inherit all things; and I will be his God, and he shall be my son." (Revelation 21:7)

Now, with regard to the world and its proceedings beyond the body of Christ (the church), Christian (Christ Centered) organizations ought to be at the forefront of mankind's endeavors. Christians should not have to join secular organizations in order to accomplish civic works; civic works should be among the priorities of the church's outreach. Among the endeavors in need beyond the body are administrations and operations in schools, hospitals, medicine, housing, shelters, prisons, pantries, public safety, counseling, entertainment and recreation to name a few. However, friendship and even partnership with the world is encouraged by the scriptures but not fellowship. Faith without works is no faith and there is a great need for endeavors on behalf of mankind as an outreach of the body of Christ. Our solutions and presentations, as led by the Holy Spirit, with the favor of Almighty God and in the name of our Lord and Savior, are to be victorious according to the Bible.

"Finally, brethren, whatsoever things are true, whatsoever things are honest, whatsoever things are just, whatsoever things are pure, whatsoever things are lovely, whatsoever things

are of good report; if there be any virtue, and if there be any praise, think on these things." (Philippians 4:8)

"Can two walk together, except they be agreed?" (Amos 3:3)

"Let no man deceive you with vain words: for because of these things cometh the wrath of God upon the children of disobedience. Be not ye therefore partakers with them. For ye were sometimes darkness, but now are ye light in the Lord: walk as children of light: (For the fruit of the Spirit is in all goodness and righteousness and truth;) Proving what is acceptable unto the Lord. And have no fellowship with the unfruitful works of darkness, but rather reprove them." (Ephesians 5:6-11)

"And I say unto you, Make to yourselves friends of the mammon of unrighteousness; that, when ye fail, they may receive you into everlasting habitations. He that is faithful in that which is least is faithful also in much: and he that is unjust in the least is unjust also in much. If therefore ye have not been faithful in the unrighteous mammon, who will commit to your trust the true riches? And if ye have not been faithful in that which is another man's, who shall give you that which is your own?" (Luke 16:9-12)

"What doth it profit, my brethren, though a man say he hath faith, and have not works? can faith save him? If a brother or sister be naked, and destitute of daily food, And one of you say unto them, Depart in peace, be ye warmed and filled; notwithstanding ye give them not those things which are needful to the body; what doth it profit? Even so faith, if it hath not works, is dead, being alone. Yea, a man may say, Thou hast faith, and I have works: shew me thy faith without thy works, and I will shew thee my faith by my works. Thou believest that there is one God; thou doest well: the devils also believe, and tremble. But wilt thou know, O vain man, that faith without works is dead? (James 2:14-20)

"And the King shall answer and say unto them, Verily I say unto you, Inasmuch as ye have done it unto one of the least of these my brethren, ye have done it unto me." (Matthew 25:40)

"Believest thou not that I am in the Father, and the Father in me? the words that I speak unto you I speak not of myself: but the Father that dwelleth in me, he doeth the works. Believe me that I am in the Father, and the Father in me: or else believe me for the very works' sake. Verily, verily, I say unto you, He that believeth on me, the works that I do shall he do also; and greater works than these shall he do; because I go unto my Father. And whatsoever ye shall ask in my name, that will I do, that the Father may be glorified in the Son. If ye shall ask any thing in my name, I will do it." (John 14:10-14)

It's all in the scriptures; Christians are to be the salt of the earth and even the light. We are to be, by design, a blessing from God to the world. We are given the gifts in the church, to accomplish God's purpose and thereby give him the glory. We are to exhibit Christ-like appropriateness in all situations.

"Ye are the salt of the earth: but if the salt have lost his savour, wherewith shall it be salted? it is thenceforth good for nothing, but to be cast out, and to be trodden under foot of men. Ye are the light of the world. A city that is set on an hill cannot be hid. Neither do men light a candle, and put it under a bushel, but on a candlestick; and it giveth light unto all that are in the house. Let your light so shine before men, that they may see your good works, and glorify your Father which is in heaven." (Matthew 5:13-16)

"I therefore, the prisoner of the Lord, beseech you that ye walk worthy of the vocation wherewith ye are called, With all lowliness and meekness, with longsuffering, forbearing one another in love; Endeavouring to keep the unity of the Spirit in the bond of peace." (Ephesians 4:1-3)

"And he gave some, apostles; and some, prophets; and some, evangelists; and some, pastors and teachers; For the perfecting of the saints, for the work of the ministry, for the edifying of the body of Christ: Till we all come in the unity of the faith, and of the knowledge of the Son of God, unto a perfect man, unto the measure of the stature of the fulness of Christ: That we henceforth be no more children, tossed to and fro, and carried about with every wind of doctrine, by the sleight of men, and cunning craftiness, whereby they lie in wait to deceive; But speaking the truth in love, may grow up into him in all things, which is the head, even Christ: From whom the whole body fitly joined together and compacted by that which every joint supplieth, according to the effectual working in the measure of every part, maketh increase of the body unto the edifying of itself in love." (Ephesians 4:11-16)

"Now there are diversities of gifts, but the same Spirit. And there are differences of administrations, but the same Lord. And there are diversities of operations, but it is the same God which worketh all in all. But the manifestation of the Spirit is given to every man to profit withal. For to one is given by the Spirit the word of wisdom; to another the word of knowledge by the same Spirit; To another faith by the same Spirit; to another the gifts of healing by the same Spirit; To another the working of miracles; to another prophecy; to another discerning of spirits; to another divers kinds of tongues; to another the interpretation of tongues: But all these worketh that one and the selfsame Spirit, dividing to every man severally as he will. For as the body is one, and hath many members, and all the members of that one body, being many, are one body: so also is Christ. For by one Spirit are we all baptized into one body, whether we be Jews or Gentiles, whether we be bond or free; and have been all made to drink into one Spirit. For the body is not one member, but many. Now ye are the body of Christ, and members in particular. And God hath set some in the church, first apostles, secondarily prophets, thirdly teachers, after that miracles, then gifts of healings, helps, governments, diversities of tongues." (1 Corinthians 12:4-14, 27&34)

"Let your moderation be known unto all men. The Lord is at hand." (Philippians 4:5)

"If there be therefore any consolation in Christ, if any comfort of love, if any fellowship of the Spirit, if any bowels and mercies, Fulfil ye my joy, that ye be likeminded, having the same love, being of one accord, of one mind. Let nothing be done through strife or vainglory; but in lowliness of mind let each esteem other better than themselves. Look not every man on his own things, but every man also on the things of others." (Philippians 2:1-4)

Christians are assured of an eternal victory over sin and the pitfalls of this world to include even the smarting pain of death.

"For whatsoever is born of God overcometh the world: and this is the victory that overcometh the world, even our faith. Who is he that overcometh the world, but he that believeth that Jesus is the Son of God?" (1 John 5:4)

"O sing unto the Lord a new song; for he hath done marvellous things: his right hand, and his holy arm, hath gotten him the victory. The Lord hath made known his salvation: his righteousness hath he openly shewed in the sight of the heathen. He hath remembered his

mercy and his truth toward the house of Israel: all the ends of the earth have seen the salvation of our God." (**Psalm 98:1-3**)

"Therefore shall the strong people glorify thee, the city of the terrible nations shall fear thee. For thou hast been a strength to the poor, a strength to the needy in his distress, a refuge from the storm, a shadow from the heat, when the blast of the terrible ones is as a storm against the wall. Thou shalt bring down the noise of strangers, as the heat in a dry place; even the heat with the shadow of a cloud: the branch of the terrible ones shall be brought low. And in this mountain shall the Lord of hosts make unto all people a feast of fat things, a feast of wines on the lees, of fat things full of marrow, of wines on the lees well refined. And he will destroy in this mountain the face of the covering cast over all people, and the vail that is spread over all nations. He will swallow up death in victory; and the Lord God will wipe away tears from off all faces; and the rebuke of his people shall he take away from off all the earth: for the Lord hath spoken it. And it shall be said in that day, Lo, this is our God; we have waited for him, and he will save us: this is the Lord; we have waited for him, we will be glad and rejoice in his salvation." (**Isaiah 25:3-9**)

"Behold, I shew you a mystery; We shall not all sleep, but we shall all be changed, In a moment, in the twinkling of an eye, at the last trump: for the trumpet shall sound, and the dead shall be raised incorruptible, and we shall be changed. For this corruptible must put on incorruption, and this mortal must put on immortality. So when this corruptible shall have put on incorruption, and this mortal shall have put on immortality, then shall be brought to pass the saying that is written, Death is swallowed up in victory. O death, where is thy sting? O grave, where is thy victory? The sting of death is sin; and the strength of sin is the law. But thanks be to God, which giveth us the victory through our Lord Jesus Christ. Therefore, my beloved brethren, be ye stedfast, unmoveable, always abounding in the work of the Lord, forasmuch as ye know that your labour is not in vain in the Lord." (**1 Corinthians 15:50-58**)

"And I saw another sign in heaven, great and marvellous, seven angels having the seven last plagues; for in them is filled up the wrath of God. And I saw as it were a sea of glass mingled with fire: and them that had gotten the victory over the beast, and over his image, and over his mark, and over the number of his name, stand on the sea of glass, having the harps of God. And they sing the song of Moses the servant of God, and the song of the Lamb, saying, Great and marvellous are thy works, Lord God Almighty; just and true are thy ways, thou King of saints. Who shall not fear thee, O Lord, and glorify thy name? for thou only art holy: for all nations shall come and worship before thee; for thy judgments are made manifest." (**Revelation 15:1-4**)

"Now unto him that is able to keep you from falling, and to present you faultless before the presence of his glory with exceeding joy, To the only wise God our Saviour, be glory and majesty, dominion and power, both now and ever. Amen." (**Jude 24&25**)

Christians have an assurance, in their knowledge of Almighty God, of life apart from the beggarly elements (ptochos stoicheion: pauperly, distressed, poor – arrangements, principles, rudiments) of this world. God knows his own and is edifying them, by faith, in the unity of his Spirit.

"But if any man love God, the same is known of him. " (**1 Corinthians 8:3**)

"And the work of righteousness shall be peace; and the effect of righteousness quietness and assurance for ever." (Isaiah 32:17)

"Even so we, when we were children, were in bondage under the elements of the world: But when the fulness of the time was come, God sent forth his Son, made of a woman, made under the law, To redeem them that were under the law, that we might receive the adoption of sons. And because ye are sons, God hath sent forth the Spirit of his Son into your hearts, crying, Abba, Father. Wherefore thou art no more a servant, but a son; and if a son, then an heir of God through Christ. Howbeit then, when ye knew not God, ye did service unto them which by nature are no gods. But now, after that ye have known God, or rather are known of God, how turn ye again to the weak and beggarly elements, whereunto ye desire again to be in bondage? (Galatians 4:3-9)

"Blessed be the God and Father of our Lord Jesus Christ, which according to his abundant mercy hath begotten us again unto a lively hope by the resurrection of Jesus Christ from the dead, To an inheritance incorruptible, and undefiled, and that fadeth not away, reserved in heaven for you, Who are kept by the power of God through faith unto salvation ready to be revealed in the last time." (1 Peter 3-5)

"For I would that ye knew what great conflict I have for you, and for them at Laodicea, and for as many as have not seen my face in the flesh; That their hearts might be comforted, being knit together in love, and unto all riches of the full assurance of understanding, to the acknowledgement of the mystery of God, and of the Father, and of Christ; In whom are hid all the treasures of wisdom and knowledge. And this I say, lest any man should beguile you with enticing words. Beware lest any man spoil you through philosophy and vain deceit, after the tradition of men, after the rudiments of the world, and not after Christ." (Colossians 2:1- 4&8)

There is one body, and one Spirit, even as ye are called in one hope of your calling; One Lord, one faith, one baptism, One God and Father of all, who is above all, and through all, and in you all. But unto every one of us is given grace according to the measure of the gift of Christ." (Ephesians 4:4-7)

Even in the midst of chaos, God is able to deliver the righteous in this life and even unto an eternal salvation.

"For Jerusalem is ruined, and Judah is fallen: because their tongue and their doings are against the Lord, to provoke the eyes of his glory. The shew of their countenance doth witness against them; and they declare their sin as Sodom, they hide it not. Woe unto their soul! for they have rewarded evil unto themselves. Say ye to the righteous, that it shall be well with him: for they shall eat the fruit of their doings." (Isaiah 3:8-10)

Psalm 37 (entirely)

18

TRUE FREEDOM, CHRISTIAN LIBERTY

What is the truth; can a person or a people ever be set free?

The Truth

The Bible states that we shall know the truth (Aletheia – verity in doctrine and profession) and that shall set us free (exempt from mortal liability, at liberty) through the only begotten Son.

> *"And ye shall know the truth, and the truth shall make you free. They answered him, We be Abraham's seed, and were never in bondage to any man: how sayest thou, Ye shall be made free? Jesus answered them, Verily, verily, I say unto you, Whosoever committeth sin is the servant of sin. And the servant abideth not in the house for ever: but the Son abideth ever. If the Son therefore shall make you free, ye shall be free indeed."* (John 8:32-36)

It is Jesus Christ who bears witness of the truth in the true and living God.

> *"And this is life eternal, that they might know thee the only true God, and Jesus Christ, whom thou hast sent."* (John 17:3)

> *"Pilate therefore said unto him, Art thou a king then? Jesus answered, Thou sayest that I am a king. To this end was I born, and for this cause came I into the world, that I should bear witness unto the truth. Every one that is of the truth heareth my voice. Pilate saith unto him, What is truth? And when he had said this, he went out again unto the Jews, and saith unto them, I find in him no fault at all."* (John 18:37-38)

Jesus affirms that he is indeed the Messiah who the Jews yet seek; the Messiah is the one that shall reveal all truth.

> *"The Lord thy God will raise up unto thee a Prophet from the midst of thee, of thy brethren, like unto me; unto him ye shall hearken; According to all that thou desiredst of the Lord thy God in Horeb in the day of the assembly, saying, Let me not hear again the voice of the Lord my God, neither let me see this great fire any more, that I die not. And the Lord said unto me, They have well spoken that which they have spoken. I will raise them up a*

Prophet from among their brethren, like unto thee, and will put my words in his mouth; and he shall speak unto them all that I shall command him. And it shall come to pass, that whosoever will not hearken unto my words which he shall speak in my name, I will require it of him." (Deuteronomy 18:15-19)

"The woman saith unto him, I know that Messias cometh, which is called Christ: when he is come, he will tell us all things. Jesus saith unto her, I that speak unto thee am he." (John 4:25&26)

The Holy Ghost comes forth in truth from God the Father while testifying and bearing witness of Christ.

"But the Comforter, which is the Holy Ghost, whom the Father will send in my name, he shall teach you all things, and bring all things to your remembrance, whatsoever I have said unto you. Peace I leave with you, my peace I give unto you: not as the world giveth, give I unto you. Let not your heart be troubled, neither let it be afraid." (John 15:26-27)

God seeks today as always, true worshippers which are converted from the carnal to the spiritual.

"But the hour cometh, and now is, when the true worshippers shall worship the Father in spirit and in truth: for the Father seeketh such to worship him. God is a Spirit: and they that worship him must worship him in spirit and in truth." (John 4:23-24)

God is a spirit and where the Spirit of the Lord has dominion there is liberty (freedom).

"Now the Lord is that Spirit: and where the Spirit of the Lord is, there is liberty." (2 Corinthians 3:17)

We can be, through our faith in Jesus Christ and the communion of the Holy Spirit, in oneness with the Heavenly Father.

"I have given them thy word; and the world hath hated them, because they are not of the world, even as I am not of the world. I pray not that thou shouldest take them out of the world, but that thou shouldest keep them from the evil. They are not of the world, even as I am not of the world. Sanctify them through thy truth: thy word is truth. As thou hast sent me into the world, even so have I also sent them into the world. And for their sakes I sanctify myself, that they also might be sanctified through the truth. Neither pray I for these alone, but for them also which shall believe on me through their word; That they all may be one; as thou, Father, art in me, and I in thee, that they also may be one in us: that the world may believe that thou hast sent me. And the glory which thou gavest me I have given them; that they may be one, even as we are one: I in them, and thou in me, that they may be made perfect in one; and that the world may know that thou hast sent me, and hast loved them, as thou hast loved me." (John 17:14-23)

Our Christian Liberty

The wages of sin is death; the Christian becomes by grace through faith, dead to sin.

"For the wages of sin is death; but the gift of God is eternal life through Jesus Christ our Lord." (Romans 6:23)

'Know ye not, that so many of us as were baptized into Jesus Christ were baptized into his death? Knowing this, that our old man is crucified with him, that the body of sin might be destroyed, that henceforth we should not serve sin. For he that is dead is freed from sin. Now if we be dead with Christ, we believe that we shall also live with him: Knowing that Christ being raised from the dead dieth no more; death hath no more dominion over him. For in that he died, he died unto sin once: but in that he liveth, he liveth unto God. Likewise reckon ye also yourselves to be dead indeed unto sin, but alive unto God through Jesus Christ our Lord. Let not sin therefore reign in your mortal body, that ye should obey it in the lusts thereof. Neither yield ye your members as instruments of unrighteousness unto sin: but yield yourselves unto God, as those that are alive from the dead, and your members as instruments of righteousness unto God. For sin shall not have dominion over you: for ye are not under the law, but under grace." (Romans 6:3,6-14)

"For by grace are ye saved through faith; and that not of yourselves: it is the gift of God:" (Ephesians 2:8)

In being freed from sin, the Christian is now made a servant of God.

"What then? shall we sin, because we are not under the law, but under grace? God forbid. Know ye not, that to whom ye yield yourselves servants to obey, his servants ye are to whom ye obey; whether of sin unto death, or of obedience unto righteousness? But God be thanked, that ye were the servants of sin, but ye have obeyed from the heart that form of doctrine which was delivered you. Being then made free from sin, ye became the servants of righteousness." (Romans 6:15-18)

Walking in the spirit gives us freedom from the fulfilling of lust in the flesh.

"This I say then, Walk in the Spirit, and ye shall not fulfil the lust of the flesh." (Galatians 5:16)

Jesus Christ is the complete reference with regard to our belief in the truth.

"Looking unto Jesus the author and finisher of our faith; who for the joy that was set before him endured the cross, despising the shame, and is set down at the right hand of the throne of God." (Hebrews 12:2)

Now, with regard to staying in that freedom, Jesus and him crucified needs to be what we are determined to know in matters of faith in God.

"For I determined not to know any thing among you, save Jesus Christ, and him crucified." (1 Corinthians 2:2)

"This I say therefore, and testify in the Lord, that ye henceforth walk not as other Gentiles walk, in the vanity of their mind, Having the understanding darkened, being alienated from the life of God through the ignorance that is in them, because of the blindness of their heart: Who being past feeling have given themselves over unto lasciviousness, to work all uncleanness with greediness. But ye have not so learned Christ; If so be that ye have heard

him, and have been taught by him, as the truth is in Jesus: That ye put off concerning the former conversation the old man, which is corrupt according to the deceitful lusts; And be renewed in the spirit of your mind; And that ye put on the new man, which after God is created in righteousness and true holiness." (Ephesians 4:17-24)

In order to remain in liberty, avoid falling into doctrines not of Christ. Note that when the Bible speaks of not turning away from the doctrine taught it is always speaking of the doctrine of Christ.

"Now I beseech you, brethren, mark them which cause divisions and offenses contrary to the doctrine which ye have learned; and avoid them. For they that are such serve not our Lord Jesus Christ, but their own belly; and by good words and fair speeches deceive the hearts of the simple." (Romans 16:17&18)

Now also, it is true that the Bible has condoned slavery but never where it was unlawful and not for life (note that slavery is not lawful anywhere in the world today). Note that the Jewish, and later the Christian master, was to have had benevolence towards the slave and the slave likewise an obedient service to the master.

"And if thy brother, an Hebrew man, or an Hebrew woman , be sold unto thee, and serve thee six years; then in the seventh year thou shalt let him go free from thee. And when thou sendest him out free from thee, thou shalt not let him go away empty: Thou shalt furnish him liberally out of thy flock, and out of thy floor, and out of thy winepress: of that wherewith the Lord thy God hath blessed thee thou shalt give unto him. And thou shalt remember that thou wast a bondman in the land of Egypt, and the Lord thy God redeemed thee: therefore I command thee this thing to day. And it shall be, if he say unto thee, I will not go away from thee; because he loveth thee and thine house, because he is well with thee; Then thou shalt take an aul, and thrust it through his ear unto the door, and he shall be thy servant for ever. And also unto thy maidservant thou shalt do likewise. It shall not seem hard unto thee, when thou sendest him away free from thee; for he hath been worth a double hired servant to thee, in serving thee six years: and the Lord thy God shall bless thee in all that thou doest. (Deuteronomy 15:12-18)

"Now these are the judgments which thou shalt set before them. If thou buy an Hebrew servant, six years he shall serve: and in the seventh he shall go out free for nothing. If he came in by himself, he shall go out by himself: if he were married, then his wife shall go out with him. If his master have given him a wife, and she have born him sons or daughters; the wife and her children shall be her master's, and he shall go out by himself. And if the servant shall plainly say, I love my master, my wife, and my children; I will not go out free: Then his master shall bring him unto the judges; he shall also bring him to the door, or unto the door post; and his master shall bore his ear through with an aul; and he shall serve him for ever." (Exodus 21:1-6)

"And ye shall hallow the fiftieth year, and proclaim liberty throughout all the land unto all the inhabitants thereof: it shall be a jubile unto you; and ye shall return every man unto his possession, and ye shall return every man unto his family." (Leviticus 25:10)

"Servants, be obedient to them that are your masters according to the flesh, with fear and trembling, in singleness of your heart, as unto Christ; Not with eyeservice, as menpleasers; but as the servants of Christ, doing the will of God from the heart; With good will doing

service, as to the Lord, and not to men: Knowing that whatsoever good thing any man do-eth, the same shall he receive of the Lord, whether he be bond or free. And, ye masters, do the same things unto them, forbearing threatening: knowing that your Master also is in heaven; neither is there respect of persons with him." (Ephesians 6:5-9)

"I beseech thee for my son Onesimus, whom I have begotten in my bonds: Which in time past was to thee unprofitable, but now profitable to thee and to me: Whom I have sent again: thou therefore receive him, that is, mine own bowels: Whom I would have retained with me, that in thy stead he might have ministered unto me in the bonds of the gospel: But without thy mind would I do nothing; that thy benefit should not be as it were of necessity, but willingly. For perhaps he therefore departed for a season, that thou shouldest receive him for ever; Not now as a servant, but above a servant, a brother beloved, specially to me, but how much more unto thee, both in the flesh, and in the Lord? If thou count me therefore a partner, receive him as myself." (Philemon 10-17)

Christian Liberty from the Burden (pressure) of Trials and Tribulation

Christians should be able to endure persecutions in the knowledge that God is aware of our circumstances and will recompense a just punishment to those that have perpetrated tribulation upon the righteous.

"We are bound to thank God always for you, brethren, as it is meet, because that your faith groweth exceedingly, and the charity of every one of you all toward each other aboundeth; So that we ourselves glory in you in the churches of God for your patience and faith in all your persecutions and tribulations that ye endure: Which is a manifest token of the righteous judgment of God, that ye may be counted worthy of the kingdom of God, for which ye also suffer: Seeing it is a righteous thing with God to recompense tribulation to them that trouble you; And to you who are troubled rest with us, when the Lord Jesus shall be revealed from heaven with his mighty angels, In flaming fire taking vengeance on them that know not God, and that obey not the gospel of our Lord Jesus Christ: Who shall be punished with everlasting destruction from the presence of the Lord, and from the glory of his power;" (2 Thessalonians 1:3-9)

God will execute vengeance not the believer.

"Dearly beloved, avenge not yourselves, but rather give place unto wrath: for it is written, Vengeance is mine; I will repay, saith the Lord." (Romans 12:19)

With a reassurance of the promises of God in our tribulation, the believer is able to rather glory in tribulation because of the peace in knowing patience, experience and hope are being accomplished.

"Therefore being justified by faith, we have peace with God through our Lord Jesus Christ: By whom also we have access by faith into this grace wherein we stand, and rejoice in hope of the glory of God. And not only so, but we glory in tribulations also: knowing that tribulation worketh patience; And patience, experience; and experience, hope: And hope maketh not ashamed; because the love of God is shed abroad in our hearts by the Holy Ghost which is given unto us." (Romans 5:1-5)

We can be ready to suffer even in our well doing.

"And who is he that will harm you, if ye be followers of that which is good? But and if ye suffer for righteousness' sake, happy are ye: and be not afraid of their terror, neither be troubled; But sanctify the Lord God in your hearts: and be ready always to give an answer to every man that asketh you a reason of the hope that is in you with meekness and fear: Having a good conscience; that, whereas they speak evil of you, as of evildoers, they may be ashamed that falsely accuse your good conversation in Christ. For it is better, if the will of God be so, that ye suffer for well doing, than for evil doing." (1 Peter 3:13-17)

Note that our suffering should not be as transgressors should suffer for their crimes and indiscretions.

"But let none of you suffer as a murderer, or as a thief, or as an evildoer, or as a busybody in other men's matters. Yet if any man suffer as a Christian, let him not be ashamed; but let him glorify God on this behalf." (1 Peter 4:15&16)

Those judged by God to be unrighteous (the righteous of Christ not imputed upon them) will not inherit eternal life.

"Know ye not that the unrighteous shall not inherit the kingdom of God? Be not deceived: neither fornicators, nor idolaters, nor adulterers, nor effeminate, nor abusers of themselves with mankind, Nor thieves, nor covetous, nor drunkards, nor revilers, nor extortioners, shall inherit the kingdom of God. " (1 Corinthians 6:9&10)

"But the fearful, and unbelieving, and the abominable, and murderers, and whoremongers, and sorcerers, and idolaters, and all liars, shall have their part in the lake which burneth with fire and brimstone: which is the second death. And there came unto me one of the seven angels which had the seven vials full of the seven last plagues, and talked with me, saying, Come hither, I will shew thee the bride, the Lamb's wife. And he carried me away in the spirit to a great and high mountain, and shewed me that great city, the holy Jerusalem, descending out of heaven from God," (Revelation 21:8-10)

But rather, God chastens those he loves (God so loves the world); therefore, endure chastening rather than the consequence of eternal damnation.

"And ye have forgotten the exhortation which speaketh unto you as unto children, My son, despise not thou the chastening of the Lord, nor faint when thou art rebuked of him: For whom the Lord loveth he chasteneth, and scourgeth every son whom he receiveth. If ye endure chastening, God dealeth with you as with sons; for what son is he whom the father chasteneth not? But if ye be without chastisement, whereof all are partakers, then are ye bastards, and not sons. Furthermore we have had fathers of our flesh which corrected us, and we gave them reverence: shall we not much rather be in subjection unto the Father of spirits, and live? For they verily for a few days chastened us after their own pleasure; but he for our profit, that we might be partakers of his holiness. Now no chastening for the present seemeth to be joyous, but grievous: nevertheless afterward it yieldeth the peaceable fruit of righteousness unto them which are exercised thereby." (Hebrews 12:5-11)

"We are made free from God's chastening by the process of self-examination. For if we would judge ourselves, we should not be judged. But when we are judged, we are chastened of the Lord, that we should not be condemned with the world." (1 Corinthians 11:31&32)

Also, have joy in the Lord, moderation in the world and call upon the Lord in prayer in order to enter into a peace with God beyond worldly explanation.

"Rejoice in the Lord alway: and again I say, Rejoice. Let your moderation be known unto all men. The Lord is at hand. Be careful for nothing; but in every thing by prayer and supplication with thanksgiving let your requests be made known unto God. And the peace of God, which passeth all understanding, shall keep your hearts and minds through Christ Jesus." (Philippians 4:4-7)

Christian Liberty from Tyrannical Rule

God ordains all leadership; God has the power not the worldly leaders.

"Let every soul be subject unto the higher powers. For there is no power but of God: the powers that be are ordained of God. Whosoever therefore resisteth the power, resisteth the ordinance of God: and they that resist shall receive to themselves damnation. For rulers are not a terror to good works, but to the evil. Wilt thou then not be afraid of the power? Do that which is good, and thou shalt have praise of the same: For he is the minister of God to thee for good. But if thou do that which is evil, be afraid; for he beareth not the sword in vain: for he is the minister of God, a revenger to execute wrath upon him that doeth evil. Wherefore ye must needs be subject, not only for wrath, but also for conscience sake. For for this cause pay ye tribute also: for they are God's ministers, attending continually upon this very thing. Render therefore to all their dues: tribute to whom tribute is due; custom to whom custom; fear to whom fear; honor to whom honor." (Romans 13:1-7)

God will judge all men according to their works including leadership and God's purpose in their governing.

"And I saw a great white throne, and him that sat on it, from whose face the earth and the heaven fled away; and there was found no place for them. And I saw the dead, small and great, stand before God; and the books were opened: and another book was opened, which is the book of life: and the dead were judged out of those things which were written in the books, according to their works. And the sea gave up the dead which were in it; and death and hell delivered up the dead which were in them: and they were judged every man according to their works." (Revelation 20:11-13)

God is always in control of leadership; God hardened Pharaoh's heart for example.

"And the Lord said unto Moses, When thou goest to return into Egypt, see that thou do all those wonders before Pharaoh, which I have put in thine hand: but I will harden his heart, that he shall not let the people go." (Exodus 4:21)

"For he saith to Moses, I will have mercy on whom I will have mercy, and I will have compassion on whom I will have compassion. So then it is not of him that willeth, nor of him that runneth, but of God that sheweth mercy. For the scripture saith unto Pharaoh, Even

for this same purpose have I raised thee up, that I might shew my power in thee, and that my name might be declared throughout all the earth. Therefore hath he mercy on whom he will have mercy, and whom he will he hardeneth." (Romans 9:15-18)

The believer is to pray for leadership because God's objective, regardless of the circumstances presented by disobedience and evil, is to have all men saved.

"I exhort therefore, that, first of all, supplications, prayers, intercessions, and giving of thanks, be made for all men; For kings, and for all that are in authority; that we may lead a quiet and peaceable life in all godliness and honesty. For this is good and acceptable in the sight of God our Savior; Who will have all men to be saved, and to come unto the knowledge of the truth." (1 Timothy 2:1-4)

Therefore, the believer needs to operate, while under tyrannical rule, in a wisdom rooted, to their benefit, in the word of God.

"For your obedience is come abroad unto all men. I am glad therefore on your behalf: but yet I would have you wise unto that which is good, and simple concerning evil." (Romans 16:19)

All things work together for those that love God and call upon his name certainly even for deliverance.

"For I know the thoughts that I think toward you, saith the Lord, thoughts of peace, and not of evil, to give you an expected end. Then shall ye call upon me, and ye shall go and pray unto me, and I will hearken unto you." (Jeremiah 29:11&12)

"Likewise the Spirit also helpeth our infirmities: for we know not what we should pray for as we ought: but the Spirit itself maketh intercession for us with groanings which cannot be uttered. And he that searcheth the hearts knoweth what is the mind of the Spirit, because he maketh intercession for the saints according to the will of God. And we know that all things work together for good to them that love God, to them who are the called according to his purpose." (Romans 8:26-28)

Deliverance from tyrannical rule is a matter of a nation's posture in relationship to the Lord God Almighty.

"Return, ye backsliding children, and I will heal your backslidings. Behold, we come unto thee; for thou art the Lord our God. Truly in vain is salvation hoped for from the hills, and from the multitude of mountains: truly in the Lord our God is the salvation of Israel. For shame hath devoured the labor of our fathers from our youth; their flocks and their herds, their sons and their daughters. We lie down in our shame, and our confusion covereth us: for we have sinned against the Lord our God, we and our fathers, from our youth even unto this day, and have not obeyed the voice of the Lord our God." (Jeremiah 3:22-25)

Man's Vain Attempt at Providing Liberty in the Bible

Moses murders.

"And it came to pass in those days, when Moses was grown, that he went out unto his brethren, and looked on their burdens: and he spied an Egyptian smiting an Hebrew, one of his brethren. And he looked this way and that way, and when he saw that there was no man, he slew the Egyptian, and hid him in the sand. And when he went out the second day, behold, two men of the Hebrews strove together: and he said to him that did the wrong, Wherefore smitest thou thy fellow? And he said, Who made thee a prince and a judge over us? Intendest thou to kill me, as thou killedst the Egyptian? And Moses feared, and said, Surely this thing is known. Now when Pharaoh heard this thing, he sought to slay Moses. But Moses fled from the face of Pharaoh, and dwelt in the land of Midian: and he sat down by a well." **(Exodus 2:11-15)**

King Saul shows his foolishness.

"Saul reigned one year; and when he had reigned two years over Israel, Saul chose him three thousand men of Israel; whereof two thousand were with Saul in Michmash and in mount Bethel, and a thousand were with Jonathan in Gibeah of Benjamin: and the rest of the people he sent every man to his tent. And Jonathan smote the garrison of the Philistines that was in Geba, and the Philistines heard of it. And Saul blew the trumpet throughout all the land, saying, Let the Hebrews hear. And all Israel heard say that Saul had smitten a garrison of the Philistines, and that Israel also was had in abomination with the Philistines. And the people were called together after Saul to Gilgal. And the Philistines gathered themselves together to fight with Israel, thirty thousand chariots, and six thousand horsemen, and people as the sand which is on the sea shore in multitude: and they came up, and pitched in Michmash, eastward from Bethaven.

When the men of Israel saw that they were in a strait, (for the people were distressed,) then the people did hide themselves in caves, and in thickets, and in rocks, and in high places, and in pits. And some of the Hebrews went over Jordan to the land of Gad and Gilead. As for Saul, he was yet in Gilgal, and all the people followed him trembling. And he tarried seven days, according to the set time that Samuel had appointed: but Samuel came not to Gilgal; and the people were scattered from him. And Saul said, Bring hither a burnt offering to me, and peace offerings. And he offered the burnt offering. And it came to pass, that as soon as he had made an end of offering the burnt offering, behold, Samuel came; and Saul went out to meet him, that he might salute him. And Samuel said, What hast thou done? And Saul said, Because I saw that the people were scattered from me, and that thou camest not within the days appointed, and that the Philistines gathered themselves together at Michmash; Therefore said I, The Philistines will come down now upon me to Gilgal, and I have not made supplication unto the Lord: I forced myself therefore, and offered a burnt offering. And Samuel said to Saul, Thou hast done foolishly: thou hast not kept the commandment of the Lord thy God, which he commanded thee: for now would the Lord have established thy kingdom upon Israel for ever. But now thy kingdom shall not continue: the Lord hath sought him a man after his own heart, and the Lord hath commanded him to be captain over his people, because thou hast not kept that which the Lord commanded thee." **(1 Samuel 13:1-14)**

Almighty God is the only one in control and there is none that is able to change that fact.

"See now that I, even I, am he, and there is no God with me: I kill, and I make alive; I wound, and I heal: neither is there any that can deliver out of my hand." (Deuteronomy 32:39)

Many today are teaching falsely against even the existence of God not to mention against God's able hand in delivering nations; they bring destruction rather than liberty.

"But there were false prophets also among the people, even as there shall be false teachers among you, who privily shall bring in damnable heresies, even denying the Lord that bought them, and bring upon themselves swift destruction. And many shall follow their pernicious ways; by reason of whom the way of truth shall be evil spoken of. And through covetousness shall they with feigned words make merchandise of you: whose judgment now of a long time lingereth not, and their damnation slumbereth not." (2 Peter 2:1-3)

"The Lord knoweth how to deliver the godly out of temptations, and to reserve the unjust unto the day of judgment to be punished: But chiefly them that walk after the flesh in the lust of uncleanness, and despise government. Presumptuous are they, selfwilled, they are not afraid to speak evil of dignities." (2 Peter 2:9-10)

"Righteousness exalteth a nation: but sin is a reproach to any people." (Proverbs 14:34)

"Thus saith the Lord, Stand ye in the ways, and see, and ask for the old paths, where is the good way, and walk therein, and ye shall find rest for your souls. But they said, We will not walk therein. Also I set watchmen over you, saying, Hearken to the sound of the trumpet. But they said, We will not hearken. Therefore hear, ye nations, and know, O congregation, what is among them. Hear, O earth: behold, I will bring evil upon this people, even the fruit of their thoughts, because they have not hearkened unto my words, nor to my law, but rejected it." (Jeremiah 6:6-19)

"O house of Israel, cannot I do with you as this potter? saith the Lord. Behold, as the clay is in the potter's hand, so are ye in mine hand, O house of Israel. At what instant I shall speak concerning a nation, and concerning a kingdom, to pluck up, and to pull down, and to destroy it; If that nation, against whom I have pronounced, turn from their evil, I will repent of the evil that I thought to do unto them. And at what instant I shall speak concerning a nation, and concerning a kingdom, to build and to plant it; If it do evil in my sight, that it obey not my voice, then I will repent of the good, wherewith I said I would benefit them. Now therefore go to, speak to the men of Judah, and to the inhabitants of Jerusalem, saying, Thus saith the Lord; Behold, I frame evil against you, and devise a device against you: return ye now every one from his evil way, and make your ways and your doings good." (Jeremiah 18:6-11)

God Gives True Liberty to Even a Nation from Its Enemies

There is the example of Moses sent by God to deliver the Israelites from Egypt.

"And the Lord said, I have surely seen the affliction of my people which are in Egypt, and have heard their cry by reason of their taskmasters; for I know their sorrows; And I am come down to deliver them out of the hand of the Egyptians, and to bring them up out of that land unto a good land and a large, unto a land flowing with milk and honey; unto the place of the Canaanites, and the Hittites, and the Amorites, and the Perizzites, and the

Hivites, and the Jebusites. Now therefore, behold, the cry of the children of Israel is come unto me: and I have also seen the oppression wherewith the Egyptians oppress them. Come now therefore, and I will send thee unto Pharaoh, that thou mayest bring forth my people the children of Israel out of Egypt." (Exodus 3:7-10)

The example of the prophetess Judge Deborah and Barak against the Canaanites.

"And Deborah, a prophetess, the wife of Lapidoth, she judged Israel at that time. And she dwelt under the palm tree of Deborah between Ramah and Bethel in mount Ephraim: and the children of Israel came up to her for judgment. And she sent and called Barak the son of Abinoam out of Kedeshnaphtali, and said unto him, Hath not the Lord God of Israel commanded, saying, Go and draw toward mount Tabor, and take with thee ten thousand men of the children of Naphtali and of the children of Zebulun? So God subdued on that day Jabin the king of Canaan before the children of Israel." (Judges 4:4-6, 23)

The example of Gideon and the 300 men of valor against the bondage of the Midianites.

"And the Lord said unto Gideon, The people are yet too many; bring them down unto the water, and I will try them for thee there: and it shall be, that of whom I say unto thee, This shall go with thee, the same shall go with thee; and of whomsoever I say unto thee, This shall not go with thee, the same shall not go. So he brought down the people unto the water: and the Lord said unto Gideon, Every one that lappeth of the water with his tongue, as a dog lappeth, him shalt thou set by himself; likewise every one that boweth down upon his knees to drink. And the number of them that lapped, putting their hand to their mouth, were three hundred men: but all the rest of the people bowed down upon their knees to drink water. And the Lord said unto Gideon, By the three hundred men that lapped will I save you, and deliver the Midianites into thine hand: and let all the other people go every man unto his place." (Judges 7:4-7)

The example of King Hezekiah praying and the enemies of God's chosen smitten.

"Therefore thus saith the Lord concerning the king of Assyria, He shall not come into this city, nor shoot an arrow there, nor come before it with shield, nor cast a bank against it. By the way that he came, by the same shall he return, and shall not come into this city, saith the Lord. For I will defend this city, to save it, for mine own sake, and for my servant David's sake. And it came to pass that night, that the angel of the Lord went out, and smote in the camp of the Assyrians an hundred fourscore and five thousand: and when they arose early in the morning, behold, they were all dead corpses. So Sennacherib king of Assyria departed, and went and returned, and dwelt at Nineveh." (2 Kings 19:32-36)

With God, whom shall we fear among our enemies?

"The Lord is my light and my salvation; whom shall I fear? The Lord is the strength of my life; of whom shall I be afraid? When the wicked, even mine enemies and my foes, came upon me to eat up my flesh, they stumbled and fell. Though an host should encamp against me, my heart shall not fear: though war should rise against me, in this will I be confident." (Psalm 27:1-3)

The battle belongs to God.

> *"And he said, Hearken ye, all Judah, and ye inhabitants of Jerusalem, and thou king Jehoshaphat, Thus saith the LORD unto you, Be not afraid nor dismayed by reason of this great multitude; for the battle is not yours, but God's."* (**2 Chronicles 20:15**)

Through our faith in God, we are made at liberty (overcomers) in this world.

> *"For whatsoever is born of God overcometh the world: and this is the victory that overcometh the world, even our faith. Who is he that overcometh the world, but he that believeth that Jesus is the Son of God?"* (**1 John 5:4-5**)

The Purpose in God's Granting of Liberty (Freedom)

There is an awesome divine yet simplistic purpose in God's granting of liberty to his people; we are to serve one another.

> *"For, brethren, ye have been called unto liberty; only use not liberty for an occasion to the flesh, but by love serve one another. For all the law is fulfilled in one word, even in this; Thou shalt love thy neighbour as thyself. But if ye bite and devour one another, take heed that ye be not consumed one of another.* (**Galatians 5:13-15**)

19

HOLY MATRIMONY DEFINED

What does the Bible say about marriage and is biblical marriage differentiated for secular marriage?

HOLY MATRIMONY IS predicated upon belief in the Bible/Holy Scriptures. Without this understanding, holy matrimony is meaningless.

> *"All scripture is given by inspiration of God, and is profitable for doctrine, for reproof, for correction, for instruction in righteousness: That the man of God may be perfect, throughly furnished unto all good works."* (2 Timothy 3:16-17)

Inherent in the belief of the Bible and the Trinity is a belief in the true and living God.

> *"But the Lord is the true God, he is the living God, and an everlasting king: at his wrath the earth shall tremble, and the nations shall not be able to abide his indignation. Thus shall ye say unto them, The gods that have not made the heavens and the earth, even they shall perish from the earth, and from under these heavens. He hath made the earth by his power, he hath established the world by his wisdom, and hath stretched out the heavens by his discretion. When he uttereth his voice, there is a multitude of waters in the heavens, and he causeth the vapors to ascend from the ends of the earth; he maketh lightnings with rain, and bringeth forth the wind out of his treasures. Every man is brutish in his knowledge: every founder is confounded by the graven image: for his molten image is falsehood, and there is no breath in them. They are vanity, and the work of errors: in the time of their visitation they shall perish. The portion of Jacob is not like them: for he is the former of all things; and Israel is the rod of his inheritance: The Lord of hosts is his name."* (Jeremiah 10:10-16)

Jesus revealed the true and living God as our heavenly Father.

> *"And this is life eternal, that they might know thee the only true God, and Jesus Christ, whom thou hast sent."* (John 17:3)

> *"For God so loved the world, that he gave his only begotten Son, that whosoever believeth in him should not perish, but have everlasting life. He that believeth on him is not condemned: but he that believeth not is condemned already, because he hath not believed in the name of the only begotten Son of God."* (John 3:16, 18)

Jesus is revealed as the Word (Logos – the divine expression, discourse, concerning doctrine, fame, intent, preaching, questioning, reason, utterance, work). Jesus reveals himself as our judge and the true vine (Ampelos – support).

> *"And the Word was made flesh, and dwelt among us, (and we beheld his glory, the glory as of the only begotten of the Father,) full of grace and truth. John bare witness of him, and cried, saying, This was he of whom I spake, He that cometh after me is preferred before me: for he was before me. And of his fulness have all we received, and grace for grace."* John 1:14-16

> *"For the Father judgeth no man, but hath committed all judgment unto the Son:* (John 5:22&23)

> *"I am the true vine, and my Father is the husbandman. Every branch in me that beareth not fruit he taketh away: and every branch that beareth fruit, he purgeth it, that it may bring forth more fruit."* (John 15:1-2)

> *"But these are written, that ye might believe that Jesus is the Christ, the Son of God; and that believing ye might have life through his name."* (John 20:31)

Now the believer, if he loves Jesus as the scriptures command, will then keep the commandments as given in the scriptures.

> *"If ye love me, keep my commandments."* (John 14:15)

To abide in Christ is to abide in sound doctrine (concerning marriage and anything else) in life.

> *"Neither pray I for these alone, but for them also which shall believe on me through their word; That they all may be one; as thou, Father, art in me, and I in thee, that they also may be one in us: that the world may believe that thou hast sent me. And the glory which thou gavest me I have given them; that they may be one, even as we are one: I in them, and thou in me, that they may be made perfect in one; and that the world may know that thou hast sent me, and hast loved them, as thou hast loved me."* (John 17: 20-23)

> *"Whosoever transgresseth, and abideth not in the doctrine of Christ, hath not God. He that abideth in the doctrine of Christ, he hath both the Father and the Son."* (2 John 9)

Holy matrimony is predicated upon the power emanating from the indwelled Holy Ghost/Holy Spirit of the Christian.

> *"But ye shall receive power, after that the Holy Ghost is come upon you: and ye shall be witnesses unto me both in Jerusalem, and in all Judaea, and in Samaria, and unto the uttermost part of the earth."* (Acts 1:8)

> *"What? know ye not that your body is the temple of the Holy Ghost which is in you, which ye have of God, and ye are not your own?"* (1 Corinthians 6:19)

> *"Then will I sprinkle clean water upon you, and ye shall be clean: from all your filthiness, and from all your idols, will I cleanse you. A new heart also will I give you, and a new spirit will I put within you: and I will take away the stony heart out of your flesh, and I will give you an heart of flesh. And I will put my spirit within you, and cause you to walk in my statutes, and ye shall keep my judgments, and do them."* (Ezekiel 36:25-27)

"Howbeit when he, the Spirit of truth, is come, he will guide you into all truth: for he shall not speak of himself; but whatsoever he shall hear, that shall he speak: and he will shew you things to come. He shall glorify me: for he shall receive of mine, and shall shew it unto you." (John 16:13-14)

"That he would grant you, according to the riches of his glory, to be strengthened with might by his Spirit in the inner man; That Christ may dwell in your hearts by faith; that ye, being rooted and grounded in love, May be able to comprehend with all saints what is the breadth, and length, and depth, and height; And to know the love of Christ, which passeth knowledge, that ye might be filled with all the fulness of God. Now unto him that is able to do exceeding abundantly above all that we ask or think, according to the power that worketh in us, Unto him be glory in the church by Christ Jesus throughout all ages, world without end. Amen." (Ephesians 3:16-21)

"This I say then, Walk in the Spirit, and ye shall not fulfill the lust of the flesh. For the flesh lusteth against the Spirit, and the Spirit against the flesh: and these are contrary the one to the other: so that ye cannot do the things that ye would. But if ye be led of the Spirit, ye are not under the law. Now the works of the flesh are manifest, which are these; Adultery, fornication, uncleanness, lasciviousness, Idolatry, witchcraft, hatred, variance, emulations, wrath, strife, seditions, heresies, envyings, murders, drunkenness, revellings, and such like: of the which I tell you before, as I have also told you in time past, that they which do such things shall not inherit the kingdom of God." (Galatians 5:16-21)

When I am counseling a couple prior to matrimony, there has to be an answer in the affirmative with regard to a mutual belief in all of the above before I can acknowledge that there is a reason to proceed in the Holy Matrimony Counseling Sessions.

Holy Matrimony was Instituted by Almighty God

God joins together the man and woman. Holy matrimony joins together a male and a female.

"And the Lord God caused a deep sleep to fall upon Adam, and he slept: and he took one of his ribs, and closed up the flesh instead thereof; And the rib, which the Lord God had taken from man, made he a woman, and brought her unto the man. And Adam said, This is now bone of my bones, and flesh of my flesh: she shall be called Woman, because she was taken out of Man. Therefore shall a man leave his father and his mother, and shall cleave unto his wife: and they shall be one flesh." (Genesis 2:21-24)

"And he answered and said unto them, Have ye not read, that he which made them at the beginning made them male and female, And said, For this cause shall a man leave father and mother, and shall cleave to his wife: and they twain shall be one flesh? Wherefore they are no more twain, but one flesh. What therefore God hath joined together, let not man put asunder." (Matthew 19:4-6)

The believer is really not to be joined in holy matrimony with an unbeliever.

"Be ye not unequally yoked together with unbelievers: for what fellowship hath righteousness with unrighteousness? and what communion hath light with darkness?" (2 Corinthians 6:14)

All marriage is honorable in the sight of God and the marital bedroom is undefiled (Amiantos – unsoiled, pure). Marital vows are scared to God

"Marriage is honorable in all, and the bed undefiled: but whoremongers and adulterers God will judge." (**Hebrews 13:4**)

"Whoso findeth a wife findeth a good thing, and obtaineth favour of the Lord." (**Proverbs 18:22**)

"Thus saith the Lord of hosts, the God of Israel, saying; Ye and your wives have both spoken with your mouths, and fulfilled with your hand, saying, We will surely perform our vows that we have vowed, to burn incense to the queen of heaven, and to pour out drink offerings unto her: ye will surely accomplish your vows, and surely perform your vows." (**Jeremiah 44:25**)

"Again, ye have heard that it hath been said by them of old time, Thou shalt not forswear thyself, but shalt perform unto the Lord thine oaths: But I say unto you, Swear not at all; neither by heaven; for it is God's throne: Nor by the earth; for it is his footstool: neither by Jerusalem; for it is the city of the great King. Neither shalt thou swear by thy head, because thou canst not make one hair white or black. But let your communication be, Yea, yea; Nay, nay: for whatsoever is more than these cometh of evil." (**Matthew 5:33-37**)

In no place or manner should behavior in marriage be without affection and/or injurious.

"This know also, that in the last days perilous times shall come. For men shall be lovers of their own selves, covetous, boasters, proud, blasphemers, disobedient to parents, unthankful, unholy, Without natural affection, trucebreakers, false accusers, incontinent, fierce, despisers of those that are good," (**2 Timothy 3:1-3**)

"And I thank Christ Jesus our Lord, who hath enabled me, for that he counted me faithful, putting me into the ministry; Who was before a blasphemer, and a persecutor, and injurious: but I obtained mercy, because I did it ignorantly in unbelief." (**1 Timothy 1:12&13**)

There is to be a mutual submission in marriage to each other and God. In holy matrimony, the marriage partners have given their physical bodies to each other.

"See then that ye walk circumspectly, not as fools, but as wise, Submitting yourselves one to another in the fear of God." (**Ephesians 5:15, 21**)

Let all bitterness, and wrath, and anger, and clamour, and evil speaking, be put away from you, with all malice: And be ye kind one to another, tenderhearted, forgiving one another, even as God for Christ's sake hath forgiven you. (**Ephesians 4:31&32**)

"Let the husband render unto the wife due benevolence: and likewise also the wife unto the husband. The wife hath not power of her own body, but the husband: and likewise also the husband hath not power of his own body, but the wife. Defraud ye not one the other, except it be with consent for a time, that ye may give yourselves to fasting and prayer; and come together again, that Satan tempt you not for your incontinency." (**1 Corinthians 7:3-5**)

A big part of the reason for marriage is procreation and therefore insidious is idea of same sex marriage.

*"So God created man in his own image, in the image of God created he him; male and fe-
male created he them. And God blessed them, and God said unto them, Be fruitful, and
multiply, and replenish the earth, and subdue it: and have dominion over the fish of the
sea, and over the fowl of the air, and over every living thing that moveth upon the earth."*
(Genesis 1:27-28)

God hates divorce (putting away). See Chapter 20, Divorce, What has to be Wrong,.

*"Judah hath dealt treacherously, and an abomination is committed in Israel and in
Jerusalem; for Judah hath profaned the holiness of the Lord which he loved, and hath
married the daughter of a strange God. The Lord will cut off the man that doeth this, the
master and the scholar, out of the tabernacles of Jacob, and him that offereth an offering
unto the Lord of hosts. And this have ye done again, covering the altar of the Lord with
tears, with weeping, and with crying out, insomuch that he regardeth not the offering any
more, or receiveth it with good will at your hand. Yet ye say, Wherefore? Because the Lord
hath been witness between thee and the wife of thy youth, against whom thou hast dealt
treacherously: yet is she thy companion, and the wife of thy covenant. And did not he make
one? Yet had he the residue of the spirit. And wherefore one? That he might seek a godly
seed. Therefore take heed to your spirit, and let none deal treacherously against the wife of
his youth. For the Lord, the God of Israel, saith that he hateth putting away: for one covereth violence with his garment, saith the Lord of hosts: therefore take heed to your spirit,
that ye deal not treacherously."* (Malachi 2:11-16)

Adultery is the only grounds for divorce (see Chapter 20, Divorce, What has to be Wrong).

*"But I say unto you, That whosoever shall put away his wife, saving for the cause of forni-
cation, causeth her to commit adultery: and whosoever shall marry her that is divorced
committeth adultery."* (Matthew 5:32)

The adulterer is judged by God to be in transgression and has no part in the kingdom of heaven.

*"Know ye not that the unrighteous shall not inherit the kingdom of God? Be not deceived:
neither fornicators, nor idolaters, nor adulterers, nor effeminate, nor abusers of themselves
with mankind, Nor thieves, nor covetous, nor drunkards, nor revilers, nor extortioners,
shall inherit the kingdom of God. "* (1 Corinthians 6:9-10)

*"What? know ye not that he which is joined to an harlot is one body? for two, saith he, shall
be one flesh. But he that is joined unto the Lord is one spirit. Flee fornication. Every sin
that a man doeth is without the body; but he that committeth fornication sinneth against
his own body. What? know ye not that your body is the temple of the Holy Ghost which
is in you, which ye have of God, and ye are not your own? For ye are bought with a price:
therefore glorify God in your body, and in your spirit, which are God's."* (1Corinthians
6:16-20)

"And grieve not the holy Spirit of God, whereby ye are sealed unto the day of redemption."
(Ephesians 4:30)

Marriage is not forever; there is no marriage in heaven.

"For in the resurrection they neither marry, nor are given in marriage, but are as the angels of God in heaven." (Matthew 22:30)

Marriage – The Husband

Let every man have his own wife if one has the physical desire for a woman.

"Now concerning the things whereof ye wrote unto me: It is good for a man not to touch a woman. Nevertheless, to avoid fornication, let every man have his own wife, and let every woman have her own husband." (1 Corinthians 7:1-2)

"His disciples say unto him, If the case of the man be so with his wife, it is not good to marry. But he said unto them, All men cannot receive this saying, save they to whom it is given. For there are some eunuchs, which were so born from their mother's womb: and there are some eunuchs, which were made eunuchs of men: and there be eunuchs, which have made themselves eunuchs for the kingdom of heaven's sake. He that is able to receive it, let him receive it." (Matthew 19:10-12)

The man was created in the image and glory of God and the woman created for the man according to the Bible.

"For the man is not of the woman: but the woman of the man. Neither was the man created for the woman; but the woman for the man." (1 Corinthians 11:8-9)

The woman in creation is the weaker (Ara – inferior) vessel; godly men need this to know and understand.

"Likewise, ye husbands, dwell with them according to knowledge, giving honor unto the wife, as unto the weaker vessel, and as being heirs together of the grace of life; that your prayers be not hindered." (1 Peter 3:7)

The husband is to the head of the wife. Husbands, rule your homes.

"But I would have you know, that the head of every man is Christ; and the head of the woman is the man; and the head of Christ is God." (1 Corinthians 11:3)

"A bishop then must be blameless, the husband of one wife, vigilant, sober, of good behaviour, given to hospitality, apt to teach; Not given to wine, no striker, not greedy of filthy lucre; but patient, not a brawler, not covetous; One that ruleth well his own house, having his children in subjection with all gravity; (For if a man know not how to rule his own house, how shall he take care of the church of God?)" (1Timothy 3:2-5)

The husband's care of his wife is likened to Christ's care of the church and a man's care of his own body.

"So ought men to love their wives as their own bodies. He that loveth his wife loveth himself. For no man ever yet hated his own flesh; but nourisheth and cherisheth it, even as the Lord the church: For we are members of his body, of his flesh, and of his bones. For this cause shall a man leave his father and mother, and shall be joined unto his wife, and they two shall be one flesh. This is a great mystery: but I speak concerning Christ and the

church. Nevertheless let every one of you in particular so love his wife even as himself; and the wife see that she reverence her husband." (**Ephesians 5:28-33**)

"The married man is to be mindful of how he may please his wife. But I would have you without carefulness. He that is unmarried careth for the things that belong to the Lord, how he may please the Lord: But he that is married careth for the things that are of the world, how he may please his wife." (**1 Corinthians 7:32-33**)

"Husbands, love your wives, and be not bitter against them." (**Colossians 3:19**)

Marriage – The Wife

Even as the husband and the wife should be submissive to each other, the wife is to be even more so submissive to her husband.

> *"And be not drunk with wine, wherein is excess; but be filled with the Spirit; Speaking to yourselves in psalms and hymns and spiritual songs, singing and making melody in your heart to the Lord; Giving thanks always for all things unto God and the Father in the name of our Lord Jesus Christ; Submitting yourselves one to another in the fear of God. Wives, submit yourselves unto your own husbands, as unto the Lord. For the husband is the head of the wife, even as Christ is the head of the church: and he is the savior of the body. Therefore as the church is subject unto Christ, so let the wives be to their own husbands in every thing."* (**Ephesians 5:18-24**)

Older women are to train young women to love and care for her family with love and obedience to her husband.

> *"The aged women likewise, that they be in behavior as becometh holiness, not false accusers, not given to much wine, teachers of good things; That they may teach the young women to be sober, to love their husbands, to love their children, To be discreet, chaste, keepers at home, good, obedient to their own husbands, that the word of God be not blasphemed."* (**Titus 2:3-5**)

> *"Unto the woman he said, I will greatly multiply thy sorrow and thy conception; in sorrow thou shalt bring forth children; and thy desire shall be to thy husband, and he shall rule over thee."* (**Genesis 3:16**)

The wife is to reverence her husband in the manner as Sarah reverenced Abraham. An odious wife is one that is disruptive to tranquility in marriage.

> *"Nevertheless let every one of you in particular so love his wife even as himself; and the wife see that she reverence her husband."* (**Ephesians 5:33**)

> *"Likewise, ye wives, be in subjection to your own husbands; that, if any obey not the word, they also may without the word be won by the conversation of the wives; While they behold your chaste conversation coupled with fear. Whose adorning let it not be that outward adorning of plaiting the hair, and of wearing of gold, or of putting on of apparel; But let it be the hidden man of the heart, in that which is not corruptible, even the ornament of a meek and quiet spirit, which is in the sight of God of great price. For after this manner in the old time the holy women also, who trusted in God, adorned themselves, being in sub-*

jection unto their own husbands: Even as Sara obeyed Abraham, calling him Lord: whose daughters ye are, as long as ye do well, and are not afraid with any amazement." (**1 Peter 3:1-6**)

For three things the earth is disquieted, and for four which it cannot bear: For a servant when he reigneth; and a fool when he is filled with meat; For an odious woman when she is married; and an handmaid that is heir to her mistress." (**Proverbs 30:21-23**)

The unmarried woman is to be mindful of how she may please God while the married woman is to be mindful of how she may please her husband.

"There is difference also between a wife and a virgin. The unmarried woman careth for the things of the Lord, that she may be holy both in body and in spirit: but she that is married careth for the things of the world, how she may please her husband." (**1 Corinthians 7:34**)

Marriage – The Children

Christian parents are responsible to spiritually educate and train their children.

"And thou shalt love the Lord thy God with all thine heart, and with all thy soul, and with all thy might. And these words, which I command thee this day, shall be in thine heart: And thou shalt teach them diligently unto thy children, and shalt talk of them when thou sittest in thine house, and when thou walkest by the way, and when thou liest down, and when thou risest up. And thou shalt bind them for a sign upon thine hand, and they shall be as frontlets between thine eyes. And thou shalt write them upon the posts of thy house, and on thy gates. And it shall be, when the Lord thy God shall have brought thee into the land which he sware unto thy fathers, to Abraham, to Isaac, and to Jacob, to give thee great and goodly cities, which thou buildedst not, And houses full of all good things, which thou filledst not, and wells digged, which thou diggedst not, vineyards and olive trees, which thou plantedst not; when thou shalt have eaten and be full; Then beware lest thou forget the Lord, which brought thee forth out of the land of Egypt, from the house of bondage. Thou shalt fear the Lord thy God, and serve him, and shalt swear by his name. Ye shall not go after other gods, of the gods of the people which are round about you; (For the Lord thy God is a jealous God among you) lest the anger of the Lord thy God be kindled against thee, and destroy thee from off the face of the earth. Ye shall not tempt the Lord your God, as ye tempted him in Massah. Ye shall diligently keep the commandments of the Lord your God, and his testimonies, and his statutes, which he hath commanded thee. And thou shalt do that which is right and good in the sight of the Lord: that it may be well with thee, and that thou mayest go in and possess the good land which the Lord sware unto thy fathers, To cast out all thine enemies from before thee, as the Lord hath spoken. And when thy son asketh thee in time to come, saying, What mean the testimonies, and the statutes, and the judgments, which the Lord our God hath commanded you? Then thou shalt say unto thy son, We were Pharaoh's bondmen in Egypt; and the Lord brought us out of Egypt with a mighty hand: And the Lord shewed signs and wonders, great and sore, upon Egypt, upon Pharaoh, and upon all his household, before our eyes: And he brought us out from thence, that he might bring us in, to give us the land which he sware unto our fathers. And the Lord commanded us to do all these statutes, to fear the Lord our God, for our good always, that he might preserve us alive, as it is at this day. And it shall be our righteous-

ness, if we observe to do all these commandments before the Lord our God, as he hath commanded us." (Deuteronomy 6:5-25)

"The fear of the Lord is the beginning of wisdom: and the knowledge of the holy is understanding." (Proverbs 10:13)

"Train up a child in the way he should go: and when he is old, he will not depart from it." (Proverbs 22:6)

The purpose of the rod of correction is to give understanding in a physical manner. The Bible is mute concerning time out and detention punishments.

"Foolishness is bound in the heart of a child; but the rod of correction shall drive it far from him." (Proverbs 22:15)

"The rod and reproof give wisdom: but a child left to himself bringeth his mother to shame." (Proverbs 29:15)

Children are to obey their parents. Children are to honor their parents to the child's great benefit and parents are not to abuse their children.

"Children, obey your parents in the Lord: for this is right. Honour thy father and mother; (which is the first commandment with promise;) That it may be well with thee, and thou mayest live long on the earth." (Ephesians 6:1-3)

"And, ye fathers, provoke not your children to wrath: but bring them up in the nurture and admonition of the Lord." (Ephesians 6:4)

Marriage – Further Particulars

There is biblical justification for the family being physically protected and defended.

"Or else how can one enter into a strong man's house, and spoil his goods, except he first bind the strong man? and then he will spoil his house." (Matthew 12:29)

"If it be possible, as much as lieth in you, live peaceably with all men." (Romans 12:18)

Those <u>not</u> providing for their families (relatives) are judged by God to be worst than unbelievers.

"But if any provide not for his own, and specially for those of his own house, he hath denied the faith, and is worse than an infidel." (1 Timothy 5:8)

In the case of the marriage of a believer and an unbeliever, the believer can be relied upon to sanctify the marriage and the offsprings.

"And the woman which hath an husband that believeth not, and if he be pleased to dwell with her, let her not leave him. For the unbelieving husband is sanctified by the wife, and the unbelieving wife is sanctified by the husband: else were your children unclean; but now are they holy. But if the unbelieving depart, let him depart. A brother or a sister is not under bondage in such cases: but God hath called us to peace. For what knowest thou, O wife, whether thou shalt save thy husband? or how knowest thou, O man, whether thou shalt save thy wife?" (1 Corinthians 7:13-16)

20

DIVORCE; WHAT HAS TO BE WRONG

Are there any grounds upon which divorce would be allowed in the Bible?

THE BIBLE TEACHES that God hates divorce and that he commands all mankind not to be involved in bringing about a divorce.

> *"Yet ye say, Wherefore? Because the Lord hath been witness between thee and the wife of thy youth, against whom thou hast dealt treacherously: yet is she thy companion, and the wife of thy covenant. And did not he make one? Yet had he the residue of the spirit. And wherefore one? That he might seek a godly seed. Therefore take heed to your spirit, and let none deal treacherously against the wife of his youth. For the Lord, the God of Israel, saith that he hateth putting away: for one covereth violence with his garment, saith the Lord of hosts: therefore take heed to your spirit, that ye deal not treacherously. Ye have wearied the Lord with your words. Yet ye say, Wherein have we wearied him? When ye say, Every one that doeth evil is good in the sight of the Lord, and he delighteth in them; or, Where is the God of judgment?"* (Malachi 2:14-17)

> *"The Pharisees also came unto him, tempting him, and saying unto him, Is it lawful for a man to put away his wife for every cause? And he answered and said unto them, Have ye not read, that he which made them at the beginning made them male and female, And said, For this cause shall a man leave father and mother, and shall cleave to his wife: and they twain shall be one flesh? Wherefore they are no more twain, but one flesh. What therefore God hath joined together, let not man put asunder."* (Mathew 19:3-6)

There is only one biblical grounds for divorce; adultery is the only grounds for divorce. The Bible does not condemn separation especially with a mindset towards reconciliation.

> *"And I say unto you, Whosoever shall put away his wife, except it be for fornication, and shall marry another, committeth adultery: and whoso marrieth her which is put away doth commit adultery."* (Matthew 19:9)

> *"And unto the married I command, yet not I, but the Lord, Let not the wife depart from her husband: But and if she depart, let her remain unmarried or be reconciled to her husband: and let not the husband put away his wife."* (1 Corinthians 7:10 & 11)

Yet still, the Bible commands the husband to consider taking a wife back in even the transgression of adultery and just as God has taken back a disobedient people.

"Plead with your mother, plead: for she is not my wife, neither am I her husband: let her therefore put away her whoredoms out of her sight, and her adulteries from between her breasts; Lest I strip her naked, and set her as in the day that she was born, and make her as a wilderness, and set her like a dry land, and slay her with thirst. And I will not have mercy upon her children; for they be the children of whoredoms. For their mother hath played the harlot: she that conceived them hath done shamefully: for she said, I will go after my lovers, that give me my bread and my water, my wool and my flax, mine oil and my drink. Therefore, behold, I will hedge up thy way with thorns, and make a wall, that she shall not find her paths. And she shall follow after her lovers, but she shall not overtake them; and she shall seek them, but shall not find them: then shall she say, I will go and return to my first husband; for then was it better with me than now." **(Hosea 2:2-7)**

"Therefore, behold, I will allure her, and bring her into the wilderness, and speak comfortably unto her. And I will give her her vineyards from thence, and the valley of Achor for a door of hope: and she shall sing there, as in the days of her youth, and as in the day when she came up out of the land of Egypt. And it shall be at that day, saith the Lord, that thou shalt call meIshi; and shalt call me no more Baali. For I will take away the names of Baalim out of her mouth, and they shall no more be remembered by their name." **(Hosea 2:14-17)**

"Then said the Lord unto me, Go yet, love a woman beloved of her friend, yet an adulteress, according to the love of the Lord toward the children of Israel, who look to other gods, and love flagons of wine. So I bought her to me for fifteen pieces of silver, and for an homer of barley, and an half homer of barley: And I said unto her, Thou shalt abide for me many days; thou shalt not play the harlot, and thou shalt not be for another man: so will I also be for thee. For the children of Israel shall abide many days without a king, and without a prince, and without a sacrifice, and without an image, and without an ephod, and without teraphim: Afterward shall the children of Israel return, and seek the Lord their God, and David their king; and shall fear the Lord and his goodness in the latter days." **(Hosea 3:1-5)**

Only through God can most men reconcile adultery on the part of a wife.

"Men do not despise a thief, if he steal to satisfy his soul when he is hungry; But if he be found, he shall restore sevenfold; he shall give all the substance of his house. But whoso committeth adultery with a woman lacketh understanding: he that doeth it destroyeth his own soul. A wound and dishonor shall he get; and his reproach shall not be wiped away. For jealousy is the rage of a man: therefore he will not spare in the day of vengeance. He will not regard any ransom; neither will he rest content, though thou givest many gifts." **(Proverbs 6:30-35)**

"Ah Lord God! behold, thou hast made the heaven and the earth by thy great power and stretched out arm, and there is nothing too hard for thee:" **(Jeremiah 32:17)**

"And he said, The things which are impossible with men are possible with God." **(Luke 18:27)**

Herein lies a remarkable scriptural quandary concerning those divorced. Those divorced for a reason other than adultery, commit adultery if they remarry according to the Bible.

> *"And I say unto you, Whosoever shall put away his wife, except it be for fornication, and shall marry another, committeth adultery: and whoso marrieth her which is put away doth commit adultery."* (Matthew 19:9)

> *"The wife is bound by the law as long as her husband liveth; but if her husband be dead, she is at liberty to be married to whom she will; only in the Lord."* (1 Corinthians 7:39)

The Law of Moses was much more lenient concerning divorce and God had a reason for it so being.

> *"They say unto him, Why did Moses then command to give a writing of divorcement, and to put her away? He saith unto them, Moses because of the hardness of your hearts suffered you to put away your wives: but from the beginning it was not so."* (Matthew 19:7 & 8)

There is the expectation in the Bible that as long as either the husband or the wife is pleased to be in the marital relationship, notwithstanding their faith, there should be the commitment of partner to remain.

> *"But to the rest speak I, not the Lord: If any brother hath a wife that believeth not, and she be pleased to dwell with him, let him not put her away. And the woman which hath an husband that believeth not, and if he be pleased to dwell with her, let her not leave him."* (1 Corinthians 7: 12 & 13)

Lastly, the Holy Spirit shall guide the believer in all truth. Christians should be different from unbelievers in their marital commitment to Almighty God. Many issues, concerning the world in general, such as incompatibility, abuse or abandonment, should not enter into the Christian marital union. However, if issues do enter, the solution lies in commitment, repentance, prayer and counseling. Separation is not prohibited by the Bible. Living faithfully under different roofs, although not necessarily a good idea, is not prohibited by the Bible. Know this that God is not involved in the business of breaking up marriages but rather that serpent Satan. Therefore, the use of an investigative agency to determine the source, which is usually the case, of the infidelity that is bringing on the incompatibility, abuse or abandonment, is not prohibited by the Bible as well. Upon identifying the infidelity, then by all means, let's talk divorce if so desired.

> *"Howbeit when he, the Spirit of truth, is come, he will guide you into all truth: for he shall not speak of himself; but whatsoever he shall hear, that shall he speak: and he will shew you things to come."* (John 16:13)

> *"Be ye therefore followers of God, as dear children; And walk in love, as Christ also hath loved us, and hath given himself for us an offering and a sacrifice to God for a sweetsmelling savour. But fornication, and all uncleanness, or covetousness, let it not be once named among you, as becometh saints; Neither filthiness, nor foolish talking, nor jesting, which are not convenient: but rather giving of thanks."* (Ephesians 5:1-4)

> *"Behold, I send you forth as sheep in the midst of wolves: be ye therefore wise as serpents, and harmless as doves."* (Matthew 10:16)

21

A Christian Basis for Child Rearing and Discipline

Does the Bible tell me how to rear and discipline my child in a manner that is now contrary to civil law?

Child Rearing

Education should begin in the home with a Christian education according to the Bible.

"Hear, O Israel: The Lord our God is one Lord: And thou shalt love the Lord thy God with all thine heart, and with all thy soul, and with all thy might. And these words, which I command thee this day, shall be in thine heart: And thou shalt teach them diligently unto thy children, and shalt talk of them when thou sittest in thine house, and when thou walkest by the way, and when thou liest down, and when thou risest up. And thou shalt bind them for a sign upon thine hand, and they shall be as frontlets between thine eyes. And thou shalt write them upon the posts of thy house, and on thy gates. And it shall be, when the Lord thy God shall have brought thee into the land which he sware unto thy fathers, to Abraham, to Isaac, and to Jacob, to give thee great and goodly cities, which thou buildedst not, " (Deuteronomy 6:4-10)

"Know ye therefore that they which are of faith, the same are the children of Abraham." (Galatians 3:7)

"Only take heed to thyself, and keep thy soul diligently, lest thou forget the things which thine eyes have seen, and lest they depart from thy heart all the days of thy life: but teach them thy sons, and thy sons' sons; Specially the day that thou stoodest before the Lord thy God in Horeb, when the Lord said unto me, Gather me the people together, and I will make them hear my words, that they may learn to fear me all the days that they shall live upon the earth, and that they may teach their children." (Deuteronomy 4:9&10)

Live as Christian examples before your children.

"Now then we are ambassadors for Christ, as though God did beseech you by us: we pray you in Christ's stead, be ye reconciled to God." (2 Corinthians 5:20)

"This I say then, Walk in the Spirit, and ye shall not fulfill the lust of the flesh." (Galatians 5:16)

"If there be therefore any consolation in Christ, if any comfort of love, if any fellowship of the Spirit, if any bowels and mercies, Fulfil ye my joy, that ye be likeminded, having the same love, being of one accord, of one mind." (Philippians 2:1-2)

"But speak thou the things which become sound doctrine:That the aged men be sober, grave, temperate, sound in faith, in charity, in patience. The aged women likewise, that they be in behavior as becometh holiness, not false accusers, not given to much wine, teachers of good things; That they may teach the young women to be sober, to love their husbands, to love their children, To be discreet, chaste, keepers at home, good, obedient to their own husbands, that the word of God be not blasphemed. Young men likewise exhort to be sober minded. In all things shewing thyself a pattern of good works: in doctrine shewing uncorruptness, gravity, sincerity, Sound speech, that cannot be condemned; that he that is of the contrary part may be ashamed, having no evil thing to say of you." (Titus 2:1-8)

Christians are to obey God as dear children and a child should be able to see the parent's obedience to Almighty God as the example.

"Be ye therefore followers of God, as dear children; And walk in love, as Christ also hath loved us, and hath given himself for us an offering and a sacrifice to God for a sweetsmelling savor. But fornication, and all uncleanness, or covetousness, let it not be once named among you, as becometh saints; Neither filthiness, nor foolish talking, nor jesting, which are not convenient: but rather giving of thanks. For this ye know, that no whoremonger, nor unclean person, nor covetous man, who is an idolater, hath any inheritance in the kingdom of Christ and of God. Let no man deceive you with vain words: for because of these things cometh the wrath of God upon the children of disobedience. Be not ye therefore partakers with them. For ye were sometimes darkness, but now are ye light in the Lord:walk as children of light:" (Ephesians 5:1-8)

Parents are charged by the Bible to train up the child and not the reverse. Inherent in this training is the building up of the body of Christ. It does not "take a whole village" to raise a Christian child; the village may stand against the beliefs of the parents and the child

"Train up a child in the way he should go: and when he is old, he will not depart from it." (Proverbs 22:6)

"And the Lord said, Shall I hide from Abraham that thing which I do; Seeing that Abraham shall surely become a great and mighty nation, and all the nations of the earth shall be blessed in him? For I know him, that he will command his children and his household after him, and they shall keep the way of the Lord, to do justice and judgment; that the Lord may bring upon Abraham that which he hath spoken of him." (Genesis 18:17-19)

"Blessed are ye, when men shall hate you, and when they shall separate you from their company, and shall reproach you, and cast out your name as evil, for the Son of man's sake. Rejoice ye in that day, and leap for joy: for, behold, your reward is great in heaven: for in the like manner did their fathers unto the prophets." (Luke 6:22&23)

God rewards respect for parents.

"Honor thy father and mother; which is the first commandment with promise; That it may be well with thee, and thou mayest live long on the earth." (**Ephesians 6:2&3**)

"Honour thy father and thy mother, as the Lord thy God hath commanded thee; that thy days may be prolonged, and that it may go well with thee, in the land which the Lord thy God giveth thee." (**Deuteronomy 5:16**)

Rebellion on the part of children is an abomination in the sight of God.

"For rebellion is as the sin of witchcraft, and stubbornness is as iniquity and idolatry." (**1 Samuel 15:23a**)

"And he caused his children to pass through the fire in the valley of the son of Hinnom: also he observed times, and used enchantments, and used witchcraft, and dealt with a familiar spirit, and with wizards: he wrought much evil in the sight of the Lord, to provoke him to anger." (**2 Chronicles 33:6**)

"Now the works of the flesh are manifest, which are these; Adultery, fornication, uncleanness, lasciviousness, Idolatry, witchcraft, hatred, variance, emulations, wrath, strife, seditions, heresies, Envyings, murders, drunkenness, revellings, and such like: of the which I tell you before, as I have also told you in time past, that they which do such things shall not inherit the kingdom of God." (**Galatians 5:19-21**)

"My son, fear thou the Lord and the king: and meddle not with them that are given to change: For their calamity shall rise suddenly; and who knoweth the ruin of them both?" (**Proverbs 24:21&22**)

Child Discipline

It is of the utmost importance that children obey their parents in a Christian home.

"Children, obey your parents in the Lord: for this is right." (**Ephesians 6:1**)

"My son, hear the instruction of thy father, and forsake not the law of thy mother: For they shall be an ornament of grace unto thy head, and chains about thy neck." (**Proverbs 1:8&9**)

God will deal with disobedience through chastisement; this is an example to parents in handling children.

"For whom the Lord loveth he chasteneth, and scourgeth every son whom he receiveth. If ye endure chastening, God dealeth with you as with sons; for what son is he whom the father chasteneth not? But if ye be without chastisement, whereof all are partakers, then are ye bastards, and not sons. Furthermore we have had fathers of our flesh which corrected us, and we gave them reverence: shall we not much rather be in subjection unto the Father of spirits, and live? For they verily for a few days chastened us after their own pleasure; but he for our profit, that we might be partakers of his holiness. Now no chastening for the present seemeth to be joyous, but grievous: nevertheless afterward it yieldeth the peaceable fruit of righteousness unto them which are exercised thereby." (**Hebrews 12:6-11**)

"My son, despise not the chastening of the Lord; neither be weary of his correction:" (Proverbs 3:11)

Certainly abuse, whether physical or mental, is in error.

"And, ye fathers, provoke not your children to wrath: but bring them up in the nurture and admonition of the Lord." (Ephesians 6:4)

Reference Appendix 8, Title 89 Social Services Chapter III Department of Children and Family Services Subchapter a Service Delivery Part 300 Reports of Child Abuse and Neglect, with regard to lawful parental behavior. Note that the key to lawful physical disciplining of a child is found under Section 300.20 Definitions. Christians should certainly have no problem of remaining within the limits of corporal punishment (note as undefined in Part 300) as understood by this author.

I am persuaded that the use of a command voice, as in the military, is the most effective voice when disciplining children. A command voice is used in the military and it has to be akin to the shout that is to be used by Jesus upon his return.

"But I would not have you to be ignorant, brethren, concerning them which are asleep, that ye sorrow not, even as others which have no hope. For if we believe that Jesus died and rose again, even so them also which sleep in Jesus will God bring with him. For this we say unto you by the word of the Lord, that we which are alive and remain unto the coming of the Lord shall not prevent them which are asleep. For the Lord himself shall descend from heaven with a shout, with the voice of the archangel, and with the trump of God: and the dead in Christ shall rise first: Then we which are alive and remain shall be caught up together with them in the clouds, to meet the Lord in the air: and so shall we ever be with the Lord." (1 Thessalonians 4:13-17)

As in all things, the believer should be led spiritually; this includes child discipline.

"Howbeit when he, the Spirit of truth, is come, he will guide you into all truth: for he shall not speak of himself; but whatsoever he shall hear, that shall he speak: and he will shew you things to come." (John 16:13)

God has ordained physical correction not reasoning and confinement. Have you noticed or heard of children trying to physically correct their parents? Embrace physical correction of your children if you really love them.

"Foolishness is bound in the heart of a child; but the rod of correction shall drive it far from him." (Proverbs 22:15)

"In the lips of him that hath understanding wisdom is found: but a rod is for the back of him that is void of understanding." (Proverbs 10:13)

"The rod and reproof give wisdom: but a child left to himself bringeth his mother to shame. Correct thy son, and he shall give thee rest; yea, he shall give delight unto thy soul." (Proverbs 29:15&17)

"My son, despise not the chastening of the Lord; neither be weary of his correction: For whom the Lord loveth he correcteth; even as a father the son in whom he delighteth." (Proverbs 3:11&12)

"He that spareth his rod hateth his son: but he that loveth him chasteneth him betimes." (Proverbs 13:24)

Physical correction plays a part in a child's salvation.

"Withhold not correction from the child: for if thou beatest him with the rod, he shall not die. Thou shalt beat him with the rod, and shalt deliver his soul from hell." (Proverbs 23:13&14)

God's view is different from society's view and probably in no case is it more surprisingly different than with regard to physical correction; God's thoughts are not our thoughts.

"Trust in the Lord with all thine heart; and lean not unto thine own understanding." (Proverbs 3:5)

"Correction is grievous unto him that forsaketh the way: and he that hateth reproof shall die. Hell and destruction are before the Lord: how much more then the hearts of the children of men? A scorner loveth not one that reproveth him: neither will he go unto the wise." (Proverbs 15:10-12)

Warning, don't physically discipline your children in public.

"Behold, I send you forth as sheep in the midst of wolves: be ye therefore wise as serpents, and harmless as doves." (Matthew 10:16)

22

WEALTH AND PROSPERITY: THE RICH IN GOD'S SIGHT

Can the rich please God and live godly lives?

THE BIBLE EXHORTS those that are rich to be not arrogant in trusting in their riches but rather be humble and trust in the living God. It is God that has given riches to be enjoyed not purely on self indulgence but rather in good works (ergo - toil, deeds, doings, labor). Some of the wealth of the rich needs to be distributed and in doing so build up treasures in heaven.

> "Charge them that are rich in this world, that they be not highminded, nor trust in uncertain riches, but in the living God, who giveth us richly all things to enjoy; that they do good, that they be rich in good works, ready to distribute, willing to communicate; laying up in store for themselves a good foundation against the time to come, that they may lay hold on eternal life." (1 Timothy 6:17-19)

God has no problem with the rich and famous that would bless his name. Abraham and Job are prime examples from the Bible.

> "Now the Lord had said unto Abram, Get thee out of thy country, and from thy kindred, and from thy father's house, unto a land that I will shew thee: and I will make of thee a great nation, and I will bless thee, and make thy name great; and thou shalt be a blessing: and I will bless them that bless thee, and curse him that curseth thee: and in thee shall all families of the earth be blessed. So Abram departed, as the Lord had spoken unto him; and Lot went with him: and Abram was seventy and five years old when he departed out of Haran. And Abram took Sarai his wife, and Lot his brother's son, and all their substance that they had gathered, and the souls that they had gotten in Haran; and they went forth to go into the land of Canaan; and into the land of Canaan they came." (Genesis 12:1-5)

> "And Abimelech took sheep, and oxen, and menservants, and womenservants, and gave them unto Abraham, and restored him Sarah his wife. And Abimelech said, Behold, my land is before thee: dwell where it pleaseth thee. And unto Sarah he said, Behold, I have given thy brother a thousand pieces of silver: behold, he is to thee a covering of the eyes, unto all that are with thee, and with all other: thus she was reproved." (Genesis 20:14-16)

"There was a man in the land of Uz, whose name was Job; and that man was perfect and upright, and one that feared God, and eschewed evil. And there were born unto him seven sons and three daughters. His substance also was seven thousand sheep, and three thousand camels, and five hundred yoke of oxen, and five hundred she asses, and a very great household; so that this man was the greatest of all the men of the east." (**Job 1:1-3**)

"And Satan answered the Lord, and said, Skin for skin, yea, all that a man hath will he give for his life. But put forth thine hand now, and touch his bone and his flesh, and he will curse thee to thy face. And the Lord said unto Satan, Behold, he is in thine hand; but save his life. So went Satan forth from the presence of the Lord, and smote Job with sore boils from the sole of his foot unto his crown. And he took him a potsherd to scrape himself withal; and he sat down among the ashes. Then said his wife unto him, Dost thou still retain thine integrity? curse God, and die. But he said unto her, Thou speakest as one of the foolish women speaketh. What? shall we receive good at the hand of God, and shall we not receive evil? In all this did not Job sin with his lips." (**Job 2:4-10**)

"And the Lord turned the captivity of Job, when he prayed for his friends: also the Lord gave Job twice as much as he had before. So the Lord blessed the latter end of Job more than his beginning: for he had fourteen thousand sheep, and six thousand camels, and a thousand yoke of oxen, and a thousand she asses. He had also seven sons and three daughters. And he called the name of the first, Jemima; and the name of the second, Kezia; and the name of the third, Kerenhappuch. And in all the land were no women found so fair as the daughters of Job: and their father gave them inheritance among their brethren. After this lived Job an hundred and forty years, and saw his sons, and his sons' sons, even four generations. So Job died, being old and full of days." (**Job 42:10, 12-17**)

The Bible teaches us that God will supply our need through his heavenly riches through Jesus Christ. If we understand that then, whether we are poor or wealthy, we can overcome all things through Christ who is able to strengthen us.

"But my God shall supply all your need according to his riches in glory by Christ Jesus." (**Philippians 4:19**)

"I know both how to be abased, and I know how to abound: every where and in all things I am instructed both to be full and to be hungry, both to abound and to suffer need. I can do all things through Christ which strengtheneth me." (**Philippians 4:12-13**)

One is not to work to become rich. Riches can be fleeting. As for the rich man, he glories in his riches rather than in the Lord.

"Labour not to be rich: cease from thine own wisdom. Wilt thou set thine eyes upon that which is not? for riches certainly make themselves wings; they fly away as an eagle toward heaven." (**Proverbs 23:4-5**)

"Thus saith the Lord, Let not the wise man glory in his wisdom, neither let the mighty man glory in his might, let not the rich man glory in his riches: but let him that glorieth glory in this, that he understandeth and knoweth me, that I am the Lord which exercise loving-kindness, judgment, and righteousness, in the earth: for in these things I delight, saith the Lord." (**Jeremiah 9:23-24**)

God is able to transfer wealth from the ungodly to the godly.

> *"Wealth gotten by vanity shall be diminished: but he that gathereth by labour shall increase. A good man leaveth an inheritance to his children's children: and the wealth of the sinner is laid up for the just."* (Proverbs 13:11&22)

The rich should have pity on the poor and in doing so they build up an indebtedness owed by God according to the Bible.

> *"He that hath pity upon the poor lendeth unto the Lord; and that which he hath given will he pay him again."* (Proverbs 19:17)

> *"Then said he also to him that bade him, When thou makest a dinner or a supper, call not thy friends, nor thy brethren, neither thy kinsmen, nor thy rich neighbours; lest they also bid thee again, and a recompence be made thee. But when thou makest a feast, call the poor, the maimed, the lame, the blind: and thou shalt be blessed; for they cannot recompense thee: for thou shalt be recompensed at the resurrection of the just."* (Luke 14:12-14)

> *"For the poor shall never cease out of the land: therefore I command thee, saying, Thou shalt open thine hand wide unto thy brother, to thy poor, and to thy needy, in thy land."* (Deuteronomy 15:11)

> *"And Cornelius said, Four days ago I was fasting until this hour; and at the ninth hour I prayed in my house, and, behold, a man stood before me in bright clothing, And said, Cornelius, thy prayer is heard, and thine alms are had in remembrance in the sight of God."* (Acts 10:30&31)

Now, every Christian should understand that a tenth of our income is holy to the Lord. If the tithe, or a portion thereof, is used rather than given to the Lord, then that amount used plus 20% belongs to God. This is tithing as the Bible teaches. There is another avenue of giving referred to as the offering (minchah - donation, tribute, sacrificial gift or present). The offering does not have a percentage requirement yet there is no limitation on the amount of the offering. How much more should the rich be able to give an offering? Incidentally, giving is out of our increase (tebuwah - fruit, gain, revenue), therefore, after taxes with tax refunds becoming revenue all over again (just compare the 10% of the take home income of a person with a tax exempt income versus a person that has taxable income).

> *"Will a man rob God? Yet ye have robbed me. But ye say, Wherein have we robbed thee? In tithes and offerings. Ye are cursed with a curse: for ye have robbed me, even this whole nation. Bring ye all the tithes into the storehouse, that there may be meat in mine house, and prove me now herewith, saith the Lord of hosts, if I will not open you the windows of heaven, and pour you out a blessing, that there shall not be room enough to receive it. And I will rebuke the devourer for your sakes, and he shall not destroy the fruits of your ground; neither shall your vine cast her fruit before the time in the field, saith the Lord of hosts."* (Malachi 3:8-11)

> *"And if it be a beast, whereof men bring an offering unto the Lord, all that any man giveth of such unto the Lord shall be holy. He shall not alter it, nor change it, a good for a bad, or a bad for a good: and if he shall at all change beast for beast, then it and the exchange thereof shall be holy. And if it be any unclean beast, of which they do not offer a sacrifice*

unto the Lord, then he shall present the beast before the priest: And the priest shall value it, whether it be good or bad: as thou valuest it, who art the priest, so shall it be. But if he will at all redeem it, then he shall add a fifth part thereof unto thy estimation." (Leviticus 27:9-13)

"And all the tithe of the land, whether of the seed of the land, or of the fruit of the tree, is the Lord's: it is holy unto the Lord. And if a man will at all redeem ought of his tithes, he shall add thereto the fifth part thereof. And concerning the tithe of the herd, or of the flock, even of whatsoever passeth under the rod, the tenth shall be holy unto the Lord." (Leviticus 27:30-32)

"Honour the Lord with thy substance, and with the firstfruits of all thine increase: So shall thy barns be filled with plenty, and thy presses shall burst out with new wine." (Proverbs 3:9&10)

There is an inherent tendency by mankind to consume riches upon our lusts. The Bible declares that it is easier for a camel to go through the eye of a needle than for a rich man to enter into the Kingdom of Heaven, however, with God it is possible.

"From whence come wars and fightings among you? Come they not hence, even of your lusts that war in your members? Ye lust, and have not: ye kill, and desire to have, and cannot obtain: ye fight and war, yet ye have not, because ye ask not. Ye ask, and receive not, because ye ask amiss, that ye may consume it upon your lusts." (James 4:1-3)

"But they that will be rich fall into temptation and a snare, and into many foolish and hurtful lusts, which drown men in destruction and perdition. For the love of money is the root of all evil: which while some coveted after, they have erred from the faith, and pierced themselves through with many sorrows. But thou, O man of God, flee these things; and follow after righteousness, godliness, faith, love, patience, meekness. Fight the good fight of faith, lay hold on eternal life, whereunto thou art also called, and hast professed a good profession before many witnesses." (1 Timothy 6:9-12)

"Then said Jesus unto his disciples, Verily I say unto you, That a rich man shall hardly enter into the kingdom of heaven. And again I say unto you, It is easier for a camel to go through the eye of a needle, than for a rich man to enter into the kingdom of God. When his disciples heard it, they were exceedingly amazed, saying, Who then can be saved? But Jesus beheld them, and said unto them, With men this is impossible; but with God all things are possible." (Matthew 19:23-26)

"Go to now, ye rich men, weep and howl for your miseries that shall come upon you. Your riches are corrupted, and your garments are motheaten. Your gold and silver is cankered; and the rust of them shall be a witness against you, and shall eat your flesh as it were fire. Ye have heaped treasure together for the last days. Behold, the hire of the labourers who have reaped down your fields, which is of you kept back by fraud, crieth: and the cries of them which have reaped are entered into the ears of the Lord of sabaoth. Ye have lived in pleasure on the earth, and been wanton; ye have nourished your hearts, as in a day of slaughter. Ye have condemned and killed the just; and he doth not resist you. Be patient therefore, brethren, unto the coming of the Lord. Behold, the husbandman waiteth for the precious fruit of the earth, and hath long patience for it, until he receive the early and lat-

ter rain. Be ye also patient; stablish your hearts: for the coming of the Lord draweth nigh."
(James 5:1-8)

Woe unto the rich, for the rich characteristically is living in comfort with a lack of concern and faith in God. Beware of a consuming desire for money.

"But woe unto you that are rich! For ye have received your consolation. Woe unto you that are full! For ye shall hunger. Woe unto you that laugh now! For ye shall mourn and weep." (Luke 6:24-25)

"Perverse disputings of men of corrupt minds, and destitute of the truth, supposing that gain is godliness: from such withdraw thyself. But godliness with contentment is great gain. For we brought nothing into this world, and it is certain we can carry nothing out. And having food and raiment let us be therewith content. But they that will be rich fall into temptation and a snare, and into many foolish and hurtful lusts, which drown men in destruction and perdition. For the love of money is the root of all evil: which while some coveted after, they have erred from the faith, and pierced themselves through with many sorrows." (1 Timothy 6:5-10)

What has a man achieved in life if he loses his soul?

"And the Lord God formed man of the dust of the ground, and breathed into his nostrils the breath of life; and man became a living soul." (Genesis 2:7)

"For what is a man profited, if he shall gain the whole world, and lose his own soul? Or what shall a man give in exchange for his soul? For the Son of man shall come in the glory of his Father with his angels; and then he shall reward every man according to his works." (Matthew 16:26-27)

Faith without works is not faith. The rich are in a position to do so much work.

"What doth it profit, my brethren, though a man say he hath faith, and have not works? Can faith save him? If a brother or sister be naked, and destitute of daily food, and one of you say unto them, Depart in peace, be ye warmed and filled; notwithstanding ye give them not those things which are needful to the body; what doth it profit? Even so faith, if it hath not works, is dead, being alone. Yea, a man may say, Thou hast faith, and I have works: shew me thy faith without thy works, and I will shew thee my faith by my works. Thou believest that there is one God; thou doest well: the devils also believe, and tremble. But wilt thou know, O vain man, that faith without works is dead? Was not Abraham our father justified by works, when he had offered Isaac his son upon the altar? Seest thou how faith wrought with his works, and by works was faith made perfect? And the scripture was fulfilled which saith, Abraham believed God, and it was imputed unto him for righteousness: and he was called the Friend of God. Ye see then how that by works a man is justified, and not by faith only. Likewise also was not Rahab the harlot justified by works, when she had received the messengers, and had sent them out another way? For as the body without the spirit is dead, so faith without works is dead also." (James 2:14-26)

The rich should cheerfully give their tithes and offerings; in doing so God will bless even more.

"And Jesus sat over against the treasury, and beheld how the people cast money into the treasury: and many that were rich cast in much. And there came a certain poor widow, and she threw in two mites, which make a farthing. And he called unto him his disciples, and saith unto them, Verily I say unto you, That this poor widow hath cast more in, than all they which have cast into the treasury: For all they did cast in of their abundance; but she of her want did cast in all that she had, even all her living." (**Mark 12:41-44**)

"But this I say, He which soweth sparingly shall reap also sparingly; and he which soweth bountifully shall reap also bountifully. Every man according as he purposeth in his heart, so let him give; not grudgingly, or of necessity: for God loveth a cheerful giver. And God is able to make all grace abound toward you; that ye, always having all sufficiency in all things, may abound to every good work: (As it is written, He hath dispersed abroad; he hath given to the poor: his righteousness remaineth for ever. Now he that ministereth seed to the sower both minister bread for your food, and multiply your seed sown, and increase the fruits of your righteousness;) being enriched in every thing to all bountifulness, which causeth through us thanksgiving to God. For the administration of this service not only supplieth the want of the saints, but is abundant also by many thanksgivings unto God; whiles by the experiment of this ministration they glorify God for your professed subjection unto the gospel of Christ, and for your liberal distribution unto them, and unto all men; and by their prayer for you, which long after you for the exceeding grace of God in you. Thanks be unto God for his unspeakable gift." (**2 Corinthians 9:6-15**)

"I have shewed you all things, how that so labouring ye ought to support the weak, and to remember the words of the Lord Jesus, how he said, It is more blessed to give than to receive." (**Acts 20:35**)

The rich should be proactive in the care of their relatives. Those of us with the abilities to care for our relatives are no more than heathens if we do not.

"But if any provide not for his own, and specially for those of his own house, he hath denied the faith, and is worse than an infidel." (**1 Timothy 5:8**)

It is good for us to enjoy the rewards of our labors but at the same time we should make an effort to do things worthy of heavenly reward. How much more are the rich able to be philanthropic in their efforts? How much more is God due the praise?

"Behold that which I have seen: it is good and comely for one to eat and to drink, and to enjoy the good of all his labour that he taketh under the sun all the days of his life, which God giveth him: for it is his portion. Every man also to whom God hath given riches and wealth, and hath given him power to eat thereof, and to take his portion, and to rejoice in his labour; this is the gift of God. For he shall not much remember the days of his life; because God answereth him in the joy of his heart." (**Ecclesiastes 5:18-20**)

"And he spake a parable unto them, saying, The ground of a certain rich man brought forth plentifully: and he thought within himself, saying, What shall I do, because I have no room where to bestow my fruits? And he said, This will I do: I will pull down my barns, and build greater; and there will I bestow all my fruits and my goods. And I will say to my soul, Soul, thou hast much goods laid up for many years; take thine ease, eat, drink, and be merry. But God said unto him, Thou fool, this night thy soul shall be required of thee: then

whose shall those things be, which thou hast provided? So is he that layeth up treasure for himself, and is not rich toward God." (Luke 12:16-21)

"Finally, brethren, whatsoever things are true, whatsoever things are honest, whatsoever things are just, whatsoever things are pure, whatsoever things are lovely, whatsoever things are of good report; if there be any virtue, and if there be any praise, think on these things." (Philippians 4:8)

23

A CHRISTIAN WORK ETHIC

In what regard is labor held in the Bible?

CHRISTIANS ARE TO be honest in the workplace and to live peaceable and hospitable lives.

> *"That no man go beyond and defraud his brother in any matter: because that the Lord is the avenger of all such, as we also have forewarned you and testified. And that ye study to be quiet, and to do your own business, and to work with your own hands, as we commanded you; That ye may walk honestly toward them that are without, and that ye may have lack of nothing."* (I Thessalonians 4:6, 11-12)

> *"Let love be without dissimulation. Abhor that which is evil; cleave to that which is good. Be kindly affectioned one to another with brotherly love; in honour preferring one another; Not slothful in business; fervent in spirit; serving the Lord; Rejoicing in hope; patient in tribulation; continuing instant in prayer; Distributing to the necessity of saints; given to hospitality."* (Romans 12:9-13)

Understanding of a primary biblical principle would help to alleviate the pressure of competition in the workplace; Christians are not to labor to become rich but rather for a quality of life for ourselves, our families, the world and the glory of God.

> *"Labor not to be rich: cease from thine own wisdom."* (Proverbs 23:4)

> *"The labor of the righteous tendeth to life: the fruit of the wicked to sin."* (Proverbs 10:16)

> *"But if any provide not for his own, and specially for those of his own house, he hath denied the faith, and is worse than an infidel."* (I Timothy 5:8)

> *"And whatsoever ye do in word or deed, do all in the name of the Lord Jesus, giving thanks to God and the Father by him. And whatsoever ye do, do it heartily, as to the Lord, and not unto men; Knowing that of the Lord ye shall receive the reward of the inheritance: for ye serve the Lord Christ. But he that doeth wrong shall receive for the wrong which he hath done: and there is no respect of persons."* (Colossians 3:17, 23-25)

Even in the workplace, Christian reliance should be upon God and a spiritual walk as opposed to self-willed direction.

"Go to now, ye that say, To day or to morrow we will go into such a city, and continue there a year, and buy and sell, and get gain: Whereas ye know not what shall be on the morrow. For what is your life? It is even a vapor, that appeareth for a little time, and then vanisheth away. For that ye ought to say, If the Lord will, we shall live, and do this, or that. But now ye rejoice in your boastings: all such rejoicing is evil. Therefore to him that knoweth to do good, and doeth it not, to him it is sin." (James 4:13-17)

"And he spake a parable unto them, saying, The ground of a certain rich man brought forth plentifully: And he thought within himself, saying, What shall I do, because I have no room where to bestow my fruits? And he said, This will I do: I will pull down my barns, and build greater; and there will I bestow all my fruits and my goods. And I will say to my soul, Soul, thou hast much goods laid up for many years; take thine ease, eat, drink, and be merry. But God said unto him, Thou fool, this night thy soul shall be required of thee: then whose shall those things be, which thou hast provided? So is he that layeth up treasure for himself, and is not rich toward God." (Luke 12:16-21)

The Bible puts the responsibility of work in the marital relationship upon men (husbands) not women (wives).

"And unto Adam he said, Because thou hast hearkened unto the voice of thy wife, and hast eaten of the tree, of which I commanded thee, saying, Thou shalt not eat of it: cursed is the ground for thy sake; in sorrow shalt thou eat of it all the days of thy life; Thorns also and thistles shall it bring forth to thee; and thou shalt eat the herb of the field; In the sweat of thy face shalt thou eat bread, till thou return unto the ground; for out of it wast thou taken: for dust thou art, and unto dust shalt thou return." (Genesis 3:17-19)

The Bible puts the responsibility of work upon the husband. However, there is no restriction upon a wife as the help meet (ezer - aid) in terms of occupation, income or any other sense.

"And the Lord God said, It is not good that the man should be alone; I will make him an help meet for him. And out of the ground the Lord God formed every beast of the field, and every fowl of the air; and brought them unto Adam to see what he would call them: and whatsoever Adam called every living creature, that was the name thereof. And Adam gave names to all cattle, and to the fowl of the air, and to every beast of the field; but for Adam there was not found an help meet for him. And the Lord God caused a deep sleep to fall upon Adam, and he slept: and he took one of his ribs, and closed up the flesh instead thereof; And the rib, which the Lord God had taken from man, made he a woman, and brought her unto the man. And Adam said, This is now bone of my bones, and flesh of my flesh: she shall be called Woman, because she was taken out of Man. Therefore shall a man leave his father and his mother, and shall cleave unto his wife: and they shall be one flesh." (Genesis 2:18-24)

Note that God gives the wife the responsibility of loving their husbands, loving their children and keeping (olkouros – domestically inclined) the home. God does not relieve a career woman of love for her husband, children, and concern for the home.

"The aged women likewise, that they be in behavior as becometh holiness, not false accusers, not given to much wine, teachers of good things; That they may teach the young women

to be sober, to love their husbands, to love their children, To be discreet, chaste, keepers at home, good, obedient to their own husbands, that the word of God be not blasphemed." (Titus 2: 3-5)

Herein lies the balance, which should be established during courtship and the notion of being equally yoked in faith. I am persuaded that the notion of being equally yoked in faith, goes even further (by common sense) to life issues as Christians should walk in light not darkness. There should be honesty and not fraud in the marital relationship. However, the husband is required to know his wife regardless.

"Be ye not unequally yoked together with unbelievers: for what fellowship hath righteousness with unrighteousness? and what communion hath light with darkness? And what concord hath Christ with Belial? or what part hath he that believeth with an infidel? And what agreement hath the temple of God with idols? for ye are the temple of the living God; as God hath said, I will dwell in them, and walk in them; and I will be their God, and they shall be my people." (2 Corinthians 6: 14-16)

"Defraud ye not one the other, except it be with consent for a time, that ye may give yourselves to fasting and prayer; and come together again, that Satan tempt you not for your incontinency." (1 Corinthians 7:5)

"Likewise, ye husbands, dwell with them according to knowledge, giving honour unto the wife, as unto the weaker vessel, and as being heirs together of the grace of life; that your prayers be not hindered." (1 Peter 3:7)

The Bible reinforces the notion of men earning a living by going to the extent to say that if a man will not earn a living then he should not eat.

"Now we command you, brethren, in the name of our Lord Jesus Christ, that ye withdraw yourselves from every brother that walketh disorderly, and not after the tradition which he received of us. For yourselves know how ye ought to follow us: for we behaved not ourselves disorderly among you; Neither did we eat any man's bread for nought; but wrought with labor and travail night and day, that we might not be chargeable to any of you: Not because we have not power, but to make ourselves an ensample unto you to follow us. For even when we were with you, this we commanded you, that if any would not work, neither should he eat. For we hear that there are some which walk among you disorderly, working not at all, but are busybodies. Now them that are such we command and exhort by our Lord Jesus Christ, that with quietness they work, and eat their own bread." (II Thessalonians 3:6-12)

A worker is worthy of the things he earns as this is applied even to the minister.

"For the scripture saith, Thou shalt not muzzle the ox that treadeth out the corn. And, The laborer is worthy of his reward." (I Timothy 5:18)

The Christian is assured of a certain level of success in whatever direction God leads.

"Only be thou strong and very courageous, that thou mayest observe to do according to all the law, which Moses my servant commanded thee: turn not from it to the right hand or to the left, that thou mayest prosper withersoever thou goest. This book of the law shall not

depart out of thy mouth; but thou shalt meditate therein day and night, that thou mayest observe to do according to all that is written therein: for then thou shalt make thy way prosperous, and then thou shalt have good success." (Joshua 1:7-8)

"The Lord shall open unto thee his good treasure, the heaven to give the rain unto thy land in his season, and to bless all the work of thine hand: and thou shalt lend unto many nations, and thou shalt not borrow. And the Lord shall make thee the head, and not the tail; and thou shalt be above only, and thou shalt not be beneath; if that thou hearken unto the commandments of the Lord thy God, which I command thee this day, to observe and to do them: And thou shalt not go aside from any of the words which I command thee this day, to the right hand, or to the left, to go after other gods to serve them." (Deuteronomy 28:12-14)

"But my God shall supply all your need according to his riches in glory by Christ Jesus." (Philippians 4:19)

"Be strong and of a good courage: for unto this people shalt thou divide for an inheritance the land, which I swear unto their fathers to give them. Only be thou strong and very courageous, that thou mayest observe to do according to all the law, which Moses my servant commanded thee: turn not from it to the right hand or to the left, that thou mayest prosper withersoever thou goest. This book of the law shall not depart out of thy mouth; but thou shalt meditate therein day and night, that thou mayest observe to do according to all that is written therein: for then thou shalt make thy way prosperous, and then thou shalt have good success. Have not I commanded thee? Be strong and of a good courage; be not afraid, neither be thou dismayed: for the Lord thy God is with thee whithersoever thou goest." (Joshua 1: 6-9)

"Not that I speak in respect of want: for I have learned, in whatsoever state I am, therewith to be content. I know both how to be abased, and I know how to abound: every where and in all things I am instructed both to be full and to be hungry, both to abound and to suffer need. I can do all things through Christ which strengtheneth me." (Philippians 4:11-13)

"A little that a righteous man hath is better than the riches of many wicked. For the arms of the wicked shall be broken: but the Lord upholdeth the righteous. The Lord knoweth the days of the upright: and their inheritance shall be for ever. They shall not be ashamed in the evil time: and in the days of famine they shall be satisfied. But the wicked shall perish, and the enemies of the Lord shall be as the fat of lambs: they shall consume; into smoke shall they consume away. The wicked borroweth, and payeth not again: but the righteous sheweth mercy, and giveth. For such as be blessed of him shall inherit the earth; and they that be cursed of him shall be cut off. The steps of a good man are ordered by the Lord: and he delighteth in his way. Though he fall, he shall not be utterly cast down: for the Lord upholdeth him with his hand. I have been young, and now am old; yet have I not seen the righteous forsaken, nor his seed begging bread." (Psalm 37: 16-25)

God provides for mankind a day that is to be regarded as a day of worship and rest.

"And God blessed the seventh day, and sanctified it: because that in it he had rested from all his work which God created and made." (Genesis 2:3)

"Remember the sabbath day, to keep it holy." (Exodus 20:8)

"And it came to pass, that he went through the corn fields on the sabbath day; and his disciples began, as they went, to pluck the ears of corn. And the Pharisees said unto him, Behold, why do they on the sabbath day that which is not lawful? And he said unto them, Have ye never read what David did, when he had need, and was an hungred, he, and they that were with him? How he went into the house of God in the days of Abiathar the high priest, and did eat the shewbread, which is not lawful to eat but for the priests, and gave also to them which were with him? And he said unto them, The sabbath was made for man, and not man for the sabbath: Therefore the Son of man is Lord also of the sabbath." (Mark 2:23-28)

"And you, being dead in your sins and the uncircumcision of your flesh, hath he quickened together with him, having forgiven you all trespasses; Blotting out the handwriting of ordinances that was against us, which was contrary to us, and took it out of the way, nailing it to his cross; And having spoiled principalities and powers, he made a shew of them openly, triumphing over them in it. Let no man therefore judge you in meat, or in drink, or in respect of an holyday, or of the new moon, or of the sabbath days: Which are a shadow of things to come; but the body is of Christ." (Colossians 2:13-17)

Our success as Christians is based upon blessings not vanity (hebel - emptiness, transitory, vain).

"Wealth gotten by vanity shall be diminished: but he that gathereth by labor shall increase." (Proverbs 13:11)

"Righteous art thou, O Lord, when I plead with thee: yet let me talk with thee of thy judgments: Wherefore doth the way of the wicked prosper? wherefore are all they happy that deal very treacherously?" (Jeremiah 12:1)

"He that loveth silver shall not be satisfied with silver; nor he that loveth abundance with increase: this is also vanity." (Ecclesiastes 5:10)

Our benefit, or if you will profit, is as a result of being made partakers of God's holiness. Do not forget that "the earth is the Lord's and the fullness thereof."

"For they verily for a few days chastened us after their own pleasure; but he for our profit, that we might be partakers of his holiness." (Hebrews 12:10)

"Behold that which I have seen: it is good and comely for one to eat and to drink, and to enjoy the good of all his labour that he taketh under the sun all the days of his life, which God giveth him: for it is his portion. Every man also to whom God hath given riches and wealth, and hath given him power to eat thereof, and to take his portion, and to rejoice in his labour; this is the gift of God. For he shall not much remember the days of his life; because God answereth him in the joy of his heart." (Ecclesiastes 5:18-20)

"The earth is the Lord's, and the fulness thereof; the world, and they that dwell therein. For he hath founded it upon the seas, and established it upon the floods. Who shall ascend into the hill of the Lord? or who shall stand in his holy place? He that hath clean hands, and a pure heart; who hath not lifted up his soul unto vanity, nor sworn deceitfully. He shall receive the blessing from the Lord, and righteousness from the God of his salvation." (Psalm 24:1-5)

24

OUR APPEARANCE AS CHRISTIANS

Does my appearance matter? The clothes I wear isn't what matters but rather it's my heart.

AS BELIEVERS, OUR bodies physically have undergone a spiritual conversion in becoming now a residence of the third person of the Trinity of God, the Holy Ghost/Holy Spirit.

> *"What? know ye not that your body is the temple of the Holy Ghost which is in you, which ye have of God, and ye are not your own?"* (1 Corinthians 6:19)

> *"Know ye not that ye are the temple of God, and that the Spirit of God dwelleth in you? If any man defile the temple of God, him shall God destroy; for the temple of God is holy, which temple ye are."* (1 Corinthians 3: 16-17)

> *"And what agreement hath the temple of God with idols? for ye are the temple of the living God; as God hath said, I will dwell in them, and walk in them; and I will be their God, and they shall be my people."* (2 Corinthians 6:16)

As we are indwelled by the Holy Spirit, we are to exhibit godly reverence and appropriateness (moderation (epiekes) – appropriate, gentle, patient).

> *"Let your moderation be known unto all men. The Lord is at hand."* (Philippians 4:5)

The believer is to walk in the world with a different mind set (circumspectly) from that of the unsaved.

> *"See then that ye walk circumspectly, not as fools, but as wise, Redeeming the time, because the days are evil. Wherefore be ye not unwise, but understanding what the will of the Lord is."* (Ephesians 5:15-17)

As believers, we are to abstain from even the look of evil. If we are indeed holy temples of God, how can we then decorate our bodies with ungodliness or excess of any kind even religious? Christians should inherently train up their boys and their girls in how to look in their physical appearance.

> *"Abstain from all appearance of evil."* (1 Thessalonians 5:22)

"Ye shall not round the corners of your heads, neither shalt thou mar the corners of thy beard. Ye shall not make any cuttings in your flesh for the dead, nor print any marks upon you: I am the Lord." (Leviticus 19:27-28)

Also, a godly cleanliness is to be exuded by Christians.

"Now the works of the flesh are manifest, which are these; Adultery, fornication, uncleanness, lasciviousness, Idolatry, witchcraft, hatred, variance, emulations, wrath, strife, seditions, heresies, Envyings, murders, drunkenness, revellings, and such like: of the which I tell you before, as I have also told you in time past, that they which do such things shall not inherit the kingdom of God." (Galatians 5:19-21)

"Wherefore lay apart all filthiness and superfluity of naughtiness, and receive with meekness the engrafted word, which is able to save your souls." (James 1:21)

Now, below are some very specific aspects of Christian appearance for men and women. The unisex look is not of God.

"The woman shall not wear that which pertaineth unto a man, neither shall a man put on a woman's garment: for all that do so are abomination unto the Lord thy God." (Deuteronomy 22:5)

Males

Preachers and godly men have no need of a head covering(s) in worship.

"Every man praying or prophesying, having his head covered, dishonoureth his head. But every woman that prayeth or prophesieth with her head uncovered dishonoureth her head: for that is even all one as if she were shaven. For if the woman be not covered, let her also be shorn: but if it be a shame for a woman to be shorn or shaven, let her be covered. For a man indeed ought not to cover his head, forasmuch as he is the image and glory of God: but the woman is the glory of the man." (1 Corinthians 11:4-7)

Homosexuality is condemned by the Bible (see Chapter 36, Homosexuality). Gay men are fond of broadcasting their lifestyle with earrings. Biblically the connotation of earrings is of high mindedness, the bondage of sin and/or a willingness to submit to physical slavery. Among heterosexual men, although there is not necessarily a ready distinction, the connotation is of male sexuality, prowess and/or a strange outlook today.

"And Aaron said unto them, Break off the golden earrings, which are in the ears of your wives, of your sons, and of your daughters, and bring them unto me. And all the people brake off the golden earrings which were in their ears, and brought them unto Aaron." (Exodus 32:2&3)

"And God said unto Jacob, Arise, go up to Bethel, and dwell there: and make there an altar unto God, that appeared unto thee when thou fleddest from the face of Esau thy brother. Then Jacob said unto his household, and to all that were with him, Put away the strange gods that are among you, and be clean, and change your garments: And let us arise, and go up to Bethel; and I will make there an altar unto God, who answered me in the day of my distress, and was with me in the way which I went. And they gave unto Jacob all the

strange gods which were in their hand, and all their earrings which were in their ears; and Jacob hid them under the oak which was by Shechem." (**Genesis 35:1-4**)

"And if the servant shall plainly say, I love my master, my wife, and my children; I will not go out free: Then his master shall bring him unto the judges; he shall also bring him to the door, or unto the door post; and his master shall bore his ear through with an aul; and he shall serve him for ever." (**Exodus 21:5&6**)

"And if thy brother, an Hebrew man, or an Hebrew woman, be sold unto thee, and serve thee six years; then in the seventh year thou shalt let him go free from thee. And when thou sendest him out free from thee, thou shalt not let him go away empty: Thou shalt furnish him liberally out of thy flock, and out of thy floor, and out of thy winepress: of that wherewith the Lord thy God hath blessed thee thou shalt give unto him. And thou shalt remember that thou wast a bondman in the land of Egypt, and the Lord thy God redeemed thee: therefore I command thee this thing to day. And it shall be, if he say unto thee, I will not go away from thee; because he loveth thee and thine house, because he is well with thee; Then thou shalt take an aul, and thrust it through his ear unto the door, and he shall be thy servant for ever. And also unto thy maidservant thou shalt do likewise." (**Deuteronomy 15:12-17**)

Long hair and braided hair is a feature prescribed biblically to women as a crowning glory to their physical bodies. I am aware also of the Nazarite; are you a Nazarite?

"Doth not even nature itself teach you, that, if a man have long hair, it is a shame unto him? But if a woman have long hair, it is a glory to her: for her hair is given her for a covering. But if any man seem to be contentious, we have no such custom, neither the churches of God. Now in this that I declare unto you I praise you not, that ye come together not for the better, but for the worse." (**1 Corinthians 11:14-17**)

And the Lord spake unto Moses, saying, Speak unto the children of Israel, and say unto them, When either man or woman shall separate themselves to vow a vow of a Nazarite, to separate themselves unto the Lord: He shall separate himself from wine and strong drink, and shall drink no vinegar of wine, or vinegar of strong drink, neither shall he drink any liquor of grapes, nor eat moist grapes, or dried. All the days of his separation shall he eat nothing that is made of the vine tree, from the kernels even to the husk. All the days of the vow of his separation there shall no rasor come upon his head: until the days be fulfilled, in the which he separateth himself unto the Lord, he shall be holy, and shall let the locks of the hair of his head grow." (**Numbers 6:1-5**)

Females

Hair styling, jewelry and beauty are biblical attributes ascribed to the woman even in terms of the physical attributes of her body.

"Behold, Rebekah is before thee, take her, and go, and let her be thy master's son's wife, as the Lord hath spoken. And it came to pass, that, when Abraham's servant heard their words, he worshipped the Lord, bowing himself to the earth. And the servant brought forth jewels of silver, and jewels of gold, and raiment, and gave them to Rebekah: he gave also to her brother and to her mother precious things." (**Genesis 24:51-53**)

"Thou hast also taken thy fair jewels of my gold and of my silver, which I had given thee, and madest to thyself images of men, and didst commit whoredom with them, And I will also give thee into their hand, and they shall throw down thine eminent place, and shall break down thy high places: they shall strip thee also of thy clothes, and shall take thy fair jewels, and leave thee naked and bare." (Ezekiel 16:17, 39)

"And I will visit upon her the days of Baalim, wherein she burned incense to them, and she decked herself with her earrings and her jewels, and she went after her lovers, and forgat me, saith the Lord." (Hosea 2:13)

"Thy cheeks are comely with rows of jewels, thy neck with chains of gold." (Song of Solomon 1:10)

"How beautiful are thy feet with shoes, O prince's daughter! The joints of thy thighs are like jewels, the work of the hands of a cunning workman. I am my beloved's and his desire is toward me." (Song of Solomon 7:1&10)

"I will greatly rejoice in the Lord, my soul shall be joyful in my God; for he hath clothed me with the garments of salvation, he hath covered me with the robe of righteousness, as a bridegroom decketh himself with ornaments, and as a bride adorneth herself with her jewels." (Isaiah 61:10)

Of no doubt, Christian women are to be in their appearance a sensual attraction to their husbands but not without a reverence to God. Christian women are to be enveloped in a modesty that would not reasonably be construed as sluttish or whorish. Also, Christian women should not be adorned in a high level (costly array) of finery; note our moderation as Christians to be appropriate not overbearing.

"Likewise, ye wives, be in subjection to your own husbands; that, if any obey not the word, they also may without the word be won by the conversation of the wives; While they behold your chaste conversation coupled with fear. Whose adorning let it not be that outward adorning of plaiting the hair, and of wearing of gold, or of putting on of apparel; But let it be the hidden man of the heart, in that which is notcorruptible, even the ornament of a meek and quiet spirit, which is in the sight of God of great price. For after this manner in the old time the holy women also, who trusted in God, adorned themselves, being in subjection unto their own husbands: Even as Sara obeyed Abraham, calling him Lord: whose daughters ye are, as long as ye do well, and are not afraid with any amazement." (1 Peter 3:1-6)

"In like manner also, that women adorn themselves in modest apparel, with shamefacedness and sobriety; not with broided hair, or gold, or pearls, or costly array; But (which becometh women professing godliness) with good works." (1 Timothy 2:9-10)

25

LEGAL MATTERS AMONG CHRISTIANS

The courts are there to solve our legal disputes. Why bother to go through all the strife concerning legalities in the fellowship; I'll see you in court?

"DO UNTO OTHERS as you would have them do unto you". The world's golden rule, as just stated, is so very similar to the biblical statement by Jesus with regard to love for our enemies. Mankind in general would be in a much better condition if people lived by, if nothing more than, the golden rule. Mankind is without excuse; endowed in creation itself, we know better.

> *"Therefore all things whatsoever ye would that men should do to you, do ye even so to them: for this is the law and the prophets."* (Matthew 7:12)

> *"For there is no respect of persons with God. For as many as have sinned without law shall also perish without law: and as many as have sinned in the law shall be judged by the law; (For not the hearers of the law are just before God, but the doers of the law shall be justified. For when the Gentiles, which have not the law, do by nature the things contained in the law, these, having not the law, are a law unto themselves: which shew the work of the law written in their hearts, their conscience also bearing witness, and their thoughts the mean while accusing or else excusing one another;) In the day when God shall judge the secrets of men by Jesus Christ according to my gospel."* (Romans 2:11-16)

Even more, among Christians, there should be a unity of the spirit which brings about a like-mindedness in Christ that should lead toward reconciliation among the brethren long before litigation.

> *"I therefore, the prisoner of the Lord, beseech you that ye walk worthy of the vocation wherewith ye are called, with all lowliness and meekness, with longsuffering, forbearing one another in love; endeavouring to keep the unity of the Spirit in the bond of peace. There is one body, and one Spirit, even as ye are called in one hope of your calling; one Lord, one faith, one baptism, one God and Father of all, who is above all, and through all, and in you all."* (Ephesians 4:1-6)

> *"If there be therefore any consolation in Christ, if any comfort of love, if any fellowship of the Spirit, if any bowels and mercies, fulfil ye my joy, that ye be likeminded, having the same love, being of one accord, of one mind. Let nothing be done through strife or vainglory;*

but in lowliness of mind let each esteem other better than themselves. Look not every man on his own things, but every man also on the things of others." (Philippians 2:1-4)

God has been clear from the Law of Moses that his people should consider and repent of their trespasses [paraptoma - a sideslip, unintentional error or willful offence, sin] against one another as they believe the good news (the gospel).

"And the Lord spake unto Moses, saying, Speak unto all the congregation of the children of Israel, and say unto them, Ye shall be holy: for I the Lord your God am holy. Ye shall not steal, neither deal falsely, neither lie one to another. And ye shall not swear by my name falsely, neither shalt thou profane the name of thy God: I am the Lord. Thou shalt not defraud thy neighbour, neither rob him: the wages of him that is hired shall not abide with thee all night until the morning. Thou shalt not curse the deaf, nor put a stumblingblock before the blind, but shalt fear thy God: I am the Lord. Ye shall do no unrighteousness in judgment: thou shalt not respect the person of the poor, nor honour the person of the mighty: but in righteousness shalt thou judge thy neighbour. Thou shalt not go up and down as a talebearer among thy people: neither shalt thou stand against the blood of thy neighbour: I am the Lord. Thou shalt not hate thy brother in thine heart: thou shalt in any wise rebuke thy neighbour, and not suffer sin upon him. Thou shalt not avenge, nor bear any grudge against the children of thy people, but thou shalt love thy neighbour as thyself: I am the Lord." (Leviticus 19:1, 2, 11-18)

"And when ye stand praying, forgive, if ye have ought against any: that your Father also which is in heaven may forgive you your trespasses." (Mark 11:25)

"And you hath he quickened, who were dead in trespasses and sins; wherein in time past ye walked according to the course of this world, according to the prince of the power of the air, the spirit that now worketh in the children of disobedience: among whom also we all had our conversation in times past in the lusts of our flesh, fulfilling the desires of the flesh and of the mind; and were by nature the children of wrath, even as others." (Ephesians 2:1-3)

"Now after that John was put in prison, Jesus came into Galilee, preaching the gospel of the kingdom of God, and saying, The time is fulfilled, and the kingdom of God is at hand: repent ye, and believe the gospel." (Mark 1:14-15)

Christians are admonished by God that whereas the saints shall judge the world with Christ in the Millennium, why should any of the just, having a matter against another, not go to settle it before the saints?

"Dare any of you, having a matter against another, go to law before the unjust, and not before the saints? Do ye not know that the saints shall judge the world? And if the world shall be judged by you, are ye unworthy to judge the smallest matters? Know ye not that we shall judge angels? How much more things that pertain to this life? If then ye have judgments of things pertaining to this life, set them to judge who are least esteemed in the church. I speak to your shame. Is it so, that there is not a wise man among you? No, not one that shall be able to judge between his brethren? But brother goeth to law with brother, and that before the unbelievers. Now therefore there is utterly a fault among you, because ye go to law one with another. Why do ye not rather take wrong? Why do ye not rather suffer yourselves to be defrauded? Nay, ye do wrong, and defraud, and that your brethren." (1 Corinthians 6:1-8)

"And I saw thrones, and they sat upon them, and judgment was given unto them: and I saw the souls of them that were beheaded for the witness of Jesus, and for the word of God, and which had not worshipped the beast, neither his image, neither had received his mark upon their foreheads, or in their hands; and they lived and reigned with Christ a thousand years. But the rest of the dead lived not again until the thousand years were finished. This is the first resurrection. Blessed and holy is he that hath part in the first resurrection: on such the second death hath no power, but they shall be priests of God and of Christ, and shall reign with him a thousand years." **(Revelation 20:4-6)**

Lawyers are not presented in a very satisfactory manner in the Bible; rather God's people are to consider God's commandments in all of their affairs.

"Then answered one of the lawyers, and said unto him, Master, thus saying thou reproachest us also. And he said, Woe unto you also, ye lawyers! For ye lade men with burdens grievous to be borne, and ye yourselves touch not the burdens with one of your fingers. Woe unto you! for ye build the sepulchres of the prophets, and your fathers killed them. Truly ye bear witness that ye allow the deeds of your fathers: for they indeed killed them, and ye build their sepulchres. Therefore also said the wisdom of God, I will send them prophets and apostles, and some of them they shall slay and persecute: that the blood of all the prophets, which was shed from the foundation of the world, may be required of this generation; from the blood of Abel unto the blood of Zacharias, which perished between the altar and the temple: verily I say unto you, It shall be required of this generation. Woe unto you, lawyers! For ye have taken away the key of knowledge: ye entered not in yourselves, and them that were entering in ye hindered." **(Luke 11:45-52)**

"And the Lord spake unto Moses, saying, Speak unto the children of Israel, and say unto them, I am the Lord your God. After the doings of the land of Egypt, wherein ye dwelt, shall ye not do: and after the doings of the land of Canaan, whither I bring you, shall ye not do: neither shall ye walk in their ordinances. Ye shall do my judgments, and keep mine ordinances, to walk therein: I am the Lord your God. Ye shall therefore keep my statutes, and my judgments: which if a man do, he shall live in them: I am the Lord." **(Leviticus 18:1-5)**

26

SICKNESS, ILLNESS AND BIRTH DEFECTS

Should a believer rely solely upon God for the healing of aliments without consulting a physician and/or taking any medication? What has God said or promised with regard to illness and treatment?

WE ARE BORN as God has so desired.

> *"And Moses said unto the Lord, O my Lord, I am not eloquent, neither heretofore, nor since thou hast spoken unto thy servant: but I am slow of speech, and of a slow tongue. And the Lord said unto him, Who hath made man's mouth? or who maketh the dumb, or deaf, or the seeing, or the blind? have not I the Lord?"* **(Exodus 4:10-11)**

> *"For thou hast possessed my reins: thou hast covered me in my mother's womb. I will praise thee; for I am fearfully and wonderfully made: marvellous are thy works; and that my soul knoweth right well. My substance was not hid from thee, when I was made in secret, and curiously wrought in the lowest parts of the earth. Thine eyes did see my substance, yet being unperfect; and in thy book all my members were written, which in continuance were fashioned, when as yet there was none of them. How precious also are thy thoughts unto me, O God! how great is the sum of them! If I should count them, they are more in number than the sand: when I awake, I am still with thee."* **(Psalm 139:13-18)**

> *"Understand, ye brutish among the people: and ye fools, when will ye be wise? He that planted the ear, shall he not hear? he that formed the eye, shall he not see? He that chastiseth the heathen, shall not he correct? he that teacheth man knowledge, shall not he know? The Lord knoweth the thoughts of man, that they are vanity."* **(Psalm 94:8-11)**

Everyone is given at least one spiritual gift in creation for the edification of the body of Christ. Physicians would fall into the category of healers and there are some without medical training who can heal through their touch and/or intercessory prayer.

> *"Now there are diversities of gifts, but the same Spirit. And there are differences of administrations, but the same Lord. And there are diversities of operations, but it is the same God which worketh all in all. But the manifestation of the Spirit is given to every man to profit withal. For to one is given by the Spirit the word of wisdom; to another the word of knowledge by the same Spirit; To another faith by the same Spirit; to another the gifts of healing by the same Spirit; To another the working of miracles; to another prophecy; to another discerning of spirits; to another divers kinds of tongues; to another the interpretation*

of tongues: but all these worketh that one and the selfsame Spirit, dividing to every man severally as he will. For as the body is one, and hath many members, and all the members of that one body, being many, are one body: so also is Christ." (**1 Corinthians 12:4-12**)

"And it came to pass, as Jesus sat at meat in the house, behold, many publicans and sinners came and sat down with him and his disciples. And when the Pharisees saw it, they said unto his disciples, Why eateth your Master with publicans and sinners? But when Jesus heard that, he said unto them, They that be whole need not a physician, but they that are sick. But go ye and learn what that meaneth, I will have mercy, and not sacrifice: for I am not come to call the righteous, but sinners to repentance." (**Matthew 9:10-13**)

"Luke, the beloved physician, and Demas, greet you." (**Colossians 4: 14**)

"And Joseph fell upon his father's face, and wept upon him, and kissed him. And Joseph commanded his servants the physicians to embalm his father: and the physicians embalmed Israel." (**Genesis 50:1-2**)

"Is any among you afflicted? let him pray. Is any merry? let him sing psalms. Is any sick among you? let him call for the elders of the church; and let them pray over him, anointing him with oil in the name of the Lord: and the prayer of faith shall save the sick, and the Lord shall raise him up; and if he have committed sins, they shall be forgiven him. Confess your faults one to another, and pray one for another, that ye may be healed. The effectual fervent prayer of a righteous man availeth much." (**James 5:13-16**)

God desires to bless those that would be a righteous people unto himself, with fruitfulness and good health. As a part of being properly trained and submitting as a child, God wants to give the reward of a long life to every individual.

"Thou shalt therefore keep the commandments, and the statutes, and the judgments, which I command thee this day, to do them. Wherefore it shall come to pass, if ye hearken to these judgments, and keep, and do them, that the Lord thy God shall keep unto thee the covenant and the mercy which he sware unto thy fathers: and he will love thee, and bless thee, and multiply thee: he will also bless the fruit of thy womb, and the fruit of thy land, thy corn, and thy wine, and thine oil, the increase of thy kine, and the flocks of thy sheep, in the land which he sware unto thy fathers to give thee. Thou shalt be blessed above all people: there shall not be male or female barren among you, or among your cattle. And the Lord will take away from thee all sickness, and will put none of the evil diseases of Egypt, which thou knowest, upon thee; but will lay them upon all them that hate thee. And thou shalt consume all the people which the Lord thy God shall deliver thee; thine eye shall have no pity upon them: neither shalt thou serve their gods; for that will be a snare unto thee. If thou shalt say in thine heart, These nations are more than I; how can I dispossess them?" (**Deuteronomy 7:11-17**)

"Honour thy father and thy mother: that thy days may be long upon the land which the Lord thy God giveth thee." (**Exodus 20:12**)

"Children, obey your parents in the Lord: for this is right. Honour thy father and mother; (which is the first commandment with promise;) That it may be well with thee, and thou mayest live long on the earth." (**Ephesians 6:1-3**)

God has never had such an obedient people or nation as to incline him to completely

wipe out all sickness and to make them completely fruitful.

"And God saw that the wickedness of man was great in the earth, and that every imagination of the thoughts of his heart was only evil continually. And it repented the Lord that he had made man on the earth, and it grieved him at his heart. And the Lord said, I will destroy man whom I have created from the face of the earth; both man, and beast, and the creeping thing, and the fowls of the air; for it repenteth me that I have made them. But Noah found grace in the eyes of the Lord." (**Genesis 6:5-8**)

"And Moses and Aaron said unto all the children of Israel, At even, then ye shall know that the Lord hath brought you out from the land of Egypt: and in the morning, then ye shall see the glory of the Lord; for that he heareth your murmurings against the Lord: and what are we, that ye murmur against us? And Moses said, This shall be, when the Lord shall give you in the evening flesh to eat, and in the morning bread to the full; for that the Lord heareth your murmurings which ye murmur against him: and what are we? your murmurings are not against us, but against the Lord. And Moses spake unto Aaron, Say unto all the congregation of the children of Israel, Come near before the Lord: for he hath heard your murmurings. And it came to pass, as Aaron spake unto the whole congregation of the children of Israel, that they looked toward the wilderness, and, behold, the glory of the Lord appeared in the cloud. And the Lord spake unto Moses, saying, I have heard the murmurings of the children of Israel: speak unto them, saying, At even ye shall eat flesh, and in the morning ye shall be filled with bread; and ye shall know that I am the Lord your God." (**Exodus 16:6-12**)

"And I, brethren, could not speak unto you as unto spiritual, but as unto carnal, even as unto babes in Christ. I have fed you with milk, and not with meat: for hitherto ye were not able to bear it, neither yet now are ye able. For ye are yet carnal: for whereas there is among you envying, and strife, and divisions, are ye not carnal, and walk as men?" (**1 Corinthians 3:1-3**)

"Beloved, when I gave all diligence to write unto you of the common salvation, it was needful for me to write unto you, and exhort you that ye should earnestly contend for the faith which was once delivered unto the saints. For there are certain men crept in unawares, who were before of old ordained to this condemnation, ungodly men, turning the grace of our God into lasciviousness, and denying the only Lord God, and our Lord Jesus Christ. I will therefore put you in remembrance, though ye once knew this, how that the Lord, having saved the people out of the land of Egypt, afterward destroyed them that believed not. And the angels which kept not their first estate, but left their own habitation, he hath reserved in everlasting chains under darkness unto the judgment of the great day. Even as Sodom and Gomorrha, and the cities about them in like manner, giving themselves over to fornication, and going after strange flesh, are set forth for an example, suffering the vengeance of eternal fire. Likewise also these filthy dreamers defile the flesh, despise dominion, and speak evil of dignities. Yet Michael the archangel, when contending with the devil he disputed about the body of Moses, durst not bring against him a railing accusation, but said, The Lord rebuke thee. But these speak evil of those things which they know not: but what they know naturally, as brute beasts, in those things they corrupt themselves. Woe unto them! for they have gone in the way of Cain, and ran greedily after the error of Balaam for reward, and perished in the gainsaying of Core. These are spots in your feasts of charity, when they feast with you, feeding themselves without fear: clouds they are with-

out water, carried about of winds; trees whose fruit withereth, without fruit, twice dead, plucked up by the roots; raging waves of the sea, foaming out their own shame; wandering stars, to whom is reserved the blackness of darkness for ever. And Enoch also, the seventh from Adam, prophesied of these, saying, Behold, the Lord cometh with ten thousands of his saints, To execute judgment upon all, and to convince all that are ungodly among them of all their ungodly deeds which they have ungodly committed, and of all their hard speeches which ungodly sinners have spoken against him. These are murmurers, complainers, walking after their own lusts; and their mouth speaketh great swelling words, having men's persons in admiration because of advantage. But, beloved, remember ye the words which were spoken before of the apostles of our Lord Jesus Christ; How that they told you there should be mockers in the last time, who should walk after their own ungodly lusts. These be they who separate themselves, sensual, having not the Spirit. But ye, beloved, building up yourselves on your most holy faith, praying in the Holy Ghost, Keep yourselves in the love of God, looking for the mercy of our Lord Jesus Christ unto eternal life." (Jude 3-21)

"For, brethren, ye have been called unto liberty; only use not liberty for an occasion to the flesh, but by love serve one another. For all the law is fulfilled in one word, even in this; Thou shalt love thy neighbour as thyself. But if ye bite and devour one another, take heed that ye be not consumed one of another. This I say then, Walk in the Spirit, and ye shall not fulfil the lust of the flesh. For the flesh lusteth against the Spirit, and the Spirit against the flesh: and these are contrary the one to the other: so that ye cannot do the things that ye would. But if ye be led of the Spirit, ye are not under the law." (Galatians 5:13-18)

There does comes a time to die in this flesh as determined by Almighty God.

"To every thing there is a season, and a time to every purpose under the heaven: A time to be born, and a time to die; a time to plant, and a time to pluck up that which is planted;" (Ecclesiastes 3:1&2)

"And as it is appointed unto men once to die, but after this the judgment: So Christ was once offered to bear the sins of many; and unto them that look for him shall he appear the second time without sin unto salvation." (Hebrews 9:27)

"In those days was Hezekiah sick unto death. And the prophet Isaiah the son of Amoz came to him, and said unto him, Thus saith the Lord, Set thine house in order; for thou shalt die, and not live. Then he turned his face to the wall, and prayed unto the Lord, saying, I beseech thee, O Lord, remember now how I have walked before thee in truth and with a perfect heart, and have done that which is good in thy sight. And Hezekiah wept sore. And it came to pass, afore Isaiah was gone out into the middle court, that the word of the Lord came to him, saying, Turn again, and tell Hezekiah the captain of my people, Thus saith the Lord, the God of David thy father, I have heard thy prayer, I have seen thy tears: behold, I will heal thee: on the third day thou shalt go up unto the house of the Lord. And I will add unto thy days fifteen years; and I will deliver thee and this city out of the hand of the king of Assyria; and I will defend this city for mine own sake, and for my servant David's sake. And Isaiah said, Take a lump of figs. And they took and laid it on the boil, and he recovered." (2 Kings 20:1-7)

We are called into righteousness and holiness and God is able to provide our need.

"This I say therefore, and testify in the Lord, that ye henceforth walk not as other Gentiles walk, in the vanity of their mind, Having the understanding darkened, being alienated from the life of God through the ignorance that is in them, because of the blindness of their heart: Who being past feeling have given themselves over unto lasciviousness, to work all uncleanness with greediness. But ye have not so learned Christ; If so be that ye have heard him, and have been taught by him, as the truth is in Jesus: That ye put off concerning the former conversation the old man, which is corrupt according to the deceitful lusts; And be renewed in the spirit of your mind; And that ye put on the new man, which after God is created in righteousness and true holiness." **(Ephesians 4:17-24)**

"But my God shall supply all your need according to his riches in glory by Christ Jesus. Now unto God and our Father be glory for ever and ever. Amen." **(Philippians 4:19-20)**

There is sin unto death or death because of sin.

"For as often as ye eat this bread, and drink this cup, ye do shew the Lord's death till he come. Wherefore whosoever shall eat this bread, and drink this cup of the Lord, unworthily, shall be guilty of the body and blood of the Lord. But let a man examine himself, and so let him eat of that bread, and drink of that cup. For he that eateth and drinketh unworthily, eateth and drinketh damnation to himself, not discerning the Lord's body. For this cause many are weak and sickly among you, and many sleep. For if we would judge ourselves, we should not be judged." **(1 Corinthians 11:26-31)**

God wants a healthy and fruitful remnant.

"I am the true vine, and my Father is the husbandman. Every branch in me that beareth not fruit he taketh away: and every branch that beareth fruit, he purgeth it, that it may bring forth more fruit. Now ye are clean through the word which I have spoken unto you. Abide in me, and I in you. As the branch cannot bear fruit of itself, except it abide in the vine; no more can ye, except ye abide in me. I am the vine, ye are the branches: He that abideth in me, and I in him, the same bringeth forth much fruit: for without me ye can do nothing. If a man abide not in me, he is cast forth as a branch, and is withered; and men gather them, and cast them into the fire, and they are burned. If ye abide in me, and my words abide in you, ye shall ask what ye will, and it shall be done unto you. Herein is my Father glorified, that ye bear much fruit; so shall ye be my disciples." **(John 15:1-8)**

"See now that I, even I, am he, and there is no god with me: I kill, and I make alive; I wound, and I heal: neither is there any that can deliver out of my hand. For I lift up my hand to heaven, and say, I live for ever." **(Deuteronomy 32: 39-40)**

"Only be thou strong and very courageous, that thou mayest observe to do according to all the law, which Moses my servant commanded thee: turn not from it to the right hand or to the left, that thou mayest prosper whithersoever thou goest. This book of the law shall not depart out of thy mouth; but thou shalt meditate therein day and night, that thou mayest observe to do according to all that is written therein: for then thou shalt make thy way prosperous, and then thou shalt have good success." **(Joshua 1:7&8)**

God is love

"And we have known and believed the love that God hath to us. God is love; and he that dwelleth in love dwelleth in God, and God in him." (1 John 4:16)

"For I know the thoughts that I think toward you, saith the Lord, thoughts of peace, and not of evil, to give you an expected end. Then shall ye call upon me, and ye shall go and pray unto me, and I will hearken unto you. And ye shall seek me, and find me, when ye shall search for me with all your heart." (Jeremiah 29:11-13)

Almighty God is a God of vengeance as well. He will visit (punish) the sins of the parents upon their children and subsequent generations. This punishment can be eliminated by turning to God.

"And God spake all these words, saying, I am the Lord thy God, which have brought thee out of the land of Egypt, out of the house of bondage. Thou shalt have no other gods before me. Thou shalt not make unto thee any graven image, or any likeness of any thing that is in heaven above, or that is in the earth beneath, or that is in the water under the earth: thou shalt not bow down thyself to them, nor serve them: for I the Lord thy God am a jealous God, visiting the iniquity of the fathers upon the children unto the third and fourth generation of them that hate me; and shewing mercy unto thousands of them that love me, and keep my commandments." (Exodus 20:1-6)

"And fear not them which kill the body, but are not able to kill the soul: but rather fear him which is able to destroy both soul and body in hell." (Matthew 10:28)

God is not mocked. We need to examine our desire in prayer and examine our faithfulness. Sickness and illness can be our chastisement and regardless God can be glorified by the outcome.

"Be not deceived; God is not mocked: for whatsoever a man soweth, that shall he also reap. For he that soweth to his flesh shall of the flesh reap corruption; but he that soweth to the Spirit shall of the Spirit reap life everlasting." (Galatians 6: 7-8)

"Ye lust, and have not: ye kill, and desire to have, and cannot obtain: ye fight and war, yet ye have not, because ye ask not. Ye ask, and receive not, because ye ask amiss, that ye may consume it upon your lusts." (James 4:2-3)

"My son, despise not the chastening of the Lord; neither be weary of his correction: For whom the Lord loveth he correcteth; even as a father the son in whom he delighteth." (Proverbs 3:11&12)

"And ye have forgotten the exhortation which speaketh unto you as unto children, My son, despise not thou the chastening of the Lord, nor faint when thou art rebuked of him: For whom the Lord loveth he chasteneth, and scourgeth every son whom he receiveth. If ye endure chastening, God dealeth with you as with sons; for what son is he whom the father chasteneth not? But if ye be without chastisement, whereof all are partakers, then are ye bastards, and not sons. Furthermore we have had fathers of our flesh which corrected us, and we gave them reverence: shall we not much rather be in subjection unto the Father of spirits, and live? For they verily for a few days chastened us after their own pleasure; but he for our profit, that we might be partakers of his holiness. Now no

chastening for the present seemeth to be joyous, but grievous: nevertheless afterward it yieldeth the peaceable fruit of righteousness unto them which are exercised thereby. Wherefore lift up the hands which hang down, and the feeble knees; And make straight paths for your feet, lest that which is lame be turned out of the way; but let it rather be healed." (**Hebrews 12:5-13**)

"And as Jesus passed by, he saw a man which was blind from his birth. And his disciples asked him, saying, Master, who did sin, this man, or his parents, that he was born blind? Jesus answered, Neither hath this man sinned, nor his parents: but that the works of God should be made manifest in him. I must work the works of him that sent me, while it is day: the night cometh, when no man can work. As long as I am in the world, I am the light of the world. When he had thus spoken, he spat on the ground, and made clay of the spittle, and he anointed the eyes of the blind man with the clay, And said unto him, Go, wash in the pool of Siloam, (which is by interpretation, Sent.) He went his way therefore, and washed, and came seeing. The neighbours therefore, and they which before had seen him that he was blind, said, Is not this he that sat and begged? Some said, This is he: others said, He is like him: but he said, I am he. Therefore said they unto him, How were thine eyes opened? He answered and said, A man that is called Jesus made clay, and anointed mine eyes, and said unto me, Go to the pool of Siloam, and wash: and I went and washed, and I received sight." (**John 9:1-11**)

"For ye see your calling, brethren, how that not many wise men after the flesh, not many mighty, not many noble, are called: but God hath chosen the foolish things of the world to confound the wise; and God hath chosen the weak things of the world to confound the things which are mighty; and base things of the world, and things which are despised, hath God chosen, yea, and things which are not, to bring to nought things that are: that no flesh should glory in his presence. But of him are ye in Christ Jesus, who of God is made unto us wisdom, and righteousness, and sanctification, and redemption: that, according as it is written, He that glorieth, let him glory in the Lord." (**1 Corinthians 1: 26-31**)

Also, we are able to walk in power and favor in our households; God answers the prayers of the righteous and will not forsake them.

"Simon Peter, a servant and an apostle of Jesus Christ, to them that have obtained like precious faith with us through the righteousness of God and our Saviour Jesus Christ: Grace and peace be multiplied unto you through the knowledge of God, and of Jesus our Lord, According as his divine power hath given unto us all things that pertain unto life and godliness, through the knowledge of him that hath called us to glory and virtue: Whereby are given unto us exceeding great and precious promises: that by these ye might be partakers of the divine nature, having escaped the corruption that is in the world through lust." (**2 Peter 1:1-4**)

"Now therefore fear the Lord, and serve him in sincerity and in truth: and put away the gods which your fathers served on the other side of the flood, and in Egypt; and serve ye the Lord. And if it seem evil unto you to serve the Lord, choose you this day whom ye will serve; whether the gods which your fathers served that were on the other side of the flood, or the gods of the Amorites, in whose land ye dwell: but as for me and my house, we will serve the Lord." (**Joshua 24:14-15**)

"And Jesus entered and passed through Jericho. And, behold, there was a man named Zacchaeus, which was the chief among the publicans, and he was rich. And he sought to see Jesus who he was; and could not for the press, because he was little of stature. And he ran before, and climbed up into a sycomore tree to see him: for he was to pass that way. And when Jesus came to the place, he looked up, and saw him, and said unto him, Zacchaeus, make haste, and come down; for to day I must abide at thy house. And he made haste, and came down, and received him joyfully. And when they saw it, they all murmured, saying, That he was gone to be guest with a man that is a sinner. And Zacchaeus stood, and said unto the Lord; Behold, Lord, the half of my goods I give to the poor; and if I have taken any thing from any man by false accusation, I restore him fourfold. And Jesus said unto him, This day is salvation come to this house, forsomuch as he also is a son of Abraham. For the Son of man is come to seek and to save that which was lost." (Luke 19:1-10)

"The steps of a good man are ordered by the Lord: and he delighteth in his way. Though he fall, he shall not be utterly cast down: for the Lord upholdeth him with his hand. I have been young, and now am old; yet have I not seen the righteous forsaken, nor his seed begging bread." (Psalms 37: 23-25)

"Beloved, I wish above all things that thou mayest prosper and be in health, even as thy soul prospereth. For I rejoiced greatly, when the brethren came and testified of the truth that is in thee, even as thou walkest in the truth. I have no greater joy than to hear that my children walk in truth." (3 John 2-4)

Now, if you hear of a healer in your area that is believed to be real, not shown to be suspect and most certainly if your physicians have offered no cure for your affliction, do not be so skeptical as to not believe in Almighty God for a miracle. Your healing is as a result of your faith in God and as he so wills.

"And these signs shall follow them that believe; In my name shall they cast out devils; they shall speak with new tongues; They shall take up serpents; and if they drink any deadly thing, it shall not hurt them; they shall lay hands on the sick, and they shall recover." (Mark 16:17&18)

"And God wrought special miracles by the hands of Paul: So that from his body were brought unto the sick handkerchiefs or aprons, and the diseases departed from them, and the evil spirits went out of them." (Acts 19:11&12)

"And he went out from thence, and came into his own country; and his disciples follow him. And when the sabbath day was come, he began to teach in the synagogue: and many hearing him were astonished, saying, From whence hath this man these things? and what wisdom is this which is given unto him, that even such mighty works are wrought by his hands? Is not this the carpenter, the son of Mary, the brother of James, and Joses, and of Juda, and Simon? and are not his sisters here with us? And they were offended at him. But Jesus said unto them, A prophet is not without honour, but in his own country, and among his own kin, and in his own house. And he could there do no mighty work, save that he laid his hands upon a few sick folk, and healed them. And he marvelled because of their unbelief. And he went round about the villages, teaching." (Mark 6:1-6)

"And when they had passed over, they came into the land of Gennesaret, and drew to the shore. And when they were come out of the ship, straightway they knew him, And ran through that whole region round about, and began to carry about in beds those that were sick, where they heard he was. And whithersoever he entered, into villages, or cities, or country, they laid the sick in the streets, and besought him that they might touch if it were but the border of his garment: and as many as touched him were made whole." (**Mark 6:53-56**)

27

CHRISTIAN SEXUAL MORALITY

What does the Bible consider to be sexual immorality in light of today's openness towards sex and the instability of marital relationships?

TWO THINGS CONCERNING this matter the Bible makes very clear, (1) sexual relations outside of marriage is fornification (porneia from proneuo - harlotry, idolatry, act like a harlot , indulge in unlawful lust) and (2) sex outside of the marital relationship is adultery (moichos (male), moichalis (female) - sexual infidelity of husband or wife, apostate). Both are sinful and can lead to condemnation.

> *"For this is the will of God, even your sanctification, that ye should abstain from fornication: That every one of you should know how to possess his vessel in sanctification and honour; Not in the lust of concupiscence, even as the Gentiles which know not God: That no man go beyond and defraud his brother in any matter: because that the Lord is the avenger of all such, as we also have forewarned you and testified. For God hath not called us unto uncleanness, but unto holiness."* (1 Thessalonians 4:3-7)

> *"Thou knowest the commandments, Do not commit adultery, Do not kill, Do not steal, Do not bear false witness, Defraud not, Honour thy father and mother."* (Mark 10:19)

> *"And he said, That which cometh out of the man, that defileth the man. For from within, out of the heart of men, proceed evil thoughts, adulteries, fornications, murders, Thefts, covetousness, wickedness, deceit, lasciviousness, an evil eye, blasphemy, pride, foolishness: All these evil things come from within, and defile the man."* (Mark 7:20-23)

> *"Now the works of the flesh are manifest, which are these; Adultery, fornication, uncleanness, lasciviousness, Idolatry, witchcraft, hatred, variance, emulations, wrath, strife, seditions, heresies, Envyings, murders, drunkenness, revellings, and such like: of the which I tell you before, as I have also told you in time past, that they which do such things shall not inherit the kingdom of God."* (Galatians 5:19-21)

> *But fornication, and all uncleanness, or covetousness, let it not be once named among you, as becometh saints; Neither filthiness, nor foolish talking, nor jesting, which are not convenient: but rather giving of thanks. For this ye know, that no whoremonger, nor unclean person, nor covetous man, who is an idolater, hath any inheritance in the kingdom of Christ and of God. Let no man deceive you with vain words: for because of these things*

cometh the wrath of God upon the children of disobedience. Be not ye therefore partakers with them." (Ephesians 5:3-7)

"Know ye not that the unrighteous shall not inherit the kingdom of God? Be not deceived: neither fornicators, nor idolaters, nor adulterers, nor effeminate, nor abusers of themselves with mankind, Nor thieves, nor covetous, nor drunkards, nor revilers, nor extortioners, shall inherit the kingdom of God. And such were some of you: but ye are washed, but ye are sanctified, but ye are justified in the name of the Lord Jesus, and by the Spirit of our God." (1 Corinthians 6:9-11)

Premeditated sexual conquest is condemned by the Bible as if the sexual mischief has already occurred.

"Ye have heard that it was said by them of old time, Thou shalt not commit adultery: But I say unto you, That whosoever looketh on a woman to lust after her hath committed adultery with her already in his heart." (Matthew 5:27&28)

The martial bed (koite- couch, cohabitation chambering) is reserved for lawful lust. The husband is to gratify the wife and the wife is to gratify the husband. The physical body of each is to belong lovingly to the other and without causing injury.

"Marriage is honourable in all, and the bed undefiled: but whoremongers and adulterers God will judge." (Hebrews 13:4)

"Let the husband render unto the wife due benevolence: and likewise also the wife unto the husband. The wife hath not power of her own body, but the husband: and likewise also the husband hath not power of his own body, but the wife. Defraud ye not one the other, except it be with consent for a time, that ye may give yourselves to fasting and prayer; and come together again, that Satan tempt you not for your incontinency. But I speak this by permission, and not of commandment." (1 Corinthians 7:3-6)

"And I thank Christ Jesus our Lord, who hath enabled me, for that he counted me faithful, putting me into the ministry; Who was before a blasphemer, and a persecutor, and injurious: but I obtained mercy, because I did it ignorantly in unbelief." (1 Timothy 1:12-13)

Whoremongers (pornos: male prostitutes, libertines, fornicators) are to be left out of the kingdom of heaven.

"Know ye not that your bodies are the members of Christ? shall I then take the members of Christ, and make them the members of an harlot? God forbid. What? know ye not that he which is joined to an harlot is one body? for two, saith he, shall be one flesh. But he that is joined unto the Lord is one spirit. Flee fornication. Every sin that a man doeth is without the body; but he that committeth fornication sinneth against his own body. What? know ye not that your body is the temple of the Holy Ghost which is in you, which ye have of God, and ye are not your own? For ye are bought with a price: therefore glorify God in your body, and in your spirit, which are God's." (Corinthians 6:15-20)

"Blessed are they that do his commandments, that they may have right to the tree of life, and may enter in through the gates into the city. For without are dogs, and sorcerers, and

whoremongers, and murderers, and idolaters, and whosoever loveth and maketh a lie." (Revelation 22:14&15)

Men are not to lie with men as they would with women (See Chapter 36, Homosexuality). Men are not to prey sexually upon women.

"Thou shalt not lie with mankind, as with womankind: it is abomination." (Leviticus 18:22)

"For the wrath of God is revealed from heaven against all ungodliness and unrighteousness of men, who hold the truth in unrighteousness; Because that which may be known of God is manifest in them; for God hath shewed it unto them. For the invisible things of him from the creation of the world are clearly seen, being understood by the things that are made, even his eternal power and Godhead; so that they are without excuse: Because that, when they knew God, they glorified him not as God, neither were thankful; but became vain in their imaginations, and their foolish heart was darkened. Professing themselves to be wise, they became fools, And changed the glory of the uncorruptible God into an image made like to corruptible man, and to birds, and fourfooted beasts, and creeping things. Wherefore God also gave them up to uncleanness through the lusts of their own hearts, to dishonour their own bodies between themselves: Who changed the truth of God into a lie, and worshipped and served the creature more than the Creator, who is blessed for ever. Amen. For this cause God gave them up unto vile affections: for even their women did change the natural use into that which is against nature: And likewise also the men, leaving the natural use of the woman, burned in their lust one toward another; men with men working that which is unseemly, and receiving in themselves that recompence of their error which was meet. And even as they did not like to retain God in their knowledge, God gave them over to a reprobate mind, to do those things which are not convenient; Being filled with all unrighteousness, fornication, wickedness, covetousness, maliciousness; full of envy, murder, debate, deceit, malignity; whisperers, Backbiters, haters of God, despiteful, proud, boasters, inventors of evil things, disobedient to parents, Without understanding, covenantbreakers, without natural affection, implacable, unmerciful: Who knowing the judgment of God, that they which commit such things are worthy of death, not only do the same, but have pleasure in them that do them." (Romans 1:18-32)

"For men shall be lovers of their own selves, covetous, boasters, proud, blasphemers, disobedient to parents, unthankful, unholy, Without natural affection, trucebreakers, false accusers, incontinent, fierce, despisers of those that are good, Traitors, heady, highminded, lovers of pleasures more than lovers of God; Having a form of godliness, but denying the power thereof: from such turn away. For of this sort are they which creep into houses, and lead captive silly women laden with sins, led away with divers lusts, Ever learning, and never able to come to the knowledge of the truth." (2 Timothy 3:2-7)

Sexual relations with animals are immoral.

"Neither shalt thou lie with any beast to defile thyself therewith: neither shall any woman stand before a beast to lie down thereto: it is confusion." (Leviticus 18:23)

Child molesters are in tremendous jeopardy.

> *"But whoso shall offend one of these little ones which believe in me, it were better for him that a millstone were hanged about his neck, and that he were drowned in the depth of the sea."* (Matthew 18:6)

The 18th Chapter of the Book of Leviticus establishes a sexual morality that is applicable to Christians.

28

SIN BY BIBLICAL DEFINITION

I want to live an acceptable life before God. How can I do that with so many things being called sin?
What is sin according to the Bible?

THE BIBLE DEFINES whatsoever that is not of faith (Pitis - Religious truth especially reliance upon Christ for salvation, assurance and belief in Christ) as sin. Belief in Jesus Christ allows for the remission of sin by his blood that was shed on the cross.

> *"Hast thou faith? have it to thyself before God. Happy is he that condemneth not himself in that thing which he alloweth. And he that doubteth is damned if he eat, because he eateth not of faith: for whatsoever is not of faith is sin."* (Romans 14: 22-23)

> *"Therefore being justified by faith, we have peace with God through our Lord Jesus Christ: By whom also we have access by faith into this grace wherein we stand, and rejoice in hope of the glory of God. And not only so, but we glory in tribulations also: knowing that tribulation worketh patience; And patience, experience; and experience, hope: And hope maketh not ashamed; because the love of God is shed abroad in our hearts by the Holy Ghost which is given unto us. For when we were yet without strength, in due time Christ died for the ungodly. For scarcely for a righteous man will one die: yet peradventure for a good man some would even dare to die. But God commendeth his love toward us, in that, while we were yet sinners, Christ died for us. Much more then, being now justified by his blood, we shall be saved from wrath through him."* (Romans 5:1-9)

> *"But Christ being come an high priest of good things to come, by a greater and more perfect tabernacle, not made with hands, that is to say, not of this building; Neither by the blood of goats and calves, but by his own blood he entered in once into the holy place, having obtained eternal redemption for us. For if the blood of bulls and of goats, and the ashes of an heifer sprinkling the unclean, sanctifieth to the purifying of the flesh: How much more shall the blood of Christ, who through the eternal Spirit offered himself without spot to God, purge your conscience from dead works to serve the living God? And for this cause he is the mediator of the new testament, that by means of death, for the redemption of the transgressions that were under the first testament, they which are called might receive the promise of eternal inheritance. For where a testament is, there must also of necessity be the death of the testator. For a testament is of force after men are dead: otherwise it is of no strength at all while the testator liveth. Whereupon neither the first testament was dedicated without blood. For when Moses had spoken every precept to all the people ac-*

cording to the law, he took the blood of calves and of goats, with water, and scarlet wool, and hyssop, and sprinkled both the book, and all the people, Saying, This is the blood of the testament which God hath enjoined unto you. Moreover he sprinkled with blood both the tabernacle, and all the vessels of the ministry. And almost all things are by the law purged with blood; and without shedding of blood is no remission. It was therefore necessary that the patterns of things in the heavens should be purified with these; but the heavenly things themselves with better sacrifices than these. For Christ is not entered into the holy places made with hands, which are the figures of the true; but into heaven itself, now to appear in the presence of God for us: Nor yet that he should offer himself often, as the high priest entereth into the holy place every year with blood of others; For then must he often have suffered since the foundation of the world: but now once in the end of the world hath he appeared to put away sin by the sacrifice of himself." (Hebrews 9:11-26)

"He that believeth on him is not condemned: but he that believeth not is condemned already, because he hath not believed in the name of the only begotten Son of God." (John 3:18)

Jesus Christ declares that, "if you love me then keep my commandments". You must be spiritually born again; believe and be baptized.

"If ye love me, keep my commandments." (John 14:15)

"He that saith, I know him, and keepeth not his commandments, is a liar, and the truth is not in him. But whoso keepeth his word, in him verily is the love of God perfected: hereby know we that we are in him. He that saith he abideth in him ought himself also so to walk, even as he walked. Brethren, I write no new commandment unto you, but an old commandment which ye had from the beginning. The old commandment is the word which ye have heard from the beginning. Again, a new commandment I write unto you, which thing is true in him and in you: because the darkness is past, and the true light now shineth. He that saith he is in the light, and hateth his brother, is in darkness even until now. He that loveth his brother abideth in the light, and there is none occasion of stumbling in him. But he that hateth his brother is in darkness, and walketh in darkness, and knoweth not whither he goeth, because that darkness hath blinded his eyes. I write unto you, little children, because your sins are forgiven you for his name's sake. I write unto you, fathers, because ye have known him that is from the beginning. I write unto you, young men, because ye have overcome the wicked one. I write unto you, little children, because ye have known the Father. I have written unto you, fathers, because ye have known him that is from the beginning. I have written unto you, young men, because ye are strong, and the word of God abideth in you, and ye have overcome the wicked one. Love not the world, neither the things that are in the world. If any man love the world, the love of the Father is not in him. For all that is in the world, the lust of the flesh, and the lust of the eyes, and the pride of life, is not of the Father, but is of the world. And the world passeth away, and the lust thereof: but he that doeth the will of God abideth for ever." (2 John 2:3-17)

"He that believeth and is baptized shall be saved; but he that believeth not shall be damned." (Mark 16:16)

Now the Bible clearly states the greatest commandment, which is a summation of the Law of Moses as well as what the prophets proclaimed to the people.

"Master, which is the great commandment in the law? Jesus said unto him, Thou shalt love the Lord thy God with all thy heart, and with all thy soul, and with all thy mind. This is the first and great commandment. And the second is like unto it, Thou shalt love thy neighbour as thyself. On these two commandments hang all the law and the prophets." (Matthew 22:36-40)

"Owe no man any thing, but to love one another: for he that loveth another hath fulfilled the law. For this, Thou shalt not commit adultery, Thou shalt not kill, Thou shalt not steal, Thou shalt not bear false witness, Thou his saying, shalt not covet; and if there be any other commandment, it is briefly comprehended in tnamely, Thou shalt love thy neighbour as thyself. Love worketh no ill to his neighbour: therefore love is the fulfilling of the law." (Romans 13:8-10)

In order not to sin, we must walk in the Spirit of God, the Holy Ghost, rather than walk to fulfill the lust of the flesh.

"For, brethren, ye have been called unto liberty; only use not liberty for an occasion to the flesh, but by love serve one another. For all the law is fulfilled in one word, even in this; Thou shalt love thy neighbour as thyself. But if ye bite and devour one another, take heed that ye be not consumed one of another. This I say then, Walk in the Spirit, and ye shall not fulfil the lust of the flesh. For the flesh lusteth against the Spirit, and the Spirit against the flesh: and these are contrary the one to the other: so that ye cannot do the things that ye would. But if ye be led of the Spirit, ye are not under the law." (Galatians 5:13-18)

"The night is far spent, the day is at hand: let us therefore cast off the works of darkness, and let us put on the armour of light. Let us walk honestly, as in the day; not in rioting and drunkenness, not in chambering and wantonness, not in strife and envying. But put ye on the Lord Jesus Christ, and make not provision for the flesh, to fulfil the lusts thereof." (Romans 13:12-14)

"Therefore to him that knoweth to do good, and doeth it not, to him it is sin." (James 4:17)

We put on Christ after the spiritual regeneration of our minds by accepting Christ as our redeemer and spiritually put on his likeness in baptism.

"For as many of you as have been baptized into Christ have put on Christ. There is neither Jew nor Greek, there is neither bond nor free, there is neither male nor female: for ye are all one in Christ Jesus. And if ye be Christ's, then are ye Abraham's seed, and heirs according to the promise." (Galatians 3:27-29)

"Know ye not, that so many of us as were baptized into Jesus Christ were baptized into his death? Therefore we are buried with him by baptism into death: that like as Christ was raised up from the dead by the glory of the Father, even so we also should walk in newness of life. For if we have been planted together in the likeness of his death, we shall be also in the likeness of his resurrection: Knowing this, that our old man is crucified with him, that the body of sin might be destroyed, that henceforth we should not serve sin. For he that is dead is freed from sin. Now if we be dead with Christ, we believe that we shall also live with him: Knowing that Christ being raised from the dead dieth no more; death hath no more dominion over him. For in that he died, he died unto sin once: but in that he liveth, he liveth unto God." (Romans 6:3-10)

"And have put on the new man, which is renewed in knowledge after the image of him that created him: Where there is neither Greek nor Jew, circumcision nor uncircumcision, Barbarian, Scythian, bond nor free: but Christ is all, and in all. Put on therefore, as the elect of God, holy and beloved, bowels of mercies, kindness, humbleness of mind, meekness, longsuffering; Forbearing one another, and forgiving one another, if any man have a quarrel against any: even as Christ forgave you, so also do ye. And above all these things put on charity, which is the bond of perfectness. And let the peace of God rule in your hearts, to the which also ye are called in one body; and be ye thankful." (Colossians 3:10-15)

The lusts of the flesh are sin. To be indulged in a life of lusts is sinful. The lusts of the flesh are: adultery (moichos (male), moichalis (female) - sexual infidelity of husband or wife, a postate), fornication (pornelia from porneno - harlotry, idolatry, act like a hariot, indulge in unlawful lust an sex) uncleanness (akatmarsia - physical or moral impurity), lasciviousness (aselgeia - licentiousness, filthy, wantonness), idolatry (eidololatres - image worshipping, worshipper of an heathen god), witchcraft (pharmakeia - magic, sorcery), hatred (echthra and echthrus - feminine and musculine hostility, enmity, odious or act hostile and adversary, enemy, and especially as Satan), variance (eris - quarreling, wrangling, contention, debate, strife), emulations (zelos - jealousy, malice, indignation), wrath (thumos - fierceness with a passion, indignation), strife (eritheia - friction, contention), seditious (dichostasia - make apart, set assunder, divide, dissension), heresies (hairesis - sects, to take or borrow from a cognate), envyings (phithonos – spiteful jealously, ill-willed pincing), murders (phonos - to slay, slaughter), drunkenness (methe - intoxication) and revellings (kamos - carousing, letting loose, rioting).

"Now the works of the flesh are manifest, which are these; Adultery, fornication, uncleanness, lasciviousness, Idolatry, witchcraft, hatred, variance, emulations, wrath, strife, seditions, heresies, Envyings, murders, drunkenness, revellings, and such like: of the which I tell you before, as I have also told you in time past, that they which do such things shall not inherit the kingdom of God." (Galatians 5:19-21)

Now, maybe I should not mention this but, there are a couple of tiny loopholes for those of us jockeying for the title of "chieftain of sin" while we would do good. And, put up a resistance to the devil always!

"For that which I do I allow not: for what I would, that do I not; but what I hate, that do I. If then I do that which I would not, I consent unto the law that it is good. Now then it is no more I that do it, but sin that dwelleth in me. For I know that in me (that is, in my flesh,) dwelleth no good thing: for to will is present with me; but how to perform that which is good I find not. For the good that I would I do not: but the evil which I would not, that I do. Now if I do that I would not, it is no more I that do it, but sin that dwelleth in me. I find then a law, that, when I would do good, evil is present with me. For I delight in the law of God after the inward man: But I see another law in my members, warring against the law of my mind, and bringing me into captivity to the law of sin which is in my members. O wretched man that I am! who shall deliver me from the body of this death? I thank God through Jesus Christ our Lord. So then with the mind I myself serve the law of God; but with the flesh the law of sin." (Romans 7:15-25)

"Brethren, if any of you do err from the truth, and one convert him; Let him know, that he which converteth the sinner from the error of his way shall save a soul from death, and shall hide a multitude of sins." (James 5:19-20)

"But the end of all things is at hand: be ye therefore sober, and watch unto prayer. And above all things have fervent charity among yourselves: for charity shall cover the multitude of sins. Use hospitality one to another without grudging. As every man hath received the gift, even so minister the same one to another, as good stewards of the manifold grace of God." (1 Peter 4:7-8)

"Ye adulterers and adulteresses, know ye not that the friendship of the world is enmity with God? whosoever therefore will be a friend of the world is the enemy of God. Do ye think that the scripture saith in vain, The spirit that dwelleth in us lusteth to envy? But he giveth more grace. Wherefore he saith, God resisteth the proud, but giveth grace unto the humble. Submit yourselves therefore to God. Resist the devil, and he will flee from you. Draw nigh to God, and he will draw nigh to you. Cleanse your hands, ye sinners; and purify your hearts, ye double minded. Be afflicted, and mourn, and weep: let your laughter be turned to mourning, and your joy to heaviness. Humble yourselves in the sight of the Lord, and he shall lift you up." (James 4:4-10)

No flesh can be justified (dikaioo - to render innocent, free, righteous) in the presence of God.

"For I through the law am dead to the law, that I might live unto God. I am crucified with Christ: nevertheless I live; yet not I, but Christ liveth in me: and the life which I now live in the flesh I live by the faith of the Son of God, who loved me, and gave himself for me. I do not frustrate the grace of God: for if righteousness come by the law, then Christ is dead in vain." (Galatians 2:19-21)

"Now we know that what things soever the law saith, it saith to them who are under the law: that every mouth may be stopped, and all the world may become guilty before God. Therefore by the deeds of the law there shall no flesh be justified in his sight: for by the law is the knowledge of sin. But now the righteousness of God without the law is manifested, being witnessed by the law and the prophets; Even the righteousness of God which is by faith of Jesus Christ unto all and upon all them that believe: for there is no difference: For all have sinned, and come short of the glory of God; Being justified freely by his grace through the redemption that is in Christ Jesus: Whom God hath set forth to be a propitiation through faith in his blood, to declare his righteousness for the remission of sins that are past, through the forbearance of God; To declare, I say, at this time his righteousness: that he might be just, and the justifier of him which believeth in Jesus." (Romans 3:19-26)

"Now unto him that is able to keep you from falling, and to present you faultless before the presence of his glory with exceeding joy, To the only wise God our Saviour, be glory and majesty, dominion and power, both now and ever." Amen." (Jude 24-25)

Walking in the Holy Spirit, we become servants of righteousness and are therefore judged by God as sinless.

"Let not sin therefore reign in your mortal body, that ye should obey it in the lusts thereof. Neither yield ye your members as instruments of unrighteousness unto sin: but yield your-

selves unto God, as those that are alive from the dead, and your members as instruments of righteousness unto God. For sin shall not have dominion over you: for ye are not under the law, but under grace. What then? shall we sin, because we are not under the law, but under grace? God forbid. Know ye not, that to whom ye yield yourselves servants to obey, his servants ye are to whom ye obey; whether of sin unto death, or of obedience unto righteousness? But God be thanked, that ye were the servants of sin, but ye have obeyed from the heart that form of doctrine which was delivered you. Being then made free from sin, ye became the servants of righteousness." (Romans 6: 12-18)

"Then Peter and the other apostles answered and said, We ought to obey God rather than men. The God of our fathers raised up Jesus, whom ye slew and hanged on a tree. Him hath God exalted with his right hand to be a Prince and a Saviour, for to give repentance to Israel, and forgiveness of sins. And we are his witnesses of these things; and so is also the Holy Ghost, whom God hath given to them that obey him." (Acts 5:29-32)

Walking according to the desires of the world, we stand to be judged by God as in sin and therefore children of disobedience.

"Wherein in time past ye walked according to the course of this world, according to the prince of the power of the air, the spirit that now worketh in the children of disobedience: Among whom also we all had our conversation in times past in the lusts of our flesh, fulfilling the desires of the flesh and of the mind; and were by nature the children of wrath, even as others. But God, who is rich in mercy, for his great love wherewith he loved us, Even when we were dead in sins, hath quickened us together with Christ, (by grace ye are saved;) And hath raised us up together, and made us sit together in heavenly places in Christ Jesus: That in the ages to come he might shew the exceeding riches of his grace in his kindness toward us through Christ Jesus. For by grace are ye saved through faith; and that not of yourselves: it is the gift of God: Not of works, lest any man should boast." (Ephesians 2:2-9)

"But God commendeth his love toward us, in that, while we were yet sinners, Christ died for us. Much more then, being now justified by his blood, we shall be saved from wrath through him. For if, when we were enemies, we were reconciled to God by the death of his Son, much more, being reconciled, we shall be saved by his life. And not only so, but we also joy in God through our Lord Jesus Christ, by whom we have now received the atonement. Wherefore, as by one man sin entered into the world, and death by sin; and so death passed upon all men, for that all have sinned: (For until the law sin was in the world: but sin is not imputed when there is no law. Nevertheless death reigned from Adam to Moses, even over them that had not sinned after the similitude of Adam's transgression, who is the figure of him that was to come. But not as the offence, so also is the free gift. For if through the offence of one many be dead, much more the grace of God, and the gift by grace, which is by one man, Jesus Christ, hath abounded unto many. And not as it was by one that sinned, so is the gift: for the judgment was by one to condemnation, but the free gift is of many offences unto justification. For if by one man's offence death reigned by one; much more they which receive abundance of grace and of the gift of righteousness shall reign in life by one, Jesus Christ.) Therefore as by the offence of one judgment came upon all men to condemnation; even so by the righteousness of one the free gift came upon all men unto justification of life." (Romans 5:8-19)

"Be ye therefore followers of God, as dear children; And walk in love, as Christ also hath loved us, and hath given himself for us an offering and a sacrifice to God for a sweetsmelling savour. But fornication, and all uncleanness, or covetousness, let it not be once named among you, as becometh saints; Neither filthiness, nor foolish talking, nor jesting, which are not convenient: but rather giving of thanks. For this ye know, that no whoremonger, nor unclean person, nor covetous man, who is an idolater, hath any inheritance in the kingdom of Christ and of God. Let no man deceive you with vain words: for because of these things cometh the wrath of God upon the children of disobedience. Be not ye therefore partakers with them. For ye were sometimes darkness, but now are ye light in the Lord: walk as children of light: (For the fruit of the Spirit is in all goodness and righteousness and truth;) Proving what is acceptable unto the Lord." **(Ephesians 5:1-10)**

"Set your affection on things above, not on things on the earth. For ye are dead, and your life is hid with Christ in God. When Christ, who is our life, shall appear, then shall ye also appear with him in glory. Mortify therefore your members which are upon the earth; fornication, uncleanness, inordinate affection, evil concupiscence, and covetousness, which is idolatry: For which things' sake the wrath of God cometh on the children of disobedience: In the which ye also walked some time, when ye lived in them. But now ye also put off all these; anger, wrath, malice, blasphemy, filthy communication out of your mouth." **(Colossians 3:2-8)**

So now, should we continue to sin in order for God to give more grace? No, for we stand in danger of being judged by God as servants of sin. To be servants of sin is to be reprobate (adokimos - unapproved, rejected, worthless, castaway). Should we be willfully in sin?

"What shall we say then? Shall we continue in sin, that grace may abound? God forbid. How shall we, that are dead to sin, live any longer therein?" **(Romans 6:1-2)**

"Let not sin therefore reign in your mortal body, that ye should obey it in the lusts thereof. Neither yield ye your members as instruments of unrighteousness unto sin: but yield yourselves unto God, as those that are alive from the dead, and your members as instruments of righteousness unto God. For sin shall not have dominion over you: for ye are not under the law, but under grace. What then? shall we sin, because we are not under the law, but under grace? God forbid. Know ye not, that to whom ye yield yourselves servants to obey, his servants ye are to whom ye obey; whether of sin unto death, or of obedience unto righteousness? But God be thanked, that ye were the servants of sin, but ye have obeyed from the heart that form of doctrine which was delivered you. Being then made free from sin, ye became the servants of righteousness." **(Romans 6: 12-18)**

"My little children, these things write I unto you, that ye sin not. And if any man sin, we have an advocate with the Father, Jesus Christ the righteous: And he is the propitiation for our sins: and not for ours only, but also for the sins of the whole world. And hereby we do know that we know him, if we keep his commandments. He that saith, I know him, and keepeth not his commandments, is a liar, and the truth is not in him. But whoso keepeth his word, in him verily is the love of God perfected: hereby know we that we are in him. He that saith he abideth in him ought himself also so to walk, even as he walked." **(1 John 2:1-6)**

"Beloved, now are we the sons of God, and it doth not yet appear what we shall be: but we know that, when he shall appear, we shall be like him; for we shall see him as he is. And

every man that hath this hope in him purifieth himself, even as he is pure. Whosoever committeth sin transgresseth also the law: for sin is the transgression of the law. And ye know that he was manifested to take away our sins; and in him is no sin. Whosoever abideth in him sinneth not: whosoever sinneth hath not seen him, neither known him. Little children, let no man deceive you: he that doeth righteousness is righteous, even as he is righteous. He that committeth sin is of the devil; for the devil sinneth from the beginning. For this purpose the Son of God was manifested, that he might destroy the works of the devil. Whosoever is born of God doth not commit sin; for his seed remaineth in him: and he cannot sin, because he is born of God." **(1 John 3:2-9)**

"Unto the pure all things are pure: but unto them that are defiled and unbelieving is nothing pure; but even their mind and conscience is defiled. They profess that they know God; but in works they deny him, being abominable, and disobedient, and unto every good work reprobate." **(Titus 1:15-16)**

"For if we sin wilfully after that we have received the knowledge of the truth, there remaineth no more sacrifice for sins, But a certain fearful looking for of judgment and fiery indignation, which shall devour the adversaries.He that despised Moses' law died without mercy under two or three witnesses: Of how much sorer punishment, suppose ye, shall he be thought worthy, who hath trodden under foot the Son of God, and hath counted the blood of the covenant, wherewith he was sanctified, an unholy thing, and hath done despite unto the Spirit of grace? For we know him that hath said, Vengeance belongeth unto me, I will recompense, saith the Lord. And again, The Lord shall judge his people. It is a fearful thing to fall into the hands of the living God." **(Hebrews 10:26-31)**

Lastly, God does not tempt us with sin but rather out of his mercy, God provides us with an escape out of that sin.

"Blessed is the man that endureth temptation: for when he is tried, he shall receive the crown of life, which the Lord hath promised to them that love him. Let no man say when he is tempted, I am tempted of God: for God cannot be tempted with evil, neither tempteth he any man: But every man is tempted, when he is drawn away of his own lust, and enticed. Then when lust hath conceived, it bringeth forth sin: and sin, when it is finished, bringeth forth death." **(James 1:12-15)**

"There hath no temptation taken you but such as is common to man: but God is faithful, who will not suffer you to be tempted above that ye are able; but will with the temptation also make a way to escape, that ye may be able to bear it." **(1 Corinthians 10:13)**

ABOMINATIONS IN THE SIGHT OF GOD

God is love. Can there be certain things that are as so utterly sinful, loathing, and disgusting to God as to risk eternal life?

The Almighty God of the Bible has indeed certain things that are as utterly sinful, loathing, and disgusting as not only to incur his judgment upon persons but even whole nations. Now there are specific pagan abominations [towedah - disgusting custom or thing] include: 1) human sacrifice, 2) divination [anan - soothsayer], 3) observer of times [soothsayer, sorcerer], 4) enchanter [nachash- whisper of magic spells, prognosticator], 5) witchcraft [kashaph- perform incantations, cast spells or practice magic], 6) charmer [chabal - charm with spells, enchantment], 7) consultant with familiar spirits [shalowm owb - friendly mumbles (spiritual)], 8) wizard [yiddoniy - conjurer], and 9) necromancer [darash & muwth - seek for, inquire of the dead]; these are most certainly abominations to the Almighty.

> "When thou art come into the land which the Lord thy God giveth thee, thou shalt not learn to do after the abominations of those nations. There shall not be found among you any one that maketh his son or his daughter to pass through the fire, or that useth divination, or an observer of times, or an enchanter, or a witch, or a charmer, or a consulter with familiar spirits, or a wizard, or a necromancer. For all that do these things are an abomination unto the Lord: and because of these abominations the Lord thy God doth drive them out from before thee. Thou shalt be perfect with the Lord thy God. For these nations, which thou shalt possess, hearkened unto observers of times, and unto diviners: but as for thee, the Lord thy God hath not suffered thee so to do." (Deuteronomy 18:9-14)

There are possibly no things more abominable than those things presented as the customs in the nations driven out before a chosen people (chosen people in Old Testament is Israel and a nation keep Christ's commandments in the New Testament).

> "Thou shalt not lie with mankind, as with womankind: it is abomination. Neither shalt thou lie with any beast to defile thyself therewith: neither shall any woman stand before a beast to lie down thereto: it is confusion. Defile not ye yourselves in any of these things: for in all these the nations are defiled which I cast out before you: and the land is defiled: therefore I do visit the iniquity thereof upon it, and the land itself vomiteth out her inhabitants. Ye shall therefore keep my statutes and my judgments, and shall not commit any of these abominations; neither any of your own nation, nor any stranger that sojourneth among you: (For all these abominations have the men of the land done, which were

before you, and the land is defiled;) that the land spue not you out also, when ye defile it, as it spued out the nations that were before you. For whosoever shall commit any of these abominations, even the souls that commit them shall be cut off from among their people. Therefore shall ye keep mine ordinance, that ye commit not any one of these abominable customs, which were committed before you, and that ye defile not yourselves therein: I am the Lord your God." (Leviticus 18: 22-30)

"For thou art an holy people unto the Lord thy God: the Lord thy God hath chosen thee to be a special people unto himself, above all people that are upon the face of the earth. The Lord did not set his love upon you, nor choose you, because ye were more in number than any people; for ye were the fewest of all people: but because the Lord loved you, and because he would keep the oath which he had sworn unto your fathers, hath the Lord brought you out with a mighty hand, and redeemed you out of the house of bondmen, from the hand of Pharaoh king of Egypt. Know therefore that the Lord thy God, he is God, the faithful God, which keepeth covenant and mercy with them that love him and keep his commandments to a thousand generations; and repayeth them that hate him to their face, to destroy them: he will not be slack to him that hateth him, he will repay him to his face. Thou shalt therefore keep the commandments, and the statutes, and the judgments, which I command thee this day, to do them. Wherefore it shall come to pass, if ye hearken to these judgments, and keep, and do them, that the Lord thy God shall keep unto thee the covenant and the mercy which he sware unto thy fathers: and he will love thee, and bless thee, and multiply thee: he will also bless the fruit of thy womb, and the fruit of thy land, thy corn, and thy wine, and thine oil, the increase of thy kine, and the flocks of thy sheep, in the land which he sware unto thy fathers to give thee. Thou shalt be blessed above all people: there shall not be male or female barren among you, or among your cattle. And the Lord will take away from thee all sickness, and will put none of the evil diseases of Egypt, which thou knowest, upon thee; but will lay them upon all them that hate thee. And thou shalt consume all the people which the Lord thy God shall deliver thee; thine eye shall have no pity upon them: neither shalt thou serve their gods; for that will be a snare unto thee."
(Deuteronomy 7:6-16)

"Know ye therefore that they which are of faith, the same are the children of Abraham. And the scripture, foreseeing that God would justify the heathen through faith, preached before the gospel unto Abraham, saying, In thee shall all nations be blessed. So then they which be of faith are blessed with faithful Abraham." (Galatians 3:7-9)

"Concerning his Son Jesus Christ our Lord, which was made of the seed of David according to the flesh; and declared to be the Son of God with power, according to the spirit of holiness, by the resurrection from the dead: by whom we have received grace and apostleship, for obedience to the faith among all nations, for his name...." (Romans 1: 3-5)

"And ye shall hear of wars and rumours of wars: see that ye be not troubled: for all these things must come to pass, but the end is not yet. For nation shall rise against nation, and kingdom against kingdom: and there shall be famines, and pestilences, and earthquakes, in divers places. All these are the beginning of sorrows. Then shall they deliver you up to be afflicted, and shall kill you: and ye shall be hated of all nations for my name's sake. And then shall many be offended, and shall betray one another, and shall hate one another. And many false prophets shall rise, and shall deceive many. And because iniquity shall abound, the love of many shall wax cold. But he that shall endure unto the end, the same

shall be saved. And this gospel of the kingdom shall be preached in all the world for a witness unto all nations; and then shall the end come." (**Matthew 24: 6-14**)

"No servant can serve two masters: for either he will hate the one, and love the other; or else he will hold to the one, and despise the other. Ye cannot serve God and mammon.' And the Pharisees also, who were covetous, heard all these things: and they derided him. And he said unto them, 'Ye are they which justify yourselves before men; but God knoweth your hearts: for that which is highly esteemed among men is abomination in the sight of God.'" (Luke 16: 13-15)

The Bible goes further to personalize abominations. Seven such abominations are lumped together in the Bible with a warning that those that do these things are subject to sudden calamity and/or fatal injury.

"These six things doth the Lord hate: yea, seven are an abomination unto him: a proud look, a lying tongue, and hands that shed innocent blood, an heart that deviseth wicked imaginations, feet that be swift in running to mischief, a false witness that speaketh lies, and he that soweth discord among brethren." (**Proverbs 6:16-19**)

"A naughty person, a wicked man, walketh with a froward mouth. He winketh with his eyes, he speaketh with his feet, he teacheth with his fingers; Frowardness is in his heart, he deviseth mischief continually; he soweth discord. Therefore shall his calamity come suddenly; suddenly shall he be broken without remedy." (**Proverbs 6:12-15**)

"Devise not evil against thy neighbour, seeing he dwelleth securely by thee. Strive not with a man without cause, if he have done thee no harm. Envy thou not the oppressor, and choose none of his ways. For the froward is abomination to the Lord: but his secret is with the righteous." (**Proverbs 3:29-32**)

God hates measuring [by balance] dishonesty, lying, lips, wickedness, arrogance, and the sacrifices of the wicked.

"Divers weights, and divers measures, both of them are alike abomination to the Lord." (**Proverbs 20:10**)

"Wisdom crieth without; she uttereth her voice in the streets: she crieth in the chief place of concourse, in the openings of the gates: in the city she uttereth her words, saying, How long, ye simple ones, will ye love simplicity? and the scorners delight in their scorning, and fools hate knowledge? Turn you at my reproof: behold, I will pour out my spirit unto you, I will make known my words unto you." (**Proverbs 1:20-23**)

"Lying lips are abomination to the Lord: but they that deal truly are his delight." (**Proverbs 12:22**)

"The way of the wicked is an abomination unto the Lord: but he loveth him that followeth after righteousness...The thoughts of the wicked are an abomination to the Lord: but the words of the pure are pleasant words." (**Proverbs 15:9 & 26**)

"Every one that is proud in heart is an abomination to the Lord: though hand join in hand, he shall not be unpunished." (**Proverbs 16:5**)

"The sacrifice of the wicked is abomination: how much more, when he bringeth it with a wicked mind?" (**Proverbs 21:27**)

Rebellion against God is as witchcraft. Rather, resist the devil and draw closer to God. This applies to individuals and nations.

"And Samuel said, Hath the Lord as great delight in burnt offerings and sacrifices, as in obeying the voice of the Lord? Behold, to obey is better than sacrifice, and to hearken than the fat of rams. For rebellion is as the sin of witchcraft, and stubbornness is as iniquity and idolatry. Because thou hast rejected the word of the Lord, he hath also rejected thee from being king." (1 Samuel 15:22-23)

"Submit yourselves therefore to God. Resist the devil, and he will flee from you. Draw nigh to God, and he will draw nigh to you. Cleanse your hands, ye sinners; and purify your hearts, ye double minded." (James 4:7-8)

"The fool hath said in his heart, There is no God. Corrupt are they, and have done abominable iniquity: there is none that doeth good. God looked down from heaven upon the children of men, to see if there were any that did understand, that did seek God. Every one of them is gone back: they are altogether become filthy; there is none that doeth good, no, not one. Have the workers of iniquity no knowledge? who eat up my people as they eat bread: they have not called upon God." There were they in great fear, where no fear was: for God hath scattered the bones of him that encampeth against thee: thou hast put them to shame, because God hath despised them." (Psalm 53:1-5)

Lastly, the Bible says that eternal damnation is reserved for the abominable among others.

"But the fearful, and unbelieving, and the abominable, and murderers, and whoremongers, and sorcerers, and idolaters, and all liars, shall have their part in the lake which burneth with fire and brimstone: which is the second death." (Revelation 21:8)

"And the devil that deceived them was cast into the lake of fire and brimstone, where the beast and the false prophet are, and shall be tormented day and night for ever and ever. And I saw a great white throne, and him that sat on it, from whose face the earth and the heaven fled away; and there was found no place for them. And I saw the dead, small and great, stand before God; and the books were opened: and another book was opened, which is the book of life: and the dead were judged out of those things which were written in the books, according to their works. And the sea gave up the dead which were in it; and death and hell delivered up the dead which were in them: and they were judged every man according to their works. And death and hell were cast into the lake of fire. This is the second death. And whosoever was not found written in the book of life was cast into the lake of fire." (Revelation 20:10-15)

30

DAMNATION

What is damnation and for what things could a God that is love possibly damn a person?

DAMNATION [KRIMA - a decision of condemnation for or against crime, condemnation; krisis - decision for or against a tribunal, justice against an accusation, condemnation; apoleia - destruction, death, perdition, perish, waste] is clearly spoken of in the Bible in what is herein to be indicated as eight areas. Foremost in damnation is unbelief; this unbelief is based upon rejection of the preaching of the gospel.

> *"And as Moses lifted up the serpent in the wilderness, even so must the Son of man be lifted up: that whosoever believeth in him should not perish, but have eternal life. For God so loved the world, that he gave his only begotten Son, that whosoever believeth in him should not perish, but have everlasting life. For God sent not his Son into the world to condemn the world; but that the world through him might be saved. He that believeth on him is not condemned: but he that believeth not is condemned already, because he hath not believed in the name of the only begotten Son of God. And this is the condemnation, that light is come into the world, and men loved darkness rather than light, because their deeds were evil. For every one that doeth evil hateth the light, neither cometh to the light, lest his deeds should be reproved. But he that doeth truth cometh to the light, that his deeds may be made manifest, that they are wrought in God." (John 3:14-21)*

> *"Jesus cried and said, 'He that believeth on me, believeth not on me, but on him that sent me. And he that seeth me seeth him that sent me. I am come a light into the world, that whosoever believeth on me should not abide in darkness. And if any man hear my words, and believe not, I judge him not: for I came not to judge the world, but to save the world. He that rejecteth me, and receiveth not my words, hath one that judgeth him: the word that I have spoken, the same shall judge him in the last day. For I have not spoken of myself; but the Father which sent me, he gave me a commandment, what I should say, and what I should speak. And I know that his commandment is life everlasting: whatsoever I speak therefore, even as the Father said unto me, so I speak." (John 12:44-50)*

> *"Now after that John was put in prison, Jesus came into Galilee, preaching the gospel of the kingdom of God, and saying, 'The time is fulfilled, and the kingdom of God is at hand: repent ye, and believe the gospel." (Mark 1:14-15)*

> *"And he said unto them, 'Go ye into all the world, and preach the gospel to every creature. He that believeth and is baptized shall be saved; but he that believeth not shall be damned."* (Mark 16:15-16)

Now, notwithstanding the condemnation of damnation, the Bible speaks of a greater [perissoteros - more abundant, overmuch] damnation. There are those such as the Pharisees and scribes, who in their religious hypocrisy devour the assets of God's people and as they are operating outside the Kingdom of God, they shut it up, thereby preventing others from entering as well.

> *"'But woe unto you, scribes and Pharisees, hypocrites! For ye shut up the kingdom of heaven against men: for ye neither go in yourselves, neither suffer ye them that are entering to go in. Woe unto you, scribes and Pharisees, hypocrites! For ye devour widows' houses, and for a pretence make long prayer: therefore ye shall receive the greater damnation. Woe unto you, scribes and Pharisees, hypocrites! For ye compass sea and land to make one proselyte, and when he is made, ye make him twofold more the child of hell than yourselves. Woe unto you, ye blind guides, which say, Whosoever shall swear by the temple, it is nothing; but whosoever shall swear by the gold of the temple, he is a debtor! Ye fools and blind: for whether is greater, the gold, or the temple that sanctifieth the gold? And, Whosoever shall swear by the altar, it is nothing; but whosoever sweareth by the gift that is upon it, he is guilty. Ye fools and blind: for whether is greater, the gift, or the altar that sanctifieth the gift? Whoso therefore shall swear by the altar, sweareth by it, and by all things thereon. And whoso shall swear by the temple, sweareth by it, and by him that dwelleth therein. And he that shall swear by heaven, sweareth by the throne of God, and by him that sitteth thereon. Woe unto you, scribes and Pharisees, hypocrites! For ye pay tithe of mint and anise and cummin, and have omitted the weightier matters of the law, judgment, mercy, and faith: these ought ye to have done, and not to leave the other undone. Ye blind guides, which strain at a gnat, and swallow a camel. Woe unto you, scribes and Pharisees, hypocrites! For ye make clean the outside of the cup and of the platter, but within they are full of extortion and excess. Thou blind Pharisee, cleanse first that which is within the cup and platter, that the outside of them may be clean also. Woe unto you, scribes and Pharisees, hypocrites! For ye are like unto whited sepulchres, which indeed appear beautiful outward, but are within full of dead men's bones, and of all uncleanness. Even so ye also outwardly appear righteous unto men, but within ye are full of hypocrisy and iniquity. Woe unto you, scribes and Pharisees, hypocrites! Because ye build the tombs of the prophets, and garnish the sepulchres of the righteous, and say, If we had been in the days of our fathers, we would not have been partakers with them in the blood of the prophets. Wherefore ye be witnesses unto yourselves, that ye are the children of them which killed the prophets.'"* (Matthew 23:13-31)

[note the entire 23rd chapter of Matthew as well]

Damnation is to be the end to those that have done evil [phalos - wicked].

> *"Marvel not at this: for the hour is coming, in the which all that are in the graves shall hear his voice, And shall come forth; they that have done good, unto the resurrection of life; and they that have done evil, unto the resurrection of damnation."* (John 5:28-29)

"Keep thee far from a false matter; and the innocent and righteous slay thou not: for I will not justify the wicked." (**Exodus 23:7**)

"God judgeth the righteous, and God is angry with the wicked every day." (**Psalm 7:11**)

Thou hast rebuked the heathen, thou hast destroyed the wicked, thou hast put out their name for ever and ever...The heathen are sunk down in the pit that they made: in the net which they hid is their own foot taken. The Lord is known by the judgment which he executeth: the wicked is snared in the work of his own hands. Higgaion. Selah. The wicked shall be turned into hell, and all the nations that forget God." (**Psalm 9:5, 15-17**)

"Many sorrows shall be to the wicked: but he that trusteth in the Lord, mercy shall compass him about." (**Psalm 32:10**)

"A good man obtaineth favour of the Lord: but a man of wicked devices will he condemn. A man shall not be established by wickedness: but the root of the righteous shall not be moved." (**Proverbs 12:2-3**)

"For our exhortation was not of deceit, nor of uncleanness, nor in guile: but as we were allowed of God to be put in trust with the gospel, even so we speak; not as pleasing men, but God, which trieth our hearts. For neither at any time used we flattering words, as ye know, nor a cloke of covetousness; God is witness: nor of men sought we glory, neither of you, nor yet of others, when we might have been burdensome, as the apostles of Christ. But we were gentle among you, even as a nurse cherisheth her children: so being affectionately desirous of you, we were willing to have imparted unto you, not the gospel of God only, but also our own souls, because ye were dear unto us. For ye remember, brethren, our labour and travail: for labouring night and day, because we would not be chargeable unto any of you, we preached unto you the gospel of God. Ye are witnesses, and God also, how holily and justly and unblameably we behaved ourselves among you that believe: as ye know how we exhorted and comforted and charged every one of you, as a father doth his children, that ye would walk worthy of God, who hath called you unto his kingdom and glory." (**1 Thessalonians 2:3-12**)

"For the wrath of God is revealed from heaven against all ungodliness and unrighteousness of men, who hold the truth in unrighteousness; because that which may be known of God is manifest in them; for God hath shewed it unto them. For the invisible things of him from the creation of the world are clearly seen, being understood by the things that are made, even his eternal power and Godhead; so that they are without excuse: because that, when they knew God, they glorified him not as God, neither were thankful; but became vain in their imaginations, and their foolish heart was darkened. Professing themselves to be wise, they became fools, and changed the glory of the uncorruptible God into an image made like to corruptible man, and to birds, and fourfooted beasts, and creeping things. Wherefore God also gave them up to uncleanness through the lusts of their own hearts, to dishonour their own bodies between themselves: who changed the truth of God into a lie, and worshipped and served the creature more than the Creator, who is blessed for ever. Amen." (**Romans 1:18-25**)

"When the Son of man shall come in his glory, and all the holy angels with him, then shall he sit upon the throne of his glory: and before him shall be gathered all nations: and he shall separate them one from another, as a shepherd divideth his sheep from the goats: and he shall set the sheep on his right hand, but the goats on the left. Then shall the King say

unto them on his right hand, Come, ye blessed of my Father, inherit the kingdom prepared for you from the foundation of the world: for I was an hungred, and ye gave me meat: I was thirsty, and ye gave me drink: I was a stranger, and ye took me in: naked, and ye clothed me: I was sick, and ye visited me: I was in prison, and ye came unto me. Then shall the righteous answer him, saying, Lord, when saw we thee an hungred, and fed thee? or thirsty, and gave thee drink? When saw we thee a stranger, and took thee in? or naked, and clothed thee? Or when saw we thee sick, or in prison, and came unto thee? And the King shall answer and say unto them, Verily I say unto you, Inasmuch as ye have done it unto one of the least of these my brethren, ye have done it unto me. Then shall he say also unto them on the left hand, Depart from me, ye cursed, into everlasting fire, prepared for the devil and his angels: for I was an hungred, and ye gave me no meat: I was thirsty, and ye gave me no drink: I was a stranger, and ye took me not in: naked, and ye clothed me not: sick, and in prison, and ye visited me not. Then shall they also answer him, saying, Lord, when saw we thee an hungred, or athirst, or a stranger, or naked, or sick, or in prison, and did not minister unto thee? Then shall he answer them, saying, Verily I say unto you, Inasmuch as ye did it not to one of the least of these, ye did it not to me. And these shall go away into everlasting punishment: but the righteous into life eternal. **Matthew 25:31- 46**

Holy Communion requires self-examination. Included in this self examination should be an assessment of our faith in Christ. Those lacking faith but persistent in the taking of communion are not discerning Christ and thereby bring damnation upon themselves in their hypocrisy.

For as often as ye eat this bread, and drink this cup, ye do shew the Lord's death till he come. Wherefore whosoever shall eat this bread, and drink this cup of the Lord, unworthily, shall be guilty of the body and blood of the Lord. But let a man examine himself, and so let him eat of that bread, and drink of that cup. For he that eateth and drinketh unworthily, eateth and drinketh damnation to himself, not discerning the Lord's body. For this cause many are weak and sickly among you, and many sleep. For if we would judge ourselves, we should not be judged. But when we are judged, we are chastened of the Lord, that we should not be condemned with the world. **1 Corinthians 11:26-32**

"He answered and said unto them, 'Well hath Esaias prophesied of you hypocrites, as it is written, This people honoureth me with their lips, but their heart is far from me. Howbeit in vain do they worship me, teaching for doctrines the commandments of men. For laying aside the commandment of God, ye hold the tradition of men, as the washing of pots and cups: and many other such like things ye do.' And he said unto them, 'Full well ye reject the commandment of God, that ye may keep your own tradition." **(Mark 7:6-9)**

"And whosoever shall speak a word against the Son of man, it shall be forgiven him: but unto him that blasphemeth against the Holy Ghost it shall not be forgiven." **(Luke 12:10)**

"And grieve not the holy Spirit of God, whereby ye are sealed unto the day of redemption." **(Ephesians 4:30)**

"Quench not the Spirit." **(1 Thessalonians 5:19)**

Insurrectionists bring about their own eternal destruction. God has ordained all that rule. To go against the ruling powers is to go against the will of God.

"Let every soul be subject unto the higher powers. For there is no power but of God: the powers that be are ordained of God. Whosoever therefore resisteth the power, resisteth the ordinance of God: and they that resist shall receive to themselves damnation. For rulers are not a terror to good works, but to the evil. Wilt thou then not be afraid of the power? Do that which is good, and thou shalt have praise of the same: for he is the minister of God to thee for good. But if thou do that which is evil, be afraid; for he beareth not the sword in vain: for he is the minister of God, a revenger to execute wrath upon him that doeth evil." (Romans 13:1-4)

False teachers are heading towards damnation according to the Bible.

"But there were false prophets also among the people, even as there shall be false teachers among you, who privily shall bring in damnable heresies, even denying the Lord that bought them, and bring upon themselves swift destruction. And many shall follow their pernicious ways; by reason of whom the way of truth shall be evil spoken of. And through covetousness shall they with feigned words make merchandise of you: whose judgment now of a long time lingereth not, and their damnation slumbereth not.)" (2 Peter 2:1-3)

[reference the entire 2nd chapter of 2 Peter]

"Beware of false prophets, which come to you in sheep's clothing, but inwardly they are ravening wolves. Ye shall know them by their fruits. Do men gather grapes of thorns, or figs of thistles? Even so every good tree bringeth forth good fruit; but a corrupt tree bringeth forth evil fruit. A good tree cannot bring forth evil fruit, neither can a corrupt tree bring forth good fruit. Every tree that bringeth not forth good fruit is hewn down, and cast into the fire. Wherefore by their fruits ye shall know them. Not every one that saith unto me, Lord, Lord, shall enter into the kingdom of heaven; but he that doeth the will of my Father which is in heaven. Many will say to me in that day, Lord, Lord, have we not prophesied in thy name? And in thy name have cast out devils? And in thy name done many wonderful works? And then will I profess unto them, I never knew you: depart from me, ye that work iniquity." (Matthew 7:15-23)

There is a category among the Jews coming out of captivity that the scriptures have declared forbidden into God's rest (eternal salvation)

"Harden not your hearts, as in the provocation, in the day of temptation in the wilderness: when your fathers tempted me, proved me, and saw my works forty years. Wherefore I was grieved with that generation, and said, They do always err in their heart; and they have not known my ways. So I sware in my wrath, They shall not enter into my rest.) Take heed, brethren, lest there be in any of you an evil heart of unbelief, in departing from the living God. But exhort one another daily, while it is called To day; lest any of you be hardened through the deceitfulness of sin. For we are made partakers of Christ, if we hold the beginning of our confidence stedfast unto the end; while it is said, To day if ye will hear his voice, harden not your hearts, as in the provocation." (Hebrews 3:8-15)

"Let us therefore fear, lest, a promise being left us of entering into his rest, any of you should seem to come short of it. For unto us was the gospel preached, as well as unto them: but the word preached did not profit them, not being mixed with faith in them that heard it. For we which have believed do enter into rest, as he said, As I have sworn in my wrath, if

they shall enter into my rest: although the works were finished from the foundation of the world." (Hebrews 4:1- 3)

In order to be forgiven we must forgive. Jesus presented this principle to us in the model prayer and he emphasized it in his teachings.

"And forgive us our debts, as we forgive our debtors. And lead us not into temptation, but deliver us from evil: for thine is the kingdom, and the power, and the glory, for ever. Amen. For if ye forgive men their trespasses, your heavenly Father will also forgive you: but if ye forgive not men their trespasses, neither will your Father forgive your trespasses." (Matthew 6:12-15)

"And when ye stand praying, forgive, if ye have ought against any: that your Father also which is in heaven may forgive you your trespasses. But if ye do not forgive, neither will your Father which is in heaven forgive your trespasses." (Mark 11:25-26)

"Judge not, and ye shall not be judged: condemn not, and ye shall not be condemned: forgive, and ye shall be forgiven:" (Luke 6:37)

"Therefore is the kingdom of heaven likened unto a certain king, which would take account of his servants. And when he had begun to reckon, one was brought unto him, which owed him ten thousand talents. But forasmuch as he had not to pay, his lord commanded him to be sold, and his wife, and children, and all that he had, and payment to be made. The servant therefore fell down, and worshipped him, saying, Lord, have patience with me, and I will pay thee all. Then the lord of that servant was moved with compassion, and loosed him, and forgave him the debt. But the same servant went out, and found one of his fellowservants, which owed him an hundred pence: and he laid hands on him, and took him by the throat, saying, Pay me that thou owest. And his fellowservant fell down at his feet, and besought him, saying, Have patience with me, and I will pay thee all. And he would not: but went and cast him into prison, till he should pay the debt. So when his fellowservants saw what was done, they were very sorry, and came and told unto their lord all that was done. Then his lord, after that he had called him, said unto him, O thou wicked servant, I forgave thee all that debt, because thou desiredst me: shouldest not thou also have had compassion on thy fellowservant, even as I had pity on thee? And his lord was wroth, and delivered him to the tormentors, till he should pay all that was due unto him. So likewise shall my heavenly Father do also unto you, if ye from your hearts forgive not every one his brother their trespasses. " (Matthew 18:23- 35)

The reprobate (adokimos - worthless, castaway, rejected) are those tares, goats and servants of sin rather than righteousness, as judged by God. We are all saved from eternal damnation by God's grace through our faith. The reprobate are judged void of faith.

"For by grace are ye saved through faith; and that not of yourselves: it is the gift of God: Not of works, lest any man should boast." (Ephesians 2:8&9)

"Likewise reckon ye also yourselves to be dead indeed unto sin, but alive unto God through Jesus Christ our Lord. Let not sin therefore reign in your mortal body, that ye should obey it in the lusts thereof. Neither yield ye your members as instruments of unrighteousness unto sin: but yield yourselves unto God, as those that are alive from the dead, and your members as instruments of righteousness unto God. For sin shall not have dominion over

you: for ye are not under the law, but under grace. What then? shall we sin, because we are not under the law, but under grace? God forbid. Know ye not, that to whom ye yield yourselves servants to obey, his servants ye are to whom ye obey; whether of sin unto death, or of obedience unto righteousness?" **(Romans 6:11-16)**

"Examine yourselves, whether ye be in the faith; prove your own selves. Know ye not your own selves, how that Jesus Christ is in you, except ye be reprobates? But I trust that ye shall know that we are not reprobates. Now I pray to God that ye do no evil; not that we should appear approved, but that ye should do that which is honest, though we be as reprobates." **(2 Corinthians 13:5-7)**

31

RACISM

Why one can not love God while harboring racism.

CHRISTIANS ABOVE ALL others should know and understand that all mankind are descendants in creation from Adam the first man and Eve the first woman. All mankind is of the same blood, just different blood types notwithstanding that there is even a universal blood type.

> *"And Adam called his wife's name Eve; because she was the mother of all living."* (Genesis 3:20)

> *"Have we not all one father? hath not one God created us? why do we deal treacherously every man against his brother, by profaning the covenant of our fathers?"* (Malachi 2:10)

> *"God that made the world and all things therein, seeing that he is Lord of heaven and earth, dwelleth not in temples made with hands; Neither is worshipped with men's hands, as though he needed any thing, seeing he giveth to all life, and breath, and all things; And hath made of one blood all nations of men for to dwell on all the face of the earth, and hath determined the times before appointed, and the bounds of their habitation; That they should seek the Lord, if haply they might feel after him, and find him, though he be not far from every one of us: For in him we live, and move, and have our being; as certain also of your own poets have said, For we are also his offspring."* (Acts 17:24-28)

The Bible accounts for all of the human races.

Refer to Genesis Chapter 10

The human race is a brotherhood to be loved and not hated; to hate your brother is to murder. Racists are murderers; it is impossible for a Christian to be a Klansman, Skinhead or a part of any other hate group.

> *"Thou shalt not avenge, nor bear any grudge against the children of thy people, but thou shalt love thy neighbor as thyself: I am the Lord."* (Leviticus 19:18)

> *"These are the things that ye shall do; Speak ye every man the truth to his neighbor; execute the judgment of truth and peace in your gates: And let none of you imagine evil in your*

hearts against his neighbor; and love no false oath: for all these are things that I hate, saith the Lord." (**Zechariah 8:16&17**)

"Honor thy father and thy mother: and, Thou shalt love thy neighbor as thyself." (**Matthew 19:19**)

"But when the Pharisees had heard that he had put the Sadducees to silence, they were gathered together. Then one of them, which was a lawyer, asked him a question, tempting him, and saying, Master, which is the great commandment in the law? Jesus said unto him, Thou shalt love the Lord thy God with all thy heart, and with all thy soul, and with all thy mind. This is the first and great commandment. And the second is like unto it, Thou shalt love thy neighbor as thyself. On these two commandments hang all the law and the prophets." (**Matthew 22: 34-40**)

"And one of the scribes came, and having heard them reasoning together, and perceiving that he had answered them well, asked him, Which is the first commandment of all? And Jesus answered him, The first of all the commandments is, Hear, O Israel; The Lord our God is one Lord: And thou shalt love the Lord thy God with all thy heart, and with all thy soul, and with all thy mind, and with all thy strength: this is the first commandment. And the second is like, namely this, Thou shalt love thy neighbor as thyself. There is none other commandment greater than these. And the scribe said unto him, Well, Master, thou hast said the truth: for there is one God; and there is none other but he: And to love him with all the heart, and with all the understanding, and with all the soul, and with all the strength, and to love his neighbor as himself, is more than all whole burnt offerings and sacrifices. And when Jesus saw that he answered discreetly, he said unto him, Thou art not far from the kingdom of God. And no man after that durst ask him any question." (**Mark 12:28-34**)

Owe no man any thing, but to love one another: for he that loveth another hath fulfilled the law. For this, Thou shalt not commit adultery, Thou shalt not kill, Thou shalt not steal, Thou shalt not bear false witness, Thou shalt not covet; and if there be any other commandment, it is briefly comprehended in this saying, namely, Thou shalt love thy neighbor as thyself. Love worketh no ill to his neighbor: therefore love is the fulfilling of the law." (**Romans 13:8-10**)

"In this the children of God are manifest, and the children of the devil: whosoever doeth not righteousness is not of God, neither he that loveth not his brother. For this is the message that ye heard from the beginning, that we should love one another." (**1 John 3:10&11**)

"Whosoever believeth that Jesus is the Christ is born of God: and every one that loveth him that begat loveth him also that is begotten of him. By this we know that we love the children of God, when we love God, and keep his commandments." (**1 John 5:1&2**)

"If a man say, I love God, and hateth his brother, he is a liar: for he that loveth not his brother whom he hath seen, how can he love God whom he hath not seen? And this commandment have we from him, That he who loveth God love his brother also." (**1 John 4:20&21**)

"For, brethren, ye have been called unto liberty; only use not liberty for an occasion to the flesh, but by love serve one another. For all the law is fulfilled in one word, even in this; Thou shalt love thy neighbor as thyself." (**Galatians 5:13 &14**)

"If ye fulfil the royal law according to the scripture, Thou shalt love thy neighbor as thyself, ye do well: But if ye have respect to persons, ye commit sin, and are convinced of the law as transgressors." (James 2:8&9)

"We know that we have passed from death unto life, because we love the brethren. He that loveth not his brother abideth in death. Whosoever hateth his brother is a murderer: and ye know that no murderer hath eternal life abiding in him." (1 John 3:15&16)

Christians are rather to do good to one another (mankind in general) and especially those of the household faith (Christian fellowship).

"Be not deceived; God is not mocked: for whatsoever a man soweth, that shall he also reap. For he that soweth to his flesh shall of the flesh reap corruption; but he that soweth to the Spirit shall of the Spirit reap life everlasting. And let us not be weary in well doing: for in due season we shall reap, if we faint not. As we have therefore opportunity, let us do good unto all men, especially unto them who are of the household of faith." (Galatians 6:7-10)

"Let no man deceive you with vain words: for because of these things cometh the wrath of God upon the children of disobedience. Be not ye therefore partakers with them. For ye were sometimes darkness, but now are ye light in the Lord: walk as children of light: (For the fruit of the Spirit is in all goodness and righteousness and truth;) Proving what is acceptable unto the Lord. And have no fellowship with the unfruitful works of darkness, but rather reprove them." (Ephesians 5:6-11)

The kingdom of heaven will consist of the righteous/believers of all races.

And after these things I saw four angels standing on the four corners of the earth, holding the four winds of the earth, that the wind should not blow on the earth, nor on the sea, nor on any tree. And I saw another angel ascending from the east, having the seal of the living God: and he cried with a loud voice to the four angels, to whom it was given to hurt the earth and the sea, Saying, Hurt not the earth, neither the sea, nor the trees, till we have sealed the servants of our God in their foreheads. And I heard the number of them which were sealed: and there were sealed an hundred and forty and four thousand of all the tribes of the children of Israel. Of the tribe of Juda were sealed twelve thousand. Of the tribe of Reuben were sealed twelve thousand. Of the tribe of Gad were sealed twelve thousand. Of the tribe of Aser were sealed twelve thousand. Of the tribe of Nephthalim were sealed twelve thousand. Of the tribe of Manasses were sealed twelve thousand. Of the tribe of Simeon were sealed twelve thousand. Of the tribe of Levi were sealed twelve thousand. Of the tribe of Issachar were sealed twelve thousand. Of the tribe of Zabulon were sealed twelve thousand. Of the tribe of Joseph were sealed twelve thousand. Of the tribe of Benjamin were sealed twelve thousand. After this I beheld, and, lo, a great multitude, which no man could number, of all nations, and kindreds, and people, and tongues, stood before the throne, and before the Lamb, clothed with white robes, and palms in their hands; And cried with a loud voice, saying, Salvation to our God which sitteth upon the throne, and unto the Lamb. (Revelation 7:1-10)

And we shall see our savior face to face which, judging from the biblical physical description may be unsettling to some.

> *"And I turned to see the voice that spake with me. And being turned, I saw seven golden candlesticks; And in the midst of the seven candlesticks one like unto the Son of man, clothed with a garment down to the foot, and girt about the paps with a golden girdle. His head and his hairs were white like wool, as white as snow; and his eyes were as a flame of fire; And his feet like unto fine brass, as if they burned in a furnace; and his voice as the sound of many waters. And he had in his right hand seven stars: and out of his mouth went a sharp twoedged sword: and his countenance was as the sun shineth in his strength. And when I saw him, I fell at his feet as dead. And he laid his right hand upon me, saying unto me, Fear not; I am the first and the last: I am he that liveth, and was dead; and, behold, I am alive for evermore, Amen; and have the keys of hell and of death."* (Revelation 1:12-18)

32

SATAN
(A.K.A. THE DEVIL)

Does Satan really exist? Who or what is Satan and from where did he come?

THE SCRIPTURE DECLARE that God has created everything including evil. Satan, called Lucifer, was created as a glorious angel who then sought to exalt himself over God.

"I form the light, and create darkness: I make peace, and create evil: I the Lord do all these things." (Isaiah 45:7)

"How art thou fallen from heaven, O Lucifer, son of the morning! How art thou cut down to the ground, which didst weaken the nations! For thou hast said in thine heart, I will ascend into heaven, I will exalt my throne above the stars of God: I will sit also upon the mount of the congregation, in the sides of the north: I will ascend above the heights of the clouds; I will be like the most High. Yet thou shalt be brought down to hell, to the sides of the pit. They that see thee shall narrowly look upon thee, and consider thee, saying, Is this the man that made the earth to tremble, that did shake kingdoms; that made the world as a wilderness, and destroyed the cities thereof; that opened not the house of his prisoners?" (Isaiah 14:12-17)

Satan (Satanas: the accuser, i.e. the devil) is identified as Lucifer, Beelzebub, and the Devil as well.

"And he was casting out a devil, and it was dumb. And it came to pass, when the devil was gone out, the dumb spake; and the people wondered. But some of them said, He casteth out devils through Beelzebub the chief of the devils. And others, tempting him, sought of him a sign from heaven. But he, knowing their thoughts, said unto them, 'Every kingdom divided against itself is brought to desolation; and a house divided against a house falleth. If Satan also be divided against himself, how shall his kingdom stand? Because ye say that I cast out devils through Beelzebub. And if I by Beelzebub cast out devils, by whom do your sons cast them out? Therefore shall they be your judges. But if I with the finger of God cast out devils, no doubt the kingdom of God is come upon you. When a strong man armed keepeth his palace, his goods are in peace: but when a stronger than he shall come upon him, and overcome him, he taketh from him all his armour wherein he trusted, and divideth his spoils." (Luke 11:14- 22)

"Then Peter opened his mouth, and said, Of a truth I perceive that God is no respecter of persons: But in every nation he that feareth him, and worketh righteousness, is accepted with him. The word which God sent unto the children of Israel, preaching peace by Jesus Christ: (he is Lord of all:) That word, I say, ye know, which was published throughout all Judaea, and began from Galilee, after the baptism which John preached; How God anointed Jesus of Nazareth with the Holy Ghost and with power: who went about doing good, and healing all that were oppressed of the devil; for God was with him." (**Acts 10:34-38**)

"And the great dragon was cast out, that old serpent, called the Devil, and Satan, which deceiveth the whole world: he was cast out into the earth, and his angels were cast out with him." (**Revelation 12:9**)

Satan spiritually roams the earth and is able to stand in the presence of God to make accusations against the saints.

"Be sober, be vigilant; because your adversary the devil, as a roaring lion, walketh about, seeking whom he may devour: whom resist stedfast in the faith, knowing that the same afflictions are accomplished in your brethren that are in the world." (**1 Peter 5:8-9**)

"Now there was a day when the sons of God came to present themselves before the Lord, and Satan came also among them. And the Lord said unto Satan, Whence comest thou? Then Satan answered the Lord, and said, From going to and fro in the earth, and from walking up and down in it." (**Job 1:6-7**)

"And he shewed me Joshua the high priest standing before the angel of the Lord, and Satan standing at his right hand to resist him. And the Lord said unto Satan, The Lord rebuke thee, O Satan; even the Lord that hath chosen Jerusalem rebuke thee: is not this a brand plucked out of the fire? Now Joshua was clothed with filthy garments, and stood before the angel. And he answered and spake unto those that stood before him, saying, Take away the filthy garments from him. And unto him he said, Behold, I have caused thine iniquity to pass from thee, and I will clothe thee with change of raiment." (**Zechariah 3:1-4**)

Satan was the tempter of mankind in the Garden of Eden and he was a tempter of Christ.

"Now the serpent was more subtil than any beast of the field which the Lord God had made. And he said unto the woman, Yea, hath God said, Ye shall not eat of every tree of the garden? And the woman said unto the serpent, We may eat of the fruit of the trees of the garden: but of the fruit of the tree which is in the midst of the garden, God hath said, Ye shall not eat of it, neither shall ye touch it, lest ye die. And the serpent said unto the woman, Ye shall not surely die: for God doth know that in the day ye eat thereof, then your eyes shall be opened, and ye shall be as gods, knowing good and evil." (**Genesis 3:1-5**)

"And Jesus being full of the Holy Ghost returned from Jordan, and was led by the Spirit into the wilderness, being forty days tempted of the devil. And in those days he did eat nothing: and when they were ended, he afterward hungered. And the devil said unto him, If thou be the Son of God, command this stone that it be made bread. And Jesus answered him, saying, 'It is written, That man shall not live by bread alone, but by every word of God.' And the devil, taking him up into an high mountain, shewed unto him all the kingdoms of the world in a moment of time. And the devil said unto him, All this power will I give thee,

and the glory of them: for that is delivered unto me; and to whomsoever I will I give it. If thou therefore wilt worship me, all shall be thine. And Jesus answered and said unto him, 'Get thee behind me, Satan: for it is written, Thou shalt worship the Lord thy God, and him only shalt thou serve.' And he brought him to Jerusalem, and set him on a pinnacle of the temple, and said unto him, If thou be the Son of God, cast thyself down from hence: for it is written, He shall give his angels charge over thee, to keep thee: and in their hands they shall bear thee up, lest at any time thou dash thy foot against a stone. And Jesus answering said unto him, 'It is said, Thou shalt not tempt the Lord thy God.' And when the devil had ended all the temptation, he departed from him for a season." **(Luke 4:1-13)**

Satan is the prince of the power of the air of this world, according to the scriptures. He is noted as the prince of all devils, father of all liars, and therefore, it is no surprise that some would worship him. He is manifested in the pulpit of some of our churches.

"And you hath he quickened, who were dead in trespasses and sins; wherein in time past ye walked according to the course of this world, according to the prince of the power of the air, the spirit that now worketh in the children of disobedience: among whom also we all had our conversation in times past in the lusts of our flesh, fulfilling the desires of the flesh and of the mind; and were by nature the children of wrath, even as others." **(Ephesians 2:1-3)**

"But when the Pharisees heard it, they said, This fellow doth not cast out devils, but by Beelzebub the prince of the devils." **(Matthew 12:24)**

"Jesus said unto them, 'If God were your Father, ye would love me: for I proceeded forth and came from God; neither came I of myself, but he sent me. Why do ye not understand my speech? Even because ye cannot hear my word. Ye are of your father the devil, and the lusts of your father ye will do. He was a murderer from the beginning, and abode not in the truth, because there is no truth in him. When he speaketh a lie, he speaketh of his own: for he is a liar, and the father of it. And because I tell you the truth, ye believe me not." **(John 8:42-45)**

"But what I do, that I will do, that I may cut off occasion from them which desire occasion; that wherein they glory, they may be found even as we. For such are false apostles, deceitful workers, transforming themselves into the apostles of Christ. And no marvel; for Satan himself is transformed into an angel of light. Therefore it is no great thing if his ministers also be transformed as the ministers of righteousness; whose end shall be according to their works." **(2 Corinthians 11:12-15)**

Satan wants to hinder and even destroy the saints.

"But we, brethren, being taken from you for a short time in presence, not in heart, endeavoured the more abundantly to see your face with great desire. Wherefore we would have come unto you, even I Paul, once and again; but Satan hindered us." **(1 Thessalonians 2:17-18)**

"And lest I should be exalted above measure through the abundance of the revelations, there was given to me a thorn in the flesh, the messenger of Satan to buffet me, lest I should be exalted above measure. For this thing I besought the Lord thrice, that it might depart from me. And he said unto me, My grace is sufficient for thee: for my strength is made per-

fect in weakness. Most gladly therefore will I rather glory in my infirmities, that the power of Christ may rest upon me." (**2 Corinthians 12:7-9**)

"And the Lord said, 'Simon, Simon, behold, Satan hath desired to have you, that he may sift you as wheat: but I have prayed for thee, that thy faith fail not: and when thou art converted, strengthen thy brethren." (**Luke 22:31-32**)

"Be sober, be vigilant; because your adversary the devil, as a roaring lion, walketh about, seeking whom he may devour: Whom resist stedfast in the faith, knowing that the same afflictions are accomplished in your brethren that are in the world. But the God of all grace, who hath called us unto his eternal glory by Christ Jesus, after that ye have suffered a while, make you perfect, stablish, strengthen, settle you." (**1 Peter 5:8-10**)

Christ in his coming again, is to bring down Satan and subject him to imprisonment. Satan is doomed.

"Let no man deceive you by any means: for that day shall not come, except there come a falling away first, and that man of sin be revealed, the son of perdition; who opposeth and exalteth himself above all that is called God, or that is worshipped; so that he as God sitteth in the temple of God, shewing himself that he is God. Remember ye not, that, when I was yet with you, I told you these things? And now ye know what withholdeth that he might be revealed in his time. For the mystery of iniquity doth already work: only he who now letteth will let, until he be taken out of the way. And then shall that Wicked be revealed, whom the Lord shall consume with the spirit of his mouth, and shall destroy with the brightness of his coming: even him, whose coming is after the working of Satan with all power and signs and lying wonders, and with all deceivableness of unrighteousness in them that perish; because they received not the love of the truth, that they might be saved. And for this cause God shall send them strong delusion, that they should believe a lie: that they all might be damned who believed not the truth, but had pleasure in unrighteousness." (**2 Thessalonians 2:3-12**)

"And I saw an angel come down from heaven, having the key of the bottomless pit and a great chain in his hand. And he laid hold on the dragon, that old serpent, which is the Devil, and Satan, and bound him a thousand years, and cast him into the bottomless pit, and shut him up, and set a seal upon him, that he should deceive the nations no more, till the thousand years should be fulfilled: and after that he must be loosed a little season." (**Revelation 20:1-3**)

The believer has power over Satan through the Holy Ghost.

"But ye shall receive power, after that the Holy Ghost is come upon you: and ye shall be witnesses unto me both in Jerusalem, and in all Judaea, and in Samaria, and unto the uttermost part of the earth." (**Acts 1:8**)

"Submit yourselves therefore to God. Resist the devil, and he will flee from you." (**James 4:7**)

"Finally, my brethren, be strong in the Lord, and in the power of his might. Put on the whole armour of God, that ye may be able to stand against the wiles of the devil. For we wrestle not against flesh and blood, but against principalities, against powers, against the rulers of the darkness of this world, against spiritual wickedness in high places. Wherefore

take unto you the whole armour of God, that ye may be able to withstand in the evil day, and having done all, to stand. Stand therefore, having your loins girt about with truth, and having on the breastplate of righteousness; and your feet shod with the preparation of the gospel of peace; above all, taking the shield of faith, wherewith ye shall be able to quench all the fiery darts of the wicked. And take the helmet of salvation, and the sword of the Spirit, which is the word of God: praying always with all prayer and supplication in the Spirit, and watching thereunto with all perseverance and supplication for all saint; And for me, that I may open my mouth boldly, to make known the mystery of the gospel."
(Ephesians 6:10-19)

A lake of fire and brimstone is reserved for the eternal imprisonment of Satan.

"And the devil that deceived them was cast into the lake of fire and brimstone, where the beast and the false prophet are, and shall be tormented day and night for ever and ever."
(Revelation 20:10)

33

RESISTING THE DEVIL

Knowing of Satan and his biblically acknowledged powers, how can he be resisted?

THE CHRISTIAN IS commanded to submit to God and to resist the devil; in doing so the devil is set back but not bound.

> *"Submit yourselves therefore to God. Resist the devil, and he will flee from you."* (James 4:7)

> *"Be careful for nothing; but in every thing by prayer and supplication with thanksgiving let your requests be made known unto God. And the peace of God, which passeth all understanding, shall keep your hearts and minds through Christ Jesus."* (Philippians 4:6 & 7)

> *He that committeth sin is of the devil; for the devil sinneth from the beginning. For this purpose the Son of God was manifested, that he might destroy the works of the devil. Whosoever is born of God doth not commit sin; for his seed remaineth in him: and he cannot sin, because he is born of God.In this the children of God are manifest, and the children of the devil: whosoever doeth not righteousness is not of God, neither he that loveth not his brother. For this is the message that ye heard from the beginning, that we should love one another."* (1 John 3:8-11)

> *"And when the devil had ended all the temptation, he departed from him for a season."* (Luke 4:13)

Christians, use Christ as your example in bashing and rebuking the devil in the power of the Holy Spirit and the Word of God.

> *"For this cause I bow my knees unto the Father of our Lord Jesus Christ, Of whom the whole family in heaven and earth is named, That he would grant you, according to the riches of his glory, to be strengthened with might by his Spirit in the inner man; That Christ may dwell in your hearts by faith; that ye, being rooted and grounded in love, May be able to comprehend with all saints what is the breadth, and length, and depth, and height; And to know the love of Christ, which passeth knowledge, that ye might be filled with all the fulness of God. Now unto him that is able to do exceeding abundantly above all that we ask or think, according to the power that worketh in us,"* (Ephesians 3:14-20)

"That at the name of Jesus every knee should bow, of things in heaven, and things in earth, and things under the earth; And that every tongue should confess that Jesus Christ is Lord, to the glory of God the Father." (Philippians 2:10 & 11)

"But he turned, and said unto Peter, Get thee behind me, Satan: thou art an offense unto me: for thou savorest not the things that be of God, but those that be of men." (Matthew 16:23)

"Then was Jesus led up of the spirit into the wilderness to be tempted of the devil. And when he had fasted forty days and forty nights, he was afterward an hungred. And when the tempter came to him, he said, If thou be the Son of God, command that these stones be made bread. But he answered and said, It is written, Man shall not live by bread alone, but by every word that proceedeth out of the mouth of God. Then the devil taketh him up into the holy city, and setteth him on a pinnacle of the temple, And saith unto him, If thou be the Son of God, cast thyself down: for it is written, He shall give his angels charge concerning thee: and in their hands they shall bear thee up, lest at any time thou dash thy foot against a stone. Jesus said unto him, It is written again, Thou shalt not tempt the Lord thy God. Again, the devil taketh him up into an exceeding high mountain, and sheweth him all the kingdoms of the world, and the glory of them; And saith unto him, All these things will I give thee, if thou wilt fall down and worship me. Then saith Jesus unto him, Get thee hence, Satan: for it is written, Thou shalt worship the Lord thy God, and him only shalt thou serve. Then the devil leaveth him, and, behold, angels came and ministered unto him." (Matthew 4:1-11)

The indwelling of the Christian by God's Holy Spirit is the key in operating in a power to resist Satan. No plan for the eternal destruction against a Christian, even by Satan, shall be successful.

But ye shall receive power, after that the Holy Ghost is come upon you: and ye shall be witnesses unto me both in Jerusalem, and in all Judaea, and in Samaria, and unto the uttermost part of the earth. (Acts 1:8)

"Blessed be the God and Father of our Lord Jesus Christ, who hath blessed us with all spiritual blessings in heavenly places in Christ: According as he hath chosen us in him before the foundation of the world, that we should be holy and without blame before him in love: Having predestinated us unto the adoption of children by Jesus Christ to himself, according to the good pleasure of his will,

To the praise of the glory of his grace, wherein he hath made us accepted in the beloved. In whom we have redemption through his blood, the forgiveness of sins, according to the riches of his grace; Wherein he hath abounded toward us in all wisdom and prudence; Having made known unto us the mystery of his will, according to his good pleasure which he hath purposed in himself: That in the dispensation of the fulness of times he might gather together in one all things in Christ, both which are in heaven, and which are on earth; even in him: In whom also we have obtained an inheritance, being predestinated according to the purpose of him who worketh all things after the counsel of his own will: That we should be to the praise of his glory, who first trusted in Christ. In whom ye also trusted, after that ye heard the word of truth, the gospel of your salvation: in whom also after that ye believed, ye were sealed with that holy Spirit of promise," (Ephesians 1:3-13)

"No weapon that is formed against thee shall prosper; and every tongue that shall rise against thee in judgment thou shalt condemn. This is the heritage of the servants of the Lord, and their righteousness is of me, saith the Lord." (Isaiah 54:17)

"Finally, my brethren, be strong in the Lord, and in the power of his might. Put on the whole armour of God, that ye may be able to stand against the wiles of the devil. For we wrestle not against flesh and blood, but against principalities, against powers, against the rulers of the darkness of this world, against spiritual wickedness in high places. Wherefore take unto you the whole armour of God, that ye may be able to withstand in the evil day, and having done all, to stand. Stand therefore, having your loins girt about with truth, and having on the breastplate of righteousness; And your feet shod with the preparation of the gospel of peace; Above all, taking the shield of faith, wherewith ye shall be able to quench all the fiery darts of the wicked. And take the helmet of salvation, and the sword of the Spirit, which is the word of God: Praying always with all prayer and supplication in the Spirit, and watching thereunto with all perseverance and supplication for all saints; And for me, that utterance may be given unto me, that I may open my mouth boldly, to make known the mystery of the gospel, For which I am an ambassador in bonds: that therein I may speak boldly, as I ought to speak." (Ephesians 6:10-18)

"For whatsoever is born of God overcometh the world: and this is the victory that overcometh the world, even our faith. Who is he that overcometh the world, but he that believeth that Jesus is the Son of God? This is he that came by water and blood, even Jesus Christ; not by water only, but by water and blood. And it is the Spirit that beareth witness, because the Spirit is truth. For there are three that bear record in heaven, the Father, the Word, and the Holy Ghost: and these three are one. And there are three that bear witness in earth, the Spirit, and the water, and the blood: and these three agree in one." (1 John 5:4-8)

Therefore, give no reverence whatsoever to the devil, not even in your personal appearance.

"Neither give place to the devil." (Ephesians 4:27)

"Abstain from all appearance of evil." (1 Thessalonians 5:22)

The night is far spent, the day is at hand: let us therefore cast off the works of darkness, and let us put on the armor of light. Let us walk honestly, as in the day; not in rioting and drunkenness, not in chambering and wantonness, not in strife and envying. But put ye on the Lord Jesus Christ, and make not provision for the flesh, to fulfil the lusts thereof." (Romans 13:12-14)

We are made new creatures in Christ and therefore we are able to operate in a manner contrary to our behavior in the past.

"And you hath he quickened, who were dead in trespasses and sins; Wherein in time past ye walked according to the course of this world, according to the prince of the power of the air, the spirit that now worketh in the children of disobedience: Among whom also we all had our conversation in times past in the lusts of our flesh, fulfilling the desires of the flesh and of the mind; and were by nature the children of wrath, even as others. But God, who is rich in mercy, for his great love wherewith he loved us, Even when we were dead in sins,

hath quickened us together with Christ, (by grace ye are saved;) And hath raised us up together, and made us sit together in heavenly places in Christ Jesus:" (**Ephesians 2:1-6**)

"This I say therefore, and testify in the Lord, that ye henceforth walk not as other Gentiles walk, in the vanity of their mind, Having the understanding darkened, being alienated from the life of God through the ignorance that is in them, because of the blindness of their heart: Who being past feeling have given themselves over unto lasciviousness, to work all uncleanness with greediness. But ye have not so learned Christ; If so be that ye have heard him, and have been taught by him, as the truth is in Jesus: That ye put off concerning the former conversation the old man, which is corrupt according to the deceitful lusts; And be renewed in the spirit of your mind; And that ye put on the new man, which after God is created in righteousness and true holiness. Wherefore putting away lying, speak every man truth with his neighbor: for we are members one of another. Be ye angry, and sin not: let not the sun go down upon your wrath: Neither give place to the devil. Let him that stole steal no more: but rather let him labor, working with his hands the thing which is good, that he may have to give to him that needeth. Let no corrupt communication proceed out of your mouth, but that which is good to the use of edifying, that it may minister grace unto the hearers. And grieve not the holy Spirit of God, whereby ye are sealed unto the day of redemption. Let all bitterness, and wrath, and anger, and clamor, and evil speaking, be put away from you, with all malice: And be ye kind one to another, tenderhearted, forgiving one another, even as God for Christ's sake hath forgiven you." (**Ephesians 4:17-32**)

Be not ignorant of Satan, our adversary, and his devices. Satan seeks out, riddles, fathers the disobedient, tricks, enters, entices, and possesses.

"Humble yourselves therefore under the mighty hand of God, that he may exalt you in due time: Casting all your care upon him; for he careth for you. Be sober, be vigilant; because your adversary the devil, as a roaring lion, walketh about, seeking whom he may devour: Whom resist stedfast in the faith, knowing that the same afflictions are accomplished in your brethren that are in the world." (**1 Peter 5:6-9**)

"And the Lord said, Simon, Simon, behold, Satan hath desired to have you, that he may sift you as wheat:" (**Luke 22:31**)

"And you hath he quickened, who were dead in trespasses and sins; Wherein in time past ye walked according to the course of this world, according to the prince of the power of the air, the spirit that now worketh in the children of disobedience:

Among whom also we all had our conversation in times past in the lusts of our flesh, fulfilling the desires of the flesh and of the mind; and were by nature the children of wrath, even as others." (**Ephesians 2:1-3**)

"Now the feast of unleavened bread drew nigh, which is called the Passover. And the chief priests and scribes sought how they might kill him; for they feared the people. Then entered Satan into Judas surnamed Iscariot, being of the number of the twelve. And he went his way, and communed with the chief priests and captains, how he might betray him unto them. And they were glad, and covenanted to give him money. And he promised, and sought opportunity to betray him unto them in the absence of the multitude." (**Luke 22:1-6**)

"Blessed is the man that endureth temptation: for when he is tried, he shall receive the crown of life, which the Lord hath promised to them that love him. Let no man say when he is tempted, I am tempted of God: for God cannot be tempted with evil, neither tempteth he any man: But every man is tempted, when he is drawn away of his own lust, and enticed. Then when lust hath conceived, it bringeth forth sin: and sin, when it is finished, bringeth forth death." (James 1:12-15)

"Then was brought unto him one possessed with a devil, blind, and dumb: and he healed him, insomuch that the blind and dumb both spake and saw. And all the people were amazed, and said, Is not this the son of David? But when the Pharisees heard it, they said, This fellow doth not cast out devils, but by Beelzebub the prince of the devils. And Jesus knew their thoughts, and said unto them, Every kingdom divided against itself is brought to desolation; and every city or house divided against itself shall not stand: And if Satan cast out Satan, he is divided against himself; how shall then his kingdom stand? And if I by Beelzebub cast out devils, by whom do your children cast them out? therefore they shall be your judges. But if I cast out devils by the Spirit of God, then the kingdom of God is come unto you. Or else how can one enter into a strong man's house, and spoil his goods, except he first bind the strong man? and then he will spoil his house." (Matthew 12:22-29)

"When the unclean spirit is gone out of a man, he walketh through dry places, seeking rest, and findeth none. Then he saith, I will return into my house from whence I came out; and when he is come, he findeth it empty, swept, and garnished. Then goeth he, and taketh with himself seven other spirits more wicked than himself, and they enter in and dwell there: and the last ." (Matthew 12:43-45)

"For to this end also did I write, that I might know the proof of you, whether ye be obedient in all things. To whom ye forgive any thing, I forgive also: for if I forgave any thing, to whom I forgave it, for your sakes forgave I it in the person of Christ; Lest Satan should get an advantage of us: for we are not ignorant of his devices." (2 Corinthians 2:9-11)

All power has been given in heaven and earth to the Lord and Savior of the church, Jesus Christ, and we are able to operate in all power when abiding in Jesus by the power of the Holy Spirit.

"And what is the exceeding greatness of his power to us-ward who believe, according to the working of his mighty power, Which he wrought in Christ, when he raised him from the dead, and set him at his own right hand in the heavenly places, Far above all principality, and power, and might, and dominion, and every name that is named, not only in this world, but also in that which is to come: And hath put all things under his feet, and gave him to be the head over all things to the church, Which is his body, the fulness of him that filleth all in all." (Ephesians 1:19-23)

"But God, who is rich in mercy, for his great love wherewith he loved us, Even when we were dead in sins, hath quickened us together with Christ, (by grace ye are saved;) And hath raised us up together, and made us sit together in heavenly places in Christ Jesus: That in the ages to come he might shew the exceeding riches of his grace in his kindness toward us through Christ Jesus." (Ephesians 2:4-7)

"And this is his commandment, That we should believe on the name of his Son Jesus Christ, and love one another, as he gave us commandment. And he that keepeth his command-

ments dwelleth in him, and he in him. And hereby we know that he abideth in us, by the Spirit which he hath given us." (1 John 3:23 & 24)

God will overcome Satan and evil.

"Why boasted thou thyself in mischief, O mighty man? The goodness of God endureth continually." (Psalm 52:1)

"Let love be without dissimulation. Abhor that which is evil; cleave to that which is good. Be not overcome of evil, but overcome evil with good." (Romans 12:9 & 21)

"And then shall that Wicked be revealed, whom the Lord shall consume with the spirit of his mouth, and shall destroy with the brightness of his coming: Even him, whose coming is after the working of Satan with all power and signs and lying wonders, And with all deceivableness of unrighteousness in them that perish; because they received not the love of the truth, that they might be saved. And for this cause God shall send them strong delusion, that they should believe a lie: That they all might be damned who believed not the truth, but had pleasure in unrighteousness." (2 Thessalonians 2:8-12)

34

SPEAKING OF THE ANTICHRIST AND ANTICHRISTS

I have no clue what people are talking about concerning the Antichrist or antichrists and whether it's a good or bad thing.

BY DEFINITION, TO be Antichrist (Anticristos - an opponent of the Messiah) is to be in denial of Jesus as the Christ. Note that the Bible calls the Antichrist(s) a liar/deceiver and Satan the father of all liars.

> *"Who is a liar but he that denieth that Jesus is the Christ? He is antichrist, that denieth the Father and the Son."* (1 John 2:22)

> *"Ye are of your father the devil, and the lusts of your father ye will do. He was a murderer from the beginning, and abode not in the truth, because there is no truth in him. When he speaketh a lie, he speaketh of his own: for he is a liar, and the father of it."* (John 8:44)

> *"For many deceivers are entered into the world, who confess not that Jesus Christ is come in the flesh. This is a deceiver and an antichrist."* (2 John 7)

The Bible has declared that the spirit of Antichrist as already in the world and that this fact affirms that we are in the last days.

> *"If there arise among you a prophet, or a dreamer of dreams, and giveth thee a sign or a wonder, And the sign or the wonder come to pass, whereof he spake unto thee, saying, Let us go after other gods, which thou hast not known, and let us serve them; Thou shalt not hearken unto the words of that prophet, or that dreamer of dreams: for the Lord your God proveth you, to know whether ye love the Lord your God with all your heart and with all your soul. Ye shall walk after the Lord your God, and fear him, and keep his commandments, and obey his voice, and ye shall serve him, and cleave unto him."* (Deuteronomy 13:1-4)

> *"And every spirit that confesseth not that Jesus Christ is come in the flesh is not of God: and this is that spirit of antichrist, whereof ye have heard that it should come; and even now already is it in the world."* (1 John 4:3)

"Little children, it is the last time: and as ye have heard that antichrist shall come, even now are there many antichrists; whereby we know that it is the last time." (1 John 2:18)

"For many deceivers are entered into the world, who confess not that Jesus Christ is come in the flesh. This is a deceiver and an antichrist. Look to yourselves, that we lose not those things which we have wrought, but that we receive a full reward." (2 John 7&9)

Satan physically roams the earth today in the spiritual realm and is able to transform himself and his ministers to appear righteous.

"Be sober, be vigilant; because your adversary the devil, as a roaring lion, walketh about, seeking whom he may devour: Whom resist stedfast in the faith, knowing that the same afflictions are accomplished in your brethren that are in the world." (1 Peter 5:8&9)

"For such are false apostles, deceitful workers, transforming themselves into the apostles of Christ. And no marvel; for Satan himself is transformed into an angel of light. Therefore it is no great thing if his ministers also be transformed as the ministers of righteousness; whose end shall be according to their works." (2 Corinthians 11:13-15)

A deceiver (planos - impostor, misleader, seducer) comes today in the form of a false prophet.

"If there arise among you a prophet, or a dreamer of dreams, and giveth thee a sign or a wonder, And the sign or the wonder come to pass, whereof he spake unto thee, saying, Let us go after other gods, which thou hast not known, and let us serve them; Thou shalt not hearken unto the words of that prophet, or that dreamer of dreams: for the Lord your God proveth you, to know whether ye love the Lord your God with all your heart and with all your soul. Ye shall walk after the Lord your God, and fear him, and keep his commandments, and obey his voice, and ye shall serve him, and cleave unto him." (Deuteronomy 13:1-4)

"But the prophet, which shall presume to speak a word in my name, which I have not commanded him to speak, or that shall speak in the name of other gods, even that prophet shall die. And if thou say in thine heart, How shall we know the word which the Lord hath not spoken? When a prophet speaketh in the name of the Lord, if the thing follow not, nor come to pass, that is the thing which the Lord hath not spoken, but the prophet hath spoken it presumptuously: thou shalt not be afraid of him." (Deuteronomy 18:20-22))

"And many false prophets shall rise, and shall deceive many." (Matthew 24:11)

"For there shall arise false Christs, and false prophets, and shall shew great signs and wonders; insomuch that, if it were possible, they shall deceive the very elect." (Matthew 24:24)

"Beware of false prophets, which come to you in sheep's clothing, but inwardly they are ravening wolves. Ye shall know them by their fruits. Do men gather grapes of thorns, or figs of thistles? Even so every good tree bringeth forth good fruit; but a corrupt tree bringeth forth evil fruit. A good tree cannot bring forth evil fruit, neither can a corrupt tree bring forth good fruit. Every tree that bringeth not forth good fruit is hewn down, and cast into the fire. Wherefore by their fruits ye shall know them. Not every one that saith unto me, Lord, Lord, shall enter into the kingdom of heaven; but he that doeth the will of my Father

which is in heaven. Many will say to me in that day, Lord, Lord, have we not prophesied in thy name? and in thy name have cast out devils? and in thy name done many wonderful works? And then will I profess unto them, I never knew you: depart from me, ye that work iniquity." (Matthew 7:15-23)

Further, the Bible delineates, in a symbolic manner, "the antichrist" from "the false prophet" and "the Devil" which is Satan. Note also that the Bible interchanges the beast with the antichrist, a second beast with the false prophet and the dragon with Satan. The beast/Antichrist obtains his power from the dragon/Satan. The Bible identifies a second beast who shall proclaim the Antichrist. This person is to appear and deceive a multitude that will join in league with him and attempt to make war with Jesus Christ upon his second appearance on earth.

"And I saw three unclean spirits like frogs come out of the mouth of the dragon, and out of the mouth of the beast, and out of the mouth of the false prophet. For they are the spirits of devils, working miracles, which go forth unto the kings of the earth and of the whole world, to gather them to the battle of that great day of God Almighty." (Revelation 16:13)

"And I stood upon the sand of the sea, and saw a beast rise up out of the sea, having seven heads and ten horns, and upon his horns ten crowns, and upon his heads the name of blasphemy. And the beast which I saw was like unto a leopard, and his feet were as the feet of a bear, and his mouth as the mouth of a lion: and the dragon gave him his power, and his seat, and great authority. And I saw one of his heads as it were wounded to death; and his deadly wound was healed: and all the world wondered after the beast. And they worshipped the dragon which gave power unto the beast: and they worshipped the beast, saying, Who is like unto the beast? who is able to make war with him?" (Revelation 13:1-4)

"And I beheld another beast coming up out of the earth; and he had two horns like a lamb, and he spake as a dragon. And he exerciseth all the power of the first beast before him, and causeth the earth and them which dwell therein to worship the first beast, whose deadly wound was healed. And he doeth great wonders, so that he maketh fire come down from heaven on the earth in the sight of men, And deceiveth them that dwell on the earth by the means of those miracles which he had power to do in the sight of the beast; saying to them that dwell on the earth, that they should make an image to the beast, which had the wound by a sword, and did live. And he had power to give life unto the image of the beast, that the image of the beast should both speak, and cause that as many as would not worship the image of the beast should be killed. And he causeth all, both small and great, rich and poor, free and bond, to receive a mark in their right hand, or in their foreheads: And that no man might buy or sell, save he that had the mark, or the name of the beast, or the number of his name. Here is wisdom. Let him that hath understanding count the number of the beast: for it is the number of a man; and his number is Six hundred threescore and six." (Revelation 13:11-18)

"And I saw the beast, and the kings of the earth, and their armies, gathered together to make war against him that sat on the horse, and against his army. And the beast was taken, and with him the false prophet that wrought miracles before him, with which he deceived them that had received the mark of the beast, and them that worshipped his image. These both were cast alive into a lake of fire burning with brimstone. And the remnant were slain with the sword of him that sat upon the horse, which sword proceeded out of his mouth: and all the fowls were filled with their flesh. And I saw an angel come down

from heaven, having the key of the bottomless pit and a great chain in his hand. And he laid hold on the dragon, that old serpent, which is the Devil, and Satan, and bound him a thousand years, And cast him into the bottomless pit, and shut him up, and set a seal upon him, that he should deceive the nations no more, till the thousand years should be fulfilled: and after that he must be loosed a little season." (Revelation 19:19 - 20:3)

Note the ending for Satan, the Antichrist and the False Prophet. The personal question with which to wrestle herein is, am I to believe this as true?

"And the beast was taken, and with him the false prophet that wrought miracles before him, with which he deceived them that had received the mark of the beast, and them that worshipped his image. These both were cast alive into a lake of fire burning with brimstone." (Revelation 19:20)

"And the devil that deceived them was cast into the lake of fire and brimstone, where the beast and the false prophet are, and shall be tormented day and night for ever and ever." (Revelation 20:10)

Now, what should be the Christian's comportment towards opponents of Christ? Christians should love the opponents of Christ even as we would love all of our enemies (see Chapter 12, Christian Tolerance) and seek their soul's salvation. However, there is no fellowship with those that, in spite of our evangelism, reject Jesus Christ.

"For this is the message that ye heard from the beginning, that we should love one another." (1 John 3:11)

"Brethren, if any of you do err from the truth, and one convert him; Let him know, that he which converteth the sinner from the error of his way shall save a soul from death, and shall hide a multitude of sins." (James 5:19&20)

"Let no man deceive you with vain words: for because of these things cometh the wrath of God upon the children of disobedience. Be not ye therefore partakers with them. For ye were sometimes darkness, but now are ye light in the Lord: walk as children of light: (For the fruit of the Spirit is in all goodness and righteousness and truth;) Proving what is acceptable unto the Lord. And have no fellowship with the unfruitful works of darkness, but rather reprove them. For it is a shame even to speak of those things which are done of them in secret. But all things that are reproved are made manifest by the light: for whatsoever doth make manifest is light. Wherefore he saith, Awake thou that sleepest, and arise from the dead, and Christ shall give thee light. See then that ye walk circumspectly, not as fools, but as wise, Redeeming the time, because the days are evil. Wherefore be ye not unwise, but understanding what the will of the Lord is." (Ephesians 5:6-17)

"This then is the message which we have heard of him, and declare unto you, that God is light, and in him is no darkness at all. If we say that we have fellowship with him, and walk in darkness, we lie, and do not the truth: But if we walk in the light, as he is in the light, we have fellowship one with another, and the blood of Jesus Christ his Son cleanseth us from all sin." (1 John 1:5-7)

As Christians, we are called upon to be kind in the spreading of the gospel. I am persuaded that an exception is made when there is someone with whom we are particularly

familiar; with those we are given more license by God to point the way.

> *"And the servant of the Lord must not strive; but be gentle unto all men, apt to teach, patient, In meekness instructing those that oppose themselves; if God peradventure will give them repentance to the acknowledging of the truth; And that they may recover themselves out of the snare of the devil, who are taken captive by him at his will."* (**2 Timothy 2:24**)

> *"What man of you, having an hundred sheep, if he lose one of them, doth not leave the ninety and nine in the wilderness, and go after that which is lost, until he find it? And when he hath found it, he layeth it on his shoulders, rejoicing. And when he cometh home, he calleth together his friends and neighbors, saying unto them, Rejoice with me; for I have found my sheep which was lost. I say unto you, that likewise joy shall be in heaven over one sinner that repenteth, more than over ninety and nine just persons, which need no repentance."* (**Luke 15:4-7**)

> *"But, beloved, remember ye the words which were spoken before of the apostles of our Lord Jesus Christ; How that they told you there should be mockers in the last time, who should walk after their own ungodly lusts. These be they who separate themselves, sensual, having not the Spirit. But ye, beloved, building up yourselves on your most holy faith, praying in the Holy Ghost, Keep yourselves in the love of God, looking for the mercy of our Lord Jesus Christ unto eternal life. And of some have compassion, making a difference: And others save with fear, pulling them out of the fire; hating even the garment spotted by the flesh. Now unto him that is able to keep you from falling, and to present you faultless before the presence of his glory with exceeding joy, To the only wise God our Saviour, be glory and majesty, dominion and power, both now and ever. Amen."* (**Jude 17-25**)

Then there is a particular breed, and I would like to think of myself as included in that number, who are called out by God to evangelize in a more robust manner as to come against those that would subvert whole families. The Bible says that "their mouths must be stopped" and that is of course by the spreading of the gospel (good news).

> *For there are many unruly and vain talkers and deceivers, specially they of the circumcision: Whose mouths must be stopped, who subvert whole houses, teaching things which they ought not, for filthy lucre's sake."* (**Titus 1:10&11**)

> *"How should one chase a thousand, and two put ten thousand to flight, except their Rock had sold them, and the Lord had shut them up? For their rock is not as our Rock, even our enemies themselves being judges. For their vine is of the vine of Sodom, and of the fields of Gomorrah: their grapes are grapes of gall, their clusters are bitter: Their wine is the poison of dragons, and the cruel venom of asps. Is not this laid up in store with me, and sealed up among my treasures? To me belongeth vengeance and recompence; their foot shall slide in due time: for the day of their calamity is at hand, and the things that shall come upon them make haste. For the Lord shall judge his people, and repent himself for his servants, when he seeth that their power is gone, and there is none shut up, or left. And he shall say, Where are their gods, their rock in whom they trusted, Which did eat the fat of their sacrifices, and drank the wine of their drink offerings? let them rise up and help you, and be your protection. See now that I, even I, am he, and there is no God with me: I kill, and I make alive; I wound, and I heal: neither is there any that can deliver out of my hand. For I lift up my hand to heaven, and say, I live for ever."* (**Deuteronomy 32:30-40**)

35

Capital Punishment under Scriptural Examination

God has said in the Ten Commandments that thou shall not kill. How then can we possibly justify capital punishment?

FROM THE BEGINNING of mankind there has been the shedding of innocent blood. Cain killed Abel and there remain those that by their unchanged nature kill and even entice others to kill their fellow man.

"And Cain talked with Abel his brother: and it came to pass, when they were in the field, that Cain rose up against Abel his brother, and slew him. And the Lord said unto Cain, Where is Abel thy brother? And he said, I know not: Am I my brother's keeper? And he said, What hast thou done? the voice of thy brother's blood crieth unto me from the ground." (Genesis 4:8-10)

"My son, if sinners entice thee, consent thou not. If they say, Come with us, let us lay wait for blood, let us lurk privily for the innocent without cause: Let us swallow them up alive as the grave; and whole, as those that go down into the pit: We shall find all precious substance, we shall fill our houses with spoil: Cast in thy lot among us; let us all have one purse: My son, walk not thou in the way with them; refrain thy foot from their path: For their feet run to evil, and make haste to shed blood. Surely in vain the net is spread in the sight of any bird." (Proverbs 1:10-17)

"The wicked, through the pride of his countenance, will not seek after God: God is not in all his thoughts. His ways are always grievous; thy judgments are far above out of his sight: as for all his enemies, he puffeth at them. He hath said in his heart, I shall not be moved: for I shall never be in adversity. His mouth is full of cursing and deceit and fraud: under his tongue is mischief and vanity. He sitteth in the lurking places of the villages: in the secret places doth he murder the innocent: his eyes are privily set against the poor." (Psalm 10:4-8)

"Behold, the Lord's hand is not shortened, that it cannot save; neither his ear heavy, that it cannot hear: But your iniquities have separated between you and your God, and your sins have hid his face from you, that he will not hear. For your hands are defiled with blood, and your fingers with iniquity; your lips have spoken lies, your tongue hath muttered perverseness. None calleth for justice, nor any pleadeth for truth: they trust in vanity, and

speak lies; they conceive mischief, and bring forth iniquity. They hatch cockatrice' eggs, and weave the spider's web: he that eateth of their eggs dieth, and that which is crushed breaketh out into a viper. Their webs shall not become garments, neither shall they cover themselves with their works: their works are works of iniquity, and the act of violence is in their hands. Their feet run to evil, and they make haste to shed innocent blood: their thoughts are thoughts of iniquity; wasting and destruction are in their paths. The way of peace they know not; and there is no judgment in their goings: they have made them crooked paths: whosoever goeth therein shall not know peace." (**Isaiah 59:1-8**)

"But those things which proceed out of the mouth come forth from the heart; and they defile the man. For out of the heart proceed evil thoughts, murders, adulteries, fornications, thefts, false witness, blasphemies:" (**Matthew 15:18 & 19**)

God has commanded that "thou shalt not kill"(ratsach: murder). God knows the darkness of man and is able to take vengeance upon the wicked and shedders of innocent blood.

"Thou shalt not kill." (**Exodus 20:13**)

"O Lord God, to whom vengeance belongeth; O God, to whom vengeance belongeth, shew thyself. Lift up thyself, thou judge of the earth: render a reward to the proud. Lord, how long shall the wicked, how long shall the wicked triumph? How long shall they utter and speak hard things? and all the workers of iniquity boast themselves? They break in pieces thy people, O Lord, and afflict thine heritage. Shall the throne of iniquity have fellowship with thee, which frameth mischief by a law? They gather themselves together against the soul of the righteous, and condemn the innocent blood. But the Lord is my defence; and my God is the rock of my refuge. And he shall bring upon them their own iniquity, and shall cut them off in their own wickedness; yea, the Lord our God shall cut them off." (**Psalm 94:1-5, 20-23**)

"A naughty person, a wicked man, walketh with a froward mouth. He winketh with his eyes, he speaketh with his feet, he teacheth with his fingers; Frowardness is in his heart, he deviseth mischief continually; he soweth discord. Therefore shall his calamity come suddenly; suddenly shall he be broken without remedy." (**Proverbs 6:12-15**)

God has in the Bible prescribed punishment [muwth: put to death, kill one worthy of death] to the Israelites to fit the capital crime of murder as well as other transgressions; this was under the tutelage of the law as was "an eye for an eye".

"He that smiteth a man, so that he die, shall be surely put to death. And if a man lie not in wait, but God deliver him into his hand; then I will appoint thee a place whither he shall flee. But if a man come presumptuously upon his neighbor, to slay him with guile; thou shalt take him from mine altar, that he may die. And he that smiteth his father, or his mother, shall be surely put to death. And he that stealeth a man, and selleth him, or if he be found in his hand, he shall be surely put to death. And he that curseth his father, or his mother, shall surely be put to death." (**Exodus 21:12-17**)

"If an ox gore a man or a woman, that they die: then the ox shall be surely stoned, and his flesh shall not be eaten; but the owner of the ox shall be quit. But if the ox were wont to push with his horn in time past, and it hath been testified to his owner, and he hath not

kept him in, but that he hath killed a man or a woman; the ox shall be stoned, and his owner also shall be put to death." (**Exodus 21:28-29**)

"Sanctify yourselves therefore, and be ye holy: for I am the Lord your God. And ye shall keep my statutes, and do them: I am the Lord which sanctify you. For every one that curseth his father or his mother shall be surely put to death: he hath cursed his father or his mother; his blood shall be upon him. And the man that committeth adultery with another man's wife, even he that committeth adultery with his neighbor's wife, the adulterer and the adulteress shall surely be put to death. And the man that lieth with his father's wife hath uncovered his father's nakedness: both of them shall surely be put to death; their blood shall be upon them. And if a man lie with his daughter in law, both of them shall surely be put to death: they have wrought confusion; their blood shall be upon them. If a man also lie with mankind, as he lieth with a woman, both of them have committed an abomination: they shall surely be put to death; their blood shall be upon them. And if a man take a wife and her mother, it is wickedness: they shall be burnt with fire, both he and they; that there be no wickedness among you. And if a man lie with a beast, he shall surely be put to death: and ye shall slay the beast. And if a woman approach unto any beast, and lie down thereto, thou shalt kill the woman, and the beast: they shall surely be put to death; their blood shall be upon them. A man also or woman that hath a familiar spirit, or that is a wizard, shall surely be put to death: they shall stone them with stones: their blood shall be upon them." (**Leviticus 20:7-16, 27**)

"If there be found among you, within any of thy gates which the Lord thy God giveth thee, man or woman, that hath wrought wickedness in the sight of the Lord thy God, in transgressing his covenant, And hath gone and served other gods, and worshipped them, either the sun, or moon, or any of the host of heaven, which I have not commanded; And it be told thee, and thou hast heard of it, and enquired diligently, and, behold, it be true, and the thing certain, that such abomination is wrought in Israel: Then shalt thou bring forth that man or that woman, which have committed that wicked thing, unto thy gates, even that man or that woman, and shalt stone them with stones, till they die. At the mouth of two witnesses, or three witnesses, shall he that is worthy of death be put to death; but at the mouth of one witness he shall not be put to death. The hands of the witnesses shall be first upon him to put him to death, and afterward the hands of all the people. So thou shalt put the evil away from among you." (**Deuteronomy 17:2-7**)

"And if a man have committed a sin worthy of death, and he be to be put to death, and thou hang him on a tree: His body shall not remain all night upon the tree, but thou shalt in any wise bury him that day; (for he that is hanged is accursed of God;) that thy land be not defiled, which the LORD thy God giveth thee for an inheritance." (**Deuteronomy 21:22&23**)

"If men strive, and hurt a woman with child, so that her fruit depart from her, and yet no mischief follow: he shall be surely punished, according as the woman's husband will lay upon him; and he shall pay as the judges determine. And if any mischief follow, then thou shalt give life for life, Eye for eye, tooth for tooth, hand for hand, foot for foot, Burning for burning, wound for wound, stripe for stripe." (**Exodus 21:22-25**)

The Bible supports government and laws. It also supports justice and mercy; would not that be fairness? An eye for an eye has yielded to grace and mercy, however, it is under-

stood by the Bible that there are transgressions, that as government determines, worthy of the punishment of death.

"Who is a God like unto thee, that pardoneth iniquity, and passeth by the transgression of the remnant of his heritage? he retaineth not his anger for ever, because he delighteth in mercy. He will turn again, he will have compassion upon us; he will subdue our iniquities; and thou wilt cast all their sins into the depths of the sea." (Micah 7:18&19)

"But let none of you suffer as a murderer, or as a thief, or as an evildoer, or as a busybody in other men's matters. Yet if any man suffer as a Christian, let him not be ashamed; but let him glorify God on this behalf." (1 Peter 4:15&16)

"For rulers are not a terror to good works, but to the evil. Wilt thou then not be afraid of the power? do that which is good, and thou shalt have praise of the same: For he is the minister of God to thee for good. But if thou do that which is evil, be afraid; for he beareth not the sword in vain: for he is the minister of God, a revenger to execute wrath upon him that doeth evil. Wherefore ye must needs be subject, not only for wrath, but also for conscience sake." (Romans 13:3-5)

"Put them in mind to be subject to principalities and powers, to obey magistrates, to be ready to every good work, To speak evil of no man, to be no brawlers, but gentle, shewing all meekness unto all men." (Titus 3:1&2)

"But God commendeth his love toward us, in that, while we were yet sinners, Christ died for us. Much more then, being now justified by his blood, we shall be saved from wrath through him. For if, when we were enemies, we were reconciled to God by the death of his Son, much more, being reconciled, we shall be saved by his life. And not only so, but we also joy in God through our Lord Jesus Christ, by whom we have now received the atonement. Wherefore, as by one man sin entered into the world, and death by sin; and so death passed upon all men, for that all have sinned: (For until the law sin was in the world: but sin is not imputed when there is no law. Nevertheless death reigned from Adam to Moses, even over them that had not sinned after the similitude of Adam's transgression, who is the figure of him that was to come. But not as the offence, so also is the free gift. For if through the offence of one many be dead, much more the grace of God, and the gift by grace, which is by one man, Jesus Christ, hath abounded unto many. And not as it was by one that sinned, so is the gift: for the judgment was by one to condemnation, but the free gift is of many offences unto justification. For if by one man's offence death reigned by one; much more they which receive abundance of grace and of the gift of righteousness shall reign in life by one, Jesus Christ.) Therefore as by the offence of one judgment came upon all men to condemnation; even so by the righteousness of one the free gift came upon all men unto justification of life. For as by one man's disobedience many were made sinners, so by the obedience of one shall many be made righteous. Moreover the law entered, that the offence might abound. But where sin abounded, grace did much more abound: That as sin hath reigned unto death, even so might grace reign through righteousness unto eternal life by Jesus Christ our Lord." (Romans 5:8-21)

"Therefore all things whatsoever ye would that men should do to you, do ye even so to them: for this is the law and the prophets." (Matthew 7:12)

"He hath shewed thee, O man, what is good; and what doth the Lord require of thee, but to do justly, and to love mercy, and to walk humbly with thy God?" (Micah 6:8)

"As every man hath received the gift, even so minister the same one to another, as good stewards of the manifold grace of God." (1Peter 4:10)

It is obvious that God has no objection to capital punishment being justified for certain offenses as deemed so by government. According to the Bible, God has sentenced murderers and other sinners to an eternal death [second death, damnation]. God's judgments are just and if punishment is purely for vengeance, that determination belongs to God and he will be faithful to carryout that judgment in the end.

"And surely your blood of your lives will I require; at the hand of every beast will I require it, and at the hand of man; at the hand of every man's brother will I require the life of man. Whoso sheddeth man's blood, by man shall his blood be shed: for in the image of God made he man." (Genesis 9:5&6)

"And Moses took half of the blood, and put it in basons; and half of the blood he sprinkled on the altar. And he took the book of the covenant, and read in the audience of the people: and they said, All that the Lord hath said will we do, and be obedient." (Exodus 24:6&7)

"Whosoever hateth his brother is a murderer: and ye know that no murderer hath eternal life abiding in him." (1 John 3:15)

"He that overcometh shall inherit all things; and I will be his God, and he shall be my son. But the fearful, and unbelieving, and the abominable, and murderers, and whoremongers, and sorcerers, and idolaters, and all liars, shall have their part in the lake which burneth with fire and brimstone: which is the second death." (Revelation 21:7&8)

"Blessed are they that do his commandments, that they may have right to the tree of life, and may enter in through the gates into the city. For without are dogs, and sorcerers, and whoremongers, and murderers, and idolaters, and whosoever loveth and maketh a lie." (Revelation 22:14&15)

"And the devil that deceived them was cast into the lake of fire and brimstone, where the beast and the false prophet are, and shall be tormented day and night for ever and ever. And I saw a great white throne, and him that sat on it, from whose face the earth and the heaven fled away; and there was found no place for them. And I saw the dead, small and great, stand before God; and the books were opened: and another book was opened, which is the book of life: and the dead were judged out of those things which were written in the books, according to their works. And the sea gave up the dead which were in it; and death and hell delivered up the dead which were in them: and they were judged every man according to their works. And death and hell were cast into the lake of fire. This is the second death. And whosoever was not found written in the book of life was cast into the lake of fire." (Revelation 20:10-15)

"Dearly beloved, avenge not yourselves, but rather give place unto wrath: for it is written, Vengeance is mine; I will repay, saith the Lord." (Romans 12:19)

"Justice and judgment are the habitation of thy throne: mercy and truth shall go before thy face." (Psalm 89:14)

36

HOMOSEXUALITY

What is wrong with a person being a homosexual and why should they be limited in any way? Should we celebrate our diversity even in the pulpit of the church?

THE BIBLE STATES that God has created us the way we are. Therefore, some homosexuals are most assuredly born. God gets the glory out of us overcoming. I have no doubt in the fact of some homosexuals being born as such because of two reasons: (1) there are persons that are born with both male and female genitals and/or chromosomes (intersexed) and (2) I was born a womanizer with a double cleft palate. In spite of my condition at birth, I am today a preacher and have been happily married to the same woman for more than three decades.

"And the Lord said unto him, Who hath made man's mouth? Or who maketh the dumb, or deaf, or the seeing, or the blind? Have not I the Lord?" (**Exodus 4:11**)

"We then that are strong ought to bear the infirmities of the weak, and not to please ourselves. Let every one of us please his neighbour for his good to edification. For even Christ pleased not himself; but, as it is written, The reproaches of them that reproached thee fell on me. For whatsoever things were written aforetime were written for our learning, that we through patience and comfort of the scriptures might have hope." (**Romans 15:1-4**)

"Set your affection on things above, not on things on the earth. For ye are dead, and your life is hid with Christ in God. When Christ, who is our life, shall appear, then shall ye also appear with him in glory. Mortify therefore your members which are upon the earth; fornication, uncleanness, inordinate affection, evil concupiscence, and covetousness, which is idolatry: for which things' sake the wrath of God cometh on the children of disobedience: in the which ye also walked some time, when ye lived in them." (**Colossians 3:2-7**)

"Christ is become of no effect unto you, whosoever of you are justified by the law; ye are fallen from grace. For we through the Spirit wait for the hope of righteousness by faith." (**Galatians 5:4-5**)

"For whatsoever is born of God overcometh the world: and this is the victory that overcometh the world, even our faith. Who is he that overcometh the world, but he that believeth that Jesus is the Son of God?" (**1 John 5:4-5**)

"But now thus saith the Lord that created thee, O Jacob, and he that formed thee, O Israel, Fear not: for I have redeemed thee, I have called thee by thy name; thou art mine. When thou passest through the waters, I will be with thee; and through the rivers, they shall not overflow thee: when thou walkest through the fire, thou shalt not be burned; neither shall the flame kindle upon thee. For I am the Lord thy God, the Holy One of Israel, thy Saviour: I gave Egypt for thy ransom, Ethiopia and Seba for thee. Since thou wast precious in my sight, thou hast been honourable, and I have loved thee: therefore will I give men for thee, and people for thy life. Fear not: for I am with thee: I will bring thy seed from the east, and gather thee from the west; I will say to the north, Give up; and to the south, Keep not back: bring my sons from far, and my daughters from the ends of the earth; Even every one that is called by my name: for I have created him for my glory, I have formed him; yea, I have made him. Bring forth the blind people that have eyes, and the deaf that have ears. Let all the nations be gathered together, and let the people be assembled: who among them can declare this, and shew us former things? let them bring forth their witnesses, that they may be justified: or let them hear, and say, It is truth. Ye are my witnesses, saith the Lord, and my servant whom I have chosen: that ye may know and believe me, and understand that I am he: before me there was no God formed, neither shall there be after me. I, even I, am the Lord; and beside me there is no saviour. I have declared, and have saved, and I have shewed, when there was no strange god among you: therefore ye are my witnesses, saith the Lord, that I am God. Yea, before the day was I am he; and there is none that can deliver out of my hand: I will work, and who shall let it? Thus saith the Lord, your redeemer, the Holy One of Israel; For your sake I have sent to Babylon, and have brought down all their nobles, and the Chaldeans, whose cry is in the ships. I am the Lord, your Holy One, the creator of Israel, your King." (Isaiah 43:1-15)

There is a God, who has created us in his image, that is jealous (qanna – envious) yet merciful. God will curse the iniquity (avon - perversity, evil fault, punishment of sin) of the fathers upon the children, which may explain why some abnormalities occur at birth and then maybe not. There is nothing that can deliver us out of God's will.

"Take heed to thyself, lest thou make a covenant with the inhabitants of the land whither thou goest, lest it be for a snare in the midst of thee: but ye shall destroy their altars, break their images, and cut down their groves: for thou shalt worship no other god: for the Lord, whose name is Jealous, is a jealous God: lest thou make a covenant with the inhabitants of the land, and they go a whoring after their gods, and do sacrifice unto their gods, and one call thee, and thou eat of his sacrifice; and thou take of their daughters unto thy sons, and their daughters go a whoring after their gods, and make thy sons go a whoring after their gods." (Exodus 34:12-16)

"And the Lord passed by before him, and proclaimed, The Lord, The Lord God, merciful and gracious, longsuffering, and abundant in goodness and truth, keeping mercy for thousands, forgiving iniquity and transgression and sin, and that will by no means clear the guilty; visiting the iniquity of the fathers upon the children, and upon the children's children, unto the third and to the fourth generation." (Exodus 34:6-7)

"And God spake all these words, saying, I am the Lord thy God, which have brought thee out of the land of Egypt, out of the house of bondage. Thou shalt have no other gods before me. Thou shalt not make unto thee any graven image, or any likeness of any thing that is in heaven above, or that is in the earth beneath, or that is in the water under the earth: Thou

shalt not bow down thyself to them, nor serve them: for I the Lord thy God am a jealous God, visiting the iniquity of the fathers upon the children unto the third and fourth generation of them that hate me; And shewing mercy unto thousands of them that love me, and keep my commandments. Thou shalt not take the name of the Lord thy God in vain; for the Lord will not hold him guiltless that taketh his name in vain." (Exodus 20:1-7)

"And as Jesus passed by, he saw a man which was blind from his birth. And his disciples asked him, saying, Master, who did sin, this man, or his parents, that he was born blind? Jesus answered, Neither hath this man sinned, nor his parents: but that the works of God should be made manifest in him." (John 9:1-3)

"See now that I, even I, am he, and there is no god with me: I kill, and I make alive; I wound, and I heal: neither is there any that can deliver out of my hand. For I lift up my hand to heaven, and say, I live for ever." (Deuteronomy 32:39-40)

Now the Bible has declared homosexuality as an abomination. Homosexuals are to have no part in the kingdom. Many have been given over to their homosexual tendencies according to the Bible.

"Thou shalt not lie with mankind, as with womankind: it is abomination." (Leviticus 18:22)

"Know ye not that the unrighteous shall not inherit the kingdom of God? Be not deceived: neither fornicators, nor idolaters, nor adulterers, nor effeminate, nor abusers of themselves with mankind, nor thieves, nor covetous, nor drunkards, nor revilers, nor extortioners, shall inherit the kingdom of God. And such were some of you: but ye are washed, but ye are sanctified, but ye are justified in the name of the Lord Jesus, and by the Spirit of our God." (1 Corinthians 6:9-11)

"For the wrath of God is revealed from heaven against all ungodliness and unrighteousness of men, who hold the truth in unrighteousness; because that which may be known of God is manifest in them; for God hath shewed it unto them. For the invisible things of him from the creation of the world are clearly seen, being understood by the things that are made, even his eternal power and Godhead; so that they are without excuse: because that, when they knew God, they glorified him not as God, neither were thankful; but became vain in their imaginations, and their foolish heart was darkened. Professing themselves to be wise, they became fools, and changed the glory of the uncorruptible God into an image made like to corruptible man, and to birds, and fourfooted beasts, and creeping things. Wherefore God also gave them up to uncleanness through the lusts of their own hearts, to dishonour their own bodies between themselves: who changed the truth of God into a lie, and worshipped and served the creature more than the Creator, who is blessed for ever. Amen. For this cause God gave them up unto vile affections: for even their women did change the natural use into that which is against nature: and likewise also the men, leaving the natural use of the woman, burned in their lust one toward another; men with men working that which is unseemly, and receiving in themselves that recompence of their error which was meet. And even as they did not like to retain God in their knowledge, God gave them over to a reprobate mind, to do those things which are not convenient; being filled with all unrighteousness, fornication, wickedness, covetousness, maliciousness; full of envy, murder, debate, deceit, malignity; whisperers, backbiters, haters of God, despiteful, proud, boasters, inventors of evil things, disobe-

dient to parents, without understanding, covenantbreakers, without natural affection, implacable, unmerciful: who knowing the judgment of God, that they which commit such things are worthy of death, not only do the same, but have pleasure in them that do them." (Romans 1:18-32)

To anyone that would call homosexuality acceptable, consider the conflict with both God and nature in the matter of same sex unions. The species dies with same sex unions being the rule. Homosexuality, if practiced by everyone, is effectively genocide upon the human species.

"And God created great whales, and every living creature that moveth, which the waters brought forth abundantly, after their kind, and every winged fowl after his kind: and God saw that it was good. And God blessed them, saying, Be fruitful, and multiply, and fill the waters in the seas, and let fowl multiply in the earth. And the evening and the morning were the fifth day. And God said, Let the earth bring forth the living creature after his kind, cattle, and creeping thing, and beast of the earth after his kind: and it was so. And God made the beast of the earth after his kind, and cattle after their kind, and every thing that creepeth upon the earth after his kind: and God saw that it was good...So God created man in his own image, in the image of God created he him; male and female created he them. And God blessed them, and God said unto them, Be fruitful, and multiply, and replenish the earth, and subdue it: and have dominion over the fish of the sea, and over the fowl of the air, and over every living thing that moveth upon the earth." (Genesis 1: 21-25, 27-28)

With regard to the office in the church of bishop (episkope, episkopos - office of, officer as in general charge of, superintendent of, overseer), this cannot be a homosexual. The overseer is not to lord over the flock but is to rather be the example. The Bible is not vague in terms of the qualifications and expectations with regard to the office of bishop.

"This is a true saying, If a man desire the office of a bishop, he desireth a good work. A bishop then must be blameless, the husband of one wife, vigilant, sober, of good behaviour, given to hospitality, apt to teach; not given to wine, no striker, not greedy of filthy lucre; but patient, not a brawler, not covetous; one that ruleth well his own house, having his children in subjection with all gravity;(For if a man know not how to rule his own house, how shall he take care of the church of God?)" (1Timothy 3:1-5)

"If any be blameless, the husband of one wife, having faithful children not accused of riot or unruly. For a bishop must be blameless, as the steward of God; not selfwilled, not soon angry, not given to wine, no striker, not given to filthy lucre; but a lover of hospitality, a lover of good men, sober, just, holy, temperate; holding fast the faithful word as he hath been taught, that he may be able by sound doctrine both to exhort and to convince the gainsayers." (Titus 1:6-9)

"Feed the flock of God which is among you, taking the oversight thereof, not by constraint, but willingly; not for filthy lucre, but of a ready mind; Neither as being lords over God's heritage, but being ensamples to the flock. And when the chief Shepherd shall appear, ye shall receive a crown of glory that fadeth not away." (1 Peter 5:2-4)

"Know ye not that they which run in a race run all, but one receiveth the prize? So run, that ye may obtain. And every man that striveth for the mastery is temperate in all things. Now

they do it to obtain a corruptible crown; but we an incorruptible. I therefore so run, not as uncertainly; so fight I, not as one that beateth the air: but I keep under my body, and bring it into subjection: lest that by any means, when I have preached to others, I myself should be a castaway." (**1 Corinthians 9:24-27**)

37

ABORTION

Notwithstanding the issues of women's rights or "right to life", what does the Bible have to say about abortion?

THE BELIEVER IS to understand that children are a gift of God and the fruit of our bodies. God has also commanded that we should not kill. Pregnant women do not have to be told of the life growing inside of their bodies.

> *"And it shall come to pass, if thou shalt hearken diligently unto the voice of the Lord thy God, to observe and to do all his commandments which I command thee this day, that the Lord thy God will set thee on high above all nations of the earth: And all these blessings shall come on thee, and overtake thee, if thou shalt hearken unto the voice of the Lord thy God. Blessed shalt thou be in the city, and blessed shalt thou be in the field. Blessed shall be the fruit of thy body, and the fruit of thy ground, and the fruit of thy cattle, the increase of thy kine, and the flocks of thy sheep."* (Deuteronomy 28:1-4)

> *"Thou shalt not kill."* (Exodus 20:13)

Also, there is a tremendous difference between conception and birth; birth is of course not assured as a result of conception.

> *"And the Egyptians made the children of Israel to serve with rigor: And they made their lives bitter with hard bondage, in morter, and in brick, and in all manner of service in the field: all their service, wherein they made them serve, was with rigor. And the king of Egypt spake to the Hebrew midwives, of which the name of the one was Shiphrah, and the name of the other Puah: And he said, When ye do the office of a midwife to the Hebrew women, and see them upon the stools; if it be a son, then ye shall kill him: but if it be a daughter, then she shall live. But the midwives feared God, and did not as the king of Egypt commanded them, but saved the men children alive. And the king of Egypt called for the midwives, and said unto them, Why have ye done this thing, and have saved the men children alive? And the midwives said unto Pharaoh, Because the Hebrew women are not as the Egyptian women; for they are lively, and are delivered ere the midwives come in unto them. Therefore God dealt well with the midwives: and the people multiplied, and waxed very mighty. And it came to pass, because the midwives feared God, that he made them houses."* (Exodus 1:13-21)

"And Job spake, and said, Why died I not from the womb? why did I not give up the ghost when I came out of the belly?" (Job 3:2&11)

"Wherefore then hast thou brought me forth out of the womb? Oh that I had given up the ghost, and no eye had seen me! I should have been as though I had not been; I should have been carried from the womb to the grave." (Job 10:18-19)

There are those that would want to fight for the rights of those in their mother's womb and yet born alive. God is always in control and is able to deliver even the unborn.

"Lord, how long wilt thou look on? rescue my soul from their destructions, my darling from the lions." (Psalm 35:17)

"He delivereth and rescueth, and he worketh signs and wonders in heaven and in earth, who hath delivered Daniel from the power of the lions." (Daniel 6:27)

The true battlefield in the issue of abortion is in the hearts and minds of the mothers.

"Create in me a clean heart, O God; and renew a right spirit within me. Cast me not away from thy presence; and take not thy Holy Spirit from me. Restore unto me the joy of thy salvation; and uphold me with thy free spirit. Then will I teach transgressors thy ways; and sinners shall be converted unto thee. Deliver me from bloodguiltiness, O God, thou God of my salvation: and my tongue shall sing aloud of thy righteousness. O Lord, open thou my lips; and my mouth shall shew forth thy praise. For thou desirest not sacrifice; else would I give it: thou delightest not in burnt offering. The sacrifices of God are a broken spirit: a broken and a contrite heart, O God, thou wilt not despise." (Psalm 51:10-17)

A mind that would regard oneself as Mary, the mother of Jesus, did finding herself pregnant while espoused, a situation punishable by death, is to be desired. Mary regarded herself as a handmaiden of God.

"Now the birth of Jesus Christ was on this wise: When as his mother Mary was espoused to Joseph, before they came together, she was found with child of the Holy Ghost. Then Joseph her husband, being a just man, and not willing to make her a publick example, was minded to put her away privily." (Matthew 1:18&19)

"And the angel said unto her, Fear not, Mary: for thou hast found favor with God. And, behold, thou shalt conceive in thy womb, and bring forth a son, and shalt call his name JESUS. He shall be great, and shall be called the Son of the Highest: and the Lord God shall give unto him the throne of his father David: And he shall reign over the house of Jacob for ever; and of his kingdom there shall be no end. Then said Mary unto the angel, How shall this be, seeing I know not a man? And the angel answered and said unto her, The Holy Ghost shall come upon thee, and the power of the Highest shall overshadow thee: therefore also that holy thing which shall be born of thee shall be called the Son of God. And Mary said, Behold the handmaid of the Lord; be it unto me according to thy word. And the angel departed from her." (Luke 1:30-35,38)

Even a pregnancy as a result of evil doing, can be made for good by God. What is to be understood by women is that according to the Bible, there is a divine purpose in any pregnancy and that being in bringing forth fruit. God is able to take care of the circumstances because with him nothing is impossible. God would have young married women to have children. There is also a divine purpose in the childless woman and the barren women.

"So God created man in his own image, in the image of God created he him; male and fe-male created he them. And God blessed them, and God said unto them, Be fruitful, and multiply, and replenish the earth, and subdue it: and have dominion over the fish of the sea, and over the fowl of the air, and over every living thing that moveth upon the earth." (Genesis 1:27&28)

"Ah Lord God! behold, thou hast made the heaven and the earth by thy great power and stretched out arm, and there is nothing too hard for thee: Thou shewest lovingkindness unto thousands, and recompensest the iniquity of the fathers into the bosom of their children after them: the Great, the Mighty God, the Lord of hosts, is his name, Great in counsel, and mighty in work: for thine eyes are open upon all the ways of the sons of men: to give every one according to his ways, and according to the fruit of his doings:" (Jeremiah 32: 17-19)

"For with God nothing shall be impossible." (Luke 1: 37)

"Now there was a certain man of Ramathaim-zophim, of mount Ephraim, and his name was Elkanah, the son of Jeroham, the son of Elihu, the son of Tohu, the son of Zuph, an Ephrathite: And he had two wives; the name of the one was Hannah, and the name of the other Peninnah: and Peninnah had children, but Hannah had no children. And this man went up out of his city yearly to worship and to sacrifice unto the Lord of hosts in Shiloh. And the two sons of Eli, Hophni and Phinehas, the priests of the Lord, were there. And when the time was that Elkanah offered, he gave to Peninnah his wife, and to all her sons and her daughters, portions. But unto Hannah he gave a worthy portion; for he loved Hannah: but the Lord had shut up her womb. And her adversary also provoked her sore, for to make her fret, because the Lord had shut up her womb. So Hannah rose up after they had eaten in Shiloh, and after they had drunk. Now Eli the priest sat upon a seat by a post of the temple of the Lord. And she was in bitterness of soul, and prayed unto the Lord, and wept sore. And they rose up in the morning early, and worshipped before the Lord, and returned, and came to their house to Ramah: and Elkanah knew Hannah his wife; and the Lord remembered her. Wherefore it came to pass, when the time was come about after Hannah had conceived, that she bare a son, and called his name Samuel, saying, Because I have asked him of the Lord." (1 Samuel 1:1-6, 9&10, 19&20)

"But as for you, ye thought evil against me; but God meant it unto good, to bring to pass, as it is this day, to save much people alive." (Genesis 50:20)

"I will therefore that the younger women marry, bear children, guide the house, give none occasion to the adversary to speak reproachfully." (1Timothy 5:14)

"He maketh the barren woman to keep house, and to be a joyful mother of children. Praise ye the Lord." (Psalms 113:9)

Barring a choice having to be made with regard to the survival of the mother versus the child, abortion needs to be seen as <u>not</u> an option in the mind of a Christian woman. The battle in this case is without question spiritual and not in the carnality of the legal system.

"(For the weapons of our warfare are not carnal, but mighty through God to the pulling down of strong holds;)" (2 Corinthians 10:4)

"For they that are after the flesh do mind the things of the flesh; but they that are after the Spirit the things of the Spirit. For to be carnally minded is death; but to be spiritually minded is life and peace. Because the carnal mind is enmity against God: for it is not subject to the law of God, neither indeed can be. So then they that are in the flesh cannot please God." (Romans 8:5-8)

God recognizes the body as a temple that should by choice be indwelled by his Spirit. The Bible does not force upon anyone spiritual/moral choices and neither should man with regard to abortion. Please note also, that in this age, there are those that would want to demand when an abortion should be performed as well.

"Know ye not that ye are the temple of God, and that the Spirit of God dwelleth in you?" (1 Corinthians 3:16)

"But the word is very nigh unto thee, in thy mouth, and in thy heart, that thou mayest do it. See, I have set before thee this day life and good, and death and evil; In that I command thee this day to love the Lord thy God, to walk in his ways, and to keep his commandments and his statutes and his judgments, that thou mayest live and multiply: and the Lord thy God shall bless thee in the land whither thou goest to possess it. But if thine heart turn away, so that thou wilt not hear, but shalt be drawn away, and worship other gods, and serve them; I denounce unto you this day, that ye shall surely perish, and that ye shall not prolong your days upon the land, whither thou passest over Jordan to go to possess it. I call heaven and earth to record this day against you, that I have set before you life and death, blessing and cursing: therefore choose life, that both thou and thy seed may live: That thou mayest love the Lord thy God, and that thou mayest obey his voice, and that thou mayest cleave unto him: for he is thy life, and the length of thy days: that thou mayest dwell in the land which the Lord sware unto thy fathers, to Abraham, to Isaac, and to Jacob, to give them." (Deuteronomy 30:14-20)

"For we ourselves also were sometimes foolish, disobedient, deceived, serving divers lusts and pleasures, living in malice and envy, hateful, and hating one another. But after that the kindness and love of God our Savior toward man appeared, Not by works of righteousness which we have done, but according to his mercy he saved us, by the washing of regeneration, and renewing of the Holy Ghost; Which he shed on us abundantly through Jesus Christ our Savior; That being justified by his grace, we should be made heirs according to the hope of eternal life." (Titus 3: 3-7)

"Fulfil ye my joy, that ye be likeminded, having the same love, being of one accord, of one mind." (Philippians 2:2)

Truth also remains as a powerful weapon against the evils of abortion with regard to the unrestricted right of abortion from conception to birth, methods of abortion, born alive abortions and mental health issues. Christians need to be made aware of the dark and barbaric side of abortion in order to make wise personal and communal decisions with regard to abortion.

"Thou shalt not kill." (Exodus 20:13)

"And he that sent me is with me: the Father hath not left me alone; for I do always those things that please him. As he spake these words, many believed on him. Then said Jesus to those Jews which believed on him, If ye continue in my word, then are ye my disciples indeed; And ye shall know the truth, and the truth shall make you free. They answered him, We be Abraham's seed, and were never in bondage to any man: how sayest thou, Ye shall be made free? Jesus answered them, Verily, verily, I say unto you, Whosoever committeth sin is the servant of sin. And the servant abideth not in the house for ever: but the Son abideth ever. If the Son therefore shall make you free, ye shall be free indeed." **(John 8:29-36)**

"This I say then, Walk in the Spirit, and ye shall not fulfill the lust of the flesh." **(Galatians 5:16)**

38

A NATION FROM A BIBLICAL PERSPECTIVE

Does God differentiate between nations? Does Almighty God discern Christian nations?

THE BIBLICAL QUOTATION, "Blessed is the Nation who's God is the Lord", surely is clear in declaring Almighty God's willingness to bless a faithful nation.

> *"Blessed is the nation whose God is the Lord; and the people whom he hath chosen for his own inheritance." (Psalm 33:12)*

> *"Now therefore, if ye will obey my voice indeed, and keep my covenant, then ye shall be a peculiar treasure unto me above all people: for all the earth is mine: And ye shall be unto me a kingdom of priests, and an holy nation. These are the words which thou shalt speak unto the children of Israel." (Exodus 19: 5&6)*

> *"Now to him that is of power to stablish you according to my gospel, and the preaching of Jesus Christ, according to the revelation of the mystery, which was kept secret since the world began, But now is made manifest, and by the scriptures of the prophets, according to the commandment of the everlasting God, made known to all nations for the obedience of faith: To God only wise, be glory through Jesus Christ for ever. Amen." (Romans 16:25-27)*

God differentiates between righteousness and sin in a nation according to the Bible. See Appendix 9, Emancipation Day Sermon in Toccoa, Georgia – God's Emancipating Word.

> *"Righteousness exalteth a nation: but sin is a reproach to any people." (Proverbs 14:34)*

> *And it shall come to pass, if thou shalt hearken diligently unto the voice of the Lord thy God, to observe and to do all his commandments which I command thee this day, that the Lord thy God will set thee on high above all nations of the earth: and all these blessings shall come on thee, and overtake thee, if thou shalt hearken unto the voice of the Lord thy God. Blessed shalt thou be in the city, and blessed shalt thou be in the field. Blessed shall be the fruit of thy body, and the fruit of thy ground, and the fruit of thy cattle, the increase of thy kine, and the flocks of thy sheep. Blessed shall be thy basket and thy store. Blessed shalt thou be when thou comest in, and blessed shalt thou be when thou goest out. The Lord shall cause thine enemies that rise up against thee to be smitten before thy face: they shall come out against thee one way, and flee before thee seven ways. The Lord shall command the blessing upon thee in thy storehouses, and in all that thou settest thine hand*

unto; and he shall bless thee in the land which the Lord thy God giveth thee. The Lord shall establish thee an holy people unto himself, as he hath sworn unto thee, if thou shalt keep the commandments of the Lord thy God, and walk in his ways. And all people of the earth shall see that thou art called by the name of the Lord; and they shall be afraid of thee. And the Lord shall make thee plenteous in goods, in the fruit of thy body, and in the fruit of thy cattle, and in the fruit of thy ground, in the land which the Lord sware unto thy fathers to give thee. The Lord shall open unto thee his good treasure, the heaven to give the rain unto thy land in his season, and to bless all the work of thine hand: and thou shalt lend unto many nations, and thou shalt not borrow. And the Lord shall make thee the head, and not the tail; and thou shalt be above only, and thou shalt not be beneath; if that thou hearken unto the commandments of the Lord thy God, which I command thee this day, to observe and to do them: And thou shalt not go aside from any of the words which I command thee this day, to the right hand, or to the left, to go after other gods to serve them.” (Deuteronomy 28:1-14)

“But thou shalt remember the Lord thy God: for it is he that giveth thee power to get wealth, that he may establish his covenant which he sware unto thy fathers, as it is this day. And it shall be, if thou do at all forget the Lord thy God, and walk after other gods, and serve them, and worship them, I testify against you this day that ye shall surely perish. As the nations which the Lord destroyeth before your face, so shall ye perish; because ye would not be obedient unto the voice of the Lord your God.” (Deuteronomy 8:18-20)

“And the Lord spake unto Moses, saying, Speak unto the children of Israel, and say unto them, I am the Lord your God. After the doings of the land of Egypt, wherein ye dwelt, shall ye not do: and after the doings of the land of Canaan, whither I bring you, shall ye not do: neither shall ye walk in their ordinances. Ye shall do my judgments, and keep mine ordinances, to walk therein: I am the Lord your God. Ye shall therefore keep my statutes, and my judgments: which if a man do, he shall live in them: I am the Lord.” (Leviticus 18:1-5)

“Incline your ear, and come unto me: hear, and your soul shall live; and I will make an everlasting covenant with you, even the sure mercies of David. Behold, I have given him for a witness to the people, a leader and commander to the people. Behold, thou shalt call a nation that thou knowest not, and nations that knew not thee shall run unto thee because of the Lord thy God, and for the Holy One of Israel; for he hath glorified thee. Seek ye the Lord while he may be found, call ye upon him while he is near: Let the wicked forsake his way, and the unrighteous man his thoughts: and let him return unto the Lord, and he will have mercy upon him; and to our God, for he will abundantly pardon. For my thoughts are not your thoughts, neither are your ways my ways, saith the Lord. For as the heavens are higher than the earth, so are my ways higher than your ways, and my thoughts than your thoughts.” (Isaiah 55:3-9)

The Bible had prophesied and history has validated the annihilation of Tyrus (Tyre) and the humbling of Egypt by Almighty God.

“Thus saith the Lord God to Tyrus; Shall not the isles shake at the sound of thy fall, when the wounded cry, when the slaughter is made in the midst of thee? Then all the princes of the sea shall come down from their thrones, and lay away their robes, and put off their broidered garments: they shall clothe themselves with trembling; they shall sit upon the ground, and shall tremble at every moment, and be astonished at thee. And they shall take

up a lamentation for thee, and say to thee, How art thou destroyed, that wast inhabited of seafaring men, the renowned city, which wast strong in the sea, she and her inhabitants, which cause their terror to be on all that haunt it! Now shall the isles tremble in the day of thy fall; yea, the isles that are in the sea shall be troubled at thy departure. For thus saith the Lord God; When I shall make thee a desolate city, like the cities that are not inhabited; when I shall bring up the deep upon thee, and great waters shall cover thee; When I shall bring thee down with them that descend into the pit, with the people of old time, and shall set thee in the low parts of the earth, in places desolate of old, with them that go down to the pit, that thou be not inhabited; and I shall set glory in the land of the living; I will make thee a terror, and thou shalt be no more: though thou be sought for, yet shalt thou never be found again, saith the Lord God." (Ezekiel 26:15-21)

"And I will make the land of Egypt desolate in the midst of the countries that are desolate, and her cities among the cities that are laid waste shall be desolate forty years: and I will scatter the Egyptians among the nations, and will disperse them through the countries. Yet thus saith the Lord God; At the end of forty years will I gather the Egyptians from the people whither they were scattered: And I will bring again the captivity of Egypt, and will cause them to return into the land of Pathros, into the land of their habitation; and they shall be there a base kingdom. It shall be the basest of the kingdoms; neither shall it exalt itself any more above the nations: for I will diminish them, that they shall no more rule over the nations. And it shall be no more the confidence of the house of Israel, which bringeth their iniquity to remembrance, when they shall look after them: but they shall know that I am the Lord God." (Ezekiel 29:12-16)

The Bible has declared that everything on the planet belongs to God. Almighty God created man and determined mankind's habitation of origin. He has prophesized with regard to nations at-large in the scriptures.

"The earth is the Lord's, and the fulness thereof; the world, and they that dwell therein. For he hath founded it upon the seas, and established it upon the floods. Who shall ascend into the hill of the Lord? or who shall stand in his holy place? He that hath clean hands, and a pure heart; who hath not lifted up his soul unto vanity, nor sworn deceitfully. He shall receive the blessing from the Lord, and righteousness from the God of his salvation. This is the generation of them that seek him, that seek thy face, O Jacob. Selah." (Psalm 24:1-6)

"Then Paul stood in the midst of Mars' hill, and said, Ye men of Athens, I perceive that in all things ye are too superstitious. For as I passed by, and beheld your devotions, I found an altar with this inscription, TO THE UNKNOWN GOD. Whom therefore ye ignorantly worship, him declare I unto you. God that made the world and all things therein, seeing that he is Lord of heaven and earth, dwelleth not in temples made with hands; Neither is worshipped with men's hands, as though he needed any thing, seeing he giveth to all life, and breath, and all things; And hath made of one blood all nations of men for to dwell on all the face of the earth, and hath determined the times before appointed, and the bounds of their habitation; That they should seek the Lord, if haply they might feel after him, and find him, though he be not far from every one of us: For in him we live, and move, and have our being; as certain also of your own poets have said, For we are also his offspring. Forasmuch then as we are the offspring of God, we ought not to think that the Godhead is like unto gold, or silver, or stone, graven by art and man's device. And the times of this

ignorance God winked at; but now commandeth all men every where to repent: Because he hath appointed a day, in the which he will judge the world in righteousness by that man whom he hath ordained; whereof he hath given assurance unto all men, in that he hath raised him from the dead." (Acts 17:22-31)

"Ho, every one that thirsteth, come ye to the waters, and he that hath no money; come ye, buy, and eat; yea, come, buy wine and milk without money and without price. Wherefore do ye spend money for that which is not bread? and your labour for that which satisfieth not? hearken diligently unto me, and eat ye that which is good, and let your soul delight itself in fatness. Incline your ear, and come unto me: hear, and your soul shall live; and I will make an everlasting covenant with you, even the sure mercies of David. Behold, I have given him for a witness to the people, a leader and commander to the people. Behold, thou shalt call a nation that thou knowest not, and nations that knew not thee shall run unto thee because of the Lord thy God, and for the Holy One of Israel; for he hath glorified thee. Seek ye the Lord while he may be found, call ye upon him while he is near: Let the wicked forsake his way, and the unrighteous man his thoughts: and let him return unto the Lord, and he will have mercy upon him; and to our God, for he will abundantly pardon. For my thoughts are not your thoughts, neither are your ways my ways, saith the Lord. For as the heavens are higher than the earth, so are my ways higher than your ways, and my thoughts than your thoughts. For as the rain cometh down, and the snow from heaven, and returneth not thither, but watereth the earth, and maketh it bring forth and bud, that it may give seed to the sower, and bread to the eater: So shall my word be that goeth forth out of my mouth: it shall not return unto me void, but it shall accomplish that which I please, and it shall prosper in the thing whereto I sent it." (Isaiah 55:1-11)

"And when Abram was ninety years old and nine, the Lord appeared to Abram, and said unto him, I am the Almighty God; walk before me, and be thou perfect. And I will make my covenant between me and thee, and will multiply thee exceedingly. And Abram fell on his face: and God talked with him, saying, As for me, behold, my covenant is with thee, and thou shalt be a father of many nations. Neither shall thy name any more be called Abram, but thy name shall be Abraham; for a father of many nations have I made thee. And I will make thee exceeding fruitful, and I will make nations of thee, and kings shall come out of thee. And I will establish my covenant between me and thee and thy seed after thee in their generations for an everlasting covenant, to be a God unto thee, and to thy seed after thee." (Genesis 17:1-7)

"And Abraham said unto God, O that Ishmael might live before thee! And God said, Sarah thy wife shall bear thee a son indeed; and thou shalt call his name Isaac: and I will establish my covenant with him for an everlasting covenant, and with his seed after him. And as for Ishmael, I have heard thee: Behold, I have blessed him, and will make him fruitful, and will multiply him exceedingly; twelve princes shall he beget, and I will make him a great nation. But my covenant will I establish with Isaac, which Sarah shall bear unto thee at this set time in the next year." (Genesis 17:18-21)

"And in the days of these kings shall the God of heaven set up a kingdom, which shall never be destroyed: and the kingdom shall not be left to other people, but it shall break in pieces and consume all these kingdoms, and it shall stand for ever. Forasmuch as thou sawest that the stone was cut out of the mountain without hands, and that it brake in pieces the iron, the brass, the clay, the silver, and the gold; the great God hath made known to the king

what shall come to pass hereafter: and the dream is certain, and the interpretation thereof sure. Then the king Nebuchadnezzar fell upon his face, and worshipped Daniel, and commanded that they should offer an oblation and sweet odours unto him. The king answered unto Daniel, and said, Of a truth it is, that your God is a God of gods, and a Lord of kings, and a revealer of secrets, seeing thou couldest reveal this secret." (Daniel 2:44-47)

Obviously, nations have to make a choice with regard to spiritual trust and faith as do people. The choice is reflected in origin of its constitutions, statues, laws, morality, customs, benevolence and justice. God is jealous even over a nation. Separation between State (government) and a government sponsored Church is one thing but separation between State and faith is wholly detrimental. To this extent, the civilization and institutions of many countries, to include the United States of America, are emphatically Christian and are in grave need of that recognition and adherence today (See Appendix 10, Proposed 28th Amendment to the United States Constitution as Revised 1/20/09 – Right of Acknowledgement).

"Now therefore fear the Lord, and serve him in sincerity and in truth: and put away the gods which your fathers served on the other side of the flood, and in Egypt; and serve ye the Lord. And if it seem evil unto you to serve the Lord, choose you this day whom ye will serve; whether the gods which your fathers served that were on the other side of the flood, or the gods of the Amorites, in whose land ye dwell: but as for me and my house, we will serve the Lord. And the people answered and said, God forbid that we should forsake the Lord, to serve other gods; For the Lord our God, he it is that brought us up and our fathers out of the land of Egypt, from the house of bondage, and which did those great signs in our sight, and preserved us in all the way wherein we went, and among all the people through whom we passed: And the Lord drave out from before us all the people, even the Amorites which dwelt in the land: therefore will we also serve the Lord; for he is our God. And Joshua said unto the people, Ye cannot serve the Lord: for he is an holy God; he is a jealous God; he will not forgive your transgressions nor your sins. If ye forsake the Lord, and serve strange gods, then he will turn and do you hurt, and consume you, after that he hath done you good. And the people said unto Joshua, Nay; but we will serve the Lord. And Joshua said unto the people, Ye are witnesses against yourselves that ye have chosen you the Lord, to serve him. And they said, We are witnesses. Now therefore put away, said he, the strange gods which are among you, and incline your heart unto the Lord God of Israel. And the people said unto Joshua, The Lord our God will we serve, and his voice will we obey." (Joshua 24:14-24)

"I am the Lord thy God, which brought thee out of the land of Egypt, from the house of bondage. Thou shalt have none other gods before me. Thou shalt not make thee any graven image, or any likeness of any thing that is in heaven above, or that is in the earth beneath, or that is in the waters beneath the earth: Thou shalt not bow down thyself unto them, nor serve them: for I the Lord thy God am a jealous God, visiting the iniquity of the fathers upon the children unto the third and fourth generation of them that hate me, And shewing mercy unto thousands of them that love me and keep my commandments. Thou shalt not take the name of the Lord thy God in vain: for the Lord will not hold him guiltless that taketh his name in vain." (Deuteronomy 5:6-11)

"And they rose up early on the morrow, and offered burnt offerings, and brought peace offerings; and the people sat down to eat and to drink, and rose up to play. And the Lord

said unto Moses, Go, get thee down; for thy people, which thou broughtest out of the land of Egypt, have corrupted themselves: They have turned aside quickly out of the way which I commanded them: they have made them a molten calf, and have worshipped it, and have sacrificed thereunto, and said, These be thy gods, O Israel, which have brought thee up out of the land of Egypt. And the Lord said unto Moses, I have seen this people, and, behold, it is a stiffnecked people: Now therefore let me alone, that my wrath may wax hot against them, and that I may consume them: and I will make of thee a great nation. And Moses besought the Lord his God, and said, Lord, why doth thy wrath wax hot against thy people, which thou hast brought forth out of the land of Egypt with great power, and with a mighty hand? Wherefore should the Egyptians speak, and say, For mischief did he bring them out, to slay them in the mountains, and to consume them from the face of the earth? Turn from thy fierce wrath, and repent of this evil against thy people. Remember Abraham, Isaac, and Israel, thy servants, to whom thou swarest by thine own self, and saidst unto them, I will multiply your seed as the stars of heaven, and all this land that I have spoken of will I give unto your seed, and they shall inherit it for ever. And the Lord repented of the evil which he thought to do unto his people." **(Exodus 32: 6-14)**

"Ye shall therefore keep all my statutes, and all my judgments, and do them: that the land, whither I bring you to dwell therein, spue you not out. And ye shall not walk in the manners of the nation, which I cast out before you: for they committed all these things, and therefore I abhorred them. But I have said unto you, Ye shall inherit their land, and I will give it unto you to possess it, a land that floweth with milk and honey: I am the Lord your God, which have separated you from other people." **(Leviticus 20:22-24)**

"When thou art come into the land which the Lord thy God giveth thee, thou shalt not learn to do after the abominations of those nations." **(Deuteronomy 18:9)**

"Ye also, as lively stones, are built up a spiritual house, an holy priesthood, to offer up spiritual sacrifices, acceptable to God by Jesus Christ. Wherefore also it is contained in the scripture, Behold, I lay in Sion a chief corner stone, elect, precious: and he that believeth on him shall not be confounded. Unto you therefore which believe he is precious: but unto them which be disobedient, the stone which the builders disallowed, the same is made the head of the corner, And a stone of stumbling, and a rock of offence, even to them which stumble at the word, being disobedient: whereunto also they were appointed. But ye are a chosen generation, a royal priesthood, an holy nation, a peculiar people; that ye should shew forth the praises of him who hath called you out of darkness into his marvellous light: Which in time past were not a people, but are now the people of God: which had not obtained mercy, but now have obtained mercy." **(1 Peter 2: 5-10)**

"The wicked shall be turned into hell, and all the nations that forget God." **(Psalm 9:17)**

Now God is able to raise up in the midst of a crooked and perverse nation those that would cry out to bring a nation to repentance.

"Now the word of the Lord came unto Jonah the son of Amittai, saying, Arise, go to Nineveh, that great city, and cry against it; for their wickedness is come up before me." **(Jonah 1:1-2)**

"Then the word of the Lord came unto me, saying, Before I formed thee in the belly I knew thee; and before thou camest forth out of the womb I sanctified thee, and I ordained thee

a prophet unto the nations. Then said I, Ah, Lord God! behold, I cannot speak: for I am a child. But the Lord said unto me, Say not, I am a child: for thou shalt go to all that I shall send thee, and whatsoever I command thee thou shalt speak. Be not afraid of their faces: for I am with thee to deliver thee, saith the Lord. Then the Lord put forth his hand, and touched my mouth. And the Lord said unto me, Behold, I have put my words in thy mouth. See, I have this day set thee over the nations and over the kingdoms, to root out, and to pull down, and to destroy, and to throw down, to build, and to plant." (Jeremiah 1:4-10)

"Moreover the word of the Lord came to me, saying, Go and cry in the ears of Jerusalem, saying, Thus saith the Lord; I remember thee, the kindness of thy youth, the love of thine espousals, when thou wentest after me in the wilderness, in a land that was not sown. Israel was holiness unto the Lord, and the firstfruits of his increase: all that devour him shall offend; evil shall come upon them, saith the Lord. Hear ye the word of the Lord, O house of Jacob, and all the families of the house of Israel: Thus saith the Lord, What iniquity have your fathers found in me, that they are gone far from me, and have walked after vanity, and are become vain? Neither said they, Where is the Lord that brought us up out of the land of Egypt, that led us through the wilderness, through a land of deserts and of pits, through a land of drought, and of the shadow of death, through a land that no man passed through, and where no man dwelt? And I brought you into a plentiful country, to eat the fruit thereof and the goodness thereof; but when ye entered, ye defiled my land, and made mine heritage an abomination." (Jeremiah 2:1-7)

"For they are a nation void of counsel, neither is there any understanding in them. O that they were wise, that they understood this, that they would consider their latter end! How should one chase a thousand, and two put ten thousand to flight, except their Rock had sold them, and the Lord had shut them up? For their rock is not as our Rock, even our enemies themselves being judges. For their vine is of the vine of Sodom, and of the fields of Gomorrah: their grapes are grapes of gall, their clusters are bitter: Their wine is the poison of dragons, and the cruel venom of asps. Is not this laid up in store with me, and sealed up among my treasures? To me belongeth vengeance, and recompence; their foot shall slide in due time: for the day of their calamity is at hand, and the things that shall come upon them make haste. For the Lord shall judge his people, and repent himself for his servants, when he seeth that their power is gone, and there is none shut up, or left. And he shall say, Where are their gods, their rock in whom they trusted, Which did eat the fat of their sacrifices, and drank the wine of their drink offerings? let them rise up and help you, and be your protection. See now that I, even I, am he, and there is no god with me: I kill, and I make alive; I wound, and I heal: neither is there any that can deliver out of my hand. For I lift up my hand to heaven, and say, I live for ever. If I whet my glittering sword, and mine hand take hold on judgment; I will render vengeance to mine enemies, and will reward them that hate me. I will make mine arrows drunk with blood, and my sword shall devour flesh; and that with the blood of the slain and of the captives, from the beginning of revenges upon the enemy. Rejoice, O ye nations, with his people: for he will avenge the blood of his servants, and will render vengeance to his adversaries, and will be merciful unto his land, and to his people." (Deuteronomy 32:28-43)

"For it is God which worketh in you both to will and to do of his good pleasure. Do all things without murmurings and disputings: That ye may be blameless and harmless, the sons of God, without rebuke, in the midst of a crooked and perverse nation, among whom

ye shine as lights in the world; Holding forth the word of life; that I may rejoice in the day of Christ, that I have not run in vain, neither laboured in vain." (**Philippians 2:13-16**)

"And it shall be, if thou do at all forget the Lord thy God, and walk after other gods, and serve them, and worship them, I testify against you this day that ye shall surely perish. As the nations which the Lord destroyeth before your face, so shall ye perish; because ye would not be obedient unto the voice of the Lord your God." (**Deuteronomy 8:19-20**)

"God be merciful unto us, and bless us; and cause his face to shine upon us; Selah. That thy way may be known upon earth, thy saving health among all nations. Let the people praise thee, O God; let all the people praise thee. O let the nations be glad and sing for joy: for thou shalt judge the people righteously, and govern the nations upon earth. Selah. Let the people praise thee, O God; let all the people praise thee. Then shall the earth yield her increase; and God, even our own God, shall bless us. God shall bless us; and all the ends of the earth shall fear him." (**Psalm 67**)

God is also able to heal (rapha - to cure, physician to cure, to repair, thoroughly make whole) the land of a righteous people. I am persuaded that the healing can be both the state of the people and the natural tendencies of the land. The process of healing can be accomplished with or without mankind's involvement.

"And the Lord appeared to Solomon by night, and said unto him, I have heard thy prayer, and have chosen this place to myself for an house of sacrifice. If I shut up heaven that there be no rain, or if I command the locusts to devour the land, or if I send pestilence among my people; If my people, which are called by my name, shall humble themselves, and pray, and seek my face, and turn from their wicked ways; then will I hear from heaven, and will forgive their sin, and will heal their land. Now mine eyes shall be open, and mine ears attent unto the prayer that is made in this place." (**2 Chronicles 7:12-15**)

39

THE ERROR IN THE CIVIL RIGHTS MOVEMENT

Many want the Church today to be as proactive in civil affairs as it was during the civil rights era with Dr. Martin Luther King.

THE BIBLE TEACHES civil obedience rather than civil disobedience in the form of either violent or non-violent civil disobedience; God is sovereign over all government.

> *"Put them in mind to be subject to principalities and powers, to obey magistrates, to be ready to every good work, To speak evil of no man, to be no brawlers, but gentle, shewing all meekness unto all men." (*Titus 3:1&2)

> *"Let every soul be subject unto the higher powers. For there is no power but of God: the powers that be are ordained of God." (*Romans 13:1)

God in his sovereignty, has ordained (Tasso – arranged in orderly manner, assigned, disposed, set, approved, determined) all leadership for his purposes as exampled by Pharaoh.

> *"For rulers are not a terror to good works, but to the evil. Wilt thou then not be afraid of the power? do that which is good, and thou shalt have praise of the same: For he is the minister of God to thee for good. But if thou do that which is evil, be afraid; for he beareth not the sword in vain: for he is the minister of God, a revenger to execute wrath upon him that doeth evil." (*Romans 13:3-4)

> *"And the Lord said unto Moses, See, I have made thee a God to Pharaoh: and Aaron thy brother shall be thy prophet. Thou shalt speak all that I command thee: and Aaron thy brother shall speak unto Pharaoh, that he send the children of Israel out of his land. And I will harden Pharaoh's heart, and multiply my signs and my wonders in the land of Egypt. But Pharaoh shall not hearken unto you, that I may lay my hand upon Egypt, and bring forth mine armies, and my people the children of Israel, out of the land of Egypt by great judgments. And the Egyptians shall know that I am the Lord, when I stretch forth mine hand upon Egypt, and bring out the children of Israel from among them." (*Exodus 7:1-5)

Insurrectionists are in error because they are actually resisting God not man.

"Whosoever therefore resisteth the power, resisteth the ordinance of God: and they that resist shall receive to themselves damnation." (Romans 13:2)

It is important for the visible church to understand God's sovereignty over governmental rulers because the sheep are to obey their pastors as well.

"Obey them that have the rule over you, and submit yourselves: for they watch for your souls, as they that must give account, that they may do it with joy, and not with grief: for that is unprofitable for you. Pray for us: for we trust we have a good conscience, in all things willing to live honestly." (Hebrews 13:17-18)

The people of God are to maintain a reputation of civil obedience and rendering to Caesar what belongs to Caesar.

"For your obedience is come abroad unto all men. I am glad therefore on your behalf: but yet I would have you wise unto that which is good, and simple concerning evil." (Romans 16:19)

"Tell us therefore, What thinkest thou? Is it lawful to give tribute unto Caesar, or not? But Jesus perceived their wickedness, and said, Why tempt ye me, ye hypocrites? Shew me the tribute money. And they brought unto him a penny. And he saith unto them, Whose is this image and superscription? They say unto him, Caesar's. Then saith he unto them, Render therefore unto Caesar the things which are Caesar's; and unto God the things that are God's." (Matthew 22:17-21)

The people of God need not be entangled in a struggle but rather prayerful with regard to rulers or slavemaster. Now that entanglement can eventually become unavoidable and Christians need to be Spirit led to recognize the point of unavoidability.

"Thou therefore endure hardness, as a good soldier of Jesus Christ. No man that warreth entangleth himself with the affairs of this life; that he may please him who hath chosen him to be a soldier." (2 Timothy 2:3-4)

"For rulers are not a terror to good works, but to the evil. Wilt thou then not be afraid of the power? do that which is good, and thou shalt have praise of the same: For he is the minister of God to thee for good. But if thou do that which is evil, be afraid; for he beareth not the sword in vain: for he is the minister of God, a revenger to execute wrath upon him that doeth evil." (Romans 13:3-4)

Masters, give unto your servants that which is just and equal; knowing that ye also have a Master in heaven. **Colossians 4:1**

"Thou therefore, my son, be strong in the grace that is in Christ Jesus. And the things that thou hast heard of me among many witnesses, the same commit thou to faithful men, who shall be able to teach others also. Thou therefore endure hardness, as a good soldier of Jesus Christ." (1 Timothy 2:1-3)

"Now I beseech you, brethren, mark them which cause divisions and offences contrary to the doctrine which ye have learned; and avoid them. For they that are such serve not our

Lord Jesus Christ, but their own belly; and by good words and fair speeches deceive the hearts of the simple." (**Romans 16:17&18**)

"To every thing there is a season, and a time to every purpose under the heaven: A time to be born, and a time to die; a time to plant, and a time to pluck up that which is planted; A time to kill, and a time to heal; a time to break down, and a time to build up; A time to weep, and a time to laugh; a time to mourn, and a time to dance; A time to cast away stones, and a time to gather stones together; a time to embrace, and a time to refrain from embracing; A time to get, and a time to lose; a time to keep, and a time to cast away; A time to rend, and a time to sew; a time to keep silence, and a time to speak; A time to love, and a time to hate; a time of war, and a time of peace." (**Ecclesiastes 3:1-8**)

Our real battle is against spiritual wickedness in our nations and ourselves.

"For we wrestle not against flesh and blood, but against principalities, against powers, against the rulers of the darkness of this world, against spiritual wickedness in high places. Wherefore take unto you the whole armor of God, that ye may be able to withstand in the evil day, and having done all, to stand." (**Ephesians 6:12-13**)

"Now I beseech you, brethren, mark them which cause divisions and offences contrary to the doctrine which ye have learned; and avoid them. For they that are such serve not our Lord Jesus Christ, but their own belly; and by good words and fair speeches deceive the hearts of the simple." (**Deuteronomy 9:1-6**)

"Being then made free from sin, ye became the servants of righteousness. I speak after the manner of men because of the infirmity of your flesh: for as ye have yielded your members servants to uncleanness and to iniquity unto iniquity; even so now yield your members servants to righteousness unto holiness. For when ye were the servants of sin, ye were free from righteousness. What fruit had ye then in those things whereof ye are now ashamed? For the end of those things is death. But now being made free from sin, and become servants to God, ye have your fruit unto holiness, and the end everlasting life. For the wages of sin is death; but the gift of God is eternal life through Jesus Christ our Lord." (**Romans 6:18-23**)

The weapons in our warfare are not carnal (pertaining to flesh, bodily, temporal, not regenerated) by rather spiritual in nature (godly).

"For though we walk in the flesh, we do not war after the flesh: (For the weapons of our warfare are not carnal, but mighty through God to the pulling down of strong holds;)" (**2 Corinthians 10:3-4**)

When we are in a right relationship with God, he is willing and able to handle our enemies.

"The Lord is my light and my salvation; whom shall I fear? The Lord is the strength of my life; of whom shall I be afraid? When the wicked, even mine enemies and my foes, came upon me to eat up my flesh, they stumbled and fell. Though an host should encamp against me, my heart shall not fear: though war should rise against me, in this will I be confident. One thing have I desired of the Lord, that will I seek after; that I may dwell in the house of the Lord all the days of my life, to behold the beauty of the Lord, and to enquire in his

temple. For in the time of trouble he shall hide me in his pavilion: in the secret of his tabernacle shall he hide me; he shall set me up upon a rock." (**Psalm 27:1-5**)

"And he said, Hearken ye, all Judah, and ye inhabitants of Jerusalem, and thou king Jehoshaphat, Thus saith the Lord unto you, Be not afraid nor dismayed by reason of this great multitude; for the battle is not yours, but God's." (**2 Chronicles 20:15**)

"See now that I, even I, am he, and there is no God with me: I kill, and I make alive; I wound, and I heal: neither is there any that can deliver out of my hand." (**Deuteronomy 32:39**)

"Be strong and of a good courage: for unto this people shalt thou divide for an inheritance the land, which I swear unto their fathers to give them. Only be thou strong and very courageous, that thou mayest observe to do according to all the law, which Moses my servant commanded thee: turn not from it to the right hand or to the left, that thou mayest prosper withersoever thou goest. This book of the law shall not depart out of thy mouth; but thou shalt meditate therein day and night, that thou mayest observe to do according to all that is written therein: for then thou shalt make thy way prosperous, and then thou shalt have good success. Have not I commanded thee? Be strong and of a good courage; be not afraid, neither be thou dismayed: for the Lord thy God is with thee whithersoever thou goest." (**Joshua 1:6-9**)

"But thanks be to God, which giveth us the victory through our Lord Jesus Christ. Therefore, my beloved brethren, be ye stedfast, unmoveable, always abounding in the work of the Lord, forasmuch as ye know that your labor is not in vain in the Lord." **1 Corinthians 15:57-58**

If we are to suffer, let us do it for the cause of Christ not as lawbreakers.

"Let him eschew evil, and do good; let him seek peace, and ensue it. For the eyes of the Lord are over the righteous, and his ears are open unto their prayers: but the face of the Lord is against them that do evil. And who is he that will harm you, if ye be followers of that which is good? But and if ye suffer for righteousness' sake, happy are ye: and be not afraid of their terror, neither be troubled; But sanctify the Lord God in your hearts: and be ready always to give an answer to every man that asketh you a reason of the hope that is in you with meekness and fear: Having a good conscience; that, whereas they speak evil of you, as of evildoers, they may be ashamed that falsely accuse your good conversation in Christ. For it is better, if the will of God be so, that ye suffer for well doing, than for evil doing." (**1 Peter 3:11-17**)

"Beloved, think it not strange concerning the fiery trial which is to try you, as though some strange thing happened unto you: But rejoice, inasmuch as ye are partakers of Christ's sufferings; that, when his glory shall be revealed, ye may be glad also with exceeding joy. If ye be reproached for the name of Christ, happy are ye; for the spirit of glory and of God resteth upon you: on their part he is evil spoken of, but on your part he is glorified. But let none of you suffer as a murderer, or as a thief, or as an evildoer, or as a busybody in other men's matters. Yet if any man suffer as a Christian, let him not be ashamed; but let him glorify God on this behalf." (**1 Peter 4:12-16**)

"Yea, and all that will live godly in Christ Jesus shall suffer persecution. But evil men and seducers shall wax worse and worse, deceiving, and being deceived." (**2 Timothy 3:12-13**)

Let us also not to have to be chastened anymore than we need to be by God.

"And ye have forgotten the exhortation which speaketh unto you as unto children, My son, despise not thou the chastening of the Lord, nor faint when thou art rebuked of him: For whom the Lord loveth he chasteneth, and scourgeth every son whom he receiveth. If ye endure chastening, God dealeth with you as with sons; for what son is he whom the father chasteneth not? But if ye be without chastisement, whereof all are partakers, then are ye bastards, and not sons. Furthermore we have had fathers of our flesh which corrected us, and we gave them reverence: shall we not much rather be in subjection unto the Father of spirits, and live? For they verily for a few days chastened us after their own pleasure; but he for our profit, that we might be partakers of his holiness. Now no chastening for the present seemeth to be joyous, but grievous: nevertheless afterward it yieldeth the peaceable fruit of righteousness unto them which are exercised thereby." (Hebrews 12:5-11)

God knows those, in the midst of affliction and social injustices, that are calling upon his name and he is able to deliver in a manner whereby he gets the glory.

"For I know the thoughts that I think toward you, saith the Lord, thoughts of peace, and not of evil, to give you an expected end. Then shall ye call upon me, and ye shall go and pray unto me, and I will hearken unto you. And ye shall seek me, and find me, when ye shall search for me with all your heart. And I will be found of you, saith the Lord: and I will turn away your captivity, and I will gather you from all the nations, and from all the places whither I have driven you, saith the Lord; and I will bring you again into the place whence I caused you to be carried away captive." (Jeremiah 29:11-14)

"And the Lord said, I have surely seen the affliction of my people which are in Egypt, and have heard their cry by reason of their taskmasters; for I know their sorrows; And I am come down to deliver them out of the hand of the Egyptians, and to bring them up out of that land unto a good land and a large, unto a land flowing with milk and honey; unto the place of the Canaanites, and the Hittites, and the Amorites, and the Perizzites, and the Hivites, and the Jebusites. Now therefore, behold, the cry of the children of Israel is come unto me: and I have also seen the oppression wherewith the Egyptians oppress them." (Exodus 3:7-9)

"Deliver me from bloodguiltiness, O God, thou God of my salvation: and my tongue shall sing aloud of thy righteousness." (Psalm 51:14)

The child of God and the people of God are to be put in the position of leading not following, always. The position of leadership comes from obeying God, not men, which in and of itself can create conflict.

"And the Lord shall make thee the head, and not the tail; and thou shalt be above only, and thou shalt not be beneath; if that thou hearken unto the commandments of the Lord thy God, which I command thee this day, to observe and to do them: And thou shalt not go aside from any of the words which I command thee this day, to the right hand, or to the left, to go after other gods to serve them." (Deuteronomy 28:13&14)

"Then went the captain with the officers, and brought them without violence: for they feared the people, lest they should have been stoned. And when they had brought them, they set them before the council: and the high priest asked them, Saying, Did not we straitly command you that ye should not teach in this name? and, behold, ye have filled Jerusalem

with your doctrine, and intend to bring this man's blood upon us. Then Peter and the other apostles answered and said, We ought to obey God rather than men." (Acts 5:26-29)

Now we as believers are embattled for the cause of Christ and that battle can be viewed as unjust or injustice.

"But we have this treasure in earthen vessels, that the excellency of the power may be of God, and not of us. We are troubled on every side, yet not distressed; we are perplexed, but not in despair; Persecuted, but not forsaken; cast down, but not destroyed; Always bearing about in the body the dying of the Lord Jesus, that the life also of Jesus might be made manifest in our body." (2 Corinthians 4:7-10)

"This know also, that in the last days perilous times shall come. For men shall be lovers of their own selves, covetous, boasters, proud, blasphemers, disobedient to parents, unthankful, unholy, Without natural affection, trucebreakers, false accusers, incontinent, fierce, despisers of those that are good, Traitors, heady, highminded, lovers of pleasures more than lovers of God;" (2 Timothy 3:1-4)

We battle/struggle recognizing a nobility and lawfulness in the struggle (fighting according to God's word).

"Thou therefore endure hardness, as a good soldier of Jesus Christ. No man that warreth entangleth himself with the affairs of this life; that he may please him who hath chosen him to be a soldier. And if a man also strive for masteries, yet is he not crowned, except he strive lawfully." (2 Timothy 2:3-5)

"In all things shewing thyself a pattern of good works: in doctrine shewing uncorruptness, gravity, sincerity, Sound speech, that cannot be condemned; that he that is of the contrary part may be ashamed, having no evil thing to say of you." (Titus 2:7-8)

God recognizes also the difference between the spiritual warfare raging and physical oppression/confrontation with war as the ultimate end.

"This I say then, Walk in the Spirit, and ye shall not fulfil the lust of the flesh. For the flesh lusteth against the Spirit, and the Spirit against the flesh: and these are contrary the one to the other: so that ye cannot do the things that ye would." (Galatians 5:16-17)

"Now the Lord is that Spirit: and where the Spirit of the Lord is, there is liberty." (2 Corinthians 3:17)

"Recompense to no man evil for evil. Provide things honest in the sight of all men. If it be possible, as much as lieth in you, live peaceably with all men. Dearly beloved, avenge not yourselves, but rather give place unto wrath: for it is written, Vengeance is mine; I will repay, saith the Lord. Therefore if thine enemy hunger, feed him; if he thirst, give him drink: for in so doing thou shalt heap coals of fire on his head. Be not overcome of evil, but overcome evil with good." (Romans 12:17-21)

"Give ear to my prayer, O God; and hide not thyself from my supplication. Attend unto me, and hear me: I mourn in my complaint, and make a noise; Because of the voice of the enemy, because of the oppression of the wicked: for they cast iniquity upon me, and in wrath they hate me. My heart is sore pained within me: and the terrors of death are fallen

upon me. Fearfulness and trembling are come upon me, and horror hath overwhelmed me. And I said, Oh that I had wings like a dove! for then would I fly away, and be at rest." (Psalm 55:1-6)

"And ye shall hear of wars and rumours of wars: see that ye be not troubled: for all these things must come to pass, but the end is not yet." (Matthew 24:6)

"From whence come wars and fightings among you? come they not hence, even of your lusts that war in your members? Ye lust, and have not: ye kill, and desire to have, and cannot obtain: ye fight and war, yet ye have not, because ye ask not. Do ye think that the scripture saith in vain, The spirit that dwelleth in us lusteth to envy?" (James 4:1-2, 5)

God is able to exercise supernatural ability in delivering his people on the battlefield. See Appendix 11, "Franklin D. Roosevelt's D-Day Prayer June 6, 1944.

"Then came Amalek, and fought with Israel in Rephidim. And Moses said unto Joshua, Choose us out men, and go out, fight with Amalek: tomorrow I will stand on the top of the hill with the rod of God in mine hand. So Joshua did as Moses had said to him, and fought with Amalek: and Moses, Aaron, and Hur went up to the top of the hill. And it came to pass, when Moses held up his hand, that Israel prevailed: and when he let down his hand, Amalek prevailed. But Moses hands were heavy; and they took a stone, and put it under him, and he sat thereon; and Aaron and Hur stayed up his hands, the one on the one side, and the other on the other side; and his hands were steady until the going down of the sun. And Joshua discomfited Amalek and his people with the edge of the sword." (Exodus 17:8-13)

"And when Judah looked back, behold, the battle was before and behind: and they cried unto the Lord, and the priests sounded with the trumpets. Then the men of Judah gave a shout: and as the men of Judah shouted, it came to pass, that God smote Jeroboam and all Israel before Abijah and Judah. And the children of Israel fled before Judah: and God delivered them into their hand. And Abijah and his people slew them with a great slaughter: so there fell down slain of Israel five hundred thousand chosen men. Thus the children of Israel were brought under at that time, and the children of Judah prevailed, because they relied upon the Lord God of their fathers." (2 Chronicles 13:14-18)

"Then spake Joshua to the Lord in the day when the Lord delivered up the Amorites before the children of Israel, and he said in the sight of Israel, Sun, stand thou still upon Gibeon; and thou, Moon, in the valley of Ajalon. And the sun stood still, and the moon stayed, until the people had avenged themselves upon their enemies. Is not this written in the book of Jasher? So the sun stood still in the midst of heaven, and hasted not to go down about a whole day. And there was no day like that before it or after it, that the Lord hearkened unto the voice of a man: for the Lord fought for Israel." (Joshua 10:12-13)

"Therefore thus saith the Lord concerning the king of Assyria, He shall not come into this city, nor shoot an arrow there, nor come before it with shield, nor cast a bank against it. By the way that he came, by the same shall he return, and shall not come into this city, saith the Lord. For I will defend this city, to save it, for mine own sake, and for my servant David's sake. And it came to pass that night, that the angel of the Lord went out, and smote in the camp of the Assyrians an hundred fourscore and five thousand: and when they arose

early in the morning, behold, they were all dead corpses. So Sennacherib king of Assyria departed, and went and returned, and dwelt at Nineveh." (2 Kings 19:32-36)

"And the Lord said unto Gideon, The people are yet too many; bring them down unto the water, and I will try them for thee there: and it shall be, that of whom I say unto thee, This shall go with thee, the same shall go with thee; and of whomsoever I say unto thee, This shall not go with thee, the same shall not go. So he brought down the people unto the water: and the Lord said unto Gideon, Every one that lappeth of the water with his tongue, as a dog lappeth, him shalt thou set by himself; likewise every one that boweth down upon his knees to drink. And the number of them that lapped, putting their hand to their mouth, were three hundred men: but all the rest of the people bowed down upon their knees to drink water. And the Lord said unto Gideon, By the three hundred men that lapped will I save you, and deliver the Midianites into thine hand: and let all the other people go every man unto his place." (Judges 7:4-7)

"O our God, wilt thou not judge them? for we have no might against this great company that cometh against us; neither know we what to do: but our eyes are upon thee. And all Judah stood before the Lord, with their little ones, their wives, and their children. Then upon Jahaziel the son of Zechariah, the son of Benaiah, the son of Jeiel, the son of Mattaniah, a Levite of the sons of Asaph, came the Spirit of the Lord in the midst of the congregation; And he said, Hearken ye, all Judah, and ye inhabitants of Jerusalem, and thou king Jehoshaphat, Thus saith the Lord unto you, Be not afraid nor dismayed by reason of this great multitude; for the battle is not yours, but God's. Tomorrow go ye down against them: behold, they come up by the cliff of Ziz; and ye shall find them at the end of the brook, before the wilderness of Jeruel. Ye shall not need to fight in this battle: set yourselves, stand ye still, and see the salvation of the Lord with you, O Judah and Jerusalem: fear not, nor be dismayed; to morrow go out against them: for the Lord will be with you."
(2 Chronicles 20:12-17)

"And when the servant of the man of God was risen early, and gone forth, behold, an host compassed the city both with horses and chariots. And his servant said unto him, Alas, my master! how shall we do? And he answered, Fear not: for they that be with us are more than they that be with them. And Elisha prayed, and said, Lord, I pray thee, open his eyes, that he may see. And the Lord opened the eyes of the young man; and he saw: and, behold, the mountain was full of horses and chariots of fire round about Elisha." (2 Kings 6:15-17)

God is able to rise up and deliver battlefield generals, bring down an entire nation on behalf of his people and/or withdraw leadership in a time of judgment.

"And it came to pass, when the children of Israel cried unto the Lord because of the Midianites, That the Lord sent a prophet unto the children of Israel, which said unto them, Thus saith the Lord God of Israel, I brought you up from Egypt, and brought you forth out of the house of bondage; And I delivered you out of the hand of the Egyptians, and out of the hand of all that oppressed you, and drave them out from before you, and gave you their land; And I said unto you, I am the Lord your God; fear not the gods of the Amorites, in whose land ye dwell: but ye have not obeyed my voice. And there came an angel of the Lord, and sat under an oak which was in Ophrah, that pertained unto Joash the Abiezrite: and his son Gideon threshed wheat by the winepress, to hide it from theMidianites. And

the angel of the Lord appeared unto him, and said unto him, The Lord is with thee, thou mighty man of valour." (**Judges 6:7-12**)

"For, behold, the Lord, the Lord of hosts, doth take away from Jerusalem and from Judah the stay and the staff, the whole stay of bread, and the whole stay of water. The mighty man, and the man of war, the judge, and the prophet, and the prudent, and the ancient, The captain of fifty, and the honorable man, and the counsellor, and the cunning artificer, and the eloquent orator. And I will give children to be their princes, and babes shall rule over them. (**Isaiah 3:1-4**)

The key to God's action on the part of his people is our obedience in what he requires. God is able to lift up and deliver those that love him!

"He hath shewed thee, O man, what is good; and what doth the Lord require of thee, but to do justly, and to love mercy, and to walk humbly with thy God? (**Micah 6:8**)

Who shall ascend into the hill of the Lord? or who shall stand in his holy place? He that hath clean hands, and a pure heart; who hath not lifted up his soul unto vanity, nor sworn deceitfully. He shall receive the blessing from the Lord, and righteousness from the God of his salvation. This is the generation of them that seek him, that seek thy face, O Jacob. Selah. Lift up your head, O ye gates; and be ye lift up, ye everlasting doors; and the King of glory shall come in. Who is this King of glory? The Lord strong and mighty, the Lord mighty in battle. Lift up your heads, O ye gates; even lift them up, ye everlasting doors; and the King of glory shall come in. Who is this King of glory? The Lord of hosts, he is the King of glory. Selah." (**Psalms 24:3-10**)

A CHRISTIAN PERSPECTIVE ON CERTAIN CELEBRATIONS AND HOLIDAYS

What is a Biblical perspective with regard to some of our celebrations and/or holidays in the United States of America?

Birthdays and Anniversaries

No Biblical prohibition.

> *"Rejoice with them that do rejoice, and weep with them that weep."* (**Romans 12:15**)

Weddings

No Biblical prohibition. Jesus attended a wedding in Cana and there performed his first miracle.

> *"And the third day there was a marriage in Cana of Galilee; and the mother of Jesus was there: And both Jesus was called, and his disciples, to the marriage. And when they wanted wine, the mother of Jesus saith unto him, They have no wine. Jesus saith unto her, Woman, what have I to do with thee? mine hour is not yet come. His mother saith unto the servants, Whatsoever he saith unto you, do it. And there were set there six waterpots of stone, after the manner of the purifying of the Jews, containing two or three firkins apiece. Jesus saith unto them, Fill the waterpots with water. And they filled them up to the brim. And he saith unto them, Draw out now, and bear unto the governor of the feast. And they bare it. When the ruler of the feast had tasted the water that was made wine, and knew not whence it was: (but the servants which drew the water knew;) the governor of the feast called the bridegroom. And saith unto him, Every man at the beginning doth set forth good wine; and when men have well drunk, then that which is worse: but thou hast kept the good wine until now. This beginning of miracles did Jesus in Cana of Galilee, and manifested forth his glory; and his disciples believed on him. After this he went down to Capernaum, he, and his mother, and his brethren, and his disciples: and they continued there not many days."* (John 2:1-12)

Thanksgiving

From Webster's II New Riverside University Dictionary, "Thanksgiving Day is a national holiday set apart for giving thanks to God, celebrated on the fourth Thursday of November in the United States and on the second Monday of October in Canada". See Appendix 12, Holiday Proclamations, for the Abraham Lincoln proclamation concerning Thanksgiving Day.

> *"This is the day which the Lord hath made; we will rejoice and be glad in it."* (**Psalms 118:24**)

> *"Praise ye the Lord. O give thanks unto the Lord; for he is good: for his mercy endureth for ever. Who can utter the mighty acts of the Lord? who can shew forth all his praise? Blessed are they that keep judgment, and he that doeth righteousness at all times. Remember me, O Lord, with the favour that thou bearest unto thy people: O visit me with thy salvation; That I may see the good of thy chosen, that I may rejoice in the gladness of thy nation, that I may glory with thine inheritance."* (**Psalms106:1-5**)

Christmas

From Webster's II New Riverside University Dictionary, "Christmas is December 25th celebrated by Christians as the birth of Jesus". The celebration of the birth of Christ is recorded in the Bible". I personally am going to continue the tradition. My tradition is inclusive of joyful Christian celebration, feasting (fellowship in the breaking of bread and sharing), giving and decorations without a Christmas tree.

> *"And Joseph also went up from Galilee, out of the city of Nazareth, into Judaea, unto the city of David, which is called Bethlehem; (because he was of the house and lineage of David:) To be taxed with Mary his espoused wife, being great with child. And so it was, that, while they were there, the days were accomplished that she should be delivered. And she brought forth her firstborn son, and wrapped him in swaddling clothes, and laid him in a manger; because there was no room for them in the inn. And there were in the same country shepherds abiding in the field, keeping watch over their flock by night. And, lo, the angel of the Lord came upon them, and the glory of the Lord shone round about them: and they were sore afraid. And the angel said unto them, Fear not: for, behold, I bring you good tidings of great joy, which shall be to all people. For unto you is born this day in the city of David a Saviour, which is Christ the Lord. And this shall be a sign unto you; Ye shall find the babe wrapped in swaddling clothes, lying in a manger. And suddenly there was with the angel a multitude of the heavenly host praising God, and saying, Glory to God in the highest, and on earth peace, good will toward men. And it came to pass, as the angels were gone away from them into heaven, the shepherds said one to another, Let us now go even unto Bethlehem, and see this thing which is come to pass, which the Lord hath made known unto us. And they came with haste, and found Mary, and Joseph, and the babe lying in a manger."* (**Luke 2:4-16**)

> *"Now when Jesus was born in Bethlehem of Judaea in the days of Herod the king, behold, there came wise men from the east to Jerusalem, Saying, Where is he that is born King of the Jews? for we have seen his star in the east, and are come to worship him. When Herod the king had heard these things, he was troubled, and all Jerusalem with him. And when he had gathered all the chief priests and scribes of the people together, he demanded of them where Christ should be born. And they said unto him, In Bethlehem of Judaea: for thus it is written by the prophet, And thou Bethlehem, in the land of Juda, art not the least among the princes of Juda: for out of thee shall come a Governor, that shall rule my people Israel. Then Herod, when he had privily called the wise men, inquired of them diligently*

what time the star appeared. And he sent them to Bethlehem, and said, Go and search diligently for the young child; and when ye have found him, bring me word again, that I may come and worship him also. When they had heard the king, they departed; and, lo, the star, which they saw in the east, went before them, till it came and stood over where the young child was. When they saw the star, they rejoiced with exceeding great joy. And when they were come into the house, they saw the young child with Mary his mother, and fell down, and worshipped him: and when they had opened their treasures, they presented unto him gifts; gold, and frankincense, and myrrh." **(Matthew 2:1-11)**

"For the customs of the people are vain: for one cutteth a tree out of the forest, the work of the hands of the workman, with the axe. They deck it with silver and with gold; they fasten it with nails and with hammers, that it move not." **(Jeremiah 10:3&4)**

Kwanzaa

Reinforced during the seven day celebration of Kwanzaa, are the Seven Principals of Blackness (Nguzo Saba) of which Dr. Maulana Ron Karenga is the author. In Swahahili, the seven principals of Kwanzaa are Umoja, Kujichagulia, Ujima, Nia, Kuumba and Imani (unity, self-determination, collective work with responsibility, cooperative economics, purpose, creativity and faith in English).

MAJOR PROBLEM:

I have been fully aware of Kwanzaa from its introduction to the public following its first celebration in December of 1966. As a teenager in Washington, D.C., I saw Dr. Maulana Ron Karenga on television promoting his invented holiday as a substitute for Christmas. Kwanzaa was to be a black alternative to Christmas as he felt that Christmas was commercialized to the point that blacks were spending what we could not afford at Christmas time. From a secular standpoint, he made some sense; however, from a spiritual standpoint, I felt in 1966 that this was an abomination. Christians have no business substituting anything in place of celebrating the birth of our Lord and Savior.

MINOR PROBLEM:

Christians should be very careful with regard to especially three of the seven (7) principals of Kwanzaa.

> **Umosa (OO-MO-JAH) Unity** - *Stresses the importance of togetherness for the family and the community, which is reflected in the African saying, "I am we", or "I am because we are".*

> **Christian Doctrinal Conflict** - *"I therefore, the prisoner of the Lord, beseech you that ye walk worthy of the vocation wherewith ye are called, With all lowliness and meekness, with longsuffering, forbearing one another in love; Endeavouring to keep the unity of the Spirit in the bond of peace. There is one body, and one Spirit, even as ye are called in one hope of your calling; One Lord, one faith, one baptism, One God and Father of all, who is above all, and through all, and in you all."* (Ephesians 4:1-6)

> **NIA (NEE-YAH) Purpose** - *Encourages us to look within ourselves and to set personal goals that are beneficial for the community.*

Christian Doctrinal Conflict – *"Even every one that is called by my name: for I have created him for my glory, I have formed him; yea, I have made him."* (**Isaiah 43:7**)

Imani (EE-MAH-NEE) Faith – *Focuses on honoring the best of our traditions, draws upon the best in ourselves, and helps us strive for a higher level of life for humankind, by affirming our self-worth and confidence in our ability to succeed and triumph in righteous struggle.*

Christian Doctrinal Conflict – *"O foolish Galatians, who hath bewitched you, that ye should not obey the truth, before whose eyes Jesus Christ hath been evidently set forth, crucified among you? This only would I learn of you, Received ye the Spirit by the works of the law, or by the hearing of faith? Are ye so foolish? having begun in the Spirit, are ye now made perfect by the flesh? Have ye suffered so many things in vain? if it be yet in vain. He therefore that ministereth to you the Spirit, and worketh miracles among you, doeth he it by the works of the law, or by the hearing of faith? Even as Abraham believed God, and it was accounted to him for righteousness. Know ye therefore that they which are of faith, the same are the children of Abraham. And the scripture, foreseeing that God would justify the heathen through faith, preached before the gospel unto Abraham, saying, In thee shall all nations be blessed. So then they which be of faith are blessed with faithful Abraham."* (**Galatians 3:1-9**)

PARTING COMMENT:

Now, do you want to know what I "really think" as a black Christian man? My people of the faith, how are we so easily duped into a celebration <u>contrived</u> to conflict with our Christmas celebration (there has never been a December harvest celebration anywhere in the world) that is bogus in its African origin? Kwanzaa is created out of an antichrist spirit whereas Dr. Karenga expressed in his 1980 book, Kawaida Theory, his belief in religion's diminishing of numerous humanistic traits and the mythical nature of Christianity and Judaism. Note that the seven principals of Kawanzaa were also the same seven principals represented in the seven–headed cobra that symbolized the revolutionary principals of the murderous Symbionese Liberation Army (SLA) of the 1970s. Further, Dr. Maulana Ron Karenga was released from prison in 1975 after being sentenced in 1971 for the brutal torturing over a two day period of two black women.

"And he gave some, apostles; and some, prophets; and some, evangelists; and some, pastors and teachers; For the perfecting of the saints, for the work of the ministry, for the edifying of the body of Christ:Till we all come in the unity of the faith, and of the knowledge of the Son of God, unto a perfect man, unto the measure of the stature of the fulness of Christ: That we henceforth be no more children, tossed to and fro, and carried about with every wind of doctrine, by the sleight of men, and cunning craftiness, whereby they lie in wait to deceive; But speaking the truth in love, may grow up into him in all things, which is the head, even Christ: From whom the whole body fitly joined together and compacted by that which every joint supplieth, according to the effectual working in the measure of every part, maketh increase of the body unto the edifying of itself in love." (**Ephesians 4:11-16**)

"My people are destroyed for lack of knowledge: because thou hast rejected knowledge, I will also reject thee, that thou shalt be no priest to me: seeing thou hast forgotten the law of thy God, I will also forget thy children." (**Hosea 4:6**)

"Beware of false prophets, which come to you in sheep's clothing, but inwardly they are ravening wolves." (**Matthew 7:15**)

"But there were false prophets also among the people, even as there shall be false teachers among you, who privily shall bring in damnable heresies, even denying the Lord that bought them, and bring upon themselves swift destruction. And many shall follow their pernicious ways; by reason of whom the way of truth shall be evil spoken of." (**2 Peter 2:1&2**)

Easter (Christian Passover) and Good Friday

Mistakenly, the Christian Easter is defined as follows by the Webster's II New Riverside University Dictionary: "Word history: The word Easter, although the name of a Christian festival, has its origins in pagan times. Eastre or Eostre, the Old English spelling of Easter, was originally the name of a Germanic goddess who was worshipped at a festival at the spring equinox. Her name is closely related to Latin aurora and Greek eos, both of which mean "dawn". Easter is also derived from the same root word as east, the direction of the sunrise.

However, by the grace of Almighty God, the word Easter (pascha - the Passover (the meal the day), the festival or the special sacrifices connected with the Passover), is used once in the Bible. Christians have made the mistake of associating the Pagan holiday with the Jewish Passover of the first century church. However, the temple Christ spoke of, his body, was destroyed and then resurrected on a Sunday morning with all of the significance of the passion (suffering in the crucifixion). Not the least in the significance of the passion of Christ is the shedding of his blood, as the Lamb of God, for the remission of mankind's sin. The Bible says that, "whosoever believeth in him should not perish but have eternal life". "For God so loved the world that he gave his only begotten Son", to take away man's sin. According to the Bible, anyone not believing and thereby passed over by God's wrath shall be resurrected from death to eternal damnation rather than eternal life. Now, Good Friday becomes a good day, for mankind, because Jesus pays on that day the wages of sin.

> *"And because he saw it pleased the Jews, he proceeded further to take Peter also. (Then were the days of unleavened bread.) And when he had apprehended him, he put him in prison, and delivered him to four quaternions of soldiers to keep him; intending after Easter to bring him forth to the people."* (**Acts 12:3&4**) *"And it came to pass, when Jesus had finished all these sayings, he said unto his disciples, Ye know that after two days is the feast of the passover, and the Son of man is betrayed to be crucified."* (**Matthew 26:1&2**)

> *"Then Moses called for all the elders of Israel, and said unto them, Draw out and take you a lamb according to your families, and kill the passover. And ye shall take a bunch of hyssop, and dip it in the blood that is in the bason, and strike the lintel and the two side posts with the blood that is in the bason; and none of you shall go out at the door of his house until the morning. For the Lord will pass through to smite the Egyptians; and when he seeth the blood upon the lintel, and on the two side posts, the Lord will pass over the door, and will not suffer the destroyer to come in unto your houses to smite you. And ye shall observe this thing for an ordinance to thee and to thy sons for ever. And it shall come to pass, when ye be come to the land which the Lord will give you, according as he hath promised, that ye shall keep this service. And it shall come to pass, when your children*

shall say unto you, What mean ye by this service? That ye shall say, It is the sacrifice of the Lord's passover, who passed over the houses of the children of Israel in Egypt, when he smote the Egyptians, and delivered our houses. And the people bowed the head and worshipped." (**Exodus 12:21-27**)

"For the life of the flesh is in the blood: and I have given it to you upon the altar to make an atonement for your souls: for it is the blood that maketh an atonement for the soul." (**Leviticus 17:11**)

"The next day John seeth Jesus coming unto him, and saith, Behold the Lamb of God, which taketh away the sin of the world." (**John 1:29**)

"This is the covenant that I will make with them after those days, saith the Lord, I will put my laws into their hearts, and in their minds will I write them; And their sins and iniquities will I remember no more. Now where remission of these is, there is no more offering for sin. Having therefore, brethren, boldness to enter into the holiest by the blood of Jesus, By a new and living way, which he hath consecrated for us, through the veil, that is to say, his flesh; And having an high priest over the house of God; Let us draw near with a true heart in full assurance of faith, having our hearts sprinkled from an evil conscience, and our bodies washed with pure water." (**Hebrews 10:16-22**)

"Jesus answered and said unto them, Destroy this temple, and in three days I will raise it up." (**John 2:19**)

"But one of the soldiers with a spear pierced his side, and forthwith came there out blood and water." (**John 19:34**)

"For God so loved the world, that he gave his only begotten Son, that whosoever believeth in him should not perish, but have everlasting life. For God sent not his Son into the world to condemn the world; but that the world through him might be saved. He that believeth on him is not condemned: but he that believeth not is condemned already, because he hath not believed in the name of the only begotten Son of God." (**John 3:16-18**)

"Jesus, when he had cried again with a loud voice, yielded up the ghost. And, behold, the veil of the temple was rent in twain from the top to the bottom; and the earth did quake, and the rocks rent; And the graves were opened; and many bodies of the saints which slept arose, And came out of the graves after his resurrection, and went into the holy city, and appeared unto many. Now when the centurion, and they that were with him, watching Jesus, saw the earthquake, and those things that were done, they feared greatly, saying, Truly this was the Son of God." (**Matthew 27:50-54**)

"Enter ye in at the strait gate: for wide is the gate, and broad is the way, that leadeth to destruction, and many there be which go in thereat: Because strait is the gate, and narrow is the way, which leadeth unto life, and few there be that find it." (**Matthew 7:13&14**)

"For the wages of sin is death; but the gift of God is eternal life through Jesus Christ our Lord." (**Romans 6:23**)

"And shall come forth; they that have done good, unto the resurrection of life; and they that have done evil, unto the resurrection of damnation." (**John 5:29**)

"Then said Jesus unto his disciples, If any man will come after me, let him deny himself, and take up his cross, and follow me. For whosoever will save his life shall lose it: and who-

soever will lose his life for my sake shall find it. For what is a man profited, if he shall gain the whole world, and lose his own soul? or what shall a man give in exchange for his soul? For the Son of man shall come in the glory of his Father with his angels; and then he shall reward every man according to his works. Verily I say unto you, There be some standing here, which shall not taste of death, till they see the Son of man coming in his kingdom." (Matthew 16:24-27)

Halloween

All Saints and All Souls remembrance is the essence of Halloween. There is to some even, the entire month of November celebration of the Month of the Dead. This celebration is widely believed to have begun by the pagan Celtic tribes of modern day Ireland, Scotland, Wales and Brittany. The Celtics believed that the dead returned among the living during their summer's end festivals and that masks needed to be worn by the living in order to scare away the dead.

Halloween grew out of a feast that celebrated all Martyrs. The feast on November 1st became know as All Hallows for "one who is holy. The eve of the feast became known as All Hallows Eve or Halloween many pagan practices instituted. Halloween is not for Christians.

> *"When thou art come into the land which the Lord thy God giveth thee, thou shalt not learn to do after the abominations of those nations. There shall not be found among you any one that maketh his son or his daughter to pass through the fire, or that useth divination, or an observer of times, or an enchanter, or a witch, Or a charmer, or a consulter with familiar spirits, or a wizard, or a necromancer. For all that do these things are an abomination unto the Lord: and because of these abominations the Lord thy God doth drive them out from before thee. Thou shalt be perfect with the Lord thy God."* (Deuteronomy 18:9-13)

> *"Neither give place to the devil."* (Ephesians 4:27)

Appendix 1

Brief Outline of the History of the Bible

BASICS REGARDING THE BIBLE

The Bible that exists as a Cannon of 66 Books (Note the Catholic Church Apocryha contains 14 other Bible Books not considered reliable) by 40 writers over a period of approximately 1500 years. Exhaustive evidence exists as to its reliability to include actual copies of what we consider the Old Testament scriptures, that pre-date the birth of Christ.

EARLIEST BIBLE CANNONS

The 39 books of present day Hebrew Bible were compiled at the council of Jamnia in A.D. 90. There existed at the time of Christ the Septuagint Bible consisting of the 39 books of the Old Testament along with the 14 books of the Apocrypha mixed throughout. This Bible dates back to 285 B.C. according to some sources. Two other ancient versions of the Bible existed as the Samaritan Pentateuch (written B.C. with Samaritan Characters) and the Peschito (or Syria) Bible which was used in parts of Syria and contained the Old and New Testament in as early as the First Century A.D. The New Testament was written from about 50 A.D. to 95 A.D. The New Testament of 27 books was first canonized in the Easter Letter of Athanasius in 367 A.D. The Finalization of the Cannon of 27 books for the New Testament was accomplished towards the end of 397 A.D. by a decree from the Council of Carthage.

THE LATIN BIBLE STANDARD FOR THE CATHOLIC CHURCH

The Vulgate Bible from approximately 400 A.D., became the standard for the Catholic Church for more that 100 years. This Bible was authored by a bible scholar named Jerome who wrote this Bible in Latin. Also, there are three other Bible manuscripts for the sake of irrefutable evidence of Bible reliability. They are the following: The CODEX SINAS US, the CODEX VATICAN US and the CODEX ALEXANDRIN US (all Greek translations).

EARLIEST LATER TRANSLATIONS OF THE BIBLE

The John Wycliffe Bible of 1380 exists as the earliest complete English translations of the Bible. Note that this existed before the printing press was invented in 1450. In 1534, Martin Luther first separated the Apocrypha from the 66 other books of the Bible in his German bible. This translation prompted Protestant versions of the Bible into other languages to include

French, Dutch and English. The first printed English translation of the Bible was the Myles Coverdale Bible in 1535. The King James version of the Bible was translated from the original languages rather that Latin, in 1611. See Appendix 2, dedicatory of the King James Version of the Bible.

Appendix 2

THE EPISTLE DEDICATORY OF THE
KING JAMES VERSION OF THE BIBLE

TO THE MOST High and Mighty Prince James by the Grace of God King of Great Britain, France and Ireland. Defendant of the Faith & c. The Translators of the Bible wish Grace, Mercy, and Peace through Jesus Christ our Lord

Great and manifold were the blessings, most dread Sovereign, which Almighty God, the Father of all mercies, bestowed upon us the people of England, when first he sent Your Majesty's Royal Person to rule and reign over us. For whereas it was the expectation of many, who wished not well unto our Sion, that upon the setting of the bright Occidental Star, Queen Elizabeth of most happy memory, some thick and palpable clouds of darkness would so have overshadowed this Land, that men should have been in doubt which way they were to walk; and that it should hardly be known, who was to direct the unsettled State; the appearance of Your Majesty, as of the Sun in his strength, instantly dispelled those supposed and surmised mists, and gave unto all that were well affected exceeding cause of comfort; especially when we beheld and Government established in Your Highness, and Your hopeful Seed, by an un-doubted Title, and this also accompanied with peace and tranquility at home and abroad.

But among our joys, there was no one that more filled our hearts, than the blessed continu-ance of the preaching of God's sacred Word among us; which is that inestimable treasure, which excelleth all the riches of the earth; because the fruit thereof extendeth itself, not only to the time spent in this transitory world, but directeth and disposeth men unto the eternal happiness which is above in heaven.

Then not suffer this to fall to the ground, but rather to take it up, and to continue it in that state, wherein the famous Predecessor of Your Highness did leave it: nay, to go forward with confidence and resolution of a Man in maintaining the truth of Christ, and propagating it far and near, is that which hath so bound and firmly knit the hearts of all Your Majesty's loyal and religious people unto You, that Your very name is precious among them: their eye doth behold You with comfort, and they bless You in their hearts, as that sanctified Person who, under God is the immediate Author of their true happiness. And this their contentment doth not diminish or decay, but every day increaseth and taketh strength, when they observe, that the zeal of Your Majesty toward the house of God doth not slack or go backward, but is more and more kindled, manifesting itself abroad in the farthest parts of Christendom, by writing in a defence of the Truth, (which hath given such a blow unto that man of sin, as will not be healed,) and every day a home, by religious and learned discourse, by frequenting the house of God, by hearing the Word preached, by cherishing the Teachers thereof, by caring for the Church, as most tender and loving nursing Father.

There are infinite arguments of this right Christian and religious affection in Your Majesty; but none is more forcible to declare it to others than the vehement and perpetuated desire of accomplishing and publishing of this work, which now with all humility we present unto Your Majesty. For when Your Highness had once out of deep judgment apprehended how convenient it was, that out of the Original Sacred Tongues, together with comparing of the labors, both in our own, and other foreign Languages, of many worthy men who went before us, there should be one more exact Translation of the body Scriptures into the English Tongue; Your Majesty did never desist to urge and to excite those to whom it was commended, that the work might be hastened, and that the business might be expedited in so decent a manner, as a matter of such importance might justly require.

And now at last, by the mercy of God, and the continuance of our labours, it being brought unto such a conclusion, as that we have great hopes that the Church of England shall reap good fruit thereby; we hold it our duty to offer it to Your Majesty, not only as to our King and Sovereign, but as to the principal Mover and Author of the work: humbly craving of Your most Sacred Majesty, that since things of this quality have ever been subject to the censures of illmeaning and discontented persons, it may receive approbation and patronage from so learned and judicious a Prince as Your Highness is, whose allowance and acceptance of our labours shall more honour and encourage us, than all the calumniations and hard interpretations of other men shall dismay us. So that if, on the one side we shall be traduced by Popish Persons at home or abroad, who therefore will malign us, because we are poor instruments to the make of God's holy Truth to be yet more and more known unto the people, whom they desire still to keep in ignorance and darkness; or if, on the other side, we shall be maligned by selfconceited Brethren, who run their own ways, and give liking onto nothing, but what is framed by themselves, and hammered on their anvil; we may rest secure, supported within by the truth and innocency of good conscience, having walked the ways of simplicity and integrity, as before the Lord; and sustained without by the powerful protection of Your Majesty's grace and favour, which will ever give countenance to honest and Christian endeavours against bitter censures and uncharitable imputations.

The Lord of heaven and earth bless Your Majesty with many and happy days, that, as his heavenly hand hath enriched Your Highness with many singular and extraordinary graces, so You may be the wonder of the world in this later age for happiness and true felicity, to the honour of that great GOD, and the good of the Church, through Jesus Christ our Lord and only Savior.

(Note that the Authorized King James Version is the Holy Bible Old and New Testaments translated out of the original tongues with previous translations diligently compared and revised by His Majesty's special command.)

Appendix 3

THE HISTORY OF THE BAPTIST CHURCH
(GREATLY ABBREVIATED)

ORIGIN IN THE PENTECOST (30 A.D.)

To say the Baptist Church has its origin in John the Baptist would be technically in error. John's Baptism was to repentance only. With the dispensation of the Holy Ghost on the Day of Pentecost, the Baptism that John spoke of as in Jesus Christ became possible. Those that were baptized on the Day of Pentecost were most probably baptized as the Baptist Church does today in obedience to the instructions of Jesus in the Book of Matthew. In combining the manner of baptism and the biblically sound doctrinal statement of the Baptist Articles of Faith, the Baptist Church can indeed claim itself to be of a day of Pentecost and New Testament church in origin (a true church).

EARLY GROWTH WITH TOLERANCE TURNING TO PERSECUTION UNDER ROMAN RULE

Roman Emperor's were gods and New Testament churches believed contrary to this, yet, the Christian Religion was considered harmless to the greatest extend. In the early years of the Christian Church, persecution of Christians was at a low level and came basically from specific emperors or aristocrats pointing blame at the Christians in circumstances where the emperor or as it was felt that the Roman gods were offended by the Christians. The church grew and flourished during this early period and despite the martyring of every one of the Apostles. Churches were founded beginning in Jerusalem and throughout Palestine, Asia Minor and Macedonia. The church in Jerusalem may have grown to as many as 50 thousand members during this period notwithstanding persecution from the Jews as well. Nero conversely severely persecuted the early Christian church beginning in 64 A.D. after he blamed those of the faith for the burning of Rome.

There were numerous other periods of horrible persecution to the point of extermination, of the early church by various Roman emperors who blamed the decline of the Roman Empire upon the Christians offending the Roman gods. Yet, growth continued throughout the Roman Empire and the known world during the first 300 years of the Early Christian Church, to the extent that a congregation where established in every city or town, due to what was considered the harmless nature of the church. In addition, just as the church in Jerusalem had grown, other large congregations had come into existence with the soon to follow establishment of governing hierarchies and corruption within the original democratic policy with regard to the government of the church. The Bible makes reference in the Book of Revelation to the Churches of Ephesus, Smyrna, Pergamos, Thyatira, Sardis, Philadelphia and Laodicea in Asia. The Apostle Paul sent epistles to the Church in Rome, Corrinth, Ephesus, Galatia, Philippi, Thessalonica and Clossae. In this climate, there arose the false teaching of "baptismal regeneration". This is a doctrine of belief in salvation in baptism alone (baptismal regeneration) and false doctrine led to the erroneous practice of infant baptism as one among many errors. This period extends from 64 A.D. until roughly 313 A.D.

THE ORIGIN OF THE ROMAN CATHOLIC CHURCH AND THE DAWN OF ITS PERSECUTION OF THE TRUE CHURCHES (CHURCHES LOYAL TO THE SCRIPTURES)

It is an historical fact that while in battle in 312 A.D., the Emperor Constantine had a vision of a flaming cross with the words above it, "BY THIS SIGN THOU SHALT CONQUER". Emperor Constantine became victorious from that time on while fighting battles under the banner of the cross. For all purposes, the Roman Catholic Church came into existence in 312 A.D. when the Emperor Constantine gave a call for the Christian churches to come together as one church and he pronounced himself as the head. The body of church rulers and the errors of Catholicism were organized into a definite system in 313 A.D. with the exclusion of the true churches by their election. Roman Catholicism became the religion of the state and all Christians were by law compelled to become a part of the state Christian church. The True Churches were then persecuted as a result for not becoming a part of Roman Catholicism. The Baptist Church as later identified as one of the contingency of True Churches of the era, was never a part of Roman Catholicism as it came into existence and departed from a loyalty to the scriptures. Some of the names of the churches that refused to become a part of Roman Catholicism were the Montanist, Paulician, Novationist, Paterines, Donatist, Albigenses and the Anabaptists. These churches, labeled also as New Testament Churches, were considered as heretics by the Roman Catholic Church; which by definition was anyone disagreeing with the Roman Catholic Church.

THE ROMAN CATHOLIC PERSECUTION OF THE TRUE CHURCHES FROM FORMATION TO REFORMATION

Severe persecution began and continued as the Roman Catholic Church became entrenched in government as the "State Church" and attempted to exterminate any Christian church that opposed her. Bloody times of persecution ensued as many of the false doctrines of the Catholic church began to take root. Now as the Roman Catholic Church in the west grew in supremacy to the Apostate Churches in the east, the persecution to the True Churches continued for centuries. A "dark age" for the True Churches, to include the Baptist Church, was to extend from 313 A.D. through the split of the Roman Catholic Church from the Eastern Orthodox Church in 1064 and beyond. The True Churches continued to rely upon the scriptures as authority in the church and practicing the two ordinances of the Church, baptizing and the "Lord's Supper".

From a period of shortly after the beginnings of the Roman Catholic Church in 312 A.D. until 1198 A.D., there was horrific persecution of the True Churches as Catholicism organized into a definitive and compelling system. There was no longer the persecution from the pagan Roman Empire but from within the within Christianity. This persecution was with governmental support and sought to eliminate all other Christian Churches.

Then there arose in 1198 an Inquisition out of the Roman Catholic Churches that began with Pope Innocent III. The Inquisition established a Church Court in which the Roman Catholic Popes would try and punish heretics which were in fact all of those that did not agree with Roman Catholicism. Punishment with unspeakable cruelty resulted in the near obscurity of the Baptist Church as people and church records were destroyed. The Inquisition lasted 500 years yet the Baptist Church, a True Church, continued to exist. During this period of time, the Catholic Church became so corrupt that reformers began to surface from within the Roman Catholic Church. John Wycliffe (1320-1384) opposed the teachings of the Roman Catholic Church and became the main precursor of the Protestant Reformation. In 1380 he translated the first English language Bible from the Latin Vulgate Bible. John Wycliffe and his followers, the Lollards, produced dozens of English language manuscripts of the Bible prior to the invention of the printing press in 1450. Within the Inquisition timeframe, other reformers to become known as Protestants came forth as voices of protest to Roman Catholicism. Among these voices were John Huss (1373-1415) Savonarola (1452-1498), Zwingli (1484), Martin Luther (1483-1546), John Knox (1505-1572) and John Calvin (1509-1564).

Another to usher in the Reformation of the Roman Catholic Church was King Henry VII of England. In 1534, King Henry established apart from the Roman Catholic Church, the Church of England with himself as head-"Defender of the Faith". This was done in order for him to divorce his wife. This helped the Reformation in that the English people turned away from the burden of the Roman Catholic Church as the nominally Protestant Church of England grew in membership and religious tolerance.

PERIOD OF INITIAL BAPTIST CHURCH TOLERATION 1644 A.D. TO 1689 A.D.

Having identified the Baptist Church as within the Church established on the day of Pentecost, there were New Testament Churches operating over the period of 313 A.D. to 1644 A.D. that had adopted Baptist Principles. The Peteobrusians, the Paulicians, the Bogmils, the Waldeness and the Anabaptists comprised the list of True Churches (New Testament Churches) of the time period. In 1644 seven Baptist Churches in London joined forces to produce the Church Confession. Undoubtedly, this leads many to establish this as the undeniable beginning of the Baptist Church in the 17th Century. In 1689 the Toleration Act, which included stated Baptist beliefs, ended the centuries of persecution of the Baptist in England.

BAPTIST TAKE ROOT IN AMERICA

The earliest Baptist Church in America was established in 1638 in Newport, Rhode Island. The Baptist Church has suffered persecution even in America and as a result of that persecution was instrumental in the passing of the First Amendment to the United States Constitution: "Congress shall make no law respecting an establishment of Religion, or prohibiting the free exercise, thereof, or abridging the freedom of speech or the Press, or the Rights of the People Peaceably to assemble and to petition the government for a repress of grievances."

Appendix 4
Baptist Church Covenant

HAVING BEEN LED, as we believe, by the Spirit of God to receive the Lord Jesus Christ as our Savior, and on the profession of our faith, having been baptized in the name of the Father, and of the Son, and of the Holy Spirit, we do now in the presence of God, angels and this assembly, most solemnly and joyfully enter into covenant with one another, as one body in Christ.

We engage, therefore, by the aid of the Holy Spirit, to walk together in Christian love; to strive for the advancement of this church in knowledge and holiness; to give it a place in our affections, prayers and services above every organization of human origin; to sustain its worship, ordinances, discipline and doctrine; to contribute cheerfully and regularly, as God has prospered us, towards its expenses, for the support of a faithful and evangelical ministry among us, the relief of the poor and the spread of the Gospel throughout the world. In case of difference of opinion in the church, we will strive to avoid a contentious spirit, and if we cannot unanimously agree, we will cheerfully recognize the right of the majority of govern.

We also engage to maintain family and secret devotion; to study diligently the word of God; to religiously educate our children; to seek the salvation of our kindred and acquaintance; to walk circumspectly in the world; to be kind and just to those in our employ, and faithful in the service we promise others; endeavoring in the purity of heart and good will towards all men to exemplify and commend our holy faith.

We further engage to watch over, to pray for, to exhort and stir up each other unto every good word and work; to guard each other's reputation, not needlessly exposing the infirmities of others; to participate in each other's joy, and with tender sympathy bear one another's burdens and sorrows; to cultivate Christian courtesy; to be slow to give or take offense, but always ready for reconciliation, being mindful of the rules of the Savior in the eighteenth chapter of Matthew, to secure it without delay; and thought life, amid evil report, and good report, to seek to live to the glory of God, who hath called out of darkness into his marvelous light.

When we remove from this place, we engage as soon as possibly to unite with some other church where we can carry out the spirit of this covenant and the principles of God's word.

Note: There is another version of this Covenant that prohibits the sell or use of alcohol as a beverage.

Appendix 5

PRAYER MEETING OUTLINE

Song or Hymn
Scripture
Opening Prayer
Song or Hymn
Opening Remarks - Minister or Deacon
Testimonies and Prayer Requests
Response to Prayer Requests and Laying on of Hands for the Sick
Song or Hymn

Corporate Prayers for:

(Basis: 1 Timothy 2:8 and Isaiah 56:4-8)

Mankind/World Problems*
(Basis: John 17:20&21, James 4:1-3 Matthew 5:44&45 and Matthew 6:9&10)
Nation/Government/Rulers*
(Basis: 1 Timothy 2:1-6 and Hebrews 13:18)
Community*
(Basis: 2 Chronicles 30:18-20, James 5:16 and Acts 1:13&14)
Sick & Shut-ins*
(Basis: James 5:13-15)
Ourselves & Our Families
(Basis: Jeremiah 29:11-13, Romans 10:13, Ephesians 6:17&18, 1 Thessalonians 5:23-25, 1 Peter 3:12, John 15:16 and Mark 11:22-25)

Closing Prayer and Benediction
* Intercessory prayer by various participants on basis of news items used in the supplications.

Appendix 6

MY CALLING

I grew up in the Greater First Baptist Church of Mount Pleasant Plaines in Washington, D.C. My mother and father joined in 1957 and I came forward to be baptized on Mother's Day of 1959 at the age on nine. Let me mention that I was a pew baby as my parents had attended two other churches in Washington, D.C. One of my earliest memories is looking down from the balcony upon the pulpit at the Metropolitan Baptist Church of Washington, D.C. Now, having been baptized in the Greater First Baptist Church, I continued to attend Sunday school and the Baptist Training Union. I served on the Junior Usher Board and was a Junior Deacon for numerous Youth Days. I sang with and became President of the Chancel (Young Adult) Choir. Upon starting my sophomore year in electrical engineering at Howard University in the fall of 1969, I auditioned and became one of the Charter Members of the Howard Gospel Choir that included as one of the musicians/directors, Richard Smallwood. There were saints at the Greater First Baptist Church that went to their graves assuring my mother that I would become a preacher and to that I paid no attention.

DREAM OF RAISING A PREACHER NOT BECOMING A PREACHER AND ALL IN A NAME:

My son and firstborn is Minister Preston Nathaniel Tolliver, III. Probably three (3) months before he was born, I saw my son in a dream and then later there came a revelation that I might raise a preacher. Many years later, I began to teach Sunday school at the Lilydale Progressive Missionary Baptist Church in Chicago, my firstborn never attended classes with the children, but rather attended my adult class. My son as of today is an associate minister in the pulpit of the Rev. Marvin G. Parker, Broadview Missionary Baptist Church, Broadview, Illinois.

Now, I had learned in grammar school that Preston meant "priestly and/or church dweller" in old English. Our middle name Nathaniel, I have come to understand while writing this book over the last few years, is from the Hebrew name Nathan which means "gift of God". How about my own definition of Tolliver as an advocate/enabler of life ("to live")?

THE INITIAL CALLING:

I had always been to a great extent a loner and an impersonal type of person. I had no desire to preach, not withstanding the fact that without any great revelation, I was being obedient to God by teaching Sunday school. Then one Saturday morning in August of 1991, as I lay partially awake beside my wife, very vividly I was lifted into a pulpit. At that point, as similar to

Zechariah 3:1-4, my garments were changed as I was then clothed in a white robe and began to preach. Upon commencing to preach, a crushing pressure came upon me and I struggled with the pressure to the extent that I awoke my wife. All of this occurred as I was aware that I was in my bedroom, therefore, it was a vision not a dream. As I came out of the vision and the pressure upon me ceased, I told my wife, "I think that I am being called to preach".

Following the initial vision, I lay awake in my bedroom on the next Saturday morning and from a corner in the bedroom which was twenty stories up in the air in the South Tower of Regents Park, Chicago, a voice called out "Preston". I asked my wife, if she heard the voice which was sharp but not loud. Then, probably the next Saturday, the same thing occurred again only this time the voice called "Preston, Preston". This time, I went into prayer in a manner similar to 1 Samuel 3:2-10. Unlike any other experience in private or public, when I closed my eyes I could see a vision similar to an old television set with a snowy picture during the non-broadcast hours. There was nothing else and I interpreted this I mean that Lord would make the picture clearer to me later.

Indeed, a short time later, the Lord began dealing with me with regard to an initial sermon. The subject was concerning my confidence in Christ. Deacon Billy March of the Lilydale Progressive Missionary Baptist Church approached me in church as asked if I would speak at that year's Annual Men's Day Prayer Breakfast. To his surprise, I readily accepted. Deacon March told me many month's later that he had asked others (understandable since I had only joined Lilydale Progressive with my entire family in May of 1989), however, everything seemed to have been pointing to me all along as speaker for that prayer breakfast. I know that my initial sermon was actually delivered at the Men's Day Prayer Breakfast at the Lilydale Progressive Missionary Baptist Church in 1991. The message was already prepared when asked. Not only this, but as I had put the finishing touches on that first sermon, I had began preparation on a second sermon, not knowing for what it was intended as I had told my wife. As I traveled the Lake Street elevated train in Chicago, I picked up a newspaper and upon looking at the article I began, as led by the Holy Ghost, preparing another sermon. When I preached the first sermon for the Men's Day Breakfast, I actually had two sermons already prepared and was approached by a Pastor in attendance to speak at his first annual banquet that next Friday night. I informed him that I was not a preacher and he informed me that I had just preached and that it was just like a cup of Maxwell House coffee, "good to the last drop". To that Pastor's amazement, I accepted the invitation right on the spot. I was asked if I needed time to think about the sermon to which I responded that I did not. The late Rev. Abraham Patterson Jackson, Pastor of the Liberty Baptist Church of Chicago, was in attendance at the banquet and he made it a point to encourage me every time I saw him thereafter, up until his passing a few years later.

God affirms callings. I was startled one Sunday at the Lilydale Progressive Missionary Baptist Church, where my eventual Father in the Ministry, the late Rev. Lawrence E. Mosley, Sr., had been Pastor for a number of years at the time. One of the oldest members of the church spotted me in the aisle and told me that I had been called to preach at that she was never wrong. I just asked for her prayers and told no one of my calling which was by then to me pretty obvious.

TRIP TO WASHINGTON, D.C. AND THE LATE REV. DR. EDWARD THOMAS.

I had doctrinal misgivings concerning Rev. Mosley. And the Lord revealed in a dream that I should go to Washington, D.C. to meet with Rev. Dr. Edward Thomas. Dr. Thomas, who had two (2) earned doctorates in religion and a professor at the Howard University School of Religion, had been my pastor since the age of seven. Rev. Thomas had baptized me at the age of nine. Now note that I graduated from the Howard University School of Engineering in December of 1972 (BSEE) and was immediately hired by Commonwealth Edison in Chicago, in January of 1973. Do the math; at a minimum of 28 sermons per year (Rev. Thomas never preached on 4th Sundays and allowing another 12 Sundays missed/year by me), I have under my belt 420 plus sermons from Rev. Dr. Thomas.

Due to a strange financial difficulty at the time, I was unable to make the trip to Washington, D.C. until September of 1992. I traveled to meet with Rev. Thomas without prior contact. In spite of my feeling of assurance that he would be present in church on that Sunday morning, I had been told that he was off to the Annual National Baptist Convention Conference as usual. Rev. Thomas surprised everyone by choosing not to attend the conference that year and I was indeed able to meet and pray with him with my father in attendance. Rev. Dr. Thomas, unbeknownst to me, had ordained the late Rev. Dr. A.W. Johnson, the late Pastor of the Saint John Church Baptist, Chicago, as a deacon and then a minister. Rev. Thomas referred me to Rev. Johnson in Chicago who in turn referred me with specific instruction back to my pastor at the Lilydale Progressive Church.

SIGNS AND WONDERS

Traveling the Lake Street Elevated to and from a start up business operation on the Westside of Chicago, the Lord spoke to me in a still voice while heading home prior to my meeting with Pastor Mosley. I could barely contain myself as he spoke to me saying to "preach my word over all that you see" of the West Side of Chicago. I had set up an appointment to meet with Pastor Mosley and had stepped on a long and sharp nail on a federal government construction site at the Grand Rapids International Airport. The nail went into the middle of the sole of my shoe, unexplainably bent and came out of the side of the sole. Thinking that it was a spec of concrete on the side of my shoe, I cut my finger as I attempted to pluck it off. The nail was broken off, embedded in the sole of my shoe and I could not pull it out. There was nothing to have prevented it from passing through my foot (it fell out many months later in the presence of Pastor Mosley).

Upon meeting with Pastor Mosley, it was agreed that my calling would be announced to the Church and that I would do an initial/trial sermon in January of 1993.

GRAND RAPIDS, MICHIGAN AND THE INITIAL SERMON

I had just been hired by the FAA in July of 1992 and given my first assignment as a Resident (field) Engineer in September. I was the resident engineer on site for the building of the ASR-9 radar installation, just outside the southeastern edge of the Grand Rapids International Airport. I passed by the Zondervan Publishing Company each day and was initially unaware that they were among, if not the largest, Bible and Christian book publishers in the world. I had my radio in the construction trailer tuned into the Moody Bible Radio Station most of the day and I had not had the opportunity to do so before or since my project in Grand Rapids. I studied and worked on my trial sermon during my off hours and observed the seemingly visible fireworks of a spiritual warfare going on in my hotel room during many nights. One night something violently pounded the wall right at my headboard. I worked on my initial sermon, "Let the Good Times Roll", from the scriptural text of Luke 4:18-19. I also heard within a 2-3 day span in Grand Rapids, two different sermons from the text of John 21:18&19; this I believe has affirmed another revelation I have concerning my calling.

I came back to Chicago from Grand Rapids with an unexplained tear in my lower abdomen, a hernia, which I had correctly diagnosed before any medical examination, and it had to be immediately repaired. I preached my initial sermon in January 1993 and was ordained in September of that year. In spite of the fact that I am on my way there, I have yet to set foot in a seminary.

Appendix 7

OPEN LETTER TO MINISTER FARRAKHAN

Dear Minister Farrakhan,

I come to you as a humble servant of the Lord, ordained within recent years in the Baptist Church and led by the Holy Ghost in this communication. I know that you are being drawn by the truth in Christ because it is obvious in your public presentations; after all, on Savior's Day in 1995 you preached that "Jesus Saves". Let this be a sign to you, in 1950 this ex-concertmaster was born in the Freedmen's Hospital which was to become the Howard University Hospital, the only hospital you trusted to save your life. This is to save your soul to life eternal.

Having studied the Qur'an and spent nearly five years in Saudi Arabia (as an engineer with ARAMCO), I also know that if you were to proclaim in Mecca some of the things that you have elsewhere as of late, you would be thrown out on your head. You are fond of quoting the scriptures because you believe; flesh and blood has not revealed this to me but rather the Holy Spirit. There is in you some sense of the qualities of Gideon, a mighty man of valor.

> "And there came an angel of the Lord, and sat under an oak which was in Ophrah, that pertained unto Joash the Abi-ezrite: and his son Gideon threshed wheat by the winepress, to hide it from the Midianites. And the angel of the Lord appeared unto him, and said unto him, The Lord is with thee, thou mighty man of valour." (Judges 6:11-12)

However, you are caught between two opinions; whether to preach Christ or to preach Islam.

> "And Elijah came unto all the people, and said, How long halt ye between two opinions? if the Lord be God, follow him: but if Baal, then follow him. And the people answered him not a word." (1 Kings 18:21)

You may not answer a word now as you read, but the Lord is speaking to you in many ways and this is definitely one of the ways. You are being required to make a choice. Muhammad, the Prophet of Islam, more than 600 years after the resurrection made his choice; he was by biblical definition an antichrist and is counted as among the deceivers according to a portion of scriptures in the Bible's New Testament of which you are so fond of quoting.

> "For many deceivers are entered into the world, who confess not that Jesus Christ is come in the flesh. This is a deceiver and an antichrist." (2 John 1:7)

However, Minister Farrakhan, you are different. I believe that you believe in the scriptures for their truth has been revealed to you.

> "All scripture is given by inspiration of God, and is profitable for doctrine, for reproof, for correction, for instruction in righteousness: That the man of God may be perfect, throughly furnished unto all good works." (2 Timothy 3:16-17)

The scriptures reveal the Christ in the Old Testament as Jesus can be quoted.

> "Search the scriptures; for in them ye think ye have eternal life: and they are they which testify of me." (John 5:39)

The scriptures reveal Christ in the New Testament.

> "This is the disciple which testifieth of these things, and wrote these things: and we know that his testimony is true. And there are also many other things which Jesus did, the which, if they should be written every one, I suppose that even the world itself could not contain the books that should be written. Amen." (John 21:24-25)

Jesus is Alpha and Omega according to the scriptures in which you believe; according to the scriptures, this excludes the Prophet Muhammad, a successor of Jesus the Christ.

> *"I am Alpha and Omega, the beginning and the ending, saith the Lord, which is, and which was, and which is to come, the Almighty." (Revelation 1:8)*

And as we accept Jesus as Alpha and Omega, we go astray when we allow some other doctrine to be mixed in with the scriptures that proclaim Christ as the incarnate word!

> "In the beginning was the Word, and the Word was with God, and the Word was God. The same was in the beginning with God. All things were made by him; and without him was not any thing made that was made. In him was life; and the life was the light of men. And the light shineth in darkness; and the darkness comprehended it not. And the Word was made flesh, and dwelt among us, (and we beheld his glory, the glory as of the only begotten of the Father,) full of grace and truth. John bare witness of him, and cried, saying, This was he of whom I spake, He that cometh after me is preferred before me: for he was before me. And of his fulness have all we received, and grace for grace. For the law was given by Moses, but grace and truth came by Jesus Christ. No man hath seen God at any time; the only begotten Son, which is in the bosom of the Father, he hath declared him. That was the true Light, which lighteth every man that cometh into the world. He was in the world, and the world was made by him, and the world knew him not. He came unto his own, and his own received him not. But as many as received him, to them gave he power to become the sons of God, even to them that believe on his name: Which were born, not of blood, nor of the will of the flesh, nor of the will of man, but of God." (John 1:1-5, 14-18 & 9-13)

"For I determined not to know any thing among you, save Jesus Christ, and him crucified." (1 Corinthians 2:2)

Even Rev. Dr. Martin Luther King, Jr. strayed in that as he became entangled in the affairs
of this world, he began preaching, unbeknownst to many not paying strict attention at the
time, Mahatma Gandhi/Henry David Thoreau mixed in with Christ. Minister Farrakhan, I
marveled at your doctrine; hear now sound doctrine from the scriptures -

"Knowing this first, that no prophecy of the scripture is of any private interpretation.
For the prophecy came not in old time by the will of man: but holy men of God spake
as they were moved by the Holy Ghost." (2 Peter 1:20-21)

In the manner as did the saints of Berea.

"And the brethren immediately sent away Paul and Silas by night unto Berea: who
coming thither went into the synagogue of the Jews. These were more noble than
those in Thessalonica, in that they received the word with all readiness of mind, and
searched the scriptures daily, whether those things were so." (Acts 17:10-11)

You spoke of atonement at the "Million Man March". According to the Bible, Christ is our
atonement to God; our faith in Christ imputes his righteousness to us and he is thereby our
propitiation.

"For when we were yet without strength, in due time Christ died for the ungodly. For
scarcely for a righteous man will one die: yet peradventure for a good man some would
even dare to die. But God commendeth his love toward us, in that, while we were yet
sinners, Christ died for us. Much more then, being now justified by his blood, we shall
be saved from wrath through him. For if, when we were enemies, we were reconciled
to God by the death of his Son, much more, being reconciled, we shall be saved by his
life. And not only so, but we also joy in God through our Lord Jesus Christ, by whom
we have now received the atonement." (Romans 5:6-11)

"My little children, these things write I unto you, that ye sin not. And if any man sin,
we have an advocate with the Father, Jesus Christ the righteous: And he is the propitiation for our sins: and not for ours only, but also for the sins of the whole world. And
hereby we do know that we know him, if we keep his commandments. He that saith, I
know him, and keepeth not his commandments, is a liar, and the truth is not in him.
But whoso keepeth his word, in him verily is the love of God perfected: hereby know
we that we are in him. He that saith he abideth in him ought himself also so to walk,
even as he walked." (1 John 2:1-6)

"To wit, that God was in Christ, reconciling the world unto himself, not imputing
their trespasses unto them; and hath committed unto us the word of reconciliation.
Now then we are ambassadors for Christ, as though God did beseech you by us: we
pray you in Christ's stead, be ye reconciled to God. For he hath made him to be sin
for us, who knew no sin; that we might be made the righteousness of God in him." (2
Corinthians 5:19-21)

I am thankful for salvation, which is to escape from God's wrath, by the blood shed by

Christ on the cross (by an eyewitness account there was no substitution on the cross) for the whole world.

> 'Then Peter said unto them, Repent, and be baptized every one of you in the name of Jesus Christ for the remission of sins, and ye shall receive the gift of the Holy Ghost." (Acts 2:38)

> "And he said unto them, These are the words which I spake unto you, while I was yet with you, that all things must be fulfilled, which were written in the law of Moses, and in the prophets, and in the psalms, concerning me. Then opened he their understanding, that they might understand the scriptures, And said unto them, Thus it is written, and thus it behoved Christ to suffer, and to rise from the dead the third day: And that repentance and remission of sins should be preached in his name among all nations, beginning at Jerusalem. And ye are witnesses of these things." (Luke 24:44-48)

> "But Christ being come an high priest of good things to come, by a greater and more perfect tabernacle, not made with hands, that is to say, not of this building; Neither by the blood of goats and calves, but by his own blood he entered in once into the holy place, having obtained eternal redemption for us. For if the blood of bulls and of goats, and the ashes of an heifer sprinkling the unclean, sanctifieth to the purifying of the flesh: How much more shall the blood of Christ, who through the eternal Spirit offered himself without spot to God, purge your conscience from dead works to serve the living God? And for this cause he is the mediator of the new testament, that by means of death, for the redemption of the transgressions that were under the first testament, they which are called might receive the promise of eternal inheritance. For where a testament is, there must also of necessity be the death of the testator. For a testament is of force after men are dead: otherwise it is of no strength at all while the testator liveth. Whereupon neither the first testament was dedicated without blood. For when Moses had spoken every precept to all the people according to the law, he took the blood of calves and of goats, with water, and scarlet wool, and hyssop, and sprinkled both the book, and all the people, Saying, This is the blood of the testament which God hath enjoined unto you. Moreover he sprinkled with blood both the tabernacle, and all the vessels of the ministry. And almost all things are by the law purged with blood; and without shedding of blood is no remission. It was therefore necessary that the patterns of things in the heavens should be purified with these; but the heavenly things themselves with better sacrifices than these. For Christ is not entered into the holy places made with hands, which are the figures of the true; but into heaven itself, now to appear in the presence of God for us: Nor yet that he should offer himself often, as the high priest entereth into the holy place every year with blood of others; For then must he often have suffered since the foundation of the world: but now once in the end of the world hath he appeared to put away sin by the sacrifice of himself. And as it is appointed unto men once to die, but after this the judgment: So Christ was once offered to bear the sins of many; and unto them that look for him shall he appear the second time without sin unto salvation." (Hebrews 9:11-28)

> "For the law having a shadow of good things to come, and not the very image of the things, can never with those sacrifices which they offered year by year continually make the comers thereunto perfect. For then would they not have ceased to be offered? because that the worshippers once purged should have had no more con-

science of sins. But in those sacrifices there is a remembrance again made of sins every year. For it is not possible that the blood of bulls and of goats should take away sins. Wherefore when he cometh into the world, he saith, Sacrifice and offering thou wouldest not, but a body hast thou prepared me: In burnt offerings and sacrifices for sin thou hast had no pleasure. Then said I, Lo, I come (in the volume of the book it is written of me,) to do thy will, O God. Above when he said, Sacrifice and offering and burnt offerings and offering for sin thou wouldest not, neither hadst pleasure therein; which are offered by the law; Then said he, Lo, I come to do thy will, O God. He taketh away the first, that he may establish the second. By the which will we are sanctified through the offering of the body of Jesus Christ once for all." (Hebrews 10:1-10)

"When Jesus therefore had received the vinegar, he said, It is finished: and he bowed his head, and gave up the ghost. The Jews therefore, because it was the preparation, that the bodies should not remain upon the cross on the sabbath day, (for that sabbath day was an high day,) besought Pilate that their legs might be broken, and that they might be taken away. Then came the soldiers, and brake the legs of the first, and of the other which was crucified with him. But when they came to Jesus, and saw that he was dead already, they brake not his legs: But one of the soldiers with a spear pierced his side, and forthwith came there out blood and water. And he that saw it bare record, and his record is true: and he knoweth that he saith true, that ye might believe. For these things were done, that the scripture should be fulfilled, A bone of him shall not be broken. And again another scripture saith, They shall look on him whom they pierced." (John 19:30-37)

In the Baptist Church, we sing the hymn, "Jesus Paid It All". All that is not of faith in Christ is sin, according to the scriptures.

"Hast thou faith? have it to thyself before God. Happy is he that condemneth not himself in that thing which he alloweth. And he that doubteth is damned if he eat, because he eateth not of faith: for whatsoever is not of faith is sin." (Romans 14:22&23)

Minister Farrakhan, be not double minded.

"A double minded man is unstable in all his ways." (James 1:8)

Jesus remains the same, consider him as you consider your ways.

"Jesus Christ the same yesterday, and to day, and for ever." (Hebrews 13:8)

"Now therefore thus saith the Lord of hosts; Consider your ways. Ye have sown much, and bring in little; ye eat, but ye have not enough; ye drink, but ye are not filled with drink; ye clothe you, but there is none warm; and he that earneth wages earneth wages to put it into a bag with holes. Thus saith the Lord of hosts; Consider your ways. Go up to the mountain, and bring wood, and build the house; and I will take pleasure in it, and I will be glorified, saith the Lord."(Haggai 1:5-8)

And, having been led into the truth, to be willingly ignorant is to be a scoffer (mocker).

"Knowing this first, that there shall come in the last days scoffers, walking after their own lusts, And saying, Where is the promise of his coming? for since the fathers fell asleep, all things continue as they were from the beginning of the creation. For this they willingly are ignorant of, that by the word of God the heavens were of old, and the earth standing out of the water and in the water: Whereby the world that then was, being overflowed with water, perished: But the heavens and the earth, which are now, by the same word are kept in store, reserved unto fire against the day of judgment and perdition of ungodly men." (2 Peter 3:3-7)

"Be not deceived; God is not mocked: for whatsoever a man soweth, that shall he also reap. For he that soweth to his flesh shall of the flesh reap corruption; but he that soweth to the Spirit shall of the Spirit reap life everlasting." (Galatians 6:7&8)

You cannot continue to deny the truth that you see in the Word of God. God will not allow you to do so without severe judgment.

"But there were false prophets also among the people, even as there shall be false teachers among you, who privily shall bring in damnable heresies, even denying the Lord that bought them, and bring upon themselves swift destruction. And many shall follow their pernicious ways; by reason of whom the way of truth shall be evil spoken of. And through covetousness shall they with feigned words make merchandise of you: whose judgment now of a long time lingereth not, and their damnation slumbereth not. For if God spared not the angels that sinned, but cast them down to hell, and delivered them into chains of darkness, to be reserved unto judgment; These are wells without water, clouds that are carried with a tempest; to whom the mist of darkness is reserved for ever. For when they speak great swelling words of vanity, they allure through the lusts of the flesh, through much wantonness, those that were clean escaped from them who live in error. While they promise them liberty, they themselves are the servants of corruption: for of whom a man is overcome, of the same is he brought in bondage. For if after they have escaped the pollutions of the world through the knowledge of the Lord and Saviour Jesus Christ, they are again entangled therein, and overcome, the latter end is worse with them than the beginning. For it had been better for them not to have known the way of righteousness, than, after they have known it, to turn from the holy commandment delivered unto them." (2 Peter 2:1-4, 17-21)

The Bible demands a choice as shown by Joshua's commandment to the people of Israel.

"Now therefore fear the Lord, and serve him in sincerity and in truth: and put away the gods which your fathers served on the other side of the flood, and in Egypt; and serve ye the Lord. And if it seem evil unto you to serve the Lord, choose you this day whom ye will serve; whether the gods which your fathers served that were on the other side of the flood, or the gods of the Amorites, in whose land ye dwell: but as for me and my house, we will serve the Lord. And the people answered and said, God forbid that we should forsake the Lord, to serve other gods;" (Joshua 24:14-16)

The unbeliever by the Word of God is condemned.

"He that believeth on him is not condemned: but he that believeth not is condemned already, because he hath not believed in the name of the only begotten Son of God." (John 3:18)

Minister Farrakhan, do you love darkness rather than light?

> "And this is the condemnation, that light is come into the world, and men loved darkness rather than light, because their deeds were evil. For every one that doeth evil hateth the light, neither cometh to the light, lest his deeds should be reproved." (John 3:19-20)

You speak of the chief cornerstone as Christ; you speak well. I have heard you do so.

> "Jesus saith unto them, Did ye never read in the scriptures, The stone which the builders rejected, the same is become the head of the corner: this is the Lord's doing, and it is marvellous in our eyes?" (Matthew 21:42)

You speak of the believer in Christ as a part of that stone; again, you speak well. I have heard you do so.

> "Ye also, as lively stones, are built up a spiritual house, an holy priesthood, to offer up spiritual sacrifices, acceptable to God by Jesus Christ. Wherefore also it is contained in the scripture, Behold, I lay in Sion a chief corner stone, elect, precious: and he that believeth on him shall not be confounded." (1 Peter 2:5-6)

The scriptures state that you must have Christ's doctrine in order to have the Father.

> "Whosoever transgresseth, and abideth not in the doctrine of Christ, hath not God. He that abideth in the doctrine of Christ, he hath both the Father and the Son." (2 John 9)

Who is the Father?

> "And this is life eternal, that they might know thee the only true God, and Jesus Christ, whom thou hast sent. I have glorified thee on the earth: I have finished the work which thou gavest me to do. And now, O Father, glorify thou me with thine own self with the glory which I had with thee before the world was. I have manifested thy name unto the men which thou gavest me out of the world: thine they were, and thou gavest them me; and they have kept thy word. Now they have known that all things whatsoever thou hast given me are of thee. For I have given unto them the words which thou gavest me; and they have received them, and have known surely that I came out from thee, and they have believed that thou didst send me. I pray for them: I pray not for the world, but for them which thou hast given me; for they are thine. And all mine are thine, and thine are mine; and I am glorified in them. And now I am no more in the world, but these are in the world, and I come to thee. Holy Father, keep through thine own name those whom thou hast given me, that they may be one, as we are." (John 17:3-11)

Minister Farrakhan, please come to understand that the Bible is Christ. Consider the remorse to be experienced by those working in iniquity and not keeping Christ's commandments.

> "There shall be weeping and gnashing of teeth, when ye shall see Abraham, and Isaac, and Jacob, and all the prophets, in the kingdom of God, and you yourselves thrust out." (Luke 13:28)

False teachers have the promise of eternal damnation according to the Bible.

> "And to you who are troubled rest with us, when the Lord Jesus shall be revealed from heaven with his mighty angels, In flaming fire taking vengeance on them that know not God, and that obey not the gospel of our Lord Jesus Christ: Who shall be punished with everlasting destruction from the presence of the Lord, and from the glory of his power; When he shall come to be glorified in his saints, and to be admired in all them that believe (because our testimony among you was believed) in that day." (2 Thessalonians 1:7-10)

You are not rightly dividing the word of the Bible or the Qur'an. I have read the Qur'an and in the Qur'an Christ is said to be a good man and a prophet. In the Bible, Christ proclaims that he came down from heaven.

> "But I said unto you, That ye also have seen me, and believe not. All that the Father giveth me shall come to me; and him that cometh to me I will in no wise cast out. For I came down from heaven, not to do mine own will, but the will of him that sent me." (John 6:36-38)

You proclaimed in Washington, DC, Christ to be the Son of God; those <u>rightfully</u> dividing the Bible have Jesus as the <u>author</u> and <u>finisher</u> of their faith.

> "Wherefore seeing we also are compassed about with so great a cloud of witnesses, let us lay aside every weight, and the sin which doth so easily beset us, and let us run with patience the race that is set before us, Looking unto Jesus the author and finisher of our faith; who for the joy that was set before him endured the cross, despising the shame, and is set down at the right hand of the throne of God." (Hebrews 12:1-2)

The Bible is revealed as the truth to them and <u>through</u> them because the Holy Spirit testifies in all situations of Jesus Christ.

> "But when the Comforter is come, whom I will send unto you from the Father, even the Spirit of truth, which proceedeth from the Father, he shall testify of me: And ye also shall bear witness, because ye have been with me from the beginning." (John 15:26&27)

All judgment is committed unto the Son who is the author of eternal salvation.

> "For the Father judgeth no man, but hath committed all judgment unto the Son:" (John 5:22)

> "And being made perfect, he became the author of eternal salvation unto all them that obey him; Called of God an high priest after the order of Melchisedec." (Hebrews 5:9&10)

Minister Farrakhan, let us reason together. God has made provision here for your salvation. You cannot serve two masters; you are beginning to hate Islam because you are beginning to embrace Christ as (1) the Son of God and (2) the savior of the whole world. Christianity and Islam are contrary; one has the light while the other has to be void of that light. The Bible declares Christ is the light and the only door to the true and living God our Heavenly Father, the Creator and the Almighty.

"I am the door: by me if any man enter in, he shall be saved, and shall go in and out, and find pasture." (John 10:9)

"And God said unto Moses, I AM THAT I AM: and he said, Thus shalt thou say unto the children of Israel, I AM hath sent me unto you. And God said moreover unto Moses, Thus shalt thou say unto the children of Israel, The Lord God of your fathers, the God of Abraham, the God of Isaac, and the God of Jacob, hath sent me unto you: this is my name for ever, and this is my memorial unto all generations. Go, and gather the elders of Israel together, and say unto them, The Lord God of your fathers, the God of Abraham, of Isaac, and of Jacob, appeared unto me, saying, I have surely visited you, and seen that which is done to you in Egypt:" (Exodus 3:14&15)

Come, let us reason together as the prophet Isaiah proposed; let us build scripture upon scripture and precept upon precept.

"Whom shall he teach knowledge? and whom shall he make to understand doctrine? them that are weaned from the milk, and drawn from the breasts. For precept must be upon precept, precept upon precept; line upon line, line upon line; here a little, and there a little: For with stammering lips and another tongue will he speak to this people. To whom he said, This is the rest wherewith ye may cause the weary to rest; and this is the refreshing: yet they would not hear. But the word of the Lord was unto them precept upon precept, precept upon precept; line upon line, line upon line; here a little, and there a little; that they might go, and fall backward, and be broken, and snared, and taken. Wherefore hear the word of the Lord, ye scornful men, that rule this people which is in Jerusalem. Because ye have said, We have made a covenant with death, and with hell are we at agreement; when the overflowing scourge shall pass through, it shall not come unto us: for we have made lies our refuge, and under falsehood have we hid ourselves:Therefore thus saith the Lord God, Behold, I lay in Zion for a foundation a stone, a tried stone, a precious corner stone, a sure foundation: he that believeth shall not make haste." (Isaiah 28:9-16)

I invite you to join me at the Safer Crossroads Correctional Facility at 0900hrs. on any Sunday or at 1900 hrs. on any Wednesday. We can, of course, meet elsewhere; I will come to your Mosque or meet you anywhere. I am praying as I invite you into a true fellowship with God as Father and son.

"That which we have seen and heard declare we unto you, that ye also may have fellowship with us: and truly our fellowship is with the Father, and with his Son Jesus Christ. And these things write we unto you, that your joy may be full. This then is the message which we have heard of him, and declare unto you, that God is light, and in him is no darkness at all. If we say that we have fellowship with him, and walk in darkness, we lie, and do not the truth: But if we walk in the light, as he is in the light, we have fellowship one with another, and the blood of Jesus Christ his Son cleanseth us from all sin." (1 John 1:3-7)

Yours in Christ,

Rev. Preston N. Tolliver, Jr.

Evangelist

P.S. I perceive that you have been baptized. **"Grieve not the Holy Spirit"** (Ephesians 4:30) **and, even more importantly, "quench not the Spirit"** (1 Thessalonians 5:19).

Appendix 8

TITLE 89: SOCIAL SERVICES CHAPTER III: DEPARTMENT OF CHILDREN AND FAMILY SERVICES SUBCHAPTER A: SERVICE DELIVERY PART 300 REPORTS OF CHILD ABUSE AND NEGLECT

Section

300.10 Purpose

300.20 Definitions

300.30 Reporting Child Abuse or Neglect to the Department

300.40 Content of Child Abuse or Neglect Reports

300.50 Transmittal of Child Abuse or Neglect Reports

300.60 Special Types of Reports (Recodified)

300.70 Referrals to the Local Law Enforcement Agency and State's Attorney

300.80 Delegation of the Investigation

300.90 Time Frames for the Investigation

300.100 Initial Investigation

300.110 The Formal Investigative Process

300.120 Taking Children into Temporary Protective Custody

300.130 Notices Whether Child Abuse or Neglect Occurred

300.140 Transmittal of Information to the Illinois Department of Professional Regulation
and to School Superintendents

300.150 Referral for Other Services

300.160 Special Types of Reports

300.170 Child Death Review Teams

APPENDIX A Acknowledgment of Mandated Reporter Status

APPENDIX B Child Abuse and Neglect Allegations

AUTHORITY: Implementing and authorized by the Abused and Neglected Child Reporting Act [325 ILCS 5] and Section 3 of the Consent by Minors to Medical Procedures Act [410 ILCS 210/3].

SOURCE: Adopted and codified as 89 Ill. Adm. Code 302 at 5 Ill. Reg. 13188, effective November 30, 1981; amended at 6 Ill. Reg. 15529, effective January 1, 1983; recodified at 8 Ill. Reg. 992; peremptory amendment at 8 Ill. Reg. 5373, effective April 12, 1984; amended at 8 Ill. Reg. 12143, effective July 9, 1984; amended at 9 Ill. Reg. 2467, effective March 1, 1985; amended at 9 Ill. Reg. 9104, effective June 14, 1985; amended at 9 Ill. Reg. 15820, effective November 1, 1985; amended at 10 Ill. Reg. 5915, effective April 15, 1986; amended at 11 Ill. Reg. 1390, effective January 13, 1987; amended at 11 Ill. Reg. 1151, effective January 14, 1987; amended at 11 Ill. Reg. 1829 effective January 15, 1987; recodified from 89 Ill. Adm. Code 302.20, 302.100, 302.110, 302.120, 302.130, 302.140, 302.150, 302.160, 302.170, 302.180, 302.190, and Appendix A at 11 Ill. Reg. 3492; emergency amendments at 11 Ill. Reg. 4058, effective February 20, 1987, for a maximum of 150 days;

amended at 11 Ill. Reg. 12619, effective July 20, 1987; recodified at 11 Ill. Reg. 13405; amended at 13 Ill. Reg. 2419, effective March 1, 1989; emergency amendment at 14 Ill. Reg. 11356, effective July 1, 1990, for a maximum of

150 days; amended at 14 Ill. Reg. 17558, effective October 15, 1990; amended at 14 Ill. Reg. 19827, effective November 28, 1990; emergency amendment at 15 Ill. Reg. 14285, effective September 25, 1991; amended at 15 Ill. Reg. 17986, effective December 1, 1991; emergency amendment at 17 Ill. Reg. 15658, effective September 10, 1993, for a maximum of 150 days; emergency expired on February 7, 1994; amended at 18 Ill. Reg. 8377, effective May 31, 1994; amended at 18 Ill. Reg. 8601, effective June 1, 1994; amended at 19 Ill. Reg. 3469, effective March 15,1995; amended at 19 Ill. Reg. 10522, effective July 1, 1995; amended at 20 Ill. Reg. 10328, effective July 19, 1996; amended at 22 Ill. Reg.18847, effective October 1, 1998; amended at 23 Ill. Reg. 13590, effective November 15, 1999; amended at 24 Ill. Reg. 7707, effective June 1, 2000; amended at 25 Ill. Reg., 12781, effective October

1, 2001; amended at 26 Ill. Reg. 7435, effective May 15, 2002; amended at 26 Ill. Reg. 11730, effective August 1, 2002, amended at 27 Ill. Reg. effective January 15, 2003.

Section 300.10 Purpose

The purpose of this Part is to describe how the Department of Children and Family Services (Department) administers and provides child protective services through a State Central Register and local child protective service units. This Part governs how child abuse and neglect is reported and how such reports are handled and investigated. (Source: Added at 11 Ill. Reg. 12619, effective July 20, 1987)

Section 300.20 Definitions

"Abused child" means a child whose parent or immediate family member, or any person responsible for the child's welfare, or any individual residing in the same home as the child, or a paramour of the child's parent:

inflicts, causes to be inflicted, or allows to be inflicted upon such child physical or

mental injury, by other than accidental means, which causes death, disfigurement,

impairment of physical or emotional health, or loss or impairment of any bodily function;

creates a substantial risk of physical or mental *injury to such child by other than*

accidental means which would be likely to cause death, disfigurement, impairment of

physical or emotional health, or loss of or impairment of any bodily function;

commits or allows to be committed any sex offense against such child, as such sex

offenses are defined in the Criminal Code of 1961, as amended, and extending those

definitions of sex offenses to include children under 18 years of age;

commits or allows to be committed an act or acts of torture upon such child; or

inflicts excessive corporal punishment; or

commits or allows to be committed the offense of female genital mutilation, as defined

in Section 12-34 of the Criminal Code of 1961, against the child. [325 ILCS 5/3]

"Caregiver" means the child's parents, guardian, custodian or relative with whom the child lives and who has primary responsibility for the care and supervision of the child.

"Child" means any person under the age of 18 years, unless legally emancipated by reason of

marriage or entry into a branch of the United States armed services. [20 ILCS 515/107]

"Child care facility" means any person, group of persons, agency, association or organization,

whether established for gain or otherwise, who or which receives or arranges for care or

placement of one or more children, unrelated to the operator of the facility, apart from the

parents, with or without the transfer of the right of custody in any facility as defined in the Child Care Act of 1969, estab-

lished and maintained for the care of children. Child care facility includes a relative who is licensed as a foster family

home under Section 4 of the Child Care

Act of 1969 [225 ILCS 10/2.05].

"Child Protective Service Unit" (CPS) means certain specialized State employees of the

Department assigned by the Director or his designee to perform the duties and responsibilities as provided under this Part. They are also known as investigative staff. [325 ILCS 5/3]

"Children for whom the Department is legally responsible" means children for whom the Department has temporary protective custody, custody or guardianship via court order, or children whose parents have signed an adoptive surrender or voluntary placement agreement with the Department.

"Collateral contact" means obtaining information concerning a child, parent, or other person responsible for the child from a person who has knowledge of the family situation but was not directly involved in referring the child or family to the Department for services.

"Credible evidence of child abuse or neglect" means that the available facts when viewed in light of surrounding circumstances would cause a reasonable person to believe that a child was abused or neglected.

"Delegation of an investigation" means the investigation of a report of child abuse or neglect has been deferred to another authority. The Department maintains responsibility for determining whether the report is indicated or unfounded, entering information about the report in the State Central Register and notifying the subjects of the report and mandated reporters of the results of the investigation.

"Department" means the Department of Children and Family Services.

"Determination" means a final Department decision about whether there is credible evidence that child abuse or neglect occurred. A determination must be either "indicated" or "unfounded."

"Disfigurement" means a serious or protracted blemish, scar, or deformity that spoils a person's appearance or limits bodily functions.

"Formal investigation" means those activities conducted by Department investigative staff necessary to make a determination as to whether a report of suspected child abuse or neglect is indicated or unfounded. Such activities shall include: *an evaluation of the environment of the child named in the report and any other children in the same environment; a determination of the risk to such children if they continue to remain in the existing environments, as well as a determination of the nature, extent and cause of any condition enumerated in such report, the name, age and condition of other children in the environment; and an evaluation as to whether there would be an immediate and urgent necessity to remove the child from the environment if appropriate family preservation services were provided. After seeing to the safety of the child or children, the Department shall forthwith notify the subjects of the report in writing, of the existence of the report and their rights existing under* the *Act in regard to amendment or expungement.* [325 ILCS 5/3]

"Godparent" is a person who sponsors a child at baptism or one in whom the parents have entrusted a special duty that includes assisting in raising a child if the parent cannot raise the child. The worker shall verify the godparent/godchild relationship by contacting the parents to confirm the fact that they did, in fact, designate the person as the godparent. If the parents are unavailable, the worker should contact other close family members to verify the relationship. If the person is considered to be the child's godparent, in order for placement to occur, the same placement selection criteria as contained in 89 Ill. Adm. Code. 301.60 (Placement Selection) must be met. If the godparent is not a licensed foster parent, all the conditions currently in effect for placement with relatives in 89 Ill. Adm. Code. 301.80 must be met.

"Indicated Report" means any report of child abuse or neglect made to the Department for which it is determined, after an investigation, that credible evidence of the alleged abuse or neglect exists.

"Initial Investigation" means those activities conducted by Department investigative staff to determine whether a report of suspected child abuse or neglect is a good faith indication of abuse or neglect and, therefore, requires a formal investigation. Good faith in this context means that the report was made with the honest intention to identify actual child abuse or neglect.

"Initial Oral Report" means a report alleging child abuse or neglect for which the State Central Register has no prior records on the family.

"Involved Subject" means a child who is the alleged victim of child abuse or neglect or a person who is the alleged perpetrator of the child abuse or neglect.

"Local law enforcement agency" means the police of a city, town, village or other incorporated area or the sheriff of an unincorporated area or any sworn officer of the Illinois Department of State Police.

"Mandated reporters" means those individuals required to report suspected child abuse or neglect to the Department. A list of these persons and their associated responsibilities is provided in Section 300.30 of this Part.

"Neglected child" means any child who is not receiving the proper or necessary nourishment or medically indicated treatment including food or care not provided solely on the basis of present or anticipated mental or physical impairment as determined by a physician acting alone or in consultation with other physicians or otherwise is not receiving the proper or necessary support or medical or other remedial care recognized under State law as necessary for a child's well-being (including where there is harm or substantial risk of harm to the child's health or welfare), *or other care necessary for a child's well-being, including adequate food, clothing and shelter; or who is abandoned by his or her parents or other person responsible for the child's welfare without a proper plan of care; or who is a newborn infant whose blood, urine or meconium contains any amount of controlled substance as defined in subsection (f) of Section 102 of the Illinois Controlled Substances Act or a metabolite thereof, with the exception of a controlled substance or metabolite thereof whose presence in the newborn infant is the result of medical treatment administered to the mother or newborn infant. A child shall not be considered neglected for the sole reason that the child's parent or other person responsible for his or her welfare has left the child in the care of an adult relative for any period of time. A child shall not be considered neglected or abused for the sole reason that such child's parent or other person responsible for his or her welfare depends upon spiritual means through prayer alone for the treatment or cure of disease or remedial care under Section 4 of* the Abused and Neglected Child Reporting Act. Where the circumstances indicate harm or substantial risk of harm to the child's health or welfare and necessary medical care is not being provided to treat or prevent that harm or risk of harm because such parent or other person responsible for the child's welfare depends upon spiritual means alone for treatment or cure, such child is subject to the requirements of this Act for the reporting of, investigation of, and provision of protective services with respect to such child and his health needs, and in such cases spiritual means through prayer alone for the treatment or cure of disease or for remedial care will not be recognized as a substitute for such necessary medical care, if the Department or, as necessary, a juvenile court determines that medical care is necessary. *A child shall not be considered neglected or abused solely because the child is not attending school in accordance with the requirements of Article 26 of The School Code.* [325 ILCS 5/3]

"Perpetrator" means a person who, as a result of investigation, has been determined by the Department to have caused child abuse or neglect.

"Person responsible for the child's welfare" means the child's parent, guardian, foster parent, relative caregiver, an operator, supervisor, or employee of a public or private residential agency or institution or public or private profit or not-for-profit child care facility; or any other person responsible for the child's welfare at the time of the alleged abuse or neglect, or any person who came to know the child through an official capacity or position of trust, including but not limited to health care professionals, educational personnel, recreational supervisors,

and volunteers or support personnel in any setting where children may be subject to abuse or neglect. [325 ILCS 5/3]

"Private Guardianship" means an individual person appointed by the court to assume the responsibilities of the guardianship of the person as defined in Section 1-3 of the Juvenile Court Act of 1987 [705 ILCS 405/1-3] or Article XI of the Probate Act of 1975 [755 ILCS 5/Art. XI].

"Relative", for purposes of placement of children for whom the Department is legally responsible, *means any person, 21 years of age or over, other than the parent, who:*
is currently related to the child in any of the following ways by blood or adoption: grandparent, sibling, great-grandparent, uncle, aunt, nephew, niece, first cousin, first cousin once removed (children of one's first cousin to oneself), second cousin (children of first cousins are second cousins to each other), godparent *(as defined in this Section)*, great-uncle, or great-aunt, or
is the spouse of such a relative, or
is the child's step-father, step-mother, or adult step-brother or step-sister,
Relative also includes a person related in any of the foregoing ways to a sibling of a child, even though the person is not related to the child, when the child and its sibling are placed together with that person. [20 ILCS 505/7(b)]

"Subject of a report" means any child reported to the child abuse/neglect State Central Register, and his or her parent, personal guardian or other person responsible for the child's welfare who is named in the report.

"Temporary protective custody" means custody within a hospital or other medical facility or a place previously designated by the Department, subject to review by the Court. Temporary protective custody cannot exceed 48 hours excluding Saturdays, Sundays and holidays.

"Undetermined report" means any report of child abuse or neglect made to the Department in which it was not possible to complete an investigation within 60 days on the basis of information provided to the Department.

"Unfounded report" means any report of child abuse or neglect for which it is determined, after an investigation, that no credible evidence of the alleged abuse or neglect exists.

(Source: Amended at 26 Ill. Reg. 11730, effective August 1, 2002)

Section 300.30 Reporting Child Abuse or Neglect to the Department

a) Reports of suspected child abuse or neglect may be immediately made to the State Central Register via its toll-free number [1-800-25A-BUSE] at any time, day or night, or on any day of the week. Reports may also be made to the nearest Department office. The Department encourages use of the toll-free hotline number.

b) Persons Mandated to Report Child Abuse or Neglect

1) Types of Mandated Reporters

Any of the following individuals who have reasonable cause to believe that a child known to them in their professional or official capacity may be abused or neglected shall immediately report or cause a report to be made to the Department. These mandated reporters include:

A) physicians, residents, and interns;

B) hospitals;

C) hospital administrators and personnel engaged in the examination, care and treatment of persons;

D) surgeons;

E) dentists;

F) dentist hygienists;

G) osteopaths;

H) chiropractors;

I) podiatrists;

J) Christian Science practitioners;

K) coroners;

L) medical examiners;

M) emergency medical technicians;

N) crisis line or hotline personnel;

O) school personnel;

P) educational advocate assigned to a child pursuant to the School Code;

Q) truant officers;

R) social workers;

S) social services administrators;

T) domestic violence program personnel;

U) registered nurses;

V) licensed practical nurses, advanced practice nurses, home health aides;

W) directors or staff assistants of nursery schools or child day care centers;

X) recreational program or facility personnel;

Y) law enforcement officers;

Z) registered psychologists;

AA) assistants working under the direct supervision of a psychologist or psychiatrist;

BB) field personnel of the Illinois Departments of Public Aid, Public Health, Mental Health and Developmental Disabilities, Corrections, Children and Family Services, Human Rights or Rehabilitation Services;

CC) probation officers;

DD) foster parents, homemakers or any other child care worker;

EE) supervisors and administrators of General Assistance under the Illinois Public Aid Code;

FF) substance abuse treatment personnel; or

GG) funeral home directors or their employees.

2) Acknowledgment of Reporting Responsibility

A) Individuals who became mandated reporters on or after July 1, 1986, by virtue of their employment shall sign statements acknowledging that they are mandated to report suspected child abuse and neglect in accordance with Section 4 of the Abused and Neglected Child Reporting Act [325 ILCS 5/4]. The statement shall be on a form prescribed by the Department, but provided by the employer. (See Appendix A.) The statement shall be signed before beginning employment and shall be retained by the employer as a permanent part of the personnel record.

B) The Department shall provide, upon request at a reasonable cost of $.50 each, copies of the Abused and Neglected Child Reporting Act to all employers employing persons who are mandated to report under this Act.

3) Interference with Reporting Prohibited

A) *Mandated reporters who report instances of child abuse or neglect in their capacity as members of the staff of a medical or other public or private institution, school, facility or agency, may also notify the person in charge or designee of such institution, school, facility or agency that a report has been made. However, the person in charge or designee may not exercise any control, restraint, modification or other change in the report or the forwarding of such report to the Department.* [325 ILCS 5/4]

B) *Any person who knowingly and willfully violates any provision of this Section shall be guilty of a Class A misdemeanor.* [325 ILCS 5/4]

C) *Employers shall not discriminate in any manner against employees who make good faith reports of suspected child abuse or neglect or who act as witnesses or testify in an investigation or proceeding concerning a report of suspected child abuse or neglect.* [325 ILCS 5/9.1]

4) Consequences of Failure to Report

A) The privileged quality of communication between any professional person required to report and patient or client shall not constitute grounds for failure to report suspected child abuse or neglect. Mandated reporters who willfully fail to report suspected child abuse or neglect are subject to license suspension or revocation in accordance with the following statutes:

i) Nursing and Advanced Practice Nursing Act of 1987 [225 ILCS 65];

ii) Medical Practice Act of 1987 [225 ILCS 60];

iii) Podiatric Medical Practice Act of 1987 [225 ILCS 100];

iv) Clinical Psychologist Licensing Act [225 ILCS 15];

v) Clinical Social Worker and Social Work Practice Act [225 ILCS 20];

vi) The School Code [105 ILCS 5];

vii) The Illinois Dental Practice Act [225 ILCS 25];

viii) Physician Assistant Practice Act of 1987 [225 ILCS 95];

ix) Illinois Optometric Practice Act of 1987 [225 ILCS 80];

x) Illinois Physical Therapy Act [225 ILCS 90]; and

xi) Illinois Athletic Trainers Act [225 ILCS 5].

B) *Any physician who willfully fails to report child abuse or neglect shall be referred to the Illinois State Medical Disciplinary Board for action. Any other person required to report suspected child abuse or neglect who willfully fails to report such abuse or neglect shall be guilty of a Class A misdemeanor.* [325 ILCS 5/4]

5) Written Confirmation of Reports

Mandated reporters shall confirm their telephone report in writing on a form prescribed by the Department within 48 hours of the oral report. The Department shall provide forms to mandated reporters--one for the exclusive use of medical professionals and another for use by all other mandated reporters. These confirmation reports shall be admissible as evidence in any administrative or judicial proceeding related to child abuse or neglect. Local investigative staff shall transmit confirmation reports to the State Central Register within 24 hours of receipt.

c) Other Persons May Report

Other persons may report suspected child abuse or neglect if they have reasonable cause to believe a child may be abused or neglected.

d) Consequences of False Reporting

Any person who knowingly transmits a false report to the Department commits the offense of disorderly conduct under subsection (a) (7) of Section 26-1 of the Criminal Code of 1961 [720 ILCS 5/26-1(a)(7)]. A violation of this subsection is a Class B misdemeanor, punishable by a term of imprisonment for not more than 6 months, or by a fine not to exceed $500, or both. *Any person who violates this provision a second or subsequent time shall be guilty of Class 4 felony.* [325 ILCS 5/4] The Department shall refer cases of false reporting to the local State's Attorney when the reporter is known.

e) Cooperation in Court or Administrative Hearings

Any person who makes a report or who investigates a report may be ordered by the Court to testify fully in any judicial proceeding resulting from the report about any evidence of the abuse or neglect or the cause of the abuse or neglect. Any mandated reporter listed in subsection (b)(1) who makes a report of suspected child abuse or neglect shall testify fully in any administrative hearing resulting from such report, as to any evidence of abuse or neglect or the cause thereof. No evidence shall be excluded because of any common law or statutory privilege regarding communications between the alleged perpetrator or the child subject and the person making or investigating the report.

f) Referrals to Public Health

All mandated reporters listed in subsection (b)(1) may refer to the Department of Public Health any pregnant person in Illinois who is addicted as defined in the Alcoholism and Other Drug Abuse and Dependency Act [20 ILCS 301].

g) Depending upon Spiritual Means Through Prayer Alone for the Treatment or Cure of Disease or Remedial Care

A child whose parent, guardian or custodian in good faith selects and depends upon spiritual means through prayer alone for the treatment or cure of disease or remedial care may be considered neglected or abused, but not for the sole reason that his parent, guardian, or custodian accepts and practices such beliefs. [325 ILCS 5/4] Where the circumstances indicate harm or substantial risk of harm to the child's health or welfare and medical care necessary to treat or prevent that harm or risk of harm is not being provided because a parent or other person responsible for the child's welfare depends upon such spiritual means, the child shall be subject to the requirements of the Abused and Neglected Child Reporting Act for the reporting of, investigation of, and provision of protective services with respect to the child and his health needs. (Source: Amended at 24 Ill. Reg. 7707, effective June 1, 2000)

Section 300.40 Content of Child Abuse or Neglect Reports

The State Central Register or the local report-taker shall attempt to secure the following information from the reporter:

a) family composition, including the name, age, sex, race, ethnicity, and address of the children named in the report and any other children in the environment;

b) name, age, sex, race, ethnicity and address of the children's parents, caregiver, if different from the parent(s), and if different, the relationship of the caregiver to the child(ren), and of the alleged perpetrator and his/her relationship to the child subjects;

c) the physical harm to the involved children and an estimation of the children's present physical, medical, and environmental condition. This estimation should include information concerning any previous incidents of suspected child abuse or neglect; and

d) the reporter's name, occupation and relationship to the children, actions taken by the reporter, where the reporter can be reached, and other information the reporter believes will be of assistance.

(Source: Amended at 19 Ill. Reg.10522, effective July 1, 1995)

Section 300.50 Transmittal of Child Abuse or Neglect Reports

a) The State Central Register, upon receipt of a report of suspected child abuse or neglect, shall immediately transmit to the appropriate investigative staff;

1) the contents of the report;

2) information on any previous indicated, pending, or undetermined reports involving the subjects of a current report; and

3) other pertinent information.

b) Local investigative staff shall immediately notify the State Central Register of any report (including duplicate reports and additional information) received from a source other than the State Central Register, or if the child is in danger, shall notify the State Central Register immediately after assuring the child's safety.

(Source: Recodified from 89 Ill. Adm. Code 302.120 at 11 Ill. Reg. 13405)

Section 300.70 Referrals to the Local Law Enforcement Agency and State's Attorney

The Department will immediately refer reports, including but not limited to the following types, to the local law enforcement agency and the appropriate State's Attorney for consideration of criminal investigation or other action:

a) reports regarding a child who may have died as a result of abuse or neglect;

b) reports in which the injury to the child suspected to be abused or neglected is severe; such as, but not limited to: multiple or spiral fractures, third degree burns, internal injuries, subdural hematomas, brain damage, and skull fractures;

c) indicated reports in which credible evidence is found that a child has been abused a second time, regardless of severity;

d) reports of physical injury when the evidence indicates that the child has been tortured;

e) reports in which a child is the alleged victim of sexual abuse; or

f) reports in which a child is alleged to be suffering from malnutrition.

(Source: Recodified from 89 Ill. Adm. Code 302.140 at 11 Ill. Reg. 3492)

Section 300.80 Delegation of the Investigation

The Department may delegate the investigation of the child abuse or neglect report to:

a) the local police, sheriff's office, other law enforcement agency, or the State's Attorney, when they are concurrently conducting a criminal investigation of the same incidents and allegations; or

b) a coroner or medical examiner who is investigating the cause of death of a child who may have been the victim of child abuse or neglect; or

c) private social service agencies which had been designated for this purpose by the Department prior to July 1, 1980; or

d) the Department of State Police, when the investigation involves suspected child abuse or neglect perpetrated by State employees acting in their official capacity or in State facilities or institutions.

(Source: Recodified from 89 Ill. Adm. Code 302.150 at Ill. Reg. 3492)

Section 300.90 Time Frames for the Investigation

The following activities must be completed within the time frames indicated, except as exempted in Section 300.110(d). The time the report was received at the State Central Register begins the investigative process.

a)

In-person contact with alleged child victim or in-person examination of the environment for inadequate shelter and environmental neglect reports only or in-person contact with mothers of infants who are hospitalized with controlled substances in their systems. Contact with mother of hospitalized infants shall be in the environment in which the mother intends to reside with the infant.

Good faith attempt/Begin the initial investigation. The investigation shall begin immediately if the child is believed to be in immediate danger of physical harm or it is likely that the family may flee with the child.

24 hours

b)

In-person contacts with the alleged perpetrator, the children's caretaker and the alleged child victim if not completed sooner

7 days

c)

Begin the Formal Investigation (Written)

14 days

d)

Final Determination -- Formal Investigation (Written)

60 days

e)

Preliminary Investigation Report -- If a 30-day extension to the formal investigation is necessary

60 days

(Source: Amended at 14 Ill. Reg. 19827, effective November 28, 1990)

Section 300.100 Initial Investigation

a) When a report of child abuse or neglect is received, Department investigative staff will make an initial investigation to validate whether there is reasonable cause to believe that child abuse or neglect exists.

b) The initial investigation will consist of the following steps:

1) in-person contact with all alleged child victims or in-person examination of the environment for inadequate shelter and environmental neglect reports only, and

2) in-person or telephone contact with the reporter, if the reporter's identity and whereabouts are available and

3) data checks of Departmental and law enforcement records.

4) If the initial investigation is not completed within seven days, the alleged perpetrator and the children's caretaker shall be contacted.

c) Investigative staff shall begin an investigation within 24 hours after the Department

receives a report alleging child abuse or neglect. An investigation shall begin
immediately when:

1) a child is believed to be in immediate danger of physical harm; or

2) it is likely that the family may flee with the child.

d) An investigation normally shall be started by in-person contact with all the children
alleged to have been abused or neglected. When the incident occurred in a group
setting and a number of perpetrators or children are alleged to be involved, contact
may be delayed while a comprehensive investigative plan is developed with other
investigative bodies (e.g. local law enforcement, the Department of State Police, out-ofstate
law enforcement, the Federal Bureau of Investigation) as long as the children's
safety can be assured during the delay.

e) However, in some instances, the Department's good faith attempt to contact the
children alleged to have been abused or neglected shall be sufficient to start the
investigation. The following constitute good faith attempts to begin the investigation:

1) when investigative staff learns, upon proceeding to the location given for the
children alleged to have been abused or neglected, that the children have
disappeared, the family has fled, the address does not
exist, no one is at the location, or not all of the children alleged as abused or
neglected are at the location; or

2) when the involved child subjects are not accessible; or

3) when the adult caretaker refuses to let child protective service staff see or
speak with the involved child subject.

f) Although a good faith attempt to contact the children alleged to be abused or
neglected begins the investigation, this good faith attempt does not relieve
investigative staff of the responsibility to complete the contacts required by Department
rule. Investigative staff will continue to attempt to establish in-person contact with the
alleged child victim, conducting a diligent search to locate the child.

g) Investigative staff will examine the following criteria to determine whether there is a
good faith indication to believe that abuse or neglect exists:

1) the alleged victim(s) must be less than 18 years of age; and

2) the alleged victim(s) must either have been harmed or must be in substantial
risk of harm; and

3) there must be an abusive or neglectful incident or set of circumstances as
defined in Appendix B of this Part which caused the alleged harm or substantial
risk of harm to the child.

4) for abuse, the alleged perpetrator must be the child's parent, foster parent,
guardian, immediate family member, any individual who resides in the same
house as the child, the paramour of the child's parent or any person
responsible for the child's welfare at the time of the alleged abuse;

5) for neglect, the alleged perpetrator must be the child's parent, guardian, foster
parent or any person responsible for the child's welfare at the time of the
alleged neglect.

h) If any one of the above criteria is not present, a determination will be made that the
report does not provide a good faith indication that child abuse or neglect exists, and
the investigation will be terminated. If the above criteria are present, investigative staff
will begin a formal investigation.

i) If, after the initial investigation, investigative staff determine that:

1) there is good faith indication that child abuse or neglect exists, and

2) the person who is alleged to have caused the abuse or neglect is employed or otherwise engaged in activity resulting in frequent contact with children; and

3) the alleged child abuse or neglect occurred in the course of that employment or activity; then upon commencement of the formal investigation the Department shall inform the appropriate supervisor or administrator of that employment or activity that a formal investigation has been commenced which may or may not result in an indicated report unless the Director determines that such notification would be detrimental to the Department's investigation. The Department may also notify the person being investigated, unless the Department determines that such notification would be detrimental to the Department's investigation.

j) The Department will notify the following persons when an initial investigation determines that a report does not contain a good faith indication that child abuse or neglect exists and, therefore, a formal investigation will not be commenced:

1) mandated reporters,

2) custodial parents, personal guardians and legal custodians of the alleged child victims, and

3) alleged perpetrators.

k) The subjects of the report may request that a report which was not validated by the initial investigation be retained in the Department's computer and local index files, if the subjects of the report believe that the report was made for harassment purposes. The Department shall honor all such written requests and shall retain these records for five years, as allowed in the Abused and Neglected Child Reporting Act.

(Source: Amended at 14 Ill. Reg. 17558, effective October 15, 1990)

Section 300.110 The Formal Investigative Process

a) Beginning the Formal Investigation

The formal investigation begins as soon as investigative staff make a determination following the initial investigation that there is reasonable cause to believe that child abuse or neglect exists. Any actions described below which were taken during the initial investigation need not be repeated. Any time frames listed in Section 300.90 which apply to the formal investigation mentioned below are retroactive to the beginning of the initial investigation.

b) Notifications During the Formal Investigation

1) During the first contact, after the formal investigation has begun, with the child's custodial parent, personal guardian, or legal custodian and the alleged perpetrator, the investigative staff shall notify them in writing that:

A) the Department has received a report alleging abuse or neglect of their child; and

B) the Department is legally mandated to investigate all child abuse or neglect reports; and

C) information concerning the report has been entered into the Department's files; and

D) the Department will work confidentially with them unless it becomes necessary to share information with authorized individuals or agencies as provided by law in 89 Ill. Adm. Code 431; and

E) the subjects have the right of access to the information in the report

with the exception of information which would identify the reporter or
persons who cooperated in the investigation.

2) Department investigative staff shall not give Miranda warnings to alleged
perpetrators.

c) Required Investigative Contacts

Investigative staff shall have direct, in-person contact with the alleged child victim, the
alleged perpetrator, and the child's caretaker within seven days after the date the
report was received, except in those situations noted in Section 300.110(d). If the
subjects of the report do not speak the English
language, an interpreter shall be obtained or a worker assigned who speaks the same
language as the subjects of the reports.

d) Situations Where the Contact Requirement is Waived

1) In-person contact is not required when:

A) any subject of a child abuse or neglect report refuses to meet with or
speak to the investigative worker; and

B) the worker has attempted to involve the local law enforcement agency
or the State's Attorney, but this has failed to gain cooperation.

2) In-person contact is not required when it is documented that a child abuse or
neglect subject is inaccessible.

3) In-person contact is not required when it is documented that the investigative
worker has made a good faith attempt to locate the subjects of the report, but
cannot, after a diligent search, locate them.

e) Collateral Contacts

The Department may make collateral contacts with persons other than the subjects of
the report or the reporter to obtain further information regarding suspected child abuse
or neglect. When determining whether collateral contacts should be made, the
Department shall weigh:

1) the allegations contained in the report;

2) the severity of the incident; and

3) the likelihood that the collateral contact will have relevant information about the
allegations or the incident.

f) Administrative Subpoenas

If a mandated reporter who is believed to have information about the subject of a report
is not allowed or refuses to speak with or provide documents to a child protective
service worker about the reported child or family, an administrative subpoena may be
issued to obtain the necessary information. This applies regardless of whether the
mandated reporter made the report being investigated. In addition, if a parent,
personal guardian, legal custodian, or alleged perpetrator refuses to meet with or
speak to a child protective service worker, a subpoena may be issued to obtain the
necessary information.

g) Photographs and X-rays

1) Department investigative staff may take or obtain color photographs and x-rays
of a child who is the subject of an abuse or neglect report when the child has
observable marks or injuries believed to be caused by abuse or neglect. When
the child's environment creates a substantial risk of injury or other harm,
photographs may be taken of the child's environment.

2) If the child's parents, personal guardian, or legal custodian can be located, he

or she shall be notified of the Department's intent to secure the photographs or x-rays.

h) Immunity from Liability

1) Any persons, institutions, or agencies shall have immunity from any liability if they, in good faith:

A) report suspected child abuse or neglect;

B) assist in the investigation of a child abuse or neglect report;

C) take temporary protective custody in accordance with Section 300.120; or

D) take photographs or x-rays to substantiate the abuse or neglect report.

2) For purpose of any civil or criminal liability, a person's good faith in taking the above actions shall be presumed.

i) Final Determinations Regarding Child Abuse or Neglect

1) Investigative staff in their role as mandated reporters may add allegations of abuse or neglect or subjects to a report during the course of the investigation.

2) Upon completion of a formal investigation of abuse or neglect, investigative staff shall make a final determination as to whether a child was abused or neglected. This determination shall be based upon whether the information gathered from other persons during the investigation and the direct observations made by the investigative staff during the investigation constitute credible evidence of child abuse or neglect.

3) Allegations may be determined to be indicated, undetermined, or unfounded.

A) When credible evidence of abuse or neglect has been obtained pertinent to an allegation, the allegation is indicated.

i) If any allegation of child abuse or neglect is indicated, the report is indicated;

ii) investigative staff shall not determine that a report is indicated based solely upon the existence of a prior unfounded report or reports.

iii) A court finding of child abuse or neglect shall be presumptive evidence that the report is indicated.

B) When credible evidence of abuse or neglect has not been obtained, the allegation is unfounded. If all allegations of child abuse or neglect are unfounded, the report is unfounded.

C) When investigative staff have been unable, for good cause, to gather sufficient facts to support a decision within 60 days after the date the report was received, the allegation shall be considered undetermined. Additional periods of 30 days shall then be permitted to complete the investigation, after which a determination shall be made. In the absence of credible evidence of abuse or neglect, the allegations and the report shall be designated unfounded.

D) Good cause for extending the period for making a determination an additional 30 days may include but is not limited to the following reasons:

i) State's attorneys or law enforcement officials have requested that the Department delay making a determination due to a pending criminal investigation.

ii) Medical or autopsy reports needed to make a determination
are still pending after the initial 60 day period.

iii) The report involves an out-of-state investigation and the delay
is beyond the Department's control.

iv) Multiple alleged perpetrators or victims are involved
necessitating more time in gathering evidence and conducting
interviews.

(Source: Amended at 22 Ill. Reg. 18847, effective October 1, 1998)

Section 300.120 Taking Children Into Temporary Protective Custody

a) Local law enforcement officers, Department investigative staff, and physicians treating
a child may take temporary protective custody of a child without the consent of the
persons responsible for the child's welfare, if they have reason to believe that:

1) leaving the child in the home or in the care and custody of the child's caregiver
presents an imminent danger to the child's life or health. The child shall not be
taken into protective custody for the sole reason that the child was left with a
relative, so long as the relative is willing to keep the child and the Department
has reason to believe that the relative can adequately and safely care for the
child; and

2) there is insufficient time to obtain a Juvenile Court order authorizing temporary
custody.

b) In addition to the above requirements, Department investigative staff shall ensure and
document that reasonable efforts were made to prevent or eliminate the need to
remove a child from the child's home. However, it may be that due to the individual
circumstances of the family and the child's best interest, safety and well-being, no
efforts reasonably can be made to maintain the child in the child's home. Reasonable
efforts shall not be required if there exists any of the grounds for expedited termination
of parental rights as described in 89 Ill. Adm. Code 309 (Adoption Services for Children
for Whom the Department of Children and Family Services Is Legally Responsible).
Such a determination that no efforts reasonably can be made must be documented. If
no efforts reasonably can be made to safely prevent or eliminate the removal of the
child, the child shall be taken into protective custody.

c) Local law enforcement officers or physicians who take temporary protective custody of
a child must immediately notify the Department of their action.

d) When taking temporary protective custody of a child or receiving a child who was taken
into temporary protective custody by the local law enforcement officer or by a
physician, Department investigative staff shall:

1) immediately notify the State Central Register of this action;

2) make every reasonable effort to notify the child's parents, personal guardian,
or legal custodian, and any relative caregiver from whom the child was
removed, of the action;

3) request that the Guardianship Administrator or designee authorize any
ordinary medical care or treatment necessary for those children taken into
temporary protective custody;

4) if the child needs treatment of an emergency nature and the parent or
guardian is unavailable or unwilling to provide consent, the physician or
hospital shall be asked to proceed under the Consent by Minors to Medical
Procedures Act [410 ILCS 210], which allows treatment to be given to minors

without consent; and

5) obtain a shelter care hearing under the provisions of the Juvenile Court Act within 48 hours, excluding Saturdays, Sundays, and holidays, in order to retain custody for more than 48 hours.

e) At any time during the investigation, but no later than 30 days prior to the date of the scheduled adjudicatory hearing, the investigative worker shall request a legal screening to determine whether the State's Attorney should be asked to file a petition for expedited termination of parental rights, if:

1) it becomes known that there is present one or more of the grounds for seeking expedited termination of parental rights described in 89 Ill. Adm. Code 309 (Adoption Services for Children For Whom the Department of Children and Family Services is Legally Responsible), Section 309.50(d)(1) and (2); and

2) the parents are unwilling to voluntarily surrender the child for adoption or consent to the adoption of the child by a specified person.

(Source: Amended at 22 Ill. Reg. 18847, effective October 1, 1998)

Section 300.130 Notices Whether Child Abuse or Neglect Occurred

a) Written Notices of Decision

The Department provides a written notice to mandated reporters who reported suspected child abuse or neglect as well as to the child's parent, personal guardian, or legal custodian; the Juvenile Court Judge (when a State ward is involved); and the alleged perpetrator concerning the final determination of the report.

b) Mandated Reporters

1) Mandated reporters who have reported suspected child abuse or neglect are informed via a written notice that a formal investigation was conducted. The written notice also provides an explanation of how further information on an indicated report may be secured. Department staff will notify them in writing:

A) of the name of the child who was the subject of a report of abuse or neglect;

B) whether the report was indicated or unfounded;

C) whether the Department took temporary protective custody.

2) Requests for additional information must be directed, in writing, to the State Central Register and must include:

A) the identity of the requestor;

B) the subject's name for whom the record is requested;

C) a notary public's attestation as to the identity of the requestor;

D) the purpose of the request.

3) Upon receipt of an appropriate request, only the following information will be disclosed to the mandated reporter:

A) whether a Department case has been opened for the family or children; and

B) what Department services are being provided to the family or children.

4) All requested information is sent in writing through certified mail and is deliverable only to the mandated reporter who made the request.

5) Whenever the Department determines that a reported incident of child abuse or neglect from a mandated reporter is unfounded, the mandated reporter may request a review of the investigation within ten days after the notification of the final findings. Multi-disciplinary Review Committees established in each of the

Department's regions shall conduct requested reviews.

6) Multi-disciplinary Review Committees shall draw upon the expertise of the Child Death Review Teams (See Section 300.170 of this Part). Each committee shall be composed of a health care professional, Department employee, law enforcement official, licensed social worker, and a representative of a State's Attorney's office. When appointing committee members, primary consideration shall be given to candidates with prior child abuse and neglect case experience.

7) Multi-disciplinary Review Committees will have access to all information in the Department's possession related to the case being reviewed. Committee recommendations concerning the adequacy of the investigation and accuracy of the final finding determination shall be made to the regional Child Protection Manager.

8) Department records of investigations provided to committees and committee recommendation reports shall not be public record.

c) Parents, Personal Guardians, Legal Custodians, and Alleged Perpetrators

1) Custodial and non-custodial parents, personal guardians, or legal custodians of child subjects, and alleged perpetrators shall receive notification within five calendar days after the report has been indicated or unfounded which indicate that the allegations were either:

A) unfounded, and that all identifying information in the computer and local index files will be retained in accordance with 89 Ill. Adm. Code 431 (Confidentiality of Information of Persons Served by the Department) or

B) indicated, and all Department records will be maintained intact.

2) In addition, written notices shall explain that:

A) the subjects of the report have access to the Department's records on the report, with the exception of the identity of the reporter or other persons who cooperated in the investigation;

B) the subjects of the report have the right to request a review of the determination that the report was indicated including the decision to maintain a record of the report in the Department's computer and local index files. 89 Ill. Adm. Code 336 (Appeal of Child Abuse and Neglect Investigation Findings) fully explains the Department's review and appeal process; and

C) the subjects of the report may request, within 10 days of the date on the written notice, that an unfounded report be retained in the Department's computer and local index files, if the subjects of the report believe the report was not made in good faith. All such requests will be honored.

d) Child's School

(Subsection added May 15, 2002)

1) The Department shall send a copy of final finding reports involving indicated allegations of physical or sexual abuse to the indicated victim's school within ten days after the investigation is completed. Reports completed during the summer months shall be sent to the last known school attended by the child.

2) The final finding report shall be sent confidential and the school shall ensure

that the report remains confidential in accordance with the Illinois School Student Records Act.

3) The victim's school shall purge the final finding report from the student's record and return the report to the Department upon notification from the Department that the report was overturned in an appeal or hearing or an indicated finding has been expunged from the State Central Register or that the Department has determined that the child is no longer at risk of physical or sexual harm.

e) **Other Parties**

The Department shall notify, in writing, those supervisors or administrators referenced in Section 300.100(i) of this Part whether a report involving the persons they supervise was indicated or unfounded and, if unfounded, that Section 13 of the Personnel Record Review Act [820 ILCS 40/13] requires that any record of the investigation must be expunged from the employee's personnel records. The Department shall also notify the employee, in writing, that notification has been sent to the employer informing the employer that the Department's investigation has resulted in an unfounded report. The notice to the employee shall also contain a statement of the employee's right to take the

notice to the employer to have any record of the investigation expunged from the employee's record.

f) **Child Abuse and Neglect Reports on Children in Department Custody**

1) When a child is reported to the Department as being abused or neglected while in a foster home or relative home placement, whether by the foster parent, caregiver, or any other person residing in the home, the Department shall promptly notify the following persons when the report has been made, when an investigation is pending, and when the report has been indicated or unfounded:

A) the parents or private guardians of the alleged abuse or neglect victim;
B) all Department caseworkers or case managers responsible for the alleged victim and for any other children in the same foster home or relative home placement;
C) those persons designated by the Director as responsible for evaluating the investigation and the disposition of the report;
D) Department staff responsible for licensing and making placements with the facility.

2) When a child is reported to the Department as being abused or neglected while in residential placement, the Department shall promptly notify the following persons when the report has been made, an investigation is pending, and when the report has been indicated or unfounded:

A) the parents or private guardians of the alleged abuse or neglect victim;
B) those Department caseworkers or case managers responsible for the alleged victim, for each child alleged to be a witness to the incident, and for each child alleged to be a perpetrator of the incident;
C) those persons designated by the Director responsible for evaluating the investigation and the disposition of the report.
D) Department staff responsible for licensing and making placements with the facility.

3) The Department shall notify the following when a report involving a child in

Department custody is indicated:

A) the Juvenile Court. If services are being provided by the Department or its providers, the notice shall also give the name and location of the Department office serving the children;

B) the Department's administrative case reviewer responsible for reviewing the case plans of the children involved.

4) The Department shall transmit a copy of the report to the guardian ad litem appointed under the Juvenile Court Act of 1987 when a report has been indicated, unfounded, or undetermined and the minor who is the subject of the report is also the minor for whom the guardian ad litem has been appointed.

(Source: Amended 26 Ill. Reg. 7435, effective May 15, 2002)

Section 300.140 Transmittal of Information to the Illinois Department of Professional Regulation and to School Superintendents

a) The Department will transmit to the Illinois Department of Professional Regulation information regarding perpetrators of indicated reports of child abuse or neglect who are known to be subject to licensure or registration by the Department of Professional Regulation under the following Acts:

1) Section 23 of The Illinois Dental Practice Act [225 ILCS 25/23];

2) Section 25 of The Illinois Nursing Act of 1987 [225 ILCS 65/25];

3) Section 24 of The Illinois Optometric Practice Act of 1987 [225 ILCS 80/24];

4) Section 17 of The Illinois Physical Therapy Act [225 ILCS 90/17];

5) Section 22 of the Medical Practice Act of 1987 [225 ILCS 60/22];

6) Section 21 of the Physician Assistant Practice Act of 1987 [225 ILCS 95/21];

7) Section 24 of the Podiatric Medical Practice Act of 1987 [225 ILCS 100/24];

8) Section 15 of the Clinical Psychologist Licensing Act [225 ILCS 15/15];

9) Section 19 of the Clinical Social Work and Social Work Practice Act [225 ILCS 20/19]; and

10) Section 16 of the Illinois Athletic Trainers Practice Act [225 ILCS 5/16].

b) The Department will transmit to district school superintendents in Illinois and private school administrators information regarding any persons known to be employed in a school or who otherwise come into frequent contact with children in a school who are determined to be perpetrators of indicated reports of child abuse and neglect.

c) The Department will transmit to regional superintendents and the State Superintendent of Education information that a person known to be a holder of a certificate issued by the State Board of Education has been named as a perpetrator in an indicated report of child abuse or neglect.

d) If a request for a review and fair hearing is received within 60 calendar days of the date on the written notice that the report is indicated, information regarding the request will be sent to the Department of Professional Regulation or district and regional school superintendents and the State Superintendent of Education in accord with applicable law.

e) Whenever the Department receives a report alleging that a child is a truant as defined in Section 26-2a of the School Code (Ill. Rev. Stat. 1989, ch. 122, par. 126-a), the Department shall notify the superintendent of the school district in which the child resides and the superintendent of the educational service region in which the child resides.

(Source: Amended at 14 Ill. Reg. 19827, effective November 28, 1990)

Section 300.150 Referral for Services

a) When an investigative worker determines that a report is indicated, the parents or caregivers may be given the opportunity to cooperate with the Department through services provided or arranged for by the Department. When the parents or caregivers are unwilling to cooperate, or when legal custody or guardianship through the Department is necessary to protect the child, the worker may seek court intervention.

b) When the investigative worker determines that a report is unfounded but the family, including a relative caregiver, may need services, the worker shall:

1) inform the family of available child welfare services and refer the family for services, if requested; or

2) provide information regarding other community resources.

c) If the report is unfounded and the family does not want services, the worker shall make no recommendation for additional services.

d) The Department may offer services to any child or family, including a relative caregiver, who is the subject of the report of child abuse or neglect prior to making a determination of indicated or unfounded when the family is in immediate need of services or there is an imminent danger to the child's life or health. However, the child's or family's willingness to accept services shall not be considered in making the determination of indicated or unfounded.

e) When the State Central Register does not accept a report of abuse or neglect because the sole reason for the report was that a child was left in the care of a relative, the State Central Register shall:

1) inform the relative of available child welfare services and refer the relative for services, if requested; or

2) provide information to the relative regarding other community resources.

(Source: Amended at 19 Ill. Reg.10522, effective July 1, 1995)

Section 300.160 Special Types of Reports

Five types of child abuse or neglect reports shall receive special attention as specified in subsections (a) through (e):

a) Incident Involving the Death of a Child

1) The Department shall immediately contact the appropriate medical examiner or coroner, the local law enforcement agency, and the State's Attorney when there is reasonable cause to suspect that a child has died as a result of abuse or neglect. The child protective investigator assigned to the investigation shall require a copy of the completed autopsy report from the coroner or medical examiner.

2) The Department shall refer to the child death review teams described in Section 300.170 of this Part the death of any child who is:

A) a child for whom the Department of Children and Family Services is legally responsible;

B) a child being served in an open service case either by the Department or through purchase of service contracts with private agencies;

C) the subject of a pending child abuse or neglect investigation; or

D) a child who was the subject of an abuse or neglect investigation at any time during the 12 months immediately preceding the child's death; or

E) any other child whose death is reported to the State central register as a result of alleged child abuse or neglect if the report is subsequently indicated.

3) The Department shall cooperate with the work of the Office of the Inspector General and the child death review teams by:

A) providing to the team all records and case information relevant to the review, including records and information concerning all available previous reports or investigations of suspected child abuse or neglect. Other records and case information relevant to the review include:

i) birth certificates;

ii) all relevant medical and mental health records;

iii) records of law enforcement agency investigations;

iv) records of coroner or medical examiner investigations;

v) records of the Department of Corrections concerning a person's parole;

vi) records of a probation and court services department, and records of a social service agency that provided services to the child or the child's family;

B) assisting the Office of the Inspector General and the team in its review of the child's death;

C) reporting on any follow-up interventions suggested by the Office o the Inspector General or the team;

D) providing follow-up on death cases where circumstances surrounding the death suggest other children may be at risk. Follow-up may include, but is not limited to:

i) further investigation;

ii) risk assessment;

iii) grief counseling for other children in the family;

iv) referrals for other services as appropriate;

E) providing information and consultation regarding the juvenile court process and the availability of the court to protect or intervene with surviving siblings; and

F) assisting with making arrangements for the date, time, and location of team meetings.

4) The Department shall prepare individual death review reports and issue an annual cumulative report to the Governor and General Assembly incorporating the data, appropriate findings and recommendations from the individual reports.

A) Child death review reports shall be completed no later than six months after the date of the death of the child. Upon completion of each report the Department shall notify the President of the Senate, the Minority Leader of the Senate, the Speaker of the House of Representatives, the Minority Leader of the House of Representatives, and the members of the Senate and the House of Representatives in whose district the child's death occurred. Reports shall address:

i) cause of death;

ii) identification of child protective or other services provided or actions taken regarding the child and his or her family;

iii) extraordinary or pertinent information concerning the

circumstances of the child's death;

iv) whether the child or the child's family received assistance, care, or other social services prior to the child's death;

v) actions or further investigation undertaken by the Department since the death of the child; and

vi) recommendations concerning child protective, child welfare, or prevention issues.

B) Reports shall not contain information identifying the name of the deceased child, his or her siblings, parents or other persons legally responsible for the child, or any other members of the child's household.

C) Reports concerning the death of a child and the cumulative reports shall be made available to the public after completion or submittal.

i) A child-specific request for a report may be honored by the Department when the Department determines that disclosure of the information is not contrary to the best interest of the deceased child's siblings or other children in the household.

ii) The Department shall not release or disclose to the public the substance or content of any psychological, psychiatric, therapeutic, clinical, or medical report pertaining to the deceased child or the child's family except as it may apply directly to the cause of the child's death.

D) The Department may request and shall receive in a timely fashion from departments, boards, bureaus, or other agencies of the state, or any of its political subdivisions, or any duly authorized agency, or any other agency that provided assistance, care or services to the deceased child any information they are authorized to provide to enable the Department to prepare the report.

b) Reports Involving Child Care Facilities

Reports alleging abuse or neglect of children in child care facilities shall be made and received in the same manner as other reports. The appropriate supervisor or administrator at the facility shall be notified once the formal investigation has been commenced. Department licensing staff will be notified of all reports on licensed facilities upon commencement of the formal investigation. The Department shall advise the supervisor or administrator of their responsibility to take reasonable action necessary, based on all relevant circumstances and the allegations being investigated, to insure that the alleged perpetrator of the reported abuse or neglect is restricted from contact with children in the facility during the course of the formal investigation.

c) Reports Involving Schools

When a report is received alleging abuse or neglect of a child by a school employee known to the child through the employee's official or professional capacity, the Department will take the following actions:

1) To the extent possible, conduct an investigation involving a teacher at a time when the teacher is not scheduled to conduct classes.

2) Conduct investigations involving other school employees in such a way as to minimize disruption of the school day.

3) Make reasonable efforts to conduct the initial investigation in coordination with

the employee's supervisor, if the report does not involve allegations of sexual abuse or extreme physical abuse.

4) When a report of alleged abuse involving a teacher occurred in the course of the teacher's efforts to maintain safety for other students, determine whether the teacher used reasonable force in accordance with rules established by the local board of education as authorized by the School Code [105 ILCS 5].

5) Advise school officials that they may, in accordance with the School Code, withhold from any person, information on the whereabouts of any child removed from school premises, when the child has been taken into protective custody as a victim of suspected child abuse and that they may direct persons seeking information to the Department or to the local law enforcement agency.

6) Advise school employees accused of child abuse or neglect of their due process rights, of the steps in the investigative process, and that they may have their superior, association or union representative, and attorney present at any interview or meeting at which the school employee is present.

7) Prior to indicating a report involving a school employee, the Department will take the following steps:

A) send the employee a copy of the investigative file with identifying information deleted. Any materials and evidence submitted to the Department subsequent to sending the employee a copy of the investigative file shall be sent to the employee upon receipt by the Department;

B) allow the school employee, prior to the final finding, an opportunity to:

i) present evidence to the contrary regarding the report; and

ii) request an informal conference at which the employee may present the additional evidence and/or, subject to the discretion of the Department, confront the accuser, provided the accuser is 14 years of age or older.

8) If an informal conference is requested, the Department shall schedule the conference after receipt by the employee of the copy of the investigative file, and shall:

A) conduct the conference in a neutral setting away from the school grounds during hours when school is not in session, unless requested otherwise by the school employee;

B) notify the following persons of the conference, if the purpose of the conference is merely to submit additional evidence:

i) the school employee and representative;

ii) Department representatives including the investigative worker;

C) notify the following additional persons if the employee wishes to confront the accuser and the Department has approved such a confrontation;

i) the accuser, provided the accuser is 14 years of age or older, and the accuser's parents, guardian and/or representative of a Child Advocacy Center, when involved in the case. (The accuser is the person who has made the allegation of abuse or neglect. The accuser is not necessarily the same as the reporter.);

ii) representatives of the State's Attorney's Office or law enforcement agency in the county where the alleged incident occurred, when the State's Attorney's Office or law enforcement agency are currently involved in the investigation and/or are considering filing criminal charges in the case;

iii) persons identified by the employee who have information relevant to the report, who will be included in only those portions of the conference pertaining to their testimony;

D) following the conference, allow the school employee at least five calendar days to present additional evidence to the Department;

E) make a final determination with regard to the report in accordance with Section 300.110 of the Part.

9) No such conference will be allowed when there is a criminal investigation pending and the Department has been advised by law enforcement authorities or the State's Attorney not to allow a face-to-face confrontation between the accused and the accuser.

10) When determining whether to allow the school employee to confront an accuser who is 14 years or older, the Department shall take the following into consideration:

A) whether, due to the nature of the allegation, a confrontation with the accused school employee would cause excessive trauma to the child, and

B) whether the child has a documented history of mental, emotional or developmental problems.

11) The Department shall inform the child and the child's parents in writing prior to the conference and orally at the conference that:

A) they may decline to attend or proceed with the conference, and

B) if they do attend, they may refuse to answer any questions posed, and

C) if the child attends, he or she has the right to have an attorney or other person representing his or her interests present at the conference, in addition to his or her parents or guardian.

12) Child's or parent's refusal to attend a conference or to answer questions shall not be grounds for unfounding an otherwise credible report.

13) All proceedings shall be confidential and no statement, summary, transcript, recording or other investigative product shall be released except on written order of the court, or in compliance with the confidentiality provisions of the Abused and Neglected Child Reporting Act. Violations of these provisions is a Class A misdemeanor (see 325 ILCS 5/11).

14) Whether or not an informal conference has been conducted, the school employee retains all other appeal rights provided in the Abused and Neglected Child Reporting Act [325 ILCS 5/7.16] and 89 Ill. Adm. Code 336 (Appeal of Child Abuse and Neglect Investigation Findings).

A) Reports Involving State Facilities and State Employees Acting in Their Official Capacity
When reports are received alleging abuse or neglect of children by any State of Illinois Department or any State employee acting in his or her official capacity, the report-taker will immediately notify the Director of the Department or designee. The Director or designee will transmit the details of the report to the Division of Internal Investigation,

Illinois Department of State Police.

B) Reports Involving Juvenile Alleged Perpetrators

Reports of abuse or neglect in which a juvenile (anyone under 18 years of age) has been named as the alleged perpetrator shall be handled as follows:

1) Juvenile Parents of Alleged Victims

All calls received by State Central Register (SCR) that meet the Department's criteria to be accepted for investigation, and in which the alleged perpetrator is a juvenile who is also the parent of the alleged victim, will be investigated and maintained on the State Central Register without regard to the age of the alleged perpetrator.

2) All other Children Under the Age of 18

Calls received at SCR alleging that children under the age of 18 are responsible for abuse or neglect will be accepted for investigation. SCR will consider situations in which children under the age of 18 are allegedly responsible for abuse or neglect to determine whether there is reasonable cause to suspect that the maltreatment is the result of blatant disregard on the part of an adult who is an eligible perpetrator. If so, a report will be accepted alleging inadequate supervision with the adult as the alleged perpetrator.

3) Indicated Findings

A) If after an investigation, reports are indicated and children under the age of 10 are determined to be the perpetrator, the child will not be named as the perpetrator for purposes of retaining the report in the State Central Register.

B) If after an investigation, reports are indicated and children between the ages of 10 and 18 are determined to be the perpetrator, reports that carry a five-year retention schedule will be expunged from the State Central Register after five years or at the perpetrator's twenty-first birthday, which ever is sooner.

C) In the event that the same child between the ages of 10 and 18 is determined to be an indicated perpetrator of another report that requires a five year retention schedule, the information concerning the previous report(s) and the subsequent report will be maintained at the State Central Register for a period of five years from the date of the subsequent report or at the perpetrator's twenty-first birthday, which ever is sooner.

D) Reports that carry a 20 or 50 year retention schedule will be expunged from the State Central Register after five years or at the perpetrator's twenty-third birthday, which ever is sooner.

E) In the event that the same child between the ages of 10 and 18 is subsequently determined to be an indicated perpetrator of an allegation carrying a 20 or 50 year retention schedule, the information concerning the previous reports and the subsequent report will be maintained at the State Central Register for a period of five years from the date of the subsequent report or at the perpetrator's twenty-third birthday, which ever is sooner.

(Source: Amended at 27 Ill. Reg., effective January 15, 2003)

Section 300.170 Child Death Review Teams

a) The Director of the Department shall appoint a child death review team in each subregion of the Department outside Cook County and at least one child death review team in Cook County.

b) Every child death shall be reviewed by the team in the Department subregion that has primary case management responsibility when the deceased child meets one of the criteria described in Section 300.160(a)(2) of this Part. The child death review team may, at its discretion, review other sudden, unexpected, or unexplained child deaths.

c) The purposes of the child death reviews are to:

1) assist in determining the cause and manner of the child's death, when requested;

2) evaluate means by which the death might have been prevented;

3) report its findings to appropriate agencies;

4) make recommendations that may help to reduce the number of child deaths caused by abuse or neglect;

5) promote continuing education for professionals involved in investigating, treating, and preventing child abuse and neglect as a means of preventing child deaths due to abuse or neglect; and

6) make specific recommendations to the Director and the Inspector General of the Department of Children and Family Services concerning the prevention of child deaths due to abuse or neglect and the establishment of protocols for investigating child deaths. [20 ILCS 515/20(b)]

d) *A child death review team shall review a child death as soon as practical upon receiving notification from the Department and not later than 90 days following the completion by the Department of the investigation of the death. When there has been no investigation by the Department, the child death review team shall review a child's death within 90 days after obtaining the information necessary to complete the review from the coroner, pathologist, medical examiner, or law enforcement agency, depending on the nature of the case.* [20 ILCS 515/20(c)]

e) Following the review, the team shall forward its recommendations, on forms provided by the Department, to the Director of the Department.

f) *The Director shall, within 90 days, review and reply to recommendations made by a team pursuant to subsection (c)(6) of this Section. The Director shall implement recommendations as feasible and appropriate and shall respond in writing to the death review team to explain the implementation or nonimplementation of the recommendations.* [20 ILCS 515/20(d)]

g) *A child death review team shall have access to all records and information that are relevant to the teams's review of a child's death and in the possession of a State or local government agency.* [20 ILCS 515/25(b)] Other records and case information relevant to the review include:

1) birth certificates;

2) all relevant medical and mental health records;

3) records of law enforcement agency investigations;

4) records of coroner or medical examiner investigations;

5) records of the Department of Corrections concerning a person's parole;

6) records of a probation and court services department, and records of a social service agency that provided services to the child or the child's family.

(Source: Added at 22 Ill. Reg. 18847, effective October 1, 1998)

300.APPENDIX A Acknowledgement of Mandated Reporter Status

I, (Employee name) , understand that when I am employed as a (Type of Employment), I
will become a mandated reporter under the Abused and Neglected Child Reporting Act (Ill.
Rev. Stat. 1985, ch. 23, pars. 2051 et seq.) This means that I am required to report or cause a
report to be made to the child abuse Hotline number (1-800-25A-BUSE) whenever I have
reasonable cause to believe that a child known to me in my professional or official capacity
may be abused or neglected. I understand that there is no charge when calling the Hotline
number and that the Hotline operates 24-hours per day, 7 days per week, 365 days per year.
I further understand that the privileged quality of communication between me and my patient or
client is not grounds for failure to report suspected child abuse or neglect. I know that if I
willfully fail to report suspected child abuse or neglect I may be found guilty of a Class A
misdemeanor. This does not apply to physicians who will be referred to the Illinois State
Medical Disciplinary Board for action.

I also understand that if I am subject to licensing under the Illinois Nursing Act, the Medical
Practice Act, the Psychologist Registration Act, the Social Workers Registration Act, the Illinois
Dental Practices Act, the School Code, or "AN ACT to regulate the practice of Podiatry in the
State of Illinois," I may be subject to license suspension or revocation if I willfully fail to report
suspected child abuse or neglect.

I affirm that I have read this statement and have knowledge and understanding of the reporting
requirements which apply to me under the Abused and Neglected Child Reporting Act.

_____
Signature of Applicant/Employee

_____
Date

(Source: Recodified from 89 Ill. Adm. Code 302, Appendix A, at 11 Ill. Reg. 3492)

300.APPENDIX B Child Abuse and Neglect Allegations

This Appendix describes the specific incidents of harm which must be alleged to have been caused by
the acts or omissions of the persons identified in Section 3 of the Abused and Neglected Child
Reporting Act before the Department will accept a report of child abuse or neglect. The allegation
definitions focus upon the harm or the risk of harm to the child. Many of the allegations of harm can be
categorized as resulting from either abuse or neglect. All abuse allegations of harm are coded with a
one or two digit number under 30. All neglect allegations of harm are coded with a two digit number
greater than 50. The allegations of harm are defined as follows:

Allegation # Definition

1/51 Death

Permanent cessation of all vital functions.

The following definitions of death are also commonly used:

- Total irreversible cessation of cerebral function, spontaneous function of the
respiratory system, and spontaneous function of the circulatory system.

- The final and irreversible cessation of perceptible heart beat and respiration.

Verification of death must come from a physician or coroner.

2/52 Head Injuries

Head Injury

As used in this Part head injury means a serious head injury causing skull fracture,
brain damage or bleeding on the brain, such as a subdural hematoma or shaken baby
syndrome. The following are considered head injuries:

Brain Damage

Brain damage means injury to the large, soft mass of nerve tissue contained within the cranium skull.

Skull Fracture

Skull fracture means a broken bone of the skull.

Hematoma

Hematoma means a swelling or mass of blood (usually clotted) confined to an organ, tissue or space and caused by a break in a blood vessel.

Subdural Hematoma

Subdural means beneath the dura mater (the outer membrane covering the spinal cord and brain).

A subdural hematoma is located beneath the membrane covering the brain and is usually the result of head injuries or the shaking of a small child or infant. It may result in the loss of consciousness, seizures, mental or physical damage, or death.

Shaken Baby Syndrome (Whiplash Shaken Infant Syndrome (WSIS))

Shaking of an infant causes stretching and tearing of blood vessels in the brain causing subdural hematoma, bleeding in the brain and retinal hemorrhage.

Verification of head injuries must come from a physician, preferably a neurosurgeon or radiologist.

4/54 Internal Injuries

An internal injury is an injury which is not visible from the outside, e.g., an injury to the organs occupying the thoracic or abdominal cavities. Such injury may result from a direct blow or a penetrating injury. A person so injured may be pale, cold, perspiring freely, have an anxious expression, or may seem semicomatose. Pain is usually intense at first, and may continue or gradually diminish as patient grows worse. Verification of internal injuries must come from a physician.

5/55 Burns

Burns

Tissue injury resulting from excessive exposure to thermal, chemical, electrical or radioactive agents. The effects vary according to the type, duration and intensity of the agent and the part of the body involved. Burns are usually classified as:
- First Degree (Partial Thickness)

Superficial burns, damage being limited to the outer layer of the epidermis (skin). Characterized by scorching or painful redness of the skin.
- Second Degree (Partial Thickness)

The damage extends through the outer layer of the skin into the inner layers (dermis). Blistering will be present within 24 hours.
- Third Degree (Full Thickness)

Burns in which both layers of the skin (epidermis and dermis) are destroyed with damage extending into underlying tissues, which may be charred or coagulated.
- Fourth Degree (Full Thickness)

Burns extend beyond skin and underlying tissues into bone, joints and muscles.

Scalding

A burn to the skin or flesh caused by moist heat and hot vapors, as steam.

All emersion burns (scalds) must be confirmed by a physician unless the alleged perpetrator has admitted to scalding the child.

6/56 Poison/Noxious Substances

Poison

Any substance, other than mood altering chemicals or alcohol, taken into the body by ingestion, inhalation, injection, or absorption that interferes with normal physiological functions. (Virtually any substance can be poisonous if consumed in sufficient quantity; therefore, the term poison more often implies an excessive amount rather than the existence of a specific substance.)

Noxious

Harmful, injurious, not wholesome.

Verification must come from a physician or by a direct admission from the alleged perpetrator.

7/57 Wounds

A gunshot or stabbing injury.

Verification must come from a physician, a law enforcement officer or by a direct admission from the alleged perpetrator.

9/59 Bone Fractures

A fracture is a broken bone.

Metaphyseal – Epiphyeal Fractures

Fractures at the end of bones. They are commonly described as corner fractures, chipped fractures or bucket – handle fractures.

Diaphyseal Fractures

Diaphyseal fractures are located in the bone shaft. Fractures in the shaft of long bones of the extremities are spiral (oblique) or transverse. Spiral fracture is caused by twisting or rotational force. Transverse fracture results from a direct blow or bending force.

Verification must come from a physician or radiologist.

10/60 Substantial Risk of Physical Injury/Environment Injurious to Health and Welfare

Substantial risk of physical injury means that the parent, caregiver, immediate family member aged 16 or over, other person residing in the home aged 16 or over, or the parent's paramour has created a real and significant danger of physical injury that would likely cause disfigurement, death, or impairment of physical health or loss or impairment of bodily functions (abuse). This allegation of harm is to be used when the type or extent of harm is undefined but the total circumstances lead a reasonable person to believe that the child is in substantial risk of physical injury. This allegation of harm also includes incidents of violence or intimidation directed toward the child that have not yet resulted in injury or impairment but that clearly threaten such injury or impairment (abuse) or placing a child in an environment that is injurious to the child's health and welfare (neglect).

Examples of incidents or circumstances that place the child in substantial risk of physical injury include, but are not limited to, the following:

Incidents of Maltreatment

- choking the child (abuse).
- smothering the child (abuse).
- pulling the child's hair out (abuse).
- violently pushing or shoving the child into fixed or heavy objects (abuse).
- throwing or shaking a smaller child (abuse).
- other violent or intimidating acts directed toward the child that cause excessive pain or fear (abuse).
- situations that place a child at substantial risk of harm due to environmental

issues in the home (neglect).

Circumstances

- domestic violence in the home when the child has been threatened and the threat is believable, as evidenced by a past history of violence or uncontrolled behavior (neglect).
- a perpetrator of child abuse who has been court ordered to remain out of the home returns home and has access to the abused child (abuse).
- anyone living in the home has a documented history of violence toward children (abuse).
- the circumstances surrounding the death of one child provides reason to believe that another child is at real and significant danger of physical injury (neglect).
- anyone in the home exposes child to environment that significantly affects the health and safety based on use, sale or manufacturing of illegal drugs or alcohol (neglect).
- parent's or caretaker's mental illness and behavior poses a significant danger to the child's health and safety (neglect). To indicate an allegation based on this factor, the investigator must rule out dependency as defined in the Juvenile Court Act as the presenting problem.
- parent has been adjudicated unfit by a court and the parent has not completed services that would correct the conditions which led to the court finding (abuse/neglect).

Factors to be Considered

Whether there is a real and significant danger to justify taking a report is determined by the following factors (All factors need not be present to justify taking the report. One factor alone may present sufficient danger to justify taking the report):
- the child's age .
- the child's medical condition, behavioral, mental, or emotional problems, developmental disability, or physical handicap, particularly related to his or her ability to protect himself or herself.
- the severity of the occurrence.
- the frequency of the occurrence.
- the alleged perpetrator's physical, mental and/or emotional abilities, particularly related to his or her ability to control his or her actions.
- the dynamics of the relationship between the alleged perpetrator and the child.
- the alleged perpetrator's access to the child.
- the previous history of indicated abuse or neglect.
- the current stresses/crisis in the home.
- the presence of other supporting persons in the home.

11/61 Cuts, Bruises, Welts, Abrasions and Oral Injuries

Cut

An opening, incision or break in the skin made by some external agent.

Bruise

An injury that results in bleeding under the skin, where the skin is discolored but not broken. Also referred to as a contusion.

Welt

An elevation on the skin produced by a lash, blow, or allergic stimulus. The skin is not broken and the mark is reversible.

Abrasion

A scraping away of the skin.

Oral Injuries

Injuries to the child's mouth, including broken teeth.

Factors to be Considered

Not every cut, bruise, or welt constitutes an allegation of harm. The following factors should be considered when determining whether an injury which resulted in cuts, bruises or welts constitute an allegation of harm:

- the child's age (children aged 6 and under are at a much greater risk of harm).
- child's medical condition, behavioral, mental, or emotional problems, developmental disability, or physical handicap, particularly as they relate to the child's ability to seek help.
- pattern or chronicity of similar incidents.
- severity of the cuts, bruises, welts, or abrasions (size, number, depth, extent of discoloration).
- location of the cuts, bruises, welts, or abrasions.
- whether an instrument was used on the child.
- previous history of indicated abuse or neglect.

12/62 Human Bites

A bruise, cut or indentation in the skin caused by seizing, piercing, or cutting the skin with human teeth.

13/63 Sprains/Dislocations

Sprain

Trauma to a joint that causes pain and disability depending upon the degree of injury to ligaments and/or surrounding muscle tissue. In a severe sprain, ligaments and/or muscle tissue may be completely torn. The signs are rapid swelling, heat and disability, often discoloration and limitation of function.

Dislocation

The displacement of any part, especially the temporary displacement of a bone from its normal position in a joint. Types include:

Complicated

A dislocation associated with other major injuries.

Compound

Dislocation in which the joint is exposed to the external air.

Closed

A simple dislocation.

Complete

A dislocation which completely separates the surfaces of a joint.

Verification must come from a physician, registered nurse, licensed practical nurse or by a direct admission from the alleged perpetrator.

14 Tying/Close Confinement

Unreasonable restriction of a child's mobility, actions or physical functioning by tying the child to a fixed (or heavy) object, tying limbs together or forcing the child to remain in a closely confined area which restricts physical movement.

Examples include, but are not limited to:

- locking a child in a closet or small room.

- tying one or more limbs to a bed, chair, or other object, except as authorized by a licensed physician.
- tying a child's hands behind his or her back.
- putting a child in a cage.

15/65 Substance Misuse

Option A

The consumption of a mood altering chemical capable of intoxication to the extent that it harmfully affects the child's health, behavior, motor coordination, judgment, or intellectual capability. Mood altering chemicals include cannabis (marijuana), hallucinogens, stimulants (including cocaine), sedatives (including alcohol and Valium), narcotics, or inhalants (abuse/neglect). Abuse occurs if the parent provides the substance to the child. Neglect occurs if the parent allows the use or fails to protect the child from consumption.

Option B

Fetal alcohol syndrome or drug withdrawal at birth caused by the mother's addiction to drugs is included in this definition and is considered child neglect (neglect).

Option C

Any amount of a controlled substance or a metabolite hereof, found in the blood, urine or meconium (newborn's first stool) of a newborn infant. A controlled substance is defined in subsection (f) of Section 102 of the Illinois Controlled Substances Act [720 ILCS 570/102] (neglect). The presence of such substances shall not be considered as child neglect if the presence is due to medical treatment of the mother or infant. NOTE: Methadone withdrawal or other withdrawal verified as under the auspices of a drug treatment program is not included under drug withdrawal at birth.

Examples of substance misuse include, but are not limited to:

- giving a minor (unless prescribed by a physician) any amount of heroin, cocaine, morphine, peyote, LSD, PCP, pentazocine, or methaqualone or encouraging, insisting, or permitting a minor's consumption of the above substances.
- giving any mood altering substance, including alcohol or sedatives, unless prescribed by a physician, to an infant or toddler.
- encouraging, insisting or permitting a child who has not reached puberty to consume alcohol, drugs, or another mood altering substance on a regular or frequent basis.
- encouraging, insisting or permitting an adolescent to consume alcohol, drugs, or another mood altering substance on a daily basis.
- encouraging, insisting or permitting any minor to become intoxicated by alcohol, drugs, or another mood altering substance even if on an infrequent basis.

Factors to be Considered

The following factors should be considered when determining whether a child is involved in substance misuse:

- age of the child.
- frequency of substance misuse.
- amount of substance consumption.
- whether the substance is illegal for general population use.
- degree of behavioral dysfunction, or physical impairment linked to substance

misuse.

- the child's culture, particularly as it relates to use of alcohol in religious ceremonies or on special occasions.

- whether the parent or caregiver's attempts to control an older child's substance misuse or to seek help for the child's substance misuse were reasonable under the circumstances.

- whether the parent or caregiver knew or should have known of the child's substance misuse.

16 Torture

Inflicting or subjecting the child to intense physical and/or mental pain, suffering, or agony that is severe, repetitive, increased, or prolonged.

17/67 Mental and Emotional Impairment

Injury to the intellectual, emotional or psychological development of a child as evidenced by observable and substantial impairment in the child's ability to function within a normal range of performance and behavior, with due regard to his or her culture.

Verification that a child has been mentally injured must come from a medical doctor, psychiatrist, registered psychologist, certified social worker, registered nurse, or a therapist or counselor of a community mental health agency.

18 Sexually Transmitted Diseases

A disease which was acquired originally as a result of sexual penetration or sexual conduct with an individual who is afflicted with the disease. The diseases may include, but are not limited to:

- Acquired Immune Deficiency Syndrome (AIDS)
- Balanoposthitis
- Calymmatobacterium Granulomatis
- Chancroid
- Chlamydia Trachomatis
- Genital Herpes
- Genital Warts
- Gonorrhea
- Granuloma Inquinale
- Haemophilus Ducreyi
- HIV Infection
- Lymphogranuloma Venereum
- Neisseria Gonorrhea
- Nonspecific Urethritis
- Proctitis
- Syphilis
- Treponema Pallidum
- Trichomonas Vaginalis (Symptomatic)

Sexual penetration is defined in the Illinois Criminal Sexual Assault Act as "any contact, however slight, between the sex organ or anus of one person by an object, the sex organ, mouth or anus of another person, or any intrusion, however slight, of any part of the body of one person or any animal or object into the sex organ or anus of another person, including but not limited to cunnilingus, fellatio or anal penetration."

Sexual conduct is defined in the Act as "any intentional or knowing touching or fondling

of the victim or the perpetrator, either directly or through clothing of the sex organs, anus or breast of the victim or the accused, or any part of the body of a child . . . for the purpose of sexual gratification or arousal of the victim or the accused."
Verification of sexually transmitted diseases must come from a medical source.

19 Sexual Penetration

Any contact, however slight, between the sex organ or anus of one person by an object, the sex organ, mouth or anus of another person, or any intrusion, however slight, of any part of the body of one person or any animal or object into the sex organ or anus of another person. This includes acts commonly known as oral sex (cunnilingus, fellatio), anal penetration, coition, coitus, and copulation.

20 Sexual Exploitation

Sexual use of a child for sexual arousal, gratification, advantage, or profit. This includes but is not limited to:
- indecent solicitation of a child/explicit verbal enticement.
- child pornography.
- exposing sexual organs to a child for the purpose of sexual arousal or gratification.
- forcing the child to watch sexual acts.
- self-masturbation in the child's presence.

NOTE: Sexual penetration and molestation are excluded from this allegation. They are listed as separate allegations.

21 Sexual Molestation

Sexual conduct with a child when such contact, touching or interaction is used for arousal or gratification of sexual needs or desires. Parts of the body, as used in the examples below, refer to the pars of the body described in the definition of sexual conduct found in the Illinois Criminal Sexual Assault Act [720 ILCS 5/12-12] as quoted above under Allegation 18, Sexually Transmitted Diseases. Examples include, but are not limited to:
- fondling.
- the alleged perpetrator inappropriately touching or pinching parts of the child's body generally associated with sexual activity.
- encouraging, forcing, or permitting the child to touch parts of the alleged perpetrator's body normally associated with sexual activity.

22 Substantial Risk of Sexual Injury

Substantial risk of sexual injury means that the parent, caregiver, immediate family member, other person residing in the home, or the parent's paramour has created a real and significant danger of sexual abuse, in that:

Option A

An indicated, registered, or convicted sex offender has significant access to children, and the extent/quality of supervision during contact is unknown or suspected to be deficient.

Option B

There are siblings or other children in the same household as the alleged offender of a current allegation of sexual abuse.

Option C

Persistent, highly sexualized behavior or knowledge in a very young child (e.g., under the age of five chronologically or developmentally) that is grossly age inappropriate, and there is reasonable cause to believe that the most likely manner in which this behavior or knowledge was learned is in having been sexually abused.

Note: When accepting a report based on behavioral indicators, State Central Register staff must inform the reporter that the report cannot be indicated unless the victim makes a statement regarding specific sexual abuse or a forensic evaluation or independent consultation results in a clinical finding of sexual abuse.

74 Inadequate Supervision

The child has been placed in a situation or circumstances that are likely to require judgment or actions greater than the child's level of maturity, physical condition, and/or mental abilities would reasonably dictate. *A child shall not be considered neglected for the sole reason that the child's parent or other person responsible for his or her welfare has left the child in the care of an adult relative for any period of time.* [325 ILCS 5/3] Examples include, but are not limited to:

- leaving children alone when they are too young to care for themselves.

- leaving children alone who have a condition that requires close supervision. Such conditions may include medical conditions, behavioral, mental, or emotional problems, or developmental or physical disabilities.

- leaving children in the care of an inadequate or inappropriate caregiver.

- being present but unable to supervise because of the caregiver's condition (This includes (1) the parent or caretaker who repeatedly uses drugs or alcohol to the extent that it has the effect of producing a substantial state of stupor, unconsciousness, intoxication or irrationality and (2) the parent or caretaker who cannot adequately supervise the child because of his or her medical condition, behavioral, mental, or emotional problems, or a developmental or physical disability).

- leaving children unattended in a place that is unsafe for them when their maturity, physical condition, and mental abilities are considered.

Factors to be Considered

The following factors should be considered when determining whether a child is inadequately supervised:

Child Factors

- child's age and developmental stage, particularly related to the ability to make sound judgments in the event of an emergency.

- child's physical condition, particularly related to the child's ability to care for or protect himself or herself. Is the child physically or mentally handicapped or otherwise in need of ongoing prescribed medical treatment such as periodic doses of insulin or other medications?

- child's mental abilities, particularly as related to the ability to comprehend the situation.

Caregiver Factors

- presence or accessibility of caregiver.

o How long does it take the caregiver to reach the child?

o Can the caregiver see and hear the child?

o Is the caregiver accessible by telephone?

o Has the child been given phone numbers to call in the event of an emergency?

- caregiver's capability.

o Is the caregiver mature enough to assume responsibility for the situation?

o Does the caregiver depend on extraordinary assistance to care for self and the child, i.e., meal preparation, laundry, grocery shopping, transportation? Is the caregiver without consistent or reliable assistance?

o Is the child assuming primary caregiving duties, i.e., meal preparation, laundry, grocery shopping, transportation?

- caregiver's physical condition.

o Is the caregiver physically able to care for the child? Do the caregiver's own health needs present serious obstacles to the care and well-being of the child?

- caregiver's cognitive and emotional condition.

o Is the caregiver able to make appropriate judgments on the child's behalf?

o Do the caregiver's own health needs present serious obstacles to the care and well-being of the child?

Incident Factors

- frequency of occurrence.

- duration of the occurrence (as related to the "child factors" above).

- time of the day or night when the incident occurs.

- child's location (the condition and location of the place where the minor was left without supervision).

- the weather conditions, including whether the minor was left in a location with adequate protection from the natural elements such as adequate heat or light.

- other supporting persons who are overseeing the child. (Was the child given a phone number of a person or location to call in the event of an emergency and whether the child was capable of making an emergency call?)

- whether food and other provisions were left for the child.

- other factors that may endanger the health and safety of the child.

75 Abandonment/Desertion

Abandonment

Abandonment is parental conduct that demonstrates the purpose of relinquishing all parental rights and claims to the child. Abandonment is also defined as any parental conduct that evinces a settled purpose to forego all parental duties and relinquish all parental claims to the child.

Desertion

Desertion is any conduct on the part of a parent that indicates an intention to terminate custody of the child but not to relinquish all duties to and claims on the child.

Examples of abandonment/desertion include, but are not limited to, parents who:

- leave a baby on a doorstep.

- leave a baby in a garbage can.

- leave a child with no apparent intention to return.

- leave a child with an appropriate caregiver but fail to resume care of the child, as agreed, and the caregiver cannot or will not continue to care for the child.

76 Inadequate Food

Lack of food adequate to sustain normal functioning. It is not as severe as Malnutrition or Failure to Thrive, both of which require a medical diagnosis.

Examples include:

- the child who frequently and repeatedly misses meals or who is frequently and repeatedly fed insufficient amounts of food.
- the child who frequently and repeatedly asks neighbors for food and other information substantiates that the child is not being fed.
- the child who is frequently and repeatedly fed unwholesome foods when his age, developmental stage, and physical condition are considered.

Factors to be Considered

Child Factors

- child's age.
- child's developmental stage.
- child's physical condition, particularly related to the need for a special diet.
- child's mental abilities, particularly related to his ability to obtain and prepare his own food.

Incident Factors

- frequency of the occurrence.
- duration of the occurrence.
- pattern or chronicity of occurrence.
- previous history of occurrences.
- availability of adequate food.

77 Inadequate Shelter

Lack of shelter that is safe and that protects the children from the elements. Examples of inadequate shelter include, but are not limited to:

- no housing or shelter.
- condemned housing.
- exposed, frayed wiring.
- housing with structural defects that endanger the health or safety of a child.
- housing with indoor temperatures consistently below 50 F.
- housing with broken windows in sub-zero weather.
- housing that is a fire hazard obvious to the reasonable person.
- housing with an unsafe heat source that poses a fire hazard or threat of asphyxiation.

Factors to be Considered

Child Factors

- child's age.
- child's developmental stage.
- child's physical condition, particularly when it may be aggravated by the inadequate shelter.
- child's mental abilities, particularly related to the child's ability to comprehend the dangers posed by the inadequate shelter.

Shelter Factors

- seriousness of the problem.
- frequency of the problem.
- duration of the problem.
- pattern or chronicity of the problem.
- previous history of shelter-related problems.

78 Inadequate Clothing (Priority III)

Lack of appropriate clothing to protect the child from the elements.

Factors to be Considered

Child Factors

- child's age.
- child's developmental stage.
- child's physical condition, particularly related to conditions that may be aggravated by exposure to the elements.
- child's mental abilities, particularly related to his or her ability to obtain appropriate clothing.

Incident Factors

- frequency of the incident.
- duration of the incident.
- chronicity or pattern of similar incidents.
- weather conditions such as extreme heat or extreme cold;

79 Medical Neglect

Medical or Dental Treatment

Lack of medical or dental treatment for a health problem or condition that, if untreated, could become severe enough to constitute a serious or long-term harm to the child; lack of follow-through on a prescribed treatment plan for a condition that could become serious enough to constitute serious or long-term harm to the child if the plan goes unimplemented.

Factors to be Considered

- child's age, particularly as it relates to the ability to obtain treatment.
- child's developmental stage.
- child's physical condition.
- seriousness of the current health problem.
- probable outcome if the current health problem is not treated and the seriousness of that outcome.
- generally accepted medical benefits of the prescribed treatment.
- generally recognized side effects/harms associated with the prescribed treatment.

It must be verified that the child has/had an untreated health problem, or that a prescribed treatment plan was implemented. Such verification must come from a physician, registered nurse, dentist, or by a direct admission from the alleged perpetrator. It must further be verified by a physician, registered nurse or dentist that the problem or condition, if untreated, could result in serious or long-term harm to the child.

81 Failure to Thrive (Non-Organic)

A serious medical condition most often seen in children under one year of age. The child's weight, height and motor development fall significantly short of the average growth rates of normal children (i.e., below the fifth percentile). In about 10% of these cases, there is an organic cause such as a serious kidney, heart, or intestinal disease, a genetic error of metabolism or brain damage. All other cases are a result of a disturbed parent-child relationship manifested in severe physical and emotional neglect of the child. Non-organic failure to thrive requires a medical diagnosis before it may be indicated. Verification of failure to thrive must come from a physician.

82 Environmental Neglect

The child's person, clothing, or living conditions are unsanitary to the point that the child's health may be impaired. This may include infestations of rodents, spiders, insects, snakes, etc., human or animal feces, rotten or spoiled food or rotten or spoiled garbage that the child can reach.

Factors to be Considered

Special attention should be paid to the child's physical condition and the living conditions in the home in order to determine whether the report constitutes an allegation of harm. In addition, the following factors should be considered.

Child Factors

- child's age (children aged 6 and under are more likely to be harmed).
- child's developmental stage.
- child's physical condition.
- child's mental abilities.

Incident Factors

- severity of the conditions.
- frequency of the conditions.
- duration of the conditions.
- chronicity or pattern of similar conditions.

83 Malnutrition (Non Organic)

Lack of necessary or proper food substances in the body caused by inadequate food, lack of food, or insufficient amounts of vitamin or minerals. (Also known as marasmus or kwashiorkor.) Non-organic malnutrition requires a medical diagnosis before it may be indicated. There are various physical signs of malnutrition:

- a decrease in lean body mass or fat; very prominent ribs; the child may often be referred to as skin and bones.
- the hair is often sparse, thin, dry, and is easily pulled out or falls out spontaneously.
- the child is often pale and suffers from anemia.
- excessive perspiration, especially about the head.
- the face appears lined and aged, often with a pinched and sharp appearance.
- the skin has an old, wrinkled look with poor turgor. (Classically, skin folds hang loose on the inner thigh and buttock).
- the abdomen is often protuberant.
- there are abnormal pulses, blood pressure, stool patterns, intercurrent infections, abnormal sleep patterns and a decreased level of physical and mental activity.

Verification of malnutrition must come from a physician.

84 Lock-Out

The parent or caregiver has denied the child access to the home and has refused or failed to make provisions for another living arrangement for the child.

85 Medical Neglect of Disabled Infants

The withholding of appropriate nutrition, hydration, medication or other medically indicated treatment from a disabled infant with a life-threatening condition. Medically indicated treatment includes medical care that is most likely to relieve or correct all life-threatening conditions and evaluations or consultations necessary to assure that sufficient information has been gathered to make informed medical decisions. Nutrition, hydration, and medication, as appropriate for the infant's needs, is medically indicated for all disabled infants. Other types of treatment are not medically indicated when:

- the infant is chronically and irreversibly comatose.

- the provision of the treatment would be futile and would merely prolong dying.

- the provision of the treatment would be virtually futile and the treatment itself would be inhumane under the circumstances.

In determining whether treatment will be medically indicated, reasonable medical judgments, such as those made by a prudent physician knowledgeable about the case and its treatment possibilities, will be respected. However, opinions about the infant's future "quality of life" are not to bear on whether a treatment is judged to be medically indicated.

Factors to be Considered

- infant's physical condition.

- seriousness of the current health problem.

- probable medical outcome if the current health problem is not treated and the seriousness of that outcome.

- generally accepted medical benefits of the prescribed treatment.

- generally recognized side effects associated with the prescribed treatment.

- the opinions of the Infant Care Review Committee (ICRC) (if the hospital has an ICRC).

- the judgment of the Perinatal Coordinator regarding whether treatment is medically indicated and whether there is credible evidence of medical neglect.

- parent's knowledge and understanding of the treatment and the probable medical outcome.

Verification that treatment was medically indicated must come from a physician and may come from experts in the field of neonatal pediatrics.

(Source: Amended at 25 Ill. Reg., effective October 1, 2001)

Appendix 9

EMANCIPATION DAY SERMON IN TOCCOA, GEORGIA – GOD'S EMANCIPATING WORD

Sermon at Toccoa Georgia Trinity C.M.E. Methodist Church

Toccoa Improvement Association, Inc.
39th Annual Emancipation Day Celebration
"God's" Emancipating Word"
Rev. Preston N. Tolliver, Jr.

(Message as Reconstructed from Sermon Notes)

PREFACE

I will bless the Lord at all times his praise shall continually be in my mouth. My soul shall make her boast in the Lord; thou shall hear therefore and be glad. O magnify the Lord with me and let us exalt his name together. O taste and see that the Lord is good. Blessed is the man that trusts in him.

Happy New Year! I greet you in the name of our Lord and Savior Jesus Christ!

I did a little math this morning. And, I suggest that you do the same. Now, take your birth year and subtract that number from 2005. Let everyone having breath thank God for that number of years. Has the Lord been good to you?

I greet you on this 142nd anniversary of the Emancipation Proclamation. What and honor and privilege it for me stand today before you. And, I thank your for the invitation.

I bring you greetings from the Zion Hill Missionary Baptist Church where my Pastor and Dean of Christian Education, National Baptist Conference, Inc., is the Rev. Dr. George Waddles, Sr. I greet you also from the Safer Corporation Crossroads Community Correctional Facility and the so called "In-House-Church" where I am the so-called "Pastor" for the last 8 years.

To the Toccoa Improvement Association, Inc. and Dr. Major C. Scott, Chairman. To the angel of this Church, the Reverend Keith Elison in his absence. To the Reverend Jerry H. Dodd, Pastor of the Friendship Baptist Church. To Rev. Carnes, my cousin Tina. I want you to know how happy I am to be with you on this day and the there is a word from the Lord!

I want to thank Mayor L.J. Harrison the husband of my cousin Mable for his introduction. What an influence he has been in my life. He and my cousin were high school sweethearts. He was so cool and he had a cool car yet he drove my cousins and me around. He went to church, finished college, married my cousin, raised a family, built a mansion of a home with own two hands. L.J. has been a policeman, teacher and college professor and the first black Mayor of Toccoa. What a role model for a little younger black man such as myself trying to find his way. You know Beyonce has a song out talking about finding a "soldier". Now I know that I should not judge a book by its cover looking at the young men in the video, but I came to tell you today, on Emancipation Day, that L.J. Harrison is a soldier. Dr. Major Scott is a soldier. I am looking into the face of my cousin Prather Wilson, one of the great patriarchs of this church down front, a soldier.

There is a word from the Lord here today in this the church of my grandmother Lorena Prather and we are broadcasting over Station WLET AM. There were a few technical difficulties and now I am told to take all the time I need; now, I hate to tell you that you have just made a mistake. I come here today to the church of my cousin Prather Wilson, a stalwart of this Church. To a church where I spend time as a youth (between here and Friendship Baptist Church). I come here in the presence of so many family members, friends and my wife Ruthanne of 30 years as of October, 2004. I come this day after we have just witnessed the tragedy of the Tsunami in the Indian Ocean; the greatest tragedy in the recorded history of the world. I come to Toccoa, meaning beautiful, as you know about death from raging waters from a number of years ago now, at Toccoa Falls Bible College. I learned to be quiet here in Toccoa when the Lord is speaking for I seems like during a rainy night in Georgia it is indeed raining all over the world.

Let us pray: Almighty God our Father. We come once again as you have allowed us to assemble in this place. We come thanking you for your grace and your mercy; for your tender care even now in this place. We come thanking for the liberty that is Christ Jesus. Lord we stand in great anticipation of your word. We know that you are able to use mortal man ordained as your mouthpiece. Have your way now Father is our prayer, in the name of Jesus Christ we pray. Amen!

Reading the scriptural text taken from 2 Timothy 3:16 &17: All scripture is given by inspiration of God, and is profitable for doctrine, for reproof, for correction, for instruction in righteousness: That the man of god may be perfect, thoroughly furnished unto all good works. Can you say Amen?

SERMON

"God's Emancipating Word" is the message title that has been laid upon my heart!

I am aware of the fact Bible that existed at the time of Christ, the Septuagint Bible, was basically what we know today as the Old Testament. I am aware also of the debate concerning the number books that should have defined as the cannon of scripture used in the temple yet, regardless, Christ said; "search the scriptures", the holy writ, the Grapha and you will see me there!

Today's generally accepted cannon of scripture that comprises the Bible consists of 66 books. There are books containing the law and history. There are books containing poetry and prophecy. There are books of the Bible that are recognized as the gospels and some the epistles. All of these books have one common thread; they are believed to be inspired by God. They are Holy Ghost evident, coming from approximately 40 different writers and over 2000 plus years; writers of different walks of life, yet, evidencing God having breathed on their writings. It has God as its origin; every title, every jot, every word not to be added to or taken away. Heaven and earth will pass away yet the word is proclaimed as everlasting; it will last after Heaven and earth shall pass away. It is incarnated in Christ, the Word, and the Logos. The entire Bible points to the coming, preaching of the gospel, death and resurrection of Jesus Christ.

Now, the text (1 Timothy 3:16&17) says that scripture is profitable for different purposes. In particular, it is helpful, advantageous for doctrine (Didakalia). That is to say for learning, teaching and/or philosophy of life. In spite of man's creation in the likeness of God, we learn in the scriptures of man's depravity in the flesh ("the thoughts of man being evil continually"). "In me, that is in the flesh, dwelleth no good thing". Mankind, according to the scriptures, must undergo a spiritual conversion from the flesh to the spirit in order to be brought into and acceptable relationship with an alienated God.

For God has declared that the wages of sin requires the shedding of sinless blood. For God so loved the world, that he gave his only son, begotten of sinful flesh yet sinless, as atonement for all. His name is Jesus and he is the reason for the holiday season we just celebrated the other day. Jesus came, preached the good news of the kingdom of heaven coming to earth, fulfilled the Law set forth by God (he alone has been able to do that) and was sacrificed on the cross at Calvary. He rose from the dead and sits alive at the right hand of the Father. He is our propitiation, if we die in life to the flesh. Believing and being baptized in Jesus, we are born again (as Jesus prescribed) and made partakers in his death, burial and resurrection. By a spiritual operation in God, our sinful nature is changed, reconciled to God, born again of the resurrection of Jesus Christ into eternal life. We are indwelled in this life by the Holy Ghost in order to enable us to love, have joy, have peace, suffer one another, be gentle one to another, exhibit goodness, triumph in faith, be humbly submissive to God and sober yet on a spiritual high. What a philosophy. What a doctrine for life!

All scripture is helpful, advantageous for reproof (elengkos: proof, conviction). In the beginning God created the heavens and the earth. Mankind was created with obvious godlike abilities to imagine, be creative and to choose our own destinies. "Choose now today whom you will serve; I have set before your life and death, blessing and cursing. Therefore, choose life that both thou and thy seed may live". Man is predestined to be reconciled to God not to eternal damnation. Notwithstanding, some have been chosen for God's specific purpose. "Thus saith the Lord, Isaiah, I made thee and formed thee from the womb I will help thee, fear not."

Proof and conviction of creation as presented in the scriptures. In the beginning God created the Heavens and the Earth. Mankind was created by the living God, a living omnipresent spirit. Mankind is not the evolutionary result of the "Big Bang Theory" because life cannot come from non-life. Mankind evolving from an apelike man trips over the "missing link". The scriptures explain that while the earth remaineth, seedtime and harvest, cold and heat, summer, winter, day and night shall not cease. A couple of thousand of years before it was scientifically proven, the scriptures convicted us that God "hath made of one blood all nations of men for to dwell on the face of the earth and hath determined the times before appointed, and bounds of their habitation".

All scripture is helpful, advantageous for correction (espanorthosis: straightening up again, rectification, reformation). "Be not deceived, God is not mocked, for whatsoever a man soweth that shall he also reap." "Trust in the Lord with all thine heart and lean not unto thine own understanding. In all the ways acknowledge him and he shall direct thy paths. Be not wise in thine own eyes. Fear the Lord and depart from evil." Pastoring the last 8 years in a house of corrections, I have quoted, with the intent of correction; "let him that stole steal no more but rather let him labor for that thing which is good that he may have to give to him that needeth". "Let none of you suffer as a murder, or as a thief or as an evil doer, or as a criminal or busybody". Rather as correction, "be ye holy for God is holy". Don't curse correction, even incarceration, for "whom God loveth he chastises". Rebellion, against especially God, is as witchcraft which is an abomination to God. Draw closer to God, "straighten" out yourself. All it takes is a resistance to the devil according to the scriptures, and he will flee you. And if you are saved, God has given you overcoming power through his Spirit.

All scripture is helpful, advantageous for instruction in righteousness. It only takes a little self examination to see how dark, insecure, envious, jealous, vengeful our thoughts and actions in the flesh can be. The Bible declares that our righteousness is no better than filthy rags.

Now, accepting the reality of a Living God with <u>none</u> besides him, that he wounds and heals and there is none that is able to deliver out of this hand yet, he is a rewarder of those that diligently seek him because he is able to teach sinners in this way. How does one obtain righteousness/justification in such a God's sight? The Bible reveals the answer; "blessed is the man to whom God will not impute sin". Our righteousness comes, according to the Bible, comes through our faith in Jesus Christ.

Through Faith, the righteousness of Jesus Christ is imputed (counted toward us). If we believe in Jesus Christ, "therefore being justified of faith we have peace with God through our lord Jesus Christ, by whom also we have access by faith into the grace in which we stand rejoicing in the hope of the glory of God".

The Bible is the sum total of all scripture today; "for I tell you, that many prophets and kings have desired to see those things which ye see, and have not seen them; and to hear those things which we hear and have not heard them".

Through Paul's instruction here in the third chapter of the 2nd epistle to Timothy, we are given insight to the world materializing today. Are we not in the most perilous times in the history of the world? Mankind has been caught up in a "me first" mentality. Look at what is coveted. See the pride of mankind to the point of blasphemy. Children are disobedient as never before to clueless parents. Truce breaking is the norm. Liars abound and mankind seeks pleasures rather than God. Are we not learning more than at any time in history yet never able to come into the knowledge of the True and Living God?

Yet, at a time like this, the scriptures furnish the preacher with what he needs and what he should do. "For the preaching of the cross is to them that perish foolishness; but unto us which we are saved it is the power of God". It has pleased Almighty God "by the foolishness of preaching to save them that believe". "The foolishness of God is wiser than men. The weakness of God is stronger than men"

Preaching is committed to faithful men; "and the things that thou has heard of me among many witnesses, the same commit than to faithful men, who shall be able to teach others also". The man of God is to be furnished in the mysteries of Christ. "Let a man so account of us as ministers of Christ and stewards of the mysteries of God." Such Stewards are equipped to be faithful by the bible. Obey these flames of fire of the Living God charged with watching over the souls of the sheep. Pray for the man of God as they must give account to God having lived honestly. They must give account to God as they have been examples, not lords, to the people of God and have preached in the light upon the housetops what God has revealed in the ear in darkness. "And it shall come to pass in the last days saith God, I will pour out of my spirit upon all flesh and your sons and your daughters shall prophesy."

The man of God is perfected, as are all Christians, by humbling himself under the hand of Almighty God and done God's will not his own. The Bible is the book that thoroughly provides the man of God with what is needed for the good work of the spreading of the good news. "You shall know the truth and the truth shall set you free." The truth shall emancipate the individual, the church and the nation.

So, I come today in the spirit of Titus; "For there are many unruly and vain talkers and deceiver, whose mouths must be stopped, who subvert whole houses, teaching things which they ought not, for "filthy lucre's sake".

If you are not emancipated today, let the Gospel of Jesus Christ set you free. Only where there is the spirit of the Lord is there true liberty (i.e. freedom from the bondage of sin).

Firstly, **Malachi 2: 10**

> "Have we not all one Father? Hath not one God created us? Why do we deal treacherously every man against his brother, by profaning the covenant of our fathers?"

Secondly, **John 17:3**

> "And this is life eternal that they might know Thee, the only True God and Jesus Christ whom thou hast sent!"

Thirdly, **1 John 2: 22-23**

> "Who is a liar but he that denieth that Jesus is the Christ. He is an antichrist, that deneith the Father and the Son. Whosoever denieth the Son, the same hath not the Father: (but) he that acknowledgeth the Son hath the Father also."

Fourthly, **John 5:22**

> "For the father, judgeth no man but hath committed all judgment unto the son."

Emancipate yourself today. Believe on Jesus Christ as Lord and Savior and be baptized in the name of the Father, the Son and the Holy Ghost.

Seek first the kingdom of God and its righteousness and all other substance shall be added unto you. Be born again of the water and the spirit. Indwelled by the Holy Ghost, you have received the power to be overcomers of the world. If you love Christ, then keep his commandments; don't be judged to reprobate by God for outside of the Kingdom of God are the fearful, unbelieving, abominable, murderers, sorcerers, idolaters and all liars. Their eternal place is in the lake of fire, the second death.

Let the church be set free today (emancipated). Church, don't leave your first love Christ Jesus. Suffer the persecution in the world today of the Church, as a good soldier. Keep strong the doctrine of Jesus Christ; keep strong Biblical Doctrine.

2 John 8-9

> "Look to yourselves, that we lose not those things which we have wrought, but that we receive a full reward. Whosoever transgresseth, and abideth not in the doctrine of Christ, hath not God. He that abideth in the doctrine of Christ, he hath both the Father and the Son."

Church, let us not forsake the assembling of ourselves but, with each individual being fully persuaded in sound doctrine, don't worship just any place. "How shall two walk together accept they agree?" Some churches are synagogues of Satan; more goats than sheep. More Tares than wheat. Satan is sitting in the pulpit. This is why the bible declares that judgment is to begin in the house of God first!

Be a part of the spiritual Church as you plant yourself in a fellowship (as led by God). The body of Christ, the gates of hell shall not prevail against and that body shall be presented faultless and revirginated

Emancipate yourself this great nation. This country from sea to shiny sea, with amber waves of grain and purple mountain's majesty, God done shed his grace on thee. "Blessed is the nation who's God is the Lord." God makes a nation abound and God can make it abased. "And I will bring again the captivity of Egypt, and I will cause them to return into the land of Pharaoh into the land of their habitation; and they shall be there a base kingdom. It shall be basest of the Kingdoms; neither shall it exact itself any more above the Nations; for I will diminish them, that they shall no more rule over the Nations."

When I think of the peculiarity is this nation that is a part of the New World and not even 300 years old yet it has been the savior of the entire world in two world wars. It is self sufficient and heretofore rooted and grounded in the word of God.

Emancipate yourself America. "Woe unto you lawyers of the land for you laden men with burdens to grievous to bear. The blood of all the prophets may be required of you." It is no accident that this Titus comes to Toccoa. A place called beautiful by its name and introduced in this pulpit by an historian. A place from whence World War II liberators called "A band of Brothers" helped put down a tyrant called Hitler. Nestled in the south where I was personally relegated to the theater balcony as a child. On this the 39th anniversary of your Emancipation Celebration and the 142 Anniversary of the Proclamation itself, at a time when technological breakthroughs allow an AM radio station to be heard around the world.

Recognizing that the Emancipation Proclamation of January 1, 1863 did not immediately free a single slave. It confirmed the fact that the war was for the Union (this great nation as it exists today) and a war for freedom.

As a matter of history - March 13, 1862 The Federal Government forbade all union officers to return fugitive slaves; this annihilated in effect the fugitive slave laws.

April 10, 1862 - Congress declared that the Federal Government would compensate all owners who freed their slaves.

April 16, 1862 - All Slaves in the hometown (Washington, D.C.) of this son of a Toccoan, were freed by the aforementioned April 10th declaration, by congress.

June 19, 1862 - A measure in Congress was enacted prohibiting slavery in the hometown (Washington, D.C.) of this son of a Toccoan, were freed by the aforementioned, April 10th declaration by congress.

June 19, 1862 - A Measure in Congress was enacted prohibiting slavery in the United States territories in defiance of the Supreme Court Dred Scott case which ruled that congress was powerless to regulate slavery in the territories. Woe unto you lawyers!

September 22, 1962 - President Lincoln issued a preliminary proclamation declaring this intention of declaring another Emancipation Proclamation in 100 days to free slaves in all territories deemed in rebellion at the time.

The January 1, 1863 Emancipation Proclamation conferred freedom on slaves in the states that were succeeding from the union. Therefore, freedom/emancipation for the slaves had to be secured by a military victory. It was the 13th Amendment to the U.S. Constitution in 1865 that completely abolished slavery.

We come today as men insist on calling good evil and evil good. We come today as the judges of this land would stamp out Christianity; "we battle not against flesh and blood but spiritual wickedness in high places". This preacher comes today, on this Great Anniversary, by helping to start this New Year off right with a call for a 28th amendment to the U.S. Constitution. Would you like to hear it; I have the draft in my coat pocket?

The draft reads as follows: "The right to acknowledge the fundamental morality of this nation as being established in the Christian principles of the Bible and to freely exhort those principles in the understanding of the morality of this nation and its democracy with the inclusion of other religious doctrines that are in support of areas of common agreement with regard to morality and democracy.

I'm not ashamed of the gospel of Jesus Christ! To the individual today, free yourselves today through the gospel of Jesus Christ. To the Church today, free yourselves today through the gospel of Jesus Christ. To this great nation, liberate yourself today through the gospel of Jesus Christ. May God bless you, my Father's children.

Appendix 10

PROPOSED 28ᵀᴴ AMENDMENT TO THE UNITED STATES CONSTITUTION AS REVISED 1/20/09 – RIGHT OF ACKNOWLEDGEMENT

THE RIGHT TO acknowledge the fundamental morality of this nation as being established in the Christian principles of the Bible and to freely exhort those principles in the understanding of the morality of this nation and its constitutional republic with the inclusion of other religious doctrines that are in support of areas of common agreement with regard to our moral principals and form of government.

Appendix 11

"FRANKLIN D. ROOSEVELT'S D-DAY PRAYER" JUNE 6, 1944

Almighty God: Our sons, pride of our Nation, this day have set upon a mighty endeavor, a struggle to preserve our Republic, our religion, and our civilization, and to set free a suffering humanity.

Lead them straight and true; give strength to their arms, stoutness to their hearts, steadfastness in their faith.

They will need Thy blessings. Their road will be long and hard. For the enemy is strong. He may hurl back our forces. Success may not come with rushing speed, but we shall return again and again; and we know that by Thy grace, and by the righteousness of our cause, our sons will triumph.

They will be sore tired, by night and by day, without rest-until the victory is won. The darkness will be rent by noise and flame. Men's souls will be shaken with the violence of war.

For these men are lately drawn from the ways of peace. They fight not for the lust of conquest. They fight to end conquest. They fight to liberate. They fight to let justice arise, and tolerance and good will among all Thy people. They yearn but for the end of battle and their return to the haven of home.

Some will never return. Embrace these, Father, and receive them, Thy heroic servants, into Thy kingdom.

And for us at home – fathers, mothers, children, wives, sisters, and brothers of brave men overseas, whose thoughts and prayers are ever with them – help us, Almighty God, to rededicate ourselves in renewed faith in Thee in this hour of great sacrifice.

Many people have urged that I call this Nation into a single day of special prayer. But because the road is long and the desire is great, I ask that our people devote themselves in a continuance of prayer. As we rise to each new day, and again when each day is spent, let words of prayer be on our lips, invoking Thy help to our efforts.

Give us strength, too – strength in our daily tasks, to redouble the contributions we make in the physical and the material support of our armed forces.

And let our hearts be stout, to wait out the long travail, to bear sorrows that may come, to impart our courage unto our sons whosesoever they may be.

And, O Lord, give us faith, give us faith in Thee; faith in our sons; faith in each other, faith in our united crusade. Let no the keenness of our spirit ever be dulled. Let not the impacts of temporary events, of temporal matters of but fleeting moment - let not these deter us in our unconquerable purpose.

With Thy blessing, we shall prevail over the unholy forces of our enemy. Help us to conquer the apostles of greed and racial arrogances. Lead us to the saving of our country, and with our sister Nations into a world unity that will spell a sure peace - a peace invulnerable to the schemings of unworthy men. And a peace that will let all of men live in freedom, reaping the just rewards of their honest toil.

Thy will be done, Almighty God.

Amen.

Source: Franklin D. Roosevelt Presidential Library and Museum

Appendix 12

HOLIDAY PROCLAMATIONS

Lincoln's 1863 Thanksgiving Proclamation

The year that is drawing towards its close, has been filled with the blessings of fruitful fields and healthful skies. To these bounties, which are so constantly enjoyed that we are prone to forget the source from which they come, others have been added, which are of so extraordinary a nature that they cannot fail to penetrate and soften even the heart which is habitually insensible to the ever watchful providence of Almighty God. In the midst of a civil war of unequalled magnitude and severity, which has sometimes seemed to foreign States to invite and to provoke their aggression, peace has been preserved with all nations, order has been maintained, the laws have been respected and obeyed, and harmony has prevailed everywhere except in the theatre of military conflict; while that theatre has been greatly contracted by advancing armies and navies of the Union. Needful diversions of wealth and strength from the fields of peaceful industry to the national defense have not arrested the plough, the shuttle, or the ship; the axe had enlarged the borders of our settlements, and the mines, as well of iron and coal as of the precious metals, have yielded even more abundantly than heretofore. Population has steadily increased, notwithstanding the waste that has been made in the camp, the siege and the battle-field; and the country, rejoicing in the consciousness of augmented strength and vigor, is permitted to expect continuance of years with large increase of freedom.

No human counsel hath devised nor hath any mortal hand worked out these great things. They are the gracious gifts of the Most High God, who, while dealing with us in anger for our sins, hath nevertheless remembered mercy. It has seemed to me fit and proper that they should be solemnly, reverently and gratefully acknowledged as with one heart and voice by the whole American People. I do therefore invite my fellow citizens in every part of the United States, and also those who are at sea and those who are sojourning in foreign lands, to set apart and observe the last Thursday of November next, as a day of Thanksgiving and Praise to our beneficent Father who dwelleth in the Heavens. And I recommend to them that while offering up the ascriptions justly due to Him for such singular deliverances and blessings, they do also, with humble penitence for our national perverseness and disobedience, commend to his tender care all those who have become widows, orphans, mourners or sufferers in the lamentable civil strife in which we are unavoidably engaged, and fervently implore the interposition of the Almighty Hand to heal the wounds of the nations and to restore it as soon as may be consistent with the Divine purposes to the full enjoyment of peace, harmony, tranquility and Union.

Abraham Lincoln

Christmas Holiday Stature

That the following days to wit: The first day in January, commonly called New Year's day, the fourth day of July, the twenty-fifth day of December, commonly called Christmas day, and any day appointed or recommended by the President of the United States as a day of public fast or thanksgiving, shall be holidays within the District of Columbia, and shall, for all purposes of presenting for payment o acceptance for the maturity and protest, and giving acceptance for maturity and protest, and giving notice of the dishonor of bills of exchange, bank checks and promissory notes or other negotiable or commercial paper, be treated and considered as is the first day of the week, commonly called Sunday, and all notes, drafts, checks, or other commercial or negotiable paper falling due or maturing on either of said holidays shall be deemed as having matured on the day previous.

Act of June 28, 1870, ch. 167, 16 Stat. 168.

Appendix 13

U. S. President George W. Bush's 2008 Thanksgiving Day Proclamation

Thanksgiving is a time for families and friends to gather together and express gratitude for all that we have been given, the freedoms we enjoy, and the loved ones who enrich our lives. We recognize that all of these blessings, and life itself, come not from the hand of man but from Almighty God. Every Thanksgiving, we remember the story of the Pilgrims who came to America in search of religious freedom and a better life. Having arrived in the New World, these early settlers gave thanks to the Author of Life for granting them safe passage to this abundant land and protecting them through a bitter winter.

Our nation's first president, George Washington, stated in the first Thanksgiving proclamation that "it is the duty of all nations to acknowledge the providence of Almighty God, to obey His will, to be grateful for His benefits, and humbly to implore His protection and flavor. While in the midst of the Civil War, President Abraham Lincoln revived the tradition of proclaiming a day of thanksgiving, asking God to heal our wounds and restore our country.

Today, as we look back on the beginnings of our democracy, Americans recall that we live in a land of many blessings where every person has the right to live, work, and worship in freedom. Our nation is especially thankful for the brave men and women of our armed forces who protect these rights while setting aside their own comfort and safety. Their courage keeps us free, their sacrifice makes us grateful, and their character makes us proud. Especially during the holidays, our country keeps them and their families in our thoughts and prayers.

Americans are also mindful of the need to share our gifts with others, and our nation is moved to compassionate action. We pay tribute to all caring citizens who reach out a helping hand and serve a cause larger than themselves.

On this day, let us give thanks to God who blessed our nation's first days and who blesses us today. May He continue to guide and watch over our families and our country always.

NOW THEREFORE. I, GEORGE W. BUSH, president of the Unites States of America, by virtue of the authority vested in me by the Constitution and the laws of the United States, do hereby proclaim Nov. 27, 2008, as a National Day of Thanksgiving. I encourage all Americans to gather together in their homes and places of worship with family, friends, and loved ones to strengthen the ties that bind us IN WITNESS WHEREOF, I have hereunto set my hand the 21st day of November, in the year of our Lord 2008, and of the independence of the United States of America 233rd.

GEORGE W. BUSH

REFERENCES

Hoppe, Lewis M,. *"Religions of the World"*, Glencoe Publishing, Encino, CA., 1979.

Overrbey, Edward, *"A Brief History of the Baptists"*, The Challenge Press 2001.

Robertson, Irvine, *"What the Cults Believe"*, Moody Press, Chicago, IL., 5th Edition 1991.

Trimingham, J. Spencer, *"Christianity Among the Arabs in Pre-Islamic Times"*, Longman Group Limited and Librairie du Liban 1979.

Dictionary of Christianity in America, Intervarsity Press, Downers Grove, IL., 1990.

Illustrated Dictionary & Concordance of the Bible, G.G. The Jerusalem Publishing House LTD, Jerusalem 1986.

The Holy Bible Old and New Testaments Authorized King James Version, Originally Published in 1611.

Today's English Version, New York: American Bible Society 1992 (also called Good News Translation).

Life Application Bible King James Version, Tyndale House Publishers, Inc., Wheaton, IL. 1989.

Interpretation on the Meanings of the Noble Qur'an in the English Language, A Summarized Version of At-Tabari, Al-Qurtubi and Ibn Kathir with comments from Sahih Al-Bukkari, Summarized in One Volume by Dr. Muhammad Mussin Khan and Dr. Muhammad Taqi-ud-Din-Al-Halali, Dar-us-Salam Publications, Riyadh 1995.

"Biblical Literature", The New Encyclopedia Britannica Macropedia, 1985.

"Christianity", The New Encyclopedia Britannica Macropedia, 1985.

"God in Islam", The Encyclopedia of Religion, 1985.

"The Final Call", *The Muslim Program*, Volume 26 Number 38, June 26, 2007, p. 39.

"Answering-Islam.org", *The Death of Muhammad*", Rev. C, November 28,2002.

"Citizen-Times.com", *President Bush's 2008 Thanksgiving Day Proclamation*, November 27, 2008.

"Teachervision.com", *Holidays: Religious and Secular, 2001*, December 28, 2001.

"The Dartmouth Review", *The Story of Kwaanza*, January 15, 2001.

Printed in the United States
By Bookmasters